THE MAYFLOWER READER

A Selection of Articles from
The Mayflower Descendant

By
George Ernest Bowman

Selected By
Ruth Wilder Sherman, F.A.S.G.

GENEALOGICAL PUBLISHING CO., INC.
BALTIMORE 1978

Excerpted from Volumes I-VII
of *The Mayflower Descendant* (1899-1905)

Reprinted with New Front Matter
Genealogical Publishing Co., Inc.
Baltimore, 1978

Library of Congress Catalogue Card Number 77-99092
International Standard Book Number 0-8063-0797-8

Made in the United States of America

FOREWORD

In 1897 four fledgling Mayflower societies gathered at Plymouth, Massachusetts, and formed the General Society of Mayflower Descendants. Present was a 37-year-old charter member of the Massachusetts Society, George Ernest Bowman, who was elected the General Society's first Secretary General. Two years later, Mr. Bowman issued the first of thirty-four volumes of *The Mayflower Descendant* on behalf of the Massachusetts Society.

The Mayflower Descendant contains transcriptions of important Pilgrim documents and some of the most valuable genealogical deductions made in 300 years concerning descendants of the Pilgrims. Most of these documents and articles were transcribed or written by Mr. Bowman. The publication of such invaluable material, thirty years before the founding of the modern American school of critical genealogy, certainly entitles George Ernest Bowman to the epithet of Father of Pilgrim Genealogy.

The articles were selected from the first seven volumes of *The Mayflower Descendant* because these particular volumes contain the greatest bulk of narrative literature pertaining to the Pilgrims, their children and grandchildren. These articles were chosen because they can be read by descendants, genealogists, historians, and public speakers. Read here not what others say the Pilgrims said, but their own words.

Ruth Wilder Sherman, F.A.S.G.
Secretary General, 1966-
General Society of Mayflower Descendants

PUBLISHER'S NOTE

Several of the articles reprinted here from *The Mayflower Descendant* contain footnotes which cite other articles in various volumes and issues of the journal. The citations give the original volume and page numbers, of course, and by themselves are of little help to anyone using this present work. To assist the reader in locating these references, therefore, we have incorporated the original volume, issue, and page numbers of the reprinted articles in the Contents. It should be remembered, however, that this book is a *selection* of articles from the first seven volumes of *The Mayflower Descendant* and not all the articles cited in footnotes will be found here.

CONTENTS

From Volume III (1901)

From Volume IV (1902)

From Volume V (1903)

From Volume VI (1904)

From Volume VII (1905)

THE MAYFLOWER READER

GOVERNOR BRADFORD'S LIST OF THE MAY-FLOWER PASSENGERS.

The names of those which came over first, in ye year .1620. and were (by the blesing of God) the first beginers, and (in a sort) the foundation, of all the plantations, and Colonies, in New England. (And their families.)

m^{r} John Carver. Kathrine his wife. Desire Minter;
.8. & .2. man-servants John Howland Roger Wilder. William Latham, a boy. & a maid servant. & a child y^{t} was
put to him called, Jasper More

m^{r} William Brewster. Mary his wife, with .2. sons,
whose names were Love, & Wrasling. and a boy was
.6. put to him called Richard More; and another of his
brothers the rest of his childeren were left behind &
came over afterwards.

m^{r} Edward Winslow Elizabeth his wife, & 2. men
.5. servants, caled Georg Sowle, and Elias Story; also
a litle girle was put to him caled Ellen, the sister of
Richard More.

.2. William Bradford, and Dorathy his wife, having but one child, a sone left behind, who came afterward.

m^{r} Isaack Allerton, and Mary. his wife; with .3. chil-
.6. dren Bartholmew Remember, & Mary. and a servant
boy, John Hooke.

.2. m^{r} Samuell fuller; and a servant, caled William Butten. His wife was behind & a child, which came afterwards.

.2. John Crakston and his sone John Crakston

.2. Captin Myles Standish and Rose, his wife

.4. m^{r} Christpher Martin, and his wife; and .2. servants, Salamon prower, and John Langemore

.5. m^{r} William Mullines, and his wife; and .2. children Joseph, & priscila; and a servant Robart Carter.

mr William White, and Susana his wife; and one sone
.6. caled resolved, and one borne a ship-bord caled peri-
griene; & .2. servants, named William Holbeck, &
Edward Thomson

mr Steven Hopkins, & Elizabeth his wife; and .2. children, caled Giles, and Constanta a doughter, both by a
.8. former wife. And .2. more by this wife, caled Damaris,
& Oceanus, the last was borne at sea. And .2. servants,
called Edward Doty, and Edward Litster.

.1. mr Richard Warren, but his wife and children were lefte
behind and came afterwards

4 John Billinton, and Elen his wife: and .2. sones John,
& Francis.

.4. Edward Tillie, and Ann his wife: and .2. childeren that
were their cossens; Henery Samson, and Humillity
Coper

.3. John Tillie, and his wife; and Eelizabeth their doughter

.2. Francis Cooke, and his sone John; But his wife & other
children came afterwards

.2. Thomas Rogers, and Joseph his sone; his other children
came afterwards.

.2. Thomas Tinker, and his wife, and a Sone

2. John Rigdale; and Alice his wife.

3. James Chilton, and his wife, and Mary their dougter;
they had another doughter yt was maried came afterward.

.3. Edward fuller, and his wife; and Samuell their sonne.

.3 John Turner, and .2. sones; he had a doughter came
some years after to Salem, wher she is now living.

.3. Francis Eaton. and Sarah his wife, and Samuell their
sone, a yong child

Moyses fletcher, John Goodman, Thomas Williams,
.10. Digerie Preist, Edmond Margeson, Peter Browne, Richard Britterige, Richard Clarke, Richard Gardenar, Gil-
bart Winslow

John Alden was hired for a cooper, at South-Hampton
1. wher the ship victuled ; and being a hopefull yong man was much desired, but left to his owne liking to go, or stay when he came here, but he stayed, and maryed here.

John Allerton, and Thomas Enlish were both hired, the later to goe m^r of a shalop here. and ye other was re-
.2. puted as one of ye company, but was to go back (being a seaman) for the help of others behind. But they both dyed here, before the shipe returned.

Ther were allso other .2. seamen hired to stay a year
.2. here in the country, William Trevore ; and one Ely. But when their time was out they both returned.

These bening aboute a hundred sowls came over in this first ship ; and began this worke, which god of his goodnes hath hithertoo blesed ; let his holy name have ye praise.

And seeing it hath pleased him to give me to see .30. years compleated, since these beginings. And that the great works of his providence are to be observed. I have thought it not unworthy my paines, to take a veiw of the decreasings, & Increasings of these persons, and such changs as hath pased over them, & theirs, in this thirty years. It may be of some use to such as come after ; but however I shall rest in my owne benefite.

I will therefore take them in order as they lye.

m^r Carver and his wife, dyed the first year, he in ye spring, she in ye somer ; also his man Roger, and ye litle boy Jasper, dyed before either of them, of ye commone Infection. Desire Minter, returned to her freind & proved not very well, and dyed in England. His servant boy Latham after more then .20. years stay in the country went into England ; and from thence to the
15 Bahamy Ilands in ye west Indees ; and ther with some others was stavred for want of food. His maid servant maried, & dyed a year or tow after here in this place. His servant John Howland maried the doughter of John Tillie, Elizabeth, and they are both now living ; and have .10. children now all living and their eldest dough-

ter hath .4. children And ther .2. dougter, one, all living and other of their Children mariagable. so .15. are come of them.

mr Brewster lived to very old age; about .80. years he was when he dyed, having lived some .23. or .24. years here in ye countrie. & though his wife dyed long before, yet she dyed aged. His sone Wrastle dyed a yonge man unmaried; his sone Love, lived till this year .1650. and
4. dyed, & left .4. children, now living. His doughters which came over after him, are dead but have left sundry children alive; his eldst sone is still liveing
2. and hath .9. or .10. children, one maried. who hath child, or .2.

Richard More, his brother dyed the first winter; but he
4. is maried, and hath .4. or .5. children, all living.

mr Ed: Winslow, his wife dyed the first winter; and he
2. maried with the widow of mr White, and hath .2. children living by her marigable, besids sundry that are dead. one of his servants dyed, as also the litle girle soone after the ships arivall. But his man Georg
.8 Sowle, is still living, and hath .8. children.

William Bradford, his wife dyed soone after their arivall;
4 and he maried againe; and hath .4. children, .3: wherof are maried.
who dyed 9 *of May*, 1658.*

mr Allerton his wife dyed with the first, and his servant John Hooke. his sone Bartle is maried in England but I know not how many children he hath. His doughter remember is maried at Salem & hath .3. or .4 children
.8. living. And his doughter mary is maried here, & hath .4. children. Him selfe maried againe with ye dougter of mr Brewster, & hath one sone living by here but she

* This note and that giving the date of Captain Standish's death are in the same handwriting.

Prince's note in his own copy of the New England Memorial (see p. 452 of Bradford's History, Ed. 1856) shows that these two entries must have been made before he received the manuscript. In neither entry is the year correctly stated. Governor Bradford died 9 May, 1657, and Captain Standish 3 October, 1656.

is long since dead. And he is maried againe, and hath left this place long agoe. So I account his Increase to be :8: besids his sons in England.

m^{r} ffuller, his servant dyed at sea ; and after his wife
.2. came over, he had tow children by her ; which are living and growne up to years. but he dyed some .15. years agoe.

John Crakston dyed in the first mortality ; and about some .5. or 6. years after his sone dyed, having lost him selfe in ye wodes, his feet became frosen, which put him into a feavor, of which he dyed.

Captain Standish his wife dyed in the first sicknes;
.4. and he maried againe, and hath .4. sones liveing, and some are dead.
who dyed .3. of Octob. 1655.*

m^{r} Martin, he, and all his, dyed in the first Infection ; not long after the arivall.

m^{r} Molines, and his wife, his sone, & his servant dyed the first winter. Only his dougter priscila survied, and
.15. maried with John Alden, who are both living, and have .11. children. And their eldest daughter is maried & hath five children.
See N. E. Memorial, p. 22.†

m^{r} White, and his .2. servants dyed soone after ther landing. His wife maried with m^{r} Winslow (as is
.7. before noted) His .2. sons are maried, and resolved hath .5. children ; perigrine tow, all living. So their Increase are :7

m^{r} Hopkins, and his wife are now both dead ; but they lived above .20. years in this place, and had one sone, and .4. doughters borne here. Ther sone became a sea-
.5. man, & dyed at Barbadoes, one daughter dyed here. and .2. are maried. one of them hath .2. children, and one is yet to mary. So their Increase, which still survive, are
4. .5. But his sone Giles is maried, and hath .4. children.

* See footnote under William Bradford, preceding.

† This entry is in a different hand.

.12. his doughter Constanta, is also maried, and hath .12. children all of them living, and one of them maried.

mr Richard Warren lived some .4. or .5. years, and had his wife come over to him, by whom he had .2. sons
4 before dyed; and one of them is maryed, and hath .2. children So his Increase is .4. but he had .5. doughters more came over with his wife, who are all maried, & living & have many children.

John Billinton after he had bene here .10. yers, was exe-
.8. cuted, for killing a man; and his eldest sone dyed before him; but his .2. sone is alive, and maried, & hath .8. children

Edward Tillie, and his wife both dyed soon after their
.7. arivall; and the girle Humility their cousen, was sent for into Ento England, and dyed ther. But the youth Henery Samson, is still liveing, and is maried, & hath .7. children.

John Tillie, and his wife both dyed, a litle after they came ashore; and their daughter Elizabeth maried with John Howland and hath Isue as is before noted.

Francis Cooke* is still living, a very olde man, and hath seene his childrens, children, have children: after his wife came over. (with other of his children) he hath .3.
.8. still living by her, all maried, and have .5. children so their encrease is .8. And his sone John which came
.4. over with him, is maried, and hath .4. chilldren living.

Thomas Rogers dyed in the first sicknes, but his sone
.6. Joseph is still living, and is maried, and hath .6. children. The rest of Thomas Rogers came over, & are maried, & have many children.

Thomas Tinker, and his wife, and sone, all dyed in the first sicknes.

And so did John Rigdale, and his wife.

James Chilton, and his wife also dyed in the first Infec-

* In the margin, in a different hand, is written "dyed 7 of April 1663 above 80."

.10. tion. but their daughter mary, is still living and hath .9. children ; and one daughter is maried, & hath a child ; so their Increase is .10.

Edward ffuller, and his wife dyed soon after they came
4 ashore ; but their sone Samuell is living, & maried, and hath .4. children. or more.

John Turner, and his .2. sones all dyed in the first siknes. But he hath a daugter still living, at Salem, well maried, and approved of.

Francis Eeaton, his first wife dyed in the generall sicknes; and he maried againe, & his .2. wife dyed, & he
4 maried the .3. and had by her .3. children. one of them is maried, & hath a child ; the other are living, but one of them is an Ideote. He dyed about .16. years agoe.

.1. his sone Samuell, who came over a sucking child is allso maried, & hath a child.

Moyses fletcher Thomas Williams Digerie preist John Goodman Edmond Margeson Richard Britterige Richard Clarke All these dyed sone after their arivall. in the Generall sicknes that befell. But Digerie preist had his wife & children sent hither afterwards she being m^r^ Allertons sister. But the rest left no posteritie here.

Richard Gardinar, became a seaman, and dyed in England, or at sea.

Gilbert Winslow after diverse years aboad here, returned into England and dyed ther.

Peter Browne maried twise, by his first wife he had .2. children, who are living, & both of them maried, and
6 the one of them hath .2. children. by his second wife, he had .2. more ; he dyed about 16 years since

Thomas English ; and John Allerton, dyed in the generall siknes.

John Alden maried with priscila, m^r^ Mollines his doughter, and had Isue by her as is before related.

Edward Doty, & Edward Litster the servants of m^{r} Hopkins. Litster After he was at liberty, went to Virginia, & ther dyed. But Edward Doty by a second wife hath .7. children and both he and they are living

Of these 100 persons which came first over, in this first ship together; the greater halfe dyed in the generall mortality; and most of them in .2. or three monthes time. And for those which survied though some were ancient & past procreation; & others left ye place and cuntrie. yet of those few remaining are sprunge up above .160. persons; in this .30. years. And are now living in this presente year .1650. besids many of their children which are dead and come not within this account.

And of the old stock, (of one, & other) ther are yet living this present year .1650. nere .30. persons. Let the Lord have ye praise; who is the High preserver of men.

Twelfe persons liveing of the old Stock this present yeare 1679.

Two persons liveing that come over in the first Shipe 1620 this present yeare 1690. Resolved White and Mary Chusman, the Daughter of m^{r} Alderton

and John Cooke the Son of frances Cooke that Came in the first ship is still liveing this present yeare 1694

& Mary Cushman. is still liveing this present yeare 1698

The last four entries, made many years after Governor Bradford closed his record, were written by two different persons.

It is impossible to determine the exact date of the first entry, but the writer overlooked at least two "of the old Stock." The following list contains the names of *fifteen* who were alive at the beginning of the year 1679:—

Peregrine White, died 1704; Mary (Allerton) Cushman, died 1699; John Cooke, died 1695; Resolved White, died between 1690 and 1694; Richard More, died 1690 or later; Gyles Hopkins, died 1690; Elizabeth (Tilley) Howland, died 1687; John Alden, died 1687; Francis Billington, died about 1686; Henry Samson, died 1684; Samuel Eaton, died 1684; Samuel Fuller, 2d, died 1683; Susanna (Fuller) (White) Winslow, died 1680; George Soule, died 1680; Mary (Chilton) Winslow, died 1679. The last named died early in 1679, perhaps before the entry was made.

Bradford wrote that there were "nere 30 persons" living in 1650, but he named only twenty-eight — those alive in 1679, and the following thirteen: Joseph Rogers, died 1678; Constance (Hopkins) Snow, died 1677; John Howland, died 1673; Damaris (Hopkins) Cooke, died between 1666 and 1669; Francis Cooke, died 1663; Isaac Allerton, died 1659; William Bradford, died 1657; Myles Standish, died 1656; Edward Doty, died 1655; Edward Winslow, died 1655; Remember (Allerton) Maverick, died about 1652; also Priscilla (Mullins) Alden and Bartholomew Allerton, both of whom Bradford mentions as living in 1650, but the years of their decease cannot be stated with any approach to accuracy.

OLD STYLE AND NEW STYLE DATING.

Julian and Gregorian Calendars.

By F. APTHORP FOSTER.

If an apology were needed for trying, with an attempt at succinctness, to treat of the calendar that our ancestors used when they first came to this country, and of the oı e that we now employ, which, though having had birth in 1582, was not adopted by Great Britain and her dependencies until 1752, such an apology were more than justified by the prevailing ignorance of the subject on the part of the average person. Some know that once upon a time something was done to the calendar, but so long ago as not to be worth troubling themselves about; some religiously copy double years or "O. S." and "N. S." after dates with only a vague idea of their meaning; while others, the greatest number, unfortunately, know nothing about the matter.

It is in the hope of throwing a little light on what is regarded as a puzzling subject by those who encounter it for the first time, that the following has been written. It makes no claim to originality, but is based on such trustworthy authorities as were found.*

As the calendar now in use was preceded by the Julian calendar, and that in turn by others, it may be of interest briefly to trace their succession.

To Romulus is given the credit of having, during his reign, divided the year into ten months with a total of 304 days. His successor, Numa, made changes in this method of reckoning for purposes of greater accuracy; but even so, in 452 B.C. the year had only been given 355 days, or a deficiency of a fraction over 10 days according to the solar

* For those who care to pursue the subject further the following list of books will be found useful: Saint-Allais, *L'Art de vérifier les dâtes*, Paris, 1818; Nicolas, *Chronology of History*, London, 1833; Bond, *Handy-Book of Rules and Tables for Verifying Dates with the Christian Era*, London, 1869; *Encyclopædia Britannica*, ed. 9, IV.

reckoning. Further corrections were subsequently made and the year increased to 366¼ days, or an excess of (approximately) one day per year. This error was rectified and the number of days put at 365¼. The right to alter the calendar for purposes of correction was placed in the hands of the Roman pontiffs, who so misused their power for political ends that in the time of Cæsar the vernal equinox, according to the calendar, differed from the true astronomical time by three months, and appeared in the summer.

JULIAN CALENDAR, OR OLD STYLE.

The necessity of some action to eliminate these discrepancies had become so great that Cæsar, as Pontifex Maximus, in his third consulate, inserted in the calendar two intercalary months, with a total of sixty-seven days, between November and December, and gave an additional twenty-three days to February, which, added to the 355 days of the year as previously reckoned, made a total of 445 days and brought about uniformity between the calendar and actual time, so that the vernal equinox was restored to March 25.

To form a calendar which should more nearly approximate correctness, Cæsar, with the aid of Sosigenes, a famous Egyptian scholar, based his calculations upon a (mean) solar year of 365¼ days. For purposes of intercalation a day was added every fourth year to the month of February. Such years were known as bissextile.* This new calendar went into effect in the year 45 B.C.†

* From *bissextus* = twice six. "This extra day was provided for by reckoning twice the sixth day before the calends (or first) of March, . . . the 'sixth' (or first sixth) day proper thus corresponding to February 25, according to our reckoning, and the extra 'sixth,' or 'second sixth,' to our February 24. Since 1662, when the Anglican liturgy was revised, the twenty-ninth day of February has been more conveniently regarded as the intercalated day in all English-speaking countries. In the ecclesiastical calendars of the countries of continental Europe, however, the twenty-fourth day of February is still reckoned as the bissextus or intercalary day." — *Century Dictionary.*

† The Roman year began in March, the months following in their present order, though February had at one time preceded January. March, May, July, September, November, and January had each thirty-one days: the remaining months had each thirty days with the exception of February, which in common years had twenty-nine days, and every fourth year thirty days. The lack of system in the number of days in the months as we now know them is interesting. July (previously *Quintilis*) was named after Cæsar; August (previously *Sextilis*) was called after Augustus, and to gratify the inordinate vanity of this sovereign by giving his month as many days as Cæsar's —

GREGORIAN CALENDAR, OR NEW STYLE.

In March, 1582, Pope Gregory XIII, having found the principal Catholic countries ready to adopt his views, issued a brief abolishing the Julian calendar and substituting in its place the one since generally known by his name, the author of which was one Aloysius Lilius, or Lilio Ghiraldi, a Neapolitan astronomer and physician. In order to bring the vernal equinox to March 21, as it was at the time of the Council of Nice, in 325 — for it had now retrograded to March 11 — the Pope directed that the 5th of October be reckoned the 15th, and that in future the year begin on January 1st. For purposes of intercalation, such years as were evenly divisible by four (for example, 1604, 1728, 1896, etc.), and such centesimal years as were evenly divisible by 400 (for example, 1600, 2000, etc.), were to be considered bissextile or leap years, and an extra day was to be added to February. In other, or common, years February was to have twenty-eight days.*

The new style of reckoning was promptly adopted by most Catholic countries, some coincidently with Rome, others later.†

In the cities of the Protestant Netherlands,‡ *e. g.* Rotterdam, Amsterdam, Leyden, Delft, Harlaem, and The Hague, Old style ended on Friday, December 21, 1582, and New Style began on Saturday, December 22 (January 1), 1582–3.

England, however, adhered for 170 years to the Old Style, with a pertinacity due to prejudice in favor of ancient practice against which reason and convenience seemed to have

thirty-one — February was robbed of a day. To avoid three consecutive months of thirty-one days each, September and November were reduced to thirty days and October and December were each given an extra day.

*" The Gregorian calendar gives ninety-seven intercalations in 400 years, or, reduced to days, hours, etc., an excess of twenty-six seconds a year over solar time, or one day in 3,323 years. To correct this slight error, it has been suggested that the year 4000 and its multiples be considered common years." — *Encyclopædia Britannica.*

†See especially Bond's *Handy-Book* for full tables.

‡" By Edict or Plakaet of 10 December, 1582 (entered in the Great Plakaet boek, I, 395, in the Record Office of the Hague), introduction of the New Style was fixed for the fifteenth of December, 1582; but afterwards settled by a resolution of the States of Holland, to begin on the first of January, 1583." — Bond, *op. cit.*

no weight. It was not until 1751 that the correction of the calendar was introduced by Act of Parliament (24 Geo. II, ch. 23).* It was enacted that throughout all his majesty's dominions the 1st of January, 1752, should be reckoned the first day of the year, and to correct the error of eleven days, the 3rd of September should be reckoned the 14th.

Many mistakes have been made in reducing Old Style to New Style from a misapprehension of the number of days' difference between the two. Thus the 22nd of November, 1620, N. S., has been erroneously adopted, *instead* of the 21st, for the date of the Signing of the Compact on the *Mayflower*, and the Landing of the Pilgrims has been placed (equally erroneously) on the 22nd of December, 1620, N. S., *instead* of the 21st. This mistake seems due to the idea that as eleven days were needed to reduce Old Style to New Style when the calendar was corrected in 1752, therefore eleven is the magic number to be used in all such cases, no matter what the century concerned is.

The following table shows the correct number of days to be applied to change Old Style to New Style:—

From March	1,	1399, to	February	29, 1499,	inclusive, add	9 days.
,,	,,	,, 1499, ,,	,,	,, 1599,	,, ,,	10 ,,
,,	,,	,, 1599, ,,	,,	,, 1699,	,, ,,	10 ,, †
,,	,,	,, 1699, ,,	September	2, 1752,	,, ,,	11 ,,

Russia and the Greek Church still hold to the Julian calendar, and according to our reckoning are now twelve days behind time.

* A similar attempt was made March 16, 27 Eliz., 1584–5; but after a second reading in the House of Commons it was lost sight of. (For this and the preceding, see Nicolas, *Chronology of History*, 34.)

† The lack of retrogression here is due to the fact that 1599–1600 was a leap year in both styles. The table which follows is arranged to show where the gain of a day comes in on March 1, in such years as were leap years, O. S., and common years, N. S.:—

FEBRUARY - MARCH, 1699–1700.

	Mon.	Tues.	Wed.	Thur.	Fri.	Sat.	Sun.	Mon.	Tues.	Wed.	Thur.	Fri.	Sat.	Sun.	Mon.	
O. S.	18	19	20	21	22	23	24	25	26	27	28	29	1	2	3	
Add days	10	10	10	10	10	10	10	10	10	10	10	10	11	11	11	
N. S.	28	1	2	3	4	5	6	7	8	9	10	11	12	13	14	etc.

COMMENCEMENT OF THE YEAR.

In England the year commenced as follows previous to the adoption of the New Style, 1752, when January 1 was made the legal date:—

Seventh to thirteenth centuries, on Christmas Day.

Twelfth century, by the Church, on March 25.

Fourteenth century, by civilians, on March 25.

In Holland and the Low Countries the year commenced as follows:—

Some provinces of the Low Countries, for example, Gueldres, Friesland, and Utrecht (since 1333), at Christmas.

Utrecht, previous to 1333, on March 25.

Delft, Dort, Brabant, on Good Friday.

Holland, Flanders, and Hainault, on Easter day.*

Two forms have generally existed in England for the commencement of the year, namely, (1) that which began on anuary 1 and was known as the *historical* year; (2) that which began on March 25 and was known as the *civil, legal,* and *ecclesiastical* year.

This double system has been the cause of much confusion, for some writers have used one form and some the other, yet both were equally correct from different points of view. To lessen the confusion and to avoid mistakes, it became the general custom to double-date, that is, to give both the legal, or civil, and historical years; for example:—

$$26 \text{ January, } 163\tfrac{1}{2} \begin{cases} \text{Civil and legal year,} \\ \text{Historical year;} \end{cases}$$

or, as it is often seen, 163½ or 1631–2, according to the fancy of the writer.†

* This "style notaries adopted in their acts; but to avoid mistakes, they were compelled to add, 'according to the style of the court,' or 'before Easter,' or 'more Gallicano.' In 1575 the duke of Requesens, governor of the Low Countries, ordered the year to commence on the first of January. The States of Holland had long before adopted this calculation [?], and endeavoured, as early as 1532, to bring it into general use."— Nicolas, *op. cit.*, 44, 45.

† Where Old and New Styles are designated at the same time the following methods are employed:—

$$\text{January}\frac{1}{11}\text{ 1631–2, or January 1 (11), 1631–2, or } \frac{\text{February 26, 1699}}{\text{March 8, 1700.}}$$

It was customary also to number the months and days of the week.* It should be borne in mind that in Old Style the order of the months was:—

1. March,	5. July,	9. November,
2. April,	6. August,	10. December,
3. May,	7. September,	11. January,
4. June,	8. October,	12. February.

It was usual to place the day of the month first, then the month, and lastly the year, but examples can easily be found which begin with the month. The following have been taken at random: 26—2 mo—46, ye 14 11 82, (18) (12) 1648, 6th mo. 18, 1663. A numerical abbreviation of the month is sometimes seen, as, for instance, 7^{ber}, 8^{ber}, 9^{ber}, 10^{ber}, for September, October, November, and December.

Where a single date is "given as the first month in the seventeenth century, without any surrounding entries to show the chronological position, it will almost always be safe to double-date it";† for example, if the entry reads 13 day 1 mo. 1658, add the historical year thus, 1658[-9].

CONCLUSION.

Many persons prefer (quite properly) not to trust to *copies* of records as final if they can consult the originals for their information. To these persons I would take the liberty of offering the following suggestions:—

1. "In making notes and citing references, the rule is absolute that every extract which is in the words of the author should be set off by quotation marks; and that all omissions within such a quoted extract should be shown by points or stars (. . . * * *)."‡

2. When making abstracts, preserve as far as possible the spelling and form of the original.

* The Latin names for the days of the week are: Dies Saturni, Saturday; Dies Solis, Sunday; Dies Lunæ, Monday; Dies Martis, Tuesday; Dies Mercurii, Wednesday; Dies Jovis, Thursday; Dies Veneris, Friday.

† Letter of W. H. Whitmore in Boston Record Commissioners' Report, No. 28, p. vii.

‡ Hart, *American History Told by Contemporaries*, I, 17.

3. Always copy dates in your notes as they are found. In this way you know how the record actually reads, whereas if you reduce Old Style to New Style, or take other liberties with dates, you make the original record responsible for your own interpolations.

4. If you add anything to a date for future guidance, as a result of investigation, or if within a quoted extract you insert words of your own, do not fail to use brackets [ ].

5. Do not jump at the conclusion that because 8. 9. 56 in one record means 8th day 9th mo. 56, that it means the same in another. It may just as well mean 8th mo. 9th day 56. The methods and peculiarities of each author or of each clerk's system of entries must be the only guide for your opinions.

In the name of God Amen

MARY (CHILTON) WINSLOW'S WILL AND INVENTORY.

LITERALLY TRANSCRIBED BY GEORGE ERNEST BOWMAN.

The original will of Mary (Chilton) Winslow is still preserved in the files of the Suffolk County Registry of Probate, at Boston, together with the bond of the administrators, signed by her son John Winslow and son-in-law Richard Middlecott. They were recorded in Vol. VI, pages 300 and 301, of the Probate Records.

The will was written on one side of a sheet of paper a little over eighteen by fourteen inches in size, and, as will be seen by the reproduction, is in excellent condition, except in some of the creases made by folding.

As William Tailer, the executor named in the will, came into court on the first of May and refused to serve, it is certain that Mary (Chilton) Winslow died before May, 1679, and probably only a short time before.

The original inventory is missing, and the copy has been made from Vol. XII, pp. 314, 315, of the Probate Records.

The copies of the will and bond were made from the original documents.

The will follows:

In the name of God Amen the thirty first day of July in the yeare of our Lord one thousand Six hundred seventy and Six I Mary Winslow of Boston in New England Widdow being weake of Body but of Sound and perfect memory praysed be almighty God for the same Knowing the uncertainety of this present life and being desirous to settle that outward Estate the Lord hath Lent me. I doe make this my last Will and Testam^{t} in manner and forme following (that is to say) First and principally I comend my Soule into the hands of Almighty God my Creato^{r} hopeing to receive full pardon and remission of all my sins; and Salvation through the alone merrits of Jesus Christ my redeemer: And my body to the Earth to be buried in Such Decent manner as to my Executo^{r} hereafter named shall be thought meet and convenient and as touching such worldly Estate as the Lord hath Lent me my Will and meaneing is the same shall be imployed and bestowed as hereafter in and by this my Will is Exprest.

Imp^{s} I doe hereby revoake renounce and make voide all Wills by me formerly made and declaire and apoint this my Last Will and Testam^{t} Item I will that all the Debts that I Justly owe to any manner of person or persons whatsoever shall be well and truely paid or ordained to be paid in convenient time after my decease by my Executo^{r} hereafter named — Item I give and bequeath unto my Sone John Winslow my great Square table Item I give and bequeath unto my Daughter Sarah Middlecott my Best gowne and Pettecoat and my Silver beare bowle and to each of her children a Silver Cup with an handle: Also I give unto my grandchild William Paine my Great silver tankard: Item I give unto my Daughter Susanna Latham my long Table: Six Joyned Stooles and my great Cupboard: a bedstead Bedd and furniture there unto belonging that is in the Chamber over the roome where I now Lye; my small silver Tankard: Six Silver Spoones, a case of Bottles with all my wearing apparell: (except onely what I have hereby bequeathed unto my Daughter Meddlecott & my Grandchild Susanna Latham:) Item I give and bequeath unto my Grandchild Ann Gray that trunke of Linning that I have alreddy delivered to her and is in her possession and also one Bedstead, Bedd Boulster and Pillows that are in the Chamber over the Hall: Also the sume of ten pounds in mony to be paid unto her within Six months next after my decease: Also my will is that my Executo^{r} shall pay foure pounds in mony pr ann for three yeares unto Mrs Tappin out of the Intrest of my mony now in Goodman Cleares hands for and towards the maintenance of the said

Ann Gray according to my agreem^t with Mrs Tappin: Item I give and bequeath unto Mary Winslow Daughter of my sone Edward Winslow my largest Silver Cupp with two handles: and unto Sarah Daughter of the said Edward my lesser Silver cupp with two handles: Also I give unto my Said Sone Edwards Children Six Silver Spoones to be divided between them: Item I give and bequeath unto my grandchild Parnell Winslow the Sume of five pounds in mony to be improved by my Executo^r untill he come of age: and then paid unto him with the improvem^t Item I give & bequeath unto My grandchild Chilton Latham the sum of five pounds in mony to be improved for him untill he come of Age and then paid to him with the improvem^t Item my will is that the rest of my spoones be divided among my grandchildren according to the discression of My Daughter Middlecott: Item I give unto my Grandchild Mercy Harris my White Rugg: Item I give unto my Grandchild Mary Pollard forty shillings in mony. Item I give unto my grandchild Susanna Latham my Petty Coate with the silke Lace: Item I give unto Mary Winslow Daughter of my Sone Joseph Winslow the Sume of twenty pounds in mony to be paid out of the sume my said Sone Joseph now owes to be improved by my Executo^r for the said Mary and paid unto her when She Shall attaine the Age of eighteene yeares or day of Marriage which of them shall first happen Item I give and bequeath the full remainder of my Estate whatsoever it is or wheresoever it may be found unto my children Namely John Winslow Edward Winslow Joseph Winslow Samuell Winslow: Susanna Latham and Sarah Middlecott to be equally divided betweene them Item I doe hereby nominate constitute authorize and appoint my trusty friend Mr William Tailer of Boston afores^d merchant the Sole Executo^r of this my last Will and testam^t: In Witness whereof I the said Mary Winslow have hereunto set my hand and Seale the daye and yeare first above written

Memorandum I do hereby also Give and bequeath unto Mr Thomas Thacher paster of the third Church in Boston the Sume of five pounds in mony to be pd convenient time after my decease by my Execut^r

Mary M Winslow
her marke (Seal)

Signed Sealed and Published by the above named Mary Winslow as her Last Will & testam^{t} in the presence of us after the adding of foure lines as part of her will

John Ilands
Ffrancis H Hacker
her marke
John Hayward scr

Mr Wm Tailer nominat^{d}. Exec^{r} appeared in Court pr^{o} May: 1679 and renounced his Executorship. to this will.

attests. Js^{a} : Addington Cler.

Jno Hayward and John Ilands made oath before the Honor^{ble}. Simon Bradstreet Esqr Govr and Edwd. Tyng Esqr Assist. 11th July 1679 that they did see m^{rs}. Mary Winslow Signe and Seale and heard her publish this Instrum^{t} to bee her last will and that then Shee was of disposeing minde to their best understanding.

attests. Js^{a} : Addington Cler.

24° July Ann^{o}: 1679.

present.

Simon Bradstreet Esqr. Govr.
Edw. Tyng Esqr.
Joseph Dudley Esqr.
Humphry Davie Esqr.
} Assists

By the Honor^{ble}. Governo^{r}. and magistrates then met in Boston. power of Adm^{con} of all and singular the goods Estate and Credits of m^{rs} Mary Winslow late of Boston Widdow dece^{d} intestate is granted unto John Winslow and Richard Middlecott Merch^{ts} two of her sons in behalfe of themslves and others concerned they giving Security to Administer the s^{d} Estate according to law and the declared minde of the dece^{d} annext and bringing in an Invent^{o} thereof upon Oath as attests. Js^{a} : Addington Cler.

(Bond of Administrators.)

Know all men by these presents that wee John Winslow Richard Middlecott & Elisha Hutchinson all of Boston in New-England merchts are holden and stand firmly bound and obliged unto Edward Tyng Esqr Treasuror for the County of Suffolke in the Sume of ffour hundred pounds To bee paid unto the s[d] Treasuror his Successo[rs] in s[d] Office or Assignes in currant money of New-England To the true payment whereof wee do binde our Selves our heires Exec[rs] Adm[rs] and every of them jointly and severally firmly by these presents. Sealed with our Seales Dated in Boston this 26° July. 1679.

The Condition of this present Obligation is such that if the above bound John Winslow and Richard Middlecott do well and truly Administer all and singular the Estate of their late mother m[rs] Mary Winslow Widdow dece[d] intestate according to Law and the declared minde of the dece[d] and shalbee accountable and responsable for the same unto the County Court for Suffolke when called thereunto then this Obligation to bee void and of no Effect or else to remain in full force and Virtue.

Signed Sealed & Deliv[d].
in presence of
Js[a]: Addington Cler.

John Winslow
Richard Middlecott
Elisha Hutchinson

(INVENTORY.)

Wee whose names are here underwritten, being desired by m[r] John Winslow and m[r] Richard Middlecott, do apprize the Estate of m[rs] Mary Winslow of Boston. dece[d] as followeth. July. 29th. 1679

	£	s	d
To .1. Silver beer Boule. 3£. Two Silver Cups .4£ .10	7	10	—
To .1. small Silver Tankard at 4£ .10. twelve Silver Spoons .6£	10	10	—
To .1. silver caudle Cup with two eares	2	18	—
To .1. small silver Cup at .10[s]. one case wth 9 bottles 12[s].	1	2	—
To .1. silke gowne and petticoate at	6	10	—
To .1. gowne .6. petticoates .1 : pair. body's .1. mantle .1. pair Stockins	3	15	—
To .1. Bed and boulster with fflocks and ffeathers	1	10	—

To .1. close bedsteed .2. coverlits & .2. old blankets .1. old Rugg .1. boulster .3. pillows & .1. p^{r}. curtains & vallents	4	—	—
To .2. Leather Chaires at 10^{s}. one ffeather Bed at 4£ .5	4	15	—
To : 11. old Sheets. at .35^{s}. one diaper Table Cloth .10^{s}	2	5	—
To .3. old ffustian .wastcoats at	—	7	6
To .22. old Napkins .7^{s}. Six Towels .2^{s}.	—	9	—
To .11. pillowbeers	—	11	—
To .6. Shifts at	1	18	6
To .6. white Aprons .18^{s}. Seven . neck handkercheifs 10/6	1	8	6
To .17. Linnen .Caps 8^{s}.6. ffourteen . headbands. 6^{s}.	—	14	6
To .3. Pocket handkercheifs .18^{d}. one Trunke .8^{s}.	—	9	6
To .1. old Chest 4^{s}. one round Table .10^{s}.	—	14	—
To .1. small cupboard 4^{s}. one small . Trunke .18^{d}	—	5	6
To .1 : p^{r}. of small Andirons .4/6. one old warmingpan 3/6	—	8	—
To .2. small brass kettles .15^{s}. one small Iron pot & hookes .6/6	1	1	6
To .1. gridiron .12^{d}. one great wicker chair .7/6	—	8	6
To .1. Close Stoole and a pan	—	6	6
To .1. great elbow chaire . 2/6. one brass candlestick .15^{d}.	—	3	9
To .1. voyder .18^{d}. one Iron. fender. 12^{d}	—	3	6
To .1. old bedsteed	—	3	—
To .3. great pewter dishes and .20. small peices of pewt^{r}	2	16	—
In debts by bills standing out	69	—	—
To one halfe of the house which was formerly m^{r} Joseph Winslows	67	—	—
To .1. Spit. 2/6. one p^{r} brass Scales .4/6	—	7	—
	£ 200 : 09 : 09		

At m^{r} John Winslows House

To .1. Long table and .6. joint Stooles. at	1	6	—
To .1 : p^{r}. small brass Andirons	—	16	—

To .1. old cupboard .7^{s}. one pothanger Iron Skillet and one .p^{a}. of Andirons .9^{s}.	—	16	—
To .9. Leather Chairs .36^{s}. one Bedsteed . 6^{s}	2	2	—
To .1. standing cupboard .20^{s}. one great Chest .10^{s}.	1	10	—
To .1. small table .8^{s}. two small bedsteeds .2^{s}.	—	10	—
To .3. chaires without Leathers .6^{s}. one p^{r}. ffire Irons. 3/6.	—	9	6
To .1. Scotch. blanket .5^{s}. one p^{r}. old striped stuffe curtains	—	6	—
To .1. woosted Rugg .18^{s}. one small ffeather pillow .3^{s}.	1	1	—
To .12. p^{s}. of pewter and .6. plates	2	15	—
To .1. old Trunke	—	5	6
	£212 :	11 :	9

Witness o^{r} hands

John Conney. Jarvis Ballard.

m^{r} Jno Winslow and m^{r} Richd Middlecott admitted Adm^{rs}. made oath in Court .2°. Augt. 1679. to the truth of this Inventory and w^{n}. more doth. appeare to discover it.

Js^{a}. Addington Cler.

THE MAYFLOWER COMPACT.

The Compact was drawn up and signed on board the Mayflower, 21 November, 1620 (11 November, old style).

The following copy, with the introduction, is taken literally from Bradford's "History," which does not give the names of those who signed the original document.

The earliest known list of the signers is that contained in Nathaniel Morton's "New England's Memorial," published in 1669. In the first edition of that book the names are arranged in the order here given, three columns of seven names each at the bottom of the page, and the others in three columns at the top of the next page. The line dividing the columns in the list appended indicates the bottom of the page in the "Memorial."

The remainder of An^o: 1620

I shall a litle returne backe, and begine with a combination made by them before they came ashore; being ye first foundation of their govermente in this place. Occasioned partly by ye discontented, and mutinous speeches that some of the strangers amongst them, had let fall from them in ye ship; That when they came ashore they would use their owne libertie; for none had power to comand them, the patente they had being for Virginia, and not for Newengland, which belonged to another goverment with which ye Virginia Company had nothing to doe. And partly that shuch an Acte by them done (this their condition considered) might be as firme as any patent; and in some respects more sure.

The forme was as followeth: —

In ye name of God Amen. We whose names are underwriten, the loyall subjects of our dread soveraigne lord King James, by ye grace of God, of great Britaine, Franc, & Ireland king, defender of ye faith, &c.

Haveing undertaken, for ye glorie of God, and advancemente of ye christian faith and honour of our king & countrie, a voyage to plant ye first colonie in ye Northerne parts of Virginia. Doe by these presents solemnly & mutualy in ye presence of God, and one of another; covenant, & combine our selves togeather into a civill body politick; for our better ordering, & preservation & furtherance of ye ends aforesaid; and by vertue hearof to enacte, constitute, and frame shuch just & equall lawes, ordinances, Acts, constitutions, & offices, from time to time, as shall be thought most meete & convenient for ye generall good of ye Colonie: unto which we promise all due submission and obedience. In witnes wherof we have hereunder subscribed our names at Cap-Codd y^e .11. of November, in ye year of ye raigne of our soveraigne lord king James of England, France, & Ireland ye eighteenth, and of Scotland ye fiftie fourth. Ano: Dom. 1620.

John Carver*	Samuel Fuller	Edward Tilley*
William Bradford	Christopher Martin*	John Tilley*
Edward Winslow	William Mullins*	Francis Cooke
William Brewster	William White*	Thomas Rogers*
Isaac Allerton	Richard Warren	Thomas Tinker*
Myles Standish	John Howland	John Ridgdale*
John Alden	Stephen Hopkins	Edward Fuller*
John Turner*	Degory Priest*	Richard Clarke*
Francis Eaton	Thomas Williams*	Richard Gardiner
James Chilton*	Gilbert Winslow	John Allerton*
John Crackston*	Edmund Margeson*	Thomas English*
John Billington	Peter Brown	Edward Doty
Moses Fletcher*	Richard Britteridge*	Edward Leister
John Goodman*	George Soule	

* Died the first year.

PILGRIM ANNIVERSARIES.

As the Pilgrims used "old style" in writing their dates, it is necessary to change them to "new style" in order to determine the anniversary of any event.

The following table gives the proper dates on which to celebrate the principal events which occurred before the end of the year 1621: —

August 15.	Sailed from Southampton, England.	1620
September 16.	Sailed from Plymouth, England.	1620
November 16.	William Butten died at sea.	1620
November 19.	First sighted Cape Cod.	1620
November 21.	Signed "The Compact." Anchored in Cape Cod Harbor and went ashore.	1620
November 23.	Took the shallop ashore for repairs.	1620
November 25.	First exploring party set out by land.	1620
November 26.	Discovered Truro Springs, Pamet River, Cornhill.	1620
December 7.	Second exploring party set out with the shallop.	1620
December 10.	Found the wigwams, graves, etc.	1620
December 14.	Edward Thomson died. *The first death after reaching Cape Cod.*	1620

December 16.	Third exploring party set out with the shallop.	
	Jasper More died.	1620
December 17.	Dorothy (May) Bradford died.	1620
December 18.	James Chilton died.	
	First encounter with the Indians.	
	Reached Clark's Island at night.	1620
December 20.	Third exploring party spent the Sabbath on Clark's Island.	1620
December 21.	FOREFATHERS' DAY. Third exploring party landed on Plymouth Rock, and explored the coast.	1620
December 25.	The Mayflower set sail from Cape Cod for Plymouth, but was driven back by a change in the wind.	1620
December 26.	The Mayflower arrived at Plymouth Harbor.	1620
December 27.	First Sabbath passed by the whole company in Plymouth Harbor.	1620
December 28.	A party landed and explored by land.	1620
December 29.	One party explored by land, and another in the shallop. Discovered Jones River.	1620
December 30.	Decided to settle near what is now Burial Hill.	1620
December 31.	Richard Britteridge died. *The first death after reaching Plymouth.*	1620
January 2.	Began to gather materials for building.	1621
January 3.	Solomon Prower died.	1621
January 7.	Divided the company into nineteen families and laid out lots.	1621
January 11.	Degory Priest died.	1621
January 14.	Myles Standish with a party discovered wigwams, but saw no Indians.	1621
January 18.	Christopher Martin died.	1621
January 22.	Peter Brown and John Goodman lost themselves in the woods.	1621
January 24.	The thatch on the commonhouse burned.	1621

January 29.	Began to build their storehouse.	1621
January 31.	Kept their meeting on land.	1621
February 8.	Rose Standish died.	1621
February 19.	The house for the sick people caught fire.	1621
February 26.	Indians carried off tools left in the woods by Myles Standish and Francis Cooke.	1621
February 27.	Had a meeting to establish military orders, and chose Myles Standish Captain.	1621
March 3.	Got the great guns mounted on the hill. William White, William Mullins, and two others died.	1621
March 7.	Mary (Norris) Allerton died.	1621
March 17.	Sowed some garden seeds.	1621
March 26.	Had another meeting about military orders, but were interrupted by the coming of Samoset.	1621
March 28.	Samoset came again, with five others.	1621
March 31.	Another meeting about laws and orders, interrupted by coming of Indians. The carpenter fitted the shallop " to fetch all from aboord."	1621
April 1.	Another meeting for public business, interrupted by the coming of Samoset and Squanto to announce Massasoit, with whom a treaty was made.	1621
April 2.	The laws and orders concluded. John Carver chosen Governor for the ensuing year.	1621
April 3.	Elizabeth (Barker) Winslow, wife of Edward Winslow, died.	1621
April 12.	Governor Carver certified a copy of the will of William Mullins, which was carried back to England on the Mayflower.	1621
May 22.	Edward Winslow and Susanna (Fuller) White married. *The first marriage in the colony.*	1621

July 12.	Stephen Hopkins and Edward Winslow set out to visit Massasoit.	1621
July 13.	They reached Sowams, and were welcomed by Massasoit.	1621
August 24.	Captain Standish set out for Namasket, with a party of armed men, to revenge the supposed death of Squanto.	1621
September 28.	Captain Standish set out with nine men, and Squanto and three other Indians, to visit the Massachusetts.	1621
September 30.	Landed at Squantum, in Quincy.	1621
November 20.	The Fortune arrived.	1621
December 23.	The Fortune set sail on her return to England.	1621

THE WILL OF GYLES HOPKINS.

Communicated by MISS MARY G. HINCKLEY, of Barnstable, Mass.

This will was recorded in the Probate Records of Barnstable County, at Barnstable, Mass., and is found in Volume I, page 32.

As the Codicil was signed 15 March, 1689 (new style), and the will was admitted to probate 26 April, 1690 (new style), the death of Gyles Hopkins must have occurred between these two dates.

The will follows:

To all Christian people to whome these presents shall com know y[e] that I Giles Hopkins of Eastham being sick and weak of Body and yet of perfit memory do declare this as my Last will and Testament on this ninteenth day of January in y[e] year of our Lord 1682

I bequeath my Body to y[e] grave in decent burial when this Temporal Life of mine shall have an end and my soul to god that gave it in hopes of a blessed Resurection at y[e] Last day

2ly my will is that my son Stephen Hopkins shall possess and Injoy all my upland and meadow Lying and being at Satuckit that is to say all my upland and meadow on y[e]

southerly side of ye bounds of ye Towne of eastham that is to say all my Right and title Intrest and claime to all those Lands from ye head of Namescakit to ye southermost part of ye long pond where mannomoyet cart way goes over to Satuckit and from thence to ye head of manomoyet river and so as our Line shall run over to ye south sea all ye Lands between thos bounds and ye westermost bounds of ye purchesers at satuckit river all these Lands I give unto my son Stephen Hopkins and to his heirs forever: and half my stock of cattill for and in consideration of ye above sd Land and half stock of cattel my will is that after my decease my son Stephen Hopkins shall take ye care and oversight and maintaine my son William Hopkins during his natural Life in a comfortable decent manner.

3ly my will is that all my Lands at Palmet both purchesed and unpurchesed both meadows and upland and all my Lands at Pochet and my third part of Samsons neck and what other Lands shall fall unto me as a purcheser from ye fore mentioned Bounds of my son Stephen Hopkinses Lands and potanomacot all these fore specified Lands I give unto my sons Caleb and Joshua Hopkins to be equaly devided between them: further my will is that if either of my sons Joshua or Caleb Hopkins dye having no Issew that then these Lands which I have given them to be equally devided between them fall to him that surviveth.

4ly. I give unto my wife Catorne Hopkins and to my son William Hopkins the improvment of too acres of meadow Lying at ye head of Rock Harbor during my wifes Life and ye one half of that too acres I give unto my son william during his Life and after ye decease of and after ye decease of my wife and son william I do give this above sd too acres of meadow to my son Joshua Hopkins and his heirs forever: as also after my decease I give unto my son Joshua Hopkins a parcel of meadow Lying at ye mouth of Rock Harbor according to ye bounds thereof specified in ye Towne Records of Lands: it I give unto my son Caleb Hopkins a parcel of meadow Lying at Little Nameskeket according to ye bounds thereof specified in ye Towne Book of Records of Lands.

It I give unto my wife my now dwelling House and halfe my Land and halfe my orchard that is by my house: by Land I mean half my Land that is about my house both fenced and unfenced during my wifes natural Life, and then ye abovesd housing and Lands to fall unto my son Joshua Hopkins; the other half of my Land and orchard I give to my son Joshua Hopkins after my death that is to say ye other half of my Lands Liying about my house.

It. I give unto my son Caleb Hopkins one pair of plow Irons.

It. I give unto my son Joshua Hopkins one payer of plow Irons.

It. I give unto my son Joshua Hopkins my carte and wheels.

It. I give unto my wife ye other half of my stock and moveables I say to my wife and my son William or what parte of ye moveables my wife shall see cause to bestow on my son William Hopkins.

It. I do appoint my son Stephen Hopkins to be my true and Lawful executor of this my Last will and testament to pay what is payable and Receive what is due.

And to ye truth and verity hereof I have hereunto sett my hand and seal ye day and year above written.

Signed and sealed in
presence of us, ye mark of
Jonathan Sparrow. Giles H Hopkins (seal)
Samuel Knowles.

Jonathan Sparrow and Samuel Knowles witnesses to this will made oath in Court ye: 16th: of April 1690 that they saw ye above sd Giles Hopkins signe seal and declare this to be his Last will and Testament.

Attest Joseph Lothrop. Clerk.

I ye abovesd Giles Hopkins do declare where as by ye providence of God my Life has been prolonged unto me and by Reason of age and disabillity of Body I am Incapatiated to provide for my owne support and my wifes, my will further is that my son Stephen Hopkins from this time and forward shall possess and Injoy all my stock and moveable estate provided he take effectual care for mine and my wifes Comfortable Support during our natural Lives witness my hand and seal this fifth day of march $168\frac{8}{9}$.

Witness Mark Snow Giles H (his mark) Hopkins (seal)
Jonath Sparrow.

The within mentioned Mark Snow and Jonathan Sparrow made oath in Court April y^e : 16 : 1690 that they saw Giles Hopkins within mentioned signe seal and declare y^e latter part of this will within mentioned to be his Last will and Testament. Attest. Joseph Lothrop, Clerk.

Duly Compared with the original and entered April y^e : 22 : 1690. Attest. Joseph Lothrop, Recorder.

THE WILL OF PEREGRINE WHITE.

Communicated by HERVEY N. P. HUBBARD, Curator and Librarian of the Pilgrim Society, Plymouth, Mass.

The original will of Peregrine White is in the collection at Pilgrim Hall, Plymouth, Mass. It is loaned to the Pilgrim Society by the courtesy of Mr. William T. Davis, to whom it belongs, and who has allowed it to be photographed for this magazine. The will is written on paper twelve by fifteen inches in size, and is well preserved. It was probated August 14, 1707,* and recorded in Book 2, page 48, Nathaniel Thomas being Judge of probate at that time. The copy is made from the original will.

The fourteenth day of July Anno Domini one thousand seven hundred and four.

I Peregrine White of Marshfield in ye County of Plimouth in New England Being aged and under many Weaknesses and Bodily Infirmities But of Sound disposing mind and memory praises be Rendered to Almighty God therefore yet in dayly Expectation of my Great Change Do therefore hereby make and Declare this my last Will and Testament hereby Revoking and making null any former Will or Wils by me heretofore made and declare this to be my last Will and Testament and no other —

Imprimis I Humbly Commit my Soul to Almighty God that Gave it and my Body to decent Buriall when it Shall Please him to take me hence And Touching my Worldly Estate which it hath pleased the Lord to Bless me with my Will and meaning is that y^e same Shall be Imployed and dis-

*1704 is the correct date.

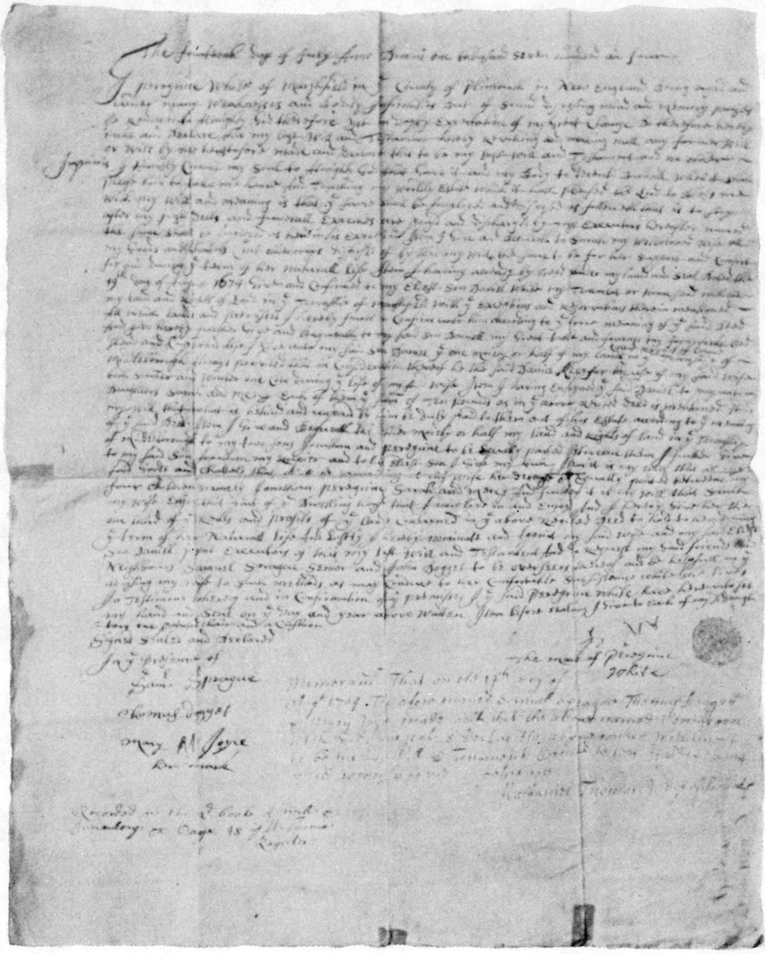
Recorded in the 2d book of wills & Inventorys on Page 18 ...

The mark of Peregrine White

Samuel Sprague

Thomas Doggett

Mary M Joyce her mark

posed as followeth that is to say after my just debts and funerall expenses are payd and discharged by my Executors hearafter named the same shall be Imployed as herein is expressed Item I Give and Bequeath to Sarah my welbeloved Wife all my Goods and Chattels not otherways disposed of by this my Will the same to be for her Support and Comfort for and during ye term of her naturall Life. Item I having already by Deed under my hand and Seal Dated the 19th day of August 1674 Given and Confirmed to my Eldest Son Daniel White my Tenement or Homestead with other my land and Rights of Land in ye Township of Marshfield with ye Exceptions and Reservations therein mentioned — All which lands and premisses I hereby further Confirm unto him according to ye true meaning of ye said Deed And I do hereby further Give and Bequeath to my said Son Daniell my Great table and fourms my Joynworke Bedstead and Cupboard Also I Give unto my said Son Daniel ye one moiety or half of my lands and Rights of land in ye Township of Middleborough Always provided that in Consideration thereof he the said Daniel Keep for the use of my said wife both Sumer and Winter one Cow during ye life of my said wife Item I having enjoyned ye said Daniel to pay unto my Daughters Sarah and Mercy each of them ye sum of Ten pounds as in ye above Recited Deed is mentioned. It is my will that what is behind and unpaid by him be duly paid to them out of his Estate according to ye meaning of ye said Deed. Item I Give and Bequeath the other moiety or half my land and Rights of land in ye Township of Middleborough to my two sons Jonathan and Peregrine to be equally parted betweene them I further Give to my said son Jonathan my Rapier and to his Eldest son I Give my Gun. Item It is my will that all my said Goods and Chattels that shall be remaining at my wife her decease be Equally parted betweene my four children namely Jonathan Peregrine Sarah and Mercy And further it is my will that Sarah my wife enjoy that part of ye Dwelling house that I now live in and enjoy And I hereby Give her the one third of ye Rents and profits of ye lands contayned in ye above Recited Deed to hold to her during ye term of her Naturall life And lastly I hereby nominate and Appoint my said Wife and my said Eldest Son Daniel joynt Executors of this my last Will and Testament And do Request my Good friends and Neighbours Samuel Sprague Senior and John Dogget to be overseers thereof and be helpfull in ye advising my wife to such methods as may conduce to her comfortable subsistance while she lives In Testimony whereof and in confirmation of ye promisses I ye said Peregrine White have hereunto set my hand and seal on ye Day and year above Written. Item before sealing I Give to Each of my sd Daughters one painted chair and a cushion.

Signed sealed and Declared **P W** (Seal)
In ye Presence of The mark of Peregrine White

Saml Sprague
Thomas Dogget
Mary **M** Joyce
her mark.

Memorand That on the 14th day of Augt 1704 The afore named Samuell Sprague Thomas Doggett & Mary Joyce made oath that the above named Perregreen White did signe seale & Declare the above written Instrument to be his last Will & Testament & that he was of Disposeing mind when he so did before me

Nathaniel Thomas
Judge of Probate

Recorded in the 2^d^ booke of wills &
Inventorys &c. Page 48 pr N Thomas
Register

THE DIVISION OF CATTLE IN 1627.

The oldest volume of the Plymouth Colony Records is entitled

"Plimouths great Book of Deeds of Lands
Enrolled : from An^{o} 1627 to An^{o} 1651 :"

On pages 50–57 of this book is entered the record of the Division of the Cattle which was made June 1, 1627, new style. This record is of great value to students of Pilgrim genealogy, as it contains the names of all members of the Pilgrim families in Plymouth on that date, including even Jonathan Brewster's little daughter Mary, born but five weeks before.*

It will be noted that forty-two of the ninety-nine persons who reached Plymouth on the Mayflower were still living there.

1627. }

At a publique court held the 22th of May it was concluded by the whole Companie, that the cattell wch were the Companies, to wit, the Cowes & the Goates should be equally devided to all the psonts of the same company & soe kept untill the expiration of ten yeares after the date above written. & that every one should well and sufficiently pvid for there owne pt under penalty of forfeiting the same.

That the old stock with halfe th increase should remaine for comon use to be devided at thend of the said terme or otherwise as ocation falleth out, & the other halfe to be their owne for ever.

* MAYFLOWER DESCENDANT, Vol. I, p. 7.

Uppon wch agreement they were equally devided by lotts soe as the burthen of keeping the males then beeing should be borne for common use by those to whose lot the best Cowes should fall & so the lotts fell as followeth. thirteene psonts being pportioned to one lot.

1 The first lot fell to ffrancis Cooke* & his Companie Joyned to him his wife Hester Cooke
3 John Cooke*
4 Jacob Cooke
5 Jane Cooke
6 Hester Cooke
7 Mary Cooke
8 Moses Simonson
9 Phillip Delanoy
10 Experience Michaell
11 John ffance
12 Joshua Pratt
13 Phinihas Pratt

To this lot fell the least of the 4 black Heyfers Came in the Jacob, and two shee goats.

2 The second lot fel to M[r] Isaac Allerton* & his Companie ioyned to him his wife ffeare Allerton.
3 Bartholomew Allerton*
4 Remember Allerton*
5 Mary Allerton*
6 Sarah Allerton
7 Godber Godberson
8 Sarah Godberson
9 Samuell Godberson
10 Marra Priest
11 Sarah Priest
12 Edward Bumpasse
13 John Crakstone*

To this lot fell the Greate Black cow came in the Ann to which they must keepe the lesser of the two steers, and two shee goats.

3 The third lot fell to Capt Standish* & his companie Joyned to him his wife
2 Barbara Standish

To this lot fell the

* Came in the Mayflower.

3 Charles Standish
4 Allexander Standish
5 John Standish
6 Edward Winslow*
7 Susanna Winslow*
8 Edward Winslow
9 John Winslow
10 Resolved White*
11 Perigrine White*
12 Abraham Peirce
13 Thomas Clarke

Red Cow wch belongeth to the poore of the Colonye to wch they must keepe her Calfe of this yeare being a Bull for the Companie. Also to this lott Came too she goats.

4 The fourth lot fell to John Howland* & his company Joyned to him his wife
2 Elizabeth Howland*
3 John Howland Junor
4 Desire Howland
5 William Wright
6 Thomas Morton Junor
7 John Alden*
8 Prissilla Alden*
9 Elizabeth Alden
10 Clemont Briggs
11 Edward Dolton*
12 Edward Holdman
13 Joh. Alden

To this lot fell one of the 4 heyfers Came in the Jacob Called Raghorne.

5 The fift lot fell to Mr Willm Brewster* & his companie Joyned to him
2 Love Brewster*
3 Wrestling Brewster*
4 Richard More*
5 Henri Samson*
6 Johnathan Brewster
7 Lucrecia Brewster
8 Willm Brewster
9 Mary Brewster
10 Thomas Prince

To this lot ffell one of the fower Heyfers Came in the Jacob Caled the Blind Heyfer & 2 shee goats.

* Came in the Mayflower.

11 Pacience Prince
12 Rebecka Prince
13 Humillyty Cooper*

6 The sixt lott fell to John Shaw & his companie Joyned
1 to him
2 John Adams
3 Eliner Adams
4 James Adams
5 John Winslow
6 Mary Winslow*
7 Willm Basset
8 Elizabeth Bassett
9 Willyam Basset Junor
10 Elyzabeth Basset Junor
11 ffrancis Sprage
12 Anna Sprage
13 Mercye Sprage

To this lot fell the lesser of the black Cowes Came at first in the Ann wth which they must keepe the bigest of the 2 steers. Also to this lott was two shee goats.

7 The seaventh lott fell to Stephen Hopkins* & his companie Joyned to him his wife
2 Elizabeth Hopkins*
3 Gyles Hopkins*
4 Caleb Hopkins
5 Debora Hopkins
6 Nickolas Snow
7 Constance Snow*
8 Willam Pallmer
9 ffrances Pallmer
10 Willm Pallmer Jnor
11 John Billington Senor*
12 Hellen Billington*
13 ffrancis Billington*

To this lott fell A Black weining Calfe to wch was aded the Calfe of this yeare to come of the black Cow, wch fell to John Shaw & his Companie, wch pveing a bull they were to keepe it ungelt 5 yeares for common use & after to make there best of it. Nothing belongeth of thes too, for ye copanye of ye first stock: but only halfe ye Increase.

* Came in the Mayflower.

To this lott ther fell two shee goats: which goats they posses on the like terms which others doe their cattell.

8 The eaight lott fell to Samuell ffuller* & his company
Joyned to him his wife
2 Bridgett ffuller
3 Samuell ffuller Junior
4 Peeter Browne*
5 Martha Browne
6 Mary Browne
7 John fford
8 Martha fford
9 Anthony Anable
10 Jane Anable
11 Sara Anable
12 Hanah Anable
13 Damaris Hopkins*

To this lott fell A Red Heyfer Came of the Cow w[ch] belongeth to the poore of the Colony & so is of that Consideration. (viz[t]) thes psonts nominated, to have halfe the Increace, the other halfe, with the ould stock, to remain for the use of the poore.

To this lott also two shee goats.

9 The ninth lot fell to Richard Warren* & his companie
Joyned wth him his wife
2 Elizabeth Warren
3 Nathaniell Warren
4 Joseph Warren
5 Mary Warren
6 Anna Warren
7 Sara Warren
8 Elizabeth Warren
9 Abigall Warren
10 John Billington*
11 George Sowle*
12 Mary Sowle
13 Zakariah Sowle

To this lott fell one of the 4 black Heyfers that came in the Jacob caled the smooth horned Heyfer and two shee goats.

*Came in the Mayflower.

10 The tenth lot fell to ffrancis Eaton* & those Joyned wth him his wife
2 Christian Eaton
3 Samuell Eaton*
4 Rahell Eaton
5 Stephen Tracie
6 Triphosa Tracie
7 Sarah Tracie
8 Rebecka Tracie
9 Ralph Wallen
10 Joyce Wallen
11 Sarah Morton
12 Robert Bartlet
13 Tho : Prence.

To this lott ffell an heyfer of the last yeare called the white belyd heyfer & two shee goats.

11 The eleventh lott ffell to the Governo[r] M[r] William Bradford* and those with him, to wit, his wife
2 Alles Bradford and
3 William Bradford, Junior
4 Mercy Bradford
5 Joseph Rogers*
6 Thomas Cushman
7 William Latham*
8 Manases Kempton
9 Julian Kempton
10 Nathaniel Morton
11 John Morton
12 Ephraim Morton
13 Patience Morton

To this lott fell An heyfer of the last yeare w[ch] was of the Greate white back cow that was brought over in the Ann, & two shee goats.

12 The twelveth lott fell to John Jene & his companie joyned to him, his wife
2 Sarah Jene
3 Samuell Jene
4 Abigall Jene
5 Sara Jene
6 Robert Hickes
7 Margret Hickes

To this lott fell the greate white backt cow w[ch] was brought over with the first in the Ann, to w[ch] cow the

* Came in the Mayflower.

8 Samuell Hickes
9 Ephraim Hickes
10 Lidya Hickes
11 Phebe Hickes
12 Stephen Deane
13 Edward Banges

keepeing of the bull was joyned for thes psonts to pvide for.

heere also two shee goats.

1627, May the 22. It was farther agreed at the same Court: That if anie of the cattell should by acsident miscarie or be lost or Hurt: that the same should be taken knowledg of by Indifferent men: and Judged whether the losse came by the neglegence or default of those betrusted and if they were found faulty, that then such should be forced to make satisfaction for the companies, as also their partners dammage:

THE DATE OF GOVERNOR BRADFORD'S PASSENGER LIST.

BY GEORGE ERNEST BOWMAN.

To the question, "When did Governor Bradford write his list of the Mayflower passengers?" the reply heretofore has been, "In 1650."

Such an answer seemed too indefinite, in regard to the record which is the foundation of all Mayflower genealogies, and I undertook to determine more closely, if possible, the time within which it must have been written. The success of the effort was greater than I expected, and the time has been reduced from one year to four weeks, as will be shown in the following notes.

In studying the records left by the Pilgrims it is necessary to keep constantly in mind the fact that they used "old style" dating, and that, according to their calendar, the year 1650 began on the twenty-fifth day of March, and ended on the twenty-fourth day of the following March.

Governor Bradford leaves no opportunity for doubt that he wrote his account of the Mayflower passengers during the year 1650, "old style," for, near the middle of the list, he writes "till this year .1650," and, in the last paragraph, "this present year .1650." * The list, therefore, must have been written before March 24, 1650, old style, that is, before April 3, 1651, new style.

Turning again to Bradford's History we find: "And seeing it hath pleased him to give me to see .30. years compleated, since these beginings. And that the great works of his providence are to be observed. I have thought it not unworthy my paines, to take a veiw of the decreasings, & Increasings of these persons, and such changs as hath pased over them, & theirs, in this thirty years." †

As Bradford distinctly says that thirty years have been "compleated, since these beginings," it is clear that he must have written this paragraph after the thirtieth anniversary of the Landing of the Pilgrims, that is, after December 21, 1650, new style. Thus Governor Bradford's own statements, in his account of the passengers, limit the time within which it was written to the three and one half months between December 21, 1650, and April 3, 1651, new style.

Continuing the investigation, a statement in the account of Elder Brewster's family attracted my attention. After mentioning the Elder and his wife, Bradford writes: "His sone Wrastle dyed a yonge man unmaried; his sone Love, lived till this year .1650. and dyed, & left .4. children, now living." ‡

As the exact date of Love Brewster's death is not known, I examined the probate records at Plymouth, and found that his will was dated October 11, 1650, new style, and his inventory was taken, by William Collier (his father-in-law) and Myles Standish, February 10, 1651, new style.§ The latter date is important, because the Pilgrims usually took an inventory of a man's property within a very few days after his death,¶ and as Love Brewster's inventory was not taken until the tenth of February, it is probable that he died very late in January, or even after the first of February. This

* MAYFLOWER DESCENDANT, Vol. I, pp. 12, 16. † Ibid. p. 11.

‡ Ibid. Vol. I, p. 12.

§ Plym. Col. Prob. Records, Vol. I, p. 89.

¶ The inventory of Henry Samson's property was taken on the day of his death.

would reduce to less than two and one half months the time within which the list could have been written.

After studying without results the other references to the deaths of the passengers, attention was turned to the children and grandchildren mentioned by Bradford, and in his account of the family of William Mullins was found the following statement: "Only his dougter priscila survied, and maried with John Alden, who are both living, and have .11. children. And their eldest daughter is maried & hath five children." *

John Alden's eldest daughter Elizabeth married on December 26, 1644, old style, William Pabodie, who was for many years the town clerk of Duxbury. While holding this office William Pabodie entered on the town records his own marriage, and the births of his children. The names of these children and the dates of their births I have copied directly from thc original record made by their father: John, October 4, 1645; Elizabeth, April 24, 1647; Mary, August 7, 1648 †; Mercy, January 2, 1649†; Martha, February 24, 1650; Priscilla, November 16, 1652 †; Priscilla, January 15, 1653 †; Sarah, August 7, 1656; Ruth, June 27, 1658; Rebecca, October 16, 1660; Hannah, October 15, 1662; William, November 24, 1664; Lydia, April 3, 1667.

It will be seen that the fifth child was Martha, who was born February 24, 1650, "old style," or March 6, 1651, "new style," and Bradford must have learned of her birth before he wrote: "And their eldest daughter is maried & hath five children."

It has therefore been demonstrated that Governor Bradford wrote his account of the Mayflower passengers and their "decreasings, & Increasings" during the four weeks between March 6, 1651, and April 3, 1651, both dates being in "new style."

* MAYFLOWER DESCENDANT, Vol. I, p. 13.

† Those not familiar with the difference between "old style" and "new style" dating will, doubtless, think it impossible that Mary should have been born August 7, 1648, and Mercy, January 2, 1649; but when we change these dates to "new style" they become respectively August 17, 1648, and January 12, 1650, and the apparent contradiction disappears. So in the case of the two children named Priscilla. The first one was born November 26, 1652, new style, and evidently died soon, for the next child, a girl, was born January 25, 1654, new style, and was also named Priscilla.

THE DIVISION OF LAND.

As the record of the division of the lands in 1623 is of interest to every Mayflower Descendant, it seems best to put it within reach of all. The text given follows that in Volume XII of the "Records of the Colony of New Plymouth," published in 1861, by the Commonwealth of Massachusetts. The paging of the *original record* is indicated in the margin.

[p. 1] The meersteads & garden plotes of (*worn*) which came first layd out 1620.

The north side		The south side
		Peeter Brown
		John Goodman
		Mr Wm Brewster
		high way
	the streete	John Billington
		Mr Isaak Allerton
		Francies Cooke
		Edward Winslow.

[p. 4] The Falles of their grounds which came first over in the May-Floure, according as thier lotes were cast .1623.

Robart Cochman	1	the number
Mr William Brewster	6	(*worn*) akers
William Bradford	3	to (*worn*) one

these lye on the South side of the brooke to the baywards.	Richard Gardener	I
	Frances Cooke	2
	George Soule	I
	Mr Isaak Alerton	7
	John Billington	3
	Peter Browen	I
	Samuell ffuller	2
	Joseph Rogers	2

these containe .29. akers.

These lye one the South side of the brook to the woodward opposite to the former.	John Howland	4
	Steven Hobkins	6
	Edward	I
	Edward	I
	Gilbard Winslow	I
	Samuell ffuller Juneor	3

these containe .16. akers besids Hobamaks ground which lyeth betwene Jo: Howlands & Hobkinses.

this .5. akers lyeth behind the forte to the litle ponde.	William White	5
these lye one the north side of the towne next adjoyning to their gardens which came in the Fortune.	Edward Winslow	4
	Richard Warren	(*worn*)
	John Goodman	(*worn*)
	John Crackston	(*worn*)
	John Alden	(*worn*)
	Marie Chilton	(*worn*)
[p. 5]	Captin Myles Standish	2
	Francis Eaton	4
	Henerie Samson	I
	Humillitie Cooper	I

[p. 6] The fales of their grounds which came in the Fortune according as their lots were cast 1623.

This ship came Novr 1621.

these lye to the sea, eastward.

These lye beyond the f(*worn*) brook to the wood we(*worn*) ward.

William Hilton	1
John Winslow	1
William Coner	1
John Adams	1
William Tench & John Cannon	2

these folowing lye beyond the .2. brooke.

Hugh Statie	1
William Beale & Thomas Cushman	2
Austen Nicolas	1
Widow Foord	4
	15. akers.

William Wright & William Pitt	2
Robart Hickes	1
Thomas Prence	1
Steven Dean	1
Moses Simonson & Philipe de la Noye	2
Edward Bompass	1
Clemente Brigges	1
James Steward	1
William Palmer	2
Jonathan Brewster	1
Benet Morgan	1
Thomas Flavell & his son,	2
Thomas Morton	1
William Bassite	2
	19. akers.

[p. 10] The fales of their grounds which came over in the shipe called the Anne according as their were cast .1623.

these to the sea eastward.

	Akers		ak(*worn*)
James Rande	1	Francis Spragge	3

these following lye beyond the brooke to Strawberie-hill.

Edmond Flood	1
Christopher Connant	1
Francis Cooke	4
Edward Burcher	2
John Jenings	5
goodwife Flavell	1
Manasseh & John Fance	2

these but against the swampe & reed-ponde

George Morton & Experience Michell	8
Christian Penn	1
Thomas Morton Junior	1
William Hiltons wife & .2. children	3

this goeth in wth a corner by ye ponde.

Allice Bradford	1
Robart Hickes his wife & children	4
Brigett Fuller	1
Ellen Newton	1
Pacience & Fear Brewster wth Robart Long	3

William Heard	1
Mrs Standish	1

These following lye on the other side of the towne towards the eele-river.

Marie Buckett adioyning to Joseph Rogers	1
Mr Ouldom & those joyned with him	10
Cudbart Cudbartsone	6
Anthony Anable	4
Thomas Tilden	3
Richard Waren	5
Bangs	4

Robart Rattlife beyonde the swampie & stonie ground	(*worn*)
These butt against Hobes Hole.	
Nicolas Snow	(*worn*)
Anthony Dixe	(*worn*)
Mr Perces .2. Ser :	(*worn*)
Ralfe Walen	(*worn*)

[p. 11] South side

Steph : Tracy three acres	3
Tho. Clarke one acre	1
Robt. Bartlet one acre	1

North side.

Edw : Holman 1. acre	.1
ffrances wife to Wil Palmer	.1. acre
Josuah Prat & Phineas Prat	2

THE WILL OF WILLIAM MULLINS.

WITH NOTES BY GEORGE ERNEST BOWMAN.

The will of William Mullins was communicated to the New England Historical and Genealogical Register (Vol. XLII, p. 62) by Henry F. Waters, A.M., in his "Genealogical Gleanings in England," and the text there given has been followed.

The will was made after the arrival of the Pilgrims in New England (then considered a part of Virginia), otherwise the words "Allsoe if my sonne William will come to Virginia" could not have been used, and, as it was evidently a nuncupative will, it was probably written 21 February, 1620, old style, the day of William Mullins' death. The date "2 : April 1621" must therefore refer to the day on which was made the copy carried back to England on the Mayflower. This date is of especial interest, as it establishes beyond question the fact that the Mayflower did not leave Plymouth, on the return voyage, until 2 April 1621 (old style), or later.

The probate record, made 23 July 1621, proves that the former residence of William Mullins was at Dorking, in the County of Surrey, and that he had left behind, in England, a married daughter, Sarah (Mullins) Blunden, who was appointed administratrix by the court. From the will we learn that his wife's given name was Alice, and that his eldest son, William, was left in England, also that the widow, Alice (——) Mullins, and her son Joseph were alive when the Mayflower sailed, as otherwise Governor Carver, in forwarding the copy of the will to be probated, would have annexed a statement of the death of these two legatees.

The second witness, Giles Heale, was the ship's surgeon and Christopher Jones was probably the captain of the Mayflower.

2: April 1621.

In the name of God Amen: I comit my soule to God that gave it and my bodie to the earth from whence it came. Alsoe I give my goodes as followeth That fforty poundes in the hand of goodman Woodes I give my wife tenn poundes, my sonne Joseph tenn poundes, my daughter Priscilla tenn poundes, and my eldest sonne tenn poundes Alsoe I give to my eldest sonne all my debtes, bonds, bills (onelye yt forty poundes excepted in the handes of goodman Wood) given as aforesaid wth all the stock in his owne handes. To my eldest daughter I give ten shillinges to be paied out of my sonnes stock Furthermore that goodes I have in Virginia as followeth To my wife Alice halfe my goodes & to Joseph and Priscilla the other halfe equallie to be devided betweene them. Alsoe I have xxj dozen of shoes, and thirteene paire of bootes wch I give into the Companies handes for forty poundes at seaven years and if thy like them at that rate. If it be thought to deare as my Overseers shall thinck good And if they like them at that rate at the divident I shall have nyne shares whereof I give as followeth twoe to my wife, twoe to my sonne William, twoe to my sonne Joseph, twoe to my daughter Priscilla, and one to the Companie. Allsoe if my sonne William will come to Virginia I give him my share of land furdermore I give to my twoe Overseers Mr John Carver and Mr Williamson, twentye shillinges apeece to see this my will performed desiringe them that he would have an eye over my wife and children to be as fathers and freindes to them; Allsoe to have a speciall eye to my man Robert wch hathe not so approved himselfe as I would he should have done.

This is a Coppye of Mr Mullens his Will of all particulars he hathe given. In witnes whereof I have sett my hande

John Carver, Giles Heale, Christopher Joanes.

Vicesimo tertio : die mensis Julii Anno Domini Millesimo sexcentesimo vicesimo primo Emanavit Commissio Sare Blunden als Mullins filie naturali et legitime dicti defuncti ad administrand bona iura et credita eiusdem defuncti iuxta tenorem et effectum testamenti suprascripti eo quod nullum in eodem testamento nominavit executorem de bene etc Jurat.

68, Dale.

Mense Julij An^o^ Dni 162j.

Vicesimo tertio die emanavit comissio Sare Blunden als Mullens filie nrali et ltime Willmi Mullens nup de Dorking in Com Surr sed in partibus ultra marinis def hentis etc ad administrand bona iura et credita ejusdem def iuxta tenorem et effcum testamenti ipsius defuncti eo quod nullum in eodem nominavit exrem de bene etc iurat.

Probate Act Book, 1621 and 1622.

(*Translation of the second Latin record.*)

In the month of July Anno Domini 1621. On the 23^d^ day issued a commission to Sarah Blunden, formerly Mullins, natural and legitimate daughter of William Mullins, late of Dorking in the County of Surrey, but deceased in parts beyond the seas, seized &c., for administering the goods, rights and credits of the said deceased, according to the tenor and effect of the will of the said deceased because in that will he named no executor. In due form &c. swears.

THE WILL AND INVENTORY OF STEPHEN HOPKINS.

Literally transcribed from the original records,

BY GEORGE ERNEST BOWMAN.

The exact date of the death of Stephen Hopkins is unknown, but he must have died at Plymouth, in the year 1644, between June 6, the day his will was made, and July 17, the day his inventory was taken.

The will and inventory were recorded in the Plymouth Colony Wills and Inventories, Volume I, folios 61, 62 and 63.

---

[61] The last Will and Testament of m^{r} Stephen Hopkins exhibited upon the Oathes of m^{r} Willm Bradford and Captaine Miles Standish at the generall Court holden at Plymouth the xxth of August Anno dm 1644 as it followeth in these wordes vizt.

The sixt of June 1644 I Stephen Hopkins of Plymouth in New England being weake yet in good and prfect memory blessed be God yet considering the fraile estate of all men I do ordaine and make this to be my last will and testament in manner and forme following and first I do committ my body to the earth from whence it was taken, and my soule to the Lord who gave it, my body to be buryed as neare as convenyently may be to my wyfe Deceased And first my will is that out of my whole estate my funerall expences be discharged secondly that out of the remayneing part of my said estate that all my lawfull Debts be payd thirdly I do bequeath by this my will to my sonn Giles Hopkins my great Bull wch is now in the hands of m^{ris} Warren Also I do give to Stephen Hopkins my sonn Giles his sonne twenty shillings in m^{ris} Warrens hands for the hire of the said Bull Also I give and bequeath to my daughter Constanc Snow the wyfe of Nicholas Snow my mare also I give unto my daughter Deborah Hopkins the brodhorned black cowe and her calf and half the Cowe called Motley Also I doe give and bequeath unto my daughter Damaris Hopkins the Cowe called Damaris heiffer and the white faced calf and half the cowe called Mottley Also I give to my daughter Ruth the Cowe called Red Cole and her calfe and a Bull at Yarmouth wch is in the keepeing of Giles Hopkins wch is an yeare and advantage old and half the curld Cowe Also I give and bequeath to my daughter Elizabeth the Cowe called Smykins and her calf and thother half of the Curld Cowe wth Ruth and an yearelinge heiffer wth-out a tayle in the keepeing of Gyles Hopkins at Yarmouth Also I do give and bequeath unto my foure daughters that is to say Deborah Hopkins Damaris Hopkins Ruth Hopkins and Elizabeth Hopkins all the mooveable goods the wch do belong to my house. as linnen wollen beds bedcloathes pott kettles pewter or whatsoevr are moveable belonging to my said house of what kynd soever and not named by their prticular names all wch said mooveables to bee equally devided amongst my said daughters foure silver spoones that is to say to eich of them one, And in case any of my said daughters should be taken away by death before they be marryed that then the part of their division to be equally devided amongst the Survivors. I do also by this my will make Caleb Hopkins my sonn and heire apparent giveing and bequeathing unto my said sonn aforesaid all my Right title and interrest to my house and lands at Plymouth wth all the Right title and interrest wch doth might or of Right doth or may hereafter belong unto mee, as also I give unto my saide heire all such lande wch of Right is Rightly due unto me and not at prsent in my reall possession wch belongs unto me by right of my first comeing into this land or by any other due Right, as by such freedome or otherwise giveing unto my said heire my full & whole and entire Right in all divisions allottments appoyntments or distributions whatsoever to all or any pt of the said lande at any tyme or tymes so to be disposed Also I do give moreover unto my foresaid heire one paire or yooke of oxen and the hyer of them wch are in the hands of Richard Church as may appeare by bill under his hand Also I do give unto my said heire Caleb Hopkins all my debts wch are now oweing unto me, or at the day of my death may be oweing unto mee either by booke bill or bills or any other way rightfully due unto mee ffurthermore my will is that my daughters aforesaid shall have free recourse to my house in

Plymouth upon any occation there to abide and remayne for such tyme as any of them shall thinke meete and convenyent & they single persons And for the faythfull prformance of this my will I do make and ordayne my aforesaid sonn and heire Caleb Hopkins my true and lawfull Executor ffurther I do by this my will appoynt and make my said sonn and Captaine Miles Standish joyntly supervisors of this my will according to the true meaneing of the same that is to say that my Executor & supervisor shall make the severall divisions parts or porcons legacies or whatsoever doth appertaine to the fullfilling of this my will It is also my will that my Execut^{r} & Supervisor shall advise devise and dispose by the best wayes & meanes they cann for the disposeing in marriage or other wise for the best advanc^{nt} of the estate of the forenamed Deborah Damaris Ruth and Elizabeth Hopkins Thus trusting in the Lord my will shalbe truly prformed according to the true meaneing of the same I committ the whole Disposeing hereof to the Lord that hee may direct you herein

June 6th 1644

Witnesses hereof By me Steven Hopkins

Myles Standish

William Bradford

[62] An Inventory of the Goods and th Cattells of m^{r} Steven Hopkins taken by Captaine Miles Standish m^{r} Thomas Willet and m^{r} John Done the xviith of July 1644. xx^{o} Cal. Re.

	£	s	d
Inpris one brod horne Cowe	05	10	00
it Mottlis Cowe	05	10	00
it Damaris heiffer	05	00	00
it Red Cowe	05	05	00
it Curld Cowe	05	05	00
it Symkins Cowe	05	00	00
it brod Hornes calf	00	12	00
it white faced calf	00	15	00
it Cooles calf	00	14	00
it Symkins calf	00	12	00
it a great Bull	08	00	00
it a mare	06	00	00
it a yeong bull	01	05	00
it a yearling heiffer wthout a tayle	01	05	00

it a yok of oxen	15 00 00
it 2 pigges	00 04 00
it poultry	00 10 00
it a bed & boulster & one pillow	03 10 00
it another bed & boulster & pillow	03 10 00
it another feathe bed & pillow	03 00 00
it another bed & bouster wth an old straw bed	02 00 00
it 3 white blankets	01 00 00
it one covering	00 12 00
it one cov^r^ing	00 04 00
it a yellow Rugg	00 08 00
it a greene Rugg	00 06 00
it 2 check^r^ blanketts	00 14 00
it curtaines & vallence	00 10 00
it a scarfe	00 06 00
it a pair of flanell sheets	00 07 00
it one old paire of sheets	00 05 00
it one paire of sheets	00 08 00
it one paire of sheets	00 08 00
it 3 sheets	00 10 00
it 4 pillow beares	00 12 00
it 5 napkins	00 03 06
it 1 diapr napkins	00 02 06
it 3 table clothes	00 04 00
it 4 dymothy caps	00 02 00
it 2 white capps	00 03 00
it 2 wrought caps	00 02 06
it 2 shirts	00 12 00
	86 06 06
it two paire of shooes	00 06 00
it p^rs^ of cotton stockings	00 02 06
it 4 spoones	01 08 00
it in money	00 00 06
it claspes	00 00 02
it a pair of garters	00 00 04
it 2 Ruffe	00 07 00
it a paire of drawers	00 00 04
it a moheire petticote	01 15 00
it a petticote of phillip & cheny	01 00 00
it a grogorm coate	01 00 00
it a prpetuam coate	01 00 00
it a cloth coate	01 00 00
it a cloake	01 10 00
it a gray cloak	01 10 00
it suit of cloth	00 08 00
it a pair of breeches	00 03 00

it an old coate & jerkine	00	10	00
it a muffe	00	06	00
it 3 cusheons & a pair of breeches	00	04	00
it a chest	00	08	00
it a chest	00	06	00
it a case & bottel & box	00	03	00
it a hogshead	00	01	00
it an old warmeing pann	00	02	00
it a frying pann	00	01	00
it 6 porringers	00	05	00
it 2 porringers	00	01	00
it 4 wine measures	00	06	00
it 3 quart potts	00	06	00
it chamber potts	00	02	00
it 2 laten candlesticks	00	01	00
it 1 puter candlestick	00	01	00
it a pestell & morter	00	03	06
it a beere bowle & wine cup	00	01	06
it a beaker	00	00	06
it a salt seller	00	01	00
it 2 funnells	00	01	00
it 2 basens	00	06	00
it a great dish	00	05	00
it 6 dishes	00	14	00
it a little dish	00	00	02
it earthen potts	00	00	06
it an Iron pott	00	05	00
it a bras pott	00	08	00
it a cast skellet	00	05	00
it a smale skellet	00	01	06
[63]it a great kettle	01	02	00
it a lesse kettle	00	06	00
it a smaler ketle	00	04	00
it another kettle	00	07	00
it 5 spoones	00	01	00
it 1 dossen & half trenchers	00	01	00
it two graters 2^{s}	00	02	00
it a shooeing horne	00	00	01
it a paire of bellowes	00	01	00
it 4 paire of old pothookes	00	03	00
it a fireshovell & tongs	00	04	00
it two spitts	00	03	06
it 3 paire of links	00	07	06
it a peece of a bar of Iron	00	01	06
it a gridiron	00	01	00
it 9 trayes	00	09	00

it a churne	00 04 00
it 2 chees fatts	00 01 00
it a old Cullender	00 00 02
it 2 payles	00 01 04
it wodden Mo	00 01 06
it 2 wheeles	00 07 00
it 2 chaires	00 08 00
it 2 stooles	00 02 00
it latten pans	00 00 06
it a tubb & forme	00 12 00
it a cheane	00 06 00
it a sive	00 00 06
it old chest	00 02 00
it a bakeing Tub	00 02 00
it old tubbs	00 01 00
it feathers	00 03 00
it 3 hoopes of Iron	00 01 06
it 1 sawe	00 01 06
it a cheese rack	00 04 00
it 4 skins	00 03 00
it an axe	00 01 06
it a prcell hemp	00 02 06
it scales & waights	00 05 00
it Debts	16 05 00
it Divers bookes	00 12 00
it more in Debts	01 01 00
it a hatt	00 01 00

THE WILL AND INVENTORY OF FRANCIS COOKE.

Communicated by EDITH FORRESTER PRATT.

Francis Cooke died at Plymouth, on the seventh of April, 1663, and his will and inventory were recorded in the Plymouth Colony Wills and Inventories, Volume II, Part II, folios 1 and 2.

---

[1] The last Will and Testament of ffrancis Cooke of Plymouth late Deceased: exhibited before the Court held att Plymouth aforsaid the fift day of June 1663 on the oathes of m^{r} John Aldin and m^{r} John howland;

The Last Will and Testament of ffrancis Cooke made this seaventh of the tenth month 1659

I being att p^rsent weake and Infeirme in body yett in prfect memory throw mercy Doe comitt my soule unto god that gave it and my body to the earthe; which my will is should bee Intered in a Decent and comly manner;

As for such goods and lands as I stand posessed of I Doe will and bequeath as followeth;

1 My will is that hester my Dear and loveing wife shall have all my moveable goods and all my Cattle of all kinds; viz: neat Cattle horsekind sheep and swine to be att her Dispose

2 my will is that hester my wife shall have and Injoy my lands both upland and meddow lands which att p^rsent I posesse During her life

3 I Doe ordaine and appoint my Deare wife and my son John Cooke Joynt exequitors of this my said will

Witnes ffrancis Cooke

John Aldin

John howland

An Inventory of the estate of ffrancis Cooke Deceased taken and Aprised the first Day of May 1663 by Ephraim Tinkham and Willam Crow

	£	s	d
Imp^rs 2 Iron potts & 1 Iron skillett	00	16	00
Item 2 paire of pott hookes	00	01	00
Item 7 pewter Dishes & 2 basons	00	17	06
Item 3 pewter potts	00	06	06
Item 1 pewter bason 2 porringers & 1 salt seller	00	02	00
Item 1 pewter Candlesticke	00	02	00
Item 2 Alcemy spoones	00	03	03
Item 1 lanthorn 1 gallypot	00	01	00
Item halfe a Dozen of trenchers and one stone bottle	00	01	00
Item 3 olde ladles	00	00	06
Item 1 woodden tray 6 trenchers	00	01	00
Item 1 morter and pestell	00	02	00
Item 4 wooden Dishes	00	00	08
Item 1 earthen pan and 2 earthen potts	00	00	09
Item 1 great brasse kettle	01	06	00
Item 2 smaller kettles	00	08	00
Item 3 wooden pailes	00	03	06
Item 1 pewter Chamber pott	00	02	06
Item 1 warming pan 1 frying pan	00	10	06

Item 1 thwart saw 1 hand saw	00 03 06
Item 1 paire of pincers 1 hammar	00 02 06
Item 1 Drawing Knife	00 00 06
Item 1 water Tubb	00 01 06
Item 1 axe	00 01 06
Item 1 greate Chaire	00 05 00
Item 3 smale Chaires	00 03 00
Item 1 gridiron 1 fiershovell 1 paire of tonggs	00 05 00
Item 2 paire of pothangers	00 06 00
Item 2 old musketts	00 12 00
Item 1 paire of sheers 1 paire of sissers	00 00 09
Item 1 great bible & 4 old bookes	00 10 00
Item 1 brush	00 00 02
Item 1 file and 1 paire of pincers	00 00 06
Item 1 Table & forme	00 06 00
Item 1 old bucking Tubb	00 02 06
Item 1 tubb & 2 kimnells *	00 05 00
Item 1 Chist	00 03 00
Item 1 pair of Cards and one baskett	00 01 00
Item 1 Chist	00 02 00
Item 4 earthen potts 1 Cupp 2 wooden trayes	00 05 00
Item 1 Chern 1 old Cask & four bottles	00 05 06
Item 1 old trough & a forme	00 00 06
Item 1 woolen wheele & scales	00 04 00
Item 1 Iron Driping pan	00 03 00
Item 1 sifting trough & one old trough	00 03 00
Item 1 tray 1 tubb 1 box	00 03 00
Item 2 seives	00 02 06
Item 3 paire of sheep sheers	00 03 00
Item 3 paire of old Cards	00 01 06
Item 1 Cheespresse 1 Cheesfatt	00 01 00
[2] Item 2 old ferkins & som sope	00 01 06
Item 2 old basketts & yarne	00 04 00
Item 1 feather bed & bolster	02 00 00
Item 1 paire of sheets	00 12 00
Item 1 Coverlid & blankett	01 00 00
Item 1 pound of Candles	00 00 06
Item 2 hoes	00 01 06
Item 1 Cushien	00 00 06
Item 2 Chistes & 3 boxes	01 06 00
Item 1 feather bed 1 bolster 1 pillow	03 10 00
Item 1 paire of sheets 10s 1 blankett 1 Coverlid 15	01 15 00
Item 2 old Curtaines & vallence	00 02 00
Item 2 paire of sheets	01 10 00
Item 3 halfe sheets	00 06 00

* Tubs.

Item 2 hatts	00 15 00
Item 1 long coate 25s 2 short coates 30s	02 15 00
Item 1 old coate & 1 Jerkin	00 15 00
Item 2 paire of briches 1 paire of Drawers	01 10 00
Item old clothes stockens gloves shooes	01 00 00
Item 4 shirts & smale linnine	01 10 00
Item 1 bed & beding in the loft	03 00 00
Item 20 lb of woole & 2 paire of old stockens	01 07 00
Item 8 paire of stockens	01 05 00
Item some other old lumber about the house	00 02 00
Item 2 mares & one yearling mare	26 00 00
Item 2 Cowes & one Calfe	07 10 00
Item 1 2 yeare old and 1 yearling heiffers	03 10 00
Item 16 sheep	08 00 00
Item 5 lambes	01 00 00
Item 4 smale swine	01 04 00
The sume apprised is	85 01 01
Debtes Due to the estate from severall about	04 00 00
Due from the estate of severall about	02 10 00
summa totalis	86 11 01

Besides the housing and land;

the goods and Chattels amount to eighty six pounds eleven shillin(gs) and a peney; apprised by us

Ephraim Tinkham

his E T

Willam Crow

The above written Inventory was exhibited before the Court held att Plymouth the fift of June 1663 and Attested unto upon oath by hester Cooke widdow

THE WILL AND INVENTORY OF NATHANIEL WARREN.

Literally transcribed from the original records,

BY GEORGE ERNEST BOWMAN.

Nathaniel Warren, the eldest son of Richard and Elizabeth (——) Warren, died at Plymouth in the year 1667, between the sixteenth of July, the date of the codicil to his will, and the twenty-first of October, the date on which the inventory of his estate was taken.

His will and inventory were recorded in the Plymouth Colony Wills and Inventories, Volume II, Part II, folios 46 and 47.

---

[46] The last Will and Testament of Nathaniel: Warren of Plymouth Late Deceased Exhibited to the Court held att Plymouth aforsaid the thirtyeth of October Ann^{o} Dom 1667 on the oathes of hugh Cole and Nathaniel: Morton

I, Nathaniel Warren seni^{r} of the Towne of Plymouth in New England being weake in body and ill att ease but of a Disposing mind and of a p^{r}fect memory; not knowing how soon the Lord may Call mee away out of this world; Doe ordaine this to bee my last Will and Testament in maner and forme following; Imprimis: I make ordaine and Constitute Sarah my loveing wife to be the sole exequitrx of this may last will: To Dispose of my estate according to the tenor of this my Will with the advise and approbation of the supervissors heerafter named; Item I give unto my loveing wife Sarah the full sume of fifteen pounds in goods or Chattles with my best bed and bedstead with Curtaines and vallence belonging to it: with two pillowes with two paire of pillowbeers and two paire of sheets with the best Rugg and a paire of the best blanketts; Incase shee shall and Doe alter her Condition by marriage; But incase and soe longe as shee shall remaine a widdow; that then my estate be all att her Dispose and in her hand to be Improved for her support and for the bringing up of my Children; Divers of them being young; provided that I Doe by this my Will give and bequeath unto my Children to each of them three pounds in mony to be Delivered to them att theire Day of marriage; onely incase That if through nessesity by the advise of my Supervissors afternamed my wife Doe or shall Dispose of the mony I leave or any p^rte therof That then theire p^rte therof shall not be payable whoe have not received it att the time when this is made known by my said exequitrix that she is soe Disinabled to pay it as aforsaid. further my will is and I Doe heerby Authorise and Impower my said exequitrix: with the advise of my supervissors afternamed: To make sale of Any of my lands and to give and seale Deeds for the Confeirmation therof to be Improved for the makeing good of my legacyes and engagements; which shalbe as Authenticall in law to all Intents and purposes as if I my selfe were surviveing and Did acte therin; and to be under stood that the land be sold to the full worth therof; and not as it may posibly be vallued in an Inventory; and accordingly what it shalbe sold for in the full extent of it; my will is shalbe Devided amongst my Children in such maner as is after expressed: Item my will is That as any of my Children shalbe occationed to alter theire Condition by marriage that they then shall have the sume of ten pounds to each of them Delivered to them att theire Day of marriage; or in some Convenient time soone after by my exequitrix out of my estate; and unto my eldest son then surviving the sume of twenty pounds and incase the said sumes Cannot be made good out of my goods or Chattles that then some p^rte of my lands be sold to Doe it as aforesaid; moreover my will is that incase my wife shall marry; That whatsoever of my estate either of lands goods or Chattles shalbe then extant and not expended In the bringing up of my Children and in the payment and makei(ng) good of my Ingagements and legacies shalbe equally Devided amongst my children then surviveing in equall and alike proportions onely that my eldest son then surviveing shall have a Double portion therof ; furthermore my will is That att the Decease of my wife ; if any p[r]te of my estate shalbe then left and not expended as aforsaid be it either in lands goods or Chattles ; That then it shalbe Devided in equall and alike proportions amongst my Children then surviveing ; onely my eldest son then surviveing shall have a Doubble portion thereof ; my Will is That incase my Deare Child my Daughter hope shall Continew lame and Impotent That it shalbe left unto the Descretion of my exequitrix and supervissors (after named) To Inlarge her portion as they shall see meet ; and the like alsoe for any other of my Children ; if they shalbe lame sicke or Impotent ; my Will is and I Doe heerby request my trusty and welbeloved frinds Captaine Thomas Southworth and my loveing brother Joseph Warren and Leiftenant Ephraim Morton To be the supervissors of this my last Will and Testament much Confiding in theire love and faithfulnes to be healpfull to my said exequitrix in the acting and Disposing of p[r]ticulars according to the tenore therof ; and to be Considered out of my estate for what time and charge they shalbe att in the p[r]mises ; and that they my supervissors ; shall have full power and I Doe heerby request them to advise about and take Care of my Children in reference to theire marriage ; That they bee matched with such as may be fitt for them both in reference to theire speritual and outward estate ; In witness that this is my last Will and Testament ; I the said Nathaniel Warren have heerunto sett my hand and seale ; this 29th day of June Ann[o] Dom 1667

Witnes heerunto
hugh Cole
Nathaniel : Morton ;

Nathaniel Warren
and a seale

A Supplyment to the abovwritten Will exhibited to the Court held att Plymouth the thirtyeth Day of october one Thousand six hundred sixty and seaven on the oathes of Captaine Southworth hugh Cole and Nathaniel Morton ;

I Nathaniel Warren being weake in body but of Desposing

memory Doe heerby Declare and manifest unto all unto whom these shall Come; That my will further is as an appendix and Supplyment unto my will bearing Date the 29th of June 1667 That in Reference unto the Land my mother mistris Elizabeth Warren hath Instated and posessed my beloved brother Joseph Warren and my sisters Mary Bartlett seni^{r} Ann Little Sarah Cooke Elizabeth Church and Abigaill Snow shalbe and is by these p^{r}sents fully freely and absolutly Ratifyed and Confeirmed unto them and theire heires and assignes for ever; with all and singular my Right title and Interest of and Into the same; To them and theire heires and assignes for ever; In Witnes wherof I have heerunto sett my hand this sixteenth Day of July 1667 in the p^{r}sence of

Thomas Southworth — Nathaniel : Warren
hugh Cole
Nathaniel Morton

[47] An Inventory of the goods and estate of Nathaniell Warren late Deceased taken the 21 of October 1667 and exhibited to the Court held att Plymouth the thirtyeth of October 1667 on the oath of Sarah Warren widdow;

	£	s	d
Imp^{r} his wearing apparrell	10	00	00
Item in Cash	41	10	00
Item 10 paire of pillowbeers	02	00	00
Item 19 paire of sheets	10	00	00
Item 3 Table Clothes & 2 Dozen of Napkins	02	00	00
Item 1 feather bed and bolster 2 pillowes 1 rid rugg 1 paire of blanketts with Curtaines and vallence	08	00	00
Item 4 feather beds and bolsters and five ruggs and 4 paire of blanketts and a Coverled and 1 paire of pillowes	20	00	00
Item 1 bedsteed and Cubbert with Drawers 1 longe Table and form with two Joyne stooles	10	00	00
Item six Chaires 1 Cradle with 2 pillows	01	00	00
Item 1 winescot Chist more 4 Chists	01	10	00
Item 1 Carpett & Cubbercloth & 2 Cushens	00	12	00
Item 2 old Chaire Tables & a little one	00	05	00
Item 3 brasse kittles	02	10	00
Item 1 bel mettle skillett & 1 old warming pan	00	08	00
Item 4 Iron potts 2 Iron kettles and an Iron skillett 2 paire of pothooks three hangers 1 frying pan	03	10	00
Item 2 paire of tongs 1 shovell a gridyron and spitt & an Iron ladle	00	10	00

Item 6 pewter platters 2 little ones 2 great basons 2 little ones 2 pint potts 1 great pott 1 beaker 1 winecup six porrengers 6 spoons 1 tin pan 1 bed pan 1 little bottle & a tinin lampe	02 10 00
Item 7 earthen pans & other earthen	00 06 00
Item 3 milke pans & Dishes and trayes	00 10 00
Item 1 paire off stilliyards 1 paire of sheepsheers 5 old sythes	01 10 00
Item 1 muskett & 2 swords	01 00 00
Item 1 old bedsted & a trundle bedsted	00 10 00
Item 4 spining wheels 5 paire of Cards woolen yarn & woole in Cotten yarn & woole	05 00 00
Item 12 pound of feathers 2 window Curtains 3 seives 8 pound of powder 28 pound of shott & som bulletts old lumber hogsheds & tubbs	03 00 00
Item 4 oxen	16 00 00
Item 8 Cowes	24 00 00
Item 6 two years and vantage & two 3 year old steers	17 00 00
Item 1 yearling & an half & 4 Calves	03 10 00
Item a share of horse fflesh	02 00 00
Item a saddle & pillian and panell & bridle	01 10 00
Item his p^rte of furniture belonging to the teame with axes howes & other lumber of old Iron and three wedges	03 10 00
In lands the house and land belonging to it lying att the Eelrivier with fifty acrees of land lying in the woods	140 00 00
Item lands lying on both syds Namassakett river that is to say his owne right and what hee bought of John Adams	60 00 00
Item a share of land within the Township of Dartmouth	50 00 00
Lands belonging to him att Punkateesett	06 00 00
Item in Coat beaver about 2^{lb}	13 00 00
Item in Debts owing to the estate about	22 07 06
Item Debts owing from the estate	15 16 03
Item the Corn in the barne wee Judge to be but sufficient for the families eating	
the sume totall is	475 00 00
more since Came to remembrance 1 grindstone 4 shots two hamers and a drawing knife	01 16 00
more Due from the estate 3 barrells of Tarr	

Taken by us Joseph Warren Ephraim Morton Thomas Southworth

JOHN HOWLAND'S WILL AND INVENTORY.

Transcribed from the original records,

BY GEORGE ERNEST BOWMAN.

John Howland died at Plymouth, on the twenty third of February 1672–3, and his will and inventory were recorded in the Plymouth Colony Wills and Inventories, Volume III, Part I, pages 49 to 54.

[p. 49] The Last Will and Testament of m^{r} John howland of Plymouth late Deceased, exhibited to the Court held att Plymouth the fift Day of March Ann^{o} Dom 1672 on the oathes of m^{r} Samuell ffuller and m^{r} Willam Crow as followeth

Know all men to whom these p^{r}sents shall Come That I John howland seni^{r} of the Towne of New Plymouth in the Colloni(e) of New Plymouth in New England in America, this twenty ninth Day of May one thousand six hundred seaventy and two being of whole mind, and in Good and p^{r}fect memory and Remembrance praised be God; being now Grown aged; haveing many Infeirmities of body upon mee; and not Knowing how soon God will call mee out of this world, Doe make and ordaine these p^{r}sents to be my Testament Containing herein my last Will in manor and forme following;

Imp I Will and bequeath my body to the Dust and my soule to God that Gave it in hopes of a Joyfull Resurrection unto Glory; and as Concerning my temporall estate, I Dispos(e) therof as followeth;

Item I Doe give and bequeath unto John howland my eldest sonne besides what lands I have alreddy given him, all my Right and Interest To that one hundred acrees of land graunted mee by the Court lying on the easter(n) side of Taunton River; between Teticutt and Taunton bounds and all the appurtenances and privilidges Therunto belonging, T belonge to him and his heires and assignes for ever; and if that Tract should faile, then to ha(ve) all my Right title and Interest by and in that Last Court graunt to mee in any other place, To belonge to him his heires and assignes for ever;

Item I give and bequeath unto my son Jabez howland all those my upland and Meadow That I now posesse at Satuckett and Paomett, and places adjacent, with all the appurtenances and privilidges, belonging therunto, and all my right title and Interest therin, To belonge to him his heires and assignes for ever,

Item I Give and bequeath unto my son Jabez howland all that my one peece of land that I have lying on the southsyde of the Mill brooke, in the Towne of Plymou(th) aforsaid; be it more or lesse; and is on the Northsyde of a fei(ld) that is now Gyles Rickards senir To belonge to the said Jabez his heires and assignes for ever;

Item I give and bequeath into Isacke howland my youngest sonne all those my uplands and meddowes Devided and undivided with all the appurtena(n)ce(s) and priviliges unto them belonging, lying and being in the Towne of Middlebery, and in a tract of Land Called the Majors Purchase neare Namassakett Ponds; which I have bought and purchased of Willam White of Marshfeild in the Collonie of New Plymouth; which may or shall appeer by any Deed or writing that is Given under the said Whites hand all such Deeds or writinges Together with the aformensioned prticulares To belonge to the said Isacke his heires and assignes for ever;

Item I give and bequeath unto my said son Isacke howland the one halfe of my twelve acree lott of Meddow That I now have att Winnatucsett River within the Towne of Plymouth aforsaid To belonge to him the said Isacke howland his heires and assignes for ever,

Item I Will and bequeath unto my Deare and loveing wife Elizabeth howland the use and benifitt of my now Dwelling house in Rockey nooke in the Township of Plymouth aforsaid, with the outhousing lands, That is uplands [p. 50] uplands and medlow lands and all appurtenances and privilidges therunto belonging in the Towne of Plymouth and all other Lands housing and meddowes that I have in the said Towne of Plymouth excepting what meddow and upland I have before given To my sonnes Jabez and Isacke howland During her naturall life to Injoy make use of and Improve for her benifitt and Comfort;

Item I give and bequeath unto my son Joseph howland after the Decease of my loveing wife Elizabeth howland my aforsaid Dwelling house att Rockey nooke together with all the outhousing uplands and Meddowes appurtenances and privilidges belonging therunto; and all other housing uplands and meddowes appurtenances and privilidges That I have within the aforsaid Towne of New Plymouth excepting what lands and meadowes I have before Given To my two sonnes Jabez and Isacke; To belong to him the said Joseph howland To him and his heires and assignes for ever;

Item I give and bequeath unto my Daughter Desire Gorum twenty shillings

Item I give and bequeath To my Daughter hope Chipman twenty shillings

Item I give and bequeath unto my Daughter Elizabeth Dickenson twenty shillings

Item I give and bequeath unto my Daughter Lydia Browne twenty shillings

Item I give & bequeath to my Daughter hannah Bosworth twenty shillings

Item I give and bequeath unto my Daughter Ruth Cushman twenty shillings

Item I give to my Grandchild Elizabeth howland The Daughter of my son John howland twenty shillings

Item my will is That these legacyes Given to my Daughters, be payed by my exequitrix in such species as shee thinketh meet;

Item I will and bequeath unto my loveing wife Elizabeth howland, my Debts and legacyes being first payed, my whole estate: viz: lands houses goods Chattles; or any thinge else that belongeth or appertaineth unto mee, undisposed of be it either in Plymouth Duxburrow or Middlbery or any other place whatsoever; I Doe freely and absolutly give and bequeath it all to my Deare and loveing wife Elizabeth howland whom I Doe by these prsents, make ordaine and Constitute to be the sole exequitrix of this my Last will and Testament to see the same truely and faithfully prformed according to the tenour therof; In witnes wherof I the said John howland senir have heerunto sett my hand and seale the aforsaid twenty ninth Day of May, one thousand six hundred seaventy and two 1672

Signed and sealed in the prsence of Samuell ffuller
Willam Crow

John howland
And a seale

[p. 51] A trew Inventory of all the goods Cattles and Chattles and Lands of Mr John howland lately Deceasd taken and aprised by Elder Thomas Cushman Serjeant Tinkham and Willam Crow the third of March Anno Dom 1672 and exhibited to the Court held att Plymouth the fift of March 167$\frac{2}{3}$ on the oathe of mrs Elizabeth howland widdow as followeth

In the outward or fier Rome	£	s	d
Impr 1 muskett 1 long Gun 1 Cutlas 1 belt, att	02	10	00
Item 1 Chimney Iron barr 2 paire of pot hangers	00	09	00
Item 1 fier shovell 1 paire of tonges 1 paire of Cob irons	00	07	00
Item 1 frying pan 1 smoothing box and Irons	00	05	06
Item 1 adds 2 axes 1 mortising axe 1 hoe	00	11	06
Item 3 augers 1 pikaxe	00	05	00
Item 1 hammer 1 paire of Pincers 1 Drawing knife 1 spliting kniffe	00	02	00
Item 2 Cow bells 1 old Chaine, and Divers peeces of old Iron Aules & a box	00	05	00
Item 2 presshookes 1 paire of sheep sheers 2 sickles	00	04	00
Item 1 pruning Instrument 1 peece of steele	00	02	00
Item 2 staples 1 peec of a Chaine	00	01	06
Item 2 staples 4 peeces of a chaine	00	01	06
Item 1 Dagger three knives 2 paire of sissers 1 paire of stilliyards	00	06	00
Item 1 padlock 1 thwart saw 3 wedges 1 ploughshare	00	10	00
Item 3 Iron potts 1 paire of pothookes 1 Iron kettle	01	06	00
Item 2 brasse kittles 1 warming pan	01	15	00
Item 1 skimer 1 ladle 1 sawsse pan 1 brasse skillett	00	04	06
Item 6 pewter platters 3 basons 3 smale pewter thinges	01	07	00
Item a quart pot 1 candlesticke 1 beer bowle	00	05	00
Item 3 porringers 1 Dram cupp 1 Tunell	00	03	00

Item	2 salt sellers 2 chamber potts 7 spoones	00 10 00
Item	1 Iron candlesticke 1 latten pott 1 Ironsockett	00 02 00
Item	1 shove Iron 2 washers 2 old sikles and old Iron	00 02 00
Item	4 earthen potts 1 pan and 1 Jugg and earthen ware	00 02 00
Item	1 hatchell	00 05 00
Item	1 great bible and Annotations on the 5 bookes of Moses	01 00 00
Item	m^r Tindalls workes m^r Wilsons workes 7 more bookes	01 00 00
Item	3 wheeles 1 cherne 1 straning Dish	00 13 00
Item	3 cheesfatts 11 trayes 1 kimnell	00 05 06
Item	3 pailes six tubbs 1 ladle 1 cheese ladder	00 14 06
Item	trenchers Roleing pins and some smale things	00 02 00
Item	3 Chaires stooles old barrells 3 Cushens	00 07 00
Item	3 beer vessells	00 04 00
		16 06 00

[p. 52] In the Inward Rome or bedchamber

his wearing apparell

Item	3 hatts	00 16 00
Item	3 great coates	02 00 00
Item	1 suite of cloth	03 00 00
Item	1 serge suite	01 10 00
Item	1 homespon suite and wastcoate	00 15 00
Item	1 suite	00 12 00
Item	old clothes	00 06 00
Item	2 red wastcoates	01 05 00
Item	6 paire of Stokens	01 00 00
Item	1 Jackett and one paire of Mittens	00 13 06
Item	1 holland shirt	00 12 00
Item	4 shirts	00 18 00
Item	4 holland capps 4 Dowlis capps and 4 other capps	00 10 00
Item	2 silke Neckclothes	00 07 06
Item	1 paire of bootes 2 paire of shooes	01 00 00
		15 11 00

In the said Rome

Item	4 remnants of clothe	00 19 00
Item	2 yards of serge	00 10 00
Item	3 yards $\frac{1}{2}$ of carsey	01 15 00
Item	4 Dozen of buttons $\frac{1}{2}$ 10 skines of silke 3 yards of Manchester	00 04 00
Item	17 yards of fflax and cotton cloth att	02 11 00
Item	1 peece of fine Dowlis	00 08 06
Item	1 remnant of lincye woolsey	00 08 00

Item about 16 yards of several remnants of homade Cloth vallued att	03 10 00
	10 05 06

In the aforsaid Inward Roome

Item 1 pound of woolen yerne	00 03 00
Item 1 paire of sheets	01 05 00
Item 2 paire of sheets	01 10 00
Item 1 paire of sheets 1 halfe sheet	01 05 00
Item 1 paire of sheets att	00 10 00
Item 1 paire of holland pillowbeers	00 08 09
Item 2 paire of pillowbeers	00 15 00
Item 3 pillowbeers	00 06 00
Item 1 Table cloth and 7 napkins	00 13 00
Item 10 towells	00 07 00
Item 4 smale Table clothes	00 04 00
Item 2 smale pillowbeers	00 01 6
Item 1 Table and 2 formes	00 10 0
Item 1 cobbert and a framed chaire	00 08 0
Item 4 chest and 1 settle	01 00 00
Item 1 bedsted and box and coard	00 12 0
Item 1 seifting trough and 2 seives	00 04 0
Item 1 glass 2 glasse bottles 2 earthen potts	00 03 0
Item 1 wineglasse gallipotts and spectacles	00 02 0
Item 2 paire of coards one bed cord 1 fishing line	00 05 06
Item some hobnailes & twelvepeny nailes	00 02 00
Item 5 peeces of Dresed lether one peece of taned lether	00 06 00
Item a smale p^r^cell of hemp and hopps	00 02 00
Item 3 or 4 basketts 1 brush 1 file	00 01 00
[p. 53] Item Cotton woole about a Dozen pound	00 12 00
Item 3 old caske	00 02 00
Item 1 feather bed and bolster 3 great & 2 smale pillowes	05 00 00
Item 5 blanketts	03 15 00
Item 1 rugg and one blankett	01 15 00
Item 1 blankett att	00 15 00
Item in reddy mony	01 19 00
Item a smale p^r^cell of powder shott and bulletts	00 03 00
Item 1 Inkhorn	00 00 06
	24 14 3

In the uper Roome or Chamber

Item I feather bed bolster and pillow	04 00 00
Item 2 blanketts and a Rugg	01 05 00
Item 1 woole or fflocke bed 2 feather bolsters and a pillow	02 00 00

Item 2 blanketts	00 15 00
Item 1 p^r^cell of sheeps woole about fifteene pound	00 15 00
Item 1 bedstead cord and box	00 10 00
Item a p^r^cell of feathers about 15 or 16 pound	00 15 00
Item a cupple of old hogsheds and an old candlesticke	00 02 00
Item 20 bushells or therabouts of Indian corne	03 00 00
Item 4 bushells of Mault or therabouts	00 16 00
Item 4 bushells of Rye or therabouts	00 14 00
Item 6 bushells of wheat or therabouts	01 07 00
Item 3 peckes of pease or therabouts	00 02 00
Item 2 bushells and an halfe of barly or therabouts	00 10 00
Item 2 ffliches of bacon and 1 third of a barrell of porke	02 00 00
Item 1 halfe of a barrell of beeff and 2 empty barrells	00 15 00
Item 15 pound of Tallow and Candles	00 07 06
Item 34 pound of butter & lard	00 17 00
Item 14 pound of sugare	00 07 00
Item 1 halfe hogshed	00 03 00
Item 1 pad 1 pillian 1 bridle 1 sheepskin	00 05 00
Item 6 pound of Tobacco 1 pecke of beans	00 04 00
Item 1 grindstone and handles 1 ffan	00 09 00
Item 8 baggs 15^s^ old Iron 1 shilling	00 16 00
	22 14 06

Cattle

Item 2 mares and one colt	03 00 00
Item 4 oxen 4 cowes	24 00 00
Item 2 heiffers and 3 steers of three years old	12 10 00
Item 2 two yeare old heiffers 2 yearling calves	03 10 00
Item 13 swine	04 15 00
Item 45 sheep young and old	15 00 00
Item the one halfe of a paire of Iron bound wheeles and cart and 12 bolts 2 shakles	02 02 06
Item 1 paire of hookes and a staple	00 01 06
Item 1 bullockes hyde	00 14 00
Item a cannooe	00 05 00
	65 18 00

[p. 54] Debts Due to the Testator

ffrom John Branch of Marshfeild att 2 severall payments the sume of	08 00 00
Edward Gray 1 barrell of salt	00 12 00
Item a Debt Due from a frind	00 10 00
	09 02 00
Brought from the other side	155 09 3
Sume	164 11 03

Debts owing by the Testator

To Elder Thomas Cushman	00 15 00
To Thomas Cushman Junir	00 05 00
To John Clarke	00 10 06
To Edward Gray	00 08 03
To Willam Crow	00 02 00
To John Gorum	01 12 00
To two or three smale Debts about	00 02 00
ffunerall Charges	03 08 00
Debts Deducted	07 02 02
The totale of the estate prissed	157 08 08

Wee find that the Testator Died posessed of these severall prcells of Land following;

Impr his Dwelling house with the outhousing uplands and meddow belonging therunto lying att Rockey nooke in the Towne of New Plymouth

Item a prcell of meddow att Jonses river meddow

Item the one halfe of a house and a prcell of meddow and upland belonging therunto lying and being att Colchester in the aforsaid Townshipp;

Item a prcell of meddow and upland belonging therunto; lying neare Joness river bridge in the Towne of Duxburrow

Item one house and 2 shares of a tract of land and meddow that lyeth in the Towne of Middleberry that was purchased by Captaine Thomas Southworth of and from the Indian Sachem Josias Wampatucke

Item 2 Shares of a tract of Land Called the Majors Purchase lying neare Namassakett ponds

pr nos Thomas Cushman senr
Ephraim Tinkam senir
Willam Crow

THE WILL AND INVENTORY OF GEORGE SOULE.

Literally transcribed from the original records,

BY GEORGE ERNEST BOWMAN.

George Soule died at Duxbury, probably in the month of January, 1680, since his inventory was taken 1 February, 1680 (new style). His wife died at Duxbury, in December 1676.

The will and inventory were recorded in the Plymouth Colony Wills and Inventories, Volume IV, Part I, page 50.

[p. 50] In the Name of God Amen
I Gorge Soule senir of Duxberry in the Collonie of New Plymouth in New England being aged and weake of body but of a sound mind and Memory praised be God Doe make this my last Will and Testament in Manor and forme following Imprimis I comitt my soule into the hands of Almighty God whoe Gave it and my body to be Decently buried in the place appointed for that use whensoever hee shall please to take mee hence; and for the Disposall of my outward estate which God of his Goodnes hath Given mee first I have and alreddy formerly by Deeds under my hand and seale Given unto my two sonnes Nathaniel: and Gorge All my lands in the Township of Dartmouth; Item I have formerly Given unto my Daughters Elizabeth and Patience all my lands in the Township of Middleberry

Item I Give and bequeath unto my Daughters Sussannah and Mary twelve pence a peece to be payed by my executer heerafter Named after my Decease; And forasmuch as my Eldest son John Soule and his family hath in my extreame old age and weaknes bin tender and carefull of mee and very healpfull to mee; and is likely soe to be while it shall please God to continew my life heer therfore I give and bequeath unto my said son John Soule all the Remainder of my housing and lands whatsoever to him his heires and Assignes for ever Item I Give and bequeath unto my son John Soule all my Goods And Chattles whatsoever Item I Nominate And appoint my son John Soule to be my sole Executor of this my last Will and Testament; and lastly I Doe heerby make Null and voyde all other and former wills and Testaments by mee att Any time made; and Declare this Instrument to be my last Will and Testament In Witnes wherof I the said Gorge Soule have heerunto sett my hand and seale this eleventh Day of August in the yeer of our Lord one Thousand six hundred seaventy and seaven;

Gorge Soule and a seale

The above Named Gorge Soule Did signe seale and Deliver this Instrument to be his Last Will and Testament in the p^r^sence of us

Nathaniell Thomas
The Marke **D T** of Deborah Thomas

Item the twentyeth Day of September 1677 I the above Named Gorge Soule Doe heerby further Declare that it is my will that if my son John Soule above named or his heires or Assignes or any of them shall att any time Disturbe my Daughter Patience or her heires or Assignes or any of them in peacable Posession or Injoyment of the lands I have Given her att Namassakett allies Middleberry and Recover the same from her or her heires or Assignes or any of them That then my Gift to my son John Soule shall shalbe voyd; and that then my will is my Daughter Patience shall have all my lands att Duxburrey And shee shalbe my sole executrix of this my last Will and Testament And enter into my housing lands and meddowes att Duxburrow, In Witnes wherof I have heerunto sett my hand and seale;

Gorge Soule and A seal

The above Named Gorge Soule Did Signe and seale to this addition in the p^{rs}ence of us
Nathaniell Thomas
The Marke **D T** of Deborah Thomas;

[p. 51] An Inventory taken of the estate of the Late Deceased Gorge Soule of Duxburrow in his Maties Collonie of New Plymouth in New England this twenty second of January 1679 by Edward Southworth and Thomas Delano and exhibited to the Court of his Matie holden att Plymouth the fift of March 1679:80 on the oath of John Soule

Item Dwelling house orchyard Barne and upland praised att	20 00 00
Item Meddow Land	05 10 00
Item bed and beding and wearing Clothes	10 00 00
Item a Gun	00 15 00
Item bookes	01 00 00
Item a Chest and Chaire	00 05 00
Item 2 paire of Sheers a tramell and wedge	00 06 00
Item to other old lumber	00 03 00
Item by Debts Due to the estate	03 00 00
	40 19 00

An Acompt of Debt Due unto John Soule to be payed out of his fathers estate

Anno: 1674 Imp^{r} for plowing in one bushell of wheat & one bushell of pease	00 06 00
for reaping Rye and pease	00 7 00
Item one Day plowing Greensword	00 05 00
Item for plowing in weeding	00 02 00
Item 2 Dayes and an half plowing in of Rye	00 08 06
Item to Willam Clarke	00 00 09
Item for Geting and bringing hom 3 load of hay	01 00 00
1675 Item for one Day plowing in of pease & two Days Reaping of Rye	00 07 06
Item 1 locke for a Barne Dore	00 01 06
Item for Goods taken up att Edmun Mufords att Boston viz: 4 yards 2^{l} Carsey	19 01
Item for 7 yards of penistone 2^{s} 09^{d} p^{r} yard	00 19 03
Item for 10 yards of Canves att 1^{s} 6^{d} p^{r} yard	00 15 00
Item for buttons and silke	00 01 10
Item for blew linnine	00 02 02
Item for thred browne Coullered	00 02 08
Item for four yards of Red Cotton att 2^{s} 6^{d} p^{r} yard	00 10 00

Item for three hundred of shooe Nailes	00 01 00
Item payed to Mr Mumford upon the old accoumpt	00 08 09
1676 for Drawing 13 load of Brush and hedging about a feild	00 05 00
Item for plowing in of pease and wheat 2 Dayes	00 08 00
Item for Makeing a p^{r}teing fence between the orchyard	00 08 00
Item for makeing stone wall about the orchyard	02 00 00
Item for 12 yards of teicking of William Vobes	01 10 00
Item for 20 yards of Canvis att 1^s 9^d p^r yard	01 15 00
Item for Dowlis of M^r hetman 7 yards att 2^s 3^d p^r yard	00 18 00
Item for eight yards of Osenbrigg of m^r Thomas att 1^s 2^d p^r yard	00 09 04
Item for serge for a paire of briches	00 10 00
Item for one paire of sheets	00 10 00
Item for Diett and tendance since my mother Died which was three yeer the Last December except some smale time my sister Patience Dressed his victualls	
Item for funerall charges	01 00 00

IN MEMORY OF
REV. JOHN ROBINSON, M.A.
PASTOR OF THE ENGLISH CHURCH WORSHIPING
WENT FORTH
THE PILGRIM FATHERS
TO SETTLE NEW ENGLAND
IN 1620.
BURIED UNDER THIS HOUSE OF WORSHIP 4 MAR
AE XLIX YEARS
IN MEMORIA AETERNA ERIT JUSTUS
A.D. 1891

THE JOHN ROBINSON TABLET.

By Morton Dexter.

On Friday, July 24, 1891, an event occurred in Leyden, Holland, of more than local or temporary interest. It was the unveiling and dedication of a bronze tablet in memory of Rev. John Robinson, pastor of the Pilgrim church founded in Scrooby, England, in 1606 or 1607, resident in Leyden from 1609 to 1620, emigrating then, by its minority, to America, but continuing in Leyden, by its majority, for some years longer, and perpetuated at present in Plymouth, Mass., by the Church of the Pilgrimage and the First Parish Church.

The tablet is on the outer wall of St. Peter's, the (Lutheran) cathedral church of Leyden, under which, in a grave which cannot be identified, Robinson was buried March 4, 1625. Just across the street, the Kloksteeg, is the site of the house in which Robinson lived and preached, and in the garden of which a score of smaller dwellings were built for other members of the Pilgrim company.

The tablet was erected under the auspices of the National Council of Congregational Churches of the United States. The original movers in the matter were the late Rev. Dr. Henry M. Dexter and Prof. George E. Day. At their instance the National Council, which met at Detroit in 1877, appointed a committee, of which they were members and Dr. Dexter chairman, to promote the object. But the execution of the project was delayed unavoidably for various reasons until 1891, when it was accomplished immediately after the end of the first International Congregational Council, held that summer in London. During the intervening years Dr. Dexter and others of the original committee died. As finally constituted, it included Prof. G. E. Day, ex-President S. C. Bartlett, Hon. E. W. Blatchford, Rev. Drs. J. K. McLean, C. R. Palmer, and W. A. Robinson, and Rev. Morton Dexter.

The tablet is seven feet high by six feet wide. It was cast by the Henry Bonnard Bronze Company, of New York. It was the largest, with a single exception, ever cast in one piece in

America. At the top is the device of a vessel, under which are the words, "The Mayflower. 1620." Below is the following inscription, composed by Dr. Dexter:—

IN MEMORY OF

REV. JOHN ROBINSON, M.A.

PASTOR OF THE ENGLISH CHURCH WORSHIPING OVER AGAINST THIS SPOT, A.D. 1609–1625, WHENCE AT HIS PROMPTING WENT FORTH

THE PILGRIM FATHERS

TO SETTLE NEW ENGLAND
IN 1620.

BURIED UNDER THIS HOUSE OF WORSHIP, 4 MAR. 1625
AE[T.] XLIX YEARS.

IN MEMORIA AETERNA ERIT JUSTUS.

ERECTED BY THE NATIONAL COUNCIL OF THE CONGREGATIONAL CHURCHES OF THE UNITED STATES OF AMERICA.

A.D. 1891.

There is no authentic picture of the "Mayflower," and the device upon the tablet, which was selected, after much investigation, by Prof. J. F. Weir, of Yale University, represents a typical vessel of the period, of about the size and character of the famous Pilgrim ship. All the lettering upon the tablet is raised above its surface.

The total cost of the undertaking was less than $2,500. It was easily raised by contributions from individuals and Congregational churches, and, by consent of the contributors, an unexpected surplus afterwards was added to the building fund of the John Robinson Memorial Church in Gainsborough, England.

The dedication of the tablet was in charge of Messrs. Palmer and Dexter of the committee. But a number of other Americans were present, among them Rev. Drs. F. A. Noble, A. H.

Ross, T. T. Munger, and Burdett Hart, President W. F. Slocum, Hon. S. R. Thayer, United States Minister to Holland, and Messrs. Samuel Holmes and G. H. Whitcomb. British Congregationalists were represented by Rev. Drs. Alexander Mackennal and John Brown, Principal A. M. Fairbairn, Rev. G. S. Barrett, and Henry Spicer, Esq., from England, and Principal A. Gosman, Rev. Dr. Thomas Roseby, and Josiah Mullens, Esq., from Australia. Representatives of the municipality, the Ecclesiastical Commissioners and the University of Leyden, various religious bodies within the city and the military forces stationed there also were in attendance.

The exercises attracted general interest and a large company of citizens gathered. Early in the afternoon a procession was formed at the *Hotel Lion d'Or* and marched, headed by a military band, to St. Peter's Church. The tablet had been covered by canvas and a platform erected beneath it. Above the tablet rose three flag staffs, from which hung, ready to be hoisted, the American, Dutch, and English flags.

The exercises of dedication were simple but impressive. As the city clocks struck two Dr. Palmer called the assembly around the platform to order. The secretary and treasurer of the committee, Mr. Dexter, read a brief paper, giving the history of the undertaking, after which Dr. Mackennal offered prayer. Then followed the unveiling of the tablet. Miss Edith B. Palmer let fall the canvas which had concealed it and its appearance was welcomed by prolonged applause. She also hoisted the three flags successively, the band accompanying the raising of each by its own national air, "The Star-Spangled Banner," "*Wien Neêrlandsch Bloed,*" and "God Save the Queen," respectively.

The procession then was formed again and entered the great church. As it moved forward the band played the appropriate air, "*Integer Vitae,*" which was taken up and concluded by the organ within while the audience was seating itself.

The indoor exercises were opened by the singing of the late Dr. Leonard Bacon's Pilgrim hymn, beginning

"O God, beneath thy guiding hand
Our exiled fathers crossed the sea."

The memorial address was delivered by Dr. Palmer. It was a thoughtful, felicitous and eloquent study of the age in which John Robinson lived, of the special conditions out of which the Pilgrim enterprise grew, and of the history, character, writings, and influence of Robinson himself. From its many passages which deserve to be generally read several should be quoted here. In describing the times and the country of the Pilgrims Dr. Palmer spoke thus :—

In the reign of Queen Elizabeth the seeds of liberty which a divine enlightenment had been scattering broadcast in England for fifty years began to germinate, to take root and to grow. Nowhere can these seeds be discovered so readily as in the convictions of the advanced Puritans. Their watchword was reformation, but the real outcome of their conflict with repressive power was to be religious and political freedom for untold myriads. We are bound to remember this day the particular shape this conflict assumed. Hundreds and thousands of Christian people, in whose hearts there burned a passionate desire for a spiritual church and an unadulterated gospel, felt constrained to renounce the national church of England. They believed the further reformation of religion to be imperatively needful. Hopeless of seeing this effected within the national church — because the Episcopal party, who could promote it, would not, and the Puritan party, Presbyterian in its preferences, who would promote it, could not, and the two parties were in irreconcilable antagonism — they resolved upon "reformation without tarrying for any." They separated themselves from the church by law established, and at the cost of everything which men hold dear, organized, by covenant with God and each other, what we know as Congregational churches, on what they conceived to be New Testament principles. Like other third parties, they were subject to ill will from both sides. They offended the party within the church which was zealous for further reformation no less than the opposite party who believed reformation had already gone too far. To go forth, therefore, was to challenge well-nigh universal execration. The step exposed them to be hunted as malefactors, to be persecuted, imprisoned, plundered, banished, executed. But forth they went, and the future vindicated their self-sacrifice and their faith. They became by the act the vanguard of advancing Christendom. Their heroic struggles, their unconquerable resolution in all this experience, make the period forever memorable. Nor did they struggle, dare and endure to no purpose. Posterity owes to them what it enjoys of religious liberty. Those Separatist communions were the pioneer free churches.

And of John Robinson himself he said :—

Upon his church, upon the community of Leyden, upon his generation, and through the Pilgrim Fathers upon the future of New England and of the

United States, and even upon the England which had driven him from her shores but which he never ceased to love, John Robinson made an enduring, an indelible impression — an impression not rationally to be accounted for save in one way: it must have been the impress of a grand personality, grand in its moral, its intellectual, its spiritual resources. . . .

His most imposing virtue, perhaps, was his catholicity — his large tolerance. In this he outran his time. Dr. Bushnell declares him two whole centuries in advance of his age. . . . He was free from fanaticism. . . . If in the earlier years of his ministry he was led by the intensity of his convictions into any narrowness of view, it is apparent that every year led him further from everything of the kind, and that by force of the better reason he carried men with him into the enlargement he had experienced. And to him more than to any other man of his age is traceable that ultimate development of true liberality and charity toward all which is the glory of modern Congregationalism. . . . He was characterized by a profound and spiritual piety; an intense loyalty to Christ as in all things his Master and Lord; singular reverence for the Scriptures as the rule of faith and conduct; an unconquerable trustfulness, giving him courage, fortitude, and assurance of the future; strong religious affections and unfailing sympathies; an abhorrence of cant, pretense, and indirection; an exemplary walk and a scrupulous vigilance of himself; and his saintly spirit shone ever more brightly until the last. His decisive personal influence was largely founded in his conspicuous righteousness, fidelity, and disinterestedness.

One of his concluding passages also should be cited: —

And now at length we, descendants of the Pilgrim Fathers, proud of their blood and their faith, messengers of five thousand churches and of uncounted Christian citizens in the Great Republic, are here to call to remembrance his inestimable services to Truth, to Liberty, to Civilization, to Christ's Eternal Kingdom, and by this tablet, which we are now solemnly to dedicate, to perpetuate that remembrance to coming generations. Fitly it will stand here, a silent but eloquent memorial, telling to listening posterity its story of faith and patience, of fortitude and magnanimity, of heroism and triumph! Yet it will not be John Robinson's grandest monument. That is the Great Republic itself, spanning the Western Continent, rising conspicuous among the nations, cherishing the exalted consciousness that in its broad area, and in its intense life, civil and religious freedom far transcending the fathers' aspirations reigns universal, unassailable, enthroned in the hearts of ever-multiplying millions.

Although the address was delivered in English it held the close attention of the large company present.

Rev. F. A. Noble, D.D., then offered an appropriate prayer, after which Dr. Palmer formally completed the work of dedicating the tablet in these words: —

Now, therefore, WE, Samuel C. Bartlett, Eliphalet W. Blatchford, George E. Day, Morton Dexter, John K. McLean, Charles Ray Palmer, and William A. Robinson, by authority to us intrusted, IN THE NAME OF THE NATIONAL COUNCIL OF THE CONGREGATIONAL CHURCHES IN THE UNITED STATES OF AMERICA — delegates from the Congregational Union of England and Wales and from the International Council of Congregational Churches lately assembled in London, together with representatives of Yale University, the University of Leyden, and Mansfield College in Oxford, present and assisting — do solemnly set apart and dedicate this Bronze Tablet, which we have erected, to the perpetuation of the venerable and sacred memory of the erudite scholar, the devoted minister, the saintly man, whose name it bears — JOHN ROBINSON, M.A., the pastor of the Pilgrim Church, the projector and spiritual father of the Plymouth Colony; and we declare this dedication duly and irrevocably accomplished. And for the grace vouchsafed to that blessed man, and to our forefathers, and to us their descendants and fellow servants — to God Almighty, the Father, the Son, the Holy Ghost, we give praise now and evermore! Amen.

He then formally transferred the tablet to the care of the Ecclesiastical Commissioners of the city of Leyden, a permanent body having charge of all such memorials within the municipality, in the following sentences: —

To the Honorable, the Ecclesiastical Commissioners.

GENTLEMEN, — This tablet, which we have brought from our far-away home and dedicated to the perpetual memory of John Robinson, we now take pleasure in committing to your honorable keeping. We heartily thank you for the gracious permission to erect it here. We thank you also for the kindly sympathy with us in our filial purpose, manifested by your presence with us to-day. To you, and to your successors forever, we now convey and deliver this memorial in which we feel so deeply interested, assured that our trust is by you cordially accepted and that it will be safe in your hands. Receive with it, gentlemen, assurances of the highest consideration on the part of ourselves and of the churches and institutions we have the honor to represent; and also of our best wishes and our prayers for the peace and progress of the churches of Leyden, and of all the churches of this ancient and honorable realm.

To these addresses several responses were made. Mr. E. van den Brandeler replied in behalf of the Ecclesiastical Commissioners, and Mr. E. M. De Laat de Kanter, the Burgomaster, in behalf of the city of Leyden, each expressing himself in Dutch. The eminent scholar and critic, Prof. A. Kuenen, D.D., also responded, first in Dutch and then in English, for the University of Leyden. Then Principal Fairbairn, of Mansfield College, Oxford, England, made a brief and eloquent closing address, after which the audience sang the well-known hymn by Mrs. Hemans beginning: —

> "The breaking waves dashed high
> On a stern and rock-bound coast,"

and Dr. Palmer concluded the service with the benediction.

This bare outline of the proceedings gives little more than the merest suggestion of the surpassing interest of the occasion. It is eminently fitting that this magazine should contain some record of it. As a work of art the tablet is most creditable alike to its designers, to those who erected it, to the city of Leyden, and to the memory of John Robinson. It is one of the objects which all strangers in the city are careful to visit, and it is a becoming tribute to the man who not only was, more than any one else, the inspiration of the Pilgrim enterprise, but also was an intellectual and spiritual leader far in advance of his contemporaries, and whose reputation to-day is far greater than it was during his lifetime.

THE MAYFLOWER GENEALOGIES.

I. Vital Statistics of the Mayflower Passengers.

Compiled from original sources,

By George Ernest Bowman.

Any compilation of the vital statistics of the Mayflower passengers must necessarily be very incomplete, owing to the loss of early records, but in many instances births, marriages or deaths may be shown to have occurred between two dates, and the Editor has spent a great deal of time in a critical examination and comparison of original records for the purpose of collecting facts which would assist in fixing as many such dates as possible. The results of this research have been arranged in alphabetical order for convenient reference. Lack of space forbids the insertion of the authority for each statement, but this will be given in the succeeding articles on the separate families.

All dates have been given in new style to prevent mistakes in celebrating anniversaries.

John Alden. Born about 1599. Died at Duxbury, 22 September, 1687. He married, at Plymouth, before 1624, Priscilla[2] Mullins (William[1]), who died after 1650.

Isaac Allerton. Died at New Haven, Conn., before 22 February, 1659. He married, *first,* at Leyden, 4 November, 1611, Mary Norris, who died at Plymouth, 7 March, 1621. He married, *second,* at Plymouth, between July, 1623, and 1 June, 1627, Fear[2] Brewster (William[1]), who died at Plymouth in 1634. He married, *third,* before 1644, Joanna ——, who survived him.

Mary (Norris) Allerton. Wife of Isaac.

Bartholomew[2] Allerton. Son of Isaac and Mary. Born at Leyden. He returned to England, married and had children there, and was living in 1650.

Remember[2] Allerton. Daughter of Isaac and Mary. Born at Leyden. Died at Salem, between 12 September, 1652, and 22 October, 1656. She married, before 6 May, 1635, Moses Maverick, who died at Marblehead, 7 February, 1686.

MARY[2] ALLERTON. Daughter of ISAAC and MARY. Born at Leyden. Died at Plymouth, 8 December, 1699. She married, at Plymouth, about 1636, Thomas Cushman, who was born in February, 1608, and died at Plymouth, 21 December, 1691.

JOHN ALLERTON. Not known to be related to ISAAC. Died at Plymouth, between 11 January and 10 April, 1621.

JOHN BILLINGTON. Died at Plymouth, in September, 1630. He married, before 1605, ELEANOR ——, who died after 12 March, 1643. She had married, *second*, at Plymouth, in September, 1638, Gregory Armstrong, who died at Plymouth, 15 November, 1650.

ELEANOR (——) BILLINGTON. Wife of JOHN.

JOHN[2] BILLINGTON. Eldest son of JOHN and ELEANOR. Born before 1605. Died at Plymouth, between 1 June, 1627, and September, 1630.

FRANCIS[2] BILLINGTON. Son of JOHN and ELEANOR. Born about 1606. Died at Middleborough, 13 December, 1684. He married at Plymouth, in July, 1634, Christian (Penn) Eaton (widow of FRANCIS EATON), who died at Middleborough, about 1684.

WILLIAM BRADFORD. Born at Austerfield, England, in March, 1590. Died at Plymouth, 19 May, 1657. He married, *first*, in Holland, in November or December, 1613, DOROTHY MAY, who was born about 1597, and was accidentally drowned at Cape Cod Harbor, 17 December, 1620. He married, *second*, at Plymouth, 24 August, 1623, Alice (Carpenter) Southworth (widow of Edward Southworth), who was born about 1590, and died at Plymouth, 5 or 6 April, 1670.

DOROTHY (MAY) BRADFORD. Wife of WILLIAM.

WILLIAM BREWSTER. Born in 1566 or 1567. Died at Plymouth, 20 April, 1644. He married, before 1593, MARY ——, who died at Plymouth, 27 April, 1627.

MARY (——) BREWSTER. Wife of WILLIAM.

LOVE[2] BREWSTER. Son of WILLIAM and MARY. Died at Duxbury, in January or February, 1651. He married at Plymouth 25 May, 1634, Sarah[2] Collier (*William*[1]), who died after 12 March, 1680. She had married, *second*, after 1 September, 1656, Richard Parke, of Cambridge, who died there in 1665.

WRESTLING[2] BREWSTER. Son of WILLIAM and MARY. Died, unmarried, between 1 June, 1627 and August, 1643.

RICHARD BRITTERIDGE. Died at Plymouth, 31 December, 1620. *The first death after reaching Plymouth.*

PETER BROWN. Died at Plymouth, between 4 April and 10 October, 1633. He married, *first*, at Plymouth, in 1624 or

1625, Martha (——) Ford, who died at Plymouth, between 1 June, 1627 and 1631. He married, *second*, between 1627 and 1631, Mary ——, who died after 21 November, 1633.

WILLIAM BUTTEN. Died on the Mayflower, at sea, 16 November, 1620.

ROBERT CARTER. Died at Plymouth, early in 1621, after 3 March.

JOHN CARVER. Died at Plymouth, between 12 April and 10 May, 1621. He married KATHARINE ——, who died at Plymouth, five or six weeks after her husband.

KATHARINE (——) CARVER. Wife of JOHN.

—— —— Maid servant of JOHN CARVER. (See FRANCIS EATON.)

JAMES CHILTON. Died on the Mayflower, at Cape Cod Harbor, 18 December, 1620. His wife died early in 1621, after 11 January.

—— CHILTON. Wife of JAMES.

MARY [2] CHILTON. Daughter of JAMES. Died at Boston, shortly before 11 May, 1679. She married, at Plymouth, between July, 1623, and 1 June, 1627, John Winslow, who was born at Droitwich, England, 26 April, 1597, and died at Boston, between 22 March and 31 May, 1674.

RICHARD CLARKE. Died at Plymouth, between 11 January and 10 April, 1621.

FRANCIS COOKE. Died at Plymouth, 17 April, 1663. He married, in Holland, Hester ——, who died after 18 June, 1666.

JOHN [2] COOKE. Son of FRANCIS and Hester. Died at Dartmouth, 3 December, 1695. He married, at Plymouth, 7 April, 1634, Sarah [2] Warren (RICHARD [1]), who died after 25 July, 1696.

HUMILITY COOPER. Died in England, between 1627 and 1651.

JOHN CRACKSTON. Died at Plymouth, between 11 January and 10 April, 1621.

JOHN [2] CRACKSTON. Son of JOHN. Died at Plymouth, soon after 1 June, 1627.

EDWARD DOTY. Died at Plymouth, 2 September, 1655. He married, *second*,* at Plymouth, 16 January, 1635, Faith [2] Clark (Tristram [1]), who was buried at Marshfield, 31 December, 1675. She had married, *second*, John Phillips, who was born about 1602, and died at Marshfield, between 30 October, 1691 and 19 May, 1692.

FRANCIS EATON. Died at Plymouth, between 4 and 18 November, 1633. He married, *first*, SARAH ——, who died at Plymouth, early in 1621, but after 11 January. His *second* wife, whom he married at Plymouth, was probably Governor Carver's

* Nothing is known concerning the first wife.

maid servant. He married, *third*, at Plymouth, in 1624 or 1625, Christian Penn, who died at Middleborough about 1684. She had married, *second*, FRANCIS[2] BILLINGTON (JOHN[1]).

SARAH (——) EATON. First wife of FRANCIS.

SAMUEL[2] EATON. Son of FRANCIS and SARAH. Born in 1620. Died at Middleborough, in 1684, before 8 November. He married, *first*, before 20 March, 1647, Elizabeth ——, who died before 1661. He married, *second*, at Plymouth, 20 January, 1661, Martha[3] Billington (FRANCIS[2], JOHN[1]), who died after 8 November, 1684.

—— ELY. Returned to England at the expiration of his contract for one year.

THOMAS ENGLISH. Died at Plymouth, between 11 January and 10 April, 1621.

MOSES FLETCHER. Died at Plymouth, between 11 January and 10 April, 1621. He married, *first*, Maria Evans, who died before November, 1613. He married, *second*, at Leyden, 21 December, 1613, Sarah (——) Dingby, widow of William.

EDWARD FULLER. Died at Plymouth, between 11 January and 10 April, 1621. His wife died early in 1621, after 11 January.

—— FULLER. Wife of EDWARD.

SAMUEL[2] FULLER. Son of EDWARD. Died at Barnstable, 10 November, 1683. He married, at Scituate, 18 April, 1635, Jane[2] Lothrop (John[1]), who died between 1658 and 1683.

SAMUEL FULLER (DR.). Died at Plymouth, between 9 August and 26 September, 1633. He married, *first*, Elsie Glascock, who died before 1613. He married, *second*, at Leyden, 30 April, 1613, Agnes[2] Carpenter (Alexander[1]), who died before 1617. He married, *third*, at Leyden, 27 May, 1617, Bridget Lee, who died after 11 March, 1664.

RICHARD GARDINER. Died in England or at sea, between 1623 and 1651.

JOHN GOODMAN. Died at Plymouth, before 1627.

WILLIAM HOLBECK. Died at Plymouth, early in 1621, but after 11 January.

JOHN HOOKE. Died at Plymouth, early in 1621, but after 11 January.

STEPHEN HOPKINS. Died at Plymouth, between 16 June and 27 July, 1644. Nothing is known of his *first* wife. He married, *second*, in 1618 or earlier, ELIZABETH ——, who died at Plymouth, between 1640 and 1644.

ELIZABETH (——) HOPKINS. Second wife of STEPHEN.

GYLES[2] HOPKINS. Son of STEPHEN by his first wife. Died at Eastham, in 1690, before 26 April. He married, 19 October, 1639, Katharine Wheldon, who died after 15 March, 1689.

CONSTANCE[2] HOPKINS. Daughter of STEPHEN by his first wife. Died at Eastham, in October, 1677. She married, at Plymouth, between 1623 and 1 June, 1627, Nicholas Snow, who died at Eastham, 25 November, 1676.

DAMARIS[2] HOPKINS. Daughter of STEPHEN and ELIZABETH.

OCEANUS[2] HOPKINS. Son of STEPHEN and ELIZABETH. Born on the Mayflower, between 16 September and 21 November, 1620. Died before 1 June, 1627.

JOHN HOWLAND. Born about 1593. Died at Plymouth, 5 March, 1673. He married, at Plymouth, before 1624, ELIZABETH[2] TILLEY (JOHN[1]), who was born about 1607, and died at Swansea, 31 December, 1687.

JOHN LANGMORE. Died at Plymouth, early in 1621, after 11 January.

WILLIAM LATHAM. Died at the Bahama Islands, between 7 November, 1645, and 6 March, 1651.

EDWARD LEISTER. Died in Virginia, before 6 March, 1651.

EDMUND MARGESON. Died at Plymouth, between 11 January and 10 April, 1621.

CHRISTOPHER MARTIN. Died at Plymouth, 18 January, 1621. His wife died early in 1621, after 11 January.

—— MARTIN. Wife of CHRISTOPHER.

DESIRE MINTER. Died in England, before 1651.

JASPER MORE. "A litle boy." Died on the Mayflower, at Cape Cod Harbor, 16 December, 1620.

ELLEN MORE. "A litle girle." Sister of JASPER. Died at Plymouth, early in 1621, after 11 January.

RICHARD MORE. Brother of JASPER. Born about 1614. Died after 20 May, 1690. He married, 30 October, 1636, Christian Hunt, who died at Salem, between 11 November, 1671 and 20 June, 1675.

—— MORE. Brother of JASPER. Died at Plymouth, early in 1621, after 11 January.

WILLIAM MULLINS. Died at Plymouth, 3 March, 1621. He married ALICE ——, who died at Plymouth, early in 1621, after 2 April.

ALICE (——) MULLINS. Wife of WILLIAM.

JOSEPH[2] MULLINS. Son of WILLIAM and ALICE. Died at Plymouth, early in 1621, after 2 April.

PRISCILLA[2] MULLINS. Daughter of WILLIAM and ALICE. (See JOHN ALDEN.)

SOLOMON PROWER. Died at Plymouth, 3 January, 1621.

DEGORY PRIEST. Born about 1579. Died at Plymouth, 11 January, 1621. He married, at Leyden, 4 November, 1611, Sarah (Allerton) Vincent (the widow of John Vincent), who died at Plymouth, in 1633, before 3 November.

JOHN RIGDALE. Died at Plymouth, between 11 January and 10 April, 1621. He married Alice ——, who died at Plymouth, early in 1621, after 11 January.

ALICE (——) RIGDALE. Wife of JOHN.

THOMAS ROGERS. Died at Plymouth, between 11 January and 10 April, 1621. Nothing is known of his wife.

JOSEPH[2] ROGERS. Son of THOMAS. Died at Eastham, between 12 and 25 January, 1678. He married before 1633, but nothing is known of his wife except that she was living 18 August, 1652.

HENRY SAMSON. Died at Duxbury, 3 January, 1685. He married at Plymouth, 16 February, 1636, Ann Plummer, who died between 1650 and 1685.

GEORGE SOULE. Died at Duxbury, shortly before 1 February, 1680. He married at Plymouth, before 1627, Mary ——, who died at Duxbury in December, 1676.

MYLES STANDISH. Died at Duxbury, 13 October, 1656. He married, *first*, ROSE ——, who died at Plymouth, 8 February, 1621. He married, *second*, at Plymouth, between July, 1623, and 3 April, 1624, Barbara ——, who died after 16 October, 1659.

ROSE (——) STANDISH. First wife of MYLES.

ELIAS STORY. Died at Plymouth, early in 1621, after 11 January.

EDWARD THOMSON. Died on the Mayflower, at Cape Cod Harbor, 14 December, 1620. *The first death after reaching Cape Cod.*

EDWARD TILLEY. Died at Plymouth, between 11 January and 10 April, 1621. He married ANN ——, who died at Plymouth, early in 1621, after 11 January.

ANN (——) TILLEY. Wife of EDWARD.

JOHN TILLEY. Died at Plymouth, between 11 January and 10 April, 1621. His wife died at Plymouth, early in 1621, after 11 January.

—— TILLEY. Wife of JOHN.

ELIZABETH TILLEY. Daughter of JOHN. (See JOHN HOWLAND.)

THOMAS TINKER. Died at Plymouth, between 11 January and 10 April, 1621. His wife died at Plymouth early in 1621, after 11 January.

—— TINKER. Wife of THOMAS.

—— TINKER. Son of THOMAS. Died at Plymouth, early in 1621, after 11 January.

WILLIAM TREVORE. Died after 7 May, 1650.

JOHN TURNER. Died at Plymouth, between 11 January and 10 April, 1621.

—— TURNER. Son of JOHN. Died at Plymouth, early in 1621, after 11 January.

—— TURNER. Another son of JOHN. Died at Plymouth, early in 1621, after 11 January.

RICHARD WARREN. Died at Plymouth, in 1628. He married, before 1611, Elizabeth ——, who was born about 1583 and died at Plymouth, 12 October, 1673.

WILLIAM WHITE. Died at Plymouth, 3 March, 1621. He married at Leyden, 1 February, 1612, SUSANNA FULLER, who married, *second*, EDWARD WINSLOW.

SUSANNA (FULLER) WHITE. Wife of WILLIAM.

RESOLVED[2] WHITE. Son of WILLIAM and SUSANNA. Died between 1690 and 1694. He married, *first*, 15 November, 1640, Judith[2] Vassall (*William*[1]) who was buried at Marshfield, 13 April, 1670. He married, *second*, at Salem, 15 October, 1674, Abigail (——) Lord (widow of William Lord), who died at Salem, between 25 June and 7 July, 1682.

PEREGRINE[2] WHITE. Son of WILLIAM and SUSANNA. Born on the Mayflower, at Cape Cod Harbor, between 7 and 10 December, 1620. He died at Marshfield, 31 July, 1704. He married, before 16 March, 1649, Sarah[2] Bassett (*William*[1]), who died at Marshfield, 2 February, 1712.

ROGER WILDER. Died at Plymouth, between 11 January and 12 April, 1621.

THOMAS WILLIAMS. Died at Plymouth, between 11 January and 10 April, 1621.

EDWARD WINSLOW. Born at Droitwich, England, 28 October, 1595. Died at sea, near the island of Hispaniola,* 18 May, 1655. He married, *first*, at Leyden, 16 May, 1618, ELIZABETH BARKER, who died at Plymouth, 3 April, 1621. He married, *second*, at Plymouth, 22 May, 1621, SUSANNA (FULLER) WHITE, the widow of WILLIAM WHITE.

ELIZABETH (BARKER) WINSLOW. Wife of EDWARD.

GILBERT WINSLOW. Brother of EDWARD. Born at Droitwich, England, 5 November, 1600. Died in England, before 1651.

* Now St. Domingo.

OLD BOSTON, ENGLAND.

By Edwin S. Crandon.

On the east coast of England, on the banks of the river Witham just above its juncture with the bay called the Wash in the low lands, or fen country of the county of Lincoln, is ancient Boston — St. Botolph's Town, where the first minister of the Puritan colony at Trimountain labored for a generation as the Vicar of the Church of England parish, where the Pilgrim Fathers who settled Plymouth were imprisoned for a time prior to their escape to the Netherlands and where to-day the feet of the New England Bostonian turn lovingly, although a journey considerably off the main line of travel is involved thereby. And surely the attractions of old Boston are ample to compensate for the necessary change of route involved. Few travellers in England think of the old town as worthy the loss of a day from the celebrated "Cathedral route" albeit St. Botolph's Church is far more interesting as a sample of architecture, is far more interesting from historical associations, and is considerably larger than some of the cathedrals famed in travellers' story. The average traveller gets to Lincoln, the shire town of the county, and finds much to interest him there; in truth Lincoln is one of the most interesting towns in England, but to us of Massachusetts the old town in the south east of Lincolnshire, with its old and stately Church, its quaint streets and inns, its memories of the past in connection with the Reverend John Cotton, and most of all, its name must possess an interest far greater than mere oddity, or picturesqueness. Boston has these and to spare, but to us of the New England Boston, its attraction is subtler than the mere pleas-

PRISON CELLS UNDER GUILD-HALL, OLD BOSTON.

ure of gazing at old buildings or impressive ecclesiastical architecture. Perhaps the traveller is not to be blamed for ignoring Boston — even the New England traveller, for his Baedeker says that it is famous chiefly for having given its name to our Boston, and dismisses the town with barely twenty lines of description. From this the tourist easily might gain the impression that the English Boston possesses little of interest beyond its name, surely not enough to warrant the journey thither and the consequent interruption to a well defined itinerary.

Boston is 116 miles north of London and 35 miles due east from the centre of England, say not more than 150 miles from Liverpool, but the main line of the railway from London to the North passes to the west of Boston, which is reached from Lincoln by a branch and from Nottingham by another. The country thereabouts is decidedly low; in fact the local name until recently was Holland, which meant exactly what the same name means for one of the provinces of the Netherlands on the opposite side of the North Sea, namely, hollow land. Nowadays they call that section the Lincolnshire fens, and many have been the inundations, the high tides and destruction on the English side of the North Sea, unprotected from the ocean by dikes until many years after the Dutch had solved their infinitely harder problem of forcing a country from the sea. The country is not particularly interesting after one has seen some other parts of England, but it has the same beautifully green appearance; the roads are grand and run between hedges of singularly attractive beauty to the American traveller; many poplar trees give local color to the quiet landscape and rivers and canals wind through the country diversifying the view enough to prevent its becoming tedious. Boston is on both sides of the river Witham, a narrow stream where there is one bridge and a ferry. The latter simply is a small boat and you are rowed across in a few minutes for a half penny. Along the river-side are old streets and lanes, with inns the oldest I saw anywhere in that country of famous old taverns — inns that were entertaining man and beast and ringing with hearty good cheer years before the Three Hills on Massachusetts Bay ever echoed to the sound of the Puritan's axe or became the seat of wisdom so profound as fairly to entitle it to the proud appellation of the Hub of the Universe. Old buildings, too, greet the delighted novice from America; buildings whose bulging sides give evidence of their antiquity, of the old, half-timbered, projecting upper story kind which delight us so much in foreign photographs, and all of stone or brick, for wood is too precious in Europe generally for use in building.

Old Boston has a most honorable, albeit somewhat uneventful past. From the English view-point it is a slow old town, with little to distinguish it from many others of like size. To us, however, it is associated with Rev. John Cotton, the first Pastor of the Boston, New England, Church, for he was Vicar of St. Botolph's Church in the Lincolnshire Boston for many years. Again, Boston is associated indelibly with the Pilgrim Fathers of Plymouth, for in the guild hall were imprisoned the Scrooby Pilgrims, arrested in their first attempt to escape from England's persecuting King and Prelate. Striking indeed is it that history should have linked together the Pilgrim and the Puritan thus early in the great movement which ultimately settled New England, dethroned for a time both English King and Bishop and made for the triumphant vindication of the right of freedom of worship for the English race. While the Puritan Cotton was Vicar of the Church of England parish of St. Botolph in Boston, England, the Separatist, or dissenting Pilgrims, were imprisoned in the same city, and a quarter century later the same Cotton, persecuted in his turn was fain to fly to the same New England shores and to become, like them, a Separatist, and ultimately the two — Pilgrim and Puritan — blended into the New Englander and laid the foundations of our mighty Nation. In this connection it is suggestive certainly, that the Colonel of the Plymouth County regiment of Minute-Men which responded to the Lexington Alarm, 19 April, 1775, was Theophilus Cotton, a direct lineal descendant of the Puritan Vicar of Old Boston and the first Minister of the Puritan Church of the New Boston, to which was given the name of the town in England where he had labored long and well. The Pilgrim descendants went forth to battle from the Pilgrim Colony under the Puritan's descendant — they had become one people then, the people of Massachusetts, and distinctions of Pilgrim and Puritan had passed away. But there was a sharp difference in the early years of the seventeenth century. The Pilgrim was hounded out of England a generation before the Puritan had to go. Here in the New England the two types blended, the Puritan, or Low-Churchman of the English Church adopting the Pilgrim's Separatist or Independent principles of Church government and meanwhile absorbing the little Pilgrim colony into its own more virile and enduring State.

Some traditions identify Boston as known to the Romans, but beyond possibly having a fort thereabouts there is nothing of Roman origin susceptible of the least proof. The first historical notice is the following, from the Saxon Chronicle: "St. Botolph built a monastery here A.D. 654, destroyed by the Danes, A.D. 870." But this is controverted and the good saint himself seems to be almost traditional if not mythical. The best that I have been able to find about him is that he flourished about the middle of the seventh century, being of a noble family, of German descent, famous for learning and zeal. The name "Botolph" is Saxon, and means "Boat-help" or "Help-ship," hence he was the patron saint of sailors. He is said to have been given a place for the establishment of a monastery by King Ethelmund of the South Angles, but the kingship of Ethelmund over a South Anglian kingdom is matter of dispute and the whole episode is shrouded in historic gloom. St. Botolph probably existed about that time but to distinguish from the legends and traditions what is actual fact is beyond the power of to-day. In any event the story goes that the saint did not want to dispossess anybody in establishing his monastery and desired a wilderness which nobody else could use, which is why he was accommodated with the location known as "Icanhoe," now Boston. At that time the Lincolnshire fens or marshes must have been dreary and wild indeed and well suited to the humble saint's yearnings for solitude. "Icanhoe," Saxon, means "Ox-hill"; some have endeavored to trace a parallel in the name of Boston — "bos" being Latin for "ox" and thus carrying out the Saxon name, but beyond much doubt the name of Boston is a contraction of

"Botolph's town," which was the name generally used in the middle ages, and the natural tendency of the English to clip names in pronunciation easily would make "Botolph's town" into "Bos-ton." The monastery was destroyed completely by the Danes in A.D. 870 and Boston does not reappear in English history for over two hundred years, or in the reign of William the Conqueror.

As to the Saint, all that we know is that his body was buried in his monastery and that at the Danish invasion his "relics were translated to the monastery at Ely and later to that at Thorney." William of Malmesbury says that St. Botolph's body lay in St. Edmund's monastery at Bury, and Weever is quoted: "It was usual with the monks of Bury when they wanted rain to carry about in procession a coffin with the bones of St. Botolph inclosed." The 16th of May was set for his memory and the Church of St. Botolph, Aldersgate, London, took his name in the reign of Edward III. Boston as a distinct town or centre of habitation cannot be identified prior to the twelfth century. It is not mentioned in the celebrated Domesday book and it is a fair inference that up to that time it never was a town or anything else but the traditional seat of St. Botolph's monastery in the wild, low, Lincolnshire fens. Probably in the Conqueror's reign, at the Domesday survey, the locality formed part of the town of Shirbeck, which parish indeed, nearly surrounded it at the beginning of the present century.

Under the Normans Boston fell to the earls of Richmond and became a place of considerable commercial importance prior to the reign of John, for in 1204 it paid a tax on merchants of £780, second only to that of London, with £836. This shows that Boston must have begun to rise into consequence shortly after the conquest. King John granted it a charter, dated 30 January, 1204, and in 1205 the men of Boston paid £100 to secure immunity from interference from sheriffs and the right to choose their own bailiffs. It was known generally at this time in legal documents as "The Town of St. Botolph." The Hanseatic merchants and those of Flanders carried on a very large and important traffic in Boston in the thirteenth century and its market and annual fairs thus early became celebrated. It was a walled town, but no part of the wall remains and only the names of streets — Bar-gate, Wormgate and similar names — survive. The town sent members of Parliament from the reign of Henry VIII, when it was made a free borough. It had sent members to the Councils in the reign of Edward III, 1326–53, the names of four of whom are known. From the reign of Edward VI, 1552, to the present the list of Boston's M. P.'s is complete. The list of Mayors of Boston begins with Nicholas Robinson in 1545 and also is complete to date, with over 250 names. In 1698 one of William III's Dutch friends, Henry of Nassau, was created Viscount Boston in reward for conspicuous services under the Prince of Orange, but the title became extinct in 1754.

In 1281 the town suffered from a great fire, and in 1286 the fourth great flood overtook it. The low country and the nearness to the coast — the River Witham running into the Wash but a few miles below Boston — made it liable to high tides and to overflows, and throughout its history we see constant references to its exposed condition and to the efforts made to protect it, unavailing until comparatively modern times. In 1288, during the annual fair, a most important event in mediæval Boston, the town was sacked by a company of bandits or brigands, and as illustrative of the wealth of old Boston in those times the historian tells us that "streams of gold, silver and other metal, molten, ranne into the sea." It recovered speedily and became a great wool port, gave attention to the fisheries, became a great resort for Flemish and other merchants, and in 1336 a patent was issued for the protection of a great number of German merchants and fourteen ships coming to the fair of St. Botolph. In 1359 when Edward III prepared to invade France, of the eighty-two towns assessed in proportion to their trading importance, Boston stood twelfth. In 1467 came another great flood. We have a description of the town at the middle of the sixteenth century, which has come down from a chronicler of the time:

"Botolph's towne standeth hard on the river of Lindis (the Witham). The great and chiefest part of the towne is on the este side of the ryver, where is a faire market place and a crosse with a square towre. The chief parish church was St. John's where yet is a church for the towne. St. Botolph's was but a chapel to it, but now it is so risen and adorned that it is the chiefest of the towne and for a parish church the best and fairest of all Lincolnshire, and served so with singing, and that of cunning men, as no parish in all England. The society and brotherhood (be)longing to this church causeth this and much land (be)longeth (to) this society. The steeple being *quadrata turris* and a lanthorn on it, both very high and faire and a marke both by sea and land for all the quarters thereaboute. There is a goodly fonte, whereof part is of white marble, or of stone very like to it. There be three colleges of Freeres (friars), gray, black and Augustine, also an hospital for poor men, and in the towne, or near to it, the late Lord Huse had a place with a stone tower. All the buildings of this side of the towne are fayre, and merchantes dwelle in it, and a staple for wool is used there. There is a bridge of wood to come over Lindis into this part of the towne, and a pile of stones set yn the middle of the ryver. The streame of it is sometymes as swift as it were an arrow. On the west side of Lindis is one long street and on the same side is the White Friars. The mayne se (sea) ys vi miles of Boston. Dyverse good shippes and other vessels ryde there."

Under Henry VIII the dissolution of the monasteries tended to reduce the importance and commercial prosperity of Boston, but Henry made amends by raising it to the rank of a free borough and by granting it several privileges under a charter 14 May, 1546, confirmed by Edward VI, 16 May, 1547, while Mary, 1554, endowed the corporation with lands to support the bridge and port, in a deplorable state at that time, also to establish and maintain a grammar school and for public worship. By the early years of the reign of Elizabeth the port nearly had gone to ruin, largely due to alterations in the river's mouth, but late in her reign means were taken to improve this. A violent tempest, 5 October, 1571, did immense damage, and in 1585 and again in 1603 visitations of the plague occurred. James I granted a charter 17 August, 1608, confirming former charters and endowing the corporation with new privileges and immunities. It was at this time that the Pilgrim Fathers, attempting to escape from Scrooby to the Netherlands, were imprisoned under the Boston Guild-Hall, or town hall, and soon after, in 1633, Rev. John Cotton, Vicar of St.

Botolph's, with some of the leading men of his parish, were forced by the antipathy and persecution of Archbishop Laud to leave the country, going to Winthrop's colony where they gave the name of Boston to the Puritan capital. Bradford says of the little Pilgrim company:

Although they could not stay yet were they not suffered to go, but the ports and havens were shut against them, so as they were fain to seek secret means of conveyance, and to fee the mariners and give extraordinary rates for their passages. And yet were they oftentimes betrayed, many of them, and both they and their goods intercepted and surprised, and thereby put to great trouble and charge. . . .

Bartlett, "The Pilgrim Fathers," says:

Of all the seaports on the eastern coast, the most convenient for Holland, and at that time the most important, was Boston, situated amidst the rich, level fens of Lincolnshire, intersected by ancient dykes formed by the Romans, and communicating with the sea by the sluggish river Witham. . . . To Boston the principal company of the emigrants turned their eyes and secretly hired a vessel to take them over to Holland. Brewster seems to lead the conduct of this business and of the arrangements relative to the embarkation. . . . Having reached Boston they found the Captain had not yet arrived and were compelled to remain in that town, sadly reducing their scanty funds, and exposed to the continual risk of discovery. At length the Captain made his appearance, but only to betray them. . . . They were carried into the town where they were made a spectacle to the multitude and at last "being by the catchpole officers rifled and stripped of their money, books and much other goods," they were carried before the magistrates and put into wards, and messengers were sent to inform the Lords of the Council of their capture and to inquire their pleasure concerning them.

Lincolnshire was the centre of the Puritan agitation. Douglas Campbell in his "Puritan in England, Holland and America," says:

The low districts about the Humber and the Wash, reclaimed from the ocean by the Hollanders, were always hotbeds of Nonconformity; here was the original Boston; near by was Cambridge, the home of Puritanism.

On the subject of the Pilgrims' imprisonment at Boston Dr. John Brown says:

The magistrates were not unfavorable to them, for Puritanism was too rife in Boston itself for them to think ill of those that went that way. When, a quarter of a century later nine hundred Puritan colonists sailed for Massachusetts with John Winthrop, many of the leading townsmen of Boston were among the number: Richard Bellingham, Recorder of the town from 1625 to 1633; Atherton Hough, Mayor of the borough in 1628 and Thomas Leverett, an Alderman. Thomas Dudley, second Governor of Massachusetts, made Boston, Lincolnshire, his residence at one time that he might listen to the preaching of the Reverend John Cotton. Bellingham also was Governor of Massachusetts later, and so was John Leverett.

Of the Pilgrims' treatment at Boston, Bradford says:

The magistrates used them courteously and showed them what favor they could, though they could not deliver them till order came from the Council table.

What the lords of the Council did is not known but after a month's imprisonment at Boston most of the Pilgrims were sent back to Scrooby or elsewhere in that vicinity. Brewster and six others were bound over to appear at the Assizes, but there are no records of what then occurred, and the failure to escape in the autumn of 1608 was followed by ultimate success in the following spring.

As to the name of our Boston and its being given in honor of John Cotton, authorities disagree. The tablet commemorating the restoration of the Chapel in St. Botolph's Church by New England Bostonians in 1855 asserts that this was the case, and certainly that idea is common. However, the Memorial History of Boston, New England, cites a memorandum to this effect: "At a Court held at Charlestown 7 September, 1630, it was ordered that Tri Mountain be called Boston" and this was three years before Cotton arrived. Governor Dudley says that it had been predetermined to name the settlement Boston, no matter where it should be made. So many of the prominent men of the Colony came from Boston and thereabouts and it was such a centre of Puritanism that the name certainly was a natural selection. That our Boston was named for the Lincolnshire St. Botolph's Town admits of no doubt; whether it was so named in honor of Cotton alone, or from the Puritanical associations of the Mother town, remains an open question, interesting in its suggestiveness to the seeker for odd historical facts.

OLD BOSTON, ENGLAND.

In the civil war Boston was a place of great importance. In the Parliamentary publications, under date 14 July, 1642, it is said: "Information was given that his Majesty intended putting garrisons in Lynn, Boston and other sea-towns, whereupon it was directed that a general order be drawn to oppose that illegal act." In 1643 Boston was one of the towns ordered by the king to contribute towards the illegal ship-money tax "one ship of 800 tons, 260 men at least, with double tackle, munition wages, and victuals." April 18, 1643, it was certified that Boston was very strongly fortified and sometime in that month the town passed under the Parliament's control. The two Boston members of Parliament, Sir Anthony Irby and William Ellis, had been indicted with many others in Lincolnshire for high treason in having sided with the Parliament. Boston became, in 1643, an important centre of Parliamentary military activity, General Fairfax calling it the "key of the associated counties." This means the agreement or association of the eastern counties generally in support of the Parliament against the king. Cromwell was in command in the neighborhood of Boston through the remainder of 1643 and a large army was gathered there. Numerous military operations took place in that section and the Royalists were completely defeated at Winceby Field, near by, 11 October, 1643, losing 600 killed and 800 prisoners, although they considerably outnumbered the Parliamentarians. With the end of the year Cromwell departed and this was all of Boston's participation in the war, although most of its leading men were on the side of the Roundheads and the town was a centre of opposition to the King during the whole of the war, which terminated in a tragical way for the personification of the "Divine right of Kings." Bishop Williams of Lincoln wrote in 1646:

"You see the times grow high and turbulent and no one knows where the rage and madness of them may end; I am just come from Boston where I was used very coarsely."

OLD BOSTON, ENGLAND.

On the restoration of the Stuarts in 1662, Boston was punished for its participation by the removal from office of nine Aldermen, eight Councilmen and one Sergeant-at-Mace, also the Mayor. It is gratifying to the Puritan descendants of Cromwell's Ironsides and to the New Englander generally to know that the Mother Boston stood so loyally for the rights of worship and against arbitrary taxation as exemplified by the Stuarts.

By the middle of the eighteenth century the trade of Boston again was reduced to a low ebb through the ruinous state of the river and haven caused by mismanagement and neglect. Floods, high tides and storms also caused great damage. In 1767 Parliament passed an act for improving the fens near Boston, bringing a great tract of land under cultivation and materially improving the town's trade. More high tides seem to have caused devastation periodically. One of these is famous wherever English literature is known and appreciated from the pen of a poet born in Boston, Jean Ingelow. This is her well known "High Tide on the Coast of Lincolnshire, 1571."

The great tide in 1810 (10 November) was the most calamitous of all and the town barely escaped total destruction. Since then there have been no serious difficulties, while the construction of a modern set of docks has given Boston a renewed lease of commercial life. To-day the town has a good and a growing trade and is far from being the sleepy village that some Americans think. It has the charm of antiquity, and its picturesqueness is most pleasing, but it also has modern life, and is growing well, as growth is measured in our conservative mother country. In 1565 Boston had 471 families according to the Harleian manuscript; in 1768 the population was 3470; in 1801 it was 5926; in 1811 it had grown to 8113; in 1880 it was about 15,000 and is to-day not far from 20,000. It will be seen that the percentage of growth of late has been very gratifying.

Reference has been made to John Cotton as easily the greatest man connected with old Boston's history, although John Fox was a native, and also Jean Ingelow. Cotton was Vicar of St. Botolph's Church from 1612 to 1633. He was son of Rowland Cotton, an attorney; was born at Derby 4 December, 1585; showed signs of Puritanism at Cambridge University, where he was a fellow of Emmanuel College and head lecturer, dean, and catechist, with many scholars. He settled at Boston, on invitation, 1612. He became a non-conformist, but continued twenty years in Boston during which time his house was filled with young students, some from Germany and Holland, but most from Cambridge, finishing their studies. Burnham's "Pious Memorials" quoted in an old history of Boston, published in 1818, says:

"His distinguished piety and extensive usefulness having sufficiently exposed him to the malice of the prelates, letters missive were out against him from the infamous high commission court. As he knew that if he appeared there he could expect no other than to be stifled with such a perpetual imprisonment as had already murdered Bates, Udal, etc. he concealed himself as well as he could from the search of the officers. Application was made in the mean time to the Earl of Dorset, for the fulfilling of an old engagement of his to Mr. Cotton and the Earl did intercede for him, but the Archbishop of Canterbury rendered all his intercessions both ineffectual and unseasonable. Lord Dorset therefore informed Mr. Cotton that if he had been guilty of drunkenness, uncleanness or any such lesser fault he could have obtained his pardon, but as he was guilty of Puritanism and non-conformity the crime was unpardonable, and therefore he advised him to flee for his safety. In consequence Cotton and two other ministers, Hooker and Stone, embarked on the same vessel for New England, arriving 3 September, 1633. Cotton died 23 December, 1652."

John Cotton's work and influence in New England are graven in letters of gold on the pages of our history. It is pleasant to know that in old Boston his learning, sincerity, ability and greatness are appreciated keenly and are honored more and more with the years; the various histories of the town give ready praise and on the whole a just analysis of his motives in holding to the Puritan side of the great controversy, and a becoming pride is taken in his great work in the new England and in the growth and influence of the new Boston as reflecting on the mother Boston. The New England Bostonian finds warmest welcome in the Lincolnshire Boston; the people are decidedly hospitable, and in St. Botolph's Church and the quaint little book-shop within its shadow — a building fairly bulging with age, albeit of stone — he is made to feel at home indeed. Old Boston has many old families and men and women proud of the past who delight in historical and literary research, and these appreciate warmly the eminence in literature which distinguishes the Boston of the west. The visitor from Trimountain to St. Botolph's town has no lack of courteous aid in his inquiries about the old town, and there is a delight in meeting us and in pointing out the places of interest, in talking about the history of the town and its great grown-up daughter, that is most enjoyable. The typical English conservatism and our own Boston reserve give way, and Bostonians, separated in their homes by more than 3,000 miles, get together right loyally in "the sympathy of kindred minds" in the dear old streets and quaint old buildings of the Boston of the fens. This most charming courtesy and kindliness of the people of old Boston towards the American visitor is not the least of the pleasures of a pilgrimage to the mother town.

Boston Church, otherwise the parish Church of St. Botolph, is the most prominent feature of the town. It is the second or third largest parish church in England, and while lacking transepts and other adjuncts of a cathedral, yet is larger than some of the seats of the Bishops of the English establishment and is certainly much more imposing than many of them. It has antiquity, solidity, beauty and history, with one of the most imposing spires to be seen on any church, even in Europe. This spire known locally as "The Boston Stump" gives a view of the surrounding country that is superb. The foundations were laid in 1309 at the time when Boston was at the height of its commercial prosperity, but the nave and chancel are thought to be even older. The account of the foundation of the present edifice by an old historian is interesting:

"Anno 1309 in the third yeare of King Edwarde ye 2nd, the foundation of Boston steeple, on the next Monday after Palm Sunday, was begun to be dug by many miners, and so continued till midsummer following, at which time they were deeper than the haven by 5 foot, and they found a bed of stone upon a spring of sand, and that laid upon a bed of clay, the thickness of which could not be known. Then upon the Monday, next after the feast of St. John Baptist was laid the first stone by Dame Margery Tilney, and thereon laid shee five pound sterling; Sir John Truesdale, then parson of Boston, gave also five pounds more. These were all ye great guifts at that time."

It is a most interesting building, whereof the spire is easily the most interesting part. The delicacy of the stone work is remarkable. It has been compared to the tower of the famous church of Antwerp and it does not suffer in the comparison. It is in the perpendicular style of architecture, a word usually abbreviated in the guide-books, hence the amusing error of the American lady who affected knowledge of architecture not possessed and described one of England's celebrated cathedrals as being in "perp." style, which was right as far as it went, but had a canine sound altogether out of keeping with the dignity of the subject. The main body of St. Botolph's Church is of the decorative style, and the name is well deserved in this case. Interiorly the Church shows the marks of the stern days of the Commonwealth, and many are the brasses which were pulled up and taken down; many the beautiful objects of art which fell before the Puritan's iconoclastic fury when at last he turned on the "Divine Right" of King and Prelate and demonstrated the diviner right of the Englishman and of the Christian. The Church had fallen somewhat into decay with the decadence of Boston commercially, and it is another odd coincidence that it was used as a cavalry stable by the Parliamentary army—a coincidence when the use made by the British troops in the daughter Boston of our Old South is remembered. It was not until 1840 that the work of restoration of St. Botolph's was undertaken and it was completed in 1853. Two years later the Cotton Chapel, which had been used as an engine house, was restored and named by New England Bostonians in honor of the illustrious Vicar of St. Botolph's and the first minister of the Puritan Church in the city by the Charles. The Latin inscription, written by Edward Everett, reads:

"In perpetual remembrance of John Cotton who during the reigns of James and Charles was for many years a grave, skilful, learned and laborious Vicar of this Church. Afterwards, on account of the miserable commotion amongst sacred affairs in his own country, he sought a new settlement in a new world, and remained even to the end of his life a pastor and teacher of the greatest reputation and of the greatest authority in the first church of Boston in New England, which receives this venerable name in honor of Cotton. Ccxxxv years having passed away since his migration, his descendants and the American citizens of Boston were invited to this pious work by their English brethren, in order that the name of an illustrious man, the love and honor of both worlds, might not any longer be banished from that noble temple in which he diligently, learnedly and sacredly expounded the divine oracles for so many years; and they have willingly and gratuitously caused this shrine to be restored and this tablet to be erected in the year of our recovered salvation, 1855."

The tower rises to a height of 272 feet, being surmounted by an octagonal lantern from which in former times a warning beacon guided navigators and travellers through the surrounding fens. Two hundred years are said to have been consumed in the erection of the building, extending through the reigns of ten sovereigns. It is not over and above well embellished, for reasons already indicated, but it does not inspire one with chilliness; on the contrary the spell of the great Vicar is over one, as he sees in use to-day the same pulpit which he honored for a generation, and the realization that here indeed we are at the birthplace of our great Boston and all that is meant thereby of progress, of education, of culture and of influence invests dear old St. Botolph's with a glory far greater than gorgeous stained glass, or rich treasures of art. It is hallowed by an honored past and by the sense of the mighty influence which went forth from this minister of the fens to the new world where Puritanism became sweetened and worked out to triumphant success its great part in the elevation of mankind, in the freeing of human thought and activity, religious and political.

Nevertheless St. Botolph's possesses rich chancel carvings, claimed to be surpassed by no church in England and what brasses remain are well worthy inspection. The organ, first mentioned in 1480, has been restored and entirely reconstructed. The ceiling of the tower is 140 feet high, and it is a curious fact that the Church conforms in a number of ways to the divisions of time. There are 365 steps to the summit of the tower, there are 52 windows, 12 pillars, 24 steps to the library and 60 steps leading to the chancel. From the tower one sees the beautiful river Witham, with ancient ruins, Lincoln Cathedral (on a clear day), the Wash, and the distant Norfolk hills, with little villages, church spires, and an altogether inspiring English landscape, wherein sea and fen mingle most charmingly.

"Boston Stump," as the tower of St. Botolph's is called locally, dominates the view everywhere in and around Boston, and the visitor soon comes to look for it wherever he may be in and around the town. The guild hall, or town hall, is as old as the church, probably older, and has been mentioned above as containing in its basement or cellars the cells wherein were confined the Scrooby Pilgrims after their first attempt at escape to the Netherlands. Numerous old buildings, with projecting upper stories, greet the eye almost everywhere in old Boston's streets, and the inns, particularly the Peacock, are delightful to the lover of the antique. This tavern was doing business long before the migration of Pilgrim and Puritan to New England, and to-day the descendants of those exiles delight to wander through its quaint, long corridors, its low ceilinged and musty rooms, richly wainscotted, out to the skittle-ground, where the good, old English game still goes on as it has done in the same spot for centuries. The heavily panelled coffee room, with its antique fireplace and mantel, make the New England Bostonian fairly yearn to transport, first one piece of furniture, then another, then the whole room, and finally the whole inn to our Boston. We have no such inns here, and few indeed there are in England. The Red Lion too, is a jolly old place of entertainment for man and beast, entered under an archway into the inn yard, where behind an open window in the summer days sits the typical red cheeked, plump English country bar-maid, while the villagers sit outside with their ale and pipes, contemplating the sides of bacon and the hams hung up above, with the activities of the old inn yard, fairly realizing the descriptions of Dickens in the accounts of the peregrinations of the immortal Pickwick. Would that the genial old president of that famous Pickwick Club had visited Boston as he did Rochester, and Cobham, and Ipswich and Bury St. Edmunds and the many other places celebrated as never before by the master touch of humor of the great novelist.

And Boston has pastry shops, too, if you do not want the "joint and the sweet" of the inn — shops where you may have a little back room for a quiet tea, with shrimps of the kind favored particularly by Sairey Gamp, with bread buttered for you in generous quantity and of unimpeachable quality, and all the delicacies of wondrous variety in tarts and goodies comprehended under the name of "sweets." Then from the Guild-Hall we turn down Spain Lane, full of quaint, low, old stone houses and warehouses, more than four hundred years old some of them, which is named, not in honor of our late antagonist, but for the De Spayne family, Boston merchants of the fourteenth century. A curious, half-timbered building nearer the centre of the town, Shodfriars-hall, commemorates one of the numerous monastic orders which was settled in Boston prior to the reformation, literally meaning monks or friars who wore sandals — were shod, in fact, instead of going barefooted. This hall is restored, but in harmony with the old style of architecture, after the fashion followed notably in Chester, and increasing in other English towns, and is used now for concerts and other public entertainments. Another hall, named for a prominent old Boston merchant, called Peascod, recalls memories of Shakespeare's delightful "Midsummer Night's Dream." The streets, some of them, suggest our Boston — High, West, and South and Cornhill Lane, but most of them are peculiar to Boston itself. Wormgate and Wide and Straight Bargate, Pump Square, Bridge Foot, Stanbow Lane, Mitre Lane, Greyfriars Lane, Liquorpond Street and Petticoat Lane are examples, and of course there is the Market Place, for all English towns of any size at all have a market place wherein once or twice a week country produce is bought and sold, and market days are *the* days generally on which to see Boston or any town at its best. Boston is one of the most curious old towns in England, with a large, irregular market place, quaint antique buildings and a strong suggestion of the picturesque towns on the other side of the North Sea. It is quiet enough save on the market days, when the streets swarm with country folk and the bustle has a delicious old world character most novel to the American.

Much indeed do we owe to the fair town of Lincolnshire, that it gave us of its best and noblest in manhood in the Puritan Cotton, servant of God and builder of New England; the inspiration of an honored ancestry which dared to follow conscience, and which has been most richly blessed in this new world which they won for liberty of worship and of government. Pleasant is the thought that in the old England our Pilgrim Fathers found some little softening of the almost universal rigor of their treatment in Boston town and that even then there was a sympathetic drawing together of Pilgrim and Puritan which prefigured the complete assimilation in later years in the new England of the two grandest types of Anglo-Saxon manhood. Long may the noble tower of the good St. Botolph stand not only a beacon for the traveller by sea and land but as an inspiration to us in this new Boston to holier, better living, for that we have in trust that honored name.

THE WILL AND INVENTORY OF HENRY SAMSON.

Literally transcribed from the original records,

BY GEORGE ERNEST BOWMAN.

Henry Samson died at Duxbury, 3 January, 1685, new style, or 24 December, 1684, old style, according to the Duxbury town records. His will and inventory were recorded in the Plymouth Colony Wills and Inventories, Volume IV, Part II, pages 94 and 95.

[p. 94] Duxburrow this 24th of the: 10th 1684

The Last Will and Testament of henery Sampson of Duxburrow;

In the Name of God Amen

Know all p^r^sons whom it may Concerne that I henery Sampson being in my right understanding Doe thuse will and bequeth my estate to be Disposed of, after my Death

1 I Doe Comitt and Comend my soule to God that gave it mee whom I trust hath redemed it; and my body to the earth for a season; Desiering that I may be Decently buried;

2 It is my will that all p^r^sonall Debts be payed out of my p^r^sonall estate; and that my funerall Charges before any legacyes

3 I Doe Give and bequeath unto my son Stephen one third p^r^te of my whole puchase of Land lying and being in the Township of Dartmouth;

4 I Doe Give unto my son John one thirds of my whole purchase of Lands lying and being within the Township of Dartmouth;

5 I Give and bequeath unto my son James the remaining p^r^te of the other third of my Land lying within the Towneship of Dartmouth; That is thuse Joseph Russell is to have the Land which was my son Jameses sold to him the said Russell; and I signed it taken out of the Last third; and the remainder is that which I Doe bequeath to my son James for hee had the Mony for the Land that was sold to the abovsaid Russell;

6 I Doe further give and bequeath unto my son James one shilling;
7 I Doe give and bequeath unto my son Caleb one shilling;
8 I Doe Give unto my Daughter Elizabeth now the wife of Roberd Sprout one shilling;
9 I Doe Give and bequeath unto my Daughter hannah now the wife of Josias holmes one shillinge;
10 It: I Doe give and bequeath unto my Daughter Now the wife of John hanmore ten shillings;
11 I Doe Give and bequeath unto Mary my Daughter Now the wife of John Summers; one shillinge
12 I Doe give unto my Daughter Dorcas now the wife of Thomas Bony one shillinge
13 I Doe Constitute ordaine and appoint; my son Stephen to be executor of this my Last Will and Testament to pay all my Debts and Legacyes and to receive all Dues;
14 It is my Desire that my trusty and honored frind m^{r} Wiswall would be the overseer of this my last will and Testament; Thus Desireing to waite untill my Change shalbe; and that those that come after may be att Peace; I shall subscribe with my hand and seale the Day & yeer above expressed; signed and sealed in the p^{r}sence
of the witnesses:
Thomas Delano
Joseph Channdeler

Henery Sampson } seale
his **H** marke }

Thomas Delano & Joseph Chandeler made oath in Court the 5th of March 16$\frac{84}{85}$ that they see henery Sampson signe seale and Declare this to be his Last will and Testament; and that to the best of theire Judgment hee was of a Disposeing mind when hee soe Did;

[p. 95] Duxburrow this 24 of the 12 1684
An Inventory taken of the estate of the Late Deceased henery Sampson of Duxberrow by us whose Names are under written;

Item To Land in Dartmouth	70 00 00
Item To one Cow	02 05 00
Item Armes wearing Clothes and Lyberary	04 10 00
Item To bedes and beding	12 00 00
Item To pewter brasse & Iron	10 00 00
Ite a Table and benches	01 10 00

Item to one and harnise	00 10 00
Item to Chaines and plow Irons and Glasse bottells	01 15 00
Item To one Chest three wheeles and some other Lumber	01 04 00
Item To Corne	08 00 00
The totall sume is	106 14 00

The Debts that are Due out of the estate

is first To Elizabeth Sproute	01 05 00
To mr Winge of Boston	03 10 00
To mr Thomas three Gallons of Rum And other funerall charges	00 18 04
To mr Wiswall	00 08 00
To the Country	00 04 00

Thomas Delano
Joseph Chandeler

Stephen Sampson made oath in Court the 5th of March $16\frac{84}{85}$ that this a true Inventory of the estate of henery Sampson Deceased; and that when hee knowes more hee will cause it to be added to this Inventory as Attests

Nathaniel Morton Secretary.

ISAAC ALLERTON'S WILL AND INVENTORY.

Transcribed from the original records,

BY GEORGE ERNEST BOWMAN.

Isaac Allerton died at New Haven, Conn., between 1 February 1658-9, when he appeared in court as defendant in a suit brought to compel the payment of an old debt, and the twelfth of the same month, the date on which his inventory was taken.

The will and inventory were recorded in the New Haven Probate Records, Volume I, Part I, pages 82 and 83.

[p. 82] At a Court of Magistrates Octob. 19. 59

A writeing presented as the last will & Testament of Isaac Alerton, late of Newhaven deceased, wth an account of certaine debts, dew to him; & from him;

An account of Debts at the Duch

first, 700. & odd gilders from Tho: Hall by Arbitration of Captaine Willet, & Augustine Harman; about Captaine Scarlet wch I paid out,

And there is 900 gilders owing by John Peterson the Bore, as by Georg Woolseyes booke will appeare; & severall obligations thereto,

ffrom Richard Cloufe owes, as Georg Woolseyes Booke will make appeare; I thinke 900. gilders, but his Estate being broken. I Desire that what may be gotten may be layd hold on for mee,

Due from william Goulder 270, od gilders, by his Bill appeares;

Due from John Snedecare a shoomaker 150, od gilders as by his acc^o appeares.

from the widdow of the Hanc Hancson due as by severall Bills & accounts;

Peter Cornelioussen 120. od guilders as by ye account will appeare.

Due from Henry Brasser for rent for 18 moneths, from the first October 1656. to the last of May 58: for three roomes at 3 gilders a week. I am in his Debt for worke of the old acc^o wch must be Deducted;

there is 20^{li} in George Woolseyes hand, that came fro. m^{r} Tho Mayhue for mee

There is 400. od. gilders that I owe to Nicholas, the ffrenchman, & a Cooper I owe something to, wch I would have that 20^{li} in Georg Woolseyes hand, & the rest of that in Henry Brassers hand to them two;

And now I leave my son Isaac Allerton and my wife, as Trustees to receive in my debts, & to pay what I owe, as farr as it will goe & what is overpluss I leave to my wife and my sonne Isaac, as far as they receive the Debts to pay what I owe;

In Captaine Willetts hand. a pcell of booke lace 1300 & odd. guilders wch I left in trust with Captaine Willett to take care of:

Seale

My brother Bruster owes mee foure score pounds & odd. as the obligations will appeare.

Besides all my Debts in Delloware Bay & in Virgenia wch in my booke will appeare, & in Barbadoes. what can be gott;

Witness. Isaac Allerton Senio^{r}

John Harriman

Edward Preston:

[p. 83] An Inventory of the Estate of Isaac Allerton late of Newhaven deceased taken ffeb 12. 1658

	li sh d
Imp^{r} the Dwelling house Orchard & Barne wth two acres of meadow	75:00:00
a pcell of Tubbs & other cask, & 2 boosh apples	01.12.06
8. Jarrs, a case of bottles, & 2 cases wthout bottles	01.03.00
1 pre of small stilleyards 1 old sieve, 6 stooles & 3 old chaires	01.02.00
1 chest of Drawers. 1 bedstead. wth cord, & one small chest, & 1 old booke	01.17.00
1 pre of Ondirons, & 4 potthangers, & other iron	00.08.02
1 rugg. 2 blankitts. 1 old featherbed & bolster & pillow	04.13.00
1 Drawtable, 2 chaires, & a forme & a carpet	02.06.00
a pre of blankitts of cotton & sheeps wooll	01.16.00
1 Sea chest, small box, & 2 warming pans	00.17.06
4 old skellitts. & 2 small old kettles	00.15.00
3 Iron potts, 2 frying panns, & a pcell of Tinware	01.17.04
5 brase candlesticks, & a brass chaffingdish	00.09.06
1 bolster, 1 blankett, & a remn^{t} tradingcloath.	01.10.00
a pcell of wearing cloaths	06.17.06

curtaines & vallens for a bed & a sm: turky carpet	02.06.00
2 old blankitts, a pcell of carpeting & a small old Table	01.08.00
a pcell of pewter	02.17.10
8 ounces of plate at 5^s pr.	02:00:00
a pcell of old linnen 1^{li} thread	02:07:04
2 sowes & 4 piggs	02:10:00
a bedstead, old curtaines, & a morter & pestell a chest case, & 2 old tubbs, & a pre spectacles, old hatt, & capp	01:05:06
5 cushions, some old bands, wth some other old linnen	00:11:06
brimston, & sheeps wooll	00.14:06
	118:05:02

Prisers.
Will: Andrews }
Will: Russell }

Debts Due to the Estate in Newhaven.

Mr. Goodenhouse pr Order of m^r Malbon 50^s fro wch he deducts 20^s that he saith m^r Allerton owed him, and 8^s paid m^r Mills, Rests	01.12.00
m^r Tuttle by the Rest of 40^s ord^red by m^r Malbon	00:10:00
Goodm: Hull is Dr	00:16:00
m^r Gilberts man Isaac Hall	01.00:00
Humphry Spinigh	
m^r w^m Trowbridg for his p^rdesesso^r Daniell Sillivan	

MAYFLOWER PASSENGERS AND COAT-ARMOUR.

BY F. APTHORP FOSTER.

The fad for using armorial devices on letter paper, carriages and what not has become so much a matter of unreasoning custom that a word of protest should be entered against the wholesale assumption of arms by those having no claim to them.

Many years ago in Boston an artist by the name of Cole painted coats of arms for the unsuspecting and for those who wished a final touch to their respectability. His method was much the same as that employed by the so-called "heraldic painters," stationers and die-cutters nowadays. Guillim, Burke or some other list of arms-bearing families was searched for one of the same name as his customer. The arms found were declared to be his. If there were more than one family mentioned, a description of whose arms was given, no doubt the most artistic coat was chosen. Where no armigerous family of the customer's name was found, a coat was promptly concocted. The whole method was fraudulent and worthy of the strongest condemnation, though the heraldic painter or stationer can hardly be held blameworthy when the customer insists on making a willing dupe of himself.

Let us briefly consider who are entitled to coat-armour, if any one can be said to be so entitled in a country where class distinctions and privileges have no legal recognition. In forming our opinion we must be guided by the English laws on the subject, for from England if from anywhere came the right of our English-speaking ancestors to coats of arms.

Roughly speaking, those who have legal right to coat-armour are the descendants in the *male* line from an ancestor to whom the Heralds made a grant of arms, or from one who was confirmed as an armiger by them in one or other of their various Visitations.

Women could only use their father's arms (provided he were entitled to them) in a lozenge, without helmet, crest or motto. Children did not inherit the mother's arms unless she were an heiress and then they quartered them with their paternal coat.*

These rules are violated daily, sometimes wittingly, more generally from ignorance. A case in point, which came under my observation. A young lady found an old seal which had been in her family for many years. It was not known who had claimed the arms engraved on it or to whom they were supposed to have belonged. However, she adopted them, and had a die made of the crest with the initial of her family name beneath. She was remonstrated with for using arms that she had not a shadow of a claim to, and her excuse was that she liked them, they were very pretty and no one would be the wiser if she said nothing. This is merely one example in hundreds of the gratuitous appropriation and constant misuse of arms. Small wonder that the whole subject is thereby brought into ridicule and disrepute.

Now who, if any, of the Mayflower passengers were rightfully

* See the report of the committee on heraldry of the New England Historic Genealogical Society in the Register, Vol. liii. p. 399.

possessed of coats of arms which their male descendants are today fairly entitled to by the rules mentioned in a previous paragraph? The answer based upon present knowledge is a short one — none.

A halo of sacredness has so long surrounded those worthy men and women who braved all for their conscience's sake, that it is with a feeling akin to desperation that one speaks of them in other than glowing superlatives, yet from a heraldic standpoint it should be borne in mind that, with Edward Winslow and Captain Myles Standish as exceptions, the Mayflower people were made up of yeomen and indentured servants. This fact of station alone disposes of the right of these two classes to coat-armour. Arms were an attribute of quality and distinction. Hunter, in his *Founders of New-Plymouth,* (p. 106,) says in this regard: "The yeomanry of England in the reign of Elizabeth formed the class next to those who were the acknowledged gentry using coat-armour of right."

Winslow's father was designated "esquire" * and very possibly the family was armigerous, but at present definite knowledge on the subject is lacking. The Governor used arms on his seal, but his right to do so has never been satisfactorily settled and cannot be until his descent from a recognized armigerous ancestor has been proved beyond doubt. Standish is the only other of the Mayflower passengers whom circumstantial evidence would place as one of the gentry. He claimed in his will to be of the Standishes of Standish and entitled to lands in England through a great-grandfather who was a younger son of that house. Diligent search has failed wholly to verify his statements, and with proof lacking to show who his English ancestors were, any claim to arms through him must be thrown aside.

In 1891 Mr. William S. Appleton published a list in the *New England Historic-Genealogical Register* † of "Positive Pedigrees and Authorized Arms." ‡ This has been followed by a supplementary list § bringing the number of names up to

* Pope, Pioneers of Massachusetts. † Vol. xlv. 187.

‡ The full sub-title is "Or an attempt at a List of Settlers named in Savage's Genealogical Dictionary of New England, whose Ancestors are recorded in the Heraldic Visitations of England, and whose Descendants are probably living in the United States of America."

§ Register, Vol. lii. 185.

thirty-two. Proof in each case was indisputable, and no claim was admitted without the most careful scrutiny. Neither in these lists, nor in a manuscript list of some additional settlers likely to have been armigerous, but for whose use of arms there was insufficient proof to justify printing their names, does Mr. Appleton mention any Mayflower passenger. To those who know the care with which Mr. Appleton's work was done, this in itself is sufficient proof that neither Winslow, Standish nor their fellow voyagers can be considered armigers.

THE INVENTORY OF SAMUEL[2] EATON (FRANCIS[1]) AND THE SETTLEMENT OF HIS ESTATE.

Transcribed from the Original Records,

BY GEORGE ERNEST BOWMAN.

The record of the settlement of the estate of Samuel[2] Eaton (Francis[1]) of Middleboro, which is found in the Plymouth Colony Wills and Inventories, Volume IV, Part I, page 83, is most unsatisfactory, since the meagre facts it contains serve only to show that there are probably many descendants of Francis Eaton whose connection has never been suspected and may always remain unknown.

Samuel Eaton married, first, before 1647, Elizabeth ——, who was living 5 (15) October, 1652, and Bradford's History states that she had one child living in 1651. She died before 1661, for Samuel married, second, on 10 (20) January, 1660–61, Martha[3] Billington (Francis[2], John[1]), who survived him.

The record shows that the first wife must have had at least two daughters who had married and had children living when the estate was settled, and that at least one of these daughters was dead. No other construction can be put upon the statement "and the Children of the first wife to have the sume of twenty shillings a peece & such of them as are Dead the sume to be payed amonge theire Children."

The record also proves that the surviving children by the second wife were a son and three unmarried daughters, the daughters all under age. The "Daughter provided for by her Grand father" must have been the one named in the deed dated 3(13) January 1663–64, in which Francis Billington conveyed land at Middleborough to Samuel and Martha Eaton (calling them his son-in-law and daughter) for their lifetime and then to their daughter Sarah.

An Inventory of the estate of Samuell Eaton of Middlbery Late Deceased exhibited to the Court held att Plymouth the 29th of October 1684

Item 3 Cowes	06	00	00
Item a two yeer old heiffer	01	10	00
Item a yeer old heiffer	01	00	00
Item a yeer old heiffer	01	00	00
Item 2 Colts	01	00	00
Item a Mare	01	00	00
Item a Mare	02	00	00
Item a horse	01	10	00
Item swine	02	02	00
Item a prte in a Grindstone	00	3	00
Item a Cart and whees and a yoke	01	00	00
Item plow takeling axes & hoes a spade 2 sickles	01	00	00
Item wheat and rye and fflax and Tobacco	02	03	00
Item Indian Corn upon the Ground	05	00	00
Item a Cannoo	00	05	00
Item Cotton woole and sheeps woole	01	04	00
Item Clothes and Armes	03	11	00
Item beding	03	00	00
Item bookes	00	08	00
Item potts & tramell and tonges a bridle & a saddle	02	02	00
Item old lumber	00	10	00
Item house and land Graunted by the Towne of Middlbery prised att	07	00	00
prised by us John Allin — the whole is	37	11	00
Nathaniel : Warren			
The Debts Due from the estate to marchant lake	*£*	*s*	*d*
of Boston	04	00	00
for worke of his sonnes	02	10	00
smale Debts	02	10	00

for the settleing of the estate of Samuell Eaton of Middlbery Deceased this Courts orders that the eldest shall have the house and Land that was Graunted to the said Eaton by the Towne of Middlbery after his Mothers Decease; the Daughter provided for by her Grand father; and to have ten shillings att Marriage or when shee is of age the which first happens; and the Children of the first wife to have the sume of twenty shillings a peece & such of them as are Dead the sume to be payed amonge theire Children and twenty shillings for the two youngest Children each to have theire prte att age or Marriage which shall first happen; and the widdow to have the remaindr for her releiffe;

SCROOBY MANOR-HOUSE.

IN AND ABOUT SCROOBY.

BY MORTON DEXTER.

Scrooby has become a sort of Mecca for all interested in Pilgrim history. More and more the number of its visitors increases. Some are lineal descendants of the men and women who have made the little hamlet famous. More look back to them as ecclesiastical and spiritual ancestors. Many others are drawn thither merely by that general interest which thoughtful people feel in any spot which has been a rallying point of vital forces in history.

Scrooby well rewards its visitor. It is unpretending, even more modest now in the days of its fame than it was three hundred years ago when the manor-house had not parted with its stateliness and when the voices of men eminent in Church and State used to awake its echoes. It is not picturesque. But its associations and memories cause the sensitive spirit to thrill.

Yet it is not without a real external charm. He must be phlegmatic indeed who is not impressed by the serene tranquillity of its peaceful meadows and lazy streams; the fresh, rich coloring of its banks and hedges, its nearer copses and remoter woodlands; and the gracefulness of its old church-spire and the cosiness of its cluster of red-roofed houses. It is beautiful in its own quiet way. It has that peculiar loveliness which characterizes rural scenery in England, and which, although no more delightful than that of many of our own similar landscapes, is different. Yet, as I have said, its special attractiveness is historical, and the visitor usually goes there to see certain distinct features of the village and the region.

Just where is Scrooby? It is so tiny that your map may not exhibit it. Then measure off a line of fifteen miles about due west from Gainsborough and another about ten miles due south from Doncaster and their point of intersection will be where Scrooby lies. You probably will approach it from either north or south and by the Great Northern Railroad. But, although it has a little station, very few trains stop there and you will do better to leave the cars at Bawtry, a mile and a half to the north. There make your headquarters at the Crown Inn. The host is used to American visitors, and a considerable experience enables me to certify that a large measure of modest but genuine comfort may be enjoyed under his roof. It is well worth while to remain for several days and explore the vicinity.

Bawtry is in Yorkshire. Scrooby, although so near, lies in Nottinghamshire, and a corner of Lincolnshire wedges itself in between the others, so that you may walk in three counties within a few moments, if you like. A mile and a half nearly north of Bawtry is Austerfield, the birthplace of William Bradford. A long mile northwest from the Crown Inn, and in Harworth parish, lies the large "Martin" farm, the remainder of the wide estate once owned by the Morton family, an ancient and honorable house which has furnished, in its descendants, at least one governor and one chief-justice of the Supreme Court to Massachusetts.

Two miles or so west of Bawtry is Harworth village — not that of the Brontë family — and beyond that at some distance lie Tickhill, with its ruined castle, and Rotherham. Babworth and Sutton are more to the south and over towards the east rises Gringley-on-the-hill, worth a visit for the charm of the drive thither and of the view from the summit. And all around Bawtry and Scrooby, as a centre, stretch smooth meadows dotted with grazing cattle and scattered elms or thickets of trees, with the Ryton and the Idle winding sluggishly into the distance, and with the line of the railroad in view here or there to remind one that this is the nineteenth century instead of the seventeenth.

In Bawtry itself, although Pilgrim eyes must have looked upon it daily and Pilgrim feet must have trodden its streets and lanes, there is little to recall them directly. The parish church, instead of standing prominently upon the public square, is down by the river and is a squat edifice with a square tower, having little beauty and no special historic associations. Much more interesting, although it has been "restored" out of whatever antique beauty it may have had, is the old Morton Chapel, which, although close to the houses of Bawtry, really is just over the line in Harworth. Three hundred years or more ago the Mortons, then Roman Catholics, built and endowed this chapel, and also, just across the road, two or three little cottages as refuges for poor old women. It is pleasant to know that the pious purposes of the founders have not failed to be fulfilled by their Protestant successors. Worship still is held regularly in the church, which has become a "chapel-of-ease" of the Bawtry parish church, and you may still see old women in the cottages who owe their enjoyment of homes, instead of becoming inmates of some great county asylum, to the beneficence of the past.

Bawtry Hall, naturally the residence of the lord of the manor, at present the Earl of Crewe, is within a stone's throw but is not occupied by him, as he prefers another home. It is a plain but dignified building, in pleasant grounds but invisible from the neighboring roads.

It is an enjoyable walk down to Scrooby. After passing the long front of the Bawtry Hall estate on the west and a stretch of meadows or wheat fields on the east, with scarlet poppies growing in brilliant profusion among the wheat, you find yourself on the brow of a slight descent. In front the land is thick with gorse and wild flowers. The road divides before you. The right hand branch is the turnpike continued. The left hand is a lane, hardly more than a cart-path. Each leads you in a few moments to Scrooby, the roofs and spire of which you can see among trees not far away. The former skirts the western edge of the hamlet. The latter winds through the meadows, over the Ryton, and beside the village mill into the middle of the settlement.

There are perhaps thirty houses in all, small and unpretentious but neat and comfortable, with white-curtained windows and an abundance of bright flowers. Their roofs are thatched or red-tiled. Tall elms shade some of them and the whole place looks well cared for and home-like. Passing the mill and continuing south for perhaps three minutes, at the crossing of two little roads you see the graveyard, from the middle of which rises the church, known as St. Wilfred's. Its pointed spire is well proportioned and graceful and has remained unchanged since the days of the Pilgrims. The church is peculiar in shape. Having proved at one time too small to accommodate the congregation, which draws its members from a considerable surrounding territory, it was enlarged by adding an aisle to its south side. As you stand in front of the spire, therefore, the south side of the church is of about twice the width of the north side. This alteration has been made during the present century and the interior of the edifice also has been changed considerably. But there are in the chancel some venerable pewbacks of oak, blackened by time, which bear simple yet graceful carvings of a grape-vine and its fruit which are just as they were when Brewster used to worship there Sunday by Sunday.

It is worth your while to sit down for a few moments in the church, or in the sunny graveyard, and let your fancy have free play. Picture to yourself the days of the Cavaliers and the Roundheads, and those earlier days when Elizabeth was queen, when Shakespeare was writing and acting his plays, when the Spanish Armada was a fact of yesterday, and when the Pilgrims one by one were deciding that they must separate from the corruptions of the State Church at no matter how great a cost. You can almost see these little lanes repeopled by men in doublets and hose with peaked hats and with swords at their sides as they pass from house to house, or chat by the roadside, or walk between the ancient graves and enter the church to worship. These very stones before you were there just where they are to-day. Could they but speak, what stories they could tell!

But we are lingering too long at the church. Let us pass to that which has much greater interest, the so-called manor-house. Walk back towards the mill and turn to the right, that is, towards the east, into the short lane, which you cannot miss, and enter through the gate at its end. We are in a meadow containing several acres. Its southern boundary is another lane leading from the village to the tiny railway station. Opposite to us the railway forms the eastern line of the estate. Some hundreds of feet away on our left stands an irregular row of buildings with a garden, a farm-yard and many trees, and behind them runs the narrow Ryton, which bounds the place on the north. Four or five tall Lombardy poplars rise among the fruit trees and are visible from a long distance. A few trees also are scattered about the meadow.

This area is far from comprehending the whole of the ancient estate. It merely includes the site of the manor-house and its immediate grounds. Notice this shallow ditch extending part way from the gate to the lane on the south. It also runs along the lane and is believed to reveal the line of the former moat. Notice, too, the uneven surface of the meadow. Here is a circular mound, hardly rising above the average level, yet plainly evident. There is an oblong hollow, some thirty feet square. All about are irregularities indicating a connection and plan in the long ago. During my earliest visit in 1871, I was allowed by the courtesy of the late Lord Houghton, then lord of the manor, to make borings and excavations freely. These revealed almost everywhere beneath the turf a mass of crumbled brick work, which once had formed the wall of the original manor-house. But to determine the plan of the foundation — if, indeed, that be possible — there must be systematic and thorough excavation of the larger part of the present estate. The probability of learning enough to warrant the cost is very slight.

Fortunately there are records which tell us something. As the estate belonged to the Archbishopric of York, the official documents of the period occasionally allude to it. And the old historian Leland says that in 1541 it had a moat and two court-yards, the outer being about four times as large as the inner. Its front, he adds, was of brick and the remainder of "tymbre." It had a large hall or chapel, and probably both. It appears to have been square or oblong, with its open interior divided into two parts, the courts, by a cross row of rooms. The structure was surrounded by gardens containing fish ponds, the whole being encompassed by the river and the moat. It must have been stately and handsome.

It was a convenient resting-place on the tedious journey from London to York and Edinburgh, and Queen Margaret of Scotland, Henry VIII, James I, and Cardinal Wolsey were among the eminent visitors whom it sheltered from time to time.

James I, and, it is said, Queen Elizabeth, tried to buy it, but in vain. But, probably about the middle of the seventeenth century, it proved too costly to be properly kept up and most of it was torn down. But it was not wholly demolished, as we shall see. The short wall, extending from the present house back to the edge of the Ryton, used to contain stones evidently once portions of chiselled cornices or columns, and the roof of one of the present cow-sheds is supported by carved beams which probably did the same work formerly in the hall or chapel, and must have echoed the voices of Brewster and his fellow Pilgrims when they organized their historic church and planned their escape to Holland.

To-day you see, as you walk from the gate along the cart-path towards the buildings, what at first looks like an ordinary English farmhouse. It has two stories and an attic, is long and narrow, and extends north and south almost from the bank of the Ryton to the meadow. Its walls are partly of brick and partly of rubble or rough plaster. On the east side the roof of the southern half slopes down over a little shed and several minor out-buildings stand near by. On its west side lies a small flower and fruit garden, beyond which are barns, sheds, a dove-cote and numerous trees, including the conspicuous Lombardy poplars.

What is there in this modest building to justify the belief that any part of it was included in the dignified manor-house of our fathers' time? Stand in the garden and look up at the house and you will see. Observe the wide arch sunken in the southern half of the western wall on its outside. Notice, too, the deep niche at the left of the upper part of the arch. They have no modern significance and they testify to the great age of that portion of the wall. Now enter the house, where the courteous tenants will make you welcome, and examine the windows. Note the thickness of the wall. Nobody builds such walls now. But they used to build them in the sixteenth century. Pass up the steep and narrow stairway and examine the upper rooms. Study especially — you will need a candle in the windowless room, itself a weighty proof of antiquity — the arch which has been filled up and the neighboring niche in the wall of the inner room. If that arch were not the doorway into the ancient chapel, and the niche the place for the usual vessel of holy water in the Roman Catholic days not long past in our fathers' time, it is difficult to imagine what they can have been.

"Enough is as good as a feast" runs the old proverb. It would be pleasant to have more evidence that we of to-day actually can see and touch a part of the very building which so often sheltered the Pilgrims. But such evidence as we have, although scanty, is convincing. An important part of the present farmhouse was included in the manor-house where William Brewster lived. We must be on our guard, however, as we chat with the present occupants of the farm. They are well-meaning but know little of history, and most of their traditions have no value. They are unconscious that their barns and sheds are comparatively modern, and their tale of the use of the shed, in which are the carved beams, as a Pilgrim chapel and of hasty escapes out of one door as the government officers entered to make arrests by the other door on the same side is manifestly absurd.

Here, too, imagination can build a truer structure on the foundation of the few known facts than tradition can supply. It is easy to picture to one's self Brewster and Bradford and Robinson and Clyfton, with the little company of their associates, praying and singing, preaching and listening, planning and organizing, conversing and breaking bread together, enjoying thoroughly their precious fellowship, yet ever alert lest they be suddenly interrupted and arrested. Kings and queens, cardinals and archbishops had met and feasted within the same walls. But none were nobler than the humble Pilgrims, and none have left a record in human history like that which Brewster and his company began to make in that now almost vanished edifice.

Before you leave the Pilgrim region you must not fail to visit Austerfield also. A pleasant foot-path from Bawtry station leads you to the little village in a quarter of an hour or so. It is less prepossessing than Scrooby. Here the church, St. Helen's, is the object of special interest. It is small and low and has no spire or tower, but only a little pointed belfry, holding two bells which are more noisy than musical when rung. It stands well back from the village street on the right as you go north, but is easily found. On its south side is a quaint entrance porch, and its "zigzag and beak" carving with its rude likeness of a dragon, the rough stone benches within the porch, the heavy buttresses outside, the narrow, diamond-paned windows, and the old oaken chancel rail inside, probably are about as they were when, on March 19, 1589, the young child, William Bradford, the future friend of Brewster and the governor and historian of the Plymouth Colony, was baptized by Rev. Henry Fletcher.

This church, too, has been somewhat modernized within, and recently certain ancient arches have been discovered in its northern wall, and an attempt has been made to restore them, and, I believe, to rebuild a former north aisle into which they opened from the church. As to the success of this effort I am not yet informed. But I cannot help regretting it, because the earliest history of the church, so far as known, is unimportant. The only celebrity and the special interest of the edifice is due to William Bradford's connection with it, and to leave it as nearly as possible as it was in his boyhood would be far more appropriate than to restore its previous appearance, even if this could be done certainly and well.

A few minutes' walk still farther north brings one to the so-called Bradford Cottage. The tradition that the Bradfords occupied it is generally believed and may possess some probability, but has no more solid basis. It deserves a visit, however, because of the tradition and of its interesting cellar, which is asserted to have been a Pilgrim hiding-place. As such a cellar, in case of suspicion, would have been certain to be immediately searched, however, the tradition probably is baseless.

When you visit Scrooby and its vicinity, take time enough. You can see all which is most important in a few hours, and of course a hasty inspection is better than none. But it pays one richly to linger for a few days, or even weeks, long enough to see everything thoroughly and repeatedly, long enough to enter somewhat into the spirit of the locality and the rich meaning of its vital relations to human history. The life of a true descendant of the Mayflower men and women will have a fresh inspiration forever after a reverent visit to the early home of so many among them.

LOVE BREWSTER'S WILL AND INVENTORY.

Transcribed from the original records,

By George Ernest Bowman.

Love Brewster's will and inventory are recorded in the Plymouth Colony Wills and Inventories, Volume I, folios 89, 90 and 91.

---

[89] The last Will and Testament of Love Brewster Deseassed exhibited at the generall Court holden at New Plym : the 4th of March 1650 upon the oath of Captaine Miles Standish

Witnesseth these psents that I Love Brewster of Duxburrow in New England and in the goverment of New Plym : being in pfect memory doe ordeaine & appoint this to bee my last will and Testamente And first my will is that if the lord shall please to take mee out of this life that my body bee buried in a decent mannor and that my funerall expences bee taken out of my whole estate; Next my will is; That all my Just and lawfull debts bee paied out of the Remainder of my said estate allso I give unto my Children that is to say Nathaniell Willam Wrasteling and Sara each of them a kettle and further my will is that my three sonns shall have each of them a peece that is to say a gun; allso I give and bequeath unto my beloved wife Sara Brewster all the Residue of my whole estate both goods and Chattles and land at Duxburrow for the bringing up of her and my Children the time of her life and after her desease I doe give the aforsaid lands to my eldest sonn and heire apparent Nathaniell Brewster and in Case god should take him away out of this life without Issew I give and bequeath the said lands at Duxburrow to my second sonn Willam Brewster and in like Case to my youngest sonn Wresteling Brewster; And for those books I have that my wife would destribute them to herselfe and Children at her descresion allso my will is and I doe by the same give unto my three sonns equally to bee devided amongst them all such land as is of Right due to mee by Purchase and first coming into the land Which was in the yeare 1620 allso I doe make Constitute and appoint my beloved wife Sara Brewster sole executrix of this my last will and Testament in Witnes Wherof I have put to my hand and Seale this sixt of october 1650

Wittnes heerunto — Love Brewster
Myles Standish — (seale)

A true Inventory of the estate of Love Brewster of Duxburrow late deseassed taken by m^{r} Willam Collyar and Captaine Miles Standish January the last day 1650 And exhibited to the Generall Court holden at New Plym: the 4th of March in the yeare aforsaid upon the oath of Sara Brewster

	li	*s*	*d*
videlect in the first Rome ten pewter dishes or platters			
It 3 pewter basons			
It 3 fruit dishes			
It 3 saucers			
It 2 porengers			
It one quart pott			
It one pint pott			
It one Candlestick	03	16	00
It one wine Cupp			
It one sault seller			
It one sucking bottle			
It halfe a pint pott			
It 9 spoones and a peece of plate			
It a table frame and forme	00	14	00
It 2 Cradles	00	05	00
It a payle a sifting trough and a Rowling pin	00	05	00
It a halfe bushell a peck and a table Chaire	00	05	00
It one tray	00	01	06
It one forme and 2 old stooles	00	02	00
It 9 trenchers	00	00	09
It one seive 2 Riddles	00	03	00
It one bucking tubb 2 beere Rundlets one feirken with a cover	00	10	00
It one payer of scales one spade 2 wooden spoones	00	04	06
It one dripping pan	00	10	00
It one spitt	00	02	06
It one frying pan	00	02	00
It an Iron to keep up the fier	00	02	00
It a gridiron	00	02	00
It a paier of broken tonges a broken fiershovell a fierforke		02	06
It a paier of pothanger a paire of pothookes an Iron barr one pound			00

It 3 peeces	03 06 00
It 2 powder hornes a flask a shott bagg one paier of bandeleers	00 10 00
It one pistoll	00 06 00
It 3 pound of powder	00 06 00
It 22 pound of shott	00 06 04
[90] It 3 pound of great shott	00 00 10
It 3 Iron potts	02 00 00
It 3 wedges weying 16 pound	00 08 00
It one Iron lampe one Iron stiring stick	00 02 06
It a snashell of a bridle	00 00 06
It one Rapier blade	00 05 00
It one Morter	00 02 00
It one skillet	00 02 00
It one smothing Iron	00 02 00
It one stone pott	00 00 06
Bookes	
It Mr Greenhams workes	00 10 00
It 2 books of the Comaundements by Mr Dodd	00 04 00
It Downhams Consolations	00 03 00
It Cottens Concordance	00 06 00
It one part of Mr Perkins works	00 08 00
It Calvin upon Esaiah	00 05 00
It Mr herons work	00 05 00
It the five books of Moses	00 10 00
It Downhams life everlasting	00 03 00
It Broughton on the lamentations of Jeremy	00 06 00
It of the spanish Inquisition	00 00 04
It ten smale torne books	00 02 06
It mr Baals Caticisme	00 00 06
It mr Whettunsall	00 00 06
It Duty of Constable and housholder	00 00 06
It 4 smale books at 6d pr booke	00 02 00
It Downhams Warfare	00 02 06
It Deffence of a peticion for Reformacion	00 01 06
It a Comentary on Philemon	00 01 06
It a Dicsonary	00 00 06
It a book of husbandry	00 10 06
It another smale book of husbandry	00 00 06
It Reasons descused	00 01 06
It a ffrench dicsonary and another dicsonary	00 02 00
It mr Downham on AntiChrist	00 01 00
It Jackson on unbeleefe	00 01 06
It Gorg his Armor	00 02 00
It swords Intelegencer	00 01 06
It a bible	00 12 00
It mr Ainsworth in answare to Sr ffrancis hastings	00 01 06
Clothes beding &c	
It 2 suites and a Coat	03 00 00
It 3 paier of shooes and 3 paier of stockens	01 00 00

It one pr of boots	00 13 00
It one hatt	00 05 00
It new Cloth or a suite	01 16 00
It silk & buttens	00 02 00
It a wastcoat of penestone	00 08 00
It 2 shirts	00 08 00
It lockorum for 2 shirts	00 15 00
It 4 handkerchifes six bands and six Capps	00 14 00
It 4 feather beds and boulsters	10 00 00
It 3 shagg Ruggs 3 plaine Ruggs two blankits	04 00 00
It 3 pr of sheets	03 10 00
It 2 pr of pillow beeres 2 table Clothes and seaven dosen and an halfe of napkins	02 00 00
It 3 Chists & one box	02 00 00
It one settlebedd one standing bedd one settle	02 00 00
It 3 kettles & one brase pan	05 00 00
It one warming pan one Candlestick one old kittle	00 15 00
It a Cart & an horse furniture for the Cart	01 10 00
It ten hoes 6 Reaphookes 7 augers one hatchet 3 axes and other lumber	02 00 00
It one plow Cheine one share one Ring for a Coppyeok & a double hooke	00 15 00
It a Cherne a butter Tubb an old trunck an old hoggs-head an old Chest	01 00 00
It 3 pillows	00 10 00
It 3 Cowes	15 00 00
It one yearling	01 10 00
It one sow and 2 shoats	01 10 00
It poultry	00 10 00
[91] It 9 bushells of wheat	02 00 06
It 5 bushells of Rye	00 17 06
It 14 bushells of Indian Corn	02 02 00
It one bushell of pease	00 04 00
It 3 pecks of barly	00 02 00
It one peck of naked oates	00 01 06
It halfe a bushell of Mault	00 02 00
It 2 forkes Rakes a ladder and other lumber	00 10 00
It 14 pound of Cotten woole	00 14 00
It ten pound of sheeps woole	01 00 00
It 4 pound of linnin yarne	00 08 00
It sope	00 00 04
It sault and a tubb	00 01 06
It a Case without bottles	00 02 00
It an old frying pan	00 01 00
It 3 old tubbs	00 03 00
It 3 ewesheep	04 10 00
It 3 weathers	03 00 00
Suma Totalis	97 07 01

Willam Collyar Myles Standish

GOVERNOR WILLIAM BRADFORD'S WILL AND INVENTORY.

Literally transcribed from the original records,

BY GEORGE ERNEST BOWMAN.

Governor William Bradford's will and inventory are recorded in the Plymouth Colony Wills and Inventories, Volume II, Part I, pages 53 to 59, both inclusive.

[p. 53] The last Will and Testament Nunckupative of Mr Willam Bradford seni^r^: Deceased May the Ninth 1657 and exhibited to the court held att Plymouth June 3^d^ 1657

Mr Willam Bradford seni^r^: being weake in body but in prfect memory haveing Defered the forming of his Will in hopes of haveing the healp of Mr Thomas Prence therin; feeling himselfe very weake and drawing on to the conclusion of his mortall life spake as followeth; I could have Desired abler then myselfe in the Desposing of that I have; how my estate is none knowes better then youerselfe, said hee to Lieftenant Southworth; I have Desposed to John and Willam alreddy theire proportions of land which they are possessed of;

My Will is that what I stand Ingaged to p^r^forme to my Children and others may bee made good out of my estate that my Name Suffer not;

ffurther my Will is that my son Josepth bee made in some sort equall to his brethern out of my estate;

My further Will is that my Deare & loveing wife Allice Bradford shalbee the sole Exequitrix of my estate; and for her future maintainance my Will is that my Stocke in the Kennebecke Trad bee reserved for her Comfortable Subsistence as farr as it will extend and soe further in any such way as may bee Judged best for her;

I further request and appoint my welbeloved Christian ffrinds Mr Thomas Prence Captaine Thomas Willett and Lieftenant Thomas Southworth to bee the Suppervissors for the

Desposing of my estate according to the p^r^mises Confiding much in theire faithfulnes

I comend unto youer Wisdome and Descretions some smale bookes written by my owne hand to bee Improved as you shall see meet; In speciall I Comend to you a little booke with a blacke cover wherin there is a word to Plymouth a word to Boston and a word to New England with sundry usefull verses;

These pticulars were expressed by the said Willam Bradford Govr the 9th of May 1657 in the p^{r}sence of us Thomas Cushman Thomas Southworth Nathaniell Morton; whoe were Deposed before the court held att Plymouth the 3^{d} of June 1657 to the truth of the abovesaid Will that it is the last Will and Testament of the abovesaid Mr Willam Bradford seni^{r}:

[p. 54] A Trew Inventory of the Estate of Mr Willam Bradford seni^{r}: lately Deceased taken and apprissed by us whose names are underwritte the 22^{cond} of May 1657 and exhibited to the court holden att Plymouth the 3^{d} of June 1657 on the oath of mis Allice Bradford

beding and other thinges in ye old parler	£	s	d
Imp^{r}: one feather bed and bolster	03	00	00
It a featherbed a featherbolster a featherpillow	03	00	00
It a Canvas bed with feathers and a bolster and 2 pillowes	01	15	00
It one green rugg	01	00	00
It a paire of whit blanketts	01	00	00
It one whit blankett	00	12	00
It 2 paire of old blanketts	01	00	00
It 2 old Coverlidds	01	00	00
It 1 old white rugg and an old ridd Coverlidd	01	00	00
It 1 paire of old curtaines Darnickes & an old paire of say curtaines		15	00
It a Court Cubbard	01	05	00
It a winescot bedsteed and a settle	01	10	00
It 4 lether Chaires	01	12	00
It 1 great lether Chaire	00	10	00
It 2 great wooden Chaires	00	08	00
It a Table & forme and 2 stooles	01	05	00
It a winscott Chist & Cubburd	01	05	00
It a Case with six knives	00	05	00
It 3 matchcock musketts	02	02	00
It a Snaphance Muskett	01	00	00
It a birding peece and an other smale peece	00	18	00
It a pistoll and Cutlas	00	12	00
It a Card and a platt	00	05	00

in the great rome	
It 2 great Carved Chaires	01 04 00
It a smale carved Chaire	00 06 00
It a Table and forme	01 02 00
It 3 striped Carpetts	01 05 00
It 10 Cushens	01 01 00
It 3 old Cushens	00 02 00
It a Causlett and one headpeece	01 10 00
It 1 fouling peece without a locke 3 old barrells of guns one paire of old bandeleers and a rest	00 16 00
linnin	
It 2 paire of holland sheets	02 00 00
It 1 Dowlis sheet	00 10 00
It 2 paire of Cotten and linnin Sheets	01 15 00
It 2 paire of hemp and Cotten sheets	01 15 00
It 2 paire of Canvas sheets	01 10 00
It 2 paire of old sheets	00 15 00
[p. 55] It 4 fine shirts	02 00 00
It 4 other shirts	01 00 00
It a Douzen of Cotten and linnin napkins	00 12 00
It a Douzen of Canvas Napkins	00 06 00
It a Diaper Tablecloth and a Douzen of Diaper Napkins	02 10 00
It 10 Diaper napkins of an other sort a Diaper tablecloth and a Diaper Cubburd cloth	03 00 00
It 2 holland Tableclothes	01 00 00
It 2 short Tableclothes	00 10 00
It 2 old Tableclothes	00 05 00
It a Douzen of old Napkins	00 08 00
It halfe a Dousen of Napkins	00 08
It 3 old Napkins	00 02 00
It a Douzen of Course napkins & a course tablecloth	00 06 00
It 2 fine holland Cubburd clothes	00 12 00
It 3 paire of holland pillowbeers	00 18 00
It 3 paire of Dowlis pillowbeers and an old one	00 14 00
It 4 holland Towells and a lockorum one	00 05 00
pewter	
It 14 pewter Dishes weying 47 pound att 15^{d} pr pound	02 18 09
It 6 pewter plates & 13 pewter platters weying thirty 2 pounds att 15^{d} pr pound	02 00 00
It 2 pewter plates 5 sawsers 4 basons & 5 Dishes weying eighteen pounds att 15^{d} pr pound	01 02 06
It 2 ppeplates of pewter	00 03 04
It 3 Chamberpotts	00 09 00
It 7 porrengers	00 03 06
It 2 quart potts & a pint pott	00 07 00
It 2 old fflagons an a yore	00 09 00
It a pewter Candlesticke a salt and a little pewter bottle	00 03 00
It 4 venice glasses and seaven earthen Dishes	00 10 00
In the kitchen brasse	
It 2 ffrench kittles	01 10 00

It 1 brasse kittle	00 15 00
It 2 little ffrench kittles	00 06 00
It an old warming pan	00 05 00
It 2 old brasse kittles	00 02 00
It a Duch pan	00 04 00
It 3 brasse skilletts	00 04 00
It 3 brasse Candlestickes and a brasse morter and pestle	00 07 00
It an old brasse skimmer and a ladle	00 01 00
It a paire of andjrons	00 06 00
It an old brasse stewpan	00 06 00
[p. 56] It 2 old brasse kittles	00 05 00
It 2 Iron skilletts and a Iron kittle	00 15 00
2 old great Iron pottes	01 00 00
It 2 Iron potts lesser	00 07 00
It 2 paire of pothangers 2 paire of pothookes	00 08 00
It 2 paire of tonggs and an old fier shovell	00 03 04
It one paire of Andjrons and a gridjron	00 10 00
It a spitt and an old Iron Driping pan	00 05 00
It a paire of Iron Rackes and an Iron veele and another peec of old Iron to lay before a Driping pan	00 10 00
It 4 Dozen of Trenchers	00 02 06
It 2 Juggs and 3 smale bottles	00 02 00
in the New Chamber his clothes	
It a stuffe suite with silver buttons & a Coate	04 00 00
It a Cloth Cloake faced with Taffety and lineed throw with baies	03 10 00
It a sad coullered Cloth suite	02 00 00
It a Turkey Grogorum suite and cloake	02 00 00
It a paire of blacke briches and a rid wastcoat	00 15 00
It a lead coullered cloth suit with silver buttons	02 00 00
It a sad coullered short coate and an old serge suite	01 10 00
It a black cloth coate	00 15 00
It a broad cloth Coate	01 05 00
It a light Coullered stuffe Coate	00 16 00
It an old green goune	01 00 00
It a light Cullered Cloth Cloake	01 15 00
It an old violett Coullered Cloake	01 05 00
It a short coate of Cloath	00 10 00
It 2 old Dublett and a paire of briches a short coate and an old stuffe Dublit and wastcoate	01 00 00
It 2 paire of stockens	00 07 00
It 2 hates a blacke one and a coullered one	01 10 00
It 2 old hatts	00 16 00
It 1 great Chaire and 2 wrought stooles	01 00 00
It a Carved Chist	01 00 00
It a Table	00 15 00
the plate	
It one great beer bowle	03 00 00
It an other beer bowle	02 00 00
It 2 wine Cupps	02 00 00

It a salt	03 00 00
It the trencher salt and a Drame cup	00 15 00
It 4 silver spoones	01 04 00
It 9 silver spoones	02 05 00
[p. 57] In the Studdie	
It eight paire of shooes of the 12^s	02 00 00
It 6 paire of shoes of the 10^s	01 04 00
It one paire of the eights	00 03 04
It 3 paire of the 7^s	00 09 00
It 2 paire of the sixes	00 02 08
It 1 paire of the 5^s 1 paire of the 4^s 1 paire of the 3^s	00 06 00
It 4 yards and an halfe of linncy woolcye	00 13 06
It 3 remnants of English Cotten	00 16 03
It 3 yards and an halfe of bayes	00 07 00
It 17 yards of Course English moheer	02 02 06
It 4 yards and 3 quarters of purpetuanna	01 00 00
It 18 yards of rid penistone	03 03 00
It 5 yards of broad cloth	03 15 00
It 2 yards of broad cloth	01 10 00
It 2½ yards and an halfe of olive cullered Carsye	00 15 00
It a yard and an halfe of whitish Carsey	00 07 00
It 4 yards of Gray carsye	01 04 00
It 5 yards and an halfe of rid Carsye	01 07 06
It 4 yards and a quarter of Carsy ollive coullered	01 10 00
It 7 yards of Carsye sad Cullered	02 06 08
It 10 yards of gray Carsye	02 10 00
It 6 yards and an halfe of rid plaine	01 19 00
It 9 yards and an halfe of rash	03 16 00
It 6 yards of holland	01 08 00
It a remnant of Cushening	00 05 00
It 7 smale moose skines	04 08 00
It in Cash	151 09 06
It his Deske	00 05 00
It 2 Cases with some emty bottles	00 10 00
It 3 or 4 old cases	00 03 00
his bookes in folio	
Mr Perkines workes	01 10 00
It 3 of Docter Willetts workes viz on genesis exodus & Daniell	01 00 00
It the ffrench acaddamey	00 08 00
It the Guiciardin	00 10 00
It the history of the Church	00 08 00
It bodins Comons wealth	00 06 00
It B Babbingtons workes	00 08 00
It Peter Martire Comon places	00 15 00
It Cartwright on the remish Testament	00 10 00
It the history of the Netherlands	00 15 00
It Peter Martire on the Romans	00 05 00
It Mayers workes on the New Testament	01 00 00
It Cottens Concordance	00 08 00

[p. 53] his bookes

Speeds generall Description of the world	01 10 00
Weames Christian Sinnagogue and the portrature of the Image of God in man	08 00
It Luther on the gallations	00 02 00
It the method of phiscicke	00 02 00
It Calvins harmony and Calvins Comentary on the actes	00 08 00
It Downhams 2cond pte of Christian Warfare	00 03 00
It Mr Cottens Answare to mr Willams	00 02 00
It Taylers libertie of Phrophecye	00 01 06
It Gouges Domesticall Dutyes	00 02 06
It Justification of Seperation or reasons Descused & observations Devine & morall the synode att Dort; the Apollogye	00 06 00
It Mr Ainsworths workes the Counterpoison the triing out of the truth	00 02 00
It Mr Ainsworth on geniseis Exodus & livitticus	00 04 00
It Calvin on genises	00 02 06
It Dike on the Deceitfulness of mans hart	00 01 06
It Gifford refuted	00 00 06
It Dod on the Comaundments & an other of his	00 03 00
It three and fifty smale bookes	01 06 06
It Calvine on the epistles in Duch with Divers other Duch bookes	00 15 00
It 2 bibles	01 00 00
It a paire of boots	00 05 00
It in lether	00 18 00
It 2 old Chists	00 10 00
It 6 old barrells a bucking tubb a brewing tubb & other old lumber	01 00 00
It a pcell of Cotten woole & a pcell of sheepes woole	02 10 00
It a pcell of feathers	00 12 00
It 3 ewe sheep	04 10 00
It 3 middleing sheep & a poor one	04 00 00
It a rame lambe and an halfe & half an ewe lamb	00 16 06
It the old mare	12 00 00
It a lame mare and an horse coult	14 00 00
It a horse of two yeare old and advantate	07 00 00
It an other horse coult of yeare and advantage	05 10 00
It 4 bullockes	20 00 00
It 7 Cowes	28 00 00
It a bull	04 00 00
It 2 young bulls of two year old	04 10 00
It a heifer of three yeare old not with Calfe	03 05 00
It 2 heifers of two years old	05 00 00
It 4 yearlings	06 00 00
It five Calves	03 00 00
It a sow and 2 hoggs	02 15 00
It 2 shoats	01 04 00
It five smale shoates	01 10 00

It the house and orchyard and some smale pcells of land about the towne of Plymouth	45 00 00
It 2 spining wheeles & a wether	00 16 00
[p. 59] Att the Westward in Debts upon the Duch account Consisting in Divers pcells	153 00 00
Iem Debts owing to the estate	
It the Kennebeck Stocke Consisting in goods and Debts both English and Indians	256 00 00
More Debts owing in the bay	
It in Doute the shoomakers hands	05 00 00
It in Mannsses Kemtons hands	05 00 00
It more belonging to the estate in Divers pticulars	57 00 00
Debts owing from the estate	
It to Mr Davis and mr Sheffe	05 00 00
It to Samuell Sturtivant	02 03 00
It 2 the townes land	01 12 00
It John Jourdaine about	02 00 00
It To goodman Clarke about	03 10 00
It two goodman Nelson for killing of Cattle & for veale	01 18 06
It to Willam Palmer	12 04 00
It To the Church of Plymouth	05 10 00

Som pcells of land not mencioned above belonging to Mr Willam Bradford senir:

It one pcell att Eastham and another att Bridgwater

It a smale pcell about Sawtuckett and his purchase land att Coaksett with his right in the townes land at Punckatessett

By us Thomas Cushman John Dunham

It Sundry Implements forgotten belonging to the teame

THE WILL AND INVENTORY OF SAMUEL[2] FULLER (EDWARD[1]).

Transcribed from the original records,

BY GEORGE ERNEST BOWMAN.

Samuel[2] Fuller (Edward[1]) died at Barnstable, 31 October (10 November), 1683. His will and inventory are recorded in the Plymouth Colony Wills and Inventories, Volume IV, Part II, pages 138 and 139.

[p. 138] The last Will and Testament of Samuell ffuller of Barnstable Late Deceased Exhibited to the Court held att Plymouth the fift of June 1684 on the oath of Capt: Josepth Laythorp and Mr Samuell Allin as followeth

The nine and twentyeth Day of October in the yeer of our Lord one thousand six hundred eighty and three; I Samuell ffuller senir of the Towne of Barnstable in the Govrment of New Plymouth being ancient and very weake in body but of good and Compitent memory thankes be unto allmighty God; and Calling to remembrance the uncertaine state of this transitory life and that all fflesh muste yeild unto Death when it shall please God to Call, Doe make ordaine and & Constitute & Declare this my last will and Testament in Manor and form following;

Revoking and Anulling by these presents all and every Testament and Testaments will and wills heertofore by mee made and declared either by word or wrighting; and this to be taken onely for my last will and Testament and none other;

and first I give and Comitt my soule unto almighty God my Saviour in whom and by the merritts of Jesus Christ I trust and beleive assuredly to be saved; and my body to the earth; from whence it was taken to be buried in such Decent and Christian manor as to my executors heerafter Named shalbe thought meet and Convenient; and Now for the settleing of my temporall estate and such goods Cattles and Debts as it hath pleased god farr above my Deserts to bestow upon mee; I Doe order Give and Dispose the same in Manor and forme following; That is to say first I will that all those Debts and Dutyes as I owe in right or Consience to any manor of p^r^son or p^r^sons whatsoever shalbe well and truely Contented and payed or ordained to be payed within Convenient time after my Decease by my executors heerafter Named;

Item I Give and bequeath unto my eldest son Samuell ffuller two p^r^sells of Marsh one of them I bought of m^r^ Samuell house Deceased and the other I bought of Captaine Matthew ffuller Deceased that hee had of m^r^ John ffreeman;

Item I give and bequeath to my son John ffuller four acrees of Marsh and one halfe which I bought of Peter Blossome

Item I Give and bequeath that p^r^sell of Marsh that lyes by Ralph Jones, his Marsh, To my two sones Samuell ffuller and John ffuller to be equally Devided betwixt and one p^r^sell of Marsh that lyeth on this side Scoton ffeildes to be Devided as abovesaid and the angle Lotts of Marsh att Scoton point to be equally Devided between them alsoe and alsoe the Eelcreik Lott of Marsh to be alike Devided as above specifyed and the Lott of Marsh att Sandy neck upon the same accoumpt alsoe; and all my upland upon Scoton Neck to be equally Devided betwixt them as the other above Mensioned

Item I give to my son Samuell ffuller all my upland that lyeth above my uppermost ffeild and to range quite Crosse my land upon one and the same lyne as the uppermost ffence as my upmost feild Now ranges, but alwaies to allow Cart wayes to the Comons into the Comons for his brother John ffuller his heires and assignes

Item I give and bequeath unto my son John fuller my now Dwellinghouse orchyard and all outhousing and all the rest of my upland wherever it doth lye, but alwaies to allow a Cart way into the meddowes for his brother Samuell ffuller his heires and assignes

Item I Give and bequeath to my son John ffuller one three yeer old horse runing in the woods ;

Item I Give and bequeath to my son Samuell ffuller two mares runing in the woods ;

Item I Give unto my Daughter Elizabeth Tayler five pound in Mony and two Cowes ;

Item I Give unto my Daughter hannah Bonham four pounds in Money and two Cowes ;

Item I Give unto my Daughter Mary Williams four pound in Money and two Cowes

Item I give and bequeath unto my Daughter Sarah Crowe four pounds in Mony and two Cowes

Item I Give and bequeath unto my four Daughters hannah Bonham Mary Williams Elizabeth Tayler and Sarah Crow all my houshold Stuffe to be equally Dvided betwixt them

Item I Give and bequeath to my son John ffuller the Indian Joell ; my p^r^te in the oxen the Cart and plow and the Cart and plow Geares and working tooles and one fatt Cow that is to kill and my bald faced horse ; and my Great bible ;

Item I Give and bequeath to my two sones Samuell ffuller and John ffuller all the rest of my Neat Cattle to be Devided To my son Samuell one third p^r^te ; and to my son John ffuller the other two third p^r^tes therof ; and all my sheep to be equally Devided betwixt them ;

Item I Give and bequath to my son Samuell ffuller ten pounds in mony which hee now owes to mee and hath now hath it alredy; and all the rest of my estate in what kind soever it be I Give and bequeath it to my two sones Samuell ffuller and John ffuller; to be Devided to my son Samuell ffuller one third p^r^te therof and to my son John ffuller the other two third p^r^tes therof, and by these p^r^sents make ordaine & Declare the above said Samuell and John ffuller the executors of this my last Will and Testament ; In Witness wherof I the said Samuell ffuller have heerunto sett my hand and seale the Date above written ;

Witnesse Samuell ffuller and a seal
Joseph Laythorp
Samuell Allin

Captaine Joseph Laythorpe made oth as a witnes to this will before the Court held att Plymouth the fift of March 16 $\frac{83}{84}$

Mr Samuell Allin Made oath as a witnes to this Will above written this 10th of March 16$\frac{83}{84}$ before mee Barnabas Laythorpe Assistant

[p. 139] A true Inventory of all and singular the Goods Chattles and Creditts o Samuell ffuller senir late of the Towne of Barnstable in the Govrment of New Plymouth in New England Deceased praysed att his house in Barnstable aforsaid the 14 Day of November in the year of our Lord 1683 by Joseph Laythorpe and Jededia Jones as followeth;

Impri his apparrell	08 08 00
Item in Cash	17 07 00
Item in 3 Guns amunition shooe Nailes & a peece of Lether	02 09 00
Item in Lynnin	03 10 00
Item in pewter and ten	02 05 00
Item in brasse	02 05 06
Item in trayes Chern a tubb and a spoon and an old warming pan	00 17 06
Item Iron potts tonges slice frying pan and Candlesticke	01 19 00
Item a Cobbord old Chists a box & and bedsteed	03 15 00
Item tables and Chaires bottles & old Gridjron	00 17 00
Item looking Lanthorne & buccett	00 05 06
Item a feather bed bolster and two pillowes three blanketts a Coverlid & 2 ruggs	07 00 00
Item a peece of New holland other peeces of linnin serge and Cotton and a remnant of homade Cloth	02 18 00
Item a Shirt Capps yarne sisers thrid	00 10 03
Item 2 seives a hatt and a tray	00 06 00
Item in beese and hunny	01 00 00
Item in old Cask basketts beer barrells a rundleit	00 12 00
Item in Corn in the & in the barne	03 10 00
Item in Corne in the Cribb	03 07 00
Item in butter and Cheese	04 00 00
Item in beefe and pork tallow & hyde & hoggs fatt	05 00 00
Item in sheeps woole feathers Tobbaco baggs earthen Dish brimston	01 09 00
Item in Neat Cattle	27 00 00
Item in Sheep	04 00 00
Item in swine	00 15 00
Item in horse kind	04 10 00
Item the Cart wheels plow Irons & Gears therunto belonging	01 13 00
Item saddle bridle and horse Geares	00 08 06
Item Sheep Sheers adds & other tooles	00 09 00

These sumes underneath are brought to the Inventor the 25 of ffebruary 1683 Apprised by Jedediah Jones above Mensioned Coming not to mind before;

Item in boards att	01 07 00
Item in a hatchell	00 05 00
Item in skines a paire of Scales	00 05 00
Item in bookes	01 04 00
Item in Geese	00 13 00
Item an old tecken att	00 05 00
the totall is	116 05 09

The lands & housing not prised

John ffuller made oath to the truth of this Inventory this 25 day of ffebrewary $16\frac{83}{84}$ before Thomas Hinckley Govr: John Thacher. Assistant

JOHN ALDEN'S INVENTORY AND THE SETTLEMENT OF HIS ESTATE.

Transcribed from the original records,

BY GEORGE ERNEST BOWMAN.

John Alden died at Duxbury on the twelfth of September, 1687, leaving no will, and the thirty-first of October the inventory of his estate was taken by his son Jonathan, who was appointed administrator on the eighth of November. John Alden had deeded certain parcels of land to his children during his lifetime, and since the inventory mentions no real estate it must all have been distributed before his death. This accounts for the smallness of the estate, only £49 17*s.* 6*d.*

The records here transcribed are found in the Plymouth County Probate Records, Volume I, pages 10 and 16.

[p. 10] The Eigth day of November 1687 Administration was Granted unto Leiu^{tt} Jonathan Alden to Administer upon the Estate of his father Mr John Alden late of Duxbury deceased

An Inventory taken of the Estate of the late deceased Mr John Alden october 31 day 1687

	£	*s*	*d*
Neate Cattell sheep Swine & one horse	13	..	..
one Table one forme one Carpit one Cubert & coubert Cloth	..	15	..
2 Chaires	..	.3	..
bedsteds Chests & boxes	..	15	..
Andirons pot hookes and hangers	..	.8	.6
pots Tongs one quort kettle	..	10	..

by brass ware	.1	:11	..
by 1 ads 1^s 6^d & saws 7^s	..	.8	.6
by Augurs and Chisells	..	.5	..
by wedges 5^s to Coupers tooles 1£ 2^s	.1	.7	..
one Carpenters Joynters	..	.1	.6
Cart boults Cleavie Exseta	..	13	..
driping pan & gridirons	..	.5	..
by puter ware 1 pound 12^s by old Iron 3^s	.1	15	..
by 2 old guns	..	11	..
by Table linen & other linen	.1	.12	..
To beding	.5	:12	..
one Spitt 1^s 6^d & baggs 2^s	..	.3	.6
one mortising axe	..	.1	..
marking Iron a Case of trenchers with other things	..	.7	..
hamen and winch exse	..	.2	.6
by one goume and a bitt of linnin Cloth	..	.7	..
by one horse bridle and Saddle liberary and Cash and weareing Clothes	18	.9	..
by other old lumber	..	15	..

Before Nathaniel Thomas Esqr Judge of the Inferior Court of Common Pleas the 8th day of November 1687 Leiu^t Jonathan Alden made oath that this is a true Inventory of the Estate of his father Mr John Alden deceased soe farr as he knoweth & when he knoweth more he will discover the same

Nath^{ll} Thomas Cler.

[p. 16] Wee whose names are Subscribed being p^{r}sonally Interested in the then Estate of John Alden senior of Duxbury Esqr lately deceased doe hereby acknowlege our selves to have Received Each of us our full Personall proportions thereof from Jonathan Alden Administrator & thereof Doe by these p^{r}sents for our selves our heires &c Exonerate acquitt & Discharge fully the said Jonathan Alden his heires &c for Ever of & from all Rights dues demands whatsoever Relateing to the afores^d Estate In Witness Whereof we have hereunto Subscribed & sealed this thirteenth day of June Ano Dom 1688. Jacobi 2^{di} 4to

Elexander Standish (Seal)
in ye Right of my wife
Sarah deceased
John Bass (Seal)
in y^e Right of my wife
Ruth deceased
Mary Alden (Seal)
Thomas Dillano (Seal)

John Alden (Seal)
Joseph Alden (Seal)
David Alden (Seal)
Prisilla Alden (Seal)
William Paybody (Seal)

ELDER WILLIAM BREWSTER'S INVENTORY AND THE SETTLEMENT OF HIS ESTATE.

Transcribed from the original records,

BY GEORGE ERNEST BOWMAN.

Elder William Brewster died at Plymouth, 10 April 1644, without having made a will, and on 5 June, 1644, his "onely two sonnes surviveing," Jonathan and Love, were appointed administrators of his estate. All records concerning the settlement of the estate are here collected.

[Court Orders, II : 101. Under date of 5 June, 1644.]

Lres of administacon of all the goods and cattells of m^{r} Willm Brewster deceased are graunted by the Court to Jonathan Brewster and Love Brewster And A true Inventory thereof was exhibited to the Court upon the Oathes of the said Jonathan & Love.

[Plymouth Colony Wills, I : 53.]

Lres of Administracon of all the goods and cattells of m^{r} Willm Brewster Deceased were graunted to Jonathan Brewster and Love Brewster at the gen^{r}all Court holden at Plymouth the fift Day of June in the xxth yeare of his said Ma^{s} now Raigne of England &c and a true Inventory thereof was exhibited to the

Court upon the Oathes of the said Jonathan and Love the same Court.

The Inventory followeth

	£ s d
Inpris 4 paire of stockings	00 . 04 . 00
It 3 wascoats and a paire of drawers	00 . 06 . 00
It 1 old gowne	00 . 09 . 00
It 1 blew cloth suite	00 . 15 . 00
It 1 old suite turned	00 . 05 . 00
It 1 black coate	00 . 01 . 06
It old cloathes	00 . 03 . 00
It 1 black cloth suite	00 . 06 . 06
It 1 paire of greene drawers	00 . 01 . 00
It 1 paire of leather drawers	00 . 00 . 06
It 1 list wascoate	00 . 00 . 06
It 1 trusse	00 . 00 . 06
It 1 black coate	00 . 10 . 00
It 1 black stuff suite	00 . 10 . 00
It 1 black suite & cloake	01 . 15 . 00
It 1 dublett	00 . 01 . 06
It 1 peere of stockings	00 . 01 . 00
It 1 black gowne	02 . 10 . 00
It 1 black hatt	00 . 04 . 00
It 1 old hatt	00 . 00 . 06
It 2 pere of gloves	00 . 01 . 00
It 1 paire of shooes	00 . 03 . 06
It 2 paire of shooes	00 . 01 . 00
It 1 sheete	00 . 01 . 00
It paire of canvas sheets	00 . 12 . 00
It 1 paire of old sheets	00 . 06 . 00
It 1 paire of sheets	00 . 07 . 00
It 1 old paire of canvas sheets	00 . 04 . 00
It 1 paire of little sheets	00 . 09 . 00
It 1 single sheete	00 . 06 . 06
It 1 diapr cloth	00 . 07 . 00
It 1 sherte	00 . 04 . 06
It 1 shert	00 . 01 . 00
It 1 canvas sheete	00 . 06 . 00
It 1 pillow beere	00 . 02 . 00
It 1 paire of fine sheets	00 . 15 . 00
It 1 paire of courser sheets	00 . 12 . 00
It 1 paire of pillow beers	00 . 06 . 00
It 1 towell	00 . 01 . 00
It 1 pillow beere	00 . 02 . 00
It 1 towell	00 . 01 . 00
It 12 handkercheefs	00 . 08 . 00
It 14 handkercheefs	00 . 03 . 00
It 1 fine handkercher	00 . 03 . 00
It 1 table cloth	00 . 03 . 00
It 1 little table cloth	00 . 02 . 00

It 6 towells	00.04.00
It 1 old pillowbeere	00.01.00
It 3 hand kerchers	00.00.08
It 1 wrought capp	00.06.00
It 1 laced capp	00.02.00
It 1 quilted capp	00.01.06
It 2 old capps	00.00.06
It 1 ruffe band	00.02.00
It ruff ript out	00.02.00
It 6 bands	00.01.00
It 1 red capp	00.00.08
It 1 budell of linnen raggs	00.00.04
It 2 gerdles	00.01.00
It 2 paire of thinn stockings	00.01.00
It 1 knitt cap	00.01.00
It 1 paire of garters	00.00.04
It 1 knife	00.00.03
It a table and forme	00.15.00
It 1 pistoll	00.07.00
It 1 silv^r beaker & a spoone	01.05.06
It 1 little trunck	00.00.06
It 1 bagg & a felling axe	00.00.10
It 1 little desk	00.01.00
It 1 chest	00.10.00
It 1 brod chest	00.08.00
It 3 cusheons	00.06.00
It 1 greene cusheon	00.00.06
It 1 settle bed	00.10.00
It 1 chaire	00.04.00
It 1 paire of bellowes	00.01.06
It a fire shovell & tongues	00.02.00
It 1 chamber pott	00.03.00
[54] It 1 pewter bottle	00.00.06
It 2 pewter cupp & spoons	00.02.00
It 1 combe	00.00.04
It 2 brushes	00.00.04
It 1 candle stick and snuffer	00.02.00
It 1 lampe	00.00.09
It 1 boxe	00.00.03
It sizzers	00.00.04
It 1 paire of black silk stockings	00.01.06
It a dagger & knife	00.02.00
It tobaccoe case &	00.00.03
It 1 case of bottles	00.04.00
It 2 boxes	00.02.00
It 1 rapier	00.01.00
It 2 hammers	00.00.06
It 1 earthen pott	00.00.04
It a feather bed & bolster	02.05.00
It 1 blankett	00.10.00

It 1 old white rugg	00.03.00
It 1 white rugg	00.15.00
It a feather bed boulster & pillowes	03.00.00
It 1 greene wascoate	00.02.00
It 2 blankets & rugg	00.12.00
It a peece of blankett	00.00.06
It 1 greene rugg	01.05.00
It 3 curtaines valence & rodds	00.06.00
It 1 earthen pott wth suger	00.01.06
It tobaccoe & some pipes	00.01.06
It 1 old hed peece	00.00.08
It a burneing glasse	00.00.06
It a tobaccoe box & tongs	00.00.03
It in silver	00.17.00

These goods were praised by Capt Miles Standish & m^{r} John Done May 10th 1644.

At his house at Duxborrow praised by m^{r} Thom Prence & Capt Miles Standish may 18th 1644.

Inpris a feather bed & boulster a pillow & straw bed	02.10.00
It 1 white rugg	00.10.00
It 1 old white irish blanket	00.05.00
It 1 white english blankett	00.10.00
It 1 sword	00.01.06
It 1 chamber pott	00.01.06
It 1 table wthout frame	00.03.00
It 1 bedstead & settle	00.15.00
It 1 stoole	00.00.04
It 1 deske	00.01.00
It old Iron	00.00.08
It vallens curtaines & rodds	00.03.00
It a bras hooke to hang a hat upon	00.00.04
It white capp	00.00.08
It 1 paire of sheets	00.06.00
It a towell	00.00.03
It a trusse	00.02.06
It an old trunck	00.04.00
It 1 old greene cusheon	00.00.03
It 1 pewter bottle	00.00.03
It 2 little chatachismees	00.00.04
It 1 lambeth on the will of man	00.00.02
It 1 morrall Discourse	00.00.02
It Discovery of spanish Inquisicon	00.00.03
It Johnson on 18th math	00.00.04
It remaynes of Brittaine	00.01.00
It Description of new England	00.00.04
It 1 violet color cloth coate	01.05.00
It 1 Costlett	00.10.00
It a table & forme	00.10.00
It 1 chaire	00.01.00

It a little table	00.02.00
It 1 settle bed	00.02.00
It 2 chaines	00.08.00
It 2 old shares & 1 Coulter	01.00.00
It 1 yeok of oxen 10 yeare old	16.00.00
It 2 yoke of oxen yeonger	28.00.00
It 1 two yere old stere	02.10.00
It 1 old cowe	04.10.00
It 1 red cowe	04.10.00
It 2 yeong Cowes	08.00.00
It 1 lame cowe	01.10.00
It 2 yearling heiffers	02.10.00
It 1 calf unweaned	00.08.00
It half a yeong sowe	00.08.00
It 1 shoate & a half	00.09.00
It a pigg	00.01.00

£ s d
The totall is 107 0 8

Myles Standish Tho: Prence.

[55] An Inventory of the latten books taken by m^r^ Bradford m^r^ Prence and m^r^ Reynor May 18th 1644.

	£ s d
Inpris Nova testamenti Malarato	01.04.00
It Tromelius & Junius biblia sacra	00.18.00
It Beza nova testament lat & Cre	01.00.00
It Centuria Selecta	00.08.00
It Calvin duodecim prphet	00.15.00
It Clavis scriptura flacio illirico	00.15.00
It Peter Martyr Com prio ad Corinthos	00.08.00
It Musculus Isaiam & Romanos	00.12.00
It Regneri prandini	00.02.06
It Gecolumnadij in Jeremia	00.03.00
It Crisostm mattias & Joannes	00.06.00
It Musculus Psalmos David	00.12.00
It Calvi ad Daniel	00.05.00
It Calvi on Isaye	00.15.00
It musculus ambos Epist ad Corinthos	00.08.00
It Molleri ad Psalmos	00.10.00
It Lanaterus Esechieli	00.05.00
It Zanchij ad Ephe	00.06.00
It Syntagma amudo polo Syntagmatis theologia Christianos	00.10.00
It Sulteti Isaiam	00.05.00
It Purei Hoseam	00.01.00
It Gualterin Delverin nov testa.	00.02.06
It Psalm Pagnij	00.02.06
It Pareus in Genosa	00.08.06
It Piscator in Nova Testament	00.17.00
It Pareus ad Romanos	00.05.00
It Pareus ad Priorem Corinthos	00.04.00
It Calvin Eze vigint prima	00.03.00

It Tabula Analytice Stephano	00.01.06
It Cartwrigh harma 4 Evangl	00.05.00
It Pascillia Hemnigm	00.01.00
It De vera Jes Chr. Religione	00.01.00
It Erasmus in Marcin	00.01.06
It Parkerius politica Eccle	00.05.00
It Piscator in Genesn	00.02.00
It Kykermano Systema Physica	00.03.00
It Beza Confess Christ	00.02.04
It Rollock in Dany	00.02.06
It Daven in prio Juni	00.02.00
It Thom Thomaseus Dix	00.02.00
It Bastwick Apologeticus	00.00.06
It Machavelii princeps	00.01.08
It Elenchus papistice Bastwick	00.00.06
It Rollock ad Psalmos	00.02.06
It Rainoldi de Romane Eccles	00.02.06
It Calvin in Josua	00.01.00
It Syntagma vigandus	00.01.06
It Epistola Apologetica	00.01.06
It Paraphrasa Erasmus in Luke	00.01.06
It latina gramatica	00.00.06
It Hebrew gramat	00.00.06
It Camden Brittain	00.03.00
It Rollock ad Romanos Ephes	00.03.00
It Dixtio: triglotts	00.01.06
It Buxtorff lexicon	00.04.06
It Cartwright proverbia	00.07.00
It Junij ad Ecclam Dei	00.00.03
It Tyrocinia	00.00.04
It Poemata Heringij	00.00.02
It Ad Rev^r^endismos patres eccliarm Anglicann	00.00.06
It Amesij contra Grevin Co	00.00.06
It Hypomneses	00.00.03
It Antichristus prognostica	00.00.04
It Narmonin Evangelin	00.00.06
	15.19.04

An Inventory of the English bookes taken by m^r^ Bradford & m^r^ Prence

It 1 English Bible lattin letter	00.08.00
It 1 English bible	00.06.00
It a new Testament	00.05.00
It m^r^ Ainsworths Psalmes in prose & meter	00.02.00
It 1 new testament	00.01.04
It Major Coment new testament	00.12.00
It Hexapla upon Daniell	00.05.00
It 2 volumes of m^r^ Perkins	01.10.00
It m^r^ Hernes works	00.05.00
It Babingtons works	00.08.00

It Cartwright against Remists	00 . 08 . 00
It Byfeild on Coloss	00 . 05 . 00
It Dodoner Herball	00 . 06 . 00
It mr Rogers on Judges	00 . 06 . 00
It mr Richardson on ye state of Eur	00 . 04 . 00
It Knights Concord	00 . 05 . 00
It Calvin on Isay	00 . 06 . 00
[56] It Willett on Roman	00 . 06 . 00
It Grensames workes	00 . 10 . 00
It Bodens Comon weale	00 . 08 . 00
It Willet on the 1st Samuel	00 . 04 . 00
It Surveyor by Ratborne	00 . 03 . 00
It Willet on Genesis	00 . 07 . 00
It Senaca workes	00 . 06 . 00
It Wilcocks on Psalmes	00 . 06 . 00
It Cottons Concordanc 2 volumes	00 . 12 . 00
It Scholasticall Discourse about the Crosse	00 . 04 . 00
It Taylor upon Tytus	00 . 05 . 00
It Hill upon life Ever	00 . 05 . 00
It Wilsons Dixonor	00 . 06 . 00
It Waimes Christia Synagogue	00 . 02 . 00
It Gibbines question & disputacons	00 . 02 . 06
It Calvin Harmon Evan	00 . 06 . 00
It Defence of Synod of Dort by Robin	00 . 02 . 00
It Messelina	00 . 03 . 01
It Downams Warfarr 2 prt	00 . 04 . 00
It Barlow on 2 Tymothy	00 . 02 . 06
It Cartwright agst Whitgift 2 prt	00 . 02 . 00
It Jackson agst misbeleefe	00 . 02 . 00
It Granger on Eccl	00 . 02 . 00
It Brightman Revel	00 . 05 . 00
It Birdag Anti	00 . 02 . 00
It Byfeild on 1 pet	00 . 05 . 00
It Weymes on Image of God in man	00 . 02 . 00
It Parr on Romans	00 . 05 . 00
It Robinson observacons	00 . 02 . 00
It Right way to go to worke	00 . 02 . 00
It Byfeilds sermons on 1 peter	00 . 05 . 00
It Dod on Comandts	00 . 02 . 06
It Mayor on Catholick Epistles	00 . 03 . 00
It Taylor parable on the Sower	00 . 02 . 00
It Narme of Chr : strarr	00 . 02 . 00
It Morley of truth of religion	00 . 03 . 00
It Attersons badges of christianyty	00 . 02 . 00
It Downam consolatrix	00 . 03 . 00
It Elton on 7 Romans	00 . 02 . 06
It a Declaracon of Quitill question	00 . 02 . 00
It Byfeild on 3 of peter	00 . 01 . 06
It 7 prbleames against Antechrist	00 . 01 . 00
It Dike upon Repent	00 . 01 . 06

It Sibbs Soules Comfort	00 . 03 . 06
It passions of the mynd	00 . 01 . 06
It 5 books of sermons stichet together	00 . 01 . 00
It Constitucons & Cannons of bb : of Cant	00 . 00 . 02
It Wittenhall Discovery of abuses	00 . 01 . 00
It Rollock on Thessal	00 . 02 . 00
It Heaven opened by Coopr	00 . 02 . 00
It Treasury of Similes	00 . 04 . 00
It Downefall of popery	00 . 02 . 00
It Saints by calling by Wilson	00 . 02 . 00
It Wittenhall discov^{ry} of abuses	00 . 02 . 00
It Udall on Lamentacons	00 . 01 . 04
It Dyocean Tryall	00 . 00 . 06
It Sparks agst Albin	00 . 02 . 06
It Wottons Defence of Perkins Refor Catholike	00 . 02 . 06
It Brinslow on Ezech	00 . 03 . 00
It Defenc of ministers reasons	00 . 01 . 06
Is Downam agst Bath & Wells	00 . 01 . 06
It A Discourse of troubles Chu : of Amster	00 . 01 . 00
It m^{r} Smyths 3 treatises	00 . 02 . 06
It Discourse of equivocation	00 . 01 . 06
It m^{r} Smyths paroliles	00 . 00 . 08
It a peticon for reformacon	00 . 00 . 06
It a primer of Chr : Relig	00 . 00 . 09
It a Discourse of varianc betweene pope & venet	00 . 01 . 00
It Broughton on lament	00 . 01 . 00
It Perkins on Sat Sophist	00 . 00 . 06
It a Discourse of Adoracon of Reliq^{us}	00 . 01 . 00
It Trew marks of Catholike Church	00 . 00 . 06
It a Quodlibet to bewarr of preists	00 . 00 . 04
It justifycacon of sepracon	00 . 02 . 00
It Stocks answere to Campion	00 . 02 . 00
It Dike on the heart	00 . 02 . 00
It Perkins on 11 Hebrewes	00 . 03 . 02
It Bayne on Ephes	00 . 02 . 00
It Dike on repent & Ch. temtations	00 . 02 . 00
It Bolton on true happynes	00 . 01 . 06
It Downame agst Beller	00 . 01 . 08
It Wotton on 1 John	00 . 02 . 00
It Gouge Armor of God	00 . 02 . 00
It Plea for Infants	00 . 01 . 06
It Dod on Comand^{nts}	00 . 03 . 00
It Rollock on effectuall calling	00 . 01 . 10
It Calling of Jewes by smyth	00 . 01 . 00
It Prin Antearminescnce	00 . 01 . 08
It Discovery by Barrow	00 . 03 . 00
[57] It Ainsworth Defence of scripture	00 . 01 . 06
It 2 Downams Reply agst Bath	00 . 03 . 00
It Admonition to Parli^{nt}	00 . 01 . 06
It Refutacon to Gifford	00 . 02 . 06

It Perth Assembly	00.01.06
It Defence of the Ministers reasons	00.01.06
It Treatise of ministery of England	00.01.00
It Cassander Anglicans	01.01.08
It Downams warfarr	00.05.00
It the meane of mourneing	00.03.00
It Hackhill History of Indyes	
It Sweeds Intellegencer	00.01.06
It Comunion of Saints	00.02.00
It Abridgment of ministers of Lincolne	00.01.06
It Jacob attestation	00.01.00
It modest Defence	00.03.00
It exposicon of Canticles	00.01.00
It Whitgifts answere to a libell	00.01.06
It a reply to a libell	00.02.00
It Duplesss of a Chur	00.02.00
It Perkins on Jude	00.02.00
It Downams 4 treatises	00.02.00
It Deareing on Hebrews	00.03.00
It A Collection of Englands Deliv^{r}ancs	00.01.06
It 1000 notable things	00.01.06
It Riches of elder ages	
It Dod on Comand^{nts}	00.02.06
It Sweeds Intilligencer	00.01.06
It tymes turne coate	00.00.06
It A continuacon of adventur of Don Sebastian	00.00.04
It Surveyor Dialougs	00.01.00
It Apology Chur of England agst Brownists	00.01.06
It Kings Declaracon about Parli^{nts}	00.00.02
It Scyrge of Drunkerds	00.00.02
It Syons Plea	00.02.00
It Elton of Comand^{nts}	00.02.00
It treatise of Chr Religion	00.02.00
It a battaile of Palatinate	00.01.06
It treatise 122 psalm	00.00.06
It Concordance of yeares	00.00.06
It Cesars tryumphs	00.00.02
It A Dialogue concerneing Ceremonies	00.00.04
It Essayes about a prisoner	00.00.03
It Politike Diseases	00.00.06
It Exposicon of liturgie	00.00.08
It magnifycent entertaynement of King James	00.00.06
It a modest Defence	00.00.06
It Essex practise of treason	00.00.06
It prosopeia	00.00.02
It Withers Motto	00.00.04
It Standish for woods	00.00.06
It a Recantacon of A Brownist	00.00.04
It a supply to German History	00.01.00
It of the use of silk wormes	00.00.06

It newes from verginia	00.00.06
It newes from Palatinate	00.00.04
It Hacklett	00.02.00
It Byfeild on the Oracles of God	00.03.02
It Gods Monarchy Devells Kingdome	00.00.04
It New shreds of old Share	00.00.06
It Davids musick	00.00.06
It Discharg of 5 imputacons	00.01.00
It Horne sheild of the Rightous	00.01.00
It Ruine of Rome	00.01.06
It Downame on 15 psalm	00.01.06
It Pisca Evangelica	00.01.06
It Virell on Lords prayer	00.01.06
It answere to Cartwright	00.00.06
It Broughton on Gods Divinitie	00.01.00
It Bayne tryall of Christ state	00.01.06
It Wheatley on Gods husbandry	00.01.00
It Exposicon on Revelac	00.01.00
It Perkins Reformed Catholik	00.01.06
It Johnsons & Withers works	00.02.00
It 10 sermons of the supper	00.01.06
It Civill conversacon Gnahzo	00.02.00
It Smyths Plea for infants	00.00.06
It Bacons prficiency in learneing	00.02.00
It Arguments agst seinge	00.01.06
It Theologicks	00.00.06
It Eming on James	00.01.06
It Catholike Judg	00.01.00
It the spirituall watch	00.01.00
It reasons for Reformacon of Chur of England	00.00.06
It a looking glass agst Prelates	00.01.00
It sermon of Bishop of London	00.00.06
It Resolucon for kneeleing	00.00.06
It 2 exact Discovery of Romish Doctrine	00.00.04
It warr was a blessing	00.00.06
It midland souldier	00.00.04
It humillitie Christians life	00.00.06
It Church Delivrance	00.01.00
It Coment on Ecclesiac	00.00.06
It Prerogative of Parlints	00.00.06
It Temple on 20 psalm	00.01.06
It Abbott sermon	00.00.03
It Soules implantacon	00.03.04
It a treatise of Stage pleas	00.00.03
It Apologie of Brownists	00.00.04
[58] It State mistery of Jesuits	00.00.06
It Dike schoole of affliccon	00.02.00
It Sibbs Comfort	00.01.06
It Taylor on 32 psalm	00.02.00
It Parable of the vine by Rogers	00.02.00

It Apologeticall reply by Damfort	00 . 02 . 00
It Divers books sticht together	00 . 02 . 00
It Broughton of lamentacon	00 . 00 . 06
It a good wyfe	00 . 00 . 03
It Northbrook against Images	00 . 01 . 06
It Tryall of truth by Chibbald	00 . 01 . 00
It the tryall of truth	00 . 00 . 04
It the paterne of true prayer	00 . 01 . 06
It houshold goverment	00 . 01 . 06
It Blackwells answers	00 . 00 . 04
It Aristotles probleames	00 . 00 . 06
It Symers Indictment	00 . 00 . 04
It Johnsons Psalmes in meeter	00 . 00 . 04
It Mores discovery	00 . 00 . 03
It a sermon	00 . 00 . 02
It refutacon of tolleracon	00 . 00 . 06
It Aphorismees of state	00 . 00 . 02
It of union betweene England & Scotland	00 . 00 . 06
It Rates of popes custome house	00 . 00 . 04
It of Pope Joane	00 . 00 . 04
It a dialogue betweene a gent & a preist	00 . 00 . 04
It against kneeleing	00 . 00 . 03
It Perkins on fayth	00 . 00 . 03
It Bacons Apologye	00 . 00 . 03
It a history of Mary Glover	00 . 00 . 03
It a bundle of smale books & papers	00 . 02 . 00
It Defyance of Death	00 . 01 . 00
It a christians apparelling	00 . 01 . 06
It Perkins on repentan	00 . 00 . 08
It Essays by Cornwallis	00 . 01 . 06
It Spirituall stedfastnes	00 . 00 . 08
It a manuell	00 00 . 06
It a breiffe of bible	00 . 00 . 06
It Jacob on 2^d^ Comand^nt^	00 . 00 . 04
It a pill to purg popery	00 . 00 . 02
It withers	00 . 00 . 04
It cathologue of nobillyty of England	00 . 00 . 03
It English votaryes	00 . 00 . 06
It Sibbs yea & amen	00 . 01 . 06
It Sermons by Rollock	00 . 01 . 00
It Kinges Bath	00 . 00 . 08
It Great Assise by Smyth	00 . 00 . 08
It martin on Easter	00 . 01 . 00
It Smyth on 6 of Hosea	00 . 01 . 06
It Discription of world	00 . 01 . 00
It Cantelus Cannon of Masse	00 . 01 . 00
It Perkins of Repentanc	00 . 00 . 06
It Gods m^r^cy & Jurasa misery	00 . 00 . 06
It silv^r^ watch bell	00 . 00 . 06
It 7 sermons by W B	00 . 00 . 06

It Burton ag^st^ Cholmely	00.00.06
It Sibbs Saints p^r^vilidges	00.01.01
It Sibbs Riches of mercy	00.01.01
It Regla vite	00.01.01
It Pilgrims prfession	00.00.08
It sermon at Pauls cross	00.00.04
It nature & grace	
It Perkins of Predestinacon	00.00.06
It Spirituall trumpett	00.00.08
It vox Regis	00.00.06
It Barrowes platforme	00.00.06
It exposicon of Lords prayer	00.00.06
It Comon weale of England	00.00.06
It right way of peace	00.00.06
It 4th prt of true watch	00.01.00
It Johnson on Psalmes	00.01.00
It Byfeild paterne of	00.01.00
It a help to memorye	00.00.06
It Duke prmises	00.00.06
It prposicons by John Sprint	00.00.11
It the morality of law	00.00.06
It Cases of Consciencs by Per	00.01.00
It Discovery of famyly of love	00.00.06
It Sermon of Repentanc	00.00.06
It Sermon at Pauls crosse	00.00.06
It Sibbs spirituall maxime	00.00.09
It memorable conceits	00.01.00
It God and the King	00.00.04
It Smyth on Riddle of Nebuchadnez	00.00.08
It Estey on Comandnts & 51th Psalm	00.01.00
It Christians Dayly walk	00.01.06
It exposicon of 11 & 12 Revelacon	00.00.06
It treatise of English medicines	00.00.06
It a Dialogue of Desiderias	00.00.06
It a supplycacon to the King	00.00.06
It Abba father	00.00.06
It Abrahams tryall Decouse	00.01.00
It Jacobbs ladder	00.01.06
It Perkins of Imagina	00.00.06
[59] It Burton Christi question	00.00.06
It a toyle for 2 legged foxes	00.00.06
It a Cordiall for comfort	00.00.06
It Zacheus conversion	00.02.01
It spirituall touch stone	00.00.03
It Dearings advantage	00.00.06
It Englands Summons	00.00.06
It Burton wooing his Chur	00.00.04
It goulden Key	00.01.00
It remedy against famine & warr	00.00.06

It treatise against popery	00.01.00
It treatise of Gods Religion	00.00.08
The totall of both latten & English books amounts to the sum of	42.19.11
The totall both of goods & bookes amounts in all to	150.00.07

Wm Bradford
Tho: Prence

[Plymouth Colony Deeds, I: 198]

Bradford Govr

Whereas William Brewster late of Plym gent deceased left onely two sonnes surviveing vizt Jonathan the Eldest and Love the yeonger And whereas the said William dyed intestate for ought can to this day appeare The said Jonathan and Love his sonnes when they returned from the buriall of their father to the house of Mr Willm Bradford of Plymouth in the prsence of mr Raph Partrich Pastor of Duxborrow mr John Reynor Teacher of the Church at Plymouth and mr Edward Buckley Pastor of the Church at Ma(rsh)feild and many others being exhorted to honor their Revrend father wth a peaceable pceeding about the division of his estate between them. The said Jonathan first answered for his part that although hee were the elder yet was willing to devide lands and goods equally betweene himself and brother. And if in case any differrence should arrise betweene them that it might be soone suppressed said he heere are four of my fathers deere and auncient frends vizt mr Willm Bradford then Govrnor of Plymouth mr Edward Winslow of Marshfeild mr Thomas Prence of Plymouth aforesaid and Captaine Miles Standish of Duxborrow. And if my brother please to accept my motion whereinsoevr we shall differ we will stand to their award wch shalbe as firme as if it had beene done by our father &c To all wch the said Love Brewster condiscended to the greate satisfaccon of the whole Assembly the said freinds of his father being there also prsent who willingly engaged themselves therein to the utmost of their power And whereas afterward differrence arose betweene the said brethren Jonathan and Love in divers prticulers about the late dwelling house of their said father at Duxborrow wherein the said Love dwelt and had donn from his marriage to that instant also about certaine accompt wherein Jonathan was made debtor to the estate in a large sume &c Hereupon according to prmise they referring themselves to the said speciall and most intimate frends of their said father the said Edward Winslow afterwards Gov^r^nor of Plymouth m^r^ Willm Bradford m^r^ Thomas Prence and Captaine Miles Standish aforesaid haveing heard divers thinges alleadged on Loves behalf to prove that the said House and half the Lands of the said Willm belonging thereunto aswell as any other the lands of the said Willm devided or to be devided wth an entire half part of the estate of the said Willm was given to the said Love and Sarah his wyfe upon a Covenant of Contract of marryage to be due at the death of the said Willm Brewster now deceased. All wch was offerred to be prooved legally if neede require by solemne prmise though not in writing The said Jonath(an) also offerring to take off upon oath the greatest prt of the said debts also &c The said Edwa(rd) Winslow Willm Bradford Thomas Prence & Captaine Miles Standish being well acquainted wth their said case aswell by divers thinges heard from their rev^r^end father in his life as by the evedence now offerred to be prduced on both sides determyned as followeth And first of all for the said debts wch were alleadged against the said Jonathan the elder brother by the said Love the yonger as aforesaid we conceive that if their father had not acquitted them before his death yet hee would nev^r^ have charged his Eldest sonn wth them in regard of his greate charge of children and so beleeveing it was donn actually or intentively or both we discharged Jonathan of all the said debt his brother made him debtor to the estate aforesaid except foure pounds sterling wch wee award him to pay his brother Love in consideracon of the wintering of some cattell wch the said Jonathan had the sommering upon the division and for the dyett of Isaack Allerton a grandchild of the said Willm wch he had placed wth his sonn Love to table And because hee was the first borne of his father we gave him his fathers Armes and also a two yeare old heiffer over and above his part of the devideables of the said estate. And for the Dwelling house aforesaid of the said Willm wherein the said Love Brewster resided we were so well acquainted wth the purpose of the sd Willm now deceased and the evidence offerred for proofe seemed to us so strong as wee beleeveing the said Willm had actually or intentively or both given the said house to his sonn Love and Sarah his wyfe and their heires &c Wee the Edward William Thomas and Myles awarded the said dwelling house to the said Love and Sarah his wyfe and their heires &c together wth half the said Estate of Lands goods and cattells except before excepted and aswell such other lands as are not yet divided blonging to the said Willm as a Purchaser of the Patent & Plantacon of New Plymouth aforesaid as that at Duxborrow whereon hee lived And whereas some differrence might have arrisen about the division of the said Lands at Duxborrow m[r] Willm Vassell being requested to survey the said Lands he made a division of yt in two parts being an hundred & eleaven acrees of upland or there abouts viz[t] to Jonathan Brewster an sixtie eight acrees or there abouts w[ch] lay entire together next a dwelling house w[ch] the said Jonathan had built on the said land by the leave of his said father and all the meddow on that side a creeke (w[c]h divided the greatest part of the said land) below a Bridg on the way betweene (the) houses of Jonathan and Love his brother And to Love Brewster fourty three acrees of upland or there abouts adjoyneing to his dwelling house whereof thir(ty acr)ees was cleered land and almost all in tillage the other thirteene being woodland as it was devided in the said Plott drawne by the said Surveighor and (mark)ed out and allowed by us except a prcell of land about three quarters (of an acr)ee prte in the garden of the said Jonathan and prt in a Swamp adjoyneing wherein onely the [p. 199] said Jonathan had Water to his house as it was marked and staked by us Also we gave unto Love Brewster all the meddow on that side the Creek adjoyne-(ing) to his land where he liveth and also that smale prcell w[ch] lyeth above the Bridg betweene their two houses before expressed And the reason wherefore we gave Love the lesse quantitie was and is because the quallity of Loves land in goodnes is equall to the quantitie of Jonathans as we judg And that this is the full determinacon of us the said Edward Willm Thomas and Myles upon the referrence aforesaid of the said Jonathan and Love as wee are prswaded in our consciences to be equall and just haveing to our best abillities faythfully discharged our duties towards God their deceased father our former worthy frend and towards Jonathan and Love his onely children remayneing In witnes thereof we have put to our hands and ordered it to be put upon the Records of the Goverment. ffinished at Plymouth the xxth August 1645

William Bradford | Edw: Winslow
Tho: Prence | Myles Standish

THE WILL AND INVENTORY OF JOHN[2] COOKE (FRANCIS[1]).

Transcribed from the original records,

BY GEORGE ERNEST BOWMAN.

John[2] Cooke (Francis[1]) died at Dartmouth, Mass., 23 November (3 December, new style), 1695, and his will and inventory are found in the Bristol County, Mass., Probate Records, Volume I, pages 139 and 140. But one original paper remains in the probate files—the bond of the executrix, Sarah Cooke, daughter of Richard Warren. The date of this bond, 15 July, 1696 (25 July, N. S.), is the latest on which I have found any mention of the widow Sarah.

The Last will and Testament of John Cook of the town of Dartmouth in the County of Bristoll: I being weake of Body but of sound and Perfect memory, have Disposed of my Estate which God hath been pleased to bestow: upon me in manner following that is to say In the first place I give to my Son in-law Arthur Hathaway & his wife Sarah my Daughter all my land in the point at or Near the Burying place in Dartmouth the which I bought of John Russell to them their heires and Assignes for Ever: And also I give unto my Son in-law Stephen west and his wife Mercey my Daughter one full Third part of a whole Share of lands in the Township of Dartmouth with all my houseing and Orchards thereunto belonging: with all the priviledges & appur=ces belonging to the same to them their heires & Assignes for ever They to possess the same after the Decease of my wife Sarah Allso I give unto Jonathan Delano. one Third part of a share of meadow Caled the ffreemens Meadow Lyeing within the Township of Rochester to him his heires & assignes for Ever: Allso I give to my Grandson Thomas Taber my little Island Caled & Known by the Name of Ram Island Lying in Cushnat River in Dartmouth with one third part of my Share of Meadow Called the ffreemens Meadow Lyeing in the Township of Rochester. to him his heires & assignes for Ever and I give to my said Grand son my Gun &

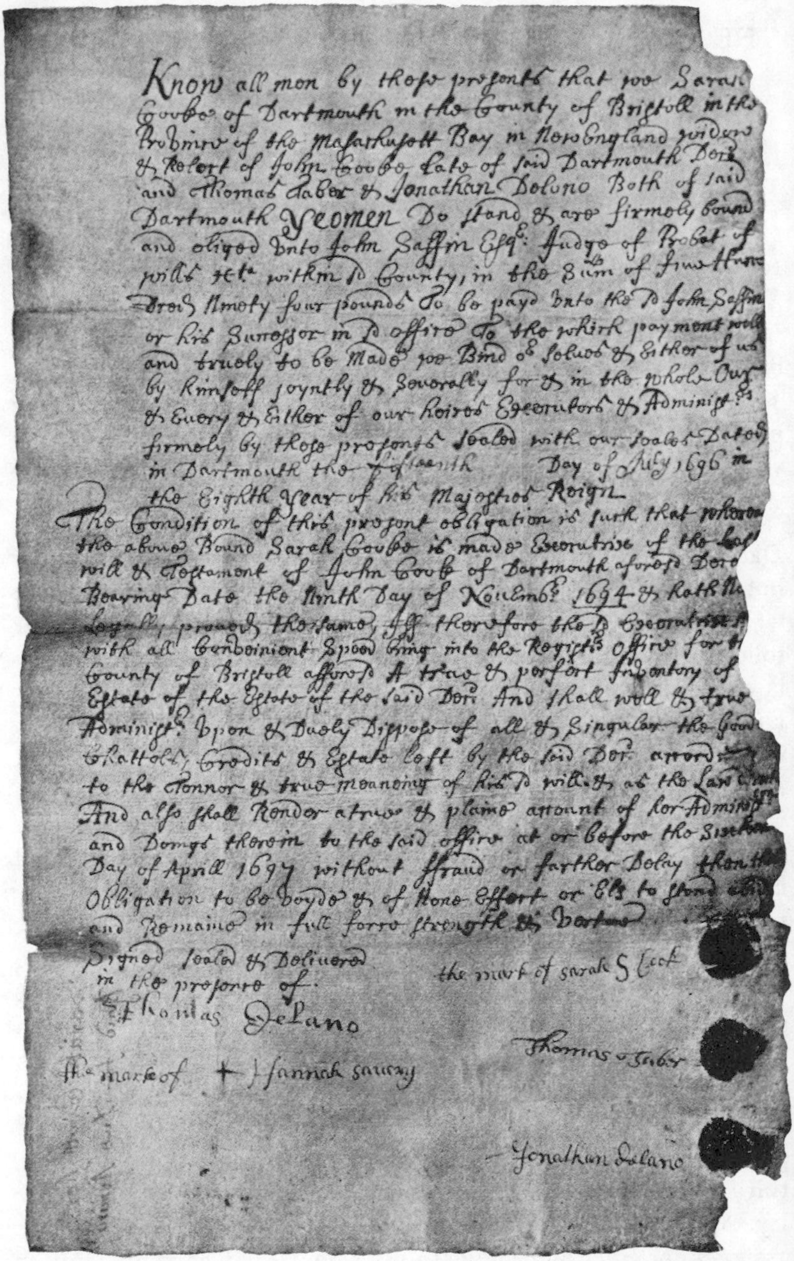

Know all men by these presents that wee Sarah
Cooke of Dartmouth in the County of Bristoll in the
Province of the Massachusett Bay in New England widow
& Relict of John Cooke late of said Dartmouth Decd
and Thomas Taber & Jonathan Delano Both of said
Dartmouth Yeomen Do stand & are firmely bound
and oliged unto John Saffin Esqr: Judge of Probat of
wills &c.a within sd County, in the Sum of five Hundred Ninety four pounds to be payd unto the sd John Saffin
or his Successor in sd office to the which payment well
and truely to be Made wee Bind os selves & Either of us
by himself joyntly & severally for & in the whole Our
& Every & Either of our heires Executors & Administrs
firmely by these presents Sealed with our seales Dated
in Dartmouth the fifteenth Day of July, 1696 in
the Eighth Year of his Majesties Reign

The Condition of this present obligation is such that whereas
the above Bound Sarah Cooke is made Executrix of the last
will & Testament of John Cooke of Dartmouth aforesd Decd
Bearing Date the Ninth Day of Novembr 1694 & hath Ne
legally proved the same, If therefore the sd Executrix [illegible]
with all Convenient Speed bring into the Registrs Office for the
County of Bristoll aforesd A true & perfect Inventory of
Estate of the Estate of the said Decd And shall well & true
Administr Upon & Duely Dispose of all & Singular the Goods
Chattels, Credits & Estate left by the said Decd according
to the Tennor & true meaning of his sd will & as the Law [illegible]
And also shall Render a true & plaine account of her Administ[illegible]
and Doings therein to the said office at or before the Sixteen[th]
Day of Aprill 1697 without ffraud or farther Delay then this
Obligation to be voyde & of None Effect or Els to stand a[nd]
and Remaine in full force strength & vertue

Signed Sealed & Delivered
in the presence of
Thomas Delano
the marke of + Hannah sawny

the mark of sarah S Cook

Thomas Taber

Jonathan Delano

sword Allso I give to my Grand Daughter Hester Perry One feather Bed & Bolster, All the Rest & Residue of Estate Goods & Chattles of what Sort or Kind so ever I Give & bequeath uto my Loveing wife Sarah to use. & Dispose of the same as she shall see good And I make my said wife Sole Executrix of this my Last will & Testament: In witness whereof I the said John Cooke have hereunto sett my hand & seale this Ninth Day of November 1694 in the presence of

Aaron Savory O his mark John Cooke (seal)
Thomas Taber

memorandum that on the 16th of Aprill 1696 Then appeared Aaron Savory & Thomas Taber both of Dartmouth, Before John Saffin Esqr Judge of Probate of wills &ca and made Oath that they were present & did see John Cooke late of Dartmouth Decd Signe seale & publish this Instrument to be his last will & testiment and yt he was of a Disposeing mind when he so did to the best of their apprehensions

Jno Saffin

John Cary Registr

Thus Entered & Engrosed may the: 8th 1696 By Jno Cary Registr

[p. 140] December the 7th 1696 *

A true Inventory of the Estate Goods & Chattels of John Cooke late of Dartmouth Deceased

	£	s	d
Imprs all his Houseing and land at	200	00	00
his Cattle of all sorts	020	00	00
In Sivir money	025	04	00
his wearing apparrel at	007	10	00
two Beds & Beding at	019	10	00
for Severall Remnants of New Cloath	002	05	00
for Pueter & Tin vessels	001	05	00
one warming Pann	000	12	00
two Bibles & Six other Books	002	00	00
two Iron pots one Iron Kettle & two old Skillets	002	00	00
five Bushels of Corn	000	15	00
for linnen yarn & flax teere	001	06	00
half a Dozen of Spoons	000	02	00
two Chains & Plow-Irons with Several other old Iron tools at	001	10	00

* This is plainly a mistake of the Register for 1695.

Due in Debts	008 00 00
One Gun a Sword & Powder & Bullets	001 10 00
one pare of Andjrons two trammils	001 10 00
two Chests one Table & a Settle	002 00 00
for lumber of all sorts at	003 00 00
	299 19 00

Taken by us the Day & year first above written

Aarther Hathaway   Thomas Tabar

April 10th 1696 the widdow Sarah Cooke made oath to ye above written Inventory

Before me   Seth Pope   Justice of peace

The above Named Sarah Cooke being a very Antient woman and unable to travile far, it was Necessary that her Deposition should be Taken as above said. to the truth of this Inventory the which I do alow and Approve and Doe hereby order it to be Recorded in the Registers Office this 16th Day of Aprill 1696

Jno Saffin   Probar

Jno Cary   Registr

Thus Entered & Engrossed May the 19th 1696 By Jno Cary Registr

[Bond of Executrix.]

Know all men by these presents that we Sarah Cooke of Dartmouth in the County of Bristoll in the Province of the Masachusett Bay in New England widow & Relect of John Cooke late of said Dartmouth Decd and Thomas Taber & Jonathan Delono Both of said Dartmouth Yeomen Do stand & are firmely bound and oliged unto John Saffin Esqr Judge of Probat of wills &ca within sd County, in the Sum of five Hundred Ninety four pounds To be payd unto the sd John Saffin or his Successor in sd office To the which payment well and truely to be Made we Bind or selves & Either of us by himself joyntly & Severally for & in the whole Our & Every & Either of our heires Executors & Administrs firmely by these presents sealed with our seales Dated in Dartmouth the fifteenth Day of July 1696 in the Eighth Year of his Majesties Reign

The Condition of this present obligation is such that whereas the above Bound Sarah Cooke is made Executrix of the Last will & Testament of John Cook of Dartmouth aforesd Dece(as^{d}) Bearing Date the Ninth Day of Novemb^{r} 1694 & hath Ne(ver) Legally proved the same, Iff therefore the sd Executrix s(hall) with all Conveinient Speed bring into the Regist^{rs} Office for th(e) County of Bristoll afforesd A true & perfect Inventory of (the) Estate of the Estate of the said Dec^{d} And shall well & true(ly) Administ^{r} upon & Duely Dispose of all & Singular the Good(s) Chattels, Credits & Estate left by the said Dec^{d} accordi(ng) to the Tennor & true meaneing of his sd will. & as the Law (di)rec(ts) And also shall Render a true & plaine account of her Administ^{con} and Doings therein to the said office at or before the Sixteen(th) Day of Aprill 1697 without ffraud or farther Delay then this Obligation to be voyde & of None Effect or Els to stand abide and Remaine in full force strength & Vertue

Signed sealed & Delivered the mark of Sarah **S** Cook
in the presence of

Thomas Delano
the mark of + Hannah Savery

Thomas Taber
Jonathan Delano

THE MAYFLOWER GENEALOGIES.

RICHARD WARREN AND HIS DESCENDANTS.

Compiled from Original Sources,
BY GEORGE ERNEST BOWMAN.

Richard Warren was from London and joined the Leyden Pilgrims in July, 1620, at Southampton, whence the Mayflower and the Speedwell first set sail for America. He was married in England, before 1611, to Elizabeth ——, whose maiden name is unknown, and had by her five daughters, Mary, Anna (born about 1612), Sarah, Elizabeth and Abigail, who were left in England and came to Plymouth with their mother in 1623. Nothing more is known of his life before he joined the Pilgrims on the Mayflower, and there are very few references to him in the Plymouth Colony records and the works of contemporary writers, doubtless owing to his early death in 1628.

Bradford's History mentions him only in the list of the Mayflower passengers,* and includes him among the few who were of enough importance to be distinguished by the title of "Mr."

Nathaniel Morton, in the New England's Memorial, published at Cambridge, Mass., in 1669, was the first to print the names of the forty-one men who signed the Compact in the cabin of the Mayflower on Saturday, 11/21 November, 1620, and Richard Warren's name appears in this list.†

The following extract from Mourt's Relation contains the only reference yet found to the place from which Richard Warren came. It also shows us that he was a member of the third exploring party sent out while the Mayflower lay at anchor in Cape Cod Harbor. This party set out in the shallop on Wednesday, 6/16 December, 1620, and after many hardships, including a fight with the Indians early Friday morning, landed at Plymouth on the following Monday, 11/21 December, 1620.

Wednesday the sixt of December, it was resolved our discoverers should set forth, for the day before was too fowle weather, and so they did, though

* Mayflower Descendant, I: 10, 14. † Ibid., I: 79.

it was well ore the day ere all things could be readie: So ten of our men were appointed who were of themselues willing to vndertake it, to wit, Captaine Standish, Maister Carver, William Bradford, Edward Winsloe, Iohn Tilley, Edward Tilley, Iohn Houland, and three of London, Richard Warren, Steeuen Hopkins and Edward Dotte, and two of our Sea-men, Iohn Alderton and Thomas English, of the Ships Company there went two of the Masters Mates, Master Clarke and Master Copin, the Master Gunner, and three Saylers. The narration of which Discovery, followes, penned by one of the Company. [Mourt's Relation, London, 1622, p. 15.]

"In the latter end of July," 1623, his wife and daughters arrived at Plymouth in the Anne, and in the Division of Land a few months later he received lots on "the north side of the towne" and "on the other side of the towne towards the eele-river." * In 1624 or 1625 his son Nathaniel was born at Plymouth,† and his second son, Joseph, must have been born there in 1626 or early in 1627, as his name appears in the division of the cattle among the "Purchasers" who in 1627 bought from the Adventurers all their rights in the Colony of New Plymouth. ‡ In this division, which was made 22 May/1 June, 1627, "The ninth lot fell to Richard Warren & his companie Joyned wth him." To this lot fell a black smooth horned heifer which came in the Jacob, and two she goats. The record of this division ‖ contains the earliest mention of the names of Richard's wife and children.

The next year, 1628, he died at Plymouth, leaving his widow to care for a family of five daughters (four of whom were under seventeen), and two sons under four. Nathaniel Morton, in writing of the year 1628, speaks of his death as follows:

This year died Mr. Richard Warren, who hath been mentioned before in this Book,§ and was an useful Instrument; and during his life bare a deep share in the Difficulties and Troubles of the first Settlement of the Plantation of New-Plimouth. [New England's Memorial, p. 68.]

There is no account of the settlement of Richard Warren's estate, but the Colony records contain abundant evidence that

* Winslow, Good Newes from New England, London, 1624, p. 51, and Mayflower Descendant, I: 14, 228–230.

† Mayflower Descendant, II: 178, 179.

‡ Bradford's History, folios 143, 144.

‖ Mayflower Descendant, I: 152.

§ As a signer of the Compact, and as a member of the third exploring party.

his widow was thoroughly competent to bring up the children and manage the property left to her care.

She is first mentioned after her husband's death in a deed dated 28 September/8 October, 1629, in which Thomas Clarke sells to William Bradford land bounded on one side by land of "widow Warren." [Plym. Col. Deeds, I: 32.]

In the tax lists made by orders of the General Court, dated 2/12 January, 1632/3 and 2/12 January 1633/4, she was taxed twelve shillings and nine shillings respectively, to be paid in corn at six shillings per bushell. [Court Orders, I: 10, 61.]

On 1/11 July, 1633, in the orders about mowing grass, Mrs. Warren and Robert Bartlett were assigned the place where they mowed the previous year, and "the marsh adjoyning, as high as Slowly Howse." [Court Orders, I: 21.]

The inventory of Godbert Godbertson, taken 24 October/3 November, 1633, mentions a debt of six shillings "To m^{rs} Warren for labor." [Mayflower Descendant, I: 157.]

Widow Mary Ring, in her will probated 28 October/7 November, 1633, gave "unto m^{rs} Warren one woodden cupp wth a foote as a token of my love."* On this last date the Court granted to Mr. Ralph Fogg a meerstead formerly granted to Richard Warren, but forfeited because not built upon, and Fogg was to pay Mrs. Warren for the fence remaining on it. [Court Orders, I: 35.]

The inventory of John Thorp, taken 15/25 November, 1633, mentions a debt of £1, 10s., 6d. to Mrs. Warren.†

Widow Warren's servant Thomas Williams was before the Court held 5/15 July, 1635, for profane and blasphemous speeches. [Court Orders, I: 80.]

On 5/15 January, 1635/6, she was sued by Thomas Clarke for £15 damages, for a boat loaned to her and lost in Eel River in an extraordinary storm. The jury found for defendant, but "for other considerations," which are not mentioned in the record, they awarded Clarke thirty shillings. [Court Orders, I: 82.]

At a general meeting about the hay grounds 14/24 March, 1635/6, Mrs. Warren, Richard Church, Thomas Little and Robert Bartlett were assigned the places they had the year before. [Court Orders, I: 89.]

* Mayflower Descendant, I: 30. † Ibid., I: 160.

The following order of the General Court under date of 7/17 March, 1636/7, is of especial interest as showing that Elizabeth Warren succeeded to her husband's rights as a "Purchaser," and because it is the first reference to the marriage of Robert Bartlett and Richard Church to her daughters. Mrs. Warren's name also appears in a list of the "Purchasers" found in the Court Orders, Vol. II, p. 244.

It is agreed upon by the consent of the whole Court That Elizabeth Warren Widdow the relict of mr Richard Warren Deceased shalbe entred and stand and bee Purchaser instead of her said husband aswell because that (hee dying before he had prformed the said bargaine) the said Elizabeth prformed the same after his decease as also for the establishing of the Lotts of land given formrly by her unto her sonnes in law Richard Church Robert Bartlett and Thomas Little in marriage wth their wives her daughters. [Court Orders, I : 107.]

On 7/17 July, 1637, the Court established the highway to Eel River. It passed west of Robert Bartlett's house, then west of Thomas Little's, east of Mrs. Warren's and east of Richard Church's. [Court Orders, I : 114.]

4/14 December, 1637, land at Eel River is confirmed to Thomas Clarke and is to be laid out so as to be least prejudicial to Thomas Little, Robert Bartlett, Mrs. Warren and others there. [Court Orders, I : 133.]

7/17 February, 1637/8, Mrs. Warren conveyed to John Cooke, who had married her daughter Sarah, land at Eel River, adjoining land she had formerly given Robert Bartlett. [Plym. Col. Deeds, I : 30.]

3/13 June, 1639, The Court of Assistants awarded Mrs. Warren ten shillings in full of all accounts between her and Mr. Andrew Hallett. [Judicial Acts, Pt. I, p. 8.]

9/19 January, 1639/40, Mrs. Warren conveyed her house and eight acres of land near Wellingsly or Hobs Hole to Anthony Snow, husband of her daughter Abigail. [Plym. Col. Deeds, I : 86.]

5/15 May, 1640, Richard Church, Robert Bartlett, Thomas Little and Mrs. Warren were granted enlargements at the heads of their lots to the foot of the Pine Hills. [Court Orders, I : 234.]

6/16 June, 1644, Stephen Hopkins, in his will, mentions his

great bull in the hands of Mrs. Warren. [Mayflower Descendant, II : 12.]

In a list dated March, 1651, of the proprietors of the lands belonging to the Town of Plymouth at Punckateesett, in what is now Little Compton, R. I., Mrs. Warren's name appears, and under date of 22 March/1 April, 1663/4, she and her son Joseph are entered as owners of the twelfth lot there. [Plym. Town Records, I : 47, 70.]

On 7/17 October, 1652, the following order reaffirmed the rights of Mrs. Warren as a "Purchaser," and the rights of those to whom she had deeded land.

Wheras a petition was prefered by Robert Bartlet unto the court holden att Plymouth the 7th of october 1652 therin requesting that wheras sundry speeches have pased from som who pretend themselves to bee the sole and right heires unto the lands on which the said Robert Bartlet now liveth att the Eelriver in the Townshipp of Plymouth; which hee the said Robert had bestowed on him by his Motherinlaw Mis Elizabeth Warren in Marriage with her Daughter by which said speeches and passages the said Robert hath ben Dishartened in his proceeding either in building ffencing &c The court haveing taken the prmises into serius consideracon and haveing serched what the court hath upon record extant; and what could bee manifested upon memory by those that then were cheife and had speciall hand in carying on and menageing the former affaires of the countrey and doe therby find that Mis Elizabeth Warren who gave the said lands unto the said Robert and others in like condition had power soe to doe as being by an order of court bearing Date March the 7th 1637 and other actes of court before envested into the state and condicon of a Purchaser as in the said order is expressed; The said court doth by these presents therfore further ratify and confeirme the aforsaid actes of court wherby the said Elizabeth Warren is declared to have right to despose of the aforsaid Lands approveing and allowing of the above said gift of land unto the said Robert Bartlet and others in like condicon with him to bee valled to his and the(ire) heires and assignes for ever; [Court Orders, III : 17.]

On 7/17 March, 1652/3, Mrs. Warren became one of the purchasers of the tract of land which afterwards became the town of Dartmouth. [Plym. Col. Deeds, II : 106, 107.]

11/21 June, 1653, Elizabeth Warren, Jane Collier and Nathaniel Warren signed an agreement concerning lands which Nathaniel claimed. [Mayflower Descendant, II : 64.]

1/11 January, 1661/2, the marks of Mrs. Warren's horses were entered on the town records as follows :

January the first 1661 these horses were entered

The markes of Mistris Elizabeth warrens horses are as followeth

viz: one rid mare about thirteen yeares old with a white blase in her face marked with two slits in the neare eare and soe the bitt cut out which marke is on the out side of the said eare and alsoe the said mare is branded with a P on topp of the buttocke;

2condly a Coult of about a yeare old of the same Couller and the same marke

3dly a Bay mare with a black tayle and maine with a li(ttle) starr in the forehead about five yeares old of the same mark

4ly a blackeish horse Coult with one white foot behind and a fayer starr in his forehead of the same marke

5ly one young mare neare two yeare old blackish with gr(a)y heires of the same marke

one blacke mare neare 4 yeare old with a few gray heres in her forehead which belonges to Nathaniell and Josepth Warren of the same marke as Mistris Warrens above said

and one Rid horse Coult with a white blasse downe his face of the same marke belonging to the said Nathaniell and Josepth Warren; [Plym. Town Records, I: 173.]

In a record of land near Manomet Ponds granted to Nathaniel Warren 27 October/6 November, 1662, land of his mother nearby is mentioned. [Plym. Town Records, I: 132.]

In the codicil to his will, dated 16 July, 1667, Nathaniel Warren mentions his mother Elizabeth Warren, his brother Joseph Warren and his sisters Mary Bartlett, senior, Anna Little, Sarah Cooke, Elizabeth Church and Abigail Snow. [Mayflower Descendant, II: 39.]

Mrs. Elizabeth Warren died at Plymouth, 2/12 October, 1673, aged above ninety years, having survived her husband forty-five years and lived to see at least seventy-five great-grandchildren. It seems impossible that her funeral should have been delayed for twenty-two days, and it is probable that there is an error in the record of her death, which follows:—

Mistris Elizabeth Warren an aged widdow aged above 90 yeares Deceased on the second of October 1673 whoe haveing lived a Godly life Cam to her Grave as a shok of Corn fully Ripe shee was honoralbey buried on the 24th of October aforsaid. [Plym. Col. Rcds, Miscellaneous, p. 39.]

No will, or inventory of her estate, is known, the only record concerning the settlement of the estate being an order of the General Court dated 4/14 March, 1673/4, as follows:—

Mary Bartlett the wife of Robert Bartlett Came into this Court and owned that shee hath received full satisfaction for whatsoever shee might Claime as Due from the estate of Mistris Elizabeth Warren Deceased; and John Cooke in the behalfe of all her sisters testifyed the same before the Court; and the Court Doth heerby settle the remainder of the said estate on Joseph Warren to bee by him Injoyed without further mollestation or Disturbance from any of them. [Court Orders, V: 97.]

Children of RICHARD and ELIZABETH (——) WARREN:

2. i. MARY[2] WARREN, born in England.
3. ii. ANNA[2] WARREN, born in England, about 1612.
4. iii. SARAH[2] WARREN, born in England.
5. iv. ELIZABETH[2] WARREN, born in England.
6. v. ABIGAIL[2] WARREN, born in England.
7. vi. NATHANIEL[2] WARREN, born at Plymouth, in 1624 or 1625.
8. vii. JOSEPH[2] WARREN, born at Plymouth, in 1626 or early in 1627.

RICHARD WARREN AND HIS DESCENDANTS.

2. MARY[2] WARREN (*Richard*[1]) was born in England, and is shown by the record of the division of cattle to have been the eldest daughter, consequently she was born before 1612.*

Her last recorded child was born in 1651, hence Mary was in all probability not born before 1606, and was between twelve and seventeen years of age when she came to Plymouth with her mother and sisters in the Anne, in July, 1623. In the same

*M. D., II: 178.

vessell came her future husband, Robert Bartlett, whose origin is unknown. In the division of land the following spring he received one acre on the south side of the town, and in the division of cattle in 1627 he was one of Francis Eaton's company, to which fell the tenth lot, a yearling heifer and two she goats. In this division Mary Warren was in her father's company.*

The date of her marriage to Robert Bartlett is unknown. It did not occur until after 22 May/1 June, 1627, since Mary Warren is named in the division of cattle on that date. Her oldest son, Benjamin, was admitted a freeman 6/16 June, 1654, which makes it certain that he was born before 6/16 June, 1633, and her daughter Rebecca was married 20/30 Dec., 1649, doubtless being at least sixteen years old at the time, which would show that she was born in 1633 or earlier. Since two children were born before the middle of 1633 it is safe to assume that Robert Bartlett and Mary Warren were married as early as 1629.

The births of but two of their children are now to be found on the records, and we can judge of the order of birth of the first four daughters only by the dates of their marriages. The approximate date of Joseph's birth is obtained from the age given on his gravestone.

Robert Bartlett died at Plymouth between 19/29 Sept., 1676, the date of his nuncupative will, and 29 Oct./8 Nov., 1676, the day his will was probated. His widow was living 13/23 Feb'y, 1677/8, as shown by her deed of that date to her son Joseph. She died before the deed from her sons Benjamin and Joseph to William Harlow, Jr., made some time in 1683.

Robert Bartlett was called a cooper in 1654 in a deed from Samuel Hicks, and in the five deeds signed by him after that date he is called either "cooper" or "wine cooper." He was evidently a man of good standing and highly respected, but was never dignified by the title "Mr.," and his public services were limited to occasional duty as a member of the grand jury, frequent service on trial juries, and several terms as surveyor of highways.

Robert Bartlett's name appears in the earliest list of freemen of Plymouth, dated 1633, and in the tax lists of 1633 and 1634 his rate was nine shillings. [C. O., I : 1a, 10, 62]

In 1633 and 1636 he had mowing ground with Mrs. Warren. [M. D., III : 47]

On 28 May/7 June, 1635, his brother-in-law Thomas Little gave him land beyond Eel River on which to build a house. [C. O., I : 79]

*M. D., I : 152, 153, 230.

On 1/11 Dec., 1635, Richard Stinnings bound himself as an apprentice to Robert Bartlett for nine years. At the end of this term he was to receive two suits of apparel and £3 in money or goods. [C. O., I : 81]

In the earliest entry of cattle marks in the Plymouth town records, made in 1636 or 1637, Robert Bartlett's are recorded as follows: (*worn*) "Bartlet a peece cut out of the right eare before and (*worn*)ece out of the left eare behind." [T. R., I : 1]

His name appears in the list of freemen dated 7/17 March, 1636/7, and on the same date he is mentioned in an order of Court as a son-in-law of Mrs. Warren. [C. O., I : 105, & M. D., III : 48]

At a general meeting held 20/30 March, 1636/7, the following assignment of hay grounds was made:

> To Richard Church Robte Bartlet & Thomas Little hey ground where they had the last yeare, and to take further supply where they can fynd yt in placs not graunted to others, and Robte Bartlet to have the Swampe or Pitt at the head of m^r Bradfords ground. [C. O., I : 111]

Robert Bartlett was one of the jury appointed 2/12 May, 1637, to establish highways about Plymouth, Duxbury and Eel River. On 9/19 May they took oath before Gov. Bradford and the next day performed their duties. Their report was made to the Court 7/17 July, 1637. The Eel River road passed west of Robert Bartlett's house. [C. O., I : 113, 114]

On 4/14 Dec., 1637, land at Eel River was ordered layed out to Thomas Clark so it would be least prejudicial to Robert Bartlett and others. [M. D., III : 48]

On 7/17 Feb'y, 1637/8, Mrs. Warren gave to John Cooke, husband of her daughter Sarah,

> one lot of land lying at the Eele River containeing eighteene acrees or there abouts and lying on the North side of Robert Bartletts lott form^rly also given the said Robert in Marriage wth Mary another of the sd m^rs Warrens Daughters wch said lott is to begin at the heigh way and so to goe in lengh & breadth wth the said Roberts lott together wth a heigh way from the said lott to the water side if it be Demaunded or requested [Col. Deeds, I : II : 30]

On 11/21 Nov., 1638,* John Cooke gave the land just mentioned to Robert Bartlett in return for a like amount at Duxbury lying between the lots of Thomas Morton and Jonathan Brewster. [Col. Deeds, I : II : 32]

On 4/14 Aug., 1638, in consideration of £6, 10s. sterling paid down, and twenty bushels of corn to be paid the next

* The record is "1637", but the date of Mrs. Warren's conveyance taken in connection with the dates of other records preceding and following this one show that an error was made in the year.

March, John Barnes made over to Robert Bartlett the unexpired time of his servant Thomas Shreeve. Thomas was to serve until 1/11 Aug., 1641, the end of his term, for £3, 6s. 8d. per year, and he agreed to serve an additional year for £5. [Col. Deeds, I : II : 40]

On 1/11 Dec., 1638, Robert Bartlett hired Edward Shaw for one year, for £8, 10s. sterling. [C. O., I : 177]

His name appears in a list of freemen made in 1639.* [Lists Fr., 2]

On 3/13 Dec., 1639, he was sued for a debt by John Atwood and was obliged to pay him £6, 1s. 6d. [J. A., 9]

On 5/15 May, 1640, he was granted an enlargement of his lot toward the Pine Hills. [M. D., III : 48]

At the General Court held 2/12 June, 1640, the grand inquest presented "all whome it may concerne" for not building a bridge at Eel River according to order. On the margin of the record is the following entry: "The ele river people is to build a bridg there & 50^{s} repayd to Rich: Church & Robt Bartlet." [C. O., I : 239]

Robert Bartlett's name appears in a list dated 30 Nov./10 Dec., 1640, but the purpose of the list is not clear. [C. O., I : 250]

He was a member of the jury in the case of John Gilbert, Jr., vs. Mr. Francis Doughty, 6/16 June, 1643. [J. A., 24]

His name appears in the list of those able to bear arms, between the ages of sixteen and sixty, in August, 1643. [Lists Fr., 30]

Under date of 29 Aug./8 Sept., 1643, is recorded the settlement of a dispute between Mr. William Thomas and William Newland, regarding the sum of £4, 10s. which the former undertook to pay to Richard Church and Robert Bartlett in behalf of the town of Marshfield. [C. O., II : 86]

On 5/15 June, 1644, Robert Bartlett was chosen a member of the grand inquest, and the same day Manasseh Kempton, Edward Bangs and Robert Bartlett were ordered by the Court to appraise two oxen belonging to William Powell which had been seized for debts to Thomas Clarke and Clement Campion. [C. O., II : 100, 101]

The town of Plymouth voted, 22 June/2 July, 1644, that in case of an alarm in time of danger companies should assemble at various places, and Robert Bartlett was assigned to the Eel River company. [T. R., I : 27]

* This date was printed "1633" in Plym. Col. Rcds., Boston, 1857, Vol. VIII, p. 174, but a careful examination of the original discloses the error. The date "1639" is also confirmed by the governor and list of assistants given, which agrees with none but that for the year 1639.

He was chosen surveyor of highways for Plymouth, 4/14 June, 1645. [C. O., II : 115]

He was on the jury 28 Oct./7 Nov., 1654, in the cases of Nathaniel Bowman vs. Morris Truant, and Roger Cooke and William Latham vs. John and Ann Barker. [J. A., 29]

On 2/12 June, 1646, he was again chosen a member of the grand inquest. [C. O., II : 137]

His name appears in two lists of Plymouth townsmen, one dated 10/20 Dec., 1646, the other undated, but apparently made between 1648 and 1659. [T. R., I : 31, 34]

On 7/17 June, 1648, he served on the jury in the trial of a part of the cases which came before that Court. [C. O., II : 168]

On Thursday, 8/18 June, 1648, Robert Bartlett's daughter Lydia was born at Plymouth. [Col. M. B. B., 2]

His team is mentioned in a list of teams, and men assigned to each, for drawing wood ; but part of the leaf is missing and the purpose is not clear. The date is also missing, but it was probably between 1648 and 1652. [Plym. T. R., I : 44]

On 9/19 April, 1649, Richard Church sold his house and land at Eel River to Robert Bartlett for £25, to be paid as follows : £8, 10s. in a red ox called "Mouse," £6 in goods at Mr. Paddy's and the remainder in the latter part of September, 1650, either in cattle, corn or merchants pay. [Col. Deeds, I : II : 271]

On 17/27 May, 1649, he was again chosen a member of the grand jury. [Plym. T. R., I : 39]

On Thursday, 20/30 Dec., 1649, Robert Bartlett's daughter Rebecca was married at Plymouth to William Harlow. [Col. M. B. B., 8]

Robert Bartlett served on the jury 6/16 March, 1649/50, in the trial of two cases, William Hedge vs. Robert Nash, and Edward Doty vs. John Shaw, Jr. [J. A., 35]

On Sunday, 10/20 March, 1650/1, his daughter Mercy was born at Plymouth. [Col. M. B. B., 11]

Under date of February, 1651/2, he was recorded as having killed two wolves, but the entry was crossed out. [Plym. T. R., I : 43]

In March, 1651, Robert Bartlett was recorded as one of the proprietors of the Plymouth lands at Punckateesett (now Little Compton, R. I.), and on 22 March/1 April, 1663/4, he and James Cole, Sr., were entered as owners of the twenty-fourth lot. On 8/18 March, 1668/9, Robert Bartlett, "cooper," sold his interest in this lot, for £3, to Mr. John Almy, merchant, of Portsmouth, R. I. [Plym. T. R., I : 47, 71, & Col. Deeds, III, 328]

On Wednesday, 10/20 Sept., 1651, his daughter Mary was married at Plymouth to Richard Foster. [Col. M. B. B., 14]

He was chosen a member of the grand inquest 3/13 June, 1652. [C. O., III : 7]

The next day, 4/14 June, 1652, Robert Bartlett, Thomas Clarke, Richard Church, Nathaniel Warren and Joseph Warren complained against the towns of Yarmouth, Barnstable and Sandwich for non-performance of a Court order to build a bridge over Eel River. [J. A., 47]

On 2/12 Aug., 1652, Thomas Little sold to Richard Foster land next to Robert Bartlett's. [M. D., I : 98]

On 7/17 Oct., 1652, Robert Bartlett petitioned the Court to settle a dispute concerning land given him by Mrs. Warren. The decision confirming his rights was printed in full on page 49 of this volume. This petition is referred to in the bond of Elizabeth Warren, Jane Collier and Nathaniel Warren dated 11/21 June, 1653. [M. D., II : 64]

On 7/17 March, 1652/3, he became one of the purchasers of what was afterwards called Dartmouth. [Col. Deeds, II : I : 106, 107]

He was a member of the juries which tried various actions on 4/14 Oct., 1653, and on 7/17 March, 1653/4, and 3/13 Oct., 1654. [J. A., 55, 58, 60]

Robert Bartlett, "wine cooper," on 30 Jan'y/9 Feb'y, 1653/4, bought of Samuel Hicks eleven acres of land on the south side of the town, lying on the bay, but was not to take possession until 15/25 Oct. 1654. [Col. Deeds, II : I : 97]

On 5/15 June, 1655, he brought suit against Thomas Pope for killing a sow, and recovered eighteen shillings. [J. A., 62]

He was a member of the grand inquest 8/18 June, 1655. [C. O., III : 77]

On Tuesday, 23 Dec./2 Jan'y, 1656/7, his daughter Sarah was married to Samuel[2] Rider (*Samuel*[1]), of Plymouth. [Col. M. B. B., 19]

His name is in a list of freemen of the town of Plymouth, made about 1658. [Lists Fr., 44]

At the General Court held 1/11 June, 1658, Lieut. Southworth, John Dunham, Sr., Robert Finney, John Barnes and Thomas Pope were appointed to determine the range between the lands on which Nathaniel Warren and Robert Bartlett lived. [C. O., III : 137]

Robert Bartlett was on the jury in several cases tried 3/13 May, 1659. [J. A., 81]

On 27 June/7 July, 1659, Robert Bartlett took a lease for ten years of the lands of his late son-in-law Richard Foster, agreeing to pay the latter's son Benjamin Foster, then aged "foure yeares or therabouts," the sum of £8 when he came of age. On the same day the widow Mary Foster and Jonathan Morey made an ante-nuptial agreement about bringing up the child Benjamin. One of the conditions was that, if Mary died before Jonathan, Benjamin should be at the disposal of Robert Bartlett, Benjamin Bartlett or William Harlow. [Col. Deeds, II : II : 28]

On Friday, 8/18 July, 1659, the widow Mary Foster and Jonathan Morey were married at Plymouth. [Col. M. B. B., 25]

On 1/11 May, 1660, Robert Bartlett was brought before the Court for speaking contemptuously of the ordinance of singing psalms. On acknowledging his error and promising not to do so again he was admonished and discharged, being required to acknowledge his fault to the persons to whom he had so spoken. [C. O., III : 188]

On 24 May/3 June, 1660, the town granted forty acres at Shifting Cove to three Indians and appointed George Watson, Robert Bartlett, Nathaniel Warren and William Cooke to lay it out. [T. R., I : 50]

On 3/13 Sept. 1660, the town granted Robert Bartlett fifty acres between the sea and the fern swamp between Eel River and Manomet Ponds, and 20 Feb'y/2 March, 1662/3, the bounds of the grant were recorded. [T. R., I : 52, 62]

On 4/14 June, 1661, he was chosen surveyor of highways for Plymouth. [C. O., III : 229]

On Thursday, 26 Dec./5 Jan'y, 1661/2, his daughter Elizabeth was married to Anthony Sprague. [Col. M. B. B., 27]

Robert Bartlett laid claim to meadow land near the Sandwich line, but the grant had not been recorded by the Court, so the town, on 30 Dec./8 Jan'y, 1663/4, granted him eight acres of meadow there, which had formerly been mowed by Thomas Butler. The town clerk evidently intended to make sure that this grant was on the records, for he entered it on two different pages. [T. R., I : 63, 67]

At a town meeting held 26 Jan'y/5 Feb'y 1663/4, he was granted an extension of his lot for a quarter of a mile towards the pine hills. At the same meeting Nathaniel and Joseph Warren were appointed to settle a dispute about lands between Robert Bartlett and Hugh Cole. [T. R., I : 65]

At a town meeting held in February, 1663/4, the town granted ten acres to Robert Bartlett adjoining his meadow that Thomas Butler had mowed. [T. R., I : 68]

He was granted a piece of swamp next to his meadow at Eel River, by a town meeting in July, 1667. [T. R., I : 84]

His wife is called Mary Bartlett, Senior, in the codicil to Nathaniel Warren's will, dated 16/26 July, 1667. [M. D., II : 39]

His daughter Mercy was married on Friday, 25 Dec./4 Jan'y, 1668/9, to John Ivey of Boston. [Col. M. B. B., 36]

His name appears in two lists of townsmen of Plymouth, one dated 15/25 Feb'y, 1668/9, the other without date. [T. R., I: 91, 95]

His name appears in a list of freemen made 29 May/8 June, 1670. [C. O., V: 200]

Robert Bartlett, "wine cooper" of Plymouth, on 14/24 July, 1670, gave "to my son in law James Barnabey Cordwinder" * of Plymouth "and my Daughter Lydia Barnabey his wife," a lot containing twenty acres on the southerly side of Eel River which was formerly the lot of Richard Church, Sr., deceased, "and by mee purchased of the said my brother in law Richard Church"; also the addition to it and four acres of upland meadow called Sandwich meadow. [Col. Deeds, III: 297]

Robert Bartlett, "cooper" of Plymouth, sold to Thomas Burge, Jr., of Newport, R. I., on 17/27 Feb'y, 1670/1, for £50 current silver money, "one Moyety or halfe in Deale" of his share of land at Acushena in Dartmouth, also "one Moyety or halfe in Deale" of a share at Pascomansucke in Dartmouth, reserving to himself one third of the last named share, "which said severall shares of land are a prte of the Purchasers land (Comonly soe called) my selfe being one of the said Purchasers," [Col. Deeds, V: 118]

On 14/24 July, 1673, Robert Bartlett, by deed of gift, conveyed to his son Joseph Bartlett his dwelling and lands at Eel River, with the condition that Joseph was not to take possession until after the death of both his father and his mother. The deed follows:

Know all men by these p^rsents, that I Robert Bartlett, of the Towne of Plymouth in the Jurisdiction of Plymouth in New England, in America wine Cooper; That for divers Good Causes and Considerations, mee therunto moveing, have out of my owne motion and out of that love Good will. and fatherly affection, which I have and doe beare unto my son Joseph Bartlett; have absolutely Given Graunted alliened enfeofed and Confeirmed; and by these presents doe Give Graunt allien enfeof and Confeirm from mee the said Robert Bartlett and my heires; To him my said son Joseph Bartlett hee his heires and assignes for ever; all that my farme Messeuage teniment and seate, which I Now live in and am possessed off, in the Township of Plymouth aforsaid; scittuate and being att a place or river Comonly calld the Eelriver: viz: all that my house and land ther; being bounded with the lands of Nathanel: Warren deceased; now in the tenor and Occupaition of Mistris Sarah warren widdow; on the Northerly syde and with the Land of Richard ffoster now in the tenor and occupation of Jonathan Morey on the southerly side, Containing two lotts or shares of land being in breadth forty pole; between the forenamed boundaries abuting on the Eelriver aforsaid and extendeth it selfe, for its length up towards the Pyne hills, To a place ordinarily Called and knowne by the Name of the Little Pyne hills; as alsoe foure acrees more or lesse, of marsh meddow appertaining therunto lying and

* Cordwainer, a shoemaker.

being att the Eelriver aforsaid; by the Riversyde against the land of Nathaniel: Warren, before mensioned; Together with a peece of ffresh or upland meddow, being two acres (be it more or lesse) lying and being att or neare Mannomett ponds, in the Township of Plymouth aforsaid; neare unto the place wher hee the said my son Joseph Bartlett, now dweleth; which was somtimes the meddow of Richard; Church lying adjoyning to a brooke Called; The beaver dam brooke, between the said brooke, and the maine brooke, extending it selfe, for the length of it up the said brooke; To have and to hold all that my said house and land, with the foure acrees more or lesse of Marsh Meddow, and the two acrees more or lesse of upland meddow; with all and singulare the appurtenances therunto belonging unto the said my son Joseph Bartlett; To him and his heires and assignes for ever; The said p^r^mises viz: all that my said ffarme with my house theron, with the said four acrees of marsh meddow, with the two acrees (more or lesse) of upland or ffresh meddow, with all and singular the houses outhouses and ffences in and upon the said farme seatt or teniment with all and singulare the woods waters profitts and privilidges emunities and emoluments, belonging therunto or to the said two p^r^sells of Meddow forenamed; and all and singulare my Right title or Interest off and Into the same, to belong and appertaine unto the onely proper use and behoof of him my said son Joseph Bartlett; To him and his heires and assignes for ever, ffree and cleare and Clearly acquitted, off and from all other and former Gifts Graunts bargaines sales Ingagments Incomberances or Intanglements whatsoever; and to be holden off our Sov^r^ Lord the Kinge as off his manor of East Greenwich in the Countey of Kent in the realme of England, in free and comon soccage, and not in capite, nor by Knights service, nor by the rents and services therof, and therby due and of Right accustomed, with warrantice against all p^r^sons that by my Right or title, might claime any Right or title off or into the said p^r^mises or any p^r^te or p^r^sell therof, alwaies provided; and that by these p^r^sents it be Clearly understood that the said my son Joseph Bartlett shall not enter upon the posession of the said my house land and meddowes, untill the decease of both mee and my wife, Mary Bartlett, or upon any p^r^te or p^r^sell therof, nor any for him; but att the decease of both mee and my said wife; hee his heires or assignes, is to have hold use occupy Inheritt and Injoy the same with all and singulare the appurtenances privilidges and emunities belonging therunto without any lawfull suite deniall Interuption or eviction or disturbance whatsoever lawfully claiming from by or under mee the said Robert Bartlett; or by my meanes acte privity Consent or procurement; and I the said Robert Bartlett doe heerby Give and Graunt libertie unto the said my son Joseph Bartlett, either by him selfe or his Attorny to Record and Inrole these p^r^sents, or to Cause them to be recorded or Inroled in his Maties court of Plymouth aforsaid, or in any other place or court of Records according to the usuall manor of Recording or Inroling deeds and evidences of land in such Case made and provided; In witnes wherof I the said Robert Bartlett have heerunto subscribed my hand and affixed my seale this fourteenth of July 1673 one Thousand six hundred seaventy and three;

Signed sealed and delivered in the
p^r^sence of Willam Clarke — Robert Bartlett **R** his marke
Nathaniel: Morton; — and a (seale)

This deed of Gift was acknowlided by Robert Bartlett seni^r^ this 14th day of July 1673 before mee — Constant Southworth Assistant;
[Col. Deeds, III: 301]

Mary (Warren) Bartlett, wife of Robert, receipted for her share of her mother's estate on 4/14 March, 1673/4. [M. D., III: 51]

On Tuesday, 19/29 Sept., 1676, Robert Bartlett made a nuncupative will, and died before 29 Oct./8 Nov., 1676, the day the will was probated. The inventory is recorded as having been taken "January the 24th 1676" and exhibited in court "the 29th of October 1676." As these dates are both old style one of them must be wrong, since January, 1676, old style, followed October, 1676, old style, and the inventory could not have been exhibited before it was taken. The will and in'entory follow:

The last Will and Testament of Robert Bartlett of Plymouth made Septem: 19: 1676 The said Robert Bartlett then being very weake in body but of sound memory and understanding; Did by word of Mouth Declare this to be his last will and Testament as followeth; I Give my wife all my estate yett undesposed of whether it be in lands or movables Goods Chattles Debts; I Give all unto my wife to be absolutly att her Dispose amonge my Children;

This will was made and Declared in the p^{r}sence of John Cotton Mordicay Ellis and exhibited to the Court held att Plymouth the 29th of October 1676 on the oathes of Mr John Cotton and Mordicay Ellis

The Inventory of the estate of Robert Bartlett exhibited to the Court held att Plymouth the 29th of October 1676 on the oath of Mary Bartlett widdow

Imp^{r} his wearing Clothes	05	00	0
Item 2 bedds 2 bolsters and 5 pillowes 3 paire of blanketts 2 ruggs	08	00	0
Item 5 paire of sheets and 3 paire of pillowbeers	05	06	0
Item 4 Napkins and a smale Table Cloth	00	06	0
Item 1 bed and bolster and a paire of blanketts and a Rugg and 5 paire of sheets	06	00	0
Item homspone Cloth 33 yards	05	00	0
Item silver mony 3^{l}	03	00	0
Item 3 Iron potts and an Iron Kettle a skillett a frying pan	01	05	0
Item pewter and spoones	01	08	0
one skillett and a warming pan	01	00	0
Item 2 hakes 2 paire of pothookes and a spitt a paire of tongues and a driping pan	01	00	0
Item 4 Chests	01	00	0
Item bookes	00	07	0
Item 2 Dwellinghouses and a barne upland and meddow	100	00	0
Item neate Cattle 2 oxen	05	10	0
Item old Cart and wheels and a plow & Chaine Copp rings and staple botts and shakells Donge forke pitch forkes syth and sickle	01	00	0
Item Cart rope and horse Geires	00	05	0
Item 7 neat Cattle	12	00	0
Item 3 horse kind 1 maire	03	00	0
Item 2 smale swine	00	06	0
Item old lumber	01	05	0
Item an old saddle and a panell	00	10	0
Item Debts Due from the estate	01	17	0
Item Debts Due to the estate	06	11	6

Taken by us January the 24th 1676 Joseph Warren Thomas ffaunce
[Col. Wills, III: II: 87]

On 6/16 March, 1676/7, "Letters of Adminnestration is Graunted by the Court unto Mary Bartlett & Joseph Bartlett to adminnester on the estate of Robert Bartlett Deceased" [C. O., V: 152]

The latest date on which the records show that Mary (Warren) Bartlett was living is 13/23 Feb'y, 1677/8, when she deeded to her son Joseph all her rights in real and personal property given her by her husband's will or reserved to her in his deed of gift to Joseph. The consideration of this deed was a bond of £300 given by Joseph for the performance of obligations not specified; but it is certain that one of them must have been his mother's maintenance while she lived. The deed follows:

To all people To whom these prsents shall Come, Mary Bartlett widdow, and Late wife unto Robert Bartlett deceased, of the Towne of New Plymouth, in the Collonie of New Plymouth, in New England England in America sendeth Greet &c:

Know yee that I the said Mary Bartlett, for and in Consideration of one bond of three hundred Pounds Sterling bearing date with these prsents, made signed sealed and delivered, unto mee by my son Joseph Bartlett, of the aforsaid Towne of New Plymouth; for the true and full prformance of severall obligations, therin expressed, and mensioned unto mee; and my order and Assignes; wherwith I doe acknowlidge my selfe to be fully satisfyed Contented and payed; have freely and absolutely bargained and sold allianated enfeofed and Confeirned; and by the prsents I doe bargaine Allianate sell Enfeoffe and Confeirm from mee the said Mary Bartlett and my heires; unto the said Joseph Bartlett hee his heires and assignes for ever; all that my Right title and Interest that I have; or may Claime, for or dureing the time of my Naturall Life, in any sort of houseing lands or meddows; which was Given or reserved to mee or for my use; by the aforsaid Robert Bartlett my husband; in his deed of Gift unto the aforsaid Joseph Bartlett Alsoe I have Bargained and sold as aforsaid all that my fifty acrees of upland be it more or lesse, that I have lying and being, neare a place Comonly Called the salt Marsh, abuting upon the sea; between the Eelriver and Mannomett Ponds, within the aforsaid Towne of New Plymouth; and fifty acrees of upland be it more or lesse; lying and being between the lands of Ephraim Morton Junir; and those lands that were James Barnabeys deceased lying att the Eelriver; and all that my one prsell of Meddow; be it more or Lesse; lying and being upon the said Eelriver; next unto the Meddow of the said Ephraim Morton; and I doe alsoe Bargaine; and sell as aforsaid, unto the aforsaid Joseph Bartlett; all that my prsonall estate; lett it be in what specue soever; That was Given unto mee by my aforsaid deceased husband Robert Bartlett; by his Last Will and Testament; which appeers by Inventory Recorded; That I Now have or shall have at the time of my decease; To be the proper estate of the said Joseph Bartlett; with all and singulare the appurtenances; and privilidges belonging unto each of the aforsaid prmises or prsells of Land; and all my Right title and Interest of and into each of the aforsaid prmises; and every prt or prsell therof; To have and to hold; all that my aforsaid Right title and Interest, of and Into any houseing Lands & meddowes Given or reserved to mee as aforsaid by my deceased husband Robert Bartlett; and all that my fifty acrees of upland; be it more or lesse; lying att the aforsaid salt Marsh abuting upon the sea; and all that my fifty acrees of upland be it more or lesse That lyeth between the Lands of Ephraim [p. 224] Morton Jur and James Barnabey deceased; and all that my one prsell of Meddow (be it more or Lesse) that lyeth upon the aforsaid Eelriver next

Ephraim Mortons meddow; And all my aforsaid prsonall estate Given unto mee by my aforsaid Robert Bartlett as it is before expressed; with all and singulare the appurtenances, and privilidges unto each of the said prmises, belonging; and all my Right title and Interest of and Into every of the said prmises and every prte and prsell therof;' unto the said Joseph Bartlett; his heires and assignes for ever; ffree and Cleare and Clearly acquitted and discharged; of all former Bargaines sales Gifts Leases; Mortgages Charges and Intanglements whatsoever; to be holden as of our Sovr Lord the Kinge; as of his Manor of East Greenwich in the Countey of Kent within the Realme of England in free and Comon soccage; and not in Capite nor by Knights service by the rents and services therof and therby due, and of Right; accustomed; to the onely proper use and behoofe of him the said Joseph Bartlett, his heires and assignes for ever; and with warrantice against all people whatsoever; for ever by these prsents from by or under mee; the said Mary Bartlett; my heires executors and Adminnestrators; and every of them; Claiming any right title or Interest; of and Into the said prmises with their appurtenances; or any prte or prsell therof; and I the said Mary Bartlett doe by these prsents authorise; The said Joseph Bartlett either by himselfe or his Attorney; to Record and Inrole these prsents or cause them to be recorded or Enroled, before the Govr of New Plymouth; or some one of his Assistants; for the time being according to the usuall manor of Recording and enroling of deeds and evidences, in his said Maties Court of New Plymouth aforsaid In Witnes wherof, I the aforsaid Mary Bartlett have heerunto sett my hand and seale; This thirteenth day of ffebruary one Thousand six hundred seaventy and seaven

Signed sealed and delivered
in the prsence of John Cotton senir
Willam Crow;
John Cotton Junir

Mary Bartlett
her **M** Marke and a seale

This deed of sale was acknowlided by Mary Bartlett widdow; the thirteenth day of ffebruary 1677 Before mee

Constant Southworth Assistant;

[Col. Deeds, IV., 223]

Some time in the year 1683 (the full date was not inserted in the deed) Benjamin and Joseph Bartlett "in Pursuance of the will of the deceased our dear Parents Robert and Mary Bartlett" confirmed to William Harlow, Jr., of Plymouth, a gift of land from his grandparents, Robert and Mary. [Plym. County Deeds, I: 132] Mary (Warren) Bartlett must have died before this deed was made and after 13/23 Feb'y 1677/8, the date of her deed to Joseph.

Children of ROBERT and MARY^{2} (WARREN) BARTLETT, all born at Plymouth:

9. i. BENJAMIN^{3} BARTLETT, m., 1st., Susanna Jenney; m., 2d., Sarah^{3} Brewster (*Love*^{2}, *William*^{1}); m., 3d., Cecilia ——.
10. ii. REBECCA^{3} BARTLETT, m., 20/30 Dec., 1649, William Harlow.
11. iii. MARY^{3} BARTLETT, m., 1st., 10/20 Sept., 1651, Richard Foster; m., 2d., 8/18 July, 1659, Jonathan Morey.
12. iv. SARAH^{3} BARTLETT, m. 23 Dec./2 Jan'y, 1656/7, Samuel^{2} Rider (*Samuel*^{1}).
13. v. JOSEPH^{3} BARTLETT, b. about 1639, m. Hannah Pope.
14. vi. ELIZABETH^{3} BARTLETT, m. 26 Dec./5 Jan'y, 1661/2, Anthony Sprague.

15. vii. LYDIA[3] BARTLETT, b. 8/18 June, 1648; m., 1st., James Barnaby; m., 2d., John Nelson.
16. viii. MERCY[3] BARTLETT, b. 10/20 March, 1650/1, m. 25 Dec./4 Jan'y, 1668/9, John Ivey of Boston.

PEREGRINE WHITE'S INVENTORY.

Transcribed from the Original Records,

BY GEORGE ERNEST BOWMAN.

Peregrine White died at Marshfield, 20/31 July, 1704. His will was dated 14/25 July, 1704. It has been printed in this magazine (Volume I, pages 129–131) and reproduced in half-tone. The inventory was dated 3/14 August, 1704, and is recorded in the Plymouth County Probate Records, Volume II, page 50.

An Inventory of the Goods Chattels & Credits of Mr Peregrine White late of Marshfield deceased Taken & Apprised the 3^d^ of August Anno Domini 1704 p^r^ John Dogget & Saml Sprague.

	lb	*s*	*d*
Imprimis His wearing Apparril	.4	..	..
His Armes & Ammunition	.1	10	..
To a joyne worke cupboard Table forme & bedstead	.6	..	..
To two painted Chaies & wrought Cushions	..	12	..
To five other Chairs	..	14	..
To an old Saddle pillion & Cloth	.1	.3	..
To a feather bed & furniture & a silk grass bed bedstead & furniture	12	..	..
To his books	..	15	..
To Table linnen & Towels	.1	..	..
To a joyne worke Chest	..	10	..

To a Hatchell	..	.6	..
To Indian Corne and Rye	..	19	..
To Pewter and Earthen vessels	.1	..	..
To an old Brass kettle	..	10	..
To 2 Iron pots & an Iron kettle	..	15	..
To a trammel Tongs & fire slice & pot hookes	..	.5	..
To a little Skillett and frame	..	.5	..
To a pair of Bellows & a meal cive	..	.5	..
To Sheeps woll and flaxteere	..	10	.6
To a frying pan 4s and a meal bagg 3s	..	.7	..
To 2 spining wheels & 3 pair of Cards	..	16	..
To a toast Iron tin and glases	..	.3	..
To wooden vessells and Lumber	.1	10	..
To ye ½ of a yoak of oxen	.3	10	..
To the half of a horse	.1	..	..
To 4 Cows at 45 shillings a cow	.9	..	..
To one Heifer of 3 years old	.1	10	..
To ½ of 3 young Cattle	.2	.5	..
To ye ½ of 10 small Swine	.1	.9	..
To 2 hives of bees	..	12	..
To 16 sheep & lambs	.3	12	..
Debts due to the Estate from the Town of Marshfield	.1	10	..
The Estate is Indebted to severall persons	.2	.1	.5
more sence come to knowledge	..	19	.3

pr Saml Sprague

Memorand: that on the 14th day of Augst Annoqu: Dom: 1704 Mrs Sarah White Relict widdow of Capt: Peregrine White late deceased & Daniel White his son made oath that the above written is a true Inventory of the Estate of the sd Capt: White so far as they know & when they know of more they will discover the same before me Nathaniel Thomas

Judge of Probates

ALICE (CARPENTER) (SOUTHWORTH) BRADFORD'S WILL AND INVENTORY.

Transcribed from the Original Records,

BY GEORGE ERNEST BOWMAN.

Alice (Carpenter) (Southworth) Bradford died at Plymouth on Saturday, 26 March/5 April, 1670, having survived her second husband, Governor William Bradford, nearly thirteen years. She was buried on the following Tuesday, and it is probable that the desire expressed in her will "that my body may be Intered as neare unto my Deceased husband; m^r^ Willam Bradford: as Conveniently may be;" was faithfully carried out.

Her will and inventory are found in the Plymouth Colony Wills and Inventories, Volume III, Part I, pages 2–5.

The Last Will and Testament of mistris Allice Bradford senir of Plymouth Deceased; exhibited to the Court held att Plymouth in New England the 7th Day of June Anno Dom 1670 on the oathes of Nathaniel: Morton and Leift: Ephraim Morton; as followeth;

I Allis Bradford senir of the Towne of Plymouth in the Jurisdiction of New Plymouth widdow: being weake in body but of Disposing mind and prfect memory blessed be God; not knowing how soone the Lord may please to take mee out of this world unto himselfe: Doe make and ordaine this to be my last Will and Testament; in manor and forme as followeth; Impr I bequeath my soule to god that gave it and my body to the Dust in hope of a Joyfull resurrection unto Glory; Desiring that my body may be Intered as neare unto my Deceased husband; mr Willam Bradford: as Conveniently may be; and as for my worldly estate I Dispose of it as followeth; Impris I give and bequeath unto my Deare sister Mary Carpenter; the bed I now lye on with the furniture: therunto belonging and a paire of sheets and a good Cow and a yearling heiffer and a younge mare Item I give and bequeath unto my son mr Constant Southworth my Land att Paomett: viz: all my Purchase land there: with all my rights p^r^ivilidges and appurtenances therunto belonging; To him and his heires and assignes for ever; Item I give and bequeath unto my said son Constant Southworth and unto my son m^r^ Joseph Bradford: the one halfe of my sheep: to be equally Devided betwixt them; and the other halfe to my son Captaine Willam Bradford Item I give unto my said son Joseph Bradford my paire of working oxen and a white heiffer; Item I give unto my honored frend m^r^ Thomas Prence one of the bookes that were my Deare husbands Library; which of them hee shall Choose; Item I give unto my Deare Grand child Elizabeth howland; the Daughter of my Deare son Captaine Thomas Southworth Deceased; the sume of seaven pounds; for the use and benifitt of her son James howland Item I give unto my servant maide Mary Smith a Cow Calfe to be Delivered her the next springe if I Decease this winter; and if I Doe not Decease this winter; my will is that shee have one Delivered to her out of my estate in som short time after my Decease; all the rest of my estate not Disposed of allreddy by this my last Will and Testament; as above said; I give and bequeath unto my sonnes m^r^ Constant Southworth Captaine Willam Bradford and m^r^ Joseph Bradford to be equally Devided amongst them in equall and alike proportions; In Witnes that this is my Last Will and Testament I the said Allice Bradford have heerunto sett my hand and seale; this twenty ninth day of December Ann^o^ Dom one Thousand six hundred sixty nine;

Signed and sealed
in the p^r^sence off
Ephraim Morton
Nathaniel: Morton Witnesses

The marke of
Allice Bradford seni^r^
And her (seale)

[p. 3] A true Inventory of the estate of mistris Allice Bradford seni^r^: Late Deceased aprised by (*worn*) names are under written this 31 of March 1670 and exhibited to the Court of his Ma(*worn*) held att New Plymouth the seaventh Day of June Ann^o^: Dom one Thousand six hundr(ed) and seaventy; on the oath of mistris Mary Carpenter;

Imp^r^ 8 Cowes	20 00 00
Item 2 yearlings	01 10 00
Item a 2 yeare old steer	01 10 00
Item a steer of 4 yeare old	02 10 00

Item 1 : 2 yeare old heiffer	01 10 00
Item 1 old horse and three mares	10 00 00
Item 17 sheep and 2 lambes	07 00 00

In the New Parlour Chamber

Item 1 bed a bolster and 2 pillowes	03 10 00
Item 1 green rugg and 1 Coverlid & 2 blanketts	03 00 00
Item a bedsteed & Curtaines and vallence	02 00 00
Item 2 Chaires	00 15 00
Item 3 wrought stooles	00 11 00
Item one Table and Carpett	01 05 00
Item a Carved Chest	01 00 00

In the outward Parlour Chamber:

a bedsteed and Curtaine and vallence and settle	01 10 00

In the old parlour Chamber;

Item a smale bed 2 blanketts 1 Coverlid & a pillow	03 10 00
Item 1 old green Cloth Goune	00 10 00
Item 8 yards of hommade Cloth	01 04 00
Item 2 Chestes	00 10 00
Item 2 Iron beames 1 hogshed 1 barrell and other old lumber	01 05 00

In the studdy in bookes

Item m^{r} Perkins two of them	01 00 00
Item 3 of Docter Willetts on genises exodus & Daniel:	01 00 00
Item Guicksarraden	00 10 00
Item the history of the Church	00 08 00
Item Peter Martirs Comon places	00 15 00
Item Cartwright on remise Testament	00 10 00
Item the history of the Netherlands	00 15 00
Item Peter Martir on the Romans	00 05 00
Item Moors workes on the New Testament	01 00 00
Item Cottons Concordance	00 08 00
Item Speeds history of the world	01 00 00
Item Weams Christian Sinnagogue & the protracture of the Image of God	00 08 00
Item the Meathod of Phisicke	00 02 00
Item Calvins harmony and his Coment on the actes	00 08 00
Item Downhams 2^{cond}: p^{r}te of Christian warfare	00 03 00
Item m^{r} Cottons answare to m^{r} Williams	00 02 00
Item Taylers libertie of Prophesye	00 01 06
Item Gouges Domesticall Dutyes	00 02 06
Item the Institutions or reasons Discused & observations Divine and morrall the synode of Dort and the Appol-ogye	00 06 00
Item m^{r} Ainsworth workes the Counterpoison & the tryall	00 02 00
Item m^{r} Ainsworth on Genises exodus & livitticus	00 04 00
Item Calvin on Genises	00 02 06
Item Dike on the Deceightfulnes of mans hart	00 01 06

Item Gifford refuted	00 00 06
Item Dod on the Comaundements and others of his	00 03 00
Item 53 smale bookes	01 06 06
Item Calvin on the epistles in Duch : and Divers other Duch bookes	00 15 00
Item 2 bibles	01 00 00
Item the actes of the Church	00 05 00
Item 3 of mr Bridgg : his workes	01 00 00
Item the Lives of the fathers	00 03 00
Item a skin of buffe	00 15 00

[p. 4] In the old Parlour

Item 1 feather bed 1 bolster 2 ruggs and a blankett	03 00 00
Item a bedsted & settle Curtaine and vallence	01 10 00
Item a Court Cubbert	01 00 00
Item a Table and forme and 2 stooles	01 05 00
Item 1 great lether Chaire	00 08 00
Item 2 great wooden Chaires	00 06 00
Item 1 great winscott Chist and a Cubbert	01 00 00
Item 2 boxes and a Deske and a wrought stoole and an old Case of bottles	00 12 00
Item 2 guns and a paire of bandaleers	01 00 00

The plate

Item the great beer bowle	03 00 00
Item another beer bowle	02 00 00
Item a wine Cupp	01 00 00
Item a salt	02 15 00
Item a trencher salt & a Drame Cupp	00 15 00
Item (*) silver spoones	02 09 00
Item a silver Dish	01 15 00
Item 2 blanketts	00 10 00
Item 1 Diaper Table Cloth and a Dozen of Diaper Napkins	02 00 00
Item another Diaper Table Cloth and 7 Diaper napkins	01 10 00
Item 2 holland Table clothes	00 15 00
Item 1 old Cubbert Cloth	00 03 00
Item 4 pillow beers	00 08 00
Item 5 towells	00 05 00
Item 3 holland sheets	01 10 00
Item 2 paire of Cotten and linnine sheets	01 05 00
Item 19 Cotton and linnine Napkins	00 15 00
Item a paire of pillowbears	00 04 00
Item a nother paire of pillowbears	00 02 06
Item 5 sheets	01 10 00
Item in shiftes and other wearing linnine	03 00 00
Item a Dingcastor hatt	01 05 00
Item her wearing Clothes and a little peece of bayes	12 00 00
Item a wicker baskett; galley potts & glasses & such smale thinges of Little vallue	00 05 00

* This appears to be a 7 written over a 4.

in the great Parlour

Item 2 great Carved Chaires	01 04 00
Item a Table and forme and Carpett	01 05 00
Item 10 Cushens	01 00 00
Item a Causlett and hedpeece	01 10 00
Item 4 great lether Chaires	01 04 00
Item in glasses and earthen ware	00 04 00
Item a Case and five knives	00 05 00
Item a rest & some other odde thinges	00 02 00

In the Kitchen

Item 24 pewter platters and a brim bason	07 00 00
Item 2 fflaggons: 2 quart potts & 3 pint potts	01 00 00
Item 6 smale pewter Dishes and a smale bason	00 10 00
Item 7 porrengers	00 06 00
Item 6 pewter plates	00 09 00
Item 2 pewter Candlestickes & a saltseller	00 06 00
Item 3 Chamber potts and three smale sawcers and pewter funnell;	00 09 00
Item 2 pye plates	00 06 00
Item a tinning pan and 2 Coverings & a lanthorne	00 02 00
[p. 5] Item 1 great Jugg and 5 smaller ones 4 earthen pans and 2 earthen potts	00 12(*)
Item 2 ffrench kettles	01 10 00
Item an old warming pan	00 03 00
Item 1 little ffrench kettle	00 03 00
Item 2 brasse kettles	00 15 00
Item a Duch pan	00 04 00
Item 3 brasse skilletts	00 04 00
Item 1 old brasse skimer and Ladle	00 01 00
Item 3 brasse Candle stickes and a brasse pestle and Mortor	00 09 00
Item a paire Andjrons	00 10 00
Item a Chafeing Dish and a stew pan	00 10 00
Item 1 Iron skillett and an Iron kettle	00 10 00
Item 2 Iron potts	00 16 00
Item 2 paire of pothangers and 2 paire of pott hookes	00 08 00
Item 2 paire of tonggs and 2 fier shovells	00 05 00
Item 2 spitts and a gridjron and an Iron Driping pan	00 10 00
Item a paire of Iron rakes	00 10 00
Item 4 Dozen of trenchers	00 02 06
Item a box Iron 2 gallon glasse bottles and three pottle bottles	00 05 00
Item a spining wheele a bucking tubb 2 pailes 2 kimnells two bowles 4 smale wooden Dishes 1 tray 2 Burchen trayes	00 16 00
Item Scales & waightes with an Iron beame	00 07 00
Item 2 beer barrells	00 04 00
Item a p^r^sell of sheepes woole	00 03 00
Item 2 smale swine	00 10 00

* Worn.

Item in Mony	00 16 00
Item a silver bodkin	00 04 00
Item in provision	01 10 00
Item one halfe hogshed and a smale p^{r}sell of salt;	00 03 00
Item one paire of oxen in Mr Joseph Bradfords hand	
prised by	sume totall 162 17 00

George Watson
Ephraim Morton
Willam harlow;

Captaine Willam Bradford and m^{r} Joseph Bradford haveing the Cattle after named in theire Costody when the estate was prised; Did give in the number and kind of them upon theire oathes as followeth;

Item 4 Cowes 2 Calves one oxe 4 yeare old; one heiffer of two yeare old and 14 sheep besides lambes; were in Captaine Bradford Costody	and hee was sworne to these June 1670
Item 2 oxen 4 Cowes 2 yearlinges one two yeare old steer 1 horse 2 mares 2 young Calves were in Mr Joseph Bradfords Custody	and hee was sworne to this June 1670

These were appertaineing to the estate and forenamed in the Inventory;

MYLES STANDISH'S WILL AND INVENTORY.

Transcribed from the Original Records,
BY GEORGE ERNEST BOWMAN.

Captain Myles Standish died at Duxbury, on Friday, 3/13 October, 1656. His will was made 7/17 March, 1655/6. It was probated 4/14 May, 1657, as is shown by the record of the inventory and by the following court order, of that date: "Mr Allexander Standish and m^r^ Josias Standish Doe accept of beeing exequitors with Mis Barbery Standish theire mother on the estate of Captaine Myles Standish Deceased;"*

The will and inventory are recorded in the Plymouth Colony Wills and Inventories, Volume II, Part I, pages 37–40.

The Last will and Testament of Captaine Myles Standish Exhibited before the court held att Plymouth (the 4th) of may 1657 on the oath of Captaine James Cudworth; and ordered to bee recorded as followeth;

Given under my hand this march the 7th 1655 Witnesseth these p^r^sents that I Myles Standish seni^r^ of Duxburrow being in prfect memory yett Deseased in my body and knowing the fraile estate of man in his best estate I Doe make this to bee my last will and Testament in manor and forme following;

1 my will is that out of my whole estate my funerall charges be taken out & my bod(y) to bee buried in Decent manor and if I Die att Duxburrow my body to bee layed as neare as Conveniently may bee to my two Daughters Lora Standish my Daugher and Mary Standish my Daughterinlaw

2 my will is that that out of the remaining prte of my whole estate that all my Jus(t) and lawfull Debts which I now owe or att the Day of my Death may owe bee paied

3 out of what remaines according to the order of this Govr-ment: my will is that my Dear and loveing wife Barbara Standish shall have the third prte

4 I have given to my son Josias Standish upon his marriage one young horse five sheep and two heiffers which I must upon that contract of marriage make forty pounds yett not knowing whether the estate will bear it att p^r^sent; my will is that the

* Court Orders, III: 112.

resedue remaine in the whole stocke and that every one of my four sons viz Allexander Standish Myles Standish Josias Standish and Charles Standish may have forty pounds appeec; if not that they may have proportionable to ye remaining prte bee it more or lesse

5 my will is that my eldest son Allexander shall have a Doubble share in land

6 my will is that soe long as they live single that the whole bee in prtenership betwix(t) them

7 I Doe ordaine and make my Dearly beloved wife Barbara Standish Allexander Standish Myles Standish and Josias Standish Joynt Exequitors of this my last will and Testament

8 I Doe by this my will make and appoint my loveing frinds m^r^ Timothy hatherley and Capt: James Cudworth Supervissors of this my last will and that they wilbee pleased to Doe the office of Christian love to bee healpfull to my poor wife and Children by theire Christian Counsell and advisse; and if any Difference should arise which I hope will not; my will i(s) that my said Supervissors shall Determine the same and that they see that m(y) poor wife shall have as comfortable maintainance as my poor state will beare the whole time of her life which if you my loveing frinds pleasse to Doe though neither they nor I shalbee able to recompenc I Doe not Doubt but the Lord will; By mee Myles Standish

further my will is that marcye Robenson whome I tenderly love for her Grandfathers sacke shall have three pounds in som thing to goe forward for her two yeares after my Decease which my will is my overseers shall see prformed

[p. 38] ffurther (m)y will is that my servant John Irish Juni^r^ have forty shillings more then his Covenant which will appeer upon the towne booke alwaies provided that hee continew till the time hee covenanted bee expired in the service of my exequitors or any of them with theire Joynt Concent

March 7th 1655 By mee Myles Standish

9 I give unto my son & heire aparent Allexander Standish all my lands as heire apparent by lawfull Decent in Ormistick Borsconge Wrightington Maudsley Newburrow Crawston and the Ile of man and given to mee as right heire by lawfull

Decent but Surruptuously Detained from mee my great G(ran)dfather being a 2^{cond} or younger brother from the house of Standish of Standish

March the 7th 1655 by mee Myles Standish

Witnessed by mee

James Cudworth

[p. 39] An Inventory of the goods and Chattles that Captaine Miles Standish gent: was possessed of att his Decease as they were shewed to us whose names are underwritten this 2^{cond} of Decembe(r) 165(6) and exhibited to the court held att Plymouth the 4 may 1657 on the oath of m^{is} Barbara Standish

	£	s	d
It one Dwelling house and outhouses with the land therunto belonging	140	00	00
It 4 oxen	24	00	00
It 2 mares to mare coults one young horse	48	00	00
It six cowes 3 heifers and one Calfe	29	00	00
It 8 ewe sheep two rames and one wether	15	00	00
It 14 swine great and smale	03	15	00
It one fowling peece 3 musketts 4 Carbines 2 smale guns one old barrell	08	01	00
It one sword one Cutles 3 belts	02	07	00
It the history of the world and the turkish history	01	10	00
It a Cronicle of England and the Countrey ffarmer	00	08	00
It ye history of queen Ellisabeth the state of Europe Vusebious Dodines earball	01	10	00
It Doctor halls workes Calvins Institutions	01	04	00
It Wilcocks workes and Mayors	01	00	00
It rogers seaven treatises and the ffrench Akadamey	00	12	00
It 3 old bibles	00	14	00
It Cecers Comentaryes Bariffes artillery	00	10	00
It Prestons Sermons Burroughes Christian contentment gosspell Conversation passions of the mind the Phisitions practice Burrowghes earthly mindednes Burroughs Descovery	01	04	00
It Ball on faith Brinssleys watch Dod on the lords Supper Sparke against herisye Davenports apollogye	00	15	00
It a reply to Doctor Cotten on baptisme the Garman history the Sweden Intelligencer reasons Discused	00	10	00
It 1 Testament one Psalmebooke Nature and grace in Conflict a law booke the mean in mourning allegation against B P of Durham Johnson against hearing	00	06	00
It a prcell of old bookes of Divers subjects in quarto	00	14	00
It an other prcell in Octavo	00	04	00
It Wilsons Dixonary homers Illiads a Comentary on James balls Cattechesmes	00	12	00
It halfe a young heiffer	(*)1	00	00

*Worn.

It one feather bed bolster and 2 pillowes	04 00 00
It 1 blankett a Coverlid and a rugg	01 05 00
It 1 feather bed blankett and great pillow	02 15 00
It one old featherbed	02 05 00
It one feather bed and bolster	04 00 00
It one blankett and 2 ruggs	01 15 00
It one feather bolster and old rugg	00 14 00
It 4 paire of sheets	03 00 00
It 1 paire of fine sheets	01 04 00
It 1 Tablecloth 4 napkins	00 10 00
It his wearing clothes	10 00 00
It 16 peeces of pewter	01 08 00
It earthen ware	00 05 00
It 3 brasse kettles one skillett	02 00 00
[p. 40] It 4 Iron potts	01 08 00
It a warming pan a frying pan and a Cullender	00 09 00
It one paire of stillyards	00 10 00
It 2 bedsteds one Table 1 forme Chaires 1 Chest and 2 boxes	02 13 0
It 1 bedsted one settle bed one box 3 Caske	01 07 00
It 1 bedsted 3 Chists 3 Casses with som bottles 1 box 4 Caske	02 06 06
It one Still	00 12 00
It 1 old settle 1 Chaire one kneading trough 2 pailes 2 traies one Dozen of trenchers 1 bowle 1 ferkin 1 beer Caske 1 Table	00 16 00
It 2 beer Caske 1 Chern 2 spining wheels one powdering tubb 2 old Caske one old flaskett	00 15 00
It 1 mault mill	02 00 00
It 2 sawes with Divers Carpenters tooles	01 19 00
It a Timber Chaine with plow Chaines	01 06 00
It 2 saddles a pillion 1 bridle	01 00 00
It old Iron	00 11 0
It 1 Chist and a bucking Tubb	00 08 0
It 1 hachell 2 tramells 2 Iron Doggs 1 spitt one fierforke 1 lamp 2 gars one lanthorn with other old lumber	02 01 0
It in woole	00 15 0
It hemp and flax	00 06 0
It eleven bushells of wheat	02 05 0
It 14 bushells of rye	02 02 0
It 30 bushells of pease	05 05 0
It 25 bushels of Indian Corn	03 15 0
It Cart and yeokes and plow Irons and 1 brake	02 05 0
It axes sickles hookes and other tooles	01 00 0
It eight Iron hoopes 1 spining wheele with other lumber	00 14 :00
	022 03 00
John Alden	055 18 00
James Cudworth	280 06 00
	358 07 00

HERE
LYETH BURIED
Y^E BODY OF CAP
RICHARD MORE
AGED 84 YEARS

THE ONLY MAYFLOWER GRAVESTONE.

By George Ernest Bowman.

It will be a great surprise to all interested in Pilgrim history to learn that there is still in existence a gravestone of a Mayflower passenger, erected at the time of his death and inscribed with his name and age; and their interest will be increased when they read that this man probably outlived John[2] Cooke (*Francis*[1]), heretofore believed to have survived all the other male passengers except Peregrine White, who was not born until the Mayflower reached Cape Cod.

The illustration facing this page shows the only known gravestone of a Mayflower passenger. This stone was erected in the old Charter Street Cemetery at Salem, Mass., to mark the last resting place of Capt. Richard More, Senior, who came to Plymouth in the Mayflower, as a boy in Elder William Brewster's family, and finally settled at Salem, where he died.

Before describing this stone, and the five others (in the same group) erected by Capt. More to mark the graves of his two wives, a son, a daughter and two grandchildren, the proof that he was a Mayflower passenger should be presented. As the object of this article is to call attention to the only existing Mayflower gravestone and to arouse an interest in Capt. Richard More which will lead others to study his family and try to prove descent from him, I shall present the evidence of his identity as briefly as possible, leaving for their proper place in the "Mayflower Genealogies" many interesting facts found on the records.

Richard More, as already stated, was a boy in Elder Brewster's family on the Mayflower.* He was still in that family at the Division of Cattle in 1627; but on 20/30 October, 1636, he married Christian Hunt, whose ancestry is not known, and on 1/11 November, 1637, he sold his house and adjoining land at Duxbury to Abraham Blush.† During the next twenty years I do not find any mention of him on the Plymouth Colony records.

A few years after this sale one Richard *Man* became an inhabitant of Scituate, and the Rev. Samuel Deane's History of Scituate, published in 1831, states that he was "a youth in Elder Brewster's family, and came to Plymouth in the Mayflower, 1620." When Bradford's History was published Deane's error was discovered, and apparently those interested thought the easiest way to reconcile the latter's statement with the fact that the name of the boy in the Elder's family was *More* would be to claim that Richard More, after selling his Duxbury house, changed his name to Man and removed to Scituate. At all events that claim has been made for many years by the descendants of Richard Man, and I have been unable to find any better foundation for it.

The Plymouth Colony records show that Richard Man was drowned early in 1656 and that his widow married John Cowin of Scituate.‡ Twenty-eight years later, in 1684, a deposition was made which proved beyond question that Richard More of the Mayflower was then living, that he was in Massachusetts Bay Colony, and that he still retained his rightful name. This deposition was found by Dr. Christopher Johnston at Annapolis, in the Records of the Provincial Court of Maryland [Liber W. R. C. No. 1], and, with other data relating to the Conant and Weston families, was printed in 1896 in the New England Historical and Genealogical Register [Vol. 50, p. 203] without any comment to indicate that its most important feature, the identification of a Mayflower passenger, had been noticed by either transcriber or editor. The following copy was taken from the "Register."

The Deposition of Richard Moore Sen[r]. aged seaventy yeares or thereabouts. Sworn saith that being in London att the House of Mr. Thomas Weston Ironmonger in the year 1620 He was from thence transported to

* M. D., I: 9. † M. D., I: 150; II: 118. ‡ Court Orders, III: 92; V: 31, 121.

New Plymouth in New England and about two yeares and a half after the said depon[ts]. arrivall at Plymo[th]. aforesaid the above mentioned Thomas Weston sent over a ship upon his p[r]per accompt with passengers to settle in the Massachusetts Bay now called Braintree but soon after they deserted the same by reason of Indians & Sicknesse And within a short space of time after the above said Weston personally came over from London to Plymouth in New England and made his aboad there some time and traded from thence to Virginia and Maryland And att that time the said deponent knew that the said Thomas Weston had and was possessed of two plantations the one in Yorke River in Virginia att a place called Cheesecake, the other in Maryland att West S[t]. Maryes by Storyes Island and heretofore were comonly known to be in the tenure & occupation of these persons here under exprest viz[t]. Mr. Wilkinson, Mr. Dent merch[t]. &c. and they all acknowledged the said Weston to be the true proprietor and lawfull owner of the said plantations And further that the said deponent knew Elizabeth Weston now Elizabeth Connant of Marblehead to be the reputed and only child of the said Thomas Weston.

Jur cor me 27 Sep[t]. 1684. } S : Bradstreet Gov[r].

It has been shown that Richard More of the Mayflower married Christian Hunt, that he was alive in Massachusetts Bay Colony in 1684, and that he was then styled "Senior." The gravestone inscriptions given later in this article, as well as numerous entries in the Essex County records, show that Capt. Richard More, Senior, of Salem had a wife Christian, who died in 1677; and the Plymouth Colony records show that he had grants of land at Swansea, Taunton and other places in that colony. For example: on 30 August, 1673, Richard More of Salem, mariner, with the consent of Christian his wife, sold his rights as a Purchaser at Swansea to Samuel Shrimpton of Boston [Plym. Col. Deeds, III : 303]. Even without the deposition already quoted, there is sufficient record evidence to prove that Richard More of the Mayflower and Capt. Richard More, Senior, of Salem were one and the same person.

I have not found any record of Capt. More's death or of the settlement of his estate. Because of his apparent uncertainty regarding his own age, as indicated by different depositions, the age eighty-four cut on his gravestone is not a reliable factor in determining the date of his death. In the deposition already quoted he called himself about seventy on 27 September, 1684, and only six years later, in 1690, he made four depositions, on 1 April, 12 July, 29 September, and 25 November, in each of which he said that he was about seventy-eight. These four depositions were made in connection with a lawsuit over land formerly the property of Richard Hollingsworth, Senior, of Salem, and are found in the Essex County Court Papers. Brief extracts of the first and last are here given:

"Richard Moore Aged aboute seventy eight yeares saith that beinge a retainer and a Labourer in the service of my ffather in Law Richard Hollingworth senio^r aboute fivety six year(es) agoe" [Vol. 49, p. 75, under date 1 Apl., 1690.]

"the deposition of Richard More Sener of Salem aged about 78 yers this deponant doth testifie and Say that my Father in law Richard Hollinsworth Sener of Salem desesed . . . . . . the widdow my mother in law Relect of said hollinsworth . . . . . . Sworne in open Court att Salem 25th 9^ber 1690 by aboves^d Capt More

attest Benj^a Gerrish Cler" [Vol. 49, p. 138. "9^ber" means "November."]

It is extremely unfortunate that the date of Richard More's death was not inscribed on his gravestone, as the difference of nearly two and one-half years in his estimates of his age, as shown by the five depositions, prevents fixing even the *year* of his death with certainty; but it is probable that the age eighty-four on the gravestone corresponds with the statements in 1690 rather than with the statement in 1684. If we accept the deposition of 1 April, 1690, as the most nearly correct, his death occurred in the year 1696. If any of the others is accepted, his death must have been at a still later date. It is probable, therefore, that Richard More outlived John Cooke, who died at Dartmouth, Mass., 23 November/3 December, 1695.*

The latest reference to Richard More I have found on the records is on 19/29 March, 1693/4, when he witnessed the bond of his daughter Susanna Dutch, who was on that day appointed administratrix of the estate of her deceased husband Samuel Dutch.†

The gravestone of Capt. Richard More is one of six stones forming a most remarkable group. This group contains not only the one Mayflower gravestone in existence, but also the

* M. D., II: 116. † Essex Co. Probate Files, Case 8420.

only gravestone of a wife of a Mayflower passenger (the gravestones of *two* wives are here), and the stones of two children and two grandchildren.

As one enters the cemetery from Charter Street the group will be found near the centre of the ground, at the left of a large willow tree. The three illustrations accompanying this article represent, respectively, the stone of Richard More; the two stones of his wives Christian and Jane, on one page; and the whole group of six stones. As one faces the group, the first wife, Christian (Hunt) More, lies nearly in the centre, with her husband at the right and a little in the rear. Still farther to the right, close to the margin of the illustration, will be seen the stone of Jane (Hollingsworth) More, the second wife. Behind Christian More's stone, and partly hidden by it, is the low square one of her son Caleb More. Next on the left and a little in front of Caleb is the double stone of the two grandchildren, Barbara Dutch (on the right half) and Samuel More (on the left half). A little farther to the left and front is the stone of Christian (More) Conant.

All these stones are remarkably well preserved, with the exception of the one marking the graves of the two grandchildren, which is split into two slabs of nearly equal thickness. It is evident that an attempt has been made to repair the stone, but it is now in as bad condition as ever and needs prompt attention.

An examination of the lettering on the four stones of Christian More and her children and grandchildren shows that these stones were all made by the same person, and it is probable that they were erected by Capt. More. The stone of Jane More, with its cherub in place of a Death's head, and its ornamental borders, is evidently the work of another man.

Richard More's stone is the smallest and plainest of the six. Its height is one foot, three and five-eighths inches; its width, one foot and one-fourth of an inch; its thickness, two inches. Its distance from Christian More's stone is four feet; from Jane More's stone, five feet, three and three-fourths inches; from Caleb's stone, three feet, eleven and one-half inches; from the stone of the grandchildren, five feet, one and one-half inches. The stonecutter evidently began to cut the inscription on what is now the back of the stone, but found he had started wrong, so turned the stone over and began again. At the top he had cut CAP^{T}, and below, RICH with part of the A.

The inscription on the face of the stone is as follows:

HERE
LYETH BURIED
Y^{e} BODY OF CAP^{T}
RICHARD MORE
AGED 84 YEARS.

Christian (Hunt) More's gravestone is one foot, nine and one-half inches in height; two feet, one and one-fourth inches in width; two and seven-eighths inches in thickness. At the top is a Death's head with wings on either side. Below is the following inscription:

HODIE MIHI CRAS TIBI
CHRISTIAN WIFE
TO RICHARD MORE
AGED 60 YEARS
DEC^{D} MARCH Y^{e} 18
1 6 7 6

The stone marking the grave of Jane (Hollingsworth) More is the most elaborate one in the group. At the top is a cherub's head with wings, and an ornamental border is cut on each side of the inscription. The stone is one foot, four inches in height; one foot, four inches wide at the base; one and fifteen-sixteenths inches thick. It is five feet and four inches from Christian More's stone. The inscription is as follows:

JANE . SECOND
WIFE . TO CAP^{T}
RICHARD , MORE
SEN^{R}, AGED , 55
YEARS . DEPARTED
THIS . LIFE Y^{e}
8 OF, OCTOBER
1 6 8 6

CHRISTIAN WIFE
TO RICHARD MORE
AGED 60 YEARS

The affidavits already quoted prove that Jane was the daughter of Richard Hollingsworth, Senior, of Salem, but I have found nothing to show whether she was unmarried or a widow when she became the second wife of Richard More. The age on her stone is probably overstated, as she is not mentioned in the list of Richard Hollingsworth's family when they came over in the "Blessing" in 1635.* She evidently had no children by Richard More.

Caleb More appears to have been unmarried, and there is no record of any settlement of his estate. His gravestone is very plain, nearly square, and much thicker than the others, its dimensions being: height, one foot, three and three-fourths inches; width, one foot, five and one-half inches; thickness, three and seven-sixteenths inches. The inscription is as follows:

CALEB MORE
AGED 34 YEARS
DEC^D^ JANUARY Y^e^
4 1 6 7 $\frac{8}{9}$

The double stone of the two grandchildren, Samuel More and Barbara Dutch, is one foot, four and one-half inches from Caleb's stone, nine inches from Christian Conant's stone, and three feet, seven inches from Christian More's stone. It is one foot, five and three-fourths inches in height; one foot, five and five-eighths inches in width; one and five-eighths inches in thickness. The stone, as already stated, is split into two slabs, one being seven-eighths of an inch, and the other three-fourths of an inch in thickness. The inscriptions on this stone, in parallel columns, are as follows:

SAMUEL SON	BARBARAH
TO RICHARD &	DAUGHTER TO
SARAH MORE	SAMUEL & SUSANA
AGED 9 DAYES	DUTCH AGED 8
DEC^D^ NOVE^R^ Y^e^ 24	MONETHS DEC^D^
1 6 7 3	APRYL Y^e^ 10
	1 6 7 8

* Hotten's Lists, p. 108.

I have made no attempt to learn the maiden name of Sarah, the wife of Richard[2] More (*Richard*[1]), or to trace his six or more children. That Richard and Sarah were both living on 11/21 September, 1691, is proved by a deed of that date signed by them. In this deed Richard[2] is called Junior.* I have found no later reference to this couple.

Capt. Richard More's daughter Susanna married first Samuel Dutch of Salem, a mariner, as is shown by a conveyance from Richard to Samuel and Susanna, dated 10/20 June, 1684.† Samuel Dutch died before 19/29 March, 1693/4, and his widow Susanna married, before 3/13 December, 1694, Richard Hutton of Wenham, who had been one of the sureties on her bond as administratrix.‡ On 3/13 February, 1695/6, Richard Hutton was appointed guardian of his wife's daughter Susanna Dutch, aged about twelve years.§ This is the latest reference to Susanna[3] Dutch (*Susanna*[2] *More, Richard*[1]) I have found, but Richard and Susanna Hutton were still living at Wenham 20/30 May, 1707, Richard being then blind.||

The gravestone of Christian (More) Conant is one foot, ten inches in height; one foot, nine inches in width; one and fifteen-sixteenths inches in thickness. Beneath a Death's head with wings on each side is the following inscription:

CHRISTIAN WIFE TO
JOSHUA CONAN & DAUGHTER
TO RICHARD MORE AGED
28 YEARS DEC^D MAY
Y^e 30 1 6 8 0

The Conant Family [p. 163] states that Joshua[3] Conant (*Joshua*[2], *Roger*[1]) married first, Christian More, on 31 August, 1676, and second, Sarah Newcomb, on 9 January, 1690/1; that he had by Christian one child Joshua, born 12 May, 1678; and that he removed to Truro, Mass., about 1700. I have not attempted to investigate this line.

As this article was not intended to form a part of "The Mayflower Genealogies," it did not seem advisable to attempt

* Essex Co. Deeds, 9: 18. ‡ Essex Co. Probate Files, Case 8420.
† Ibid., 6: 123. § Ibid., Probate Records, 305: 131. || Essex Co. Deeds, 20: 22.

such an exhaustive examination of the records at Salem as would otherwise have been made. This would have required an immense amount of time and labor, owing to the lack of indexes of *all names* on the records there. Like nearly all ancient records the indexes refer only to names of grantors and grantees, plaintiffs and defendants, testators, &c. It is, therefore, possible that evidence may yet be discovered which will determine at least the year of Richard More's death.

The complete index to *every name* in the manuscript volumes of the Plymouth Colony Wills and Inventories, the Plymouth Colony Deeds, and the Plymouth County Wills and Deeds, which I am making for the Massachusetts Society of Mayflower Descendants, has greatly simplified the task of examining those records for traces of Richard More, and it is very doubtful if anything more concerning him can be found therein.

The only gravestone of a Mayflower passenger is certain to attract a great deal of attention, and the Massachusetts Society of Mayflower Descendants, through its Committee on Marking Historic Sites, is planning to mark the spot in an appropriate manner, and to repair the damaged stone at the graves of the two infants.*

---

* Information regarding the plans of this committee may be found in the "Pilgrim Notes and Queries," in this number.

JACOB[2] COOKE'S WILL AND INVENTORY.

Transcribed from the Original Records,

By George Ernest Bowman.

Jacob[2] Cooke (*Francis*[1]) died at Plymouth between 11/21 December, 1675, the day his will was made, and 18/28 December, 1675, the day his inventory was taken. No record of his death has been found. His will and inventory are found in the Plymouth Colony Wills and Inventories, Volume III, Part II, pages 1–4. The record is very badly worn, as indicated in the following copy.

[p. 1] The last Will and Testament of Jacob Cooke seni^{r}: of Plymouth in New England late Decased exhibited to the Court held att Plymouth aforsaid the 8th Day of March 1676 on the oathes of Mr Edward Gray and Leift: Joseph howland as followeth;

Know all men to whom these p^{r}sents shall come that I Jacob Cooke seni^{r} of the Towne of Plymouth in New England; being att this p^{r}sent very weake in body through many Infeirmities and Deseas; that are upon mee; but of sound and p^r^fect understanding and memory; Doe make and ordaine this to be my last Will and Testament to Continewe for ever feirme and Inviolable; Imprimis my will is that my engagement unto my Deare and loveing wife Elizabeth Cooke att or before my marriage with her be truely and honestly p^r^formed unto her; Item I will and bequeath unto my said wife Elizabeth Cooke one yoake of oxen and one cow, towards the bringing up of my three youngest Daughters; and for her and theire more comfortable subsistence; I Give unto her my said wife Dureing her widdowhood; the use benifitt and Improvement of the orchyard that is by my Now Dwelling house; and the orchyard that I planted by or in the place I lived in att my first Marriage; alsoe During her widdowhood I Give her free Comonage for her stocke of Cattle of all sorts to Depasture in and upon those my lands att Rockey nooke; and my will is that my said wife take into her Costody the portions of my three youngest Daughters; To Cecure them untell they are of Capassitie to receive them; if shee please; Item I will and bequeath unto my eldest son Caleb Cooke; a Double portion of all my lands; that is to say one halfe of them for quantitie and quallitie; and my will is that hee shall have in his p^r^te of them, the one halfe of my meddow that lyeth att Pyny point alsoe three quarters of my two Great Lotts of meddow that lyeth in Joneses River meddow; and all my meddow that lyeth att home on Joneses River and the remainder of his proportion of lands; hee shall have them out of my Lands that I now live on; and my lands in Rockey Nooke; and my thirty acrees of wood land that lyeth att the head of my lotts; onely what meddow or Grasse I have engaged unto my wife aforsaid; shee shall have it out of his lott and halfe of Meddow att Jonses River meddow; and hee shall not Deney my said wife but lett her have ffree egresse and regresse for Pastureing on those lands in Rockey nooke which shalbe Considered to him when (*worn*)n is made; Item I will and bequeath unto my son Jacob Cooke one share of (*worn*) lands, that is one quarter p^r^te of them for quantitie and quallitie; and my (*worn*)at hee shall have in his p^r^te of them; my sixty acrees of upland that lyeth (*worn*) all that my meddow and upland that lyeth next unto (*worn*) Gave and possessed, by my brother John Thomson (*worn*)nd in Rockey nooke; alsoe hee shall have the onehalf (*worn*) lyeth next unto John Dunhames meddow att (*worn*) of mddow that lyeth in Joneses river meddow; and (*worn*) amount to his proportion for quantitie (*worn*) payed by one of his brothers (*worn*) that in mony, soe hee to alow them if otherwise (*worn*)on ffrancis Cooke one share of all my lands (*worn*)antitie and quallitie; and my will is that in his (*worn*) my forty five acrees of upland (*worn*)rother Wrights land; alsoe the onehalfe of my (*worn*) Winnatucksett next John Dunhames Meddow (*worn*) meddow; that lyeth att Jonses River meddow and (*worn*) what these severall p^r^sells shall want of (*worn*)mainder out of the lands I live upon or (*worn*)es of age; by his brother Caleb; if those to (*worn*)s my will see cause; that my son ffrancis (*worn*)ny; and that they; att the Devision Determine (*worn*) p^r^formance; Item I will and betweath unto (*worn*)s haveing Don formerly, according to (*worn*)th unto my six Daughters viz Mary (*worn*)kah Cookes my Debts and legacyes (*worn*)s monyes Debts Goods [p. 2] Cattle Chattells and whatsoever moveable estate appertaineth unto mee to be equa(lly) Devided betwixt them six onely what Corne and provision shalbe found in being shal(*worn*) be Devided; but spent by my wife and Children that are with her; and my Desire is that my executors take the best Course they Can, to Cecure theire portions, to the time of theire marriage or that they Come of age; And I Doe by these p^r^sents appoint make and ordaine my Deare and loveing wife Elizabeth Cooke; and my loveing son Caleb Cooke my executors of this my Last Will; and testament; to Adminnester upon my said estate to receive all such Debtes as are Due to mee and; to pay all such Debts and legacyes as I owe or are Given by these p^r^sents; and I Doe alsoe Impower and Authorise my said executors by these p^r^sents to give unto my Cozen Daniell Wilcockes a Deed of that land att Punckateesett; which I sold him, and hee hath payed mee for; Alsoe to Give & take a Deed of my brother John Thompson for the land and meddow that hee and my selfe exchanged, one with the other; alsoe that my executors see that my body be Decently buried, and out of my estate to Defray the Charge therof; and my will is that my loveing frinds my brother John Thompson and Willam Crow; Doe see the p^r^formance of this my last Will, and the settlement of my estate; and I Doe therefore Desire order and Impower them; for to be healpfull to my wife and Children in all theire Devisions above mensioned; and to Determine what and how any matter shalbe between them; as neare as they Can according to the true Intent of this my last Will and Testament; And by these p^r^sents I revoake all former wills; thus hopeing that this my last Will and Testament wilbe kept and p^r^formed according to the true Intent and meaning therof: I Comitt my body to the Dust and my soule to God that Gave it mee; In Witnes wherof I Jacob Cooke seni^r^: have sett to my hand and seale this eleventh Day of December one thousand six hundred seaventy and five; alsoe for my fifty acrees of Land att or about Joneses river meddow; I would have it Devided to my sonnes as my other lands, either to all of them or else to one of them hee paying his brothers for their p^{r}tes;

Signed and sealled in the presence of us to be his last will and Testament
Joseph howland
Edward Gray his marke
Isacke Wright his marke

Jacob Cooke seni^{r}:
his I C marke and a (seale)

An Inventory of the Estate of Jacob Cooke seni^{r} of the Towne of New Plymouth Deceased taken and apprised the 18th Day of December 1675, by m^{r} Thomas Cushman Leiftenant Jos(*worn*)* and serjeant Ephraim Tinkham; and exhibited to the Court of his Matie h(*worn*) aforsaid the 8th of March Ann^{o} Dom: 1675, 76, on the oath of E(*worn*)†

Imp^{r}: 1 yoake of oxen (*worn*)
Item 4 Cowes (*worn*)
Item 2 steers of 3 yeers and advantage (*worn*)
Item 1 heiffer of 2 yeers and vantage (*worn*)
Item the halfe of a Cow 20^{s} and the half (*worn*)
Item halfe of a heiffer 12^{s} 6^{d} & halfe of (*worn*)
Item 1 yeerlyng heiffer (*worn*)
Item 3 Calves (*worn*)
Item a mare and Colt or else a D(*worn*) vallued att (*worn*)
Item 1 mare 15^{s} and a yonge horse (*worn*)
Item 59 sheep and lambes att six pou(*worn*)
Item 7 sowes att 6^{s} apeece and 4 piggs (*worn*)

Takling without Dores

Item 1 winch for a Grindstone (*worn*)
Item 1 Cart and wheeles with theire Iron worke with (*worn*)
Item 1 Copp yeoke and one stinge yoake with theire Iron w(*worn*)
Item 1 plow share with a Coulter and bee (*worn*)
Item 1 Cart rope and halter (*worn*)
Item 1 Draft Cheine 5^{s} 1 logg Cheine in 2 peeces (*worn*)
Item a paire of hinges (*worn*)
Item 1 auger and handsaw (*worn*)
Item 1 Dunge forke & 2 pitch(*worn*)
Item 2 hoes 1 spade 1 axe (*worn*)
Item 1 hooke and exe; and (*worn*)
Item 1 hoop and a paire of pince(*worn*)
Item 1 old Cow bell and old Iron (*worn*)
Item 1 Gouge 6^{d} and one hechell (*worn*)
Item 1 Stocke of bees 8^{s} — 1 augur 9^{d} = 8^{s} = 9‡

* This must have been "Joseph Howland."
† This must have been "Elizabeth Cooke."
‡ This item was written on the inside margin of the page.

[p. 3] in the house the outward rome

Item 1 Tramell 4^s — 1 Tramell 3^s — 1 hanger 1^s	00 08 00
Item 1 Iron kettle 9^s 1 Iron pott and pothookes 10^s	00 19 00
Item 1 Iron pott 8^s with the pothookes to it	00 08 00
Item 1 Great brasse kettle 12^s 1 Ditto lesser kettle 7^s	00 19 00
Item 2 brasse skilletts and 1 old peece of brasse	00 02 00
Item 1 fireslice	00 01 06
Item 1 pewter platter 6^s — one pewter platter 5^s 6^d	00 11 06
Item 1 Ditto 4^s — 1 Ditto 3^s 1 Ditto 3^s	00 10 00
Item 1 Cracked pewter Dish 2^s 1 quart pott 3^s	00 05 00
Item 1 pint pott 2^s 1 pint pott 1 beaker 1 Dram Cupp 1	00 03 00
Item halfe a Dozen of spoones 3^s halfe a Dozen of spoones 2^s 6^d	00 05 06
Item 1 frying pan and one peece of a Gridjron 1 old peece of a pewterbason	00 03 00
Item 1 bread Grator 1 shill 2 milk pan 8^d	00 01 08
Item 1 longe fowling peece	01 10 00
Item 1 short Muskett	00 16 00
Item 1 Carbine 10^s — 1 Rapier 12^s	01 02 00
Item 1 backe sword 8^s — 1 spitt 3^s 6^d	00 11 06
Item 1 smoothing box and heators	00 03 00
Item 1 loome 15^s and the one halfe of 5 paire of Geers 15^s	01 10 00
Item 6 pound of bulletts 2 hornes with powder	00 04 00
Item 1 Great Iron wedge 1^s 6^d 4 pailes 4^s	00 05 06
Item 24 pound of woolen yearne	01 16 00
Item 12 pound of woolen yerne and 1 pound of Cotten yearne	01 04 00
Item 4 pound of fflax yearne	00 10 00
Item 3 Chaires 4^s one Cradle 1^s 6^d	00 05 06
Item 1 houer Glasse 9^d 1 paire of sheep sheers 15^d	00 02 00
Item 1 bible 4^s 1 Psalme book 1^s 6^d 4 old bookes 2^s	00 07 06
Item 1 Curbe bridle 3^s 1 saddl 10^s 1 pannell 8^s	01 01 00
Item 1 sickle 1^s 1 hamer 1^s	00 02 00
	16 07 02

In the bed Chamber

Impr: 1 bed and a bolster	03 00 00
Item 1 Green rugg and one white blankett	01 00 00
Item 4 paire of sheets att 16^s a paire	03 04 00
Item 2 old Chests & a box	00 06 06
	07 10 06

In the uper Chamber or loft

Item 1 bed and bolster	02 15 00
(*worn*) 1 blankett 8^s : 1 Green Rugg 5^s	00 13 00
(*worn*)ed Rugge 5^s 1 blankett 6^s	00 11 00
(*worn*)	02 15 00
(*worn*) 1 bolster 1 pillow 5^s	02 16 00
(*worn*)rabouts of sheeps woole 13^s 6^d	00 17 06
(*worn*)ole	00 03 06

(*worn*) 5^s	00 08 00
(*worn*)ke 3^s	00 06 06
(*worn*)llowes 6^s	00 07 06
	11 13 00
(*worn*) seive 3^s 6^d	00 07 06
(*worn*)rrell 2^s 6^d 1 tubb 6^d	00 04 06
(*worn*)omas Lettices	00 07 06
(*worn*)	00 03 00
(*worn*) woole att 9^d pr pound is	00 07 06
(*worn*)	00 02 00
(*worn*)	00 04 00
(*worn*)on 10^s 4 yard Cotton 9^s 4^d	00 19 04
	02 15 04

Apparrell

(*worn*)	01 00 00
(*worn*)	00 12 00
(*worn*)f breeches and one paire of Drawers 15^s	01 05 00
(*worn*)	00 04 06
(*worn*)s	00 08 00
(*worn*)	00 11 06
(*worn*)	00 04 00
(*worn*)	02 13 06
	06 18 06
[p. 4] Item 1 pewter Chamber pott	00 03 00
Item 1 brake 3^s 1 paire of Cards 1^s	00 04 00
Item 1 Iron Square	00 01 06
	00 08 00
Item Severall pticulars expended	01 00 06
Item the onethird of 2 weathers 4^s	

Debts owing to the testator

Item from Caleb Cooke	01 05 00
ffrom ffrancis Douce	00 08 00
ffrom Samuell Dunham son of John Dunham	00 03 00
ffrom John Dotey	00 07 00
ffrom Nathaniell Wood allies Attwood	00 03 00
ffrom John Bradford	00 03 00
ffrom Jacob Cooke	00 06 00
The sume of the estate is	104 16 03

Debts owing by the Testator

Item To Willam harlow	01 00 00
To Thomas Lettice	00 04 00
To Samuell Jenney	00 04 00
To Joseph Wadsworth	00 06 00
To Captaine Matthew ffuller	01 00 00
To Doctor Samell ffuller	00 07 00

To the estate of Ester Cooke Deceased	02 12 04
To Edward Gray	02 05 00
To the estate of Willam Shurtliffe Deceased	00 10 08
To Gorge Watson	01 00 00
To John Thompson	01 03 01
To Gorge Bonum	00 05 00
To Joseph howland	00 03 00
To Robertt ffinney	00 03 06
To ffunerall Charges	02 06 06
Debts owing	13 10 01
The Estate Debts Deducted is	091 00 02

Wee are Informed that the Testator Died posessed of these lands as followeth;

Impr 1 Dwelling house with the out houses therunto standing and be(*worn*) upon his two lotts off land that lyeth on the southsyde of the smelt brooke (*worn*) the Towne of Plymouth with the additions therunto belonging;

Alsoe 4 fift prtes of a prsell of lands and meddow, that were Injoyed by his Dece(ased) father ffrancis Cooke, lying and being in Rockey nooke; in the said Towne of Pl(ymouth)

Sixty acrees of upland lying att Moonponsett pond

forty five acrees of upland lying att Winnetucksett Neare Richard Wrights lan(d)

fifty acrees of upland lying att or neare the I(*worn*) (*worn*)nd(*worn*)

Three acrees of salt Marsh Meddow lying att Pyney po(*worn*)

Thirty acrees of Meddow more or lesse in three lotts lyin(*worn*)

Twelve Acrees of meddow lying att Winnatuxett; by the (*worn*)

six acrees of Meddow with a smale prsell of upland (*worn*) meddow lying att Winnatucksett;

Thirty Acrees of upland lying on the Norths(*worn*) neare a place Called the woolfe trappe;

This Inventory was Attested (*worn*) Elizabeth Cooke this 8cond* (*worn*) in open Court as

Attests J(*worn*)

* This was first written 2cond. Afterwards the 2 was made into 8 without changing the rest.

GOVERNOR EDWARD WINSLOW'S WILL.

THE will of Governor Edward Winslow, which is preserved at Somerset House, London, is one of the three existing original wills of Mayflower passengers. The others are Mary (Chilton) Winslow's and Peregrine White's, both of which we have already reproduced. The illustration of Governor Winslow's will facing this page is from a photograph made at the expense of the Foreign Research Fund and secured by the Hon. Winslow Warren, of our Committee on Publication, with the courteous assistance of the Rev. Stopford W. Brooke, of London.

No mention of Governor Winslow's death is found on the Plymouth Colony records, and we learn the date from Nathaniel Morton's New England's Memorial, under the year 1655. We reprint his account in full, from the Rev. Thomas Prince's copy of the first edition (1669), now in the Boston Public Library.

This year that Worthy and Honourable Gentleman Mr. *Edward Winslow* deceased; of whom I have had occasion to make honourable mention formerly in this Discourse. He was the Son of *Edward VVinslow* Esq; of the Town of *Draughtwich* * in the County of *Worcester:* He travelling into the *Low-Countreys*, in his Journeys fell into acquaintance with the Church of *Leyden* in *Holland*, unto whom he joyned, and with whom he continued until they parted to come into *New-England*, he comming with that part that came first over, and became a very worthy and useful Instrument amongst them, both in the place of Government and otherwise, until his last Voyage for *England*, being sent on special Imployment for the Government of the *Massachusets*, as is forementioned in this Book; and afterwards was imployed as one of the grand Commissioners in that unhappy Design against *Domingo* in *Hispaniola*, who taking grief for the ill success of that Enterprize; on which, together with some other Infirmities that were upon him, he fell sick at Sea betwixt *Domingo* and *Jamaica*, and died the eighth day of *May*, which was about the Sixty first year of his life, and his Body was honourably committed to the Sea, with the usual Solemnity of the Discharge of Fourty two Piece of Ordnance.

* Droitwich.

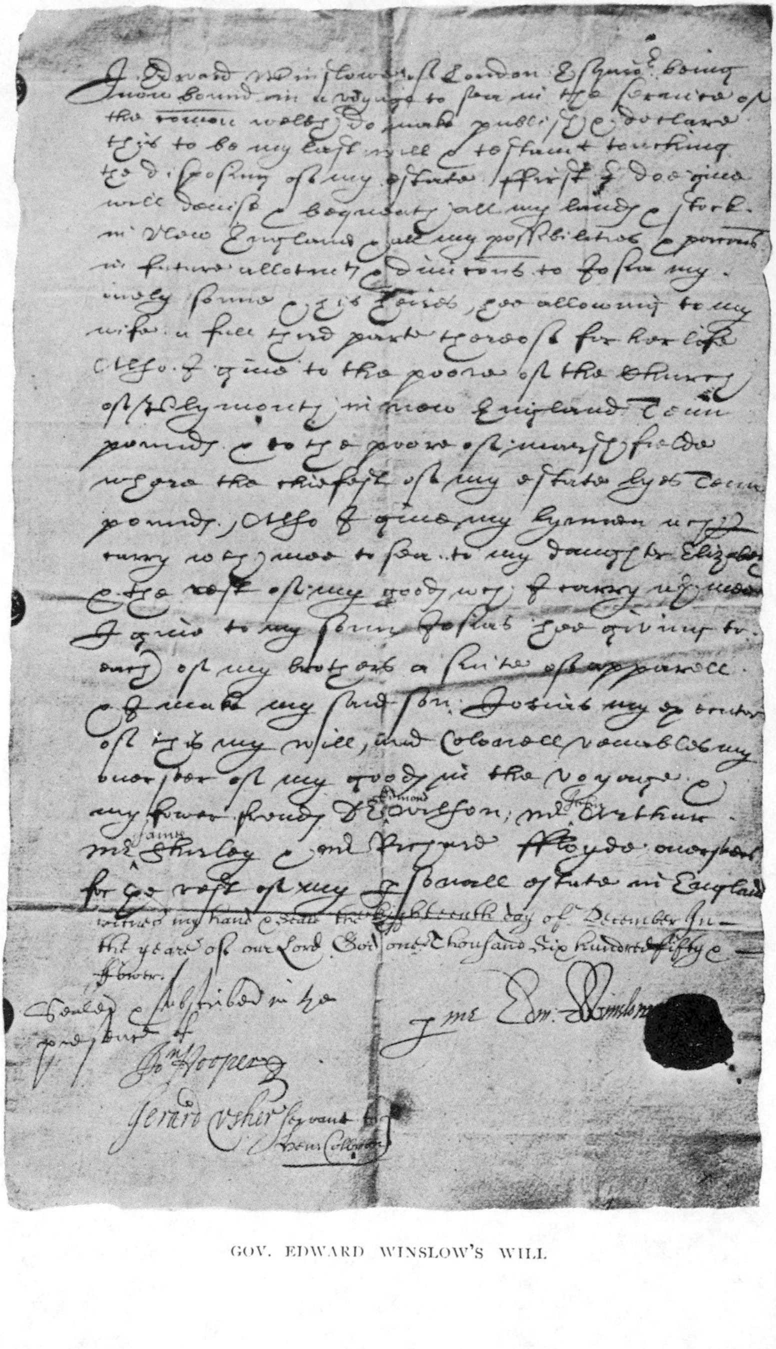

I Edward Winslow of London Esquire being
now bound in a voyage to sea in the service of
the common welth do make publish & declare
this to be my last will & testament touching
the disposing of my estate. ffirst I doe give
will devise & bequeath all my lands & stock
in New England & all my possibilities & porcons
in future allotments & divisions to Josias my
only sonne & his heires, hee allowing to my
wife a full third parte thereof for her life
Alsoe I give to the poore of the Church
of Plymouth in new England tenn
pounds & to the poore of Marshfield
where the chiefest of my estate lyes tenn
pounds. Alsoe I give my lynnen which I
carry with mee to sea to my daughter Elizabeth
& the rest of my goods which I carry with mee
I give to my sonne Josias hee giving to
each of my brothers a suite of apparell.
I make my said son Josias my executor
of this my will, and Colonell Venables my
overseer of my goods in the voyage &
my fower friends Dr Edmond Wilson, mr John Arthur
mr James Shirley & mr Richard ffloyde overseers
for the rest of my small estate in England
witnes my hand & seale the eighteenth day of December in
the yeare of our Lord God one thousand six hundred fifty &
ffower.

Sealed & subscribed in the
presence of

Edw. Winslow

Jo: Hooper

Gerard Usher servant to
Edm. Collyer

GOV. EDWARD WINSLOW'S WILL.

One of the Company who was imployed in taking notice of the Particulars of that Tragedy, gave such Testimony of the said Mr. *VVinslow*, as followeth in this Poem:

The Eighth of May, *west from* 'Spaniola *shore,*
God took from us our Grand Commissioner,
Winslow *by Name, a man in Chiefest Trust,*
VVhose Life was sweet, and Conversation just;
VVhose Parts and wisdome most men did excell:
An honour to his Place, as all can tell.

While examining the Marshfield town records some time since, the Editor discovered a vote regarding the disposition of the ten pounds bequeathed by Governor Winslow to the poor of that town. A literal transcript of this record follows the copy of the will.

I Edward Winslowe of London. Esquio^{r}. being now bound in a voyage to sea in the service of the comon welth do make publish & declare this to be my last will & testam^{t} touching the disposing of my estate. ffirst I doe give will devise & bequeath all my lands & stock. in New England & all my possibilities & porcons in future allotm^{ts} & divicons to Josia my. onely sonne & his heires, hee allowing to my wife. a full third parte thereof for her life Also. I give to the poore of the Church of Plymouth in new England Tenn pounds. & to the poore of marshfielde where the chiefest of my estate lyes Tenn pounds., Also I give my lynnen wch I carry wth me to sea. to my daughter Elizabet(h) &. the rest of. my goods wch I carry wth mee I give to my sonn Josias. hee giving to. each of my brothers a suite of apparell. & I make my said son. Josias my executor of this my will, and Colonell venables my overseer of my goods in the voyage. & my fower frends Dr Edmond wilson; m^{r} John Arthur. m^{r} James Shirley & m^{r} Richard ffloyde. overseers for the rest of my prsonall estate in England

witness my hand & Seale the Eighteenth day of December In the yeare of our Lord God one Thousand Six hundred fifty & ffower.

Sealed & subscribed pr me Edw: Winslow (seal)
in the presence of
Jo^{n} Hooper
Gerard Usher servant to Hen: Colbron

[Marshfield Records, I: 60, under date 3 Nov., 1656.]

Att ye same Townes meeting it was ordered That m^{r} Thomas Bourne and Joseph Beedell should Receave The Ten pounds which m^r^ Edward Winslow gave To The poore of This Towne by will and ye sayd prtyes so betrusted To Rec: & dispose of The stocke in The Townes behalfe have disposed one Cow To Edward Bumpus & John Branch one Cow & John Thomas The Remainder & These prtyes That is Edward & both The Johns To keepe These Cowes & To Returne at ye end of The Tea(rme) (as The Towne hath formerly lett out ye poore stocke) The princip(al) being living To ye Towne & The Third of The Increase The having Two Thirds of ye Increase Themselves.

PERMANENT CONTRIBUTIONS BY THE PILGRIMS TO THE CAUSE OF RELIGION.

[*An Address Delivered at the Second Annual Forefathers' Day Service of the Massachusetts Society of Mayflower Descendants, held at King's Chapel, Boston, December 21, 1901.*]

By Rev. Frederick Baylies Allen.

This is Forefathers' Day. Two hundred and eighty-one years ago, this 21st day of December, the Pilgrims first set foot on the shore of Plymouth and chose it as their home.

It was not the whole company, however, which did this. The Mayflower had cast anchor a month before (on the 21st day of November), in the harbor of what is now Provincetown, at the end of Cape Cod, and had remained there.

Three successive exploring parties went forth to find a place of settlement. It was the third party, composed of ten Pilgrims and eight seamen, which struggled into Plymouth Harbor, in a small shallop, late in the stormy evening of Friday, December 18th and landed on Clark's Island.

Bradford's history says that Saturday they dried their stuff, rested, gave thanks to God, and, this being the last day of the week, they prepared there to keep the Sabbath.

On Monday, the 21st (the day we are now observing), Bradford, who was one of the party, says: "They sounded the harbor and found it fit for shipping: and marched into the land and found divers cornfields and little running brooks: a place, (as they supposed) fit for situation; at least, it was the best they could find: and the season and their present necessitie made them glad to accept of it.

"So they returned to their ship again with this news to the rest of their people, which did much comfort their hearts."

That is the original account of the first Forefathers' Day.

The Mayflower reached Plymouth five days later (on the 26th). The second landing may be ascribed to December 30th, though the company left the ship gradually as houses were prepared for them, the last of the party going ashore as late as the month of April.

We, their descendants are met here today to commemorate by our service of prayer and song, those of whom James Russell Lowell said: "Next to the fugitives whom Moses led out of Egypt, the little shipload of outcasts who landed at Plymouth are destined to influence the future of the world."

We meet however, not at Plymouth, but at Boston, the capital of the Massachusetts Bay Colony, the original seat of Puritanism.

We worship moreover in a building whose early history is indelibly associated with the Church of England.

King's Chapel was erected (much against the will of the Puritans) under the auspices of the Royal Governors, for the express purpose of providing for public worship according to the liturgy of the English Book of Common Prayer.

It was, at one time, the only place in New England where the forms of the Court Church were used.

These triple associations of time and place: the Forefathers' Day, the Puritan city and the first Episcopal Church in New England have suggested the special theme to which I invite your attention: "The Permanent Contributions of the Pilgrims to the Cause of Religion: with incidental notice of the respective attitudes of the Pilgrims and of the Puritans to the Church of England."

I. I ask you to remember first that the Pilgrims were the earliest advocates of the separation of Church and State.

The Puritans when they crossed the ocean claimed loyal devotion to the National Church of England.

At the end of Queen Elizabeth's reign, through the popular antagonism of the people to the papacy, the great bulk of the country gentlemen and of the wealthier traders, of whom Parliament was chiefly composed, had become Puritans. Largely upon political grounds these Puritans acquired a bitter antagonism to those ceremonies which seemed to them allied to Roman Catholicism. Though called Non-Conformists, or as they preferred to call themselves Reformists, they felt themselves to be devoted members of the National Church. Owing to the personal antagonism of Elizabeth and James I. to Puritanism, it came about from the Union of Church and State that many of the appointees to the Church were persons practically destitute of religion. The spectacle of cruel and worldly ecclesiastics, performing the holiest rites of the church, stimulated the revolt against the liturgy.

This antagonism would have been comparatively feeble had the same ritual been administered by devout and earnest men.

It is generally conceded that if the demands of the Puritans had been met in a conciliatory spirit, they would have been content with moderate concessions.

The signers of the Millenary Petition, presented to King James at the beginning of his reign, asked for no change in the organization of the Church; but only "a reform of its courts, the removal of superstitious usages from the Book of Common Prayer, the disuse of lessons from the apocryphal books of Scripture, a more rigorous observance of Sundays and the provision and training of ministers who could preach to the people." How modest a request apparently.

In contemptuous scorn of these demands, three hundred Puritan clergymen who refused rigid conformity with the rubrics, were, in the spring of 1605, driven from their livings. The popular revolt deepened as they saw the church used as a machine to enforce slavish obedience to the royal will.

The very eagerness of the Puritans, however, to reform from within the Church of which they counted themselves the most loyal members, made them hate the Separatists, who looking deeper at the principles involved, withdrew, for conscience sake, from the Church.

Says John Richard Green: "To the zealot whose whole thought was of the fight with Rome, the position of those who rejected the very notion of a national Church and asserted the right of each congregation to perfect independence of faith and worship, seemed the claim of a right to mutiny in the camp, a right of breaking up Protestant England into a host of sects, too feeble to hold Rome at bay."

That explains the significance of the words of Francis Higginson, the Puritan minister of Salem, when he cried: "We will not say, as the Separatists were wont to say, at their leaving of England, Farewel Babylon! Farewel Rome! But we will say, Farewel Dear England! Farewel the Church of God in England, and all the Christian friends there! We do not go to New England as Separatists from the Church of England; though we cannot but separate from the corruptions in it. But we go to practise the positive part of church reformation, and propagate the Gospel in America."

And Governor Winthrop's Puritan company, as they sailed for America, spoke of themselves:

"As those who esteem it our honor to call the Church of England from whence we rise, our dear Mother; and cannot part from our native countrie where she specially resideth, without much sadness of heart and many tears in our eyes."

Turn now to the Pilgrims. We notice first that they were a very small company of men. Instead of the 20,000 who in less than a score of years came to Massachusetts Bay, they were but a few hundred in all. Only one hundred came over in the Mayflower and the portion of their company left behind in Holland was probably not more than twice as large.

But this small community were more homogeneous, more completely moulded into one spirit, than the mass of Puritans. They had been for thirteen years schooled and disciplined under many adversities by one man of singular force of character.

That man was their pastor in Leyden the Reverend John Robinson.

He had been the minister of the little congregation which under the fostering hospitality of William Brewster, had worshipped at Scrooby Manorhouse, England.

A man of rare piety, wisdom and thoughtfulness, he had, in the face of the tyranny and irreligion of the authorities, come to believe in the principle of the entire separation of Church and State. He states their position thus:

"As the Lord's free people, this congregation joined themselves, by a covenant of the Lord, into a church estate, in the fellowship of the Gospel, to walk in all His ways made known, or to be made known unto them, according to their best endeavors, whatever it should cost them; the Lord assisting them."

It cost them first their country, for in 1607 they were driven by the fierceness of the persecution to migrate to Holland, the only country in Europe where there was entire freedom of belief. For twelve years they dwelt there under the benign and penetrating influence of their noble pastor. It was he whose spiritual insight, wise leadership, and singular sagacity bred in these men that temper which for nearly a century characterized the Plymouth Colony.

At last in 1620, as the twelve years' truce between Holland and Spain approached its termination, as they found themselves in danger of losing their nationality in a foreign land; as they saw their children growing up under hardships and temptations which endangered both their health and their character, they came to the conclusion that it was their duty to remove, as they said, to "those vast and unpeopled countries of America, where they might at least lay the foundation for propagating and advancing the Gospel of the Kingdom of Christ."

We know well the story of that voyage across the ocean, the succession of obstacles which delayed it, the unspeakable hardships of the first winter and the gradual establishment upon firm foundations of the colony upon our shore.

The central element in the position of the Pilgrims as Separatists, was their repudiation of any official union of Church and State. The church polity called Independency or Congregationalism, though it was equally their faith, was another and distinct feature.

I shall confine what I have to say here to their protest against the mingling of the two spheres of religion and politics — the government of the Church with the administration of the State.

It was the enormities practised by the prelates of that day which forced the issue and drove them to deep and thorough searching of ultimate principles.

Had the Church of England been what it is now, Robinson and Brewster and Bradford would have gladly remained in her communion. But when a Bishop, by virtue of his office, could defy all legal restraints, and in the name of the king, who was the head of the Church, could cram the prisons of London with good Christians, who according to all modern ideas were perfectly innocent of any crime; clear thinking began to drive Robinson and Brewster into questioning the right of any such union of civil and religious functions.

This, then, was their conclusion: while they were never captious or controversial, while they said they would obey the king and his officers, and even his bishops in all secular matters — the things of man's deeper life, his faith in God, his privileges of worship were matters apart; which, with their consent, were never to be under the control of the State.

How consistently they adhered to this principle is manifest from the fact that when the ocean was crossed, unlike the Massachusetts Bay Colony, they never made church membership a condition of the franchise. So far as is known, even Myles Standish never joined the church, and some have believed that, at least nominally, he was a Roman Catholic. And these non-church members were from the beginning, regular legal members of the colony, who according to the compact signed on the Mayflower, had combined themselves into a civil (or secular) body politic. These two functions went on simply and naturally, side by side, just as they do today throughout our land. But they were the pioneers to first test this great principle.

When the Massachusetts Colony voted by its General Court—"That for time to come noe man shall be admitted to the freedom of this body pollitícke, but such as are members of some of the churches within the limits of the same." [Morton, p. 308.]—the Plymouth Colony dared to be true to its colors. A few of their number who had little in common with their noble leaders were still allowed equal political rights and absolute secular equality; and the time came when the strong, proud Massachusetts Bay Colonists were compelled to follow the lead of their humbler brethren to the south and absolutely sever Church and State.

We are all Separatists now. There is not one of us here who is not thankful that throughout the length and breadth of the land there is no established church.

It is largely because Protestants and Roman Catholics and Jews are all on precisely the same political level, in the sight of the law, that so kindly and charitable a spirit prevails between those of different faiths.

Let us never forget however, that we owe this benign result to our forefathers, who, when the title *Separatist* was a term of obloquy and reproach, exposing its bearer to persecution and loss, dared to be faithful to this fundamental principle.

II. The second tenet which we owe to the Pilgrims is their recognition of the *laity* as an integral part of the Church.

Robinson contended that "It is given to ministers to feed, guide and govern the Church, but not themselves to *be* the Church." *

In another place he says: "The officers of a church are not, by themselves, the Church. While there are *many* things in the settled and well ordered state of the Church which one would willingly leave to the administration of the officers thereof, they are or can be rightly and orderly done, but with the people's privity and consent."

The Pilgrims could not yield this point. "If," said they, "we should let the true practice of the gospel go, posterity after us, being brought into bondage, might justly blame and curse us, that we did not stand for the rights of the people in that which we acknowledge to be their due."

* These quotations from Robinson's writings are taken from "The Pilgrim Fathers of New England," by Rev. John Brown, D.D.

Robinson repeatedly asserts this root idea, though with a reasonableness and insight that shows how carefully he had studied the problem.

He says: "Wise men writing on this subject have approved as good and lawful three kinds of politics — monarchical, aristocratical and democratical, and all these three forms have their place in the Church of Christ. In respect of Christ the head, it is a monarchy; in respect of its officers, it is an aristocracy; and in respect of its body, a popular state. The governors of the Church must be in and of the church they govern, but they are not the *Church*."

Without endorsing the precise forms in which he applied this principle, its essence — that is, the representative character of the church and the rights of the laity to be duly considered in its administration is now acknowledged by all Protestant communions. We are so familiar with it, so assured of its justice and its wisdom, that it is hard for us to realize what an utter novelty it seemed in that day.

It had scant recognition at first in the Massachusetts Bay Colony. The eminent John Cotton of Boston, writing in 1636 to Lord Lay, declares: "Democracy I do not conceive that ever God did ordain as a fit government, either for church or commonwealth. If the people be governors, who shall be the governed?" Yet the day came when the Plymouth idea conquered the conservatism of the Puritan Colony.

How profound and far reaching has been the practical development of this germinal principle which our Pilgrim ancestors so fearlessly adopted.

Granting all the perverse and unlovely excesses to which it has often led in ignorant or untrained communities, it has now come to be recognized as an axiom, as a necessary and just law held by us as of priceless value. It may require both intelligence and piety for its best exercise, but it has now taken its due place as an essential and just requirement.

The *laity* are an integral part of a true church, fully entitled to a voice and due representation both in legislation and in the administering of its affairs.

III. Another Pilgrim principle, distinctive enough to merit notice, is the emphasis which they laid upon character as the supreme goal and test of religion.

At a time when Protestantism everywhere was suffering from an intense spirit of controversy, when every conceivable point of doctrine and church polity and ritual had been wrangled over until those who had forsaken the Church of Rome had become subdivided into multiplied warring sects and trifles had received more attention than essentials; it is wonderful what uniform stress was laid by the Pilgrims upon that which is central, upon personal religion and upon conduct.

This estimate of values was in one respect urged by Pilgrim and Puritan alike, when they both insisted that the church should not open wide her doors and offer her holiest rites and privileges to all men, utterly irrespective of character.

They both held that religion was something deeper than an external alliance with an institution. It was at its heart a matter of righteousness and purity and personal loyalty to the Lord. They were shocked that in the Church of England, men of notorious immorality and scandalous lives should be not only invited, but driven to the Holy Communion.

Robinson complains of England: "That all the natives there and subjects of the kingdom, although never such strangers from the show of true piety and goodness, and fraught never so full with many most heinous impieties and vices, are without difference compelled and enforced by most severe laws, civil and ecclesiastical, into the body of that church."

* * * * *

"Every subject of the kingdom dwelling in this or that parish, whether in city or country, whether in his own or other man's house, is thereby, *ipso facto*, made legally a member of the same parish in which that house is situated, and bound, will he nill he, fit or unfit, as with iron bounds, and all his with him, to participate in all holy things (and some unholy also), in that same parish church."

In this protest Pilgrims and Puritans, as I have said, shared alike; but where the former differed from the latter, was that their supreme reverence for goodness made them less critical and censorious than the Puritans as to irrelevant and secondary matters.

I believe the poet rightly judged them when he sung of the Pilgrims:

> What did they want, whom high and low
> Despised and persecuted so?
> Little, when understood —
> They wanted to be good.
>
> To worship God in their own way;
> To read their Bibles and to pray,
> And save their souls! Poor men —
> But poorer England then.

They proved the beauty and integrity of their religion by their example; by the lives they led before all men. Says Robinson: "God is not partial as men are; nor regards that church and chamber religion towards Him which is not accompanied in the house and in the streets with lovingkindness and mercy and all goodness towards men."

Nor was this theory merely.

Governor Bradford, recalling the days when they lived in Leyden, says: "Such was the true piety, the humble zeal and fervent love of this people towards God and his ways, and the single heartedness and the sincere affection one towards another, that they came as near the primitive pattern of the first Churches as any other Church of these later times have done according to their rank and quality."

He says in another place: "Though many of them were poor, yet there was none so poor but if they were known to be of that congregation, the Dutch (either bakers or others) would trust them in any reasonable matter when they wanted money. Because they had found by experience how careful they were to keep their word, and saw them so painful and diligent in their callings; yea, they would strive to get their custom and to employ them above others in their work, for their honesty and diligence."

This same high sense of honor and tenderness of conscience and charity towards others they carried with them into the new world. They made religion beautiful and attractive by their integrity and their cheerful kindness.

When in their sore need during one of their first explorations they took a store of corn which they found buried by the Indians, they diligently sought for the owners, and discovering them long months after, they scrupulously made them ample restitution.

The practical character of their religion is nowhere better illustrated than by their uniform fairness towards the Indians, for half a century.

Now it is not merely the fact that they were good men which is worthy of notice, but that their goodness was of so wholesome and pure a strain; so free from cant, and controversy, and perpetual argument and fault-finding. They got on amicably with all kinds of people, which was more than the so-called saints always did. They knew what was central in religion and lived it; and about the things which divided good people from one another, they were not disposed to be perpetually quarrelling.

Love towards God, purity of character, charity toward man — that was the pith of the Pilgrim faith.

IV. That brings me naturally to the remaining trait which I mention at this time, their religious tolerance.

The Pilgrims had enjoyed one advantage over the Puritans. They had sojourned for thirteen years in Holland and had seen in actual practice there, the fullest religious liberty granted to all faiths and to all nationalities.

But their practice of this principle had deeper root. Their charity to all sorts and conditions of men grew out of an openness of mind which they had learned at the feet of John Robinson. They had been taught by him to believe that they were not in the possession of all truth and that they might find something to learn from those who differed from them most fundamentally.

The memorable passage in which this hospitality to new light is enjoined, was quoted by Governor Bradford from the counsel given by John Robinson in 1620, upon the departure of the Pilgrims to America.

Familiar though it be, it can hardly be too often repeated, as it is the key to that consistent policy of religious tolerance practiced by the Plymouth Colony.

"He charged us," says Winslow, "before God and his blessed angels, to follow him no further than he followed Christ; and if God should reveal anything to us by any other instrument of His, to be as ready to receive it, as ever we were to receive any truth by his Ministry. For he was very confident the Lord had more truth and light yet to break forth out of His Holy Word."

* * * * *

"But withal he exhorted us to take heed what we received for truth: and well to examine and compare, and weigh it with other Scriptures of truth before we received it."

"For," saith he, "it is not possible the Christian world should come so lately out of such thick anti-Christian darkness; and that full perfection of knowledge should break forth at once."

Here we see how it was that these men who remembered and cherished their pastor's words were always so charitable to those of other faiths.

"Church of England people and Baptists dwelt continuously in Plymouth in peace, except such as openly sought to overturn the Independent Churches. Visitors of all beliefs and no belief were entertained (to their host's subsequent privation), for months together, so hospitable were they."

The French Jesuit Druillette, who came to Boston in 1650, improved the opportunity to spend a day at Plymouth. He especially mentions Bradford's kindness, and the fact "that, the day being Friday, the Governor gave him an excellent dinner of *fish*."

At the Lord's table the Pilgrims communed with pious Episcopalians, with Calvinists of the French and Dutch Churches, and with Presbyterians, and recognized the spiritual fraternity of all who hold the Faith.

In 1659 Massachusetts Bay forbade keeping "any such day as Christmas, either by forbearing to labor, or feasting or in any other way," under penalty of five shillings.

Plymouth never had any such narrow and contemptible restrictions, but would have allowed anyone to feast, rest, or observe the day as they wished, provided they did not interfere with those who did not care to keep it.

Their administration of law was remarkably mild for the standards of their day. At the accession of James I., England made thirty-one crimes capital. Massachusetts Bay made thirteen crimes capital; the Virginia Colony had seventeen (including Unitarianism), Plymouth had only five classes of capital crime; and of these she actually punished but two.

As Senator Hoar says: "Their good sense kept them free from witchcraft delusions. No witch was ever hung there. They established trial by jury. They treated the Indians with justice and good faith. They held no foot of land not fairly obtained by honest purchase. Their tolerance was an example to Roger Williams himself. And when at last in 1692 Plymouth was blended with Massachusetts, the days of bigotry and tolerance and superstition as a controlling force in Massachusetts — were over."

These then were the contributions, well nigh unique in their day, which our forefathers made to the cause of religion:

1. They taught and practiced the separation of Church and State.

2. They claimed that not merely the clergy but the laity were an integral part of the Church and entitled to representation.

3. They laid stress upon character as the supreme requisite in true religion:

4. And they practiced with exquisite courtesy the principle of religious tolerance.

There is not one of these four tenets which is not cherished and defended today by all our Protestant Churches, — including the Protestant Episcopal Church to which I belong.

Yet for insisting upon these things, our forefathers suffered obloquy and persecution.

They were the pioneers who, through hardship and loss, blazed a path which has now become a smooth highway for all. We tread it with too little appreciation of the humble heroes to whose clear thought, unflinching courage and pious devotion we owe our rich privilege.

If they were not the kind of men whom the world applauds, there was One who called them "blessed," for they were poor in spirit; they mourned; they were meek; they hungered and thirsted after righteousness; they were merciful; they were pure in heart; they were peacemakers; they were persecuted for righteousness sake — and great is their reward in heaven.

JOSEPH[2] WARREN'S WILL AND INVENTORY.

Literally Transcribed from the Original Records,

BY GEORGE ERNEST BOWMAN.

JOSEPH[2] WARREN (*Richard*[1]) died at Plymouth and his wife Priscilla Faunce survived him eighteen years. The following records of their deaths are taken from the Plymouth Town Records, Volume I: "Joseph Warren Senior deceased May the 4th 1689" [p. 201] — "The Widow pricila Warren Deceased on ye 15 of May 1707 being Nea(r) 74 yeares of age" [p. 204]

Joseph Warren's will and inventory are found in the Plymouth County Probate Records, Volume I, pages 38 and 39.

To all People to whome these presents shall Come etc: Know Ye that I Joseph Warren Senr of the Town of Plimouth in the County of New Plimouth in new-England being weak of body through age & Sickness but of perfect and disposing memory & Sound understanding Blessed be God. Yet not knowing how soone it may please God to Change my Sickness & life to death do therefore make and ordaine and by these presents I do make & ordaine these presents to be my last will and Testament to stand good and to Remaine firm and Inviolable for ever in maner and forme following:

Imp[rs] I Will and bequeath my Soul to God that gave it me and my body to the dust and to be decently Buried: and for that outward estate that God hath given to me I dispose of as followeth: Item I will and bequeath unto my dear and Loving wife Pricilla Warren all that my now dwelling house out housing uplands & meadow lands that I am now possessed of in the Township of Plimouth. Excepting such Lands as I shall hereafter dispose of to my Son Joseph, Together with all my household Goods and debts that is owing to me as also four Cows and two oxen which she shall have before a division of my Cattell be made, all which housing lands debts Goods and Chattels above expressed I do Give unto my dear and Loving wife Priscilla Warren to be at her disposing and for her Support during the time of her widowhoode; And farther I do give unto my loving wife all that my fifty acres of Land Lying at Monament ponds in the Township of Plimouth as alsoe Eight acres of upland at the Hoope place field So called for her to Rent out or sell if necescity Require. And I doe by these presents allow her so to doe as alsoe the one half of my uplands & meadow lands at Aggawam that is alredy divided together with a fourth part of the undivided lands. All which I do give unto my loving wife to be at her disposing to doe with it what she will during her life or widdowhoode for her Supporte and Comfort and in Case she should marrey then my will is that she shall have my best Bed and all furniture thereunto belonging to be her own for ever: Item I Give unto my son Joseph Warren all That my fifty acres of upland lying upon Sandwich Road in the Township of Plimouth this to have and possess after my decease as alsoe the one half of my share of land and meadow at Aggawam that is already divided and after my Wives decease my will is and I doe by these presents give unto my son Joseph Warren my now dwelling house outhousing uplands and meadow land that I have in the Township of Plimouth I do give to him and his Heires for ever That is begotten of his body. Item I give unto my son Benjamin Warren all my lands both uplands and meadow land that I have Lying both in Middlebury and Bridgwater Townships to belong to him and his heires for ever that is Begotten of his Body Item I give unto my daughter Mercy Bradford two Cowes. Item and it is my Will that after my Wives decease or marriage againe that then my whole Estate both movablles Chattels or debts or whatsoever or wheresoever it may be found shall be equally divided amongst four of my

Children that is to say Joseph Benjamin Patience and Elizabeth: And [p. 39] And lastly I do nominate and appoint my dear and loving wife Priscilla Warren to be the sole Executrix of this my last will and testament to administer on my s^d^ estate to pay Such debts as I owe and to Receive Such debts as is owing to me and to se that my body be decently buried and to defray the Charges thereof And I do Request my Brother Thomas ffaunce to be helpfull to my s^d^ Executrix in the acting and disposing of particulars according to the tenor hereof Thus hoping that this my last Will and Testament will be performed and kept Revoaking all other wills Either verball or written I have here unto set my hand and Seal on the 4th of May 1689:

Signed Sealed and declared to	The Mark of Joseph
be his last will and Testament	Warren Senior and a (seal)
In presence of	
Ephraim Morton sen^r^	
Ephraim Morton jun^r^	
Tho: ffaunce:	

Leiu^t^ Ephraim Morton Thomas ffaunce and Ephraim Morton jun^r^ the witnesses herein named appeared before two of the Magistrates of this County of Plimouth Viz^t^ William Bradford dep^t^ Govr and John Cushing assistant & made oath that they were present and Saw the above named Joseph Warren deceased Signe seal & heard him declare this Instrument as his last will & testament and that to ye best of their judgment he was of a disposing mind & memory when he did ye same. September ye 4th 1689:

Attest Sam'l, Sprague Clerk

An Inventory of the Estate of Joseph Warren sen^r^ of Plimouth deceased Taken and apprised by us whose names are under written: on the 15th of May 1689:

Imp^ris^ His Wearing apparrell and Books:	15 08 00
Item in Silver	28 14 00
Item in Cattell 4 oxen at	11 00 00
Item in ten Cowes at	19 00 00
Item in four three year old Steeres	07 00 00
Item in two 4 year old Steeres	04 00 00
Item in two buls and one Steere	06 10 00
Item in 4 yearlings and two 2 year olde Heiffers	06 10 00
Item in other Small Cattel and horses and Swine	02 01 00
Item in Beds and Beding Suitable to them	30 00 00
Item in Table Linnen and new Cloth	08 01 06
Item in Pewter and Brass	04 03 00

Item in Iron pots kittles Hakes and hookes	01 10 00
Item in armes and Amunition	06 00 00
Item in Carpenters Tooles Sythes and Sickles	02 10 00
Item in Earthern Vessels and Glass Bottles	00 10 00
Item in an old fflock Bed three Blankets & Cushions	02 00 00
Item in Wooden Vessels & Spinning wheels	01 10 00
Item in Tables Chaires and Chests	02 00 00
[p. 40] Item in one paire of Stillyards Iron Hachell & Steel trapp	01 0 0
Item in an old Cart and wheels and Plows and Tacklen to them	03 0 0
Item in shingle and Boltes	06 10 0
Item in Hoes Spade and and Pitchforkes	00 12 0
Item in 3 Canooes & Cartrope	03 0 0
Item in Cotton and Linnen Yarne Woolen Yarn flax teere	03 0 0
Item in Cotton & sheeps wooll	02 0 0
Item in nailes and Razor and Case of ffleams and 2 Bells	01 0 0
Item in Wheel timber old Saddle Bridle and Pannell	01 14 0
Item in Old Cask and other Lumber	00 10 0
Item in debts due to the Estate	12 8 4
Item the Estate Indebted	20 0 0

Ephraim Morton Senr
Tho ffaunce

Priscilla Relict Widdow of the above named Joseph Warren deceased appeared at Plimouth September the 4th: 1689 before the Magistrates of this County of Plimouth and Made oath that the above written is a true Inventory of the Goods & Chattels of s^d^ deceased as far as she Knows and that if more appear she will Bring it to this Inventory

Attest Sam'l, Sprague Clerk

PHINEAS PRATT OF PLYMOUTH AND CHARLESTOWN.

(*Reprinted, with additions, from " The Macdonough–Hackstaff Ancestry.*")

BY RODNEY MACDONOUGH.

THE opening up of a new country and the planting of settlements therein are usually due to commercial enterprise and activity; occasionally to political or religious expediency.

New England furnishes no exception to the general rule, and these influences will supply a raison d'ctre for each of the early settlements within her borders. Commercial enterprise, the foundation of the colonization idea, was the strongest of the three forces and naturally found expression in the establishment of numerous plantations dedicated to trade and barter. Among the earliest of these was Wessagusset, a neighbor of Plymouth. It is not the purpose of the writer to enter into the details of the settlement and subsequent history of Wessagusset, but to give what facts are known concerning one who was intimately connected with that plantation and later with Plymouth and Charlestown, Phineas Pratt.

The following brief account of the coming of Phineas and his early experiences here shows the hardships, the dangers and the sufferings undergone by those who sought new homes in a new country, and a recital of these happenings, in whatever form presented, can hardly fail to interest his descendants both because of a feeling of kinship and because of the attendant circumstances of time and place. Phineas himself has left us, in his " Declaration," a most interesting account of the affairs of the early settlers and his own experiences. The writer has quoted freely from this invaluable document, printed in the Massachusetts Historical Society Collections (Fourth Series, IV, 476), and the quotations will be readily recognized.

Phineas was one of a small party sent by Thomas Weston, a London merchant, and a Mr. Beachamp, in the Sparrow to prepare the way for the settlement of a new colony.* This party consisted of but six or seven persons. Bradford says seven.† Winslow says six or seven.‡ Phineas says "we being but 10 men," referring to the initial trip of the Sparrow's

* Bradford's History (London, 1896), 72. † Ibid., 72, 78.

‡ Winslow's " Good Newes from New England " (London, 1624), 11.

boat to Plymouth, but this number no doubt included the Master's Mate and two or three seamen of the Sparrow, thus leaving six or seven in Weston's party. It is certain that others of the Sparrow's crew besides the Master's Mate accompanied the settlers on this trip to take back the boat, for Winslow says the party "brought no more prouision for the present than serued the Boats gang for their returne to the ship."* Some sixty more men were to follow this party later.

The Sparrow sailed for Massachusetts Bay, "but wanting a pilote," writes Phineas, "we Ariued att Damoralls Cove. The men y^{t} belong to ye ship, ther fishing, had newly set up a may pole & weare very mery. We maed hast to prepare a boat fit for costing. Then said Mr. Rodgers, Master of our ship, 'heare ar Many ships & at Munhigin, but no man y^{t} does vndertake to be yor pilate; for they say y^{t} an Indian Caled Rumhigin vndertook to pilot a boat to Plimoth, but thay all lost tha^{r} Lives.' Then said Mr. Gibbs, Mast^{rs} Mate of our ship, 'I will venter my Liue wth y^{m}.' At this Time of our discouery, we first Ariued att Smithe's Ilands, first soe Caled by Capt. Smith, att the Time of his discouery of New Eingland, ... fterwards Caled Ilands of Sholes; ffrom thence to Cape Ann . . . . so Caled by Capt Mason; from thence to ye Mathechusits Bay. Ther we continued 4 or 5 days. Then we pseaued, y^{t} on the south part of the Bay, weare fewest of the natives of the Cuntry Dwelling ther. We thought best to begine our plantation, but fearing A great Company of Salvages, we being but 10 men, thought it best to see if our friends weare Living at Plimoth. Then sayling Along the Cost, not knowing the harber, thay shot of a peece of Ardinance, and at our coming Ashore, they entertaned vs wth 3 vally of shotts."

Phineas and his party reached Plymouth the last of May, 1622. The month is given by Bradford and the context shows the year. He says: — "But about y^{e} *later end of may*, they spied *a boat* at sea (which at first they thought had beene some french-man) but it proued a shalop which came from a ship which Mr Weston, & an other, had set out a fishing, at a place called Damarins-coue .40. leagues to ye eastward of them; wher were y^{t} year many more ships come a fishing. This boat brought .7. passengers; and some letters, but no uitails, nor any hope of any."† Bradford does not mention the name of the vessel to which the shallop belonged, but this omission is supplied by Winslow, who writes: — "This Boat proued to be a

* Winslow's "Good Newes from New England" (London, 1624), 11.

† Bradford's History (London, 1896), 72.

shallop that belonged to a fishing ship, called the Sparrow, set forth by Master *Thomas Weston*, late Merchant and Citizen of London, which brought six or seuen passengers at his charge, that should before haue beene landed at our Plantation, who also brought no more prouision for the present than serued the Boats gang for their returne to the ship."*

The Plymouth colonists being greatly in need of provisions at this time, the men of the Sparrow accompanied some of them to the fishing fleet at the Damariscove Islands to procure what food the ships could spare. Their friends "did what they could freely" and the party returned to Plymouth with such necessaries as the fleet could spare from its scanty store.

It has been thought that after this expedition Phineas and his companions returned from Plymouth to the Sparrow and there awaited the coming of the rest of Weston's company.† The writer does not agree with this view. Phineas himself is silent on this point, merely saying, "At this Time, on or two of them went wth vs in our vesill to ye place of ffishing to bye vicktuals." Weston plainly expected them to stay at Plymouth until the rest of the party came, for in a letter to Governor Carver delivered by the Sparrow party on their arrival he says:—". . . we haue sent *this ship*, and these pasengers on our owne accounte. Whom we desire you will frendly entertaine, & supply with shuch necesaries as you cane spare, and they wante &c. . . . To ye end our desire may be effected, which I assure my selfe will be also for your good we pray you giue them entertainmente in your houses ye time they shall be with you. That they may lose no time, but may presently goe in hand to fell trees, & cleaue them, to ye end lading may be ready and our ship stay not."‡ Bradford says:—". . . they tooke compassion of those .7. men. Which *this ship* (*which fished to ye eastward*) *had kept till planting time was ouer*, and so could set no corne. And allso wanting vitals, (for y^ey^ turned them off w^th^out any) and indeed wanted for them selues) neither was their salt-pan come, so as y^ey^ could not performe any of those things which Mr Weston. had appointed; and might haue starued if ye plantation had not succoured them, who in their wants, gaue them as good as any of their owne."§ The expression "y^ey^ turned them off," used by Bradford in connection with their leaving the Sparrow, contains the implication that they were not expected to return.

* Winslow's "Good Newes," 11.

† Phineas Pratt and Some of His Descendants, 19.

‡ Bradford's History, 72, 73. § Ibid., 75.

In a passage already quoted Winslow says the party brought no more provisions than would suffice for the return of the boat's "gang" to the ship,* thus also indicating that the boat's crew were expected to return, but not the settlers. But the most conclusive evidence we have that Phineas and his companions returned to Plymouth with the party who went to the fishing fleet for provisions and there (at Plymouth) awaited the coming of the Charity and the Swan is Bradford's statement when he writes, referring to the reception of Weston's 60 colonists by those vessels:—"So as they had receiued his former company of .7. men and vitailed them as their owne hitherto, so they also receiued these (being *aboute* .60. *lusty men*) and gaue housing for them selues, and their goods, and many being sicke they had ye best means ye place could aford them; . . ."† But one interpretation can be placed upon the words "vitailed them as their owne hitherto" and that is that Phineas and his companions had been offered, and had accepted, the hospitality of the Plymouth men after leaving the Sparrow and that they were living in Plymouth at the time of the arrival of the rest of the party in the Charity and the Swan.

"In the end of Iune, or beginning of Iuly, came into our harbour two ships of Master *Westons* aforesaid, the one called the Charitie, the other the Swan, hauing in them some fifty or sixty men sent ouer at his owne charge to plant for him."‡ There is a discrepancy of about a month between the date of the arrival of these vessels as given by Winslow and the date given by Phineas. The latter says:—"8 or 9 weeks after this, to of our ships Arived att Plimoth." By "this" he refers either to the time of the arrival of his party at Plymouth in the latter part of May, 1622, or to the subsequent trip to the fishing fleet for provisions. In either case "8 or 9 weeks after" would bring the Charity and Swan to Plymouth the end of July or the first of August, 1622.

Shortly after the arrival of these two vessels Weston's men began the settlement of Wessagusset. The leading man was Richard Greene, a brother-in-law of Weston. He died, however, on a subsequent visit to Plymouth and was succeeded by John Sanders. For a time all went well. The Wessagusset settlers, however, had never experienced the rigors of a New England winter and consequently made little or no preparation against the severe winter months. Levett says in his "Voyage into New England":—"they neither applyed themselues to planting of corne nor taking of fish, more than for their present

* "Good Newes," 11. † Bradford's History, 78, 79. ‡ "Good Newes," 13.

use, but went about to built Castles in the Aire, and making of Forts, neglecting the plentifull time of fishing. When Winter came their forts would not keepe out hunger, and they hauing no provision beforehand, and wanting both powder and shot to kill Deare and Fowle, many were starued to death, and the rest hardly escaped. There are foure of his men which escaped, now at my plantation, who haue related unto me the whole businesse."*

As the season advanced the situation of the settlers became perilous in the extreme. Provisions ran short and many of them actually died of starvation. Their loss in numbers, want of food and isolated position placed them completely in the power of the natives. Late in 1622 (old style) the Indians formed a plan to cut off the English both at Wessagusset and Plymouth on the same day. Phineas, then about 30 years old, learning of the intended massacre, resolved to warn the settlers at Plymouth and ask their assistance. No one being willing to accompany him, he determined to go alone.

Waiting for a favorable opportunity, he said good-bye to his friends and with considerable difficulty eluded the vigilance of the Indians and set out alone on his perilous undertaking. The Indians, learning of his escape, pursued him, but without success.

"I Run Southward tell 3 of ye Clock, but the snow being in many places, I was the more distresed becaus of my ffoot steps. The sonn being beclouded, I wandered, not knowing my way; but att the Goeing down of the sonn, it apeared Red; then hearing a great howling of wolfs, I came to a River; the water being depe & cold & many Rocks, I pased through wth much adoe. Then was I in great distres—ffant for want of ffood, weary with Running, ffearing to make a ffier because of y^m^ y^t^ pshued me. Then I came to a depe dell or hole, ther being much wood falen into it. Then I said in my thoughts, this is God's providence that heare I may make a fier. Then haveing maed a fier, the stars began to a pear and I saw Ursa Magor & the . . . . pole yet fearing . . . . beclouded. The day following I began to trafell . . . . . but being unable, I went back to the ficr the day ffal . . . . sonn shined & about three of the clock I came to that part . . . Plimoth bay wher ther is a Town of Later Time . . . . Duxbery. Then passing by the water on my left hand . . . cam to a brock & ther was a path. Haveing but a short Time to Consider . . . . ffearing to goe beyond the plantation, I kept Running in the path; then passing through James Ryuer I said in my thoughts, now am I as a deare Chased . . . the wolfs. If I perish, what will be the Condish. . . . of distresed Einglish men. Then finding a peec of a . . . I took it up & Caried it in my hand. Then finding a . . of a Jurkin, I Caried them under my arme. Then said I in my . . . . God hath giuen me these two tookens for my Comfort; y^t^ now he will giue me my live for a pray. Then Running down a hill J . . . an Einglish man Coming in the

* Baxter's "Christopher Levett, of York," 125, 126.

path before me. Then I sat down on a tree & Rising up to salute him said, 'Mr. Hamdin, I am Glad to see you aliue.' He said 'I am Glad & full of wonder to see you aliue: lett us sitt downe, I see you are weary.'"

Bradford says, referring to Phineas' dangerous undertaking:—"In y[e] meane time, came one of them from y[e] Massachucts with a small pack at his back, and though he knew not a foote of y[e] way yet he got safe hither, but lost his way, which was well for him for he was pursued, and so was mist. He tould them hear, how all things stood amongst them, and that he durst stay no longer, he apprehended they (by what he obserued) would be all knokt in y[e] head shortly."* "*This mans name,*" writes Nathaniel Morton, "*was* Phinehas Pratt, *who hath penned the particular of his perilous Journey, and some other things relating to this Tragedy.*"†

Phineas reached Plymouth on March 24, 1622/3. The minor dates are given by Winslow and the context gives the year. He writes:—"The three and twentith of March being now come, which is a yeerely Court-day, . . . we came to this conclusion, That Captaine *Standish* should take so many men as he thought sufficient to make his party good against all the *Indians* in the *Massachuset-bay*; . . . but on the next day before hee could goe, came one of M[r]. *Westons* Company by land vnto vs, with his packe at his backe, who made a pitifull narration of their lamentable and weake estate."‡

Two or three days after his coming, according to Phineas, and the next day (March 25, 1623),§ according to Winslow, Captain Myles Standish and his party started on the expedition which resulted in inflicting on the Indians the doom they had in store for the English and in saving the remnant of the Wessagusset colony.

It was evidently not Phineas' intention to part from his own company entirely, for when he arrived at Plymouth after his difficult and dangerous journey, he only asked that "hee might there remaine till things were better settled at the other plantation."§ After Myles Standish rescued the Wessagusset party from their perilous position and relieved their immediate necessities, a majority of them decided to abandon the settlement and make their way home, while some of them chose to return with Standish and join the Plymouth colony. "Now were M[r]. *Westons* people resolued to leaue their Plantation and goe for *Munhiggen*, hoping to get passage and returne with

* Bradford's History, 94.

† "New England's Memorial" (Boston, 1721), 57.

‡ "Good Newes," 37, 38. § Ibid., 39.

the fishing ships. . . . Some of them disliked the choyce of the body to goe to *Munhiggen*, and therfore desiring to goe with him to *Plimouth*, he tooke them into the shallop: and seeing them set sayle and cleere of the *Massachuset bay*, he tooke leaue and returned to *Plimouth*, . . ."*

As soon as he was physically able, Phineas rejoined his company at Piscataqua. Those of the Wessagusset colony who returned to Plymouth with Standish had no doubt told Phineas of the plan of the majority of the party to return to England, if they could, by way of Monhegan Island, and it is quite possible that he, too, went to Piscataqua in the hope of securing passage home in one of the fishing fleet. But whatever his plan may have been, he did not return to England and we find him a little later engaged in skirmishes with the Indians at Dorchester and at Agawam (Ipswich), but he does not tell us what took him to those places. "Three times we fought with them" he says in his petition to the General Court in 1668, referring to the encounters with the Indians at Wessagusset, Dorchester and Agawam.

"In the latter end of Iuly and the beginning of August,"† 1623, according to Winslow, the Anne and the Little James arrived at Plymouth. Some time between their arrival and the beginning of 1624 (old style) there was a division of land at Plymouth among the passengers of the Mayflower, Fortune and Anne on the basis of one acre to each person for seven years' continual use.‡ This division must have been after August 14, 1623, for William Bradford's wife, Alice Bradford, shared therein, and they were married on that date. It was probably made late in 1623 (old style), very likely in March, just before the April planting of 1624. Phineas is put down among the Anne's passengers and was assigned one acre. He must, therefore, have returned to Plymouth prior to the division and settled there.

As to why he shared in the division at all, not being a passenger by either the Mayflower, Fortune or Anne—it is very likely that when he returned to Plymouth and expressed a desire to remain there he was received as an inhabitant and permitted to share in the subsequent allotment of land. Joshua Pratt, with whom he is associated in the list of the Anne's passengers, is not known to have been related to him.

As an inhabitant of Plymouth Phineas' name occurs frequently in the colony records during his residence there and

* "Good Newes," 44, 45. † Ibid., 51.

‡ Mayflower Descendant, I: 227–230.

after he went to Charlestown. The following extracts are from the original records except in one or two cases which are indicated. It appears that he was a joiner, and he so calls himself in various deeds and in his will.

1623. Mentioned in a list which follows "The fales of their grounds which came over in the shipe called the Anne according as their were cast. 1623." *

This was the division of land among the passengers of the Mayflower, Fortune and Anne made probably in March, 1623 (old style). The probable reason why Phineas was included in this division has already been mentioned.

1627, May 22. Assigned to Francis Cooke's company in the division of cattle.

"To this lot fell the least of the 4 black Heyfers Came in the Jacob and two shee goats." †

1627. Appears on a list of "The Names of the Purchasers" of Plymouth. [Court Orders, II: 244]

1633. Mentioned in a list of "The Names of the ffreemen of the Incorporacon of Plymoth in New England An: 1633." [Court Orders, I: 1]

1633, March 25. Taxed nine shillings. [Court Orders, I: 9]

1633, October 28. "Phineas Pratt referred to further hearing at the same time about the goods of Godbert Godbertson & Zara his wife." [Court Orders, I: 35]

1633, November 11. "At this Court Phineas Prat appointed to take into his possession all the goods & chattels of Godbert Godbertson & Zarah his wife & safely to preserue them according to an Inventory presented upon oath to be true & just by m^r^ Joh Done & m^r^ Steph. Hopkins." [Court Orders, I: 37]

Godbert Godbertson was the stepfather of Mary Priest (daughter of Degory Priest) whom Phineas married.

1633/4, January 2. Taxed nine shillings. [Court Orders, I: 61]

1633/4, March 10. "Whereas Phineas Prat joyner in the behalfe of Marah his wife is possessed of thirty Acres of land neer unto the high Cliffe the said Phineas & Marah haue exchanged the fee simple thereof wth m^r^ Thomas Prence for other thirty Acres of land at Wynslows stand and next adjoyning to an other portion of land belonging to the said Phineas: But whereas there is a brooke w^th^in the said thirty acres thus

* Mayflower Descendant, I: 230. † Ibid., I: 149.

exchanged & acknowledged by mutuall consent whereat John Come Gent may freely make use of, It is granted to him his heires or assignes provided he so make use of the said water as the said phineas be not annoyed thereby. but either by convenient inclosure at the Cost of the said Joh. or otherwise shall saue harmeles the said phin. & his heires from any detri[t] or annoyance that shall or may befall them the said Phines & Marah their heires & assigne[s]" [Court Orders, I: 57]

1635/6, March 2. "At the same Court, A Jury of twelue being impaniled and charged in the moneth of ffebr foregoing to enquire after the death of John Deacon in the behalfe of our Soveraigne Lord the king. gaue in their verdict as followeth in their owne words and under their hands, viz[t]

"Having searched the dead body we finde not any blowes or wounds or any other bodily hurt. We finde that bodily weakenes caused by long fasting & wearines by going to & fro wth extream cold of the season were the causes of his death.

"Their names were John Jenny John Cooke Will Basset Joseph Rogers William Hoskins, Thomas Cushman George Partridge Stephen Tracy Abraham Peirce Richard Cluffe Tho. Clarke Phineas Pratt." [Court Orders, I: 87]

1635/6, March 14. "At a generall meeting the 14th of March concerning the hey grownds for Plymoth & Duxburrough" it was ordered "That Phineas Pratt haue between ffr Billington and his owne howse." [Court Orders, I: 88, 89]

1636, November 7. "At the same time Tristram Clarke appointed to haue eight Acres of land fowr in breadth & two in length on the south side a porcon allotted formerly to m[r] John Coombe between Phineas Pratt & widow Billington." [Court Orders, I: 96]

1636/7, January 14. "Januar 14th 1636 There is graunted this day by the Court of Assistants to James Skiffe Tenn acres of lands lying next vnto the lands graunted to Thirston Clarke (five in length & two in breadth) betweene the lands of Phineas Pratt & widdow Billington five acres whereof are part of those lands due vnto him for his service Donn to m[r] Isaack Olerton and thother fiue acres are in the right of Peter Talbott for service by Indenture prformed to Edward Doty." [Court Orders, I: 98]

1636/7, March 7. His name appears in a list of Plymouth freemen. [Court Orders, I: 104]

1636/7, March 20. There is assigned "To Phineas Pratt and m[r] Coomes the hey ground they had the last yeare." [Court Orders, I: 110]

1637, July 12. Edward Dotey sells to Richard Derby his property at the "high Cliffe" purchased of Joshua Pratt, Phineas Pratt and John Shaw. [Plym. Col. Deeds, XII: 20]

1637, October 2. Is a juryman at the meeting of the General Court. [Plym. Col. Judicial Acts, 3]

1640, June 1. Granted five acres of land.* [Court Orders, I: 236]

1640, August 3. "fforasmuch as it appeareth by the testymony of Josuah Pratt & otherwise that The two acrees of vpland lying at Wellingsly brook on the north side of the lotts giuen Godbert Godbertson, were giuen by the said Godbert Godbertson to John Combe gent & Phineas Pratt in marriage wth their wiues his Daughters The Court Doth confirme the said two acrees vnto the said John Combe & Phineas Pratt their heires and assignes for eu^{r}." [Court Orders, I: 241]

1640, August 5. "Memorand the fift day of August 1640 That John Combe gent and Phineas Pratt joyner Do acknowledg that for and in consideracon of the sum of three pounds sterl to them in hand payd by John Barnes of new Plymouth haue freely and absolutely bargained and sould vnto the said John Barnes his heires & Assignes all those two acrees of vpland wch they had of Goodbert Godbertson in marryage wth their wiues lyinge on the North side next to the Towneward of that parcell of vpland at Wellingsley brooke wch fell to him by lott in the first Diuisions, and all their right title and interrest of and into the said two acrees of vpland wth all and singuler thapp^{r}tences thereto belonging To haue & to hold the said two acrees of vpland wth all and singuler their app^{r}tences vnto the said John Barnes his heires Assignes foreuer To the onely p^{r}per vse & behoofe of him the said John Barnes his heires & Assignes for euer." [Plym. Col. Deeds, I: 101]

1640, November 2. Granted six acres of "meddowing in the North meddow by Joanes Riuer." [Court Orders, I: 249]

1642, April 5. John Combe sells to Thomas Prence "all those his two acrees of Marsh meddow lying before the house of the said Thom Prence at Joanes Riuer next to the Marsh meddow of Phineas Pratt . . ." [Plym. Col. Deeds, I: 138]

1642, May 7. Joshua Pratt sells to Edward Dotey "one acre of vpland lying at the heigh Cliff betwixt the lands of Phineas Pratt & John Shawe . . ." [Plym. Col. Deeds, I: 142]

1642, December 31. John Barnes sells to Edward Edwards

* This entry is crossed out in the original records.

certain property purchased from Thomas Hill and "the two acrees of vpland lying at wellingsly brooke lately purchased of Mr John Combe & Phineas Pratt . . ." [Plym. Col. Deeds, I: 154]

1643, August. Appears on a list of Plymouth men able to bear arms. The same year (no minor dates given) his name, crossed out and with interlinear notation "gon," appears on a list of Plymouth freemen. [Plym. Col. Records, VIII: 174, 187] His name was crossed out and the note made, of course, after he left Plymouth.

1644, June 22. "At a Townes meeting the xxiith June 1644

"In case of Alarume in tyme of warr or Danger these Divisions of the Towneship are to be observed. & these companys to repaire together

At Joanes river	mr Bradfords famyly one mr Princes one mr Hanbury one mr Howland one ffrancis Cooke one Phineas Pratt Gregory Armestrong John Winslow mr Lee"

Of the other two companies the first was ordered to assemble "At the Ele river" and the second at Wellingsly. [Plym. Town Rcds., I: 27]

1644, October 30. Edward Edwards sells to Thomas Whitney the property which was formerly Thomas Hill's and "the two acrees bought of phineas Pratt" by John Barnes and sold to him (Edwards) December 31, 1642. [Plym. Col. Deeds, I: 154]

1644, November 5. "The fift of Novembr 1644 Memorand That Thomas Bunting dwelling wth Phineas Pratt hath wth and by the consent of the said Phineas put himself as a servant to Dwell wth John Cooke Junior from the fifteenth Day of this instant Novembr for and During the terme of eight yeares now next ensuing and fully to be compleate and ended the said John Cooke fynding vnto his said servant meate drink and apparell During the said terme and in thend thereof Double to apparell him throughout and to pay him twelue bushells of Indian Corne. The said John Cooke haueing payd the said Phineas for him one melch cowe valued at v^{li} and fourty shillings in money and is to to lead the said Phineas two loades of hey yearely During the terme of seauen yeares now next ensuinge." [Court Orders, II : 106]

PHINEAS PRATT OF PLYMOUTH AND CHARLESTOWN.

1646, September 17. "The .17. of y^e .7. month .1646. phineas prate came before ye Goue^r and acknowledged the sale of his house & land, with all ye appurtenances thertoo belonging; to John Cooke, according to a deed then exhibited which they desired might be recorded Also his wife came before ye Gou^r and gaue her consente to ye same sale.

"Allso Samuell Cudberte did ye same day & year aboue writen, freely relinquish all ye claime, title, or Intrest, that he euer had, or might pretend to haue, to any parte, or parcell of ye lands afforsaid As also from those for which they were exchanged with m^r prence. And did freely giue, grante, and make ouer all ye right, and Intreste that he euer had, or hereafter, should haue, or at any time might pretend to haue, to any parte or parcell of ye lands aforesaid, and those mentioned in ye deede Insuing to Phineas Prate, & his heires, & assignes for euer ; for his, & their onely proper vse & behoofe.

William Bradford Gou^r" *

The .26. of August .1646.

These presents doe witnes that Phineas Prate of Plimoth Joyner, for & in consideration of ye sume of twenty pounds sterl: to be payed by John Cooke Jun of plimoth afforesaid planter, in maner & forme following, that is to say fiue pounds to be payed in cloathing within one month nexte after ye date hearof fiue pounds in march next, either in wheat, or comodities, fiue pounds in a milch cowe as shee shall be prised by .2. Indifferent men chosen by either party one, and ye last .5^{li}. this time twelfe months. Hath freely and absolutly barganined and sould, & by these presents doth bargaine & sell vnto the said John Cooke, all y^t his house, & howsing, and

* The autograph of Governor Bradford is appended to the original entry.

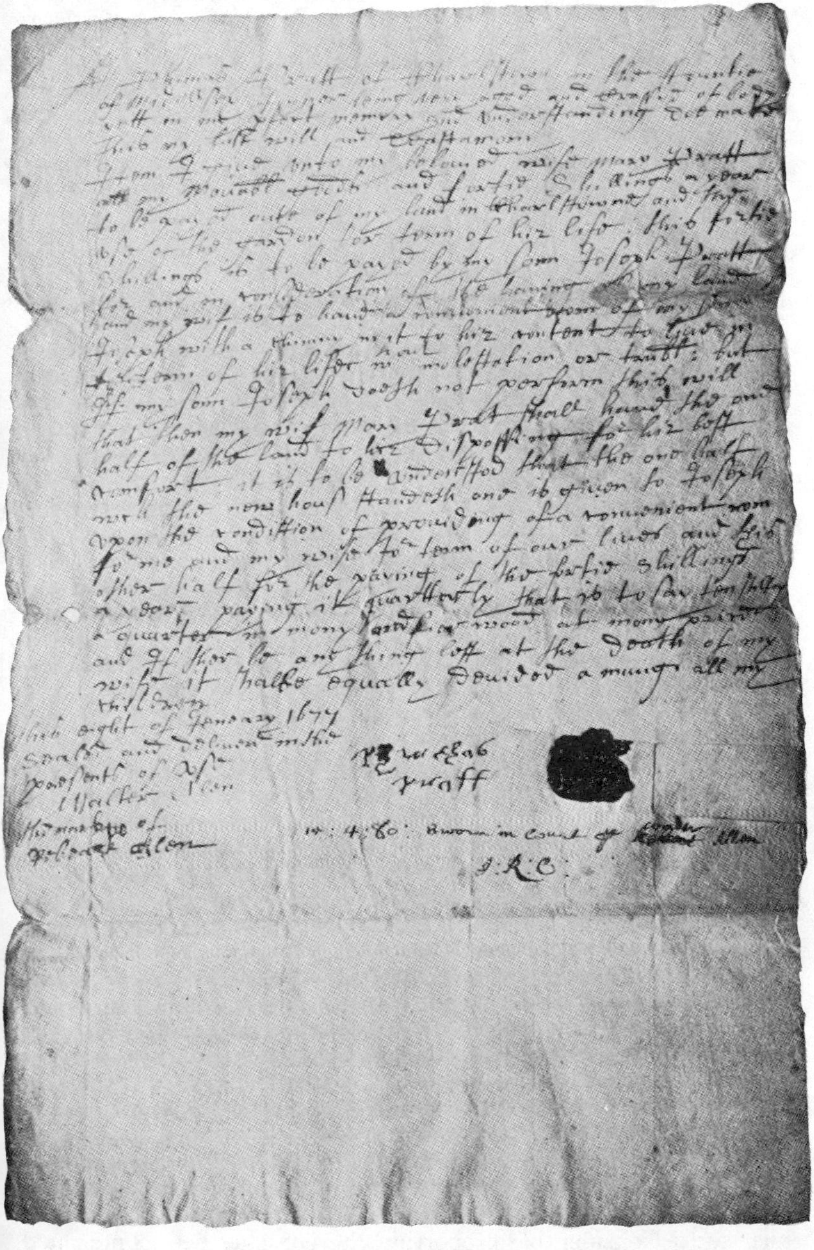
I Phinehas Pratt of Charlstown in the Countie of Middlesex being now aged and weake of body yett in [illegible] perfect memory and understanding doe make this my last will and testament
Item I give unto my beloved wife Mary Pratt all my moveable goods and fortie shillings a year to be payed out of my land in Charlstowne and the use of the garden for term of her life. this fortie shillings is to be payed by my son Joseph Pratt for and in consideration of the having of my land and my wif is to have a convenient room of my son Joseph with a chimney in it to her content to have [illegible] the term of her life without molestation or trouble; but if my son Joseph doeth not perform this will that then my wif Mary Pratt shall have the one half of the land to her disposing for her best comfort it is to be understood that the one half with the new hous standeth one is given to Joseph upon the condition of providing of a convenient room for me and my wife for term of our lives and the other half for the paying of the fortie shillings a year paying it quarterly that is to say ten shillings a quarter in mony and fier wood at mony price and if ther be any thing left at the death of my wife it shalbe equally devided amungst all my children
this eight of January 1677
sealed and delivered in the presents of us
Walter Alen
the marke of Robert Alen
Phinehas Pratt
14:4:80 Sworn in Court by [illegible] Robert Allen
J. R. C.

PHINEAS PRATT'S WILL

gardine place and orchard (excepting ye fruite trees now growing therin, or so many of them to be deliured to the said Phineas, or his assignes when he shall demande them, so it be in due time) and fiftie acres of vpland tow acres of meadow at Joanes riuer, and all and singuler the appurtenances thervnto belonging, and all his right, title, & Interest of & into ye same, & euery parte, & parcell thereof; to haue & to hold the said house, housing, garden, and orchard (excepting before excepted) the fiftie Acers of vpland, and ye .2. Acres of meadow at Joans riuer, with the sixe Acres of vpland meadow, at the great meadow with all, & euery their appurtenances, vnto the said John Cooke, his heirs, & assignes, for euer. and to the onely proper vse, & behofe of him the said John Cooke, his heires and assignes for euer, and with warranties against all people, from by or vnder him, claiming any righte, title, or Interest of, & into the said premises or any parte or parcell therof, and espetially against Samuell Cudberte his heirs, & assignes for euer by these presents; And the said Phineas Prate doth further Couenante and grant by these presents, that it shall & may be lawfull too, & for the said John Cooke either by him selfe, or his Atturney to enrole, or recorde the title or tenure of these before the Gouernour for ye time being, according to ye vsuall order & manor of enrolling & recording deeds, & euidences in his Maties Court at plimoth in shuch case made, & prouided In witnes wherof the said Phineas Prate hath herevnto sett his hand & seale the day & year first aboue writen

In ye presence of — Phineas Prate
Ralfe Whoory
William Pady
Thomas Willet
Nathanell Sowther

And in consideration of ye sume of .2s. 6d. to ye said Phineas Prate in hand paid hath freely, & absolutly bargained & sould vnto ye said John Cooke all his right title & Interest, of & into any lands lying at the head or ende, of ye afforesaid bargained premises before the sealing and delivery of these presents. [Plym. Col. Deeds, I: 224]

1650, October 24. Thomas Prence sells to John Cooke, Jr., "two acars of mersh meddow bee it more or lesse lying before the house and land of the Elder Cushman at Joaneses riuer next vnto a prcell of meddow which was samtimes Phenias Prats;" [Plym. Col. Deeds, I: 329]

The same year (no minor dates given) in recording the bounds of a grant of land in 1641 to John Cooke, Jr., at "Rockey nooke," reference is made to "the lots adioyning which the said John Cook hath bought of Phenias Prat;" [Plym. Col. Deeds, I: 350]

1658, June 5. "June the fift 1658 liberty was graunted by the Court vnto Phenias Prat or any for him to looke out a prcell or tract of land to accomodate him and his Posterite withall together with other ffreemen; or alone as hee shall think meet and to make reporte of the same vnto the Court; that soe a Considerable proportion thereof may bee Confeirmed vnto him;" [Court Orders, III: 139]

1664, June 8. "In reference vnto the Request of Phineas Pratte; and the Elder Bates in the behalfe of the Children of Clement Briggs; That wheras they the said Phineas Pratt and Clement Briggs haue not had theire proportions of land with others of this Jurisdiction formerly Called Purchassers or old Comers; That they might haue some Consideration of land in that respect in a p^r^cell or tract of land lying neare vnto the line betwixt the massachusetts Jurisdiction and vs neare vnto Waymouth; The Court Doth graunt vnto the said Phineas Pratt and vnto two of the said Clement Briggs his sonnes viz: Dauid Briggs and Remember Briggs three hundred and fifty acrees of the said lands with all and singulare the appurtenances thervnto belonging vnto them and theire heires and assignes for euer viz: vnto the said Phineas Pratt two p^r^tes of three of the said three hundred and fifty acrees; and the remainder therof vnto the two sonnes of the said Clement Briggs afornamed and this to bee layed forth for them by John Jacob of hingham and John Whitmarsh of Waymouth and incase any Indian or Indians shall heerafter lay claime vnto the said lands That the said Phineas Prat and the Elder Bates stand bound to the Court to answare the Charge of the Purchase therof and all other nessesary Charges about the said land;"

marginal note:—

"this land was layed out afterwards by order of the court by John Whitmarsh and John Jacob and is att the Path that leads from Waymouth to Bridgwater; as it is said a litle brooke running through the same" [Court Orders, IV: 75]

1664, October 4. James Lovell, of Weymouth, desires to take up land "neare the place where Phenias Prat and the sonnes of Clement Briggs were accomodated; between theire land and the line of the Pattent;" [Court Orders, IV: 82]

1665, June 7. "A Certaine p^r^cell of meddow or such swampy ground as tendeth towards meddow is graunted by the Court vnto Pheneas Pratt and James Louell lying on the westerly side of Phenias Pratts land that was graunted vnto him the last June Court neare vnto the line betwixt the Massachusetts and this Jurisdiction the said p^r^cell being about foure or fiue acrees bee it more or lesse to bee equally Deuided betwixt them the said Pheneas Pratt and James Louell to them and theire heires and assignes for euer" [Court Orders, IV: 102]

1668, October 29. "In Reference vnto the Request of James Lovell for to haue an addition of swampey land neare vnto his land hee hath in the right of m^r^ Nathaniel Souther The Court haue ordered that m^r^ Constant Southworth and Cornett Studson shall view the said land and alowe him twelue acrees therof; besides that which hee hath alreddy graunted vnto him with Phenias Pratt;" [Court Orders, V: 3]

1672/3, January 1. Phineas and Mary Pratt, of Charlestown, sell to John Shaw, Sr., of Weymouth, the land granted by the Court June 8, 1664, and June 7, 1665. [Plym. Col. Deeds, III: 271]

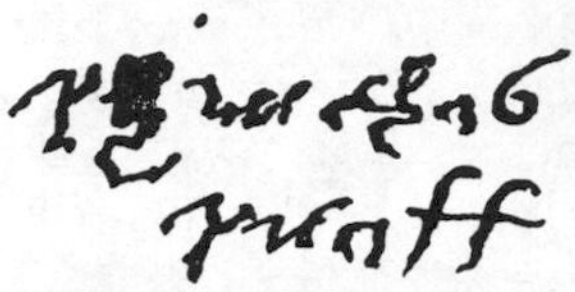

From his will dated January 8, 1677/8.

The foregoing records are interesting as determining within a comparatively brief period the time of Phineas' settling at and leaving Plymouth, as indicating the part of the town in which he lived and as showing that he was regarded as one of the "old comers" or "Purchasers" of Plymouth. But their chief interest and value is in serving to identify his wife and to fix the approximate date of his marriage. These two interesting details are dwelt upon later.

From Plymouth he removed to Charlestown, where, on May 20, 1648, he bought a house and garden from George Bunker. It is impossible to say just when he left Plymouth. He sold his home there August 26, 1646, and is described in the deed as being "of Plimoth." On September 17, three weeks later, he and his wife appeared before the Governor, he to ask to have the deed recorded and she to give her consent to the sale, so they were no doubt still living there at that time. He is described in the Charlestown deed as being an inhabitant "in the same towne" as the grantor, *i. e.*, Charlestown. He must, therefore, have left Plymouth in the interval between the recording of the Plymouth deed September 17, 1646, and the purchase of the Charlestown property May 20, 1648.

The entry made in the records by John Greene, town clerk, concerning the transfer of the Charlestown house and land is as follows:—

A sale of a House and a garden in Charltowne By George Bunker vnto Phinias Prat the 20th of the 3d month 1648.

Know all men by these presents That I George Bunker Inhabitant in Charltowne have sould assigned and set over, and by this declare that I doe sell assign and set over unto Phinias Prat Inhabitant in the same towne A House or Tenement with a garden to it adioyning: which house and garden stands and is scituate in Charltowne in the great through fare street which goes from the Neck of land into the market place, this hous and garden stands right over against the way that goes up to the windmill hill, and that way which goes intoo elbow lane, the house is bounded on the front by the street way, or by the west, and the hous and garden is bounded East by the back street which goes to the pitt where the Beasts drinke, and where the Creek begins wch runs on the back syde of the maiors garden into Charls River, and it is bounded Northward by samuell Howard, and south ward by Thomas Carter senior: Alsoe I Georg Bunker doe acknowledg my selfe to bee fully payd and satisfied for this sayd hous and garden, And I doe heer by resigne all my Right, Titell, and interest vnto the sayd house and garden vnto the sayd Phinias Prat to be his and his heigres for ever.

John Greene.

[Charlestown Book of Possessions, 117]

This property was sold April 10, 1711, to Benjamin Lawrence by Phineas' son Joseph who inherited it. [Middlesex Co. Deeds, XV: 501]

On March 1, 1657/8, there was a division of land in accordance with "The Returne of the Committee, Apoynted by the Inhabitants of Charltowne, for the division, of the wood and Commons one Mistick syde," and Phineas drew lot No. 54 containing 2½ commons and a certain proportion of woodland. [Book of Possessions, 87]

In 1662 he presented to the General Court of the Massachusetts Bay Colony that interesting and valuable paper which he called "A Decliration of the Afaires of the Einglish People [that first] Inhabited New Eingland." Either accompanying or following this document was a petition on which the General Court took the following action May 7 of the same year (1662):—

In Ansr: to. ye petition of. phineas Prat. of charls Toune. who presented this Court wth a narrative of the streights & hardships that the first planters of this Colony vnderwent in their endeavors to plant themselves at plimouth. & since wherof he was. one The Court judgeth it meet to Graunt him Three. hundred acres of land where it is to be had not hindering a plantation *

A few years later, June 1, 1665, there is the following entry in the Court records:—

Layd out to Phineas Pratt of Charls Toune three hundred acres of land (more or lesse). in the wilderness. on the East of merremack Riuer neere the vpper end of Nacooke brooke on the South East of it it begins at a great sare Pjne standing anent the midle of nacooke pond & joyneth. to the ljne of fiue hundred acres of land lately granted to the Toune of Billirrikey on the south of it ninety sixe pole & so continues a streight ljne two hundred & sixe pole further vnto a white oake bounded wth P from thence it turnes vnder the side of a great hill one hundred fifty & two pole vnto another white oake marked wth P. which stands on the North side of an other great hill. & on the south Corner of a little swampe from thence

* Mass. Bay Rcds., IV: 402.

it runns neere the west & by south. two hundred pole to a great Red oake bounded as before. from thence the closing ljne to the first Pine is two hundred & ninety pole. the exact forme of it together wth the rule of finding the exact lines is fully demonstrated by this inclosed plott taken of the same 20 8mo 1664.

By Jonathan Danforth. survejo[r]

The Court Allows & approoues of this Returne.*

In October, 1668, Phineas, then about 75 years old, presented another petition to the General Court in which, while expressing his thankfulness for the grant of land made him three years before in answer to his first petition, he refers to his physical infirmities and present lack of the actual necessities of life and entreats that he may receive some measure of support in his old age. "Yet my necessity causeth me farther to entreat you," he writes, and there is here an intimation that his first petition had not been answered quite as he expected — that he had asked for bread and had been given a stone in the shape of three hundred acres of land in the wilderness. The Court acted unfavorably on the petition now presented, not recognizing his claim to further assistance. This paper does not appear in the Court records and a careful search fails to find it among the unpublished State Archives. It is reprinted here from an article by Mr. Richard Frothingham, Jr., in the Massachusetts Historical Society Collections (Fourth Series, IV, 487), in which it was printed for the first time from the original, then evidently in Mr. Frothingham's hands, with the following prefatory note, viz: — "This Petition is printed from a manuscript of the date of 1668, as is evident from the autograph attestation of Torrey and Pyncheon, though it is so unlike the 'Declaration,' both in composition and chirography, as to make it certain that it is not in the handwriting of Pratt."

To the Honoured the Generall Court, holden at Boston, this Oct. 1668.

I acknowledg my self truly thankfull unto the Honoured Court for that they gave me at the time I presented an History called, A declaration of the affaires of the English people, that first inhabited New England. Yet my necessity causeth me farther to entreat you to consider what my service hath been unto my dread Soveraign Lord King James of famous memory. I am one of that litle number, ten men that arrived in Massachusets Bay for the setling of a Plantation, & am the remainder of the forlorn hope sixty men. We bought the south part of the Bay of Aberdecest their Sachem. Ten of our company died of famine. Then said y[e] Natives of the Countrey, let us kill them, whilst they are weak, or they will possesse our Countrey, & drive us away. Three times we fought with them, thirty miles I was pursued for my life, in time of frost, and snow, as a deer chased with wolves. Two of our men were kill'd in warr, one shot in the shoulder. It was not by the wit of man, nor by y[e] strength of the arme of flesh, that

*Ibid., IV: 471.

we prevailed against them. But God, that overrules all power, put fear in their hearts. And now seeing God hath added a New England to old Engl. and given both to our dread Soverg Lord King Charles the second, many thousand people enjoy the peace thereof; Now in times of prosperity, I beseech you consider the day of small things; for I was almost frozen in time of our weak beginnings, and now am lame. My humble request is for that may be for my subsistance the remaining time of my life. And I shall be obliged.

Your thankfull servant,

Phinehas Pratt.

The Deputyes Doe not Judge meete to graunt this petition, wth refference to the consent of o^r^ Hono^ed^ magis^ts^. hereto.

William Torrey, Cleric.

The Magistrates consent wth their bretheren the Deputys.

Jo: Pynchon, Pr Curiam.

Phineas had apparently reached a point where he required assistance. He was old and he was lame, a condition which materially impaired his ability to provide for himself. The Selectmen of Charlestown came to his relief in a most generous manner, as the following extracts from the town orders will show, and the assistance granted Phineas during his lifetime was extended to his widow.

1668/9, January 25. "Also ordered Counstab^le^. Jno. Hayman to supply Phineas Pratt with so much as his p^r^sent low Conditiō. may require." [Charlestown Town Orders, III: 96]

1669, March 26. "This day also m^r^ Rand^ll^. Nicholes was desired to deliver to Phineas Pratt 200 foote of good bords fitt for his use this on the townes Acco^tt^. to be repaid him in season." [Town Orders, III: 100]

1677, October 1. "Order to Zech. Johnson Constable to pay to ye Necessity of ffather Prat forty shillings in pay as sutablc as he can & place it to ye townes Acco^t^." [Town Orders, III: 205]

1678, December 4. "Ordered Severall Bills to be graunted viz. Two of 20^s^. Each to Tho: Smith 2d. Counts for keeping Swains Childe To Good. wf. Parker a Bill to Goodm: Clew for 20^s^ for her p^r^s^t^ relief To Goodm Pratt a Bill for 40^s^.

pr J R Recorder"*

1679, October 6. "Ord^r^d. y^t^ 20^s^. In mony be given Phenius. Pratt for his releefe. & this to be payd by Constable. Newell

By ye ord^r^ of ye Selectmen J: N R"†

1679, December 14. "Ord^r^d. y^t^ Phenius. Pratt. hath twenty shillings In mony allowed for his Releife. payd by J N:

J: N: R:"‡

* Town Orders, IV: 2. † Ibid., IV: 16. ‡ Ibid., IV: 17.

Phineas' wife was Mary, daughter of Degory and Sarah (Allerton) (Vincent) Priest. She was born in Leyden, Holland, probably within a year or two after the marriage of her parents November 4, 1611. Neither she nor her sister nor mother came with Degory Priest in the Mayflower to Plymouth in 1620. After her husband's death there on January 1, 1620/21, the widow married Godbert Godbertson at Leyden November 13, 1621, and, with her two daughters, Mary and Sarah Priest, came with him to Plymouth in the Anne in 1623.

There Mary Priest met and married Phineas Pratt. It has been frequently stated that they were married in 1630. There is not a particle of evidence in the Plymouth records to support this statement, though it must be admitted that neither is there any evidence to disprove it. The most the records prove is that they were married *after* the division of cattle May 22, 1627, and *before* Godbert Godbertson's death, which occurred prior to October 24, 1633, the date of the inventory of his estate. [Mfr. Desc., I: 154]

The division of land in 1623 contains the names of the heads of families only, but the division of cattle May 22, 1627, contains the names of all persons in the colony at the time (except possibly some of the servants), grouped in families. Thus, in the Godbertson family, we find Godbert Godbertson, Sarah Godbertson, Samuel Godbertson, Mary Priest and Sarah Priest. The order in which the names of the sisters occur indicates that Mary was the older, for, in those cases where the relative ages of the children are known, the children are found arranged in order of birth, the males first.

Phineas died in Charlestown April 19, 1680, and a stone still marks the spot where he is buried in the Old Burying Ground. He was born about 1593, as is shown by his deposition already printed in this magazine. [II: 46]. His wife survived him, dying probably just prior to July 22, 1689, for on that date there is the following entry in the town orders: —

> Then Mr Jacob Green Senr & Mr Eleazr Phillips were & are Impowered to Apprize the goods of Widd. Pratt who lately decd at Tho Barbar. and to dispose of the same for the sattisfing her Debt to Tho. Barbars wife. & as their discretion shall direct them. And so to make returne thereof to the selectmen at their next meeting
>
> By ordr of the selectMen
>
> Jno Newell *

It is evident from this item that the provision in Phineas' will for the permanent use by his widow of a room in their

* Town Orders, IV : 93.

house had, probably by an agreement between the mother and son, either not been carried out or the arrangement had been terminated.

During his long residence in Charlestown Phineas appears only once in the land records as grantor and that is on January 21, 1662/3, when he and his wife Mary sold to John Smith a wood lot in Charlestown's further common.* On December 31, 1681, Mary Pratt, Phineas' widow, and her son Joseph sold to Solomon and Samuel Phip[p]s a cow common within the limits of the Charlestown stinted common on the south side of Mystic River.† On January 1, 1681/2, Joseph sold to John Simpson a certain piece of land in Charlestown and the deed was signed not only by Joseph but also by Mary Pratt, his mother, and Dorcas Pratt, his wife, as interested parties, although Joseph is the only grantor mentioned in the body of the deed.‡ On February 14, 1680/81, there was a division "of the Stinted Comons in Charles Towne on this Side Mistick river," among the proprietors thereof and Mary and Joseph were jointly allotted one common containing an acre and a half.§

The two following items from the town orders show that the aid given Phineas was generously extended to his widow:—

1683/4, February 5. "Then orderd Twenty. Shill. vnto Widow Pratt & Twenty Shill to Wido Davie wch is for their releifes." [Town Orders, IV: 56]

1686/7, March 7. "Then Agreed yt Mr Jno Call Supply the Wido Pratt wth what she needs for her releife: Like wise to supply Tho Orton & Tho March wth Bread" [Town Orders, IV: 84]

Phineas' will‖ was made January 8, 1677/8, and probated June 15, 1680. An inventory‖ of his estate was made May 21, 1680, and presented in Court June 15, 1680. From it we learn that the widow had been appointed executrix. For some reason the 300 acres of land granted him by the General Court in 1662 and laid out in 1665 were not included in the inventory. Daniel Fletcher was appointed administrator of this portion of the estate December 28, 1722, and on May 6, 1723, Henry Farwell, Joseph Blanchard and Thomas Blanchard were ap-

* Middlesex Co. Deeds, X: 136. † Ibid., VIII: 499.

‡ Ibid., IX: 245. § Book of Possessions, 235, 236.

‖ Middlesex Co. Probate Files, First Series, No. 12,762.

pointed to appraise this property. They reported on November 25, 1723, that they valued it at £135. One of the most interesting and valuable papers connected with the settlement of the estate is that dated July 31, 1738, and endorsed "Phineas Pratts Children."* It is as follows: —

July 31. 1738.

The Return of the Commiss^{rs} appointed to apprize & Destribute the Real Estate of Phinehas Pratt late of Charlstown Dec'd — (Commission wanting) read — present, sundry of the Heirs.

memorand^{m} — say To the Children severally (if Liveing) or to their Heirs (if Deceas'd)

John is Dead }
& Peter Dead } Ergo — say only to their Heirs each to give Bond to refund, &c.

Each one his share to be allotted to him when he shall have given Bond to refund, &c,

Is p^{d} 5 settlement & 6/ for 6 Bonds. p^{d} by James Perry.

John Pratt Decd Saml Daniel Peter Decd Mary	Sureties	Saml. Pratt of Middlebury Wheelwright William Swan of Camb^{e}. Husbandman Will: Thomas of Middleborough Gentleman James Perry of Charlestown Chairmaker.

Joseph }
Aaron } their shares bought by Danl: Fletcher
Mercy }

Recd. settlement, Recording, Bond &c 14. p^{d}. by Will: Swan.

charges of settlement advanced

by Sam. Pratt	26—14—3
by Wm Thomas	10—03—0
by Wm Swan	3—14—0
by James Perry	11—15—6
	52—6—9

1/9th whereof is 5—16—$3\frac{2}{3}$.
Commission not returned.

The estate was settled in this year (1738). A remarkable feature is the unusual period, fifty-eight years, which intervened between Phineas' death and the final division.

The children of Phineas and Mary (Priest) Pratt were: —

1. John, married Ann (or Anna), daughter of John and Anna (Williams) Barker, in or before 1664. The information regarding Ann's parents was not secured until after the printing of the article on her husband, John Pratt, in the third volume of this magazine. 2. Samuel. 3. Daniel. 4. Peter. 5. Mary. 6. Joseph. 7. Aaron. 8. Mercy.

* Middlesex Co. Probate Files, First Series, No. 12,762.

WILL.*

I Phinias Pratt of Charlstown in the Countie of Midellsex Joyner being very aged and Crazye of body yett in my pfect memory and vnderstanding doe make This my last will and Teastamoen

Item I giue vnto my belouied wife Mary Pratt all my mouabl goods and fortie Shillings a year to be payed oute of my land in Charlstowne and the use of the gardon for term of hir life: this fortie Shillings is to be payed by my sonn Joseph Pratt for and in consideration of the hauing of my land and my wif is to haue a conuenient room of my sonn Joseph with a chimny in it to hir content to liue in for term of hir life. without molestation or trubl; but If my sonn Joseph doeth not perform this will that then my wif Mary Prat shall haue the one half of the land to hir Dispossing for hir best comfort: it is to be vnderstod that the one half wch the new hous standeth one is giuen to Joseph vpon the condistion of prouiding of a conuenient room for me and my wife for term of our liues and this other half for the paying of the fortie Shillings a year paying it quartterly that is to say ten shllig a quarter in mony and fier wood at mony price and If ther be any thing left at the death of my wife it shalbe equally deuided a mung all my children.

this eight of Jeneary 1677 Phinehas Pratt

Sealed and deliuerd in the
presents of Use

Walter Alen
the marke of
Rebeack Alen

15 : 4 : 80 : Sworn in Court pr Walter Allen
J : R : C :

INVENTORY.

Ann Innvytory of the Estat of Phinias Prat of Charlstown deceased

a psell of land	18	00	00
In primis in woolen clothes of his	01	10	00
It in linning shirts	00	09	00
It 8 pillober & 5 napkins	00	13	00
It 5 sheetts	01	04	00
It 4 blanckitts & 2 rugs	02	05	00
It a bed boulster & pillo	02	10	00
It a small bed	00	08	00
It 2 culbards 2 Chests one box	01	05	00
It peuter	02	02	00
It 2 bras Skillitts 5s a warmg pan 5s	00	10	00
It 2 Iorn potts on Skillit	00	09	00
It 2 Iorn keettells	01	06	00
It a tramil & fring pan	00	03	00
It a small tabell 2 chayers	00	05	00
It a pr of hose 2 bages	00	04	00
It earthen war 5 trenchers	00	02	06
It wooden ware	00	02	00
It a hachit a houldfast a froue	00	05	00

* See illustration facing page 129.

It lumber	00	16	00
It bookes	00	08	00
	16	16	06
	34	16	06

thes goods are prized by
Larenc Dowce & henery Balcom
the 21 : 3 : 1680
15 : 4 : 80 Sworn in Court by the executrix Mary Pratt
as attest, Tho : Danforth. R.
Added. 4. 12. 81. Cow comon in charlstown stinted comon. 06 00 00

GEORGE SOULE'S AUTOGRAPH.

By George Ernest Bowman.

The only autograph of George Soule of the Mayflower of which I have yet learned is his signature as a witness to the will of John Barnes of Plymouth, and was written 6/16 March, 1667/8. Soule was the first witness to sign, and fortunately "Senr" was written after his name. This proves conclusively that the witness was George Soule of the Mayflower and not his son, George^2.

An examination of the half-tone reproduction of the will, facing this page, shows that Soule wrote a very good hand, but there are evident signs of trembling, which may have been due to age.

The will is preserved in the "Scrap Book" in the Registry of Deeds at Plymouth. It is written on the first page of a four-page folio, and is in fair condition. The pages are twelve and one-fourth inches tall by seven and seven-eighths inches wide. The top of the first page has evidently been used in place of a copy book.

The second witness, Samuel Seabury, married for his second wife Martha^3 Pabodie (*Elizabeth*^{2} *Alden, John*^{1}).

In this will John Barnes calls Henry Samson's wife (Ann Plummer) his cousin. This connection will probably be helpful in finding her ancestry.

The will was recorded in the Plymouth Colony Wills and Inventories, Volume III, Part I, page 31, from which the record of the probate is taken. The transcript of the will is made from the original document.

The last Will and Testament of Mr John Barnes of Plymouth in New England late Deceased; exhibited to the court

GEORGE SOULE'S AUTOGRAPH

held att Plymouth the 29th of October anno Dom 1671 on the oathes of Mr Samuell Saberry and Samuell hunt as followeth;

New Plimoth. New England. 6th. of March. $16\frac{6}{6}\frac{7}{8}$

The Last will & Testament of John Barn's which is as follow's.

To All whome these may concern. Know you That I John Barn's being of my Sound understanding &c: doe declai^re This to be my last will and Testament. Knowing not how soon y^e lord may call me out of this world. doe theirfore labor to give noe occasio' of striffe unto those that shall Survive me: But that peace may be Among them:

1. In the first place I doe desire that my body be decently buryed all y^t all Funerall charges be Exspended out of my psonall Estate

2. That all Legacys be pay'd, before any division of my Estate be may'd

3. I doe apoynt y^t my dear wife Joan Barn's & my Sonn Jonathan Barn's be ye Executo^rs of this my last will and Testament

4. I doe Bequeath unto my wife Joan Barn's half of Every pt and pcell of all my houseing and lands y^t I doe now possess in ye Township of New Plimoth dureing The Tearm of her life.

5. I doe bequeath unto my unto my Sonn Jonathan the other half part of my sayd houseing land's &c: fforEver unles my say'd Sonn shall forfitt it on condittion's as ffollow's in an oyr* pt of this my will.

6. I doe bequeath all my land lying Near to Road Island unto my grandsonn John Marshall. as alsoe ye silver dish y^t I doe usually use to Eate in

7. I doe bequeath to my Cozen ye wife of henery Samso. forty shillings out of my Estate to be pay'd Beffore division of my Estate.

8. I doe Bequeath my moveable Estate as follow's one third to my wife for Ever in Case she shall not molest any pson to whome I have fformerly sould any Land's unto in Case she shall soe doe, y^n it shall ffall to Sonn, or grandson John Marshall. ye Next Third I doe bequeath to my sonn Jonathan In Case he doe not demand any pt of That Estate y^t fformerly I gave to my daughter Lyddyah. Now deceased. in Case he

*This is evidently a mistake for "other." The copy in the Colony Records reads: "in any one."

shall Soe doe y^n third shall ffall unto my grandson John Marshall ffor Ever The Next (t)hird I doe bequeath to my gr(an)dchildren now in being togeither wth my Kinswoman Ester Ricket to say to Each of y^m an Equall pt of y^t my Estate: hopeing That my last will may be an Instrument of peace; shall cease waiting for ye Time of my chang,

9. I doe Further Request and desire Elder Thos: Couchma L^t: Ephraem Morton and Joseph Warren to be the overseers of this my Last will and Testament

Signed and sealed In
ye p^rsence of
George Soule Senr:
Saml: Seabury
samuell hunt

his mark
John I B Barnes
(seal)

This Will is recorded according to order p^r me Nathaniel Morton Secretary see book of Wills and Inventorys recorded begining att 71; in folio 31

WILLIAM BREWSTER.

His True Position in Our Colonial History.

[*An Address Delivered before the Massachusetts Society of Mayflower Descendants, 13 February, 1902, at Boston.*]

By Hon. Lyman Denison Brewster.

The story of the Mayflower and Plymouth Rock is the story of the formation of a little Separatist or Congregational Church at Scrooby, England, its escape to Holland, its migration from thence to Plymouth, and its establishment there as the first embodiment in America of freedom in the Church and equality in the State.

William Brewster cradled the church at Scrooby, in his own home. He devoted his means to the support of its ministers and the succor of its members. After suffering fine and imprisonment and risking his life for this heresy, he helped the little flock to Holland, where his duty as elder intrusted him especially with the discipline and building up of the Church and the preservation therein of soundness of doctrine. This duty he successfully performed with great gentleness and equal firmness. While in Leyden his arrest was sought for publishing Protestant books for circulation in England and Scotland.

He was in every respect the co-equal and colleague with Robinson in all the measures for preparing the voyage to America, and shares with Carver and Cushman the honor of procuring the requisite London assistance.

That he drafted the Compact of November 21, 1620, in the cabin of the Mayflower seems almost certain. That he was the moral, religious and spiritual leader of the Colony during its first years of peril and struggle and its chief civil adviser and trusted guide until the time of his death is quite certain. But for his ecclesiastical position he would have been Governor of the Colony.

So that, while it was perhaps unfortunate, as a matter of good taste, that Rev. Ashbel Steele entitled his valuable biography "Chief of the Pilgrims: or The Life and Time of William Brewster"—unfortunate, since the modest Elder of Plymouth was the last man in the world to institute comparisons with his brethren, it is nevertheless true as a matter of history that he was indeed in the fullest sense "The Chief of the Pilgrims." And it is also true that having the rare felicity to be both the founder of the first free Church in America and also the founder of the first free colony in America, he was in a sense in which no other man, not even Roger Williams (as I shall show) can claim the honor—the first Apostle of both civil and religious liberty on this continent.

In the light of recent research he stands out more clearly than ever, the leading figure of the Mayflower and of Plymouth. In the prime of his intellectual vigor, in the 54th year of his age, the only reason why the Elder was not chosen the first Governor of the Plymouth Colony, says Hutchinson in his History, was that "He was their ruling elder, which seems to have been the bar to his being their Governor—civil and ecclesiastical office, in the same person, being then deemed incompatible." Perhaps an equally cogent reason was that an outlawed exile would hardly be "persona grata" to the officers of the Crown.

Some subsequent historians, not realizing that, as Judge Baylies says, "the power of the church was then superior to the civil power," or the true reason of the apparent but not real subordination of the Elder to the Governors (Carver and Bradford), have failed to give to the heroic Elder the supremacy he deserves over each and all, as the heart, brain and soul of the new Plymouth enterprise, without whom it could hardly have been attempted, with whom it became the most memorable and successful pioneer colonization on the American continent after its discovery by Columbus.

Let me mention some of the admirable qualities of his leadership. Not intending in the least to suggest a word in derogation or depreciation of the good qualities, nay the grand qualities of those superb fellow Pilgrims, Bradford, Winslow, Carver and Standish, I will state briefly what he was, what he accomplished.

Of gentle birth, educated at Cambridge, a courtier before he was twenty years of age, in high esteem with Her Majesty's Secretary of State, treated by him more like a son than a servant, soon a member of the English Embassy to Holland, after loyally and faithfully serving his patron Davidson who was deposed from his high position by the perfidy of the Queen, he, after suffering years of persecution in building up the Mayflower church at Scrooby, left his native land, his position and his fortune, to be an exile in Holland and a pilgrim in America.

A word each on his scholarship, his statesmanship, his saintliness and his standing among the Founders of States.

First, as to his scholarship and ability as a lay preacher. It was always known that he was a trained scholar of the greatest of English Universities, but it remained for the late Dr. Dexter to show the depth and breadth, the fulness and ripeness of his learning and wisdom. Dr. Dexter wrote to me that he regarded him as the ablest man of the first generation of New England colonists, and no man was better qualified to give that judgment. While a persecuted refugee in Leyden he published and in some instances himself printed and edited both popular and erudite theological treatises in Latin and English. While living in his log house in Plymouth, built by his own hands, he yearly received supplies of newly published books in Latin and English, and his library was inventoried at his death in 1644 at four hundred volumes.

Dr. Dexter took the brief headings of the inventory deciphered by Mr. Winsor and tracing out the books through the leading libraries of England and Europe, restored the full titles. Sixty-two were in Latin and ninety-eight commentaries on or translations of the Bible. Dr. Dexter says:

"It is my strong impression that it is very doubtful whether, for its first quarter-century, New England anywhere else had so rich a collection of exegetical literature as this."

With such a scholar to explain the Scriptures, which was the chief function of the pulpit in those days, it is no wonder that when a minister who came over in 1629 was chosen to be the Plymouth pastor, the people "finding him to be a man of low gifts and parts, they, as providence gave opportunity, improved others as his assistants." And this scholar worked with his own hands to build his house in Plymouth, and afterwards in Duxbury, and up to the age of nearly eighty helped to cultivate his own farm. And there is nothing to show, says one biographer, in the records that he ever asked for or received any salary.

But the crowning glory of this wealth of learning and knowledge was this. For thirty years it was devoted constantly, utterly and superbly to the people with whom he had cast his hazardous lot. All he could learn he freely imparted to those he taught.

He was a scholar and preacher from the people, with the people, for the people and to the people, and in their close companionship of toil and danger the people did indeed hear him gladly. Of their place of worship and order of assembling De Rasiere, a wise observer from Holland in 1627 gives this often repeated but always interesting sketch:

He says: "Upon the hill they had a large square house, with a flat roof, made of thick sawn planks, stayed with oak beams, upon the top of which they have six cannons, which shoot iron balls of four and five pounds, and command the surrounding country. The lower part they use for their church, where they preach on Sundays and the usual holidays. They assemble by beat of drum, each with his musket or firelock, in front of the captain's door; they have their cloaks on, and place themselves in order, three abreast, and are led by a sergeant without beat of drum. Behind comes the Governor, in a long robe; beside him on the right hand comes the preacher with his cloak on, and on the left hand the captain with his side-arms and cloak on, and with a small cane in his hand; and so they march in good order, and each sets his arms down near him. Thus they enter their place of worship, constantly on their guard night and day."

How much Governor Bradford, the excellent governor of the colony for over thirty years, owed not only to the guidance, but to the training, teaching and companionship of his old neighbor, comrade and life-long friend, his grateful words bear full witness. He says of Brewster that "he was foremost in our adventure in England and in Holland and here." John Brown of Bedford calls him "The Great Heart of their pilgrimage." Dr. Griffis says "from the first Brewster was the soul of the Plymouth colony."

The devout Elder was regarded with the utmost veneration and reverence in his later years by the colonists of the eight towns into which the little settlement of 1620 had grown. Hence I think the popular impression of the old patriarch pictures him with the austere severity and rigid narrowness of an old iron-sides, rather than with the "sweetness and light" of Hampden and Milton. Nothing could be further from the truth. Humblest and gentlest of men, his flock almost worshipped him because they loved him and had reason to love him, while that love was returned in full measure, and the chronicle says of his death in which he "so sweetly departed this life unto a better": "We did all grievously mourn his loss as that of a dear and loving friend."

Of his personal qualities Bradford says: "He was wise and discreet and well spoken, having a grave and deliberate utterance, of a very cheerful spirit, very sociable and pleasant amongst his friends, of an humble and modest mind, of a peaceable disposition, undervaluing himself and his own abilities, and sometimes overvaluing others; inoffensive and innocent in his life and conversation, which gained him the love of those without, as well as those within. . . . . He was tender-hearted, and compassionate of such as were in misery, but especially of such as had been of good estate and rank, and were fallen unto want and poverty, either for goodness and religion's sake, or by the injury and oppression of others. . . . . In teaching, he was moving and stirring of affections, also very plain and distinct in what he taught. . . . . He had a singular good gift in prayer, both public and private. . . . . He always thought it were better for ministers to pray oftener, and divide their prayers, than be long and tedious in the same."

"He taught twice every Sabbath, and that both powerfully and profitably, to the great contentment of his hearers, and their comfortable edification; yea, many were brought to God by his ministrie. He did more in this behalf in a year, than many that have their hundreds a year do in all their lives." Bradford's whole eulogy of his beloved friend and pastor is the most pathetic and beautiful passage in his History of New Plymouth so lately restored to the State of Massachusetts.

Next as a statesman. If the acorn is judged by the oak it produces, he had no superior in that age of great statesmen. How far-reaching the policy that foresaw that the refugees must leave Holland, if they would preserve their English morals with their English freedom! How tersely in the short Social Compact which we believe he penned, impromptu apparently, in the cabin of the Mayflower is the whole genius of "Liberty, Equality and Fraternity" put in a few lines! Well has it been called the "germ of all our American Constitutions and Declarations of Right"—"Magna Charta reinforced by the spirit of the Dutch Common-wealth."

Professor Goldwin Smith in his brilliant little book called "The United States Political History 1492–1871" tells us that the recital, in the Compact signed on the Mayflower, of the colonists' allegiance and fealty to King James was a great and serious mistake and "created a relation false from the beginning," that in it "lay the fatal seeds of misunderstanding" etc. On the contrary the mistake is all on the side of the Professor. Not to have acknowledged that fealty and allegiance would have been false and if interpreted as seriously intended would have been suicidal. It was because they intended to be English colonists and English freemen that they left Holland. In all the business of procuring their charter that fealty is assumed and this allegiance and fealty is reiterated and reaffirmed in the Plymouth Code of 1636, of whose drafters the Elder was one.

How superior the wise, peaceful, just and courageous policy of the Plymouth Colony in its treatment of the Indians and its fellow colonies! And the man who always had the last word in these important matters—the Joshua and Nestor of the plantation was Elder William Brewster. Here again see the crowning glory of his success as a political philosopher. He put his glorious theory of Equality and Fraternity into practice, and Liberty could not help being the result. The first Plymouth town meeting of equal citizens with equal rights had in it the seeds of Yorktown and Gettysburg. It was the first clear prophecy of the Republic which was to extend from ocean to ocean.

Dr. Gregory of Edinburgh in his recent work on Puritanism, cool and judicial Scotchman as he is, sums up the consensus of historians when he says "It is not too much to say that in a very real and profound sense the Mayflower carried with her the destinies of the world. Her crew (evidently the doctor means her passengers) were not only the pioneers of civil and religious liberty, they were the heralds of a faith which tested by the heroic men it has formed and heroic actions it has produced may indeed challenge comparison with any faith by which men have been moulded and inspired. The struggle they were called upon to wage was a struggle for liberty not only in the New World but in the old, and but for the planting of Puritanism in New England the victory of Puritanism in the

Mother Country would have been short lived, and shorn of its most characteristic features and products." And in spite of all criticism Bancroft states but a fact when he says that "in the cabin of the Mayflower humanity recovered its rights and instituted government on the basis of equal laws for the general good."

Dr. Gregory in summing up the influence of the Mayflower and Plymouth Rock, wisely and justly, it seems to me, merges and blends the Pilgrim Separatist and the Massachusetts colony Puritans as exerting essentially the same influence after 1630 on subsequent history, since all the Puritans of New England soon became Separatists.

Better than all, he was a saint in a church where saint worship was abolished. Of his own sincere, devout, spiritual, religious faith and practice every day of his exiled life bore witness. But what especially distinguished him as a religious leader in those days was his breadth, toleration and charity. When that sturdy and heroic heretic Roger Williams in Plymouth denounced the Mother Church in England as Anti-Christ, pronouncing it sinful to attend its worship or to fellowship with it, the more charitable Leader of the Pilgrims refused to go with him or to hold to any such nonsense. In fact the spiritual descendants of William Brewster and John Robinson were not more Jonathan Edwards and the New England Calvinists than Phillips Brooks, Horace Bushnell, Henry Ward Beecher and Charles Briggs. "The Pilgrims were neither Puritans nor Persecutors" was the motto I saw some years ago written over the spot across the street from which Elder William built his house. But in reality the Pilgrim was, as Dr. Dexter says, "The Puritan in the superlative degree."

John Robinson and Roger Williams are justly praised as the fathers and apostles of religious toleration in their age. But William Brewster was more Catholic and tolerant than either, at an earlier date.

"Paget" according to Powicke in his recent Life of Henry Barrows "says that Robinson had 'tolerated' his fellow elder 'for this long time' in this practice" and "this practice" was the custom of hearing ministers of the Church of England, and it is a touching evidence of the Elder's influence on the life and belief of his beloved pastor that there was found in the study of John Robinson after his decease a treatise on "The Lawfulness of Hearing of the Ministers of the Church of England." We have already seen how on this very point the Elder of Plymouth was more tolerant than Roger Williams in the new colony. The sturdy leader who surpassed both John Robinson and Roger Williams in true catholicity and toleration before 1620 may well stand for the Pioneer of Religious Liberty in New England and America.

The claim that the Elder was in the slightest degree blameworthy in advising the Plymouth Church to accept Roger Williams' petition for a dismissal from that church to the church in Salem will hardly pass muster with any student of history thoroughly conversant with the "chip on the shoulder" characteristics of the great Founder of Rhode Island, or who has thoughtfully read Bradford's words of tender regret at the parting — words which undoubtedly echoed the sentiments of the Elder.

It seems to me that Dr. Gregory's criticism of the unstinted laudation of the intrepid Baptist by Mr. Strauss when he puts him on a level with Luther and Cromwell is fully justified. There seems to be a lack of historical perspective.

Easily first among the Pilgrims (for Robinson the master mind of all was not a Pilgrim as he stayed on the other side of the seas and is out of the comparison), how does the scholar, teacher and sainted father of the first colony of New England stand among the founders of states? Lord Bacon puts the founders of States in the first rank of the Great Men of the world. It seems to me that depends on the motive, and method of their achievements. Where conquest and greed are the motives and treachery and bloodshed the methods, I see nothing to admire or respect. But what colony was ever founded on loftier aims, with more devoted sacrifice and by more honorable methods than that which was started in possession at Plymouth two hundred and eighty two years ago. Its free spirit has taken possession of the continent. The man whose thought originated, whose spirit pervaded, whose presence stimulated, whose counsels preserved that colony in its infancy can well bear comparison with any of the famous colonizers of the continent.

It was no accident that made William Brewster the planter of a great church, and pioneer of a great state. The long schooling in Holland after the sharp persecution in England seems to have educated the Pilgrims and their great leader to a more gracious spirit, a more Christian sense of the relations of man to man than was possessed by the subsequent New England colonists. There was less bigotry, no persecution and little of the superstition and narrowness that darkened the history of most of the other New England colonies. The bond that kept together that immortal band through flood and famine, pestilence and peril, was not commercial or primarily political. It was religious and spiritual. It was faith in God and the Gospel of the Christ. And their spiritual leader full of that faith himself, inspired his flock with his own zeal and moulded the colony not only during his own life but for a whole generation after. The very symmetry and perfection of William Brewster's character, have in a sense prevented a full and just recognition of his services to church and state.

But to my mind the entire sanity, moderation, self-restraint, the grand common-sense of the founder of Plymouth constitutes one of his most attractive characteristics. Too often, alas, have the reformers of the world, the founders of states and systems had the one-sided vehemence of a John the Baptist instead of sharing something in the serene dignity and repose of the Master. Patience, humility, indomitable fortitude, unquenchable hope, purity of life and purpose, kindliness of heart, sympathy for the weak and poor, fidelity to the death for all that is right, absolute abhorrence for all that is wrong, are they not worthy human qualities although their possessors forsooth be termed Puritans? But these pilgrims although puritans of the puritans in their moral steadfastness, were also free in a large degree from the narrowness, intolerance and vulgarity that have elsewhere sometimes characterized those who held the name. How much of this freedom must we fairly attribute to their leader and teacher? See the effectiveness as well as the quality of his work! In England he not only made of his home a Meeting house, but he provided its pastors and devoted his means and his life to his brethren who sought to reform what he and they believed the unscriptural practices of the Church established by law. When the little flock had gathered again after their hazardous flight to Holland, not only did his printing press at Leyden furnish to Scotland and England exactly the English Protestant literature which the Reformation most needed, but his wise eldership contributed no less than the genius of Robinson to preserve and shape a church worthy of being the pioneer church of New England.

In Plymouth — elder, advisor, Nestor of the little band, Dr. Dexter tells us there is every reason to believe the English books of his library were openly accessible to all and formed in reality the first Public Library of New England. A preacher who never had been a priest, a pastor who had never been an ordained clergyman, he was the fitting leader of a band of Independents who were to found a Church without a Bishop as well as a State without a King. Opposed to all ritualism and formalism, to any ceremonials not in their opinion plainly enjoined by the word of God, the Plymouth Colony, under the Elder's wise and able guidance preserved a moderation, sanity and freedom from extravagance and superstition not always prevalent in the other Puritan Colonies.

There have been many saints in Old England and in New England well beloved we may believe of God and man, but how many of his energy and of such influence on the future, who were so free from asceticism, fanaticism, ignorance and superstition? How many unembittered by such persecution, unnarrowed by such isolation? This "Chief of the Pilgrims" was a Puritan of the Puritans in all that makes puritanism a power for good, for purity, for piety, for valor, and a terror to evil doers, but in nothing else. The sourness, the barrenness, the vulgarities of puritanism seemed left out of Elder Brewster's composition.

And it is a pleasant thought, I am sure, for every member of our society to realize that the more the records are searched, the more clearly it appears that the spiritual leader of our Pilgrim Ancestors — the transplanter of the first New England Meeting House, the suggester of the first New England town-meeting, was in everything throughout his life, in everything we know of his thought and action, a noble Christian gentleman.

THE PORTIONS OF STEPHEN HOPKINS' DAUGHTERS, AND THE ESTATE OF ELIZABETH[2] HOPKINS.

Transcribed from the Original Records,

BY GEORGE ERNEST BOWMAN.

STEPHEN HOPKINS bequeathed all his movable estate, not specifically mentioned, to his four daughters, Deborah, Damaris, Ruth and Elizabeth, to be equally divided between them.* The division of this property, made by Caleb[2] Hopkins and Myles Standish, is recorded in Plymouth Colony Wills and Inventories, Volume I, folios 65 and 66.

Caleb[2] Hopkins died before 1651,† but no record of the settlement of his estate can be found on the Plymouth records. It is possible that the land sold by Elizabeth[2] Hopkins to Jacob[2] Cooke (*Francis*[1]) was a part of Caleb's estate.

The agreement concerning Elizabeth's estate shows that

* Mfr. Desc., II: 12. † Ibid., I: 13.

she had disappeared and that her relatives thought that she was probably dead.

[fol. 65] The sev^r^all porcons of the children of m^r^ Steven Hopkins Deceased as they were Devided equally by Capt Myles Standish Caleb Hopkins their brother

To Deborah Damaris Ruth and Elizabeth.

Debrahs porcon

	l	*s*	*d*
Inpris i bed boulster pillowe & a phillip & cheney petty-coate	04	10	00
It i silver spoone	00	08	00
It i wrought cov^r^ing and an old blankett	00	16	00
It 3 sheets	00	08	00
It i pillow beere	00	03	00
It i Diapr napkine	00	02	06
It i great Chest	00	08	00
It i alkemy spoone	00	00	02
It i Iron pott i bras pott i bras skellet & a Kettle	01	02	00
It 5 trenchers 2 peuter platters i bason i quart pott 2 poringers i tinnen candlestick half a pint pot	0	12	00
It i paire of scales and waights	00	05	00
It Due for hempe	00	02	00
It more for part of a cloake	00	10	00

Damaris porcon

Inpris i feather bed boulster pillow a stray bed a suite of cloathes another pettycote and a beaver muffe	04	10	00
It i silver spoone	00	08	00
It ii checker coverings	00	16	00
It i peere of linnen sheets	00	08	00
It i pillow beere	00	03	00
It 2 napkins & 2 table cloths	00	02	06
It i chest box and a Case	00	08	00
It an Alkemy spoone	00	00	02
It i great Cittell	01	02	00
It 5 trenchers 2 pewter platters 1 quart pot i pynt pott i salt 2 porringers i chamber pott i tin candlestick i earthen judg i linke & i sive	00	12	00
It i stoole	00	05	00
It Due for hemp	00	02	00
It for part of a cloake	00	10	00

Ruth Hopkins part

	l	*s*	*d*
Inpris i feather bed pillow & a cloth growne	04	10	00
It i silv^r^ spoone	00	06	00
It i greene rugg & bastable blankett	00	16	00
It i paire of sheets	00	08	00
It i pillow beere	00	03	00
It a table cloth	00	02	06
It linnen wheele i wollen wheele i joyned stoole	00	08	00
It i spoone	00	00	02
It i Kettle a Churne bellowe tonges fire shovell spitt pot hookes gridiron & an Iron to lay before the fyre	01	02	00
It 5 trenchers two platters two porringers a pewter candlestick i puter cup a chamber pot a beaker i cullender & a tinn funell	00	12	00
It i half bushell i half peck ii hand sawes 3 Iron hoopes	00	05	00
It for hemp	00	02	00
It for prt of a cloake	00	10	00

ffor Elizabeth Hopkins as followeth.

The agreement betweene Richard Sparrow on thone prt and Captaine Myles Standish and Caleb Hopkins on thother prt conc^r^ning Eliz: Hopkins

Inpris That the said Richard shall have the said Elizabeth Hopkins as his owne child untill the tyme of her marryage or untill shee be nineteene yeares of age.

2ly. In consideracon of the weaknes of the Child and her inabillytie to prforme such service as may acquite their charges in bringing of her up and that shee bee not too much oppressed now in her childhood wth hard labour It is agreed that Richard Sparrow shall have putt into his hands her whole estate and to have the use of yt for the tyme of her continuance wth him. Onely one heiffer reserved wch is now in the hands of Gyles Hopkins of Yarmouth

[the tearmes of this agreement are fully prformed by Richard Sparrow *]

3 It is agreed that if it should so fall out by the prvidence of God that Goodwyfe Sparrow should be taken away by Death Then Elizabeth Hopkins shalbe free to be Disposed off as Captaine Standish & Caleb Hopkins shall think meete & likewise her estate.

4 That if the wyfe of Richard Sparrow be taken away

* This note is on the margin of the page.

by Death wth in three yeares then he is to be allowed twelve months tyme to pay the estate back againe: if after three yeares till the expiracon of the terme then he is to be allowed nine months.

5 It is agreed that if it should please God to take away the said Elizabeth Hopkins by Death then her estate to returne to Captaine Standish and Caleb Hopkins to be Disposed of amongst the rest of her Sisters according to the Will of m^{r} Hopkins provided Richard Sparrow be allowed convenyent tyme for the payment of the same namely if in three years then twelve months if after then nine months

6. That whensoev^{r} this estate is to be returned Richard Sparrow is to pay it in a Melch Cowe a feather bed and things belonging thereto and the remaynder thone half in wheate and thother in Indian Corne wee meane by the featherbed and things belonging to the same valued and worth as now they are deliv^{r}ed. witnes our hands this xxxth of the ixth month 1644.

The estate to be returned is fifteene pounds one shilling & two pence in manner & forme abovesaid

Witnes our hands

Willm Paddy
Thomas Willet

Myles Standish
Caleb Hopkins
Rich. Sparrow.

[fol. 66] The coppy of note or writing under the hand of the said Richard Sparrow for the payment of a part of Ruth hopkins porcon This witnesseth That I Richard Sparrow of Plymouth have received the half of a Cow from Capt Miles Standish wch is Ruth Hopkins In consideracon of wch I the said Richard Sparrow am to pay to the said Capt Miles Standish in the behalf of Ruth Hopkins and for her use: two yeare old heiffers or two yeare old Steeres at the expiracon of three yeares or sooner, such as shalbe m^{r}chantable witnes my hand this xvth of the 8th 1644

Witnes

Willm Paddy.

Rich Sparrow

May the 19th 1647

These witnesseth that I have received two young steers in full Satisfaction for halfe a Cow which was Ruth hopkins which Richard Sparrow bought of mee upon such tearmes; for which I had a bill of him but this shalbee for a full Discharge, I say received two steers;

Myles Standish

Elizabeth Hopkins to Jacob Cooke.

[Plym. Col. Deeds, II : I : 196]
1657 Prence Govr:

The 10th of October 1657

Memorandum That Elizabeth hopkins Doth acknowlige that for and in Consideration of a valluable sume to her alreddy satisfyed and fully paied by Jacob Cooke of the towne of Plymouth planter shee hath fully freely and absolutly bargained allianated and sold enfeofed and Confeirmed and by these p^{r}sents Doth bargaine sell enfeofe and Confeirme unto the said Jacob Cooke all that her portion or prcell of meddow that shee hath in the great meddow att Joanses river viz ten acres of ffresh meddow bee it more or lesse lying betwixt the meddow of Capt : Thomas Willett and m^{r} John Done runing from woodside to woodside To have and to hold the said ten acres of meddow bee it more or lesse lying in the meddow Comonly Called the great meddow att Joanses river runing and being bounded as above expressed with all and singulare the appurtenances and privilidges belonging therunto ; unto the said Jacob Cooke his heires and assignes for ever The said p^{r}mises with all and singulare the privilidges belonging therunto with all the said Elizabeth hopkins her right title and Interest of and into the same or any prte or prcell therof to belong and appertaine unto the onely proper use and behoofe of him the said Jacob Cooke his heires and Assignes for ever ;

Elizabeth Hopkins' Estate Settled.

[Plym. Col. Wills, II : I : 90, 91]

[fol. 90] An Inventory of the estate of Elizabeth hopkins which is in the hands of Jacob Cooke taken this 6th of october 1659 as likewise what prte of her said estate is in the hands of Andrew Ring an Inventory therof likewise taken the Day and yeare abovesaid and attested on the oathes of the said Andrew ringe and Jacob Cooke before the Court and by the Court ordered to be recorded as followeth

	ll	*s*	*d*
Imp^{r} : one Cow	03	00	00
It a yeare and vantage heifer	01	10	00
It halfe a Cow Calfe of this yeare	00	07	00
It five ewe sheep	04	00	00
It one sheep weather	00	08	00
It one ewe lambe and an halfe	00	15	00
It one weather lambe and an halfe	00	14	00

It one kittle att 2 bushells of wheat	00 08 00
It a quart pot	00 01 00
It att Gorge Bonums one Cow	03 00 00
It halfe a yearling heiffer	00 15 00
It halfe a Calfe	00 07 00
It a rugge one pillow one bedd one blankett and bolster	05 10 00
It one warming pan one pestle and morter	00 10 00
It one brasse Skillett	00 01 00
It one bread grater and an Indian Tray	00 02 00
It 2 old silver spoones	00 10 00
It one garden spott	01 00 00
It one Cow killed the last yeare	03 00 00
It woole	00 16 00
summa	26 14 00

To some thinges remaining in Gyles hopkins hand with a smale matter in Mrs Standishes * hand;

Thomas Southworth John Morton;

[fol. 91] 1659 Prence Govr

A writing ordered by the Court to bee recorded as followeth;

These prsents Testifyeth that wee whose Names are underwritten according to our best understanding have vallued the Cattle that goeth under the Name of Elizabeth hopkinses her Cattle and are in the Custitie of Gyles hopkins and Doe vallue the one halfe of three steers and a poor Calfe att eight pounds and five shillings and one very smale poor Cow and an old Cow being Defective att six pound;

the 29th : 7m : (59) our hands John ffreeman
Edward Banges

Att the Court held att Plymouth the. 5t of october 1659 It was ordered by the Court and agreed by Andrew ringe Jacob Cooke and Gyles hopkins; that incase Elizabeth hopkins Doe Come Noe more; that the prticulars of Cattle above expressed viz: the one halfe of three steers and a poore Calfe and the poor Cow and the old Cow above expressed soe vallued as abovsaid; shalbee the said Gyles hopkins his prte and portion of the estate of Elizabeth hopkins and the said Gyles hopkins accepted therof soe to bee; and therfore these prsents Doth Declare that the said Gyles hopkins Doth heerby quitt Claime unto any more of the said estate of Elizabeth hopkins and that neither hee nor his heires are not to Demaund of; or molest the said Andrew Ringe or Jacob Cooke in the peacable enjoyment of that which they have of the estate of Elizabeth hopkins; neither them nor theire heires or assignes for ever;

* This is the latest known mention of Barbara Standish.

EPHRAIM TINKHAM'S WILL AND INVENTORY.

Transcribed from the Original Records,

BY GEORGE ERNEST BOWMAN.

EPHRAIM TINKHAM died at Plymouth between 17/27 January, 1683/4, the date of his will, and 20/30 May, 1685, the day his inventory was taken. His wife Mary was the daughter of Peter Brown of the Mayflower. The record of the will and inventory are found in the Plymouth Colony Wills and Inventories, Volume IV, Part II, pages 110 and 111.

[p.110] Know all men to whome these p^r^sents shall Come That I Epharim Tincom seni^r^ of the Towne of Plymouth in New England being at ye day of ye date hereof but weake of body, but blessed be god of sound & perfect & well disposing memory not knowing how soon it may please god to Change my Temporall life to death doe therfore make these p^r^sents to be my last will & Testament to Continue for ever firme & Inviolable in manner & forme following: Imp^rmis^ I will & bequeath unto my dear & loveing Wife Mary Tincom my now dwelling house & housing that is in Plymouth with ye orchyard belonging there unto, and all my lands meadowes with ye appurtenances & privildges belonging unto them lying & being in ye Townships of Plymouth Middlebury Dartmouth or any other place in this

Colony whatsoever that belongs to me Excepting such lands as I shall perticulerly dispose of in this my will, I give them all as afforesd unto my wife for her support & Comfort for & during her naturall life : Item I will & bequeath unto my Eldest son Epharim Tincome that hundred acre lott he lives on in ye Township of Middlebury ioyning to ye land of Samuel Wood Item I give to my son Ebenezer Tincom ye other other hundred acre lott that ioynes to my son Epharims to them & their heirs for ever. with ye meadow lands belonging to it lying in Middleburys great meadow, Item, I give & bequeath unto my son Peter Tincome that share of land he now lives on in ye Township of Middlebury neer whetstone vynyard brooke & all ye meadows belonging to it to him & to his heirs for ever, Item : I give unto my son Elkiah one third part of a share of land lying at Dartmouth to him & his heirs for ever Item I give unto my two sons John Tincum & Isaack Tincom that my now dwelling place housing orchards lands meadows & all ye privi-ledges belonging to it after their mothers decease to be equally devided between them, I say to them & their heirs for ever Item I give & bequeath unto my daughter Mary Tomson fifty acres of upland which was given me by ye Towne of Plimouth & lyes in ye Township of Plimouth neer ye place that is com-only caled Momponsett, my will is also what my wife shall leave at her decease be it good or Chattels that it shall be devided amongst my seaven Children my eldest son to have a double portion, my six guns they are already disposed of unto my six sons who have them for their proper use. Item I will & bequeath unto my dear & loveing Wife Mary Tincome my debts being first paid all my goods cattle or Chattles & debts whatsoever are due & belonging unto me & to pay all debts that they lawfully appear that I doe owe, And I doe by these presents appoint & make & ordaine my dear & loveing wife Mary Tincome to be my sole Executrix of this my last will & Testament to administer upon my said estate to pay such debts I owe & receive such debts as are due to me. & to make choyce of my son Epharim Tincome to be helpfull to her in ye same, As also to see my body be decently buried & to defray ye Charge thereof, Thus hopeing that this my last will & Testa-ment will be performed according to ye Tenure thereof. I Comitt my body to ye dust, & my soul to god that gave it By these p^r^sents ratifiing & Confirming my said wife Mary Tin-come to be my sole & lawfull Executrix revoking & makeing void all other my former wills written or verball : In witness where of I ye aforesaid Epharim Tincom seni^r^ have here unto sett my hand & seal this seventeen day of January one thousand six hundred eightie three :

Signed sealed & declared to be my last will & Testament. in presence of
William Hoskins sen^r
Jonathan Shaw sen^r :

Ephriam Tincome senio^r
his mark : **E T** & (seal)

This will was proved in ye Court held at Plymouth ye fifth of June 1685 on ye oaths of William Hoskins & Jonathan Shaw who testified upon oath that they saw Serieant Tincome sign seal & declare this to be his last will & Testament & that he was of disposing mind & memory so to doe :

[p. 111] An Inventory of ye estate of Epharim Tincome seni^r taken & apprised ye 20 day of may 1685 by us whose names ar under written

	li	*s*	*d*
Inp^{r}mis his wearing Clothes & hatt	03	17	0
Item one bible & other smale books	00	17	0
It in ye inner roome one bed & bolster 1 rug 1 pair blanketts one pair sheets	06	00	0
It one bed bolster 1 pair of sheets one pair of blanketts one rug	05	00	0
It 14 yards of Cotton & lining Cloth	01	13	0
It 2 chests & one smale Trunk 4 meal baggs	01	04	0
It one great Wheel one little wheel one hatchell 3 pair of cards	00	17	0
It in ye Kitchen one Copper Kettle	01	00	0
It one smale Table and 4 Chairs	00	10	0
It one old warming pan and litle brass Kittle	00	03	0
It 2 Iron potts one Iron Kettle & posnett	00	17	0
It 3 Tramels & Iron spitt 2 pair pott hooks one pair of tongs & gridiron	01	00	0
It 3 pewter platters one bason & Champer pott	00	13	6
It 2 old pewter pots one little pewter bottle 7 spoons	00	0*	0
It 5 pewter poringers one salt celler	00	04	0
It one lanthorne old candlestick & frying pan	00	02	6
It one earthen pan one stone iug 2 earthen potts	00	02	0
It 2 wooden boles & Trayes & other dishes	00	09	0
It one Churne 3 pailes with other smal wooden things	00	08	0
It in ye Chamber one bed one pair of sheets one pair blanketts one rug	05	10	0
It one pillow 2 pair of pillobees	00	07	0
It one sifeten trough 2 sives one washing tub on halfe bushell & other lumber	01	00	0

* Either 05 or 07.

It also Iron tools 5 sickles 2 sythes & sneath	00	10	0
It 4 axes 2 hows one spade 3 forks with severall other iron tools	02	00	0
It one Cart & plough & tackling belonging to them	03	00	0
It as to Cattell 3 yoke of oxen and 2 steers	21	00	0
It more 8 Calves 1 steer one bull 3 yeerlings	22	00	0
It 23 sheep and 5 swine	09	05	0
It 6 guns and one rapier	04	10	0
It as to his housing & lands in plimouth & lands in middlebury & dartmouth	407	10	0
the whole sum. is	500	17	9
Debts due from y^e^ estate	04	08	4
more Debts due from y^e^ estate	01	10	0

Nathaniel Southworth
Thomas Faunce

MAJOR WILLIAM BRADFORD'S WILL AND INVENTORY.

Transcribed from the Original Records,

BY GEORGE ERNEST BOWMAN.

MAJOR WILLIAM[2] BRADFORD (*Gov. William*[1]) died at Plymouth on Saturday, 20 February /2 March, 1703/4. His will and inventory are found in the Plymouth County Probate Records, Volume II, pages 40–43.

[p. 40] The Last Will & Testament of William Bradford living in the Township of Plimouth in the Province of the Massachusets Bay in New England

I the s^d^ William Bradford being Exercised with many bodily Infirmitys which gives me cause to think the time of my dissolution to be near being of a disposeing mind & memory do make ordaine & constitute this my last will & Testament as followeth.

Imp^r^: I Commit my soul to God my Creator & my body to the dust of the Earth to be decently buried in hopes of a glorious resurection through the meritts of my dear Redeemer the Lord Jesus Christ. As to what outward Estate it hath Pleased God to bless me with I dispose of the same as followeth my debts being all first faithfully fully & truly satisfied and paid.

Imp^r^: my Will is that my Loving wife Mary Bradford have her thirds in my Lands & meadows where I now dwell in the Township of Plimouth as also in all my lands or meadow which I have Elce where not by me heretofore disposed of dureing her naturall life & that she have with David Bradford my son the house in which I live with the barn & orchard by it during her life & after her decease that my s^d^ son David Bradford shall have my s^d^ house barn & orchard to him & his heirs for ever saveing that my Will is that my sons Ephraim Bradford & Hezekiah Bradford shall have so much Interest in my s^d^ house as to have liberty to dwell therein till they can provide for themselves otherwise.

ffurther my Will is that my wife before mentioned shall have a third part of all my goods & Chattells for her own forever togather with a bed & sutable furniture to it

Item to my Eldest son John Bradford I have made over tracts of Lands and meadows as p^{r} deed under my hand & seal appeareth whereon he now liveth further I give & bequeath to him my fathers manuscript viz: a Narrative of the begining of New Plimouth Pareus upon the Revelations and Barriffs Military discipline.

Item To my Grandson William Bradford the son of my son William Bradford deceased I have given tracts of Land & meadow as Appear under my hand & seal further I give to him when he shall come of age one of Mr Perkins his workes.

Item To my son Thomas Bradford I have given a portion in Lands in Norwich (which were the Lands of my brother John Bradford) as p^{r}: deed under my hand & seal may Appear.

Item To my son Samuel Bradford I have given tracts of Land under my hand & seal as may appear;

Item to my son Joseph Bradford a portion of Lands near Norwich aforesaid (which was his Mothers & part I Purchased) as may appear under hand & seal also I give to him the history of the Netherlands, & a Rapier.

Item I give & bequeath unto my four sons John Bradford Thomas Bradford Samuel Bradford & Joseph Bradford all that my Pattent Right which I have to the head of Cape Cod.

Item I give & bequeath to my son Samuel Bradford my right of Commonage or Common Right which I have in the Township of Duxborrough.

Item It is my Will that my sons Israel Bradford Ephraim Bradford David Bradford & Hezekiah Bradford shall have all that my farm or tenement whereon I now dwell togather with all the fences orchads trees and fruittrees [p. 41] ffruittrees (Except what is above Excepted) standing or growing thereon wth all other Lands meadows swamps or right of lands that I now have within the Township of Plimouth lying on the Northerly side of the brooke Commonly called stony brooke with all & singuler the previledges thereof which s^{d} lands meadows farme or tenement aboves^{d} I do by these presents give bequeath & demise to my s^{d} four sons, (that is to say Each of them an Equal part or proportion) to them & their heirs for ever not to be sold given or made away either the whole or any part thereof Except to Each other or some bearing the name of the Bradfords decended from me this I give & bequeath to them hoping they will show themselves very

Carfull of dutifull & Respectfull to my Loving wife their mother dureing her life.

Item It is my will that whereas my son Israel Bradford hath been at charge in building an house upon part of the afores^{d} farm or tenement that he the s^{d} Israel shall have & Enjoy the s^{d} house for his own togather with an acre of land thereunto Adjoining to him & his heirs forever.

Item I will & bequeath to my s^{d} son Israel Bradford my belt & Rapier.

Item I Give to my son Ephraim Bradford one of my musquetts & a table with drawrs.

Item I Give to my son David Bradford my silver Bowl after his mothers decease not to be Alienated from the family of the Bradfords.

Item I Give to my son Hezekiah Bradford my gold ring & a silver spoone.

Item I Give to my Grandson John Bradford, Dr Willets works on Gensis & Exodus.

Item I Give to my Grandson William Bradford the son of John Bradford my silver wine Cup when he Comes of age.

Item I give to my daughter Mercy Steel Hannah Riply Melatiah Steel Mary Hunt to Each of them beside what portion I have already given ten shillings a peice to be paid within a year next after my decease

Item I Give & bequeath to my daughter Alce Fitch a wrought Cushion that was her Mothers.

Item I Give unto my daughter Sarah Baker two of my biggest pewter platters & also a China bason. Also a Cow to be delivered to her within a year after my decease.

Item I Give unto my son Samuel Bradford all my Lattin bookes, to Encourage him in bringing up one of his sons to Learning which said bookes it is my Will that they shall by him be given to his s^{d} son whom he shall so bring up.

Item I Give to Every one of Daughters a good booke which they may chose out of my Liberary.

Item I give to hannah the wife of my son Samuel Bradford m^{r} Borroughs upon the Eleventh of Mathew.

Item It is my will that the rest of my bookes be safely keept by my Executors & In Case my son Samuel shall bring up one of his sons to Learning to be by s^{d} Executors delivered to him when he Comes of age.

I do Constitute & Appoint my Loving sons John Bradford Samuel Bradford & Israel Bradford as Executors of this my last Will & Testament to pay such debts as I owe, to Receive my dues and to see my body decently buried, to defray the charge thereof, And to see my will (as near as they can) in all the perticulers of it performed, thus hopeing that they will faithfully perform such a trust Committed unto them I do Revoke & make void any former will by me at any time heretofore made. I the s[d] [p. 42] I the said William Bradford have hereunto set my hand & seal this twenty ninth day of June one thousand seven hundred & three 1703

Signed Sealed & Declared to be William Bradford (Seal)
his Last Will and Testament
In presents of us
John Rogers
Thomas Loring
Ephraim Little Ju[r]:

Memorand: That on the 10th day of March Annoq: Dom: 1703 the above named Ephraim Little & Thomas Loring two of the witnesses to this Instrum[t]: made oath that they were present with Major W[m]: Bradford late deceased & saw him signe & seal & heard him declare this Instrument to be his last will & Testament & that he was then of a disposing mind & memory to the best of their Judgments And on the 29th day of the same month of march the above named John Rogers the other Witness above named made oath to the same before me.

Nathaniel Thomas Judge of Probates

Pli: ss: Nathaniel Thomas Esq: Appointed & Comisionated Judge of the Probate of Wills & Granting letters of administration &c: to all unto whome these presents shall Come Greeting Know yea that on the twenty ninth day of March in the year of our Lord one thousand seven hundred & four Before me at Plimouth in the County of Plimouth the Will of Major William Bradford late of Plimouth afores[d] deceased to these presents annexed was proved approved & allowed who haveing whilst he lived & at the time of his death Goods Chattels Rights or Creditts in the County afores[d], And the Probate of the s[d] will & power of Comitting administration of all & singuler the Goods Chattels Rights & Creditts of the s[d] deceased & also the hearing Examining & allowing the accompts of the same by virtue thereof Appertaining unto me The administration of all the goods Chattels Rights & Creditts of the s[d] deceased & his will in any manner Concerning is hereby Comitted unto John Bradford Samuel Bradford & Israel Bradford sons of the

s^{d} Deceased & Joynt Executors in the same Will named well & faithfully to Execute the s^{d} will and to administer the Estate of the s^{d} deceased according thereunto & to make a true & perfect Inventory of all & singuler the goods Chattels Rights & Creditts of the said deceased & to Exhibett the same into the Registry of the Court of Probate for the County afores^{d} at or before the twenty third day of June next Ensueing, & also to Render a plain & true accompt of their s^{d} administration upon oath, In testimony whereof I have hereunto set my hand & the Seal of the said Court of Probate, Dated at Plimouth afores^{d} the day & year first above written.
Nathaniel Thomas Register Nathaniel Thomas

Plimouth february 28 1703 The Inventory of the Estate of Major William Bradford deceased taken & apprized by us the Subscribers.

To Wearing apparrill to Cash to a Ring to arms	06 00 00
to Cattell	18 14 00
to Chares & Cushings	00 13 00
to a Chest & Cubbert & trunk	00 09 00
to mantel	00 08 00
to a Carpitt	00 03 00
to Plate	07 10 00
to pewter	01 12 00
[P. 43] To Earthen ware	00 02 06
to Iron ware	01 04 00
to table Linnen	02 00 00
to a bell	00 03 06
to a spining wheel	00 05 00
to a desk & two trunks	00 08 00
to other old Lumber	00 09 00
to bookes	15 03 00
to beds & furniture	14 08 00
to brass & bellmettle	01 08 00
	70 00 00

Thomas Loring
Elisha Wadsworth

Memorandum that on the 10th day of March 170$\frac{3}{4}$ before Nath^{ll}: Thomas Esq: Judge of the Probates &c: Major John Bradford & Samuel Bradford Executors to the last will & testament of their father Major William Bradford Deceased made oath that the above written is a true Inventory of the Estate of the s^{d} deceased so far as they know & when they know of more that they will discover the same.

Nathaniel Thomas Register

JOHN[2] SOULE'S INVENTORY AND THE SETTLEMENT OF HIS ESTATE.

Transcribed from the Original Records,

BY GEORGE ERNEST BOWMAN.

JOHN[2] SOULE (*George*[1]) died at Duxbury, but the date of his death is not known. He died intestate and his widow Hester was appointed administratrix, on 14 November, 1707, by Nathaniel Thomas, Judge of Probate. The record of this appointment is in the Plymouth County Probate Records, Volume II, page 87. The inventory is on the same page. The agreement between the heirs is found on page 91 of the same volume.

[p. 87] The Inventory of John Soul late of Duxbourrough Decease is as it was taken & apprized by us whose names are under written this 3^d^ day of December 1707.

	ll	*s*	*d*
Viz: one Cow & heifer	2	15	0
Wareing Clothes Libery & money	5	00	0
2 swine	0	10	0
beds & beding	8	10	0
Iron Houshold stuff & tools	2	4	0
Brass & Pewter	0	12	0
two Chests with other wooden lumber	1	10	0
flax & table linen	0	10	0
to a mean Cow hide & a maire hide at ye Tanners in Plimouth	0	5	6
one wheel & bag with a Cannoe & spectacles	1	14	6
The Estate of Hester Soul Widdow of John Soul aboves^d^ which she Brought with her is as follows			
Viz: 2 Iron pots with some other Lumber	1	2	0

Thomas Deleno
Abraham Samson
Ben: Deleno

Memorandum on the Ninteenth day of December 1707 before Nath^ll^ Thomas Judge of the Probate of wills &c: Appeared Hester Soul & made oath y^t^ the above written is a true Inventory of the Estate of her Husband John Soul late of Duxborrough Deceased so far as she knoweth & when she knoweth of more that she will Discover the same

Nath^ll^ Thomas Register

[p. 91] Middleborrough December 5th 1707 Whereas we whose names are hereunto Subscribed were desired by the heirs of Mr John Soul of Duxborrough Deceased, to make apprizement of the severall percels of land which the sd John Soul died seized of in the township of Middleborrough & which he had not in his life time disposed of, which we have acordingly done, according to the best of our Judgments as followeth: namely we have prized

	ll	s	d
1st The lot of Ceder Swamp in the six & twenty mens Purchase	3	0	0
2d The lot of land in Assawanset neck	5	0	0
3d The lot of the last division of upland in the sixteen shilling Purchase & the share of Ceder Swamp at Assonet Ceder Swamp & the undivided land in the sixteen shilling Purchase: all	7	0	0
4th The lot in the south Purchace being in Number the (*) lot	1	0	0
5th The lot in the South Purchace being in number the (*) lot	1	5	0
Joseph Vaughan total	17	5	0

Jacob Tomson

March the 5th 1707 The settlement of the Estate in lands of John Soul late of Duxborrough deceased Intestate. He haveing in his life time settled all his sons Portions in land by deed & his Daughter Sarah had only one Cow of her father in his life time & his Daughter Rachel & Rebecka haveing had nothing of their father, & he leaveing undisposed some small parcells of land at Middleborrough being apprised at 17ll 5s 0d is by them that is to say Adam Wright in behalf of his children which he had by the said Sarah his wife Deceased & John Cob and Rachel his wife & Rebecka the wife of Edmond Weston Mutually agreed as followeth, That is to say the said Smal parcels of land as afforesd prized at 17ll 5s 0d & the Cow said Sarah had of her father at 40 shillings makes 19ll 5s 0d which being devided in three parts makes 6ll 8s 4d to Each of them And that the Children of the said Sarah shall have the lot of the last division of upland in the sixteen shilling Purchase & the share of Ceder Swamp at Assonet Ceder Swamp & the undevidid land in the sixteen shilling Purchase all prized seven pounds to belong to the said children & their heirs the sd Adam Wright haveing paid & satisfied to the sd Rachel Cobb the sum of 2ll 11s 8d & that the said Rebecka Weston shall have the lot of land in Assawamset neck prised at five pounds & the 2 lots in the south Purchace to her & her heirs both prized at fourty

*The number of the lot was omitted.

five shillings she haveing paid her sister Rachel Cobb the sum sixteen shillings & 8 pence And the said Rachel Cobb shall have the lot of Ceder Swamp in the six & twenty mens Purchace to her & her heirs prized at three pounds which with the money she has Received make Each persons share Equall & to all their satisfactions In Witness wnereof they have hereunto set their hands & seals March the sixt 1707–8.

In presents of us
Nath^ll Thomas Ju^r:
Joseph Soul

Adam Wright (Seal)
his marke
Rebecka weston (Seal)
her marke
John Cobb (Seal)
Rachel Cobb (Seal)
her marke

Memorand: that on the sixt day of March 1707–8. all the persons hereunto Subscribed acknowledged this Instrument to be their act & deed before me

Nathaniel Thomas J: Probates.

DESIRE (HOWLAND) GORHAM'S ESTATE.

Transcribed from the Original Records,

BY GEORGE ERNEST BOWMAN.

DESIRE (Howland) GORHAM, eldest daughter of John and Elizabeth (Tilley) Howland, died at Barnstable and her death is entered on the town records [Volume I, page 414] as follows : "Mrs Desire Gorham Relict of Cap John Gorham Senr Late of Barnstable Deceas^d^ Departed this Life ye 13 Day of Octo^r^ 1683." According to the probate records her inventory was taken 3 August, 1683, more than two months earlier, and it is evident that one of these entries is incorrect. The probate record was copied from the original inventory and the town record was copied, in 1736, from the original volume now lost.*

[Plym. Col. Wills, IV : II : 63]

An Inventory of the estate of Desire Gorum taken the 3 of August 1683 and exhibited to the Court of his Mat^ie^ : held att Plymouth the sixt Day of March $16\frac{83}{84}$ on the oathes of James Gorum and John Gorum as followeth ;

Imp^r^ : 1 third of the Mill & lands meddowes and tooles belonging to the said Mill	35	00	0
Item 1 yoak of oxen	07	00	0
Item 5 Cowes	10	00	0
Item 2 steers of two yeers old and vantage	03	00	0
Item 1 yeerling	01	00	0
Item 3 Calves	01	00	0
Item 1 horse	01	10	0
Item 7 growne swine	03	00	0
Item 5 piggs	00	12	6

* Mayflower Descendant, II : 212.

Item in turkes & other foules	00	15	0
Item Cart wheeles and yoakes and Copes 10^{s} plow taklings & Copes 4^{s}	00	14	0
Item 1 Chaine and horse gear : 2 hoes & one axe	00	08	0
Item 1 pitchforke 1^{s} and one spitt 3^{s} 6^{d}; 2 pothangers one five^{s} & one 3 shillings	00	12	0
Item 1 Iron pot and pot hookes 7^{s} one frying pan 3^{s} 6^{d} and 1 2^{s} 6^{d}	00	13	0
Item 1 Iron pot 3^{s} 1 Iron skillett 3^{s} one Iron kettle 7^{s}	00	13	0
Item 1 morter & pestle 4^{s} 2 brasse skilletts 2^{s} brasse kettle 1^{s}	00	07	0
Item Scales & waights 6^{s} a paire of stilliyards 6^{s} a warming pan 5^{s}	00	17	0
Item a skimer 2^{s} 6^{d} 1 rundelett 1^{s} 1 rundelett 6^{d}	00	04	0
Item 2 milke pailes 1^{s} 6^{d} one beer Caske 1 Copper 2^{ll} 15^{s}	02	17	6
Item 1 hogshed a barrell a butter tubb 5^{s} a washing tubb 4^{s} a round measure 9	00	09	9
Item 1 Chern 1 old paile	00	01	0
Item 1 Gun 1^{ll}; 1 smoothing Iron 1 heater 1^{s} 6^{d} one Linnin wheel and reel 5^{s}	01	06	6
Item in wooden trayes 7^{s} 2 Chaire one six shill; one 4^{s} 1 Chaire 2^{s}	00	19	00
Item a sifting trough 4^{s}; 1 Chest with a rope att the end 4^{s}	00	08	00
Item pewter 12^{s} shillings 1 Chist 2^{s} and old bible and Tillinhasts book 2^{s}	00	16	00
Item 2 glasse bottles 1^{s} 3^{d} stone Juggs 6^{d} 2 gally potts 1 brush & a viall	00	02	3
Item an Iron Candle stick 9^{d} 1 wicker baskett & other basketts 1^{s}	00	02	9
Item 1 bed bolster and 2 smale pillowes, in the Chamber 3^{ll}	03	00	0
Item 1 bed bolster 1 pillow bedsted and Cord	03	10	0
Item 1 Coverlid 1^{ll} 2 white blanketts home made, 1^{ll} 2^{s}	02	02	0
Item 1 speckled blankett 9^{s} 1 Coverlid 1^{ll} 1 green rugg 8^{s}	01	17	0
Item 1 sale blankett 6^{s} & 7 pound of fflax 7	00	13	0
Item 2 old blanketts 3^{s} 1 new sheet 12^{s} 6^{d} & 1 Course 5^{s}	01	01	6
2 silver spoones and a Dram Cup 1^{ll} 1 silver beaker 3^{ll}	04	00	0
Item 1 Cokernutt 6^{d} some smale thinges in a Capp 1^{s}	00	01	6
Item 1 whiske 4^{s} 1 hood 6^{s} a black Cape and an old hood 1^{s}	00	11	0
Item 1 green apron 1^{s} 6^{d} a paire of Sleves 1^{s} 6^{d} a silke lase 3^{d} 3^{d}	00	03	5
Item 1 paire of red stockens 6^{s} 1 white apron 5^{s} 6^{d} 1 apron 3^{s} 6^{d}	00	09	6
Item 1 paire of white Gloves 3^{s} twisted yarne 9^{d}	00	03	9
Item a p^{r}sell of white linnine that is marked;	01	02	5
	0128	16	11

Item to a womans black Cloake and Claspes	01	00	00
Item 1 old Cloth hood 4^s 1 old sarge Samar 18^s 1 serge Coat 18^s	02	00	00
Item 1 New Samar 1^{ll} 18^s : 1 Moheare Coate 12^s	02	10	00
Item Curtaines and vallence 15^s an under wastcoate 1 shilling 1^s	00	16	00
Item Indian Corn 31 bushells att 2^s 6^d pr bushell & two towells 1^s	03	18	06
Item a paire of shooes 2^s 1 hat Case 2^s some Indian Basketts 5^s	00	09	00
Item to beding & sheets that tota makes use of	02	00	00
Item to a paire of wast silver buttons 3^s in mony 13^s 10^d	00	16	10
Item 5 bushells of Rye att 3^s a bushell 15^s : the wheat Not threshed 6^s	01	01	00
Item rye not threshed 18^s one shovell & peel 1^s 3^d earthen ware & trenchers 6^d	00	19	09
Item seaming pillow Coate 3^s 6^d, one 1^s 6^d, one 2 6^d a small table Cloth	00	11	00
Item 1 sheet 5^s 6^d, 1 sheet 10, 2 twowells 1 6^d one towell 6^d	00	17	09
Item 2 pillow Coates 6^s 1 sheet 10 1 sheet 5^s 1 sheet 10^s	01	11	00
Item 1 sheet 5–6 1 sheet 10 tow towells 1^s 6^d 1 towell 9^d	00	17	09
Item 1 twowell 10^d a single Neckcloth 2^s : 3 Capps	00	04	07
[p. 64] Item one small bundle of old thinges 1^s 1 handker Chiffe one & sixpence & 1 twowell 6^d	00	03	0
Item 1 Diaper Napkin 1^s one striped neckcloth 9^d a blew Apron 1^s 6^d	00	03	3
Item 1 shift 6^s one 2^s 1 paire of stockens 1^s 6^d	00	09	6
Item 1 bundle of old aprones 1^s 1 bedstead 15^s	00	16	0
Item 1 barrill att mill 1^s 6^d one straw hatt 3^s	00	04	6
Item 1 woolen wheel and Iron spindle 3^s 6^d and bridle & Crooper 1^s 6^d	00	05	0
Item 2 yards of Lutestringe in a scraff	00	10	0
Item 1 wiker Baskett 3^s; 4 Napkins six shillings 1 smale pillow Coate; 6^d	00	10	6
Item 1 shooing horn 3^d 1 powder bar 6^d six shift 6^d one thing I Can not read*	00	02	09
Item 2 Cushens 1^s 6^d 1 sheet 6^s; one sheet 8 shilling 1 sheet 6^s	01	02	06
Item 1 sheet 6^s; and 1 sheet 7^s 1 Towell two and 6^d a Diaper table Cloth 8^s	1	03	6
Item 1 Diaper table Cloth 12^s 1 paire of holland sheets 2^{ll}	02	12	0
Item 1 pillow Coate 8^s, 2 more att 12^s one Napkin Diaper 9^d	01	00	09
Item 1 winestcott Chist 10^s shilling 3 plates a porringer and sawser 4	00	14	00
Item 6 trenchers 6^d 1 looking Grasse 8^s : 3 earthen Dishes 1^s	00	09	09

* Interlined in original.

Item 1 trunk 1s 6d : one box 5s	00 06 06
Item 3 acrees of land bought of Sowashan	00 15 00
Item more 1 shift 3s 6d som old Clothing 8s	00 11 06
Item 1 pitcher 6d	00 00 06
Item Due upon bill 40ll	30 15 11
	123 16 11
Item Due upon bill as before	40 00 00
Debts Due to the estate;	*ll*
Item silver mony lent to John hawes	05 00 00
silver mony Lent to Joseph whilden	02 00 00
Debts Due from the estate as wee Doe apprehend	05 00 00

Taken and apprised by us John Thacher
John Miller

[Court Orders, VI : II : 2, under date of 5 March, 1683/4.]

In reference unto the settlement of the Estate of Desire Gorum of Yarmouth Deceased amonge the Children; It was agreed and Determined by Govr hinckley Major Bradford Deputy Govr : mr ffreeman mr Laythorp & mr Thacher Asistants alsoe with the mutuall Consent of the Children then appeering viz: James Gorum John Gorum Joseph Gorum; with the Consent likewise of the sonnes in Law as followeth;

That James Gorum have a Dubble portion of the whole estate Debts being first payed out and all the rest of the Children both sonnes and Daughters to have an equall portion; of the aforsaid estate that is John Joseph Jabez : and Shuball; Desire Temperance Elizabeth Deseased, Marsy Lidia and hannah, as Elizabeth Deceased wee Doe agree and Consent that her Children shall have an equall prte that Did belong to theire Mother as to Shuball the youngest son wheras there was fifty pound in Mony Given to his Mother to bestow upon him in Learning, wherof wee find upon account a great prte of it bestowed on him, yet wee Doe Consent and agree that hee shall have forty pound in silver mony mad up to him when hee Cometh to age out of the aforsaid estate besides his equall prte; and alsoe five pounds of his equall prte, which, to be in silver mony; which makes his 40li to be 45 pounds in mony;

THOMAS[2] DOTY'S WILL AND INVENTORY.

Transcribed from the Original Records,

By George Ernest Bowman.

Thomas[2] Doty (*Edward*[1]) died at Plymouth on the fourth or fifth of December, 1678. His nuncupative will was made on the fourth and "Comitted to writing December the 5th within 24 houres after the Death of the said Thomas Dotey." His widow, Mary, made oath to the inventory 3 March, 1678/9, the day the will was probated. The will and inventory are recorded in the Plymouth Colony Wills and Inventories, Volume IV, Part I, page 33, and a torn copy of the will, possibly the original, is on page 132 of the Scrap Book.

Thomas Dotey of Plymouth being very sicke yett haveing the use of his sences and reason Did on the fourth Day of December 1678 Declare these following words To be his last will Namly that all his estate hee Gave absolutely to his wife Mary Dotey to be wholly att her Dispose and left it all with her to Improve and make use of as shee should see best; This hee Declared to be his will as above written; In the p^r^sence of Edward Dotey and Samuell Eaton and Anne Sav[*blotted*]*; And it was Comitted to writing December the 5th within 24 houres after the Death of the said Thomas Dotey;

An Inventory of the estate of Thomas Doten Deceased taken the 28th Day of January by us whose Names are under written

Item 2 Cowes 1 Calfe 4 swine	05	12	0
Item his wearing Clothes	03	16	0
Item pewter and brasse and Iron ware	02	02	0
Item 2 Chests and a box	00	14	0
Item earthen ware trenchers and spoones & Glasses	00	07	0
Item Armes and amunition	01	13	0
Item bookes	00	04	0
Item 25 pound of sheeps woole and 19 pound and an halfe of Cotton woole	01	05	2
Item lines and ledds and hookes and spliting kniffe	00	08	0

* "Savoury" in the copy in the Scrap Book.

Item a butt & old Caske payels & tubbs	00	15	0
Item 1 shees and Napkins and blankett and other old linnine	01	01	0
Item 1 paire of boots	00	12	0
Item 1 spade 1 axe 1 paire of pitchforke tynes & other old Iron	00	06	0
Item 3 old baggs one paire of Cards 1 looking Glasse	00	03	0
Item 10 pond of feathers	00	10	0
	17	16	8

Debts Dew from the estate

Item att Boston to John Poole	01	04	0
Item To ffrancis Douce	00	12	0
Item To John Winge	00	13	06
Item To Mary ffarnum	00	16	0

Debts Due from the estate att Plymouth

To mr Thomas Clarke	01	10	0
To Grge Watson	01	10	0
To John Churchill	00	10	0
To John Bryant senir:	00	07	0
To Abraham Jackson	00	16	00

Ephram Morton
Willam harlow

These abovewritten Will and Inventory were exhibitted to the Court held att Plymouth the third of March 1678 : 79, the Inventory on the oath of Marey Dotey widdow;

GOVERNOR BRADFORD'S LETTER BOOK.

Reprinted, by permission, from the Collections of the Massachusetts Historical Society.

Governor Bradford's Letter Book is so little known it has been decided to reprint it in this magazine and make it accessible to all. Unfortunately the fragment of the original manuscript rescued by Mr. Clarke cannot now be found, and the text printed in the "Collections of the Massachusetts Historical Society," Volume III (1794), pages 27 to 76 inclusive, has been followed. From the first volume of the "Proceedings" of the same society we also reprint in full the account of the receipt of the manuscript, and notes regarding it.

[Proceedings, Vol. I, pp. 51, 52]

At a meeting of the Historical Society, on Tuesday, the thirtieth day of July, 1793, at Winthrop's or Governor's Island . . . . The following donations were received: — For the Library: — Fragment of a MS. Letter-book of Governor Bradford, of Plymouth, from 1624 to 1630, found in a grocer's shop in Halifax, Nova Scotia. From James Clarke, Esq., of Halifax.

This fragment of Governor Bradford's Letter-book was printed in Vol. III. of the Collections, making fifty pages. It appears from a note at the beginning of the printed text that the MS. of the part preserved began with "page 339, the preceding pages wanting," and covered the years 1624–1630. This shows that what was recovered was but a small part of what was lost; while it is probable that the collection originally contained also letters of a later date than 1630. Governor Bradford's History closed with the year 1646, and the letters which he had preserved to illustrate that part of the narrative, from 1630 to its conclusion, may have been included in his Letter-book, as well as those used in the earlier portion. The fragment recovered may have been one volume of a series continuously paged. The fortunate recovery of Governor Bradford's History, some sixty years after Mr. James Clarke rescued this fragment from a grocer's shop in Halifax, happily supplies to a certain extent the place of the Letter-book; for, while the author did not copy into his History all these letters, we may well suppose him, judging from the use he made of those preserved, to have used the most valuable part of them.

The finding of this manuscript in Halifax naturally suggests the thought that it left Boston at the time of the "evacuation," in March, 1776; and, it being well known that the British soldiers during the occupation of Boston had free access to the Historical Library of books and manuscripts of the Rev. Thomas Prince, kept in a room in the tower of the Old South Meeting-house, that it was taken from that collection. This is not improbable. There may be no positive evidence that Prince's Library then contained this Letter-book, yet we know that it was once in Prince's possession. For, besides the manuscripts of Bradford, which he mentions, in the preface to his Chronological History, as having had an "opportunity to search," — namely, "Bradford's History of Plymouth People and Colony," in folio, and "A Register of Governor Bradford's, in his own hand, recording some of the first deaths, marriages, and punishments at Plymouth, with three other miscellaneous volumes of his," in octavo, — he several times refers, in his notes on the margin of Bradford's manuscript History, to "Governor Bradford's Collection of Letters." See pp. 47, 61, 64, and 71 of the printed volume.*

The following is the letter of Mr. Clarke which accompanied the manuscript:

"Halifax, May 28, 1793.

"Sir, — The enclosed ancient manuscript I found some years ago in a grocer's shop in this town, of whom I obtained it with a view of saving what remained from destruction. I lament extremely that a page has been torn out; and it gives me pleasure that I now have an opportunity of placing it in your hands, — a freedom I am induced to take from your advertisement of the first of November, 1792, and from a persuasion that it may contribute in some measure to the important objects of your Society, and I could wish I might otherwise be serviceable.

"I am, respectfully, Sir, your most obedient humble servant,

"James Clarke.

"The Rev. Jeremy Belknap."

Where the writer speaks of a *page* being torn out, he probably means that one *leaf* had been torn out of the volume. Bradford may have written on one side only of the leaf in copying his letters, as he generally did in writing his History, so that one leaf would represent one page of writing. — Eds.

Governour Bradford's Letter Book.

[Page 339 — the preceding pages wanting.]

To our beloved and right well esteemed friend Mr. William Bradford Governour these, but inscribed thus:

To our beloved friends Mr. William Bradford, Mr. Isaac Allerton, Mr. Edward Winslow, and the rest whom they think fit to acquaint therewith.

Two things (beloved friends) we have endeavoured to effect, touching Plymouth plantation, first, that the planters there might live comfortably and contentedly. 2d that some returns might be made hither for the satisfying and encouragement of the adventurers, but to neither of these two can we yet attain. Nay,

* Edition of 1856.

if it be as some of them report which returned in the Catherine, it is almost impossible to hope for it, since, by their sayings, the slothfulness of one part of you, and the weakness of the other part, is such, that nothing can go well forward. And although we do not wholly credit these reports, yet surely, either the country is not good where you are, for habitation; or else there is something amiss amongst you; and we much fear the willing are too weak and the strong too idle. And because we will not stand upon the number of the objections made by them against you; we have sent them here enclosed, that you may see them and answer them. (*These are those which are inserted and answered before in this book; namely, before Liford's letters, where those letters should also have been placed, but they came not then to hand and I thought better to put them in, than to omit them.*)

As for such as will needs be upon their particulars now that they are gotten over, you must be sure to make such covenants with them, as that first or last the company be satisfied for all their charge. Neither must you proceed to these agreements and consultations with many at once, otherwise how easy might *they* make a lead in rebellion, which have so long done it in cheating and idleness.

Touching Mr. Weston, his disturbing of you about that £100 taken up for Mr. Brewer, except we conclude with Solomon that oppression maketh a wise man mad, we cannot but wonder at it, seeing under his own hand, it is apparently and particularly expressed, summed up and sold with the rest of his adventures, so as no sober man can possibly question it. 2dly, had it not been sold, Mr. Brewer might well have had it, to pay himself part of a debt which Mr. Weston oweth him for commodities sold to him, which he saith amounteth to above £100, as he can prove by good testimony. 3dly, if it had not been apparently sold, Mr. Beuchamp who is of the company also, unto whom he oweth a great deal more, had long ago attached it (as he did other's 16ths) and so he could not have demanded it, either of you or us.

And if he will not believe our testimony here about, who shall believe his, either in this, or any other matters. It is a dangerous *case*, when a man groweth naught in prosperity, and worse in adversity, and what can the end of all this be, but more and more misery. And for conclusion with him, you may shew him what we have wrote about him, and if that satisfy him not, but that he shall still follow his mad and malicious practices against you, warn him out of your precincts, and let it be upon his peril to set foot thereon; it being indeed no reason that a whole plantation should be disturbed or indamaged by the frantic humours of any one man whatsoever.

Now further for yourselves; as the power of government is fallen upon you, both by lot and desert (as we are persuaded) so your troubles and cares have been so much the more hitherto; and we would not have you think of easing yourselves till you have either made things better, or ended your warfare; for it is best that the world afford us these crosses lest we should forget the meditation of heaven.

And we pray you all even look to yourselves, and your ways; that there be not amongst you some cause or occasion of these evil men's insultings and bravery upon you, as they do, that we charge you with nothing, but are ready to make your just defence at all times against opposites; yet let it not offend you, that we wish you to look to yourselves, as first that you walk close with God, being fervent and frequent in prayer, instruction and doctrine, both openly and privately. 2dly, that you instruct and bring up your young ones in the knowledge and fear of God, restraining them from idleness and profanation of the Sabbath. 3dly, that you freely and readily entertain any honest men, into your church, estate and society, though with great infirmities and difference of judgment; taking heed of too great straitness and singularity even in that particular. 4thly, that there be fervent love and close cleaving together among you that are fearers of God, without secret whispering or undermining one of another, and without contempt or neglect of such as are weak and helpless, if honest, amongst you. This do, and in all things be humble, cheerful and thankful; that if you cannot grow rich in this world, yet you may be rich in grace; and if you can send us no other treasure, yet let all that visit you, bring from you the fame of honesty, religion and godliness, which we trust, shall comfort us more than all else you can send us in this world.

At a word, though we be detected of folly, ignorance, want of judgment, yet let no man charge us with dishonesty, looseness or unconscionableness; but though we lose our labours or adventures, or charges, yea our lives; yet let us not lose one jot of our innocence, integrity, holiness, fear and comfort with God.

And, thus ceasing for this time to trouble you further; praying God to bless and prosper you, and sanctify all your crosses and losses, that they may turn to your great profit and comfort in the end, with hearty salutations to you all, we lovingly take leave of you, from London, April 7, 1624.

Your assured lovers and friends,

James Sherley, *Thomas Fletcher,*
Thomas Brewer, *John Ling,*
William Collier, *William Thomas,*
Joseph Pocok, *Robert Reayne.*

[Now follows the first letters we received after the breach; for Mr. Thornell and the rest never replied nor writ more unto us, being partly ashamed of what they done and written.]

To our beloved friends Mr. William Bradford, Mr. Isaac Allerton, Mr. William Brewster, and the rest of the general society of Plymouth in New England, salutations.

Though the thing we feared be come upon us and the evils we strove against, have overtaken us; yet cannot we forget you, nor our friendship and fellowship, which, together we have had some years; wherein though our expressions have been small, yet our hearty affections towards you (unknown by face) have been no less than to our nearest friends, yea even to our own selves. And though your and our friend, Mr. Winslow, can tell you the estate of things here, and what hath befallen us; yet lest we should seem to neglect you, to whom by a wonderful providence of God, we are so nearly united; we have thought good once more to write unto you, and the arguments of our letter must consist of these three points, first to shew you what is here befallen, 2dly, the reason and cause of that which is fallen, 3rdly, our purposes and desires towards you hereafter.

The former course for the generality here is wholly dissolved from that course which was held. And whereas you and we, were formerly sharers, and partners in all voyages and dealings, this way is now so no more, but you and we are left to bethink ourselves, what course to take in the future, that your lives and our monies be not lost. And this, as ourselves first saw, so have we begun to practice, as we thought best for your and our safety for hereafter; and it standeth you no less in hand seriously to consider what is best to do, that you may both continue good conscience with God and procure your best safety in this world.

The reasons and causes of this alteration, have been these first and mainly, the many crosses, and losses and abuses by sea and seamen, which have caused us to run into so much charge, and debts and engagements, as our estates and means were not able to go on without impoverishing ourselves, and much hindering if not spoiling our trades and callings here; except our estates had been greater or our associates had cloven better to us. 2dly, As here hath been a faction and siding amongst us now more than two years; so now there is an utter breach and sequestration amongst us, and in two parts of us, a full dissertion, and forsaking of you, without any intent or purpose of medling more with you.

And though we are persuaded the main cause of their this doing is want of money (for need whereof men use to make many excuses) yet other things are by many pretended, and not without some colour urged, which are these: 1st, A distaste of you there, for that you are (as they affirm) Brownists, condemning all other churches, and persons but yourselves and those in your way, and you are contentious, cruel and hard hearted, among your neighbours and towards such as in all points both civil and religious, jump not with you. And that you are negligent, careless, wasteful, unthrifty, and suffer all general goods, and affairs to go at six and sevens and spend your time in idleness and talking and confering, and care not what be wasted worn and torn out, whilst all things come so easily, and so cheap unto you. 2dly, A distaste and personal contempt of us for taking your parts and striving to defend you, and make the best of all matters touching you, insomuch as it is hard to say whether you or we are least loved of them.

Now what use either you or we may make of these things, it remaineth to be considered; and the more, for that we know the hand of God to be present in all these things, and he no doubt would admonish us of something which is not yet so looked to and taken to heart as it should. And although it be now too late for us, or you, to prevent and stay these things, yet is it not too late to exercise patience, wisdom and conscience, in bearing them, and in carrying ourselves in and under them for time to come. And as we ourselves stand ready to embrace all occasions that may tend to the furtherance of so hopeful a work; rather admiring at what is, than grudging for what is not, so it must rest still in you to make all good again. And if in nothing else you can be approved, yet let your honesty and conscience be still approved, and lose not one jot of your innocence amidst your many crosses and afflictions.

And surely if you upon this alteration behave yourselves wisely and go on fairly, as men whose hopes is not in this life; you shall need no other weapon to wound your adversaries;

for when your righteousness is revealed as the light, they shall cover their faces with shame, that causelessly have sought your overthrow.

And although (we hope) you need not our council in these things, having learned of God how to behave yourselves, in all estates in this world, yet a word for your advice and direction, to spur those forward, which we hope run already.

And first, seeing our generality here is dissolved, let yours be the more firm; and do not you like carnal people (which run into inconveniences and evils by examples) but rather be warned by your harms, to cleave faster together hereafter; take heed of long and sharp disputes and oppositions, give no passage to the waters, no not a tittle; let not hatred or heartburning be harboured in the breast of any of you one moment, but forgive and forget all former failings and abuses, and renew your love and friendship together daily. There is often more sound friendship and sweeter fellowship in afflictions and crosses than in prosperity and favours; and there is reason for it, because envy flieth away when there is nothing but necessities to be looked on; but it is always a bold *guest* where prosperity shews itself.

And although we here which are hedged about with so many favours and helps in worldly things and comforts; forget friendship and love and fall out often times for trifles; yet you must not do so, but must in these things turn a new leaf and be of another spirit. We here can fall out with a friend and lose him today, and find another tomorrow; but you cannot do so, you have no such choice, you must make much of them you have, and count him a very good friend, which is not a professed enemy. We have a trade and custom of tale bearing, whispering and changing of old friends for new, and these things with us are incurable. But you which do as it were begin a new world and lay the foundation of sound piety and humanity for others to follow, must suffer no such weeds in your garden, but nip them in the head, and cast them out forever; and must follow peace and study quietness, having fervent love amongst yourselves as a perfect and entire bond to uphold you when all else fails you. And although we have written much to you heretofore to provoke to union and love as the only way to make you stand, and without which all would come to nothing; so now you are much more to be provoked thereunto, since you are left, rather to be spectators to the eye than objects to the hand, and stand most need one of another, at home when foreign help is so much decayed and weakened.

And if any amongst you, for all that, have still a withdrawing heart, and will be all to himself, and nothing to his neighbour, let him think of these things. 1st, The providence of God in bringing you there together. 2d, His marvellous preserving you from so many dangers, the particulars whereof you know and must never forget. 3d, The hopes that yet are of effecting somewhat for yourselves and more for your posterity if hand join in hand. 4th, The woful estate of him which is alone, especially in a wilderness. 5th, The succour and comfort which the generality can daily afford, having built houses, planted corn, framed boats, erected salt works, obtained cattle, swine, and pulling,* together with the diverse varieties of trades and faculties employed by sea and land, the gains of every one stretching itself unto all whilst they are in the general: but such as withdraw themselves tempting God and despising their neighbours, must look for no share or part in any of these things; but as they will be a commonwealth alone, so alone they must work, and alone they must eat, and alone they must be sick and die, or else languishing under the frustration of their vain hopes, alone return to England, and there to help all cry out of the country and the people; counting the one fruitless and the other merciless; when indeed their own folly, pride, and idleness is the cause of all which never weigh either the providence of God, the conscience of their duty, nor care for their neighbours, or themselves, further than to grate upon their friends; as if other men owed them all things, and they owed no man any thing. 6th, The conscience of making restitution, and paying those debts and charges which hath befallen to bring you there, and send those things to you, which you have had, must hold you together; and for him that withdraws himself from the general; we look upon him, as upon a man, who, having served his turn, and fulfiled his desire, cares not what becomes of others, neither maketh conscience of any debt, or duty at all, but thinketh to slide away under secret colours, to abuse and deceive his friends; and against whom we need say little, seeing the Lord will never cease to curse his course.

And albeit, the company here as a company hath lost you; you know when Saul left David, yea, and pursued him, yet David did not abuse his allegiance and loyalty to him, no more should you; the evil of us here, cannot justify any evil in you, but you must still do your duty, though we neglect ours. 2dly, Indeed we are persuaded, it is in the most of the adventurers rather want of power, than will, that maketh them break off;

* Pullen, an obsolete word for poultry.

they having gone as far as they can in the business, and are as sorry that they cannot go forward as you are offended that they do not go forward, yea, and the pretences of those which have the most colours, we are persuaded, proceed more from weakness of the purse, than fear of any thing else; and the want of money is such a grevious sickness now-a-days, as that it makes men rave and cry out, they cannot tell for what. 3dly, And in a word we think it but reason, that all such things as these, are appertaining to the general, be kept and preserved together, and rather increased daily, than any way dispersed or embezzled away, for any private ends or intents whatsoever. 4thly, That after your necessities are served, you gather together such commodities as the country yields, and send them over to pay debts and clear engagements here, which are not less than £1400. All which debts, besides adventures, have been made about general commodities and implements, and for which divers of us, stand more or less engaged. And we dare say of you, that you will do the best you can to free us, and unburden us, that for your sakes, and help, are so much hazarded in our estates, and names. 5thly, If there be any that will withdraw himself from the general, as he must not have, nor use any of the general's goods, so it is but reason that he give sufficient security for payment of so much of the debts as his part cometh to; which how much it will come to, upon a person, or family is quickly counted; and since we require but men's faithful endeavours, and cannot obtain them, let none think much if we require other security than fair words and promises, of such men as make no more conscience of their words and ways.

If any amongst you shall object against us, either our long delays in our supplies heretofore, or our too much jollity in spending sometimes at our meetings more than perhaps needed; that will prove but trifling, for we could also find fault with the idleness and sloth of many amongst you, which have made all the rest go forward slowly, as also we could find fault with your liberality, and largeness also, when it might have been otherwise; but all such matters must still be left to the discretion and conscience of either side, knowing that where many have a hand in such business, there will not want some, that are too timerous and slack; as also that in matters of note, something must be done for form and credit. And for ourselves we think there hath hardly in our days; been a business, of this note, and fame, carried by Londoners, with twice the expense in by matters that this hath been; and therefore let each man rather seek to mend himself, than hastily to cast in objections against others.

In a word, since it thus still falleth out, that all things between us, are as you see, let us all endeavour to keep a fair and honest course, and see what time will bring forth, and how God in his providence will work for us. We still are persuaded, you are the people, that must make a plantation, and erect a city in those remote places, when all others fail, and return; and your experience of God's providence and preservation of you is such, that we hope your hearts will not now fail you, though your friends should forsake you (which we ourselves shall not do whilst we live, so long as your honesty so well appeareth) yet surely help would arise from some other place, whilst you wait on God with uprightness, though we should leave you also.

To conclude, as you are especially now to renew your love one to another; so we advise you, as your friends to these particulars. First let all sharpness, reprehensions, and corrections, of opposite persons, be still used sparingly, and take no advantage against any, for any by respects; but rather wait for their mending amongst you, than to mend them yourselves by thrusting them away, of whom there is any hope of good to be had. 2d, Make your corporation, as formal as you can, under the name of the Society of Plymouth in New England, allowing some peculiar privileges, to all the members thereof, according to the tenure of the patents. 3d, Let your practises and course in religion in the church, be made complete, and full; let all that fear God amongst you, join themselves thereunto without delay; and let all the ordinances of God be used completely in the church without longer waiting upon uncertainties, or keeping the gap open for opposites. 4ly, Let the worship and service of God be strictly kept on the Sabbath, and both together, and asunder let the day be sanctified; and let your care be seen on the working days every where and upon all occasions to set forward the service of God. And lastly, be you all entreated to walk so circumspectly and carry yourselves so uprightly in all your ways, as that no man may make just exceptions against you; and more especially that the favour and countenance of God may be so towards you, as that you may find abundant joy and peace even amidst tribulations, that you may say with David, *though my father, and my mother should forsake me; yet the Lord will take me up.*

We have sent you some cattle, cloth, hose, shoes, leather, &c. but in another nature than formerly, as it stood us in hand to do; we have committed them to the custody and charge of, as our factors, Mr. Allerton and Mr. Winslow, at whose discretion they are to be sold and commodities, taken for them as is fitting. And it standeth you in need the more carefully to look to, and make much of all your commodities, by how much the more they are chargeable to you, and though we hope you shall not want things necessary, so we think the harder they are got, the more carefully they will be husbanded. Good friends, as you buy them, keep a decorum in distributing them, and let none have varieties, and things for delight, when others want for their mere necessities, and have an eye rather on your ill deservings at God's hand, than upon the failings of your friends towards you; and wait on him with patience, and good conscience; rather admiring his mercies, (than repining at his crosses,) with the assurance of faith, that what is wanting here shall be made up in glory a thousand fold. Go on good friends, comfortably pluck up your hearts cheerfully, and quit yourselves like men, in all your difficulties, that notwithstanding all displeasure and threats of men, yet the work may go on which you are about, and not be neglected, which is so much for the glory of God, and the furtherance of our Countrymen, as that a man may with more comfort spend his life in it; than live the life of Methuselah in wasting the plenty of a tilled land, or eating the fruit of a grown tree.

Thus having not time to write further unto you, leaving other things to the relation of our friends; with all hearty salutations to you all, and hearty prayers, for you all, we lovingly take our leave this 18th of December, 1624.

Your assured friends to our power,
James Sherley, (sick)
William Collier,
Thomas Fletcher,
Robert Holland.

[This letter was wrote with Mr. Cushman's hand; and it is likely was penned by him at the other's request.]

GOVERNOR BRADFORD'S LETTER BOOK.

Mr. CUSHMAN *to Gov.* BRADFORD.

SIR, *December* 22, 1624.

My hearty love remembered unto you, and unto your wife, with trust of your healths, and contentment amidst so many difficulties. I am now to write unto you, from my friend, and from myself, my friend and your friend. Mr. Sherley, who lieth even at the point of death, intreated me, even with tears, to write to excuse him, and signify how it was with him; he remembers his hearty, and as he thinks his last, salutations to you, and all the rest, who love our common cause. And if God does again raise him up, he will be more for you (I am persuaded) than ever he was. His unfeigned love towards us, hath been such, as I cannot indeed express; and though he be a man not swayed with passion, or led by uninformed affections, yet hath he cloven to us still amidst all persuasions of opposites; and could not be moved to have an evil thought of us, for all their clamours. His patience and contentment in being oppressed hath been much; he hath sometimes lent £800 at one time, for other men to adventure in this business, all to draw them on; and hath indeed by his free heartedness been the only glue of the company And if God should take him now away, I scarce think much more would be done, save as to enquire at the dividend what is to be had.

He saith he hath received the tokens you sent, and thanks you for them: he hath sent you a cheese, &c. Also he hath sent an heifer to the plantation, to begin a stock for the poor. There is also a bull and three or four jades, to be sold unto you, with many other things, for apparel and other uses; which are committed to Mr. Alerton and Mr. Winslow, who as factors are to sell them to you; and it was fitter for many reasons, to make them factors than yourself, as I hope you will easily conceive.

And I hope though the first project cease, yet it shall be never the worse for you, neither will any man be discouraged, but wait on God, using the good means you can. I have no time to write many things unto you; I doubt not but upon the hearing of this alteration some discontent may arise, but the Lord I hope will teach you the way which you shall choose. For myself as I have laboured by all means, to hold things here together, so I have patiently suffered this alteration; and do yet hope it shall be good for you all, if you be not too rash, and hasty; which if any be, let them take heed they reap not the fruit of their own vanities.

But for you, good Sir, I hope you will do nothing rashly, neither will you be swayed, by misreports, beside your ordinary course, but will persuade who may be, to patience, and peace.; and to the bearing of labours, and crosses in love together.

I hope the failings of your friends here, will make you the more friendly one to another, that so all our hopes may not be dashed. Labour to settle things, both in your civil, and religious courses, as firm, and as full as you can. Lastly, I must intreat you still, to have a care of my son, as of your own ; and I shall rest bound unto you, I pray you let him sometime practice writing. I hope the next ships to come to you; in the mean space and ever, the Lord be all your direction, and turn all our crosses and troubles to his own glory, and our comforts, and give you to walk so wisely, and holily, as none may justly say, but they have always found you honestly minded, though never so poor. Salute all our friends, and supply, I pray you, what, if failing in my letters. From London, *December* 22, *A.D.* 1624.

Thus were his last letters. And now we lost the help of a wise and faithful friend, he wrote of the sickness, and probability of the death of another; but knew not that his own was so near, what cause have we therefore ever to be ready! He purposed to be with us the next ships, but the Lord did otherwise dispose; and had appointed him a greater journey, to a better place. He was now taken from these troubles into which (by this division) we were so deeply plunged. And heer I must leave him to rest with the Lord. And will proceed to other letters which will further shew our proceedings and how things went on.

Gov. BRADFORD *to Mr.* CUSHMAN.

Loving and kind friend, I most heartily thank you; and would be right glad to see you here, with many other of our old and dear friends, that we might strengthen, and comfort one another, after our many troubles, travels, and hardships I long greatly for friends of Leyden, but I fear, I shall now scarce ever see them, save in heaven; but the will of the Lord be done. We have rid ourselves of the company of many of those, who have been so troublesome unto us; though I fear we are not yet rid of the troubles themselves. I hear Culdom * comes himself into England; the which if he do, beware of him for he is very malicious, and much threatens you; thinking he hath some advantage by some words you have spoken. Touching his factious doings here, and our proceedings with him, I refer you for it, and many other things to the relations of Captain Standish, whom we have thought most meet for sundry reasons, to send at this time. I pray you be as helpful to him

* This was unquestionably a misreading and should have been "Ouldom", *i.e.* "Oldham." — Editor.

as you can; especially in making our provisions, for therein he hath the least skill.

We have sent by this first ship, a good parcel of commodities, to wit: As much beaver and other furs, as will amount to upwards of £277, sterling, at the rates they were sold the last year. In part of payment of those goods, they and you sent to be sold to us. But except we may have things, both more serviceable, and at better rates, we shall never be able to rub through; therefore if we could have some ready money disbursed to buy things at the best hand, it would be greatly in our way. Special care is to be had of procuring us good trucking stuff, for without it we can do nothing; the reason why heretofore we have got so little is, because we never had any that was good till Mr. Winslow brought some over.

Our people will never agree, any way again to unite with the Company; who have cast them off with such reproach and contempt; and also returned their bills, and all debts upon their heads. But as for those our loving friends, who have, and still do stick to us, and are deeply engaged for us, and are most careful of our goods, for our parts we will ever be ready to do any thing, that shall be thought equal and mete.

But I think it will be best to press, a clearance with the company; either by coming to a dividend, or some other indifferent course or composition; for the longer we hang and continue in this confused and lingering condition, the worse it will be, for it takes away all heart and courage, from men, to do any thing. For notwithstanding any persuasion to the contrary, many protest they will never build houses, fence grounds, or plant fruits for those, who not only forsake them, but use them as enemies, lading them with reproach and contumely. Nay they will rather ruin that, which is done, than they should possess it. Whereas if they knew what they should trust to, the place would quickly grow and flourish with plenty, for they never felt the sweetness of the country till this year; and not only we but all planters in the land begin to do it. Let us be as little engaged about fishing, or any other projects, as you can, to draw us away from our own employments for they will be the most beneficial unto us. I suppose to spend our own salt and to employ as many of our own boats as we can, will be best for us. If we had but kept two a trading this year, it would have been twice as good as our fishing; though I hope the ships will return with good voyages.

Your son and all of us, are in good health, (blessed be God) he received the things you sent him. I hope God will make him a good man. My wife remembers her love unto you, and thanks you for her spice. Billington still rails against you, and threatens to arrest you, I know not wherefore; he is a knave and so will live and die. Mr. John Pearce wrote he would make a parliamentary matter, about our grand patent, I pray you wish our friends to look to it, for I mistrust him, I perceive there passeth intelligence between Mr. Weston, and him, by means of Mr. Hix. He is come again hither, and is not yet quiet about that £100. The Lord hath so graciously disposed, that when our opposites thought, that many would have followed their faction, they so distasted their palpable dishonest dealings, that they stuck more firmly unto us, and joined themselves to the Church. But time cuts me off, for other things; I refer you to my other more general, and larger letters, and so with my renewed salutations, and best love remembered unto you. I commend you and all our affairs, to the guidance of the Most High, and so rest, your assured loving friend,

WILLIAM BRADFORD.

New-Plymouth, June 9, 1625.

[*Mr. Cushman died before this letter arrived.*]

Next follows a letter to the Council of New England, wherein their help was supplicated.

To the right Honourable his Majesty's Council for New England these be, &c.

Right Honourable, *June* 28, *A.D.* 1625

The assurance we have of your noble dispositions to releave the oppressions of the innocent, doth cause us to fly unto you as to a sanctuary, in this our just cause. It hath pleased the divine Providence to bring us into this place where we inhabit under your government, wherein we now have resided almost these five years, having put some life, into this then dreaded design, made way for others and to all that are here, have been and still are their bulwark and defence.

Many necessities we have undergone, incident to the raw and immature beginnings of such great exertions, and yet are subject to many more. We are many people, consisting of all sorts, as well women children, as men; and are now left, and forsaken of our adventurers, who will neither supply us with necessaries for our subsistence, nor suffer others that would be willing; neither can we be at liberty to deal with others, or provide for ourselves, but they keep us tied to them, and yet they will be loose from us; they have not only cast us off, but entered into particular course of trading, and have by violence, and force, taken at their pleasure, our possession at Cape Ann. Traducing us with unjust, and dishonest clammours abroad, disturbing our peace at home; and some of them threatening, that if ever we grow to any good estate they will then nip us in the head. Which discouragements do cause us to slack our diligence, and care to build and plant, and cheerfully perform our other employments, not knowing for whom we work whether friends or enemies.

Our humble suit therefore to your good lordships and honours is, that seeing they have so unjustly forsaken us, that you would vouchsafe to convene them before you, and take such order, as we may be free from them; and they come to a division with us, that we and ours may be delivered from their evil intents against us. So shall we comfortably go forward, with the work we have in hand, as first to God's glory, and the honour of our king; so to the good satisfaction of your honours, and for our present, common, and after good of our posterity. The prosecution of this, we have committed to our agent Captain Myles Standish, who attends your Honourable pleasures.

The great God of heaven and earth, who hath put into your hearts, to travail in this honourable action, strengthen your hearts and hands hereunto; and gave his blessing answerable to your worthy endeavours. In all humbleness we commit ourselves to your honourable direction and protection. And rest with the knowledge, consent and humble request of the whole plantation ever at commandment.

WILLIAM BRADFORD, *Gov.*

But by reason of the great plague which raged this year in London, of which so many thousands died weekly, Captain Standish could do nothing either with the Council of New England, or any other hereabout, for there was no Courts kept or scarce any commerce held, the city being in a sort desolate, by the fervent pestilence, and flight of so many. So as he was forced to return; having by the help of some friends (with much ado, and great both trouble and peril to himself) procured a convenient supply; which he brought with him to save our greatest necessities.

A Letter of Mr. Fletcher's, showing his great loss of the little James; she and the beaver in her, which was sent for the goods we bought the other year, being for the most part his; and was taken by the Turks to his utter undoing.

To his loving friends Mr. BRADFORD, *Mr.* ALLERTON, *and Mr.* WINSLOW, *salutations, &c.*

London, November 25, 1625.

My last unto you, was of the death of Mr. Robinson and what else then needful, since which I have received divers letters from you, and perceive at large what things you want, and do desire, and with what grievances you have been oppressed. And had the Lord so disposed, as to have sent us the pinace home, no doubt myself would have seen you well supplied; and some of your grievances should have been removed, but so it is, that all power therein to do you good, is wholly (by God's providence) taken from me. And so I much fear, that this year you will hardly be able to do yourselves, or your friends much good, but patience, &c.

And for other affairs either touching myself, and my necessities I am put unto, besides disgrace and reproach from many; as also touching the rest of our adventurers, who fall from me like the water brooks, as Job complains. I say for all these things, and many more here passed, I refer you to your Agent, and my loving friend, Captain Standish, who can certify you all things at large; as also of the feigned and perfidious dealings of Mr. John Peirce towards me, and others, who now hath manifest himself, at least to some, not to mind that good for you, or us, as was fit, and oft pretended. But all these things, they come from God for diverse reasons as first, to humble us, and subdue our corruption; 2d, to win us from the world. 3d, to add unto our joy to come. 4th, to shew forth the great power, goodness and mercy of our God, in preserving us in, and delivering us out of the same. Wherefore let us be patient, and thankful without murmuring, Amen, Amen. And so with my hearty well wishes for you all, and your general good; for which I shall often approach to the throne of grace, and expect the like from you, and so I leave you with this salutation, fare you well, my brethren all, fare you well; and God of grace and peace, bless you, and your posterities to the coming of Jesus Christ. Amen.

Your loving friend, in what I can.

THOMAS FLETCHER.

GOVERNOR BRADFORD'S LETTER BOOK.

I WILL next insert some letters from our friends at Leyden, written this year; and first, a letter of Mr. White's to myself, in which the heavy tidings of our beloved and able pastor's death and the manner of it, is declared.

To his loving friend, Mr. WILLIAM BRADFORD, *Governour of Plymouth, in New England, these be, &c.*

Loving and kind friends, &c. I know not whether ever this will come to your hands, or miscarry, as other of my letters have done; yet in regard of the Lord's dealing with us here, I have had a great desire to write unto you; knowing your desire to bear a part with us, both in our joys and sorrows, as we do with you.

These therefore are to give you to understand, that it hath pleased the Lord to take out of this veil of tears, your, and our loving and faithful pastor, and my dear brother, Mr. John Robinson, who was sick some, eight days, beginning first to be sick on a Saturday morning, yet the next day, being the Lord's day he taught us twice, and the week after grew every day weaker, than other, yet felt no pain but weakness, all the time of his sickness; the physick he took wrought kindly, in man's judgment, yet he grew every day weaker than other, feeling little or no pain, yet sensible, till the very last. Who fell sick the twenty second of February, and departed this life the first of March. He had a continual inward ague, which brought the ——— but I thank the Lord, was free of the plague, so that all his friends could come freely to him. And if either prayers, tears, or means would have saved his life, he had not gone hence. But he having faithfully finished his course, and performed his work, which the Lord had appointed him here to perform; he now rests with the Lord, in eternal happiness. We wanting him and all church Governours, not having one at present that is a governing officer amongst us. Now for ourselves here left (I mean the whole Chruch) we still, by the mercy of God, continue and hold close together in peace and quietness, and so I hope we shall do though we be very weak; wishing (if such were the will of God) that you and we were again together in one, either there or here, but seeing it is the will of the Lord, thus to dispose of things, we must labour with patience to rest contented till it please the Lord otherwise to dispose of things.

For news at present here, is not much worth the writing, only as in England we have lost our old King who departed this life about a month ago, so here we have lost Grave Morrice, the old Prince here, who both departed this life, since my brother Robinson; and as in England we have a new King, Charles, of whom there is great hope of good; the King is making ready about one hundred sail of ships, the end is not yet certain, but they will be ready to go to sea very shortly; the King himself goes to see them once in fourteen days. So here likewise we have made Prince Hendrick General, in his brother's place, who is now with the Grave of Mansfield with a great army, close by the enemy, to free Breda, if it be possible, which the enemy hath besieged now some nine or ten months; but how it will fall out at last, is yet uncertain, the Lord give good success if it be his will. And thus fearing lest this will not come to your hands, hoping as soon as I hear of a convenient messenger, to write more at large, and to send you a letter which my brother Robinson sent to London; to have gone to some of you, but coming too late, was brought back again. And so for this time I cease further to trouble you, and rest,

Your assured loving friend,

ROGER WHITE.

Leyden, April 28, *Anno* 1625.

A letter of Thomas Blossom's to myself and Mr. Brewster, touching the same thing, as followeth.

BELOVED SIR,

Kind salutations, &c. I have thought good to write to you, concerning the cause as it standeth both with you and us; we see, alas! what frustrations and disappointments it pleaseth the Lord to send in this our course, good in itself and according to godliness taken in hand and for good and lawful ends, who yet pleaseth not to prosper us we see, for reasons best known to himself: And which also nearly concerns us to consider of, whether we have sought the Lord in it, as we ought, or not; that the Lord hath singularly preserved life in the business to great admiration, giveth me good hope that he will (if our sins hinder not) in his appointed time, give a happy end unto it. On the contrary when I consider how it pleaseth the

Lord to cross those means that should bring us together, being now as far off or farther than ever, in our apprehension; as also to take that means away, which would have been so comfortable unto us in that course, both for wisdom of council as also for our singular help in our course of godliness, whom the Lord (as it were) took away even as fruit falleth before it was ripe, (he means Mr. Robinson) when neither length of days, nor infirmity of body, did seem to call for his end. The Lord even then took him away, as it were in his anger, whom if tears would have held, he had remained to this day. The loss of his ministry was very great unto me, for I ever counted myself happy in the enjoyment of it, notwithstanding all the crosses and losses otherwise I sustained. Yet indeed the manner ot his taking away hath more troubled me, as fearing the Lord's anger in it, that, as I said, in the ordinary course of things might still have remained, as also, the singular service he might have yet done in the church of God. Alas, dear friends, our state and cause in religion! by his death being wholly destitute of any that may defend our cause as it should against our adversaries. That we may take up that doleful complaint in the Psalm, that there is no prophet left among us, nor any that knoweth how long.

Alas! you would fain have had him with you, and he would as fain have come to you; many letters and much speech hath been about his coming to you, but never any solid course propounded for his going; if the course propounded the last year had appeared to have been certain, he would have gone though with two or three families. I know no man amongst us knew his mind better than I did, about those things; he was loath to leave the church, yet I know also, that he would have accepted the worst conditions which in the largest extent of a good conscience could be taken, to have come to you. For myself and all such others as have formerly minded coming, it is much what the same, if the Lord afford means. We only know how things are with you by your letters, but how things stand in England we have received no letters of any thing, and it was November before we received yours. If we come at all unto you, the means to enable us so to do must come from you. For the state of our church, and how it is with us and of our people, it is wrote of by Mr. White. Thus praying you to pardon my boldness with you in writing as I do, I commend you to the keeping of the Lord, desiring, if he see it good, and that I might be serviceable unto the business, that I were with you. God hath taken away my son, that was with me in the ship, when I went back again; I have only two children which were born since I left you: Fare you well.

Yours to his power,

THOMAS BLOSSOM.

Leyden, December 15, *Anno* 1625.

To his very loving friend, Mr. William Bradford, Governour of Plymouth in New England, these be.

My loving and kind friend, and brother in the Lord; my own and my wife's true love and hearty salutations to yourself and yours and all the rest of our loving friends with you; hoping in the Lord of your good healths, which I beseech him long to continue for the glory of his name and good of his people. Concerning your kind letter to the church, it was read publicly; whereunto (by the church) I send you here inclosed an answer. Concerning my brother Robinson's sickness and death and our practice, I wrote you at large, some five or six months since; but lest it should miscarry, I have now written to Mr. Brewster thereof, to whom I refer you. Now concerning your course of choosing your Governours yearly, and in special of their choosing yourself year after year, as I conceive they still do, and Mr. Allerton your assistant; howsoever I think it the best way that can be, so long as it please the Lord to continue your lives, and so good Governours offer you; yet, considering man's mortality, whose breath is in his nostrils, and the evils of the times wherein we live, in which it is ordinarily seen that worse follow them that are good, I think it would be a safer course, for after time, the government was sometime removed from one to another; so the assistant one year might be Governour next and a new assistant chosen in his place, either of such as have or have not been in office; sometimes one, sometimes another, as it shall seem most fit to the corporation. My reasons are, first, because other officers that come after you, will look (especially if they be ambitiously minded) for the same privileges and continuance you have had; and if he have it not, will take great offence, as though unworthy of the place, and so greatly disgraced, whom to continue, might be very dangerous, and hazard (at least) the overthrow of all; men not looking so much at the reasons why others were so long continued as at the custom. 2dly, because others that are unexperienced in government might learn by experience; and so there might be fit and able men continually, when it pleaseth the Lord to take any away. 3dly, by this means, you may establish the things begun, or done before; for the Governour this year, that was assistant last, will in likelihood, rather ratify and confirm, and go on with that he had a hand in the beginning of, when he was assistant, than otherwise, or persuade the new to it; whereas new Governours, especially when there are factions, will many times overthrow that which is done by the former, and so scarcely any thing goeth forward for the general good; neither that I see, can this be any prejudice to the corporation; for the new may always have the counsel and advice of the old, for their direction, though they be out of office; these things I make bold to put to your godly wisdom and discretion, intreating you to pardon my boldness therein; and so leave it to your discretion to make use of as you see it fitting, not having written the least inkling hereof to any other. Now I entreat you, at your best leisure to write to me, how you think it will in likelihood go with your civil and church estate; whether there be hope of the continuance of both, or either; or whether you fear any alteration to be attempted in either; the reason of this my request is, the fear of some amongst us (the which if that hinder not, I think will come unto you) occasioned partly by your letter to your father in law, Mr. May, wherein you write of the troubles you have had with some, who it is like (having the times and friends on their sides) will work you what mischiefs they can; and that they may do much, many here do fear: And partly by reason of this king's proclamation, dated the 13th of May last, in which he saith, that his full resolution is, to the end that there may be one uniform course of government, in, and through all his whole monarchy; that the government of Virginia shall immediately depend on himself, and not be committed to any company or corporation, etc. so that some conceive he will have both the same civil and ecclesiastical government that is in England, which occasioneth their fear. I desire you to write your thoughts of these things, for the satisfying of others; for my own part and some others, we durst rely upon you for that, who we persuade ourselves, would not be thus earnest, for our pastor and church to come to you; if you feared the danger of being suppressed. Thus desiring you to pardon my boldness, and remember us in your prayers; I for this time and ever, commit you and all your affairs to the Almighty, and rest

Your assured loving friend

And brother in the Lord,

ROGER WHITE.

Leyden, Dec. 1, *Anno* 1625.

P. S. The church would entreat you to continue your writing to them, which is very comfortable.

To our most dear, and entirely beloved brethren, Mr. William Bradford and Mr. William Brewster, grace mercy and true peace be multiplied, from God our Father, through our Lord Jesus Christ. Amen.

Most dear christian friends and brethren, as it is no small grief unto you, so is it no less unto us, that we are constrained to live thus disunited each from other, especially considering our affections each unto other, for the mutual edifying and comfort of both, in these evil days wherein we live: if it pleased the Lord to bring us again together, than which as no outward thing could be more comfortable unto us, or is more desired of us, if the Lord see it good; so see we no hope of means of accomplishing the same, except it come from you, and therefore, must with patience rest in the work and will of God, performing our duties to him and you assunder; whom we are not any way able to help, but by our continual prayers to him for you, and sympathy of affections with you, for the troubles which befal you; till it please the Lord to reunite us again. But our dearly beloved brethren, concerning your kind and respective letter, howsoever written by one of you, yet as we continue with the consent (at least in affection) of you both, although we cannot answer your desire and expectation, by reason it hath pleased the Lord to take to himself out of this miserable world our dearly beloved pastor, yet for ourselves we are minded as formerly, to come unto you, when and as the Lord affordeth means, though we see little hope thereof at present, as being unable of ourselves, and that our friends will help us we see little hope. And now, brethren, what shall we say further unto you; our desires and prayers to God, is (if such were his good will and pleasure) we might be reunited for the edifying and mutual comfort of both, which, when he sees fit, he will accomplish. In the mean time, we commit you unto him and to the word of his grace; whom we beseech to guide and direct both you and us, in all his ways, according to that, his word, and to bless all our lawful endeavours, for the glory of his name and good of his people. Salute, we pray you, all the church and brethren with you to whom we would have sent this letter. If we knew it could not be prejudicial unto you, as we hope it cannot; yet fearing the worst, we thought fit either to direct it to you, our two beloved brethen, leaving it to your goodly wisdom and discretion, to manifest our mind to the rest of our loving friends and brethren, as you see most convenient. And thus intreating you to remember us in your prayers, as we also do you; we for this time commend you and all your affairs to the direction and protection of the Almighty, and rest,

Your assured loving friends
And brethren in the Lord,
FRANCIS JESSOPP,
THOMAS NASH,
THOMAS BLOSSOM,
ROGER WHITE,
RICHARD MAISTERSON.

Leyden, Nov. 30, *A.D.* 1625.

Before I pass to other things, I will here insert a letter of Mr. Robinson's, which, though it is out of place, yet coming now to hand, I thought better to put it here, than to omit it. It was written to the church as followeth:

To the church of God, at Plymouth, in New England.

Much beloved brethren, neither the distance of place, nor distinction of body, can at all either dissolve or weaken that bond of true christian affection in which the Lord by his spirit hath tied us together. My continual prayers are to the Lord for you; my most earnest desire is unto you; from whom I will not longer keep (if God will) than means can be procured to bring with me the wives and children of divers of you and the rest of your brethren, whom I could not leave behind me without great, both injury to you and them, and offence to God and all men. The death of so many our dear friends and brethren; oh! how grievous hath it been to you to bear, and to us to take knowledge of, which, if it could be mended with lamenting, could not sufficiently be bewailed; but we must go unto them and they shall not return unto us: And how many even of us, God hath taken away here, and in England, since your departure, you may elsewhere take knowledge. But the same God has tempered judgment with mercy, as otherwise, so in sparing the rest, especially those by whose godly and wise government, you may be, and (I know) are so much helped. In a battle it is not looked for but that divers should die; it is thought well for a side, if it get the victory, though with the loss of divers, if not too many or too great. God, I hope, hath given you the victory, after many difficulties, for yourselves and others; though I doubt not, but many do and will remain for you and us all to strive with. Brethren, I hope I need not exhort you to obedience unto those whom God hath set over you, in church and commonwealth, and to the Lord in them. It is a christian's honour, to give honour according to men's places; anc his liberty, to serve God in faith, and his brethren in love or derly and with a willing and free heart. God forbid, I shoulc need to exhort you to peace, which is the bond of perfection and by which all good is tied together, and without which it is scattered. Have peace with God first, by faith in his promises good conscience kept in all things, and oft renewed by repent ance; and so, one with another, for his sake, who is, though three, one; and for Christ's sake who is one, and as you are called by one spirit to one hope. And the God of peace anc grace and all goodness be with you, in all the fruits thereof plenteously upon your heads, now and for ever. All your brethren here, remember you with great love, a general toker whereof they have sent you.

Yours ever in the Lord,

Leyden, (*Holland*) *June* 30, *Anno* 1621. JOHN ROBINSON

GOVERNOR BRADFORD'S LETTER BOOK.

THIS next year being Anno. 1626, we sent Mr. Allerton into England, partly to make some supply for us, and to see if he could make any reasonable composition with the adventurers and because we well knew that nothing can be done without money, we gave him an order to procure some, binding ourselves to make payment thereof, as followeth:

Know all men by these presents, that whereas we William Bradford, Governour of Plymouth in New England, and William Brewster, Capt. Miles Standish, Isaac Allerton, Samuel Fuller, Edward Winslow, John Jeney, John Howland, and John Allden; being all inhabitants of Plymouth, aforesaid, are for ourselves, and divers others, our associates, &c. And whereas the said Isaac Allerton (by God's providence) for the necessary occasions of the colony abovesaid, is bound for England; and whereas divers of us above named, have acquainted divers of our worthy and approved friends (by our letters *) with our raw and weak estate, and want of ability of ourselves

* These letters I have not.

to manage so great an action, as the upholding of the plantation aforesaid. If therefore God shall move the heart or hearts of any of our friends, in compassion of our wants and present straits, to lend us above named, the sum of one hundred pounds sterling, for the space of two years, upon any such terms as shall be agreed upon, between him or them and the said Isaac Allerton, our partner and agent, and deliver the same into his hands for our use; that we, the said William Bradford, William Brewster, &c. together with the said Isaac Allerton, do bind ourselves, our heirs, &c. jointly and severally, for the faithful performance of such obligations, conditions, or covenants, as shall be agreed on, &c. In witness whereof, we have put to our hands and seals, this 2d of July, Anno 1626, &c.

Upon this order, he got two hundred pounds, but it was at thirty in the hundred interest, by which appears in what straits we were; and yet this was upon better terms than the goods which were sent us the year before, being at forty-five per cent. so that it was God's marvellous providence, that we were ever able to wade through things, as will better appear if God give me life and opportunity to handle them more particularly, in another treatise more at large, as I desire and purpose (if God permit) with many other things, in a better order.

Besides the obtaining of this money, he with much ado made a composition and agreement with the body of the adventurers, Mr. Allden (something now softened by my letter before mentioned) who was one of our powerfulest opposers, did not only yield thereunto, but was a furtherer of the same. I will shew the heads of it, as it was drawn in a deed as followeth:

To all christian people, to whom this present writing indented shall come greeting,

Whereas, at a meeting the 26th of October last past, divers and sundry persons, whose names to the one part of these presents are subscribed in a schedule hereunto annexed, adventurers to New-Plymouth, in New England in America, were contented and agreed (in consideration of the sum of one thousand and eight hundred pounds sterling, to be paid unto the said adventurers in manner and form following) to sell and make sale of all and every the stocks, shares, lands, merchandize and chattles whatsoever, to the said adventurers and other their fellow adventurers to New Plymouth aforesaid accruing or belonging, to the generality of the said adventurers aforesaid, as well by reasons of any sum or sums of money, or merchandize at any time heretofore adventured by them, or otherwise howsoever; for the better expression and setting forth of which said agreement, the parties to these presents subscribing, do for themselves severally, and as much as in them is, grant, bargain, alien, sell and transfer, all and every the said shares, goods, lands, merchandize and chattles to them belonging as aforesaid, unto Isaac Allerton, one of the planters resident at New Plymouth aforesaid, assigned and sent over as agent for the rest of the planters residing there, and unto such other planters at New Plymouth aforesaid, as the said Isaac Allerton, his heirs or assignees, at his, or their arrival shall by writing or otherwise think fit to join, or partake in the premises, their and every of their heirs and assigns in as large and ample and beneficial manner and form, to all intents and purposes, as the said several subscribing adventurers here could or may do, or perform; all which stocks, shares, lands, &c. to the said adventurers, in severalty alloted, apportioned or belonging; the said adventurers do warrant, and defend unto the said Isaac Allerton his heirs and assigns, against them, their heirs and assigns, by these presents: And therefore, the said Isaac Allerton for him, his heirs and assigns, doth covenant, promise, and grant to and with the said adventurers, whose names are hereunto subscribed, their heirs, &c. well and truly to pay, or cause to be paid unto the said adventurers or five of them, which were at the meeting aforesaid, nominated and deputed, viz. John Pocock, John Beauchamp, Robert Kean, Edward Bass, and James Shirley, their heirs, &c. to, and for the use of the generality of them, the sum of eighteen hundred pounds, of lawful money of England, at the place appointed for the receipts of money, on the west side of the Royal Exchange in London, by two hundred pounds yearly and every year, on the feast day of St. Michael, which shall be in the year 1628: And the said Isaac Allerton, for him, his heirs, &c. doth covenant and grant to, and with the said adventurers, their heirs, &c. to do his, and their good endeavours, to procure, obtain, and get of, and from all the planters, at New Plymouth aforesaid, or so many of them as he or they by persuasion and entreaty can or may, security by several obligations, or writing obligatory, to make payment of the said sum of eighteen hundred pounds, in form aforesaid, according to the true meaning of these presents. In testimony whereof, to this part of these presents, remaining with the said Isaac Allerton, the said subscribing adventurers have set to their names,

&c. And to the other part of these presents remaining with the said adventurers, the said Isaac Allerton hath subscribed his name, the 15th of November, Anno 1626, and in the second year of the reign of our sovereign Lord, King Charles, by the grace of God, King of England, &c: Subscribed thus as followeth:

John White,	*Samuel Sharp,*	*Thomas Hudson,*
John Pocock,	*Robert Holland,*	*Thomas Andrews,*
Robert Kean,	*James Shirley,*	*Thomas Ward,*
Edward Bass,	*Thomas Mott,*	*Fria. Newbald,*
William Hobson,	*Thomas Fletcher,*	*Thomas Heath,*
William Penington,	*Timothy Hatherly,*	*Joseph Tilden,*
William Quarles,	*Thomas Brewer,*	*William Penrin,*
Daniel Poynton,	*John Thorned,*	*Eliza Knight,*
Richard Andrews,	*Myles Knowles,*	*Thomas Coventry,*
Newman Rookes,	*William Collier,*	*Robert Allden,*
Henry Browning,	*John Revell,*	*Laurence Anthony,*
Richard Wright,	*Peter Gudburn,*	*John Knight,*
John Ling,	*Emnu. Alltham,*	*Matthew Thornhill,*
Thomas Goffe,	*John Beauchamp,*	*Thomas Millsop,*

In all forty-two.

This year, Anno 1627, Mr. Allerton was sent again as for other things, so especially to ratify and confirm this bargain; and for that end we gave him full authority under our hands, and seal, and became bound in several bonds for the payment of the money yearly: So the thing was fully concluded, and the bargain fairly engrossed in parchment, under their hands and seals, as legally and formally done, as by the learnedest lawyers could be devised, as by the deed itself will better appear; which I will not here insert, being long, but the substance may be seen in the former, to which it hath reference; only I will mention this particular clause, how we were bound thereby to forfeit thirty shillings a week, for every week that we failed of due payment, at any the several days. Thus all now is become our own, as we say in the proverb, when our debts are paid. And doubtless this was a great mercy of God unto us, and a great means of our peace and better subsistence, and wholly dashed all the plots and devises of our enemies, both there and here, who daily expected our ruin, dispersion and utter subversion by the same; but their hopes were thus far prevented, though with great care and labour, we were left to struggle with the payment of the money.

GOVERNOR BRADFORD'S LETTER BOOK.

A letter of Mr. Sherley's to myself upon this conclusion, as followeth:

To his very loving and much respected friend, Mr. William Bradford, Governour of Plymouth, in New-England, these.

Most Worthy and Beloved

SIR,

I have received your letter of the 14th of June last, by your and my loving friend, Mr. Allerton, wherein it pleaseth you to express more thankfulness than I have deserved; I confess my desire is much larger than my power, to do you and those good friends with you, the good I would. We cannot but all take notice how the Lord hath been pleased to cross our proceedings and caused many disasters to befal us therein; and sure I conceive the only cause to be, we, or *many of us here, aimed at other ends than God's glory:* But now I hope that cause is taken away, the bargain being fully concluded and, as far as our powers will reach, confirmed under our hands and seals to Mr. Allerton and the rest of his and your co-partners: But for my own part, I confess, as I was loath to hinder this bargain, being the first propounder thereof at our meeting, so, on the contrary side, I was as unwilling to set my hand to the sale, being the receiver of the most part of the adventures and a second causer of much of the engagements, and one more threatened, being most envied and aimed at (if they could find any step to ground their malice on) than any other of the adventurers whosoever: I profess I know no just cause they ever had, or have so to do, neither shall it ever be proved that I have wronged them or any of the adventurers, wittingly or willingly, one penny in the disbursement of the best part of five thousand pounds, in those two years' troubles: No, the sole cause why they malice me (as I and others have conceived) was that I would not side with them against you and the going over of the Leyden; but as I then cared not, so now I little fear what they can do; yet charge and trouble I know they may cause me to be at; and for these reasons, I would gladly have persuaded the other four to have sealed to this bargain and so have left me out; but Mr. Allerton knoweth they would not; so rather than it should now fail, Mr. Allerton having taken so much pains (as I am even ashamed to relate) I have sealed with the rest, with this proviso and promise of Mr. Allerton's, that if any troubles arise here, you are to be at half the charge: Wherefore now I doubt not but you will give your generality good content and self peace amongst yourselves, and peace with the natives, then, no doubt but the God * of peace will bless your going out and returning in, and cause all that you set your hand to to prosper: The which I shall ever pray the Lord to grant, if it be his most blessed will, and that for Jesus Christ his sake.

I acknowledge myself much obliged to you, and others with you, for your good counsel and loving respect to my kinsman; I pray you continue the same still and set it as on my score to requite when occasion is offered. My wife and I most kindly remember our loves unto you and Mrs. Bradford, desiring you to remember us in your prayers, for assuredly unless the Lord be merciful unto us and the whole land in general, our estate and condition is far worse than yours; wherefore if the Lord send persecution here (which is much to be feared) and so should put into our minds to fly for refuge, I know no place safer than to come to you, for all Europe is at variance one with another, but chiefly with us) not doubting but to find such friendly entertainment as shall be honest and conscionable, notwithstanding what hath lately passed; for I profess in the word of an honest man, had it not been to procure your peace and quiet from some turbulent spirits here, I would not have sealed to this deed, though you have given me all my adventure and debt ready down: And this I leave to your serious consideration, not questioning, but you will approve yourselves faithful and honest before God and men: And thus desiring the Lord to bless, preserve and prosper you and all with you, I for this time cease, but ever resting,

Your faithful and loving friend
to my power,
JAMES SHIRLEY.

London, Dec. 27th, Anno 1627.

* He hath hitherto done it, blessed be His name!

GOVERNOR BRADFORD'S LETTER BOOK.

THIS year we had letters sent us from the Dutch plantation, of whom we had heard much by the natives, but never could hear from them nor meet with them before themselves thus writ to us, and after sought us out; their letters were writ in a very fair hand, the one in French, and the other in Dutch, but were one *verbatim*, so far as the tongue would bear.

[*Here follows a letter in Low Dutch, from Isaac de Razier at Manhatas, in fort, Amsterdam Mar.* 9, 1627 *N. S. to the Governour of New-Plymouth.*]

I will not trouble myself to translate this letter, seeing the effect of it will be understood by the answer which now follows in English, though writ to them in Dutch.

To the Honourable and Worshipful the Director and Council of New Netherland, our very loving and worthy friends and christian neighbours.

The Governour and Council of Plymouth in New England wish your Honours and Worships all happiness, and prosperity in this life, and eternal rest and glory with Christ Jesus our Lord in the world to come.

We have received your letters wherein appeareth your good will, and friendship toward us, but is expressed with over high titles, and more than belongs to us, or than is meet for us to receive: But for your good will and congratulation of our prosperity in this small beginning of our poor colony, we are much bound unto you, and with many thanks do acknowledge the same; taking it both for a great honour done unto us, and for a certain testimony of your love, and good neighbourhood. Now these are further to give your Honours, Worships and Wisdoms to understand, that it is to us no small joy, to hear, that it hath pleased God to move his Majesty's heart, not only to confirm that ancient amity, alliance, and friendship, and other contracts formerly made, and ratified by his predecessors of famous memory; but hath himself (as you say) and we likewise have been informed, strengthened the same with a new union, the better to resist the pride of that common enemy the Spaniards, from whose cruelty the Lord keep us both, and our native countries. Now for as much as this is sufficient to unite us togather in love, and good neighbourhood in all our dealings; yet are many of us further tied by the good and courteous entreaty which we have found in your country; having lived there many years, with freedom and good content, as many of our friends do to this day; for which we are bound to be thankful, and our children after us and shall never forget the same but shall heartily desire your good and prosperity, as our own forever. Likewise for your friendly proposition and offer to accommodate and help us with any commodities or merchandize which you have and we want, either for beaver, otters or other wares, is to us very acceptable, and we doubt not but in short time, we may have profitable commerce and trade together: But you may please to understand that we are but one particular colony or plantation in this land, there being divers others besides, unto whom it hath pleased those Honourable Lords of his Majesty's Council for New England, to grant the like commission, and ample privileges to them (as to us) for their better profit and subsistence; namely to expulse, or make prize of any, either strangers or other English which shall attempt, either to trade, or plant within their limits (without their special licence and commission) which extends to forty degrees: Yet for our parts, we shall not go about to molest or trouble you in any thing, but continue all good neighbourhood and correspondence as far as we may; only we desire that you would forbear to trade with the natives in this bay, and river of Naragansett and Sowames, which is (as it were) at our doors: The which if you do, we think also no other English will go about any way to trouble or hinder you; which otherwise are resolved to solicit his Majesty for redress, if otherwise they cannot help themselves.

May it please you further to understand, that for this year we are fully supplied with all necessaries, both for clothing and other things; but it may so fall out, that hereafter we shall deal with you, if your rates be reasonable: And therefore when your people come again, we desire to know how you will take beaver by the pound, and otters by the skin, and how you will per cent. for other commodities, and what you can furnish us with; as likewise what commodities from us, may be acceptable with you, as tobacco, fish, corn, or other things, and what prices you will give.

Thus hoping that you will pardon and excuse us for our rude and imperfect writing in your language, and take it in good part; because, for want of use, we cannot so well express that we understand; nor happily understand every thing so fully as we should: And so we humbly pray the Lord, for his mercy's sake, that he will take both us and our native countries, into his holy protection and defence. Amen.

By the Governour and Council, your Honours' and Worships' very good friends and neighbours.

New-Plymouth, March 19th.

Next follows their reply to this our answer, very friendly but maintaining their right and liberty to trade in those parts, which we had desired they would forbear; alleging that as we had authority and commission from our king; so they had the like from the States of Holland, which they would defend.

August 7, 1627.

Another of theirs upon our answer to their last, which I here omit.

An answer to the former letters.

We have received your * letters dated the 7th of August, and with them a rundlet of sugar, and two Holland cheeses, by John Jacobson of Wiring; for which we give you many thanks and must remain your debtors till another time, not having any thing to send you for the present that may be acceptable: Further, you shall understand that it is also our resolution and hearty desire to hold and continue all friendship and good neighbourhood with you as far as we may and lies in our power; we desire also that we might have opportunity (according as you write) by word of mouth, to confer together touching our mutual commerce and trading in such things as our countries afford; and would now have sent one, but that one of our boats is abroad, and we have much business at home; But if by the next you would please to depute one (according as you have propounded) to come hither and to confer hereabouts, we should be glad and he should be welcome. If not, we shall send as soon as conveniently we can (after harvest) if we can know when your bark comes this way. We cannot likewise omit (out of our love and good affection toward you and the trust you repose in us) to give you warning of the danger which may befal you, that you may prevent it; for

* This was wrote in their own tongue.

if you light either in the hands of those of Virginia or the fishing ships, which come to New England, peradventure they will make prize of you, if the can, if they find you trading within those limits; as they surprised a colony of the French, not many years since, which was seated within these bounds: For howsoever you allege in your former letter, that you have navigated and traded in these parts above this twenty-six years, and that your company have now authority from the States and the Prince of Orange to do so; yet you must understand that her Majesty, Queen Elizabeth, of famous memory hath began to navigate and plant in these lands well nigh forty years ago, as appeareth by her patents and royal grants conferred upon divers of her subjects and since confirmed and enlarged by his late Majesty, and still continued by possession. Therefore it were best (in our opinion) that your masters should solicit the States that they might come to some order and agreement with the King's Majesty and State of England hereabout, before any inconvenience befal; for howsoever you may be assured for ourselves, yet we should be sorry to hear you should sustain harm from any of our nation; but more of these things when we shall speak one with another: In the mean time we commit you and your affairs to the protection of the highest.

Your loving friends, the Governour
and Council of New-Plymouth.
WILLIAM BRADFORD.
Plymouth, August 14, *Anno* 1627. *Governour, &c.*

THEIR answer to this directed to myself thus superscribed:

Monsieur Monseignieur, William Bradford, Governeur in Nieu-Plemeuen.

This I will put in English and so will end with theirs, viz.

After the wishing of all good unto you, this serves to let you understand, that we have received your (acceptable) letters dated the 14th of the last month, by John Jacobson of Wiring, who besides, by word of mouth, hath reported unto us your kind and friendly entertainment of him: For which cause (by the good-liking and approbation of the Directors and Council) I am resolved to come myself, in friendship, to visit you, that we may by word of mouth friendly communicate of things together; as also to report unto you the good will and favour that the Honourable Lords of the authorized West-Indian company bear towards you. And to show our willingness of your good accommodation, have brought with me some cloth of three sorts and colours, and a chest of white sugar, as also some *seawan*, &c. not doubting but, if any of them may be serviceable unto you, we shall agree well enough about the prices thereof. Also John Jacobson aforesaid hath told me, that he came to you overland in six hours, but I have not gone so far this three or four years; wherefore I fear my feet will fail me, so I am constrained to entreat you to afford me the easiest means that I may, with least weariness, come to congratulate with you: So leaving other things to the report of the bearer, shall herewith end; remembering my hearty salutations to yourself and friends, &c. from a-board the bark Nassau, the 4th of October; before Frenchman's point.

Your affectionate friend,

Anno 1627. ISAAC DE RAZIER.

So, according to his request, we sent our boat for him, who came honourably attended with a noise of trumpeters; he was their upper *commis*, or chief merchant and second to the Governour; a man of a fair and genteel behaviour, but soon after fell into disgrace amongst them; by reason of their factions; and thus at length we came to meet and deal together. We at this time bought sundry of their commodities, especially their *sewan* or *wampampeack*, which was the beginning of a profitable trade with us and the Indians: We further understood, that their masters were willing to have friendship with us and to supply us with sundry commodities, and offered us assistance against the French if need were. The which, though we know it was with an eye to their own profit, yet we had reason both kindly to accept it and make use of it: So after this sundry of them came often to us, and many letters passed between us, the which I will pass by, as being about particular dealings, and would not be here very pertinent; only upon this passage we wrote one to their Lords and masters; as followeth.

Right Honourable and Worthy Lords, &c.

We understand by your agent, Mr. Isaac Razier, who is at this present with us (and hath demeaned himself to your honours and his own credit) of your honourable and respective good intentions towards us, which we humbly acknowledge with all thankfulness, and shall ever be ready in the performance of all offices of good and christian neighbourhood, towards your colony and plantation here, and in all satisfactory correspondence to your Honours, so far as in us lieth and may stand with our allegiance to the King's most excellent Majesty. our Sovereign Lord the King of Great-Britain; acknowledging ourselves tied in a strict obligation unto your country and State, for the good entertainment and free liberty which we had, and our brethren and countrymen yet there have and do enjoy, under our most honourable Lords the States; and so shall be ready to accommodate ourselves to your good satisfaction: For the propositions of your agent concerning the matter of trade and commerce, we will have due and respective consideration, wishing it had been sooner propounded at the beginning of the year, before we sent our factor into England and Holland about our trade and supplies; for, till his return, we can determine of nothing, not yet knowing certainly what issue there will be of the business between the merchants our partners, and ourselves; and therefore desire suspension of our determination and resolution herein till the next year, we being not yet altogether free in respect of our engagements unto them: In the meantime we will digest it in our best cogitations; only we desire your Honours, that ye would take into your wise and honourable considerations, that which we conceive may be a hindrance to this accordation, and may be a means of much future evil, if it be not prevented, namely, that you clear the title of your planting in these parts, which his Majesty hath, by patent, granted to divers his nobles and subjects of quality; least it be a bone of division in these stirring evil times, which God forbid: We persuade ourselves, that now may be easily and seasonably done, which will be harder and with more difficulty obtained hereafter, and perhaps not without blows; so there may be assured peace and good correspondence on all parts, and ourselves more free and able to contract with your Honours. Thus commending our best service to our most noble Lords, praying for the prosperous success of your worthy designs, we rest your Lordships'

Most sincerely affected and bounden,
William Bradford.

Plymouth, Oct. 1, *Anno* 1627. *Governour, &c.*

GOVERNOR BRADFORD'S LETTER BOOK.

WE well knew likewise, that this dealing and friendship with the Dutch (though it was wholly sought of themselves) yet it would procure us envy from others in the land, and that at one time or other, our enemies would take occasion to raise slanders and frame accusations against us for it; therefore, to prevent their malice, as also to shew the sincerity of our dealing and our loyal and dutiful respect to his Majesty and the Honourable Council for New England; we sent their first letter (with our answer thereto and their reply to the same) unto the Council as may appear more particularly by our letters following.

A letter to the Council of New England.

Right Honourable,

WE held it our bounden duty to inform and acquaint your Lordships and Honours, with all such occurrences and matters of note as do here befal, and may any way concern the estate of this country, in either the good or hurt thereof, which, next his Majesty, stands under your honourable governments and protection; or which may in any sort, be worthy your wise and prudent considerations. May it please your Honours and Lordships to understand, that of late we received letters from the Dutch plantation, who using to trade near unto us, had order to stay for an answer from us; and the effect of their letters, being friendly and congratulatory, we answered them in like sort; since which time, we received another from them, but have had as yet no opportunity to give answer thereto. Their first letters were two,* but both one in effect and verbatim, so far as the proprieties of the tongues will bear; the French, with the copies both of our answer and their reply, we have here enclosed sent unto your Honour's view, that according to your honourable directions therein, we may govern ourselves, in our dealings with them. We further understand that for strength of men and fortification, they far exceed us, and all in this land. We cannot likewise forbear to complain unto your Lordships, of the irregular living of many in this

* The one in French and the other in Dutch.

land, who without either patent or licence, order or government, live, trade and truck, not with any intent to plant, but rather to forage the country and get what they can, whether by right or wrong, and then be gone: So as such as have been and are at great charge to settle plantations, will not be able to subsist, if some remedy be not provided, both with these and the inordinate course of fishermen, who begin to leave fishing, and fall wholly to trading, to the great detriment of both the small beginning here, and the State of England, by the unprofitable consuming of the victuals of the land upon these salvages: Whereas plantations might here better raise the same in the land, and so be enabled both to subsist and to return the profit thereof into England for other necessaries, which would be beneficial to the commonwealth. Our humble suits therefore to your good Lordships is, that you would take some such order, for redress herein, as shall seem best to your honourable wisdoms, for the relief of all the plantations in the land. So in all humbleness we commit ourselves to your honourable direction, and you to the protection of the Almighty, resting

Yours ever at commandment,

WILLIAM BRADFORD,

New-Plymouth, June 15, *Anno* 1627. *Governour, &c.*

Another to Sir Ferdinando Gorges, touching the same subject.

Honourable Sir,

MY humble duty remembered; we have of late received letters from the Dutch plantation and have had speech with some of them; I hold it my duty to acquaint your Worship and the rest of the Honourable Council therewith, unto whom we have likewise writ and sent the copies of their letters, that, together with their and your honourable directions, we may know how to order ourselves herein: They have used trading there this six or seven and twenty years, but have begun to plant of later time, and now have reduced their trade to some order, and confined it only to their company, which heretofore was spoiled by their seamen and interlopers, as ours is this year most notoriously, of whom we have made some complaint in our letters to the Council, not doubting but we shall find worshipful furtherance therein. We are now upon concluding with our adventurers, and shall be put upon hard straits by great payments, which we are enforced to make, for sundry years, or else to leave all, which will be to us very difficult; and, to say the truth, if these disorders of fishermen and interlopers, be not remedied, no plantations are able to stand, but will decay, whereas otherwise they may subsist and flourish: Thus in all humbleness I take leave, and rest,

At your service,
WILLIAM BRADFORD,

Plymouth, June 15, *Anno* 1627.

P. S. Besides the spoiling of the trade this last year, our boat and men had like to have been cut off by the Indians, after the fishermen were gone, for the wrongs which they did them, in stealing their skins and other abuses offered them, both the last year and this; and besides they still continue to truck pieces, powder and shot with them, which will be the overthrow of all, if it be not looked unto.

BUT I will now return to prosecute other letters out of England, touching our business and success thereof.

A letter of Mr. Shirley's.

To his worthy and loving friend, Mr. William Bradford, Governour of Plymouth, in New-England; these.

Thrice worthy and beloved Sir,

I HAVE received your letter of the 26th of May, by Mr. Gibs and Mr. Goff, and with all the barrel of skins according to the contents; for which Mr. Beauchamp and I got a bill of store, and so took them up and sold them together at £78 12*s.* sterling, and since, Mr. Allerton hath received the money, as will appear by the account. It is true as you write, your engagements are great, not only the purchase, but you are yet necessitated to take up the stock you work upon, and that not at 6 or 8 per cent. as it is here let out, but at 30, 40, yea and some 50 per cent. which were not your gains great, and God's blessing on your honest endeavours more than ordinary, it could not be that you should long subsist, in the maintaining of and upholding of your worldly affairs: And this your honest, wise, and discreet agent, Mr. Allerton, hath seriously considered and so deeply laid to mind how to ease you of it, as I know it hath much troubled him: He told me you were contented to accept of me and some few others, to join with you in the purchase, as partners; for which I kindly thank you and all the rest and do willingly accept of it; and though absent, shall willingly and readily be at such charge as you and the rest shall think meet; and this year am contented to forbear my former £50 and two years increase for the adventure, both which now makes £80, without any bargain or condition for the profit, you (I mean the generality) standing to the adventure outward and homeward: Now (not that I would seem to boast or seek for undeserved praise) I have persuaded Mr. Andrews and Mr. Beauchamp to do the like; so as you are eased of that high rate you were at the other two years, I say we leave it freely to yourselves, allow us what you please and as God shall bless: I purpose, God willing, to be at charge of sending over a man or two; and so doth Mr. Andrews and now Mr Beauchamp; for what course I run he desireth to do the same; and though he have been or seemed somewhat harsh heretofore, yet, now you shall find he is new moulded.

I also see, in your letter, your desire I should be your agent or factor here; truly Mr. Bradford and our worthy Governour, far be it from me to flatter you (for I profess to hate it) I have ever esteemed and found you so faithful, honest and upright men, as I have even resolved with myself (God assisting me) to do you all the good that lieth in my power; and therefore if you please to make choice of so weak a man, both for abilities and body, to perform your business, I promise, the Lord enabling me, to do the best I can, according to those abilities he hath given me, and wherein I fail, excuse me and blame yourselves, that you made no better choice; now, because I am sickly and we are all mortal, I have advised Mr. Allerton to join Mr. Beauchamp with me in your deputation, which I conceive to be very necessary and good for you; your charge shall be no more for it is not your salary makes me undertake your business: Sir, for your love and good counsel to my kinsman, I acknowledge myself much engaged unto you, I pray you be still the same, for I know he hath much need of it.

[The rest being news, and of sundry passages about the Parliament; I omit as not pertinent to my purpose, it was concluded as followeth.]

Thus fearing I have been troublesome in relating of things, I cease, heartily desiring the long continuance of your good health to the pleasure of the Lord, and commending you and yours, and all God's faithful people wheresoever, unto the guidance and safe protection of the Almighty, ever resting

Your faithful loving friend,

JAMES SHIRLEY.

London, Nov. 17, *Anno* 1628.

BEING thus deeply engaged, and a few only of us being bound to make payment of all, yea in a double bond; for besides our formal bonds, it was our credits and honesty, that made our friends rest and rely upon us, assuring themselves, that if we lived and it was possible, we would see them have their monies: Therefore we thought it our safest and best course to come to some agreement with the people, to have the whole trade consigned to us for some years; and so in the time to take upon us, to pay all the debts and set them free: Another reason which moved us to take this heavy burthen upon our shoulders was, our great desire to transport as many of our brethren of Leyden over unto us, as we could, but without this course we could never have done it, all here being (for peace and unity's sake) made joint purchasers with us, and every one thereby had as much interest as ourselves; and many were very opposite here against us in respect of the great charge: Again we well knew, that, except we followed our trading roundly, we should never be able to do the one or the other; therefore we sought means to have our patent enlarged, and to have some good trading places included therein; that if we could not keep them thereby wholly to ourselves, yet that none should exclude or thrust us wholly out of them, as we well knew that some would have done, if we now had not laid hold of the opportunity: Therefore Mr. Allerton was sent over to prosecute these things, and to acquaint those few of our friends in England, whom the year before were joined purchasers with us, what agreements we had made and concluded with our people, and for what ends, and so to offer them to be our partners in trade and the whole business; writing our letters unto them for that end.

The copy of the covenants made with the people here followeth; after the which were signed by them, we made division of the cattle and other things, every one having according to their proportion of shares, and so were set free from all engagements and debts, they resting wholly on our heads.

ARTICLES of agreement between the Colony of Plymouth in New England of the one party; and William Bradford, Captain Miles Standish, and Isaac Allerton, and such others as they shall take as partners and undertakers with them, on the other party, made the —

First, it is agreed and covenanted betwixt the said parties, that they the said William Bradford, Captin Miles Standish, and Isaac Allerton, and such others as they shall take unto them, have undertaken, and do by these presents covenant and agree to pay, discharge and acquit the said colony, of all the debts, both due for the purchase, or any other way belonging to the same, at the day of the date of these presents.

Secondly, the abovesaid parties are to have and freely enjoy the pinnace, the boat at Manamett, and the shallop, called the Bass Boat, with all other implements to them belonging, that is in the store of the company; with all the whole stock of furs, fells, beads, corn, wampampeak, hatchets, knives, *&c.* that is now in the store, or any way due unto the same upon account.

Thirdly, that the abovesaid parties have the whole trade to themselves their heirs and assigns, with all the privileges thereof, as the said colony doth now, or may use the same; for six full years to begin the last of September next ensuing.

Fourthly, in further consideration of the discharge of the said debts every several purchaser, doth promise and covenant yearly to pay, or cause to be payed, to the abovesaid parties, during the full term of the said six years, three bushels of corn or six pounds of tobacco, at the undertaker's choice.

Fifthly, the said undertakers shall, during the aforesaid term, bestow £50 per annum in hose and shoes, to be brought over for the colony's use, to be sold them for corn, at *6s.* per bushel.

Sixthly, that at the end of the said term of six years, the whole trade shall return to the use and benefit of the said colony, as before.

Lastly, if the aforesaid undertakers, after they have acquainted their friends in England with these covenants, do (upon the first return) resolve to perform them, and undertake to discharge the debts of the said colony according to the true meaning and intent of these presents, then they are (upon such notice given) to stand in force, otherwise all things to remain, as formerly they were, and a true account to be given to the said colony, of the disposing of all things according to the former order.

This agreement was by these subscribed; for some would not subscribe, and some were from home.

William Brewster,	Cudbert Cudbers,	William Palmer,
Stephen Hopkins,	John Adams,	Exper. Michell,
Francis Eaton,	Phineas Pratt,	Edward Bangs,
Jona. Brewster,	Stephen Trasie,	Samuel Fuller,
Manas. Kempton,	Edward Doty,	Robert Hicks,
Thomas Prince,	Joshua Pratt,	John Howland,
Anthony Anable,	Stephen Dean,	John Billington,
John Shaw,	Wm. Wright,	Peter Brown,
William Bassett,	Francis Cook,	John Fance.

The names of the undertakers, were these following, for the three before mentioned made choice of these other, and though they knew not their minds before (many of them being absent) yet they did presume they would join with them in the thing, as afterward they did.

William Bradford,	John Howland,	*And these of London*
Captain Standish,	John Allden,	James Shirley,
Isaac Allerton,	Thomas Prince,	John Beauchamp,
Edward Winslow,		Richard Andrews,
William Brewster,		Timothy Hatherly.

GOVERNOR BRADFORD'S LETTER BOOK.

THIS year sundry that pretended themselves to be planters, seeing the gain the fishermen made by trading of pieces, and powder, and shot to the Indians, and how they went on uncontrouled in the same, they began to practice the same: A principal head of whom was one Morton, who had gathered a profane crew unto him, and was himself an example of all wickedness unto them, who kept a house (or school rather of *Athesmy*) in the Massachusetts bay. He not only had offended in trading off sundry pieces to the Indians, but when he was by his neighbours gently admonished of the same, and shewed the evil consequences that would follow thereupon, he took it in great scorn, and said he would do it in the dispite of all; and for that end sent for many new pieces out of England; besides, as he and his consorts got much hereby, so they spent it as lewdly in maintaining drunkenness, riot and other evils amongst them; yea and inveigling of men's servants away from them, so as the mischief began to grow intolerable, and if it had been suffered a while longer would have become incurable; his neighbours about him grew afraid of him, and suffered many abuses at his hands, and knew not how to help it; but both they, and other of the weaker plantations, made suit to us, to help and assist them to take some order with him and that desperate company; we told them that we had no authority to do any thing, but seeing it tended to the utter ruin of all the whole country, we would join with them against so public a mischief so we sent first again to admonish him, from ourselves and the rest, and signified unto him, that besides the hurt and peril he brought upon us all, his actions was flatly against a proclama tion of the late King's Majesty, published to all his subjects, both in England and here, against the trucking of any pieces or other arms, to any of the Savages; his answer (after oaths and other contumelies) was, that proclamations were no law, nor enjoined no penalty; he was answered yes, the breakers incurred his Majesty's displeasure, which might prove a penalty too heavy for him to bear; he replied, that King was dead, and his displeasure died with him: Thus seeing no other remedy, at the earnest request of the other planters, and plantations in the land, we assisted and led in the apprehension of him (which was with danger enough, for he armed himself for resistance) and so, by the mutual consent of all the rest, he was sent prisoner into England,* to the council of New England, with letters and information against him; which letters follow:

To the Right Honourable, his Majesty's council for New England, these,

Right Honourable, and our very good Lords,

NECESSITY hath forced us, his Majesty's subjects of New England in general (after long patience) to take this course with this troublesome planter, Mr. Thomas Morton, whom we have sent unto your Honours, that you may be pleased to take that course with him, which to your honourable wisdom shall seem fit; who hath been often admonished not to trade or truck with the Indians, either pieces, powder, or shot, which yet he hath done, and duly makes provision to do, and could not be restrained, taking in high scorn (as he speaks) that any here should controul therein: Now the general weakness of us, his Majesty's subjects, the strength of the Indians, and at this time their great preparations to do some affront upon us, and the evil example which it gives unto others, and having no subordinate general government, under your Honours, in this land, to restrain such misdemeanours, causeth us to be troublesome to your Lordships, to send this party unto you for remedy and redress hereof: And not only in respect to this particular delinquent, but of the fishing ships, who make it too ordinary a practice, with whom we have neither authority nor ability to deal, and who are more encouraged when the planters themselves are so licentious herein; and therefore most humbly pray your Lordships, to take into your honourable considerations that some speedy course and remedy may be taken herein; otherwise we shall be forced to quit the country, to our great grief, and dishonour to our nation; for we shall be beaten with

* And his consorts were dispersed.

our own arms if we abide: And that which further presseth us thus to send this party, is the fear we have of the growing of him and his consorts to that strength and height, by the access of loose persons, his house be a receptacle for such, as we should not be able to restrain his inordinariness when we would, they living without all fear of God or common honesty; some of them abusing the Indian women most filthily, as it is notorious: And for further satisfaction of your Lordships we have sent some particular testifications which we aver upon the faith of christians to be true: And likewise this bearer, Mr. John Oldham, who can give your Honours further information upon his oath, if need so require whom we have sent with the prisoner, and to attend your Lordships pleasures: And thus most humbly beseeching your Lordships and Honours to make a favourable construction of our honest intendments herein, of our loyalty and respective service to his Majesty, and our care for the common good of this country, thus we cease, and most humbly commend your Lordships and honours to the protection of the highest.

Your Lordships most humble, &c.

June 9, *Anno* 1628.

This letter was subscribed by some of the chief of every plantation; but I have not their names to the copy, and therefore omit them; yet they may in part be seen by that which was at the same time underwritten (in another paper) towards the charge, as followeth; though it cost us a great deal more, and yet to little effect, as the event sheweth.

	£.	s.
From Plymouth,	2	10
From Naumkeak,	1	10
From Pascataquack,	2	10
From Mr. Jeffrey and Mr. Burslem,	2	
From Natascot,	1	10
From Mrs. Thomson,		15
From Mr. Blackston,		12
From Edward Hilton,	1	
	12	7

We wrote this following, likewise, to Sir FERDINANDO GORGES.

Honourable Sir,

AS you have ever been, not only a favourer, but also a most special beginner and furtherer of the good of this country, to your great cost and no less honour, we whose names are underwritten, being some of every plantation, in the land, deputed for the rest, do humbly crave your worship's help and best assistance, in the speedy (if not too late) redress of our almost desperate state and condition in this place, expecting daily to be overrun and spoiled by the Savages, who are already abundantly furnished with pieces, powder and shot, swords, rapers and *Jaflings;* all which arms and munition is this year plentifully and publickly sold unto them, by our own countrymen; who, under the pretence of fishing, come a trading amongst them; yea, one of them (as your worships may further understand by our particular informations) hath for his part sold twenty or twenty-one pieces, and one hundred weight of powder, by which you may conceive of the rest; for we hear the savages have above sixty pieces amongst them, besides other arms; in a word there is now almost nothing vendible amongst them, but such munition, so they have spoiled the trade, in all other things; and as vice is always fruitful; so from the greedy covetousness of the fishermen, and their evil example, the like hath began to grow amongst some, who pretend themselves to be planters, though indeed they intend nothing less, but to take opportunity of the time, and provide themselves and begone, and leave others to quench the fire which they have kindled; of which number Mr. Thomas Morton is one, being of late a dweller in the Massachusetts bay, and the head of a turbulent and seditious crew, which he had gathered unto him, who, dwelling in the midst of us, hath set up the like practice in these parts, and hath sold sundry pieces to the natives, who can use them with great dexterity, excelling our English therein, and have been vaunting with them, at Sowams, Narragansett and many other places, so as they are spread both north and south, all the land over, to the great peril of all our lives: In the beginning of this mischief we sought friendly to dissuade him from it; but he scorned us therein and prosecuted it the more; so as we were constrained for the safety of ourselves, our wives and innocent children, to apprehend him by force (though with some peril) and now have sent him to the council of New England to receive according to his demerits, and be disposed of as their Honours shall think fit, for the preventing of further mischief, the safety of our lives, and the terror of all other delinquents in the same kind: Now our hope and humble request is, that your worship, and those honourable of his Majesty's council for New England, will commiserate our case, tender our lives and pity our infants; and consider the great charges and expenses, that we, and our assistants and associates have been at, besides all the miseries and hardships, that we have broken through in these beginnings which have hitherto happily succeeded, for the planting of this country, which is hopeful, if it be cherished and protected against the cankered covetousness of these licentious men; if not, we must return and quit the country: Wherefore we beseech your Worship to afford us your favourable assistance and direction in bringing this man to his answer, before those whom it may concern; and to credit our true informations, sent by this bearer, lest by his audacious and coloured pretences, he deceive you, which know not things as we do; as likewise that such fishermen, may be called to account, for their great abuses offered this year and the last, as many as have been known to offend in this case; and that your worship for the time to come would be a means, in what you may that we may be strengthened with some authority, or good order amongst ourselves, for the redressing of the like abuses which may arise amongst us, till some general government be established in the land: Thus in hopeful assurance that your worship will make a favourable construction of these our honest intendments and humble requests, we commend you to the protection of the highest and rest

June 9, *Anno* 1628. At your service, &c.

I now will come to the year 1629.

THIS year we had divers of our friends of Leyden come to us, as had long been desired, both of them and us, and by the good providence of God end the willing mindedness of our friends, was now in part effected, as will appear by this letter following.

To my worthy and well beloved friend, Mr. WILLIAM BRADFORD, &c.

MOST loving and most respected Sir, having but two days past parted fom my dear and only daughter, by reason whereof nature forceth me to be full of grief and heaviness (though otherwise, I bless God, I have cause to rejoice) be entreated therefore, to accept these few lines: First I acknowledge myself much engaged unto you for your love and care over my kinsman; be entreated to enlarge my score, by the continuance thereof; and as you for your particular have occasion, make use of me, and I hope the Lord will direct my heart not to be unthankful, nor unmindful of your love. Here are now many of your friends from Leyden coming over, which though for the most part, they be but a weak company, yet herein is a good part of that end obtained which was first aimed at, and which hath been so strongly opposed by some of our former adventurers; but God hath his working in these things, which man cannot frustrate: With them also we have sent some servants, or in the ship that went lately (I think called the Talbot) and this, that these come in, is the May-flower. Now Mr. Andrews, Mr. Beauchamp, and myself, are with your love and liking, joined partners with you; the like is Mr. Collier, Mr. Thomas and Mr. Hatherly, but they no doubt will write unto you; but Mr. Andrews, and Mr. Beauchamp rely wholly on me; they are such as Mr. Hatherly could take up, for whose care and pains you and we, are much beholden unto him; we have disbursed the charges of setting them out and transporting them over, and what allowance or agreement, you and your assistants, please to make with us, we will accept of; nay if you think mete we should make them up two a piece, because our persons are absent, we will consent to what you do, and, upon your letter and answer, make good what we are too short, or what you desire herein; Mr. Hatherly hath bound them, some upon one condition and some upon another, as they could agree. I doubt not but beaver will continue a good price still, as 15 or 16 shillings per pound; it is daily more and more worn here; besides we have now peace with France, so as now much will be carried thither; and there is some likelihood for a peace with Spain, I pray God it may be for our good, which is much to be feared: Thus not being fit, to write at this time, I shall cease with my love, and my wife's, most kindly remembered to you and yours, &c.

Your loving friend to command,
JAMES SHIRLEY.

THESE persons were in all thirty-five, which came at this time unto us from Leyden, whose charge out of Holland into England and in England till the ship was ready, and then their transportation hither, came to a great deal of money; for besides victuals and other expenses they were all newly appareled, for there was bought for them

Of Kersey, and other cloth,	125 yards.
Of Linnen Cloth	127 ells.
Of Shoes,	66 pair.

Besides hats and other necessaries needful for them; and after their coming here, it was 16 months before they could reap any harvest, all which time they were kept at our charge which was not small: As the Lord sent these unto us, both to their and our comfort, so at the same time he sent many other godly persons into the land, as the beginning of a plentiful harvest, as will appear more fully hereafter: So as the delay of our friends was now recompensed with a large increase, to the honour of God and joy of all good men; these began to pitch at Naumkeak, since called by them Salem, to which place was come in the latter end of summer before, a worthy gentleman, Mr. John Endicott by name, and some others with him, to make some preparation for the rest; to whom (by some that came hither from thence) I had occasion to write unto him, though unknown by face, or any other way, but as I had heard of his worth, from whom I received this letter following.

To the worshipful and my right worthy friend WILLIAM BRADFORD, *Esq. Governour of New Plymouth, these,*

Right Worthy Sir,

IT is a thing not usual, that servants to one master and of the same household should be strangers; I assure you I desire it not, nay to speak more plainly, I cannot be so to you: God's people are all marked with one and the same mark, and sealed with one and the same seal, and have, for the main, one and the same heart, guided by one and the same spirit of truth; and where this is there can be no discord, nay, here must needs be sweet harmony; and the same request (with you) I make unto the Lord, that we may, as christian brethren, be united by an heavenly and unfeigned love, bending all our hearts and forces in furthering a work beyond our strengh with reverence and fear, fastening our eyes always on him that only is able to direct and prosper all our ways. I acknowledge myself much bound to you, for your kind love and care, in sending Mr. Fuller amongst us, and rejoice much that I am by him satisfied, touching your judgments, of the outward form of God's worship; it is (as far as I can yet gather) no other than is warranted by the evidence of truth, and the same which I have professed and maintained, ever since the Lord in mercy revealed himself unto me, being far differing from the common report that hath been spread of you touching that particular; but God's children must not look for less here below, and it is the great mercy of God that he strengthens them, to go through with it. I shall not need at this time to be tedious unto you, for, God willing, I purpose to see your face shortly: In the mean time I humbly take my leave of you, committing you to the Lord's blessed protection, and rest,

Your assured loving friend and servant,

JOHN ENDICOTT.

Naumkeak, May 11, *Anno* 1629.

NOW shortly after the writing of this letter came these people before mentioned, and quickly grew into church order, and set themselves roundly to walk in all the ways of God, as will appear by this letter following.

To the Worshipful, his worthy, and much respected friend, Mr. BRADFORD, *Governour of Plymouth these,*

MOST worthy and much respected friend, Mr. Bradford; I with my wife, remember our service unto you and yours, thanking you most humbly for your great kindness, when we were at Plymouth with you: Sir, I make bold to trouble you with a few lines, for to certify you, how it hath pleased God to deal with us, since you heard from us; how, notwithstanding all opposition, that hath been here and elsewhere, it hath pleased God to lay a foundation, the which I hope is agreeable to his word, in every thing: The 20th of July, it pleased God to move the heart of our Governour, to set it apart, for a solemn day of humiliation for the choice of a pastor and teacher; the former part of the day being spent in praise and teaching; the latter part was spent about the election, which was after this manner; the persons thought on (who had been ministers in England) were demanded concerning their callings; they acknowledged there was a two-fold calling, the one and inward calling, when the Lord moved the heart of a man to take that calling upon him, and fitted him with gifts for the same; the second (the outward calling) was from the people, when a company of believers are joined together in covenant, to walk together in all the ways of God, every member (being men) are to have a free voice in the choice of their officers, &c. Now we being persuaded that these two were so qualified, as the apostle speaks of to Timothy, where he saith a bishop must be blameless, sober, apt to teach, &c. I think I may say as the eunuch said unto Philip, what should let him from being baptised, seeing there was water, and he believed; so these two servants of God clearing all things by their answers (and being thus fitted) we saw no reason but that we might freely give our voices for their election after this trial: Their choice was after this manner, every fit member wrote, in a note, his name whom the Lord moved him to think was fit for a pastor, and so likewise, whom they would have for teacher; so the most voice was for Mr. Skelton to be pastor, and Mr. Higginson to be teacher; and they accepting the choice, Mr. Higginson, with three or four more of the gravest members of the church, laid their hands on Mr. Skelton, using prayers therewith. This being done, then there was imposition of hands on Mr. Higginson: Then there was proceeding in election of elders and deacons, but they were only named, and laying on of hands deferred, to see if it pleased God to send us more able men over; but since Thursday, being (as I take it the 5th of August) is appointed for another solemn day of humiliation, for the full choice of elders and deacons and ordaining them; now, good Sir, I hope, that you and the rest of God's people (who are acquainted with the ways of God) with you, will say that here was a right foundation laid, and that these two blessed servants of the Lord came in at the door, and not at the window: And thus I have made bold to trouble you with these few lines, desiring you to remember us to Mr. Brewster, Mr. Smith, Mr. Fuller, and the rest of the church; so I rest, at your service in what I may till death,

CHARLES GOTT.

Salem, July 30, *Anno* 1629.

GOVERNOR BRADFORD'S LETTER BOOK

BUT now I will return again to Mr. Shirley's letters, and see what he saith to our last agreement.

To his worthy and approved loving friend, Mr. WILLIAM BRADFORD, *Governour of Plymouth in New England, these,*

Most worthy Sir, and my continual loving friend Mr. BRADFORD,

YOUR letters of the 21st of May, from Plymouth, and of the 6th of Sept. 1629 from Salem, I have received, whereby I understand of your health and welfare, and all your friends, for which great mercies and blessings, the Lord make us thankful, for answer of your loving letter and the many thanks for small courtesies, I say, in a word, I would I had power and ability to do for you and all honest men with you, according to my will and desire; but though I came short in the former, I hope the Lord will continue my love in affection, and that you will accept of what I can do: Your deputation we have received, and the goods have been taken up and sold, by your faithful agent, Mr. Allerton, myself having been in Holland near three month this summer, at Amsterdam and other places, about my affairs: I see further the agreement you have made with the generality, in which I cannot understand but you have done very well, both for them and you, and also for your friends at Leyden; Mr. Beauchamp, Mr. Andrews, Mr. Hatherly and myself, do so like it and approve of it, as we are willing to join with you in it, and, as it shall please God to direct and enable us, will be assisting and helpful to you the best that possibly we can: Nay, had you not taken this course, I do not see how you should have accomplished the end you first aimed at, and some others endeavoured these years past: We know it must keep us from the profit, which otherwise, by the blessing of God and your endeavours, might be gained; for most of those which came in May last unto you, as also these now sent, though I hope honest and good people, yet not like to be helpful to raise profit; but rather, nay certain, must, a good while, be chargeable to you and us; at which it is likely, had not this wise and discreet course been taken, many of your generality would have grudged: Again you say well in your letter (and I make no doubt but you will perform it) that now being but few on whom the burden must be, you will both manage it the better and set to it more cheerfully, having no discontents nor contradiction, but so lovingly join together in affection and counsel, as God no doubt but will bless and prosper your honest labours and endeavours: and therefore in all respects I do not see but you have done marvellously, discreetly and advisedly, and no doubt but it gives all parties good content, I mean that are reasonable and honest men, such as make conscience in giving the best satisfaction they are able for their debt, and that regard not their own particular so much as the accomplishing of that good end for which this business was first intended.

Sir, for our business I shall refer you to our general letter, which way of advice I would entreat you to use and write a general letter, naming therein Mr. Beauchamp, Mr. Andrews, and Mr. Hatherly with myself, though, this time, they did not, nay, Mr. Hatherly would but could not write to you. Sir, I must of force break off. My wife desires to be remembered to you and yours, and I think she hath put up a small token (as a pair of stockings) for you; thus desiring the Lord to bless and prosper you, and all your, and our honest endeavours, I ever rest

Your unfeigned, and ever loving friend,
JAMES SHIRLEY.

March 8, *Anno* 1629.

P. S. Mr. Bradford, give me leave to put you in mind of one thing; here are many of your Leyden people now come over, and though I have ever had good thoughts of them, yet believe not every one, what they shall report of Mr. Allerton; he hath been a trusty honest friend to you all, either there or here: And if any do (as I know some of them are apt to speak ill of him) believe them not. Indeed they have been unreasonably chargeable, yet grudge and are not contended: Verily their indiscreet carriage here hath so abated my affection towards them, as were Mrs. Robinson well over, I would not disburse one penny for the rest.

This offence was given by some of them, which redounded to the prejudice of the whole; and indeed our friends which sent this latter company were to blame; for they now sent all the weakest and poorest, without any of note and better discretion and government amongst them, contrary to our minds and advice; for they thought, if these were got over, the other might come when they would; but partly this distaste, but especially the great charge, which both these companies came to, coming so near together, put a bar in the way: for though this company were the fewer in number, yet their charge came to an 100l more. And notwithstanding this indiscretion, yet they were such as feared God, and were to us both welcome and useful, for the most part; they were also kept at our charge eighteen months, and all new appareled and all other charges defrayed.

Another of Mr. SHIRLEY'S, *to our worthy and beloved friends Mr.* WILLIAM BRADFORD *Governour, and the rest of our loving partners, these, at Plymouth in New England.*

MOST worthy and loving friends Mr. Bradford, Mr. Brewster, Captain Standish, and Mr. Winslow, with the rest; you may marvel I join you all in one letter, having many letters from you: But Mr. Allerton may make excuse for me in this particular; it is true I have had some of your letters in July and some since by Mr. Peirce, but till our main business, the patent, was granted, I could not set my mind nor pen to writing; and Mr. Allerton was so turmoiled about it, and found so many difficulties and oppositions, as verily I would not, nay, could not, have undergone it, if I might have had a thousand pounds; but the Lord so blessed his labours (even beyond expectation in these evil days) as he obtained love and favour of great men in repute and place; he got granted from the Earl of Warwick and Sir Ferdinando Gorges all Mr. Winslow desired in his letters to me, and more also, which I leave him to relate: Then he sued to the King to confirm their grant and to make you a Corporation, and so to enable you to make and execute laws in such large and ample manner, as the Salem or Massachusetts plantation hath it, which the King graciously granted, referring it to the Lord Keeper to give order to the solicitor to to draw it up, if there were a precedent for it; so the Lord Keeper (the best of his rank) furthered it all he could, and also the solicitor; but as Festus said to Paul, with no small sum obtained I this freedom, for by the way there were many riddles which must be resolved, and many locks must be opened with the silver, nay, the golden key; then it was to come to the Lord Treasurer, to have his warrant for freeing the custom for a certain time; but he would not do it but referred it to the Council Table, and there Mr. Allerton attended, day by day, that they sat, and made great means and friends, both of Lords and secretaries, for the furtherance of it, but they were so full of other great matters, as he could not get his, or rather Mr. Bradford's petition read, and (by reason of Mr. Peirce, his being and staying with all the passengers at Bristol, even ready to set sail, and the wind good) he was forced to leave the further tending and prosecuting of it to a solicitor, and come for Bristol; but there is no fear nor doubt but it will be granted; for he hath the chief of them to friend; yet it will be marvellous needful for him to return by the first ships that come from thence, for if you had this granted, then were you complete, and might bear such sway and government, as were fit for your rank and place that God hath called you unto, and stop the mouths of base and scurrilous fellows, that are ready to question and threaten you in every action you do: And besides, if you have the custom free for seven years inward and twenty-one years outward, the charge of the patent will soon be recovered, and there is no fear of obtaining it; only such things must work by degrees, men cannot hasten it as they would; wherefore we (I write here, in the behalf of all our partners) desire you to be earnest with Mr. Allerton, and with his wife here to come, and she to spare him this one year (nay I hope but a few months more) to finish this great and weighty business, which we conceive will be much for your good and well and sure subsisting, yea, and I hope for your posterity, and for many generations to come; for I am persuaded Sir Ferdinando (how loving and friendly soever he seems to be) knows he can, nay, purposeth to overthrow, at his pleasure, all the patents he grants, but, this being obtained, he will be frustrate of his intent; and unless a Parliament should call them in (which is not likely) you need not fear, as Mr. Allerton can further certify you, and so much for this *costly and tedious business; now I see what most of your letters signify unto me, concerning the contracting of ourselves into a fewer number for the managing of our business and paying of our debts, which I confess are great and needful to be carefully considered of; and no doubt but we, joining in love, may soon overcome them, but we must follow it roundly and to purpose, for if we piddle out the time in our trade, others will step in and nose us; but we know and consider you have that acquaintance and experience as none the like in the country; wherefore, loving friends and partners, be no ways discouraged with the greatness of the debt (of which I refer you to the accounts, being the only cause of my being at Bristol, and, if time permit and God enable me, shall be brought in some good and plain form) let us not fulfil the proverb, bestow twelve pence on a purse, and put sixpence in it; but as you and we have been at great charge, and undergone much for settling of you there, and to gain experience; so, as God shall please to enable us, let us make use of it and not think with 50l. a year sent you over, to raise such means as to pay our debts.† We see a possibility of good, if you be well supplied and fully furnished, and chiefly, if you do lovingly, and as you do (and well you do) profess to be brethren, so say as Abraham said to Lot, let there be no contention because we are brethren: I know I write to godly, wise, and understanding men, such as have learned to bear one another's infirmities and rejoice at any one's prosperity; and if I were able I would press this the more, because it is hoped by some of your and our enemies, that you will fall out amongst yourselves and so overthrow our hopeful business; nay, I have heard it credibly reported, that some have said that till you be disjointed, by discontents and factions amongst yourselves, it boots not for any to go over, in hope of getting or doing good in these parts; but we hope better things of you, and that you will not only bear with one another, and persuade, and that effectually, one another to the contrary, but that you will banish such thoughts, and not suffer them to lodge in your breasts; it is certain offences will come, but wo unto them, by whom they come, and blessed is the peace maker; which blessedness I know you all desire, and God grant you may disappoint the hopes of your foes and procure the hearty desire of yourselves and friends in this particular. I am further to acquaint you

* It was costly indeed, in the conclusion.

† Here the sum of the debts and other things were blotted out again.

that we have sent you a large supply for your magazine, or trade, and also that we have thought good to join with one Edward Ashley (a man I think whom most of you know) but it is only of that place whereof he hath a patent, in Mr. Beauchamp's name; and to that end have furnished him with large provisions; now if you please to be partners with us in this, we are willing you shall, for after we understood how willing and forward, Bristol men, and, as I hear, some able men of his own kindred have been, to stock and supply him, hoping of profit, we thought fit for us to lay hold of such an opportunity, and a kind of running plantation, rather than other who have not borne the burden of settling a plantation, as we have done; and he, on the other side, like an understanding young man, thought it better to join with those that had means by a plantation, to supply and back him there, rather than strangers, that look but only after profit: Indeed the Salem partners here, as Mr. Humfries, Mr. Johnson; but chiefly Mr. Cradock and Mr. Winthrop, would fain have joined with him, and, when that could not be, with us, in that business; but we not willing, and they failing they said he would strip them of all trade in those parts; and therefore they so crossed him and us in the taking of the patent, as we could not have it, but to join their name with ours in it, though Knights, and men of good rank and near the King, spake in his behalf; and this I conceive they did only to bring it to pass, that they might join with us: Now it is not known that you are partners with him, or you and we joined partners with him, but only we four, Mr. Andrews, Mr. Beauchamp, and myself and Mr. Hatherley, who desired to have the patent in consideration of our great loss we have already sustained in settling of the first plantation there; so in conclusion we agree together to take it in both our names. And now as I said before, if you please to join with us, we are willing you should partake with us in the profits, if it please God to send any: Mr. Allerton had no power from you to make this new contract, neither was he willing to do anything therein without your consent and approbation. Mr. William Peirce is joined with us in this, and we thought it very convenient because of landing Edward Ashley and his goods there, if it please God, wind and weather serving, as I hope it will, and he will bend his course accordingly; he hath a new boat hence with him and boards to make another; and as I think four or five lusty fellows, whereof one is a carpenter: Now in case you are not willing to join in this particular with us, fearing the charge and doubting the success, yet thus much we would entreat of you to afford him all the help you can either by men, commodities or boats, yet not but that he will pay you for any thing that he hath; for I will and so desire you to keep the accounts apart, though you join with us; because there is (as you see) other partners in this, than in the other; so, for all men's wages, boats hire, or commodities which he shall have of you, make him debtor for it, and what you shall have of him, make the plantation or yourselves, debtors for it to him; and so there need be no mingling of the accounts. And now loving friends and partners, if you join in Edward Ashley's patent and business (as I cannot see but it is for your good to do) though we have laid out the money and taken up much to stock this business and the other, yet I think it conscionable and reasonable that you should bear your shares and proportion of the stock, if not by present money yet by securing us, for so much as it shall come to; for it is not barely the interest that is to be allowed, and considered of but the adventure; though I hope by the blessing of God and your honest endeavours, it may soon be payed; the years that this partnership holds is not long nor many, let all therefore lay it to heart, and make the best use of the time that possibly we can; and let every man set too his shoulder and the burden will be the lighter, for though some speak or write not of it, but are contented to do as I do, and wholly rely on me, yet I would be loath they should think themselves hardly dealt with all; but I know you are so honest and conscionable men, as you will take it into consideration and return such answer as may give good satisfaction; there is none of us would have ventured as we do, were it not to strengthen, settle, and do you good, more than our own particular profit: Mr. Fogge, Mr. Coalson, and Mr. Thomas, though they seemed earnest to be partners, yet when they saw the debt and charge fell themselves off, and left you, us, and the business; but some though honest, yet I think they minded their own particular profit so much, as both you and we may be glad we are rid of them: For Mr. Collier verily I could have wished it would have sorted with his other affairs, to have been one of us, but he could not spare money, and we thought it not reasonable to take in any partner, unless he were willing and able to spare money, and to lay down his portion of the stock; however, account of him as a sure friend, both ready and willing to do you all the offices of a firm friend. There is no possibility of doing any good in buying the debt for the purchase, I know some will not rebate the interest, and therefore let it run its course, they are to be paid yearly, and so I hope they shal. according to the agreement. I have much more to write but want time, and so must be forced abruptly to break off, desiring the Lord to bless you, and us all, and all our honest endeavours, and grant that our loves and affections, may still be united and knit together in the Lord; and so we rest your ever loving friends,

JAMES SHIRLEY,
TIMOTHY HATHERLEY.

Bristol, March 19, *Anno* 1629.

GOVERNOR BRADFORD'S LETTER BOOK

THUS it appears that our debts were now grown great about the coming over of these two companies of the Leyden people, and the large expenses about the patents, which indeed proved to be large and excessive, when we saw them: About this business of Ashley's we were forced to join in it, though we did not much like it (for the person's sake whom we feared was a knave) for if we should have furnished him with commodities and assistance, it would much have hindered our own trade; and if we should have denied this their request, we should have lost the favour of such good friends; so we thought it the safest way to join with them herein, according to their offer, though we ran a great hazard. This last company of our friends came at such a time of the year, as we were fain to keep them eighteen months at our charge ere they could reap any harvest to live upon; all which together, fell heavy upon us and made the burthen greater; that if it had not been God's mercy, it is a wonder we had not sunk under it, especially other things occuring, whereby we were greatly crossed in our supplies for trade, by which these sums should have been repaid. With this latter company of our brethren, came over many worthy and able men into the country (or rather ours with them) amongst whom was that worthy and godly gentleman, Mr. John Winthrop, Governour of the Massachusetts; and so began the plantations there, which have since much grown and increased under his godly, able, and prudent government, and the church of God, especially, to the rejoicing of our, and the hearts of all good men; of whose beginnings and proceedings something may be gathered by a letter or two of some of our own, who were then there by occasion, which follow:

A letter to myself, from SAMUEL FULLER, *being (at this time) in the bay of Massachusetts.*

SIR,

THE gentlemen here lately come over (as I suppose you understand of their arrival ere this, by Jonathan Brewster) are resolved to sit down at the head of Charles river, and they of

*Matapan purpose to go and plant with them. I have been at Matapan, at the request of Mr. Warham, and let some twenty of these people blood; I had conference with them, till I was weary. Mr. Warham holds that the visible church may consist of a mixed people, godly, and openly ungodly; upon which point we had all our conference, to which, I trust, the Lord will give a blessing. Here is come over, with these gentlemen, one Mr. Phillips (a Suffolk man) who hath told me in private, that if they will have him stand minister, by that calling which he received from the prelates in England, he will leave them: The Governour is a godly, wise, and humble gentleman, and very discreet, and of a fine and good temper. We have some privy enemies in the bay (but blessed be God) more friends; the Governour hath had conference with me, both in private and before sundry others; opposers there is not wanting, and satan is busy; but if the Lord be on our side who can be against us; the Governour hath told me he hoped we will not be wanting in helping them, so that I think you will be sent for: Here is a gentleman, one Mr. Cottington, a Boston man, who told me, that Mr. Cotton's charge at Hampton was, that they should take advice of them at Plymouth, and should do nothing to offend them: Captain Endicott (my dear friend, and a friend to us all) is a second Burrow; the Lord establish him, and us all in every good way of truth: Other things I would have writ of but time prevents me; again I may be with you before this letter; remember me unto God in your prayers, and so I take my leave, with my loving salutations to yourself and all the rest.

Yours in the Lord Christ,
SAMUEL FULLER.

Massachusetts, June 28, *Anno* 1630.

To our loving brethren and christian friends Mr. WILLIAM BRADFORD, *Mr.* RALPH SMITH, *and Mr.* WILLIAM BREWSTER, *these be.*

Beloved, &c.

BEING at Salem the 25th of July, being the Sabbath, after the evening exercise Mr. Johnson having received a letter from the Governour, Mr. Winthrop, manifesting the hand of God to be upon them, and against them, at Charlestown, in visiting them with sickness and taking divers from amongst them, not sparing the righteous, but partaking with the wicked

* Since called Dorchester.

in those bodily judgments, it was therefore by his desire, taken into the godly consideration of the best here, what was to be done to pacify the Lord's wrath; and they would do nothing without our advice, I mean those members of our church, there known unto them, viz. Mr. Fuller Mr. Allerton and myself, requiring our voices, as their own, when it was concluded, that the Lord was to be sought in righteousness; and so to that end the sixth day (being Friday) of this present week is set apart, that they may humble themselves before God, and seek him in his ordinances; and that then also such godly persons that are amongst them and known each to other, publicly at the end of their exercise, make known their godly desire, and practice the same, viz. solemnly to enter into covenant with the Lord to walk in his ways; and since they are so disposed of in their outward estates, as to live in three distinct places, each having men of ability amongst them, there to observe the day, and become three distinct bodies; not then intending rashly to proceed to the choice of officers, or the admitting of any other into their society than a few, to wit, such as are well known unto them, promising after to receive in such, by confession, as shall appear to be fitly qualified for that estate; and, as they desired to advise with us, so do they earnestly entreat that the church at Plymouth would set apart the same day, for the same ends, beseeching God as to withdraw his hand of correction, so to establish and direct them in his ways; and though the time be very short, yet since the causes are so urgent, we pray you be provoked to this godly work, wherein God will be honoured, and they and we undoubtedly have sweet comfort in so doing: Be you all kindly saluted in the Lord, together with the rest of our brethren: The Lord be with you and his spirit direct you, in this and all other actions that concern his glory and the good of his:

Your brethren in the faith of Christ,
And fellowship of the gospel, SAMUEL FULLER,
Salem July 26, *Anno* 1630. EDWARD WINSLOW.

To his loving friend, Mr. WILLIAM BRADFORD, *Governour of Plymouth, these.*

SIR,

THERE is come hither a ship (with cattle, and more passengers) on Saturday last; which brings this news out of England; that the plague is sore, both in the city and country, and that the University of Cambridge is shut up by reason thereof;

also, that there is like to be a great dearth in the land by reason of a dry season. The Earl of Pembroke is dead, and Bishop Laud is Chancellor of Oxford; and that five sundry ministers are to appear before the High Commission, amongst whom, Mr. Cotton, of Boston, is one. The sad news here is, that many are sick, and many are dead, the Lord in mercy look upon them! Some are here entered into a church covenant, the first four, namely, the Governour, Mr. John Winthrop, Mr. Johnson, Mr. Dudley, and Mr. Willson; since that, five more are joined unto them, and others it is like will add themselves to them daily. The Lord increase them, both in number and holiness, for his mercy's sake. I here but lose time and long to be at home, I can do them no good, for I want drugs, and things fitting to work with: I purpose to be at home this week (if God permit) and Mr. Johnson, and Captain Endicott will come with me; and upon their offer, I requested the Governour to bear them company, who is desirous to come, but saith he cannot be absent two hours. Mrs. Cottington is dead. Here are divers honest christians that are desirous to see us; some out of love, which they bear to us, and the good persuasion they have of us; others to see whether we be so evil, as they have heard of us. We have a name of love and holiness to God and his saints; the Lord make us answerable and that it may be more than a name, or else it will do us no good. Be you lovingly saluted, and my sisters, with Mr. Brewster, and Mr. Smith, and all the rest of our friends. The Lord Jesus bless us and the whole Israel of God. Amen.

Your loving brother in law,

Charlestown, August 2, *Anno* 1630. SAMUEL FULLER.

But this worthy gentleman, Mr. Johnson, was prevented of his journey, for shortly after he fell sick and died, whose loss was great and much bewailed.

THE SETTLEMENT OF PETER BROWNE'S ESTATE AND DEEDS OF LAND BELONGING TO HIS HEIRS.

Transcribed from the Original Records

BY GEORGE ERNEST BOWMAN.

THE material collected relating to Peter Browne's children will require so much space that it has been decided to print in this number some of the most important records, leaving the discussion of these and other records for a later issue.

The deed from Ephraim Tinkham to John Browne should be mentioned here, since it is the only known contemporary record in which the definite statement is made that Ephraim Tinkham's wife Mary was the daughter of Peter Browne. This deed seems to have escaped the notice of other investigators.

[SETTLEMENT OF PETER BROWNE'S ESTATE.*]

In this Court Mary the late wife of Peter Browne deceased who dyed w^th^out will presented an Inventory of the goods & Chattels of her said husb. upon oath & was referred for Administracon to an other Cour of Assistants to be held the on munday the 11th of Novbr next ensuing.
[Court Orders, I : 33, under date of 28 October, 1633.]

New Plym. Wynslow Govr.
1633. Novbr 11th At a Court of Assistants held the 11th of Novembr in the ninth yeare of the raigne of our Soveraigne Lord Charles by the grace of God King of Engl. Scotl. ffrance & Ireland Defender of the ffaith &c. It was ordered, that

Whereas Peter Browne dyed w^th^out will having divers children by divers wives his estate amounting to an hundred pownds or thereabouts. It is ordered that Mary his wife who is allowed the Administratrix of the said Peter foorthwith pay downe fifteen pownds for the use of Mary Browne daughter of the said Peter to m^r^ Joh. Done of Plymoth aforesaid . wth whom the said Court have placed the said Mary for nine yeares. At the end whereof the said John is to make good the said fifteen pownds to her or her heires if in case she die. Also it is

* His inventory was printed in Volume I, page 79.

further ordered that the said Widow Mary Browne pay or cause to be paid into the hands of m^r Will Gilson the full sum of fifteen pownds for the use of Prisilla Browne an other of the daughters of the said Peter the Court having placed the said Prisilla wth the said Will for 12 yeares At thend whereof the said Will is to make good the same unto her as her ffathers legacy as aforesaid, & to that end the said John & Will eithe[r] stand bound for other for pformance of the severall paym^ts as also for such other pformancs of meet drinke cloathing &c during the said terme as is meet. And for the rest of the estate the widow having two children by the said Peter together wth her owne 3^d it is allowed her for bringing up the said children. Provided that shee discharge w^tsoever debts shall be proved to be owing by the said Peter, & the legacies given by the Court. ffor pformance whereof shee & m^r Will Brewster bownd in two hundred pownds
[Court Orders, I : 37]

Willam Allen Married to Presilla Browne the 21 of March*

[Ephraim Tinkham to Henry Sampson.]

October 27th 1647.

Memorand : that Ephraim Tinkeham and mary his wife Doth acknowledge that for and in consideracon of the sum of seven pounds in hand paid by Henry Sampson of Duxborough, hath freely and absolutely bargained and solde unto Henry Sampson aforesaid all that Third pte of that Lott wch was formly the land of Peter Browne Deceased. dwelling house and buildings in and upon the same wth all and singular the app^rtences thereunto belonging (except the third pte of the whole meadow) the said third of the upland lying and being nexte adioyning unto the land of the said Henry Sampson in Duxborough aforemenconed, and all his right title & interest of and into the said Third pte of upland & p^rmisses and evy pte and pcell thereof. To have and to holde all that third pte of alottm^t of upland housings and all and singular the app^rtences thereunto belonging (except before excepted) unto the said Henry Sampson his heires and Assignes for ever to the only pp use and behoofe of him the said Henry Sampson his heires & Asss for ever pvided the said Ephraim Tinkha is doth reserve to his owne use all the fruitetrees and lib^rty to remove

* Plym. Col. Births, Marriages and Burials, p. 9, under the year 1649.

them in convenient time, as also use of all the housing for this winter.
[Plym. Col. Deeds, I : 240]

[William Allen to John Browne.]

apointed to bee Recorded the 8th of June 1650

Memorand That Willam Allin of the Towne of Sandwidg in the Colonie of New Plym. Doth acknowlidge yt for and in Consideration of the sum of five pound to him allredy paied by John Browne of Duxburrow in the Colonie aforsaid weaver; hee hath freely and absolutly barganed and sould unto the said John Browne a pcell of upland beeing about thirty acars bee it more or lesse Lyinge and being in Duxburrow aforsaid next aioyning on the one side unto the land of Mr John Reainer being the one part of three of the land which appertained unto the Children of Peeter Browne brother unto John Browne aforsaid; the said thirty acars of upland with all and singular the apurtenances therunto belonging To have and to hold unto the said John Browne his heaires and assignes for ever unto the onely proper use and behoof of him the said John Browne his heaires and assignes for ever.

And Presilla the wife of the said Willam Allin Did give her free Concent unto the sale of the aforsaid pcell of land before Mr Willam Collyar asistant

with all the apurtenances therunto belonging*

this sale was made about the last of January 1649*

[Plym. Col. Deeds, I : 309]

[Ephraim Tinkham to John Browne.]

1683 Hinckly Govr

To all to whom these prsents shall Come Ephraim Tinkham senir : of the Towne of New Plymouth in New England in America sendeth Greeting Know yee that I the said Ephraim Tinham, for and in Consideration of the some of four pounds unto mee in hand payed by John Browne of Duxborrow wherwith I Doe acknowlidge myself suffiently satisfyed Contented and payed, and therof and of every prte and prsell; theroff Doe acquitt exownarate, and Discharge the said John Browne his heires executors, and Adminnestrators, and every of them, forever by

* These two entries are on the margin of the page.

these p^{r}sents; have ffreely and absolutely, bargained and sold allianated enfeofed and Confeirmed, and by these p^{r}sents Doe bargaine sell allianate enfeof and Confeirme, from mee the said Ephraim Tinkham and my heires, unto the said John Browne and his heires and assignes for ever, all that my portion of Meddow land that lyeth and abuteth against the Land of the said John Browne that hee Now Liveth upon in the towne of Duxborrow; it being two acrees more or Lesse; The one of which acrees, I had in right of Mary my wife, daughter, of Peter Browne deacesed, the other I bought of Nathaniel: Morton; of Plymouth with all the appurtenances, and privilidges Therunto belonging; To have and to hold; The said Portion or Parsell of medow land, being two acrees more or lesse, with all the appurtenances Privilidges Rights therunto belonging, unto the said John Browne his heires and assignes for ever; To be holden of our Sov^{r} Lord the Kinge, as of his Manor of East Greenwich, in the Countey of Kent, in the Realme of England in free and Comon Sockage and Not in Capite Nor by Knightes service, nor by the rents and services therof, and therby Doe, and of right accostomed, To the onely proper use and behoffe of him the said John Browne his heires and assignes for ever; with warrantice against all people for ever by these p^{r}sents; from by or under mee the said Ephraim Tinkham; My heires executors and adminnestrators; and every of them Claiming any right title and Interst into the aforsaid p^{r}mises, or any p^{r}te or p^{r}sell therof; and I the said Ephraim Tinkham; Doe by these p^{r}sents authorise; the said John Browne or his Attorny, to record and Inrole these p^{r}sents, or Cause them to be recorded, and Inroled; before the Govr: or some one of the Majestrates of New Plymouth, for the time being, according to the usuall Manor of recording and Inroling deeds and evidences, in his said Maties Court, of New Plymouth in witnes wherof; I the aforsaid Ephraim Tinkham seni^{r}: have heerunto, sett my hand & seale this thirteenth Day of August one Thousand six hundred seaventy and nine;

Signed sealed and Delivered in the p^{r}sence of — Ephraim **E T** Tinkham his Mark and a (seal)

Easter Tinkham her **E** mark;
Willam Crow;

This Deed was acknowlidged to be the ffree acte and Deed of Ephraim Tinkham, above Mencioned; and alsoe Mary his wife, Gave her full Consent; to it the 8th of october 1679

Before mee William Bradford Assistant;

[Plym. Col. Deeds, V: 197]

[William Snow to John Browne.]

To all to whom these p^{r}sents shall Willam Snow of the Towne of Bridgwater in the Collonie of New Plymouth in New England in America husbandman sendeth Greet &c

Know yee that I the said Willam Snow for and in Consideration of the sume of five pounds Sterling to mee in hand payed by John Browne of the Towne of Duxburrow in the Collonie aforsaid yeoman wherwith I Doe acknowlidge my selfe to be fully Satisfyed Contented and payed, and therof and of every p^{r}te and p^{r}sell therof Doe acquitt exownarate and Discharge the said John Browne his heires Executors and Adminnestrators and every of them for ever by these p^{r}sents have ffreely and absolutly bargained and sold allianated enfeoffed and Confeirmed and by these p^{r}sents Doe bargaine sell allianate enfeoffe and Confeirme from mee the said William Snow and my heires unto the said John Browne and his heires and assignes for ever; all that my one third p^{r}te of five twenty acree lotts of Land which is thirty three acrees; and the one third p^{r}te of one acree more or lesse; which were the Lotts formerly of Peter Browne Deceased lying and being in the aforsaid Towne of Duxburrow; and are betwixt the Lands formerly of William Palmers Deceased; and of henery Sampson and alsoe one acree of Meddow be it more or lesse lying against the said Land with all and singulare the appurtenances and privilidges therunto belonging, and all my right title and Interest of and into the said p^{r}mises and every p^{r}te, and p^{r}sell therof; To have and to hold all that my aforsaid one third p^{r}te of five twenty acree lotts of land, which is thirty three acrees & one third p^{r}te of an acree More or lesse; and one acree of Meddow more or lesse lying as aforsaid, with all and singulare the appurtenances and privilidges To the said p^{r}mises belonging and every p^{r}te and p^{r}sell therof; unto the said John Browne his heires and assignes for ever; To be holden of our Sov^{r} Lord the Kinge, as of his Manor of East Greenwich in the Countey of Kent within the Realme of England, in ffree and Comon Soccage; and not in Capite nor by Knightes service Nor by the rents and services therof and therby Due & of Right accostomed; To the onely proper us and behoofe of him the said John Browne his heires and assignes for ever; with warrantice against all people whatsoever for ever by these p^{r}sents, from by or under mee the said Willam Snow my heires executors and adminnestrators and every of them, Claiming any Right title or Interest of or into the aforsaid p^{r}mises with theire appurtenances or any p^{r}te or p^{r}sell therof;

And I the said Willam Snow Doe by these p^r^sents Authorise the said John Browne; either by himselfe or his attorney to record or Inrole these p^r^sents or cause them to be recorded or Inroled before the Govr: of the Collonie aforsaid, or some one of his Assistants for the time being according to the usuall manor of recording and Inroling of Deeds and evidences in his said Maties Court of New Plymouth aforsaid In witnes wherof I the aforsaid Willam Snowe have heerunto sett my hand and seale This seaventh Day of November one Thousand six hundred seaventy and Nine 1679

Signed sealed and Delivered — William Snow his Marke
in the p^r^sence of David Aldin — and a (seale)
Jonathan Aldin;

Willam Snow; with the Consent of Rebeckah his wife acknowlidged this Deed this 7 of the 9 month before mee;

John Aldin Assistant

[Plym. Col. Deeds, V : 197, 198]

[William Snow to Ephraim Tinkham.]

1668 Prence Govr:

To all to whome these p^r^sents shall Come; William Snow of the Towne of Bridgwater in the Jurisdiction of New Plymouth in New England in America husbandman sendeth Greeting

Know yea That the said William Snow for and in Consideration of a valluable sume of mony to him alreddy payed by Ephraim Tinkham of the Towne of New Plymouth in the Jurisdiction aforsaid wherwith hee Doth acknowlidg himselfe to be sufficiently satisfyed Contented and fully payed and therof and of every p^r^te and p^r^sell therof Doth acquite exownarate and Discharge the said Ephraim Tinkham his heires exequitors and adminnestrators and every of them for ever by these p^r^sents hath freely and absolutely bargained and sold allianated enfeofed and confeirmed; and by these p^r^sents Doth bargaine sell allianate enfeofe and Confeirme; from him the aforsaid William Snow and his heires unto the aforsaid Ephraim Tinkham his heires and assignes for ever all that his one third p^r^te of one whole share of upland and meddow lands Devided and undevided lying in or about the now Called Towne of Dartmouth of the Jurisdiction of New Plymouth aforsaid The which aforsaid one third p^r^te was of or Did belonge unto one share of a tract of Lands which was graunted by the honored Court of the Jurisdiction aforsaid unto Peter Browne; as a Purchaser or oldcomer of the said Jurisdiction; The which afore said Tract of lands now called the Towne of Dartmouth was bought and purchased of Wosamequen and Wamsutta as by a writing Dated November the 29th one Thousand six hundred fifty and two may and Doth appeer; with all and singular the appurtenances belonging unto the said one third p^{r}te of one whole share and all his right title and Interest of and into the said p^{r}mises and every p^{r}te and p^{r}sell therof To have and to hold the aforsaid one third p^{r}te of one whole share of uplands and meddow lands Devided and alreddy lotted for and that which is not Devided nor lotted for lying and being as aforsaid within or about the said Towne of Dartmouth with all and singulare the appurtenances to the said p^{r}mises belonging and every p^{r}te and p^{r}sell therof unto the said Ephraim Tinkham his heires and assignes for ever To be holden of our Sov^{r}: Lord the Kinge as of his manor of East greenwich in the Countey of Kent within the Realme of England in free and Comon Soccage and not in Capite nor by Knights service by the rents and services therof and therby Due and of Right accustomed; To the onely proper use and behoofe of him the said Ephraim Tinkham his heires and assignes for ever; with warrantice against all people for ever by these p^{r}sents from by or under him the aforsaid William Snow his heires exequitors and Adminnestrators and every of them claiming any right title or Interest of or Into the said p^{r}mises with theire appurtenances or any p^{r}te or p^{r}sell therof and the said William Snow Doth by these p^{r}sents Authorise the said Ephraime Tinkham either by himselfe or his Attorney to record and enrowle these p^{r}sents or cause them to be recorded and enrowled before the Govr or some other Majestrates of Plymouth for the time being according to the usuall manor of recording and enrowling Deeds and evidences in his Maties Court of Plymouth aforsaid In witnes wherof the said William Snow hath heerunto sett his hand and seale this 25th Day of march one Thousand six hundred sixty and seaven or sixty eight;

Signed sealed and Delivered in the p^{r}sence of
John Willis
Samuell Allin;

The marke of William Snow
The marke of Rebeckah Snow
And theire (seale)

This Deed was by William Snow Acknowlidged before me William Bradford Assistant Ann^{o}: Dom 1667 or 1668
[Plym. Col. Deeds, III : 111]

[William Allen to Henry Tucker.]

1670 Prence Govr:

Know all men by these p^r^sents That I Willam Allin of the Towne of Sandwich in the Jurisdiction of Plymouth in New England in America plantor: Doe acknowlidge that for and in consideration of a valluable sume: viz: the sume of fifteen pounds to mee alreddy payed by henery Tucker somtimes of Unkatey allias Milton in the Jurisdiction of the Massachusetts plantor; wherwith I the said Willam Allin Doe acknowlidge my selfe to be fully satisfyed contented and fully payed; and therof and of every p^r^te and p^r^sell therof Doe exownarate acquitt and Discharge the said henery Tucker him his heires exequitors and adminnestrators for ever by these p^r^sents have ffreely and absolutely bargained allianated and sold enfeofed and Confeirmed and by these p^r^sents Doe bargaine sell enfeofe and Confeirme; from mee the said Willam Allin and my heires To him the said henery Tucker and his heires and assignes for ever; all that my one third p^r^te of one whole share of upland and meddow land Devided and undevided being in or about the now called Towne of Dartmouth in the Jurisdiction of Plymouth aforsaid; the which aforsaid one third p^r^te of Lands was off: or Did belong unto one whole share or Tract of Lands which was graunted by the honored Court of the Jurisdiction of Plymouth aforsaid unto Peter Browne Deceased, as a Purchaser or oldcomer of the said Jurisdiction the which aforesaid Township or Tract of land called Dartmouth was bought and of Woosamequen and Wamsutta Indians Sachems as by a writing Dated November the twenty ninth one Thousand six hundred fifty and two, may and Doth appeer, with all and singulare the appurtenances belonging unto one third p^r^te of one whole share of the said Tract of land; and all my title right Interest and proprietie of and into the same and every p^r^te and p^r^sell therof; To have and to hold the aforsaid one third p^r^te off one whole share of upland and meddow lands Devided and alreddy loted for; and That which is not Devided nor loted for; lying and being as aforsaid within or about the said Towne of Dartmouth with all and singulare the appurtenances to the said p^r^mises belonging: and every p^r^te and p^r^sell therof; unto him the said henery Tucker hee his heires and assignes for ever; unto the onely proper use and behoofe of him the said henery Tucker hee his heires and assignes for ever; To be holden of our Sov^r^: Lord the King as of his manor of East Greenwich in the Countey of Kent in the Realme of England; in ffree and Comon Soccage and not in Capite nor by Knight service nor by the rents and services therof and therby Due and of right accostomed; with warrantice against all people for ever by these p^r^sents that by my right or title might claime any right or title of or into the said p^r^mises or any p^r^te or p^r^sell therof whatsoever; and I the said Willam Allin; Doe heerby Covenant promise and graunt to and with the said henery Tucker that it shalbe lawfull for him: either by himselfe or his attorney to record and enrowle these p^r^sents or to cause them to be recorded and enrowled in his Maties Court att att Plymouth aforsaid before the Govr: for the time being or any other majestrate of that Jurisdiction according to the usuall manor of recording and enrowling Deeds and evidences of lands: in such Cases provided. In Witnes wherof I the said Willam Allin have heerunto sett my hand and seale this fifteenth Day of Aprill one thousand six hundred sixty and nine 1669

Signed sealed and Delivered — Willam Allin and a (seale)
in the p^r^sence of John Doane
Edward Perrey

This above written Deed acknowlidged the Day and time of sealing and Delivering by the p^r^sons Concerned heerin before mee

John ffreeman Assistant

[Plym. Col. Deeds, III: 159]

THE MAYFLOWER GENEALOGIES.

STEPHEN HOPKINS AND HIS DESCENDANTS.

Compiled from Original Sources,

BY GEORGE ERNEST BOWMAN.

"So ten of our men were appointed who were of themselues willing to vndertake it, to wit, Captaine Standish, Maister Carver, William Bradford, Edward Winsloe, Iohn Tilley, Edward Tilley, Iohn Howland, and three of London, Richard Warren, Steeuen Hopkins and Edward Dotte."

"m^{r} Steven Hopkins, & Elizabeth his wife; and . 2 . children, caled Giles, and Constanta a doughter, both by a
8 . former wife. And . 2 . more by this wife, caled Damaris, & Oceanus, the last was borne at sea. And . 2 . servants, called Edward Doty, and Edward Litster."

"m^{r} Hopkins, and his wife are now both dead; but they lived above . 20 . years in this place, and had one sone, and . 4 . doughters borne here. Ther sone be-
5 . came a seaman, & dyed at Barbadoes, one daughter dyed here . and . 2 . are maried. one of them hath . 2 . children, and one is yet to mary. So their Increase, which still survive, are . 5 . But his sone Giles is maried,
4 . and hath . 4 . children.
12 . his doughter Constanta, is also maried, and hath . 12 . children all of them living, and one of them maried."

All that we know of Stephen Hopkins and his family before they arrived at Cape Cod is contained in these brief statements from Mourt's Relation and Bradford's History.* He came from London, had been married twice, had two children by each wife and brought two servants. These meagre facts are the only ones yet discovered which are supported by absolutely trustworthy contemporary evidence. Much speculation regarding his early life has been indulged in by various writers, but all have failed to produce from contemporary sources conclusive evidence of the soundness of their claims.

Before proceeding to a chronological record of the events in Stephen Hopkins's life after the arrival at Cape Cod, it will be well to consider more particularly the statements of Bradford quoted at the beginning of this article. A critical study of his

* Mayflower Descendant, I: 10, 13, 14; III: 46.

words in connection with the will of Stephen Hopkins and the record of the division of his personal estate among his unmarried daughters, and other contemporary evidence, has convinced me that the Damaris Hopkins who came in the Mayflower died young, that the second of the four daughters said to have been born at Plymouth was named Damaris for her deceased sister, and that it was this second Damaris who, in the latter part of 1646 or early in 1647, became the wife of Jacob[2] Cooke (*Francis*[1]).

If this theory is accepted all known records can be perfectly harmonized. On any other theory a number of contemporary records are found to be contradictory and it becomes necessary to prove that at least part of them are incorrect.

For more than three years I have sought for evidence to prove that Bradford made an error in his account of the Hopkins family, for it is not a pleasant task to show descendants of Jacob Cooke that his wife Damaris did not come in the Mayflower, and I hoped that the idea that she must have been younger than Deborah, conveyed by the terms of her father's will, might be explained away. But the more I studied the records the more thoroughly convinced I became that the Mayflower Damaris died young.

I was first impressed by the order in which Stephen Hopkins mentioned his four unmarried daughters in his will.* They are three times named, and every time it is in this order: Deborah, Damaris, Ruth, Elizabeth. Again, when Caleb Hopkins and Myles Standish divided the personal estate † among these daughters they were named in the same order. Why did both the father and the brother name Deborah first if Damaris was the older?

In Bradford's "view of the decreasings, & Increasings" of the passengers he mentions, either by name or in a way which makes identification positive, all of the children on the ship with the exception of Damaris Hopkins and Oceanus Hopkins. Since the name of Oceanus does not appear in the Division of Cattle in 1627 ‡ it is certain that he died before that time. If the Mayflower Damaris was the one who married Jacob Cooke and had at least one child before 1651 why did she alone of all the Mayflower passengers fail to receive credit for her share of the "Increasings?"

Three ways of explaining this failure to make any mention of Damaris have been suggested. The first and most reason-

* Mayflower Descendant, II: 12. † Ibid., IV: 114.

‡ Ibid., I: 151.

able one seems to be that she as well as Oceanus had died very young. The second is that Bradford forgot that she was a passenger and counted her as one of the four daughters he said were born at Plymouth. The third, and least probable, explanation is that he entirely overlooked her, although he had strictly followed out his plan and had taken every family "in order as they lye." At the end of his account of the passengers he mentions the two servants brought by Hopkins. If it is claimed that he forgot them until the list was completed it only strengthens the argument that Damaris was neither forgotten nor misplaced. He could hardly have discovered the omission of the servants without noticing any error in regard to Damaris.

Bradford's distinct statement that Hopkins had four daughters born at Plymouth, of whom one had died (evidently unmarried), one was still single, one was married and had no children living, and one was married and had two living children, must be accepted as correct unless positive proof to the contrary is produced. In writing of the children and grandchildren of Stephen and Elizabeth Hopkins born after the arrival at Plymouth, he says: "So their Increase, which still survive, are . 5 ." This number he also sets in the margin. (It is important to bear in mind that by "Increase" in this connection Bradford invariably means children or grandchildren born on this side of the ocean, after the arrival at Plymouth.) He says that Hopkins had a son and four daughters born at Plymouth, and that one of these daughters had borne two children who were still living, also that the son and one of the daughters had died. Each one of the five children "borne here" is specifically mentioned, and it is impossible to believe that Bradford intentionally included the Mayflower Damaris among the four daughters.

If she was entirely forgotten who were the four daughters born at Plymouth? Four unmarried daughters, Deborah, Damaris, Ruth and Elizabeth, are mentioned in Stephen's will. It is evident from this will that there were no other unmarried daughters living in 1644, that the only married daughter then alive was Constance, the wife of Nicholas Snow, and that there were no children of a deceased daughter. If, therefore, Damaris of the Mayflower married Jacob Cooke, and there were four other daughters born at Plymouth who was the fourth one, and why does not some trace of her appear in her father's will or some other contemporary record? As not the slightest hint of such another daughter has been found and the records almost conclusively prove that there was no such daughter we may safely discard the third explanation suggested.

The second explanation offered, that Bradford made a mistake and counted the Mayflower Damaris as one of the four daughters born at Plymouth, is more reasonable, but still it requires us to assume that he made an error in a matter where he would naturally be expected to be particular, and credited Stephen Hopkins with an increase too large by one. We must also assume that the father and brother of the Damaris of the will had some reason, unknown to us, for putting the oldest of four unmarried daughters in a secondary place instead of in her natural position. We must also believe that she was not married until an age, twenty-seven or more, which was for those times very unusual, and that she bore children unusually late in life.

Let us now consider the explanation which was suggested first by myself, over three years ago. Every one who has had any experience in the examination of old records has found many cases where a child died young and another child born later was given the same name. In some of these cases no mention of the death of the first child nor of the birth of the second is found on the records, but positive proof of the facts has been discovered. The absence of any record of the early death of the Mayflower Damaris or of the birth at Plymouth of another Damaris can not therefore be considered as proof that these events did not take place, especially when we remember that the vital records of Plymouth prior to 1648 have been lost.

Since Oceanus was born on the Mayflower, between 6/16 September and 11/21 November, 1620, the Mayflower Damaris must have been born at least a year earlier and was probably born before the year 1619. The record of the Division of Cattle, 22 May /1 June, 1627, mentions Damaris, Caleb and Deborah. Since Caleb was named as the executor of his father's will he was probably of age at the time it was made, 6/16 June, 1644. He certainly was twenty-one on 28 October /7 November, 1644, when he deeded land to his brother Gyles.* The appointment of Myles Standish as "overseer" of Stephen's will does not necessarily indicate that Caleb was then under age, since it was very common for overseers to be appointed if the widow,† or a daughter, or a son who had lately reached his majority, was chosen executor, and Caleb certainly was not over

* Plym. Col. Deeds, I: 182.

† See Anthony Snow's will in this issue.

twenty-three when the will was made. It is probable, therefore, that he was born before 6/16 June, 1623, and as Oceanus was born late in 1620 and his mother doubtless suffered severely with the rest in that terrible first winter which proved fatal to so many, including probably the infant Oceanus, it is altogether unlikely that another child was born between Oceanus and Caleb. Even if Deborah was born before Caleb it is not probable that the date was earlier than the first part of 1622. The placing of her name after Caleb's in the Division of Cattle does not give us any clue to their relative ages, as it was very common in legal documents to name first all the sons, even infants, then all the daughters.

As already shown, the Mayflower Damaris must have been born early in 1619, or before. If, therefore, she was living when her father made his will she was at least three years, and was probably more than seven years, older than Deborah. The four daughters, Deborah, Damaris, Ruth and Elizabeth, were then unmarried and it is certainly a very unusual case if the father three times in his will placed a younger sister first. The will contains no intimation of favoritism towards Deborah, and as she was not married until nearly two years later it is not reasonable to suppose that approaching marriage led Stephen to name her first. If it were not known that a daughter Damaris came in the Mayflower no one would doubt that the Damaris of the will was younger than her sister Deborah.

The marriage of Jacob Cooke to Damaris Hopkins did not take place until after 10/20 June, 1646,* and if his wife came on the Mayflower she must have been over twenty-seven years of age, an unusually late marriage for a period when a girl was far more likely to marry at seventeen, and she was unusually old at the birth of her daughter Ruth, 17/27 January, 1665/6.†

It only remains to show that the four unmarried daughters mentioned in Stephen Hopkins' will in 1644 could have been the four mentioned by Bradford in 1651 as born at Plymouth.

Deborah[2] Hopkins married Andrew Ring at Plymouth on 23 April /3 June, 1646,‡ and we do not find any record of a child born to them until the birth of Elizabeth, at Plymouth, 19/29 April, 1652.§ This daughter Elizabeth is mentioned in Andrew's will ‖ as deceased, and the other daughters were clearly younger than she. William Ring is called "elder son"

* Mayflower Descendant, II: 27.

† Plym. Col. B. M. B., p. 36.

‡ Court Orders, II: 130.

§ Plym. Col. B .M. B., p. 15.

‖ Mayflower Descendant, IV: 193.

in the will. He died at Plymouth between 16/26 June, 1730, and 21/31 May, 1731, the dates of making and probating his will.* His gravestone on Burial Hill states that he died in April, 1729, in the seventy-seventh year of his age. This date cannot of course be correct and his age at death may also be an error. If we assume that the age given is correct, then William the "elder son" was certainly born after Elizabeth, in 1653 or later. Every other reference to him found on the records indicates that he was much younger. If any children were born before Elizabeth no evidence of such births can now be found on the records and they certainly died young, probably before Bradford wrote.

Damaris[2] Hopkins married Jacob[2] Cooke (*Francis*[1]) in the latter part of 1646 or early in 1647 and the first child we find recorded as born to this couple was Elizabeth Cooke, born at Plymouth, 18/28 January, 1648/9.† The second child on the records, Caleb, called "eldest son" in his father's will,‡ was born at Plymouth 29 March /8 April, 1651.§ He was born therefore after Bradford wrote.|| The daughter Elizabeth married John[2] Doty (*Edward*[1]) and died in 1692 in her forty-fourth year. Before her birth there was plenty of time for the birth of another child, who probably died after Bradford wrote.

Ruth[2] Hopkins must have been the daughter who died before Bradford wrote, as her father's will provided that in case Deborah, Damaris, Ruth or Elizabeth died unmarried her share of the personal estate should be distributed among the remaining sisters, and the settlement of Elizabeth's estate in 1659 shows that Ruth had died, unmarried, before that time. This settlement proves also that Elizabeth was the daughter described by Bradford as the one who was "yet to mary."

Although the evidence which has been presented does not prove conclusively that Damaris (Hopkins) Cooke was not a Mayflower passenger, it offers a reasonable explanation of contemporary records and statements which apparently are contradictory. If any record is found which conflicts with or disproves any part of this theory no one will be more pleased to see it than myself, since my sole aim in the compilation of the Mayflower Genealogies is to get at the facts as shown by the original records and written or printed statements of contemporary writers.

* Plym. Co. Prob. Rcds., VI: 34, 35.

† Plym. Col. B. M. B., p. 5.

‡ Mayflower Descendant, III: 237.

§ Plym. Col. B. M. B., p. 13.

|| Mayflower Descendant, I: 161.

The record of Stephen Hopkins after the arrival of the Mayflower at Cape Cod Harbor will be taken up in the next installment.

THE SETTLEMENT OF REV. SAMUEL FULLER'S ESTATE.

Literally Transcribed

BY GEORGE ERNEST BOWMAN.

REV. SAMUEL FULLER, son of Dr. Samuel Fuller of the Mayflower, died intestate at Middleborough 17 August, 1695,* and his widow Elizabeth was appointed administratrix 25 September, 1695. The record of this appointment and of the inventory taken 5 September, 1695, may be found in the Plymouth County Probate Records, Volume I, page 223. On page 224 is recorded the appointment of a guardian for the minor son Isaac, and on pages 246 and 247 is the agreement between the heirs.

The original inventory and the bond of the administratrix are still preserved in the probate files. The bond is of especial interest as it bears the autograph signatures of the widow Elizabeth Fuller and of her two bondsmen, Rev. Isaac Cushman and John Nelson. It is twelve and one-eighth by eight inches in size, and is in good condition, as will be seen by the accompanying illustration. The original inventory was used in making the copy for printing. It is somewhat worn on the right hand margin.

Contributions towards the expense of illustrating the bond have been received from Mr. Linus E. Fuller of New York and Messrs. James D. Lazell and George T. Prince of Philadelphia.

[APPOINTMENT OF ADMINISTRATRIX.]

William Bradford Esqr Commissionated &c for y^{e} Granting

* Mayflower Descendant, I: 222, and gravestone.

Know all men by these presents that we Elizabeth Fuller Relict & Widow

Elizabeth Fuller

Isaac Cushman

John Nelson

BOND OF WIDOW ELIZABETH FULLER.

of probate of wils and Letters of Administration within ye County of Plimouth &c To Elizabeth ffuller Relict & widdow of Mr Saml ffuller late of Middleborough deceased Intestate Trusting in your care & fidellity I do by these presents commit unto you full power to Administer all & singular the Goods chattels Rights and Credits of ye sd Deceased and well & faithfully to dispose of ye same according to law And also to ask gather levy Recover & Receive all and whatsoever Credits of ye sd deceased which to him while he lived and at ye time of his Death did appertain and to pay all debts in which ye deceased Stood bound so far as his goods chattels Rights and Credits can extend according to ye value thereof And to make a true & perfect Inventory of all & singular ye Goods chattels Rights & Credits of ye sd deceased & to exhibit ye same Into ye Registers office of ye aforesaid County at or before the fifteenth day of october next ensuing And to Render a plain & true account of your sd Administration upon oath at or before the twenty nineth day of September one thousand six hundred ninety and six And I do by these presents Ordaine Constitute & appoint you Administratrix of all & singular the Goods chattels Rights & credits aforesd In Testimony whereof I have hereunto set my hand & ye seal of ye sd office

Dated in plimouth ye 25th William Bradford
day of September 1695
Saml Sprague Regist^{r}
[Plym. Co. Prob. Rcds., I : 223]

[Bond of Administratrix.]

Know all men by these presents that We Elizabeth ffuller Relict & Widdow of m^{r} Samuel ffuller late of Middleborough Deceased Intestate and Isaac Cushman & John Nelson both of Plimouth within ye county of Plimouth are holden & stand firmly bound and obliged unto William Bradford Esqr in the full sum of one hundred pounds currant money of New England aforesaid to be paid to the sd Wm Bradford his Successours in ye office of Judge of the probate of Wils and Granting Administration Within ye sd county or Assigns to the true payment whereof we do bind ourselves our heirs executors & Administrato^{r}s joyntly and severally firmly by these presents Sealed with our Seals. Dated in Plimouth the 25th day of September 1695 An^{o} Regni Gulielmi Tertii Anliæ Scotiæ ffranciæ et Hiberniæ Regis Septimo.

The Condition of this present Obligation is such that if the above bounden Elizabeth ffuller Administratrix of all & singular the Goods Chattels Rights & C[redits of the] sd Deceased Intestate Do make a true and perfect Inventory of all & singu[lar y^e] Goods Chattels Rights and Credits of the sd Deceased which have or shall come to ye hands possession or knowledge of the said Administratrix or Into the hands & possession of any other person or persons for her & the same so made do exhibit Into ye Registers office of ye sd county at or before ye 25th day of october next ensuing and the same Goods Chattels Rights & Credits and all other ye Goods Chattels Rights and Credits of ye sd Deceased at ye time of his Death which at any time after shall come to ye hands or possession of the sd Administratrix or any other person or persons for her Do well & truly Administer according to law & further do make or cause to be made a just & true account of her sd Administration at or before ye twenty nineth day of September 1696. And all ye Rest & Residue of the sd Goods Chattels Rights & Credits which shall be found Remaining upon the sd Administrators account the same being first examined and allowed of by the judge or judges for ye time being of probate of Wils and Granting of Administration within ye county of Plimouth shall deliver & pay unto such person & persons Respectively as ye sd judge or judges by his or their decree or sentence pursuant to law shall limit and appoint And if it shall hereafter appear that any last will and Testament was made by ye sd deceased and the executor or executors therein Named Do exhibit ye same Into the sd court of probate making Request to have it allowed and approved accordingly If the sd Elizabeth ffuller within bounden being there unto Required do Render & deliver the said letters of Administration Approbation of such Testament being first had & made into ye Registers office of ye sd County then this obl[igation] to be voyd & of none effect or else to Remain in full for[ce]

Signed Sealed & delivered
in presence of * Elizabeth Fuller (seal)
Isaac Cushman (seal)
John nelson (seal)

[From Original Document.]

[INVENTORY]

Semtember : the 5 : 1695

this is a tru inventary of the Estate of m^r Samuell Fuller Teacher of the church of middelbury Lately deaseased prised by us whose names are under written

* The bond was not witnessed.

his wearin cloathing woollin and linnen	09 00 00
his books	04 00 0*
to beds with bedin	07 00 *
puter with table linnen	01 04 0*
a still	01 00 0*
the brase to kittells and a spise mortter	00 14 0*
A iron pot and kittell and mortter	00 16 *
tramells tongs and pot hooks	00 08 *
chests and trays and dishes and chairs	00 15 0*
tubs and pails	00 08 00
Earthen ware and glases	00 02 00
runlets and barells and a churn	00 07 *
a siften trof and a frien pan	00 04 0*
a loom and taklin	01 ·05 0*
hors taklin	00 18 00
taklin for a teem and old iron	00 12 00
a pare of oxen	05 00 *
3 cowes	04 10 00
3 heifer	03 10 00
2 Calves	00 12 00
swine	01 15 00
a hors and a mare	03 00 00
3 swarm of bees	00 08 00
at middelbury his dwellin hous and 20 Akers of Land and A full share of the six and twenty mens purshas only twenty five Akers and twelf Akers of Land near John haskels and a parsell of Land Cominly called the sixteen shillin purshas and A hous and Land Plimouth	
more to books and a bibell	00 15 00
tow pare of scalles	00 06 00
three wheells and a pare : of cards :	00 10 00
A pot and a spoon	00 07 00
A gun	00 08 00
toue yarn	00 02 00
The widdows Bed not apprised	

Josepth : vaughan
Samuell wood

Mrs Elizabeth ffuller Relict & Widdow of Mr Saml ffuller above named made oath in Plimouth September 25th : 1695 that ye above Written is a true Inventory of ye Goods Chattels Rights & Credits of ye sd Deceased so far as she knoweth & that if more shall come to her knowledge she will make it known

Before William Bradford Esqr &c.
Attest Saml Sprague Register

* Comparison with the record (Vol. I : 223) shows that in every case where we have placed asterisks the original document had ciphers.

The above written Inventory is Recorded in ye 223d page of ye first Book of wils Recorded for ye County of Plimouth.

pr Saml Sprague Register

[From Original Document.]

[Appointment of Guardian.]

Memorand ye 25 of Sept 1695

John Nelson of Plimouth appointed Guardian to Isaac ffuller Son of mr Saml ffuller late of Middleborough deceased.

pr William Bradford judge

[Plym. Co. Prob. Rcds., I : 224]

[Agreement of the Heirs.]

This agreement made betwixt the widdow Mrs Elizabeth ffuller and all the Children of Mr Samuel ffuller late Minister of Middleborough in ye County of Plimouth in New England deceased Namely Samuel ffuller & Daniel Cole and Mercy his wife James wood and Experience his wife Samuel Eaton and Elizabeth his wife Hannah ffuller and John Nelson as Guardian to Isaac ffuller ye youngest son of sd fuller deceased and John ffuller said widdow and all said children have mutually and firmly Covenanted and Agreed & do by these presents firmly Covenant and agree for themselves & every of their heirs and assigns for ever to and with each other That ye Articles herein to be mentioned shall be and are the full & satisfying division and disposall of ye estate of said mr ffuller deceased And that sd Widdow and all ye children above mentioned are & for ever will be fully satisfied & contented with this Settlement both of ye lands and all ye goods & chattels of sd estate as hereafter followeth.

Imprs It is agreed that Samuel ffuller ye eldest son of sd deceased Mr ffuller Quietly possess & enjoy for his portion to him his heirs & Assigns for Ever that seat of land in ye Town of Plimouth aforesaid which formerly was the possession of his said ffather and of late years Possessed by said Samuel his son with a house Standing thereupon with all uplands and meadows & all priviledges belonging thereunto Provided sd Samuel ffuller pay or Cause to be paid Annually to mrs Elizabeth ffuller Relict of his said father ten Shillings in Silver money at or before the first day of each October during ye time She Remains a widdow. ffurther it is agreed as aforesaid that John ffuller ye Second Son of ye said deceased have one hundred acres of land with ye meadow lying at ye foote of said land which land said

John ffuller hath now in his possession and is Butting upon Namasket River lying in ye lands purchased by Captain Thomas Southworth on ye North side of ye Road from Lakenham to Namasket River with half ye meadow lying in ye Great Meadow said lott of meadow is to be divided into two equall parts and said John ffuller to take his choyce And in that purchase one share of ye undivided lands of said Purchase And if hereafter said undivided land Shall be divided into lotts then said John ffuller is to have and choose his half of sd Divisions Also it is agreed as aforesaid that said Widdow Elizabeth ffuller Quietly have and possess the House and land which she now possesses in Middlebury Contayning Twenty acres more or less in ye Homestead Twelve acres more lying by ye lands of John Haskall and twenty acres of Land more or less lying at ye uper end of ye Great meadow in said Captain Southworths purchase together with ye one half of said meadow divided and undivided Belonging to said Purchase This housing and lands mentioned the said widdow is to enjoy wholy to her own proper use and benifit untill Isaac ffuller the youngest Son of sd ffuller deceased arrive at ye Age of twentyone years After which said Isaac ffuller is to have the one half of said House and said Widdow to have the other half And said Isaac is then to have two thirds of said Lands and sd Widdow one third during her life and after her decease said Isaac ffuller is to have and enjoy the whole house and all said lands to him his heirs and Assigns for ever It is also further agreed as aforesaid That after all ye just debts are paid the said Widdow ffuller shall have one full third part of ye moveables of sd Estate in what specie soever it be to her own proper use and benifit for ever moreover it is agreed that if said widdow dye before her son Isaac come to ye age of one and twenty years then ye Guardian of said Isaac hath full power and liberty to lease out said house and land for ye use and benifit of said Isaac till he Come of age to possess it. further more it is firmly Covenanted and Agreed as aforesaid that upon the decease of said Widdow the said House shall be apprised by persons [p. 247] Indifferently chosen by ye children concerned and ye value of it to be divided into Six equall parts and given to Mercy Cole John ffuller Experience wood Elizabeth Eaton Hannah ffuller and Isaac ffuller said Isaac ffuller Reserving his own sixth part of ye value of said House to himselfe is to pay ye Remainder of ye value of said House to his said Brother John and his said ffour sisters each of them a just proportion equally And said Isaac shall have liberty for two year before he pay said legacies to his said Brother and sisters after he comes to age if at that age of twenty one years he enter upon ye full and Intire possession of ye whole house but if it be some years after he is of age before he come fully to possess said house by ye decease of his mother then he shall be obliged to pay said legacies within a year after his taking possession of said house And if his mother dye before he sd Isaac come of age yet he shall not be obliged to pay said legacies till two years after his being of age ffurthermore it is agreed as aforesaid that for all ye lands in plymouth Township that are not before exprest in this Instrument that are part of ye estate of sd m^r ffuller deceased they are hereby granted & confirmed to Mercy Cole before named to her and her heirs for ever Particularly a Grant of land by said Plimouth Town or Court to said ffuller lying at doteys meadow in said Township And for his land in ye sixteene shilling purchase and all his Right of land in Assawamset Neck at or near Middleborough aforesaid it is mutually agreed as aforesaid That said land be herby granted and confirmed to Experience Wood Elizabeth Eaton and Hannah ffuller to them their heirs and Assigns forever to be equally divided betwixt them. It is also agreed as aforesd That ye two thirds of ye moveable Estate of sd ffuller be divided into four equall parts and to be equally divided betwixt the four sisters above named Mercy Experience Elizabeth and Hannah what each of them hath already Received being to be accounted as part of their portion and accordingly ye Remainder out of these two thirds to make each of their portions alike for ye full and firm Confirmation and Establishment of all and every of ye said Articles the widdow and children before named have set to their hand and Seals this first day of October one thousand Six hundred Ninety and five was ye day wherein sd widdow and Children made these articles of agreement.

Signed sealed and declared to be the joynt agreement of ye parties herein Concerned in presence of
William Bradford
ye Mark of Samuel Wood
Elkanah Cushman
Thomas Nelson

The **E** mark of
Elizabeth ffuller (seal)
Samuel ffuller (seal)
The mark of
Mercy Cole (seal)
John ffuller (seal)
John Nelson (seal)
James Wood
Experience Wood } (seal)
Samuel Eighton
The mark
Elizabeth Eaton } (seal)
Hannah ffuller (seal)

Elizabeth ffuller Samuel ffuller Mercy Cole John ffuller John Nelson James Wood Experience Wood Samuel Eaton Elizabeth Eaton Hannah ffuller Coming all of them personally before me 27th of July 1696 did freely own and acknowledge ye Instrument above written to be their act and deed

William Bradford. Justice of peace

Entered on Record Novembr 20th 1696.

pr Saml Sprague Register

[Plym. Co. Prob. Rcds., I : 246, 247]

GOVERNOR JOSIAH WINSLOW'S WILL AND INVENTORY.

Transcribed from the Original Records,

By George Ernest Bowman.

Governor Josiah Winslow, son of Governor Edward Winslow, died at Marshfield on 18/28 December, 1680. His will and inventory are recorded in the Plymouth Colony Wills and Inventories, Volume IV, Part II, pages 115, 116 and 117.

To all Christian people to whome these p^r^sents shall Come Josiah Winslow of Marshfeild in the Colony of New plymouth in New England sendeth greeting In the Lord god everlasting, And further Know yee. That I the said Josiah Winslow being by ye goodnes of God in Competent health, and of sound memory, but sensable of my fraylety, and that I am subiect to suddayne Changes. Revooking hereby any other or former will by me at any time made, doe declare and order this to be my last will and Testament.

Imp^r^mis I bequeath my body to the dust in decent buriall, And my soul to god that gave it, with some Comfortable perswasion of my resurrectiŏn to life and glory at the great and last day. And respecting the temporall estate wherewith it hath pleased god to bless me, My will and desier is, that all my Just debts be truely and seasonably paied and discharged by my Executrix that shall hereafter be declared

Item I give to my loveing sister Elyzabeth Corwin * my pockett watch, that was sometimes our honored fathers

Item I doe hereby Confirme unto my Kinsman John Brook (son to my said sister) all those my lands that are on pachaeg neck in the Township of Middlebery with the meadows and previledges thereunto appertaining and a hundred acres more of land layed out to me on the northerly side of Teticut River to him and to his heirs for ever.

Item I give unto my Brother Resolved White a suat and Cloak of my wearing aparrell.

Item I give to my Brother Peregrine White my spannish rapier & buffe belt with silver Claspes

* See Mayflower Descendant, I : 238–240.

Item I give to my kinsman William White a feather bed boulster rug blankett and a pair of sheets at what time he shall leave my wife & family

Item As a Testimony of my respect to her though in so smale a matter I give unto my Aunt Mrs Elyzabeth pelham two mares

Item I give to my Brother Edward pelham if he returne againe to New England a young horse for his owne riding

Item I give to the Reverend Mr Samuell Arnold such books of divinity as he now hath of mine in his possession & ye anotations on the bible by the asembly of English divines

Item I give to Elyzabeth Gray when she marrieth or leaves my wife one Cow.

Item I give to the poor of this Towne of Marshfeild one Cow.

And my debts and above mentioned legacies being paid, my will is That all the rest of my estate (viz) my houseing and lands goods Chattles and whatsoever be in the present posession and improvement of my affectionate and loveing wife Penelope Winslow (whome I here make and declare my sole Executrix) for her support and lively hood, And for the bringing up of our Children, To each of whome my desier and will is that good education may be given according to their sex and as my estate will bear

And I doe will and bequeath to my daughter Elyzabeth Winslow out of my sd estate the sum of three hundred pounds, besides what may be given her by any other frinds which three hundred pounds shall be paid to her at such time as she arives at eighteen yeers of age, or at the time of her marriage, which shall first be, if it may Conveniently be doone without selling any part of the lands wheron I live, or putting my wife and family too much to straytes, but if my wife find that she Cannot pay more then half the said sum of three hundred pounds at times above mentioned, Then my will is that the rest be paid at time of my wives decease, with ye addition of fifty pounds more for the forbearance.

And if it shall please god to lengthen out my wifes life untill our son Isack attaines to one & twenty yeers of age, My will is that the personall estate then resting (my daughters portion taken out as above) shall be equally devided between my dear wife and my said son, onely in all devisions my wife to have her Choyce, And my further will is, that as the personall estate shall be equally devided between my wife & my said son when he Comes of age, In like manner shall the house, out housing, and lands be equally devided between my wife and my said son during my wives naturall life, and that at my wives decease, The whole of my housen and lands at Marshfeild aforesaid shall be fully, freely, and absolutely to my said son Isack and to his heirs for ever, And if my said son should dye before he Come to age of one and twenty yeers not leaving lawfull issue by him begotten, or after he Comes of age if he dye without Issue (being yet posessed of the said estate) My will is, that then the estate of housen and lands shall as freely and absolutely goe unto, rest in, and settle upon my daughter Elyzabeth and her heirs for ever, but if god should take away both my above named Children, my dear wife yet surviveing [p. 116] My will is that then my whole estate shall be unto my said wife and to her heirs for ever she then paying within the Compass of a yeer, one hundred pounds in good and currant pay (viz) fifty ponds to my sisters son John Brooke if then liveing, or to his Child, or Children if he have any; And other fifty pounds to some other of my neer relations, who by their love and respect to her and hers, she shall see best deserving, And if John Brooke dye without issue the said fifty pounds not paid, that then it be paid to my sister Elyzabeth Corwin if liveing, or otherwise to some Child of hers by Captaine Georg Corwin her present husband

What other lands I have or may hereafter have at Succonett, or els where that I have not mentioned, nor disposed of I leave as Chattles at the free dispose of my Executrix, for paiment of my debts, or to make a part of my daughters portion or for other necessary occasions as she may see cause.

And my further will is that any thing above mentioned notwithstanding, It shall be lawfull for my said Executrix upon urgent necessity for the support and Comfort of her selfe and my Children, To sell a part of my lands at Marshfeild (whereon we now live) provided that a full halfe be reserved with the house and housen on it, And that in such matter of Importance she have the Concurrent advice and asistance of my overseers

And finally my request and desier is, That my respected Brother Captaine George Corwin my Cuzen Mr Peter Sergiant and my Cuzen Nathaniell Winslow will be pleased to guide and asist my said Executrix in such matters of importance as may be to weighty for her, And if any of my friends above named shall not accept of the trust which out of my good respect to them, I here nominate and appoint them unto or if after theire acceptance god should remove any of them by death or otherwise that they cannott in such a way be helpfull to her; My desier is that my wife choose some other grave and faithfull freind to supply his place for her Comfort and my childrens, In Confirmation of all and every the premises I have hereunto sett my hand and afixed my seal this second day of July in the yeer of our Lord 1675

Signed sealed and declared Josiah Winslow & a (seal)
to be my last will and Testament
In presence of
Humphrey Johnson
John Thomas.

At the Court of his Matie, held at Plymouth y^{e} 2^{d} of march $\frac{1680}{1681}$ Mr Humphry Johnson of Hingham and John Thomas made oath to y^{e} truth of this will; viz, That the Testator did Declare unto them that this will before signed and sealed by him was and is the last will and Testament of him the said Josiah Winslow Esqr. late Deceased

As Attesteth Nathaniell Morton Secretary.

[p. 117] An Inventory of the goods and Chattles of Josiah Winslow Esqr deseased Late Govr of the Colony of New Plymouth, Taken and prized by us whose names are under written the 1 day of June 1681

	li	*s*	*d*
Imp^{r}mis To his purse & Rings & Apparrell & watch	54	1	
Item To his personall Armes & horse furniture	18		
Item To his plate	45		
Item To Cash paid to his Docter and others by his Executrix	20		
Item To his Books	31	9	
Item To his household Arms and Amunition	7	15	
Item To the parlour to ye Cubbards chairs & other things	2		
Item In ye parlor Chamber to a trunk of Damask Diaper holland and other linnen	14		
Item To 3 beds and furniture in s^{d} chamber	12		
Item To a trunck with Carpet chair cases & other things	*	10	
Item To a table Cubbard cloth Andirons & other things	3		
Item To a Chest with Course old linnen in ye porch chamber	3	6	†
Item To a bed furniture in ye sd Chamber	2		
Item To 2 beds and furniture & other things in ye middle chamber	6	5	

* Worn.

† Except at this place no pence were entered. There was but one figure here, probably a "6," but the ink has eaten through the paper.

Item To a Coverled Counterpaine and other things in a Closett	2	10
The widdows bed not prised		
Item To a bed in ye Garrett and other things		15
Item To pewter bras & bell mettle in ye middle kitchin	22	15
Item To Iron and wooden ware. &c.		5
Item To Glasses Earthen ware and other things in ye seller	1	10
Item To horse furniture Carts plows chains & other takling	3	
Item To neat Cattle of all sorts	77	15
Item To Sheepe	11	4
Item To Swine	8	
Item To his horse flesh of all sorts	16	

William Bradford
Marke Eames

ZACHARIAH[2] SOULE'S INVENTORY.

Transcribed from the Original Records,

By George Ernest Bowman.

Zachariah[2] Soule (*George*[1]) was born before the Division of Cattle on 22 May /1 June, 1627,* and it is probable that he died not long before 11/21 December, 1663, the date on which his inventory was taken by John Alden and Constant Southworth. His widow, Margaret, was appointed administratrix, since her bond, dated 2 March, 1663/4, is preserved in the "Scrap Book" (p. 20) at the Plymouth Registry of Deeds. William Ford, Sr., of Marshfield was her surety and John Sutton and John Morton were the witnesses.

I have been unable to find any other record connected with the settlement of this estate and nothing to indicate that Zachariah left any children.

The inventory will be found in the Plymouth Colony Wills and Inventories, Volume II, Part II, page 18.

An Inventory of the goods and Chattles of Zacarya Soule taken this 11th of December 1663 and exhibited to the court held att Plymouth the third of March 1663 on the oath of Margarett Soule widdow;

	l	*s*	*d*
Imp[r]: 3 Cowes 1 heiffer 1 Calfe att	14	00	00
Item 1 mare att	08	00	00
Item 2 pigges att	05	00	00
Item swines flesh	03	00	00
Item 1 fowling peece and sword att	01	08	00
Item a saddle and bridle att	01	02	06
Item in Chistes	00	10	00
Item 1 Cloth coate att	01	14	00
Item 2 shirts 3 bands and 1 handkerchiffe	01	05	00
Item in pewter Dishes & bason & latten pannes	01	10	00
Item in earthen ware	00	04	00
Item 1 Iron pott potthookes 2 smale Iron kettles att	00	18	00
Item 1 old bedpan kettle & skillett	00	07	00
Item 1 frying pan & six spoones att	00	06	00
Item 1 hatt att	00	03	00
Item in severall goods new att	03	00	00

* Mayflower Descendant, I : 152.

Item in sifting trough trayes & Dishes & trenches	00 10 00
Item in wheele and cards woole & yearne & hemp	00 06 00
Item in butter and lard	00 08 00
Item in sope	00 05 00
Item 1 paire of shott moulds & sheers & handplaine & Drawing knife	00 07 00
Item tonggs and fier pan & axe & hoes	00 04 00
Item 1 pound of powder bad* & three hornes	00 02 06
Item 2 bagges att	00 03 00
Item 2 old mackerell lines & three ledds att	00 03 00
Item 2 barrells & 2 pound and an halfe of feathers	00 05 00
Item 3 bushells & 3 peckes of salt att	00 15 00
Item sythes & pitchforkes	00 03 00
Item house and land att powder point	26 00 00
Item a purchase share of land & meddow lying about Namassakett	25 00 00
Item 2 acrees of meddow lying about the gurnett	02 00 00
Item 40 acrees of upland lying in the woods	06 00 00
Item prte of a nett & ledd	00 03 00
Item about 4 load & an halfe of hay	
Item Debtes owing to the estate	01 08 09
Debts owing from the estate about 17s 00	

John Aldin
Constant Southworth

---

* Sic.

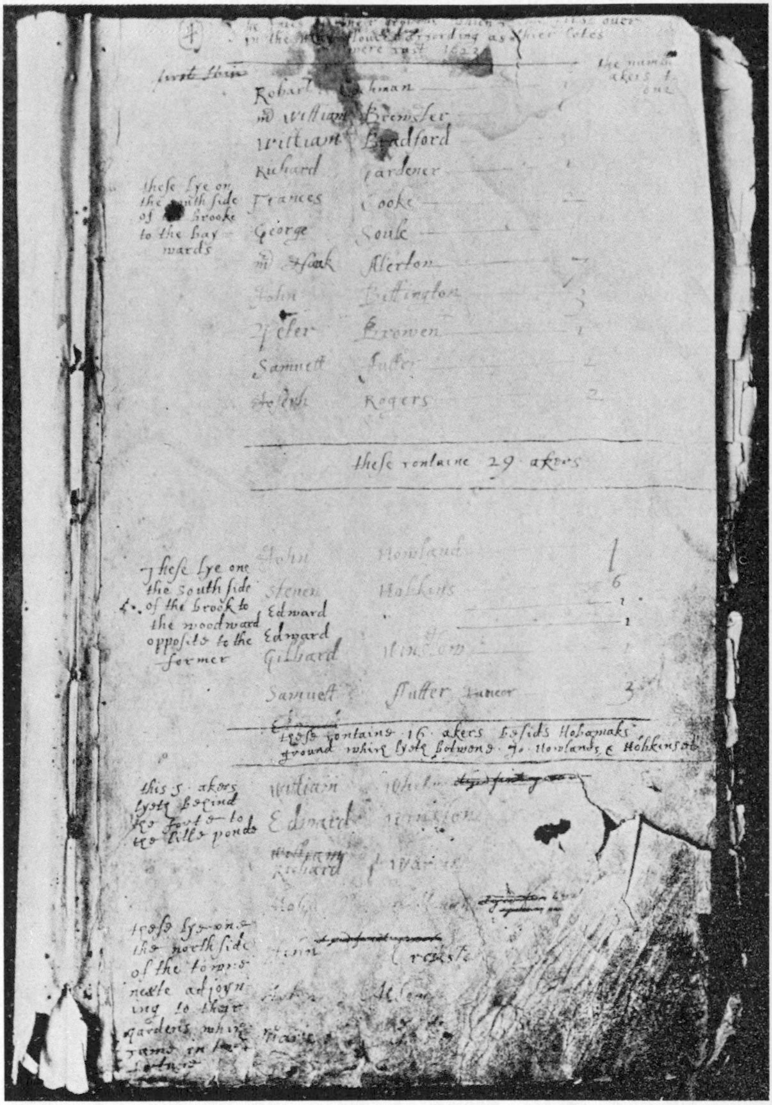
in the Mayflower according as their lotes were cast 1623

the number akers

Robart Cushman 1

mr William Brewster

William Bradford

Richard Gardener 1

these lye on the south side of the brooke to the bay wards

Frances Cooke 2

George Soule 1

mr Isaack Allerton 7

John Billington 3

Peter Browen 1

Samuell Fuller 2

Joseph Rogers 2

these containe 29 akers

these lye one the south side of the brook to the woodward opposite to the former

John Howland 1

Stephen Hobkins 6

Edward 1

Edward 1

Gilbard Winslow 1

Samuell Fuller Iunior 3

these containe 16 akers besids Hobamaks ground which lyes betwene Jo Howlands & Hobkinses

this 5 akers lyes behind the forte to the little ponds

William White

Edward Winslow

Richard Warren

these lye on the north side of the towne next adjoyning to their gardens which came in the fortune

John Crackston

EARLIEST KNOWN RECORD CONTAINING THE NAME "MAYFLOWER."

THE NAME "MAYFLOWER."

BY GEORGE ERNEST BOWMAN.

IT seems almost a waste of valuable time and space to again publish the proof that the vessel in which the Pilgrims set sail from Plymouth, England, on Wednesday, September 16, 1620 (New Style), was called the "Mayflower," but careless writers, because they do not find the name in any of the published writings of Bradford or Winslow, have jumped to the conclusion that such proof does not exist. Although the evidence was printed at least as early as 1861, and has been printed a number of times since, very few persons have had the privilege of seeing the original record, which is shown in the accompanying illustration, reproduced from a photograph. This is, we believe, the first time that a facsimile of this record has been published.

The illustration shows the fourth page of the first volume of the Plymouth Colony Records of Deeds. At the top of the page may be seen, in the well-known handwriting of Governor Bradford, the following entry:

The fales of their grounds which came first over in the Mayfloure according as thier lotes were cast . 1623.

This entry by Governor Bradford himself, in the oldest volume of the Plymouth Colony Records and written in 1623 or soon after that date, must be accepted as conclusive evidence that the Pilgrim ship was called the "Mayflower."

The earliest known mention of the name in print occurs in Nathaniel Morton's "New England's Memorial," published in 1669, and it is interesting to note that, as Secretary of Plymouth Colony from 1647 to his death in 1685, he had the custody of the records and made many entries in this first volume of deeds. He must, therefore, have been familiar with Bradford's record of the Division of Land in 1623, in which he doubtless took a lively interest as a boy of about ten years. Since Nathaniel Morton came to Plymouth with his father in the "Anne" but a few months before this division was made he must have been personally acquainted with nearly one-half of the Mayflower passengers, and two of them, John Howland and Mary (Allerton) Cushman, were still living at Plymouth when his book was written, so that even if the records had not been in his care he certainly was in a position to know the name of the first ship, and his statement of the name should have been accepted in the entire absence of any contradictory evidence.

THE WILL OF JOHN[2] ROGERS.

Transcribed from the Original Records,

BY GEORGE ERNEST BOWMAN.

JOHN ROGERS of Duxbury, the son of Thomas Rogers of the Mayflower, died between 26 August, 1691, the day his will was made, and 20 September, 1692, the day it was proved. All original documents connected with the settlement of the estate have disappeared from the files and there is no record of an inventory. The copy of the will has been made from the Plymouth County Probate Records, Volume I, page 145.

[JOHN[2] ROGERS' WILL.]

On the 26 August in the year of our Lord 1691 :

In the Name of God Amen. I John Rogers sen^{r} of Duxborough in the County of New Plimouth Being Sick and weak of Body but of Sound and perfect mind and memory Praise be therefore Given to Almighty God . Doe make and ordain this my present last will and Testament in maner and forme following that is to say first and Principally I comend my soul into the hands of Almighty God Hoping through the merits Death and Passion of my Saviour Jesus Christ to have full and free pardon and forgiveness of all my sins and to Inherit Everlasting Life. And my Body I Commit to the earth to be decently Buried at the discretion of my Executor hereafter named. And as Touching the Disposall of all Such Temporall Estate as it hath Pleased God to bestow upon me I Give and Dispose thereof as followeth . first I will that my debts and funerall charges be paid .

Item I Give unto my Grandson John Rogers all my houses and Lands Lying and being in the Township of Duxborough in the County aforesaid to him and his heires forever. I Give also unto my Grandson John Tisdall for the use of his mother Anne Terrey one half of my Land Divided and undivided lying and being in the Township of Middleborough Excepting my Right in the Majors Purchase And my Will is that this Land be disposed of according to his mothers mind. Item I Give unto my Daughter Elizabeth Williams the other half of sd tract of Land in the Township of Middleborough as aforesaid to her and heires. All my Cattell I Will that they be Equally divided Between my daughter Elizabeth Williams and my Grandson John Rogers and my Grandson John Tisdall. Item I Give all my houshold Stuff and moneys whatsoever . unto my Grandson John Rogers out of which he shall pay forty shillings to his sister Elibeth * Rogers and twenty shillings apeece to his other three sisters Hannah Bradford Ruth Rogers and Sarah Rogers. Also I Give that twenty shillings a year which is my due for fourscore acres of land which I sold to my two Grandsons Joseph Richmond and Edward Richmond which said twenty shillings a year I Give to my daughter Abigail Richmond. I Doe hereby Constitute make and appoint my Loving Son John Rogers sole Executor and Administrator of this my last Will and Testament.

Signed Sealed in John Rogers & a (seal)
the presence of
Rhodolphus Thacher
Mary Wadsworth
Elisha Wadsworth

M[r] Rhodolphus Thacher and Elisha Wadsworth two of the witness herein named made oath before the Court at Plimouth the 20th of Sep[t] 1692 that they were present and Saw and heard the above named John Rogers the Testator Sign Seal and Declare the above written to be his last will and testament and that to the best of their Judgment he was of sound mind and memory when he did the same

Attest Sam[l] Sprague Clerk

---

* Sic.

THE SETTLEMENT OF EDWARD[2] DOTY'S ESTATE.

Transcribed from the Original Records,

BY GEORGE ERNEST BOWMAN.

Edward[2] Doty (*Edward*[1]) died intestate on 8 February, 1689/90, and his wife Sarah (Faunce) Doty was appointed administratrix on 18 March 1689/90. On the third of December, 1696, the widow having married again and died in the meantime, the surviving heirs made a final settlement of the estate. The inventory, the appointment of the administratrix and the agreement of the heirs are recorded in the Plymouth County Probate Records, Volume I, pages 53 and 251. The only original document connected with this estate remaining in the files is the bond of the administratrix, which was not recorded.

[The Inventory.]

[p. 53] An Inventory of the Estate of Edward Doten Senr late of Plimouth Deceased taken and aprised by us whose names are here unto subscribed on y^{e} 3^{d} of march $16\frac{89}{90}$ his wearing cloaths and some Bedding were lost when he was Drowned.

	£	s	d
Imp^{r}s In one Bed and furniture to it at	4	. .	. .
Item in one ffeather Bed and Bedding to it at	4	. .	. .
Item in one old Bed and 5 sheets at	3	. .	. .
Item in Table linnen and Pillowbeeres at	1	6	. .
Item in armes and Amunition at	4	. .	. .
Item in Pewter and Brass at	1	19	. .
Item in Iron Pots and Kettles and one pair of stilyards at	1	3	. .
Item in Bookes	. .	10	. .
Item in fflax teere and Yarn linnen and woolen	1	5	. .
Item in new Cloath Linnen & woollen and Cotton & sheeps wooll	2	17	. .
Item in housing and all his upland and meadow in Plimouth at	60	. .	. .
Item in one great Table a Chist and Boxes at	1	17	. .
Item in a Little Table and Chaires at	. .	10	. .
Item in Box iron & heaters axes hoes tramel Pot hooks & tongs	1	. .	. .
Item in Cattle sheep swine and a horse at	19	. .	. .
Item in woodden Dishes Pailes and Glass Bottles at	. .	8	. .
Item in one Canooe horse Geeres little Plow a bridle and Saddle	2	. .	. .
Item in old Cask and old lumber at	1	. .	. .
Item in 3 Spinning wheeles and old Cards at	. .	12	. .
Item in Debts the Estate oweth	11	12	6
More the Estate oweth	5	18	. .

John Doten.
James Warrin.

Sarah Dotey Relict Widdow of Edward Dotey late of Plimouth Deceased made oath before the County Court at Plimouth the 18th of March $16\frac{89}{90}$ That the above written is a true Inventory of the Estate of the said Edward Dotey Deceased So far as she Knoweth and that if more shall be made known unto her she will Discover it

Attest Sam'^{l} Sprague Clerk

[Appointment of Administratrix.]

Administration is Granted by the Court unto Sarah Dotey Relict widdow of Edward Dotey late of Plimouth aforesd Deceased to administer on the Estate of sd Deceased She having given Bond to administer according to law and Render account of her administration to the said Court when leagally Required

Attest Sam'l Sprague Clerk

[Bond of Administratrix.]

At a County Court held at Plimouth March 18th $16\frac{89}{90}$
Memorandum.

There Came personally before the Court Sarah Dotey Relict widdow of Edward Dotey late of Plimouth Deceased and Thomas ffaunce and John Dotey all of sd Plimouth and acknowledged themselves their Executors & Administrators to stand bound unto the said Court in the Severall Sums hereafter mentioned that is to say the said Sarah as principle in the Sum of thirty pounds and the Sd Thomas and John as s[*worn*] Each of them in the Sum of fifteene pounds; to be levied on their lands Goods and Chattels : &c

On Condition that whereas the Sd Sarah Dotey hath obtained and taken power of Administration upon the Estate of her late husband Edward Dotey aforesd Deceased if there fore she the said Sarah shall Administer thereon according to law and Render up account of her sd Administration to Sd Court when leagally Required of her and in all things Do & act in sd Respect as the law Enjoins that then &c :

This Recognzance Taken before the above sd Court

Attest Sam'l Sprague Clerk

[Agreement of the Heirs.]

[p. 251] These presents Witnesseth ye Mutual agreement of Such of ye children of Edward Dotey late of Plimouth within ye County of Plimouth in New England Deceased Intestate, as are of full age and Capacity to act for themselves and ye Gaurdians of Such of them as are in their Minority Whose names are herein Expressed And who have under Subscribed Relating to a Settlement and Division of ye Estate of sd Deceased to and among his sd Children That is to say ye Agreement of James Warren and Sarah his Wife Martha Dotey Mary Dotey Tobias Oaksman and Elizabeth his Wife And Thomas ffaunce and John Dotey Gaurdians of and in the Behalf of Samuel Dotey Benjamin Dotey and Mercy Dotey as followeth that is to say that ye sd Sarah Martha Mary and Elizabeth for their full part portion and part of ye Estate of ye sd Deceased Shall have and henceforth Enjoy All that the fifty Acres of land and three acres of Meadow at or near Monponset in ye Township of Plimouth And one other parcell of land which sd Deceased while he lived bought of Mr William Crow at a place Called Atwoods Swamp in sd plimouth together also With all ye Goods and Chattels or Cattell that now Remains of ye Estate of sd Deceased And also ye Sum or value of four pounds out of ye Rents or proffits of ye Housing of sd Deceased All ye afore mentioned Lands goods & Chattels to be long and appertain unto ye said Sarah Warren Martha Dotey Mary Dotey & Elizabeth Oaksman their Severall heirs Executors Administrators and Assigns for Ever And nextly it is hereby agreed That the said Samuel Benjamin and Mercy for their full part portion & share of the Estate of sd Deceased Shall hereafter have and Enjoy all ye Residue of ye sd Estate that is to say particularly the Housing House Lott or Homestead of sd Deceased in ye Town of Plimouth aforesaid according to ye known & accustomed Boundaries of ye same Together with all that parcell of meadow pertaining to ye Estate of ye sd Deceased at ye South meadow within ye Township of plimouth aforesaid All wch aforesaid Housing Homestead and parcell of Meadow last mentioned to belong and Appertain to the said Samuel Dotey Benjamin Dotey & Mercy Dotey their Severall Heirs and Assigns for Ever In Testimony Whereof the sd James Warren and Sarah his wife Martha Dotey Mary Dotey Tobias Oaksman & Elizabeth his wife And Thomas ffaunce and John Dotey Gaurdians for & of the sd Samuel Dotey Benjamin Dotey and Mercy Dotey have here unto set their Severall hands and Seals this third Day of December In ye year of our Lord God one thousand Six hundred ninety and Six 1696.

In ye presence of	James Warren & a Seal
these Witnesses	The mark of Sarah Warren & Seal
John Morton	The mark of Martha Dotey & a seal
James Barnabee	The mark of Mary Dotey & a seal
	The mark of Tobias Oaksmand and a Seal.
	The mark of Elizabeth Oaksman & a Seal
	Thomas ffaunce and a Seal
	The mark of John Dotey and a seal

Memorandum that upon ye third Day of December 1696 the above named partyes who have hereunto sealed & Subscribed y^t^ is to say James Warren and Sarah his wife Martha Dotey

Mary Dotey Tobias Oaksman & Elizabeth his wife & Thomas ffaunce & John Dotey Gaurdians of Samuel Dotey Benjamin Dotey & Mercy Dotey Came all of them Personally before me y^{e} Subscriber judge of probate & acknowledged y^{e} abovesd Agreement to be their act & Deed and I do allow & approve of y^{e} same as a finall Settlement And partition of y^{e} Estate of y^{e} above named Edward Dotey Deceased

William Bradford.

Entered January 2^{d} $169\frac{6}{7}$ p^{r} Saml Sprague Regist^{r}.

JOSEPH^2 BRADFORD'S WILL AND THE REASONS FOR NOT APPROVING IT.

Transcribed from the Original Documents,

BY GEORGE ERNEST BOWMAN.

JOSEPH^2 BRADFORD (*Governor William*^{1}) lived in that part of Plymouth which was set off in 1726 as the town of Kingston, and he died there 10 July, 1715, in the eighty-fifth year of his age according to the inscription on his gravestone on Burial Hill at Plymouth. His wife, who survived him fifteen years, was Jael Hobart, the daughter of Rev. Peter Hobart of Hingham, Mass.

The index of the Plymouth County Probate Records and Files contained no reference to any settlement of Joseph^2 Bradford's estate, therefore I was much surprised, while examining in the Registry of Probate at Plymouth some miscellaneous papers which had never been recorded or indexed, to find a will with his autograph signature, also an inventory of his estate and the other documents which are here presented. These papers are now docketed and indexed.

The reasons for the refusal to approve the will are so clearly stated in the Memorandum of the Judge of Probate it would be superfluous to repeat them here.

[Joseph[2] Bradford's Will.]

The eight day of October in the year of Our Lord one thousand seven hundred and twelve I Joseph Bradford of the town & County of Plimoth in Her Majesties Province of ye Massachusetts bay in New England planter, being in some Measure of bodily health: of a Sound mind & Memory do make and ordain this my last will & testament in manner and forme following. In the first and Chief place I Resign & bequeth my Soul into the hands of God who gave it my body I commit to the earth to be decently buried. And as to my temporal Estate I give, bequeath and dispose thereof as followeth

Imprimis I give and bequeath to my dear and loveing wife Jael Bradford & to my Son Elisha Bradford all my household goods & debts whatsoever Item I give and bequeath unto Jael Bradford my wife her heirs and assignes forever one halfe part of all my housing and lands forever with all & every of their appurtenances . Item I give and bequeath to my son Elisha Bradford the other halfe part of all my lands and houses to him the Said Elisha Bradford his heires and assignes forever. Also I do Constitute and appoint my beloved wife Jael Bradford to be the Executrixe and my son Elisha Bradford to be the Executor of this my last will & testament finally I do hereby Revoke and disanul all former wills by me made and in testimony that this is my last will and testament I have hereunto set my hand & affixed my seale the day & yeare above written

Signed Sealed & Declared by the said Joseph Bradford to be his last will & testament in the presence of us the Subscribers

Joseph Bradford (Seal)

David Hobart
Elisha stetson
wrrastling bruster

[The Inventory.]

A Inventory of the Estate of m^r^ Joseph bradford late of Plymoth In the County of Plymoth in New england desesed taken the 27 day of July anno dominy 1715 by us hows names are underwriten

	ll	*s*	*d*
To wering Cloathes at	10	00	00
To bookes	10	00	00
To beeds and shets and other bed cloths	50	00	00
To Plate and mony	10	00	00
To bras and Peuter and Earthenware	09	18	00
To Ironware and Pots	04	00	00
To tabeel linen	06	14	00
To Hors furneiture	02	00	00
To Chiestes and tables and old lumber	06	10	00
To Sheeps wooll	01	01	00
To five pare of Stockens	01	00	00
To Neet Cattel and one mare	51	00	00
To Swine	02	05	00
To Sheepe	06	00	00
To all the lands and meddoes and housing at	1606	00	00
To two goons	01	10	00
The Sum totall at	1777	18	00

Eleazer Cushman
Joseph Stockbridge

Plim ss on the 19th day of october 1715 Mrs Jael Bradford & her son Elisha Bradford made oath that the abovewritten is a true Inventory of the Estate of Mr Joseph Bradford deceased so far as they Know & That when they Know of More will Cause it to be added

before me Nathaniel Thomas Judge of Probats

[Testimony of David Hobart.]

I David Hobart testifie that mr Joseph Bradford decesd desired me to write him a will which I did according to his directions & being Read to him he signed sealed the same & declared it to be his last will & testament, and when he so did he was of a disposing Judgment and memory to my best knowledge, the said will baring date the eight day of october one thousand seven hundred and twelve and this will was presented to the Honbl Judge of probate for the Conty of Plymoth

Taken upon oath October the 19th 1715 before me

Nathaniel Thomas Judge of Probats

[Testimony of Elisha Stetson and Wrestling Brewster.]

Elisha Stetson & Wrastling Bruster made oath That they were prsent & Saw Mr Joseph Bradford Sign seale & heard him Declare the abovewritten Instrument to be his last Will &

Testament but Can not say that when he so did he was of a disposeing mind & Memory

Taken upon oath October the 19 . 1715 before me

Nathaniel Thomas Judge of Probats

on wensday the Court in december is appointed to Argue the Probate of Mr Joseph Bradfords Will.

Memorand that Elisha Stetson & Wrestling Brewster at the first Presenting the said Will to the said Judge declared unto him; That the said Instrument was not Read to the said Joseph Bradford in their hearing at the time when he signed & sealed & Declared the same to be his Will.

[Testimony of Ephraim Little.]

I Ephraim Little Of plymouth being subpenaed Do Testify and Declare, that some years Ago Mrs Jael Bradford then the wife of Mr Joseph Bradford Came to my house & Gave mee a paper inclosed but not Sealed & Desired mee to Seal it & take it into my Custody, Telling me it was her husbands Will, I accordingly tooke it & Laid it up . but after sometime Upon Something I had heard I Opened s^{d} Will and Readd it and Indeed was very Much surprized to see that Mr Bradford having but one son should make his Will & not give any of his lands to him & thereupon resolved to Lett Mr Bradford know I had Opened the Will & Give him my thoughts about it . accordingly putt ye will into my pockett & went to Mr Bradfords . and mett wth him Walking in his pasture Alone. I presently Gave him An Acc^{t} of my business & Desired him to reconsider his Will & whether he had Just Cause to disinheritt his son he told mee he had given all his lands to his son only reserving to his Wife ye Improv^{t} Of one half during her life Upon that I told him he was und^{r} a great Mistake & took out ye will to read to him to convince him of his Mistake but he replyed No lets go into ye house & it shall be read before her. I suppose Meaning his Wife. Accordingly Wee went in & as soon as Mr Bradford came in (what sayth he! Mr Little sayth I have given all ye lands to you & seem^{d} pretty Much disturbed his Wife endeavoured to pacify him & desired mee to sit down I did so he Desired mee to read ye Will upon wch I tooke it out and was ging to read it wch Mrs Bradford Objected Against alledging it was not Convenient it should be read but Mr Bradford (wth some heat) s^{d} it shou'd be read, upon wch I desired

Mrs Bradford to give her reasons why shee thought not convenient and it may be wn wee had heard them Mr Bradford would not desire the reading of it, shee seemd not very forward in giving any Reason; Mr Bradford still Insisted upon ye reading it. & at last Mrs Bradford offered this reason that viz. that it would be more Convenient to lett it alone to another time that ye man that wrote it might read it to her husband To wch I thus Replyed, said I Mrs I do not know who ye man was that wrote this will but whoever it was I am afraid he has read it once to yr husband and read it wrong & therefore I'll now read it to him & read it right & Imediatly began to read, shee seemd Much Disturbd at it & so did Mr Bradford too wn I came to that paragraph yt related To ye disposall of ye land & Interrupted mee & said it was none of his Will & it should be burnt & that he never sett his hand to it. upon that I lookd on his name & held ye paper to him telling him I believed it was his own hand, he replyed that if so they gave him another to read & made him putt his hand to this for this was not ye paper he read, & Was very much disturbed abt ye matter, & utterly disclaimed it to be his Will After some time I having ye will still in my hands Mrs Bradford desired mee to give it to her but I refused it at wch shee seemd Angry: I told her if Mr Bradford desired it I would give it to him; shee faulted mee much for Opening it I told her I would not Justify my Opening it but If I had done amiss I must beg Mr Bradfords pardon & not hers. he replyed he was glad I Opened it & there was a good providence in it. after wee had sat a while Mr Bradford desired ye Will of mee I readily gave it to him. presently his Wife desired him to give it to her to Lay up. but he refused it; but before I came away shee obtained it of him telling him if there was any thing Amiss in it it should be rectifyed.

This is the substance of wt I know abt ys Matter.

Octobr 19. 1715 Eph. Little

Plimouth ss on the 22d day of December Annqe Dom 1715 Mr Ephraim Little made oath to the truth of the above & before written before me

Nathaniel Thomas Judge of Probates

& the sd Ephraim Little Do further Testify that being sometime the last summr at ye house of Mr Joseph Bradford deceased and having some discourse wth Mrs Bradford I heard Mr Bradford say to his wife why Do you trouble Mr Little abt it I always Intended to give my lands To my son

Plim ss on the 22ᵈ day of December . 1715 The above named EPhraim little made oath to the Truth of the above-written

before me Nathaniel Thomas Judge of Probats

[TESTIMONY OF ELEAZER CUSHMAN.]

Eleazʳ Cushman of full Age being supenaed testifyeth & Saith that sometime in Octoᵇʳ 1713 as I take it . I being in the morning at yᵉ house of Mʳ Joseph Bradford Deceased Mʳ David Hobert was there & yᵉ sᵈ hobert & I fell into discourse about the opening of sᵈ Bradfords former Will and the Misinterpretting & holding forth that yᵉ sᵈ Mʳ Bradford had given his Estate from his son to yᵉ Hobarts . and at that time I heard sᵈ hobart say he wrote sᵈ Will & did it according to Mʳ Bradfords direction and that sᵈ Bradford liked & Approved it : in our sᵈ Discourse the sᵈ Mʳ Bradford broke in upon us & sᵈ Mʳ Little had done very ill in his reporting about yᵗ Mattʳ for sᵈ he I Do Intend my son Elisha shall have all my lands and I was informed by Elisha Stetson that Mʳ Bradford had Just before signed his Will . and that he & Wrestle Brewster had signed as Witnesses to it & furthʳ sayth not

Plim ss on the 22ᵈ day of December Annoq Dom 1715 Mʳ Eliezar Cushman made oth to the truth of the abovewritten

before me Nathaniel Thomas Judge of Probates

[MEMORANDUM OF JUDGE OF PROBATE.]

Septembʳ Court 1715.
These pʳsents sheweth,

The Reasons Wherfore the Judge of Probats for the County of Plimouth Could not Approve the Instrument pʳsented to him by Mʳˢ Jael Bradford as her late Husbands Will.

Before the said Instrument was Exhibited to the said Judge Major John Bradford desired him That when his uncle Mʳ Joseph Bradfords Will was Exhibitted he might be pʳsent & hear it Read before it was Proved

Accordingly when Mʳˢ Jael Bradford Relict widow of the said Mʳ Joseph Bradford Came before the said Judge to Exhibit her said Husbands Will . Major Bradford was sent for & then the said Instrument or writing was Read. And then the said Majʳ Bradford said That Instrument or writing was not his uncles Will . but his Aunts Will . & Entred a Cavit with the Judge against the Probate therof untill he should be further heard & bring in his Witnesses against the Probate therof

Elisha Stetson & Wrestling Brewster two of the Witneses named in the said Will being p^{r}sent were asked by the Judge whether that writing was Read to Mr Joseph Bradford before he signed it they Answered it was not Read to him in their hearing

Then the Judge told Mrs Jael Bradford it was Nessesary her Brother Mr Hobart the other Witness should Come & Testify whether the said Writing was Read to her husband before he signed it And so the Matter was deferred untill Mr David Hobart should Come & on the 19th day of october 1715. the said Hobart & the other Witneses Came before the Judge & gave their severall Testimonys to the said Writing which are on file

Maj^{r} John Bradford being then p^{r}sent said some of his Witneses Could not be then had & Prayed a further time might be appointed for to Argue the Probate of the said Will before it was allowed And accordingly wenesday the Court in december was appointed for both partys to be p^{r}sent to argue & Prove what Each thought fit for & against the Probate of the said Will.

At which day Maj^{r} Bradford appearing & Mrs Jael Bradfords brother in Law & a kinsman of hers on her behalf And Maj^{r} Bradford then Produced his Witnesses who being all Sworn that Matter was Argued on both sids & a full hearing had

The said Judge Declared that he Could not approve nor allow the said Writing to be the Will of the said deceased Mr Joseph Bradford And his Reasons are as follows viz

1 because it was Evident by the Testimoney of Mr Ephraim Little that the said Mr Joseph Bradford was deceived in a former will written by the said David Hobart brother to the said Jael And the said Mrs Bradford Promoting it & declaring it to be her husbands Will. when (as he after said) it was not his Will.

2 That by this Will or writing the on half of Mr Joseph Bradfords lands will Probably fall to the Hobarts therfore the said David Hobart not so fit for a Witness or Scribe therof.

3 The other two Witnesses Cannot say he was of a disposeing mind & memory when he signed it.

4 By Mr Eliazer Cushmans Testimony (a man also of known Integrity) It is Evedent that Either he the said Mr Joseph Bradford was non Sane Memori or that he was agen deceived in this as in his former Will when he signed it. by his saying he would give all his lands to his son. when but a few hours before he had signed his Will & therin gave half his lands to his wife & her heires & asigns for Ever.

Note That M[rs] Jael Bradford nor any in her behalf ever moved to the said Judge any appeal from the afores[d] sentence.

Nathaniel Thomas J. Probats

EDWARD WINSLOW.

COMMUNICATED BY WINSLOW WARREN.

No historian of the Pilgrims of Plymouth would fail to assign to Edward Winslow a prominent place as one of their three or four great leaders. Of high social standing, well educated, of gentle and courteous manners, tactful and kind yet resolute, he combined qualities some of which were rare among the Pilgrims and of the utmost importance to the success of their settlement. No other man among them possessed such skill in diplomacy as Winslow and he was their chief and sure reliance in dealing with the perplexing questions arising with the Indians, in negotiations with the mother country, in the disputes with Massachusetts and the other colonies, and in all the trade relations with England, the Kennebec, Connecticut and other settlements. He filled many responsible positions with great ability and displayed a knowledge of men and affairs surprising in view of his lack of early training and experience.

While in practical administrative ability he may not have equalled Bradford, and while he was not a soldier like Standish, in scholarship and general culture, and in the power of adapting his knowledge to the needs and conditions of the settlement, he was approached by neither.

Although he is the only one of the Pilgrims of whom we have an authentic portrait, and memorials of him in the form of publications and coats of arms, and silver and furniture, are not rare, we really know but little of his history before his coming to Plymouth. His grandfather Kenelm Winslow lived at Kempsey in the County of Worcester, England, and his father Edward owned a family seat called Careswell at Droitwich in the same County, where the birth of the Pilgrim Edward is recorded in 1595. He was the oldest of five sons all of whom came to America, Edward and Gilbert in the Mayflower, the others later. He was educated at Droitwich and as far as we know lived there until he reached the age of twenty-two. There has been a tradition that he was educated at Cambridge University but it appears to be without foundation. There is nothing to show that in England he had any communication with the Pilgrims or that he was in any way inclined to their religious views — his family lived at a considerable distance from Scrooby or Austerfield where most of the Pilgrims met and there is no evidence of any special Puritan or Separatist movement in Worcestershire distinct from the general tendency throughout England. He first appears in history as a young man of liberal education who while travelling for pleasure upon the Continent falls in by accident with Robinson's congregation in Leyden in 1617, becomes interested in their peculiar views and joins the Pilgrim church. He was then a bachelor, but twenty-two years of age, apparently of some means but engaged in no particular business or profession. Soon after becoming a member of the Leyden congregation the records show that he was married to Elizabeth Barker, a young English girl also a member of the congregation. The three years spent in Leyden he is supposed to have been in the printing business, probably with Brewster, but we hear little of him until in the summer of 1620 we find him corresponding as one of the Pilgrim agents with Carver and Cushman in England with reference to the arrangements for the departure for America.

About August 1, 1620, he left with the others in the Speedwell from Delft Haven, shared their experiences with the leaky ships in England and sailed in the Mayflower for America September 16. His name appears on the famous compact signed in Provincetown harbor in the cabin of the Mayflower November 21. He was upon the march inland begun December 16, during which the Pilgrims had their first encounter with the Indians, and was with the party which landed on Clark's Island and "the next day being the Sabbath wee rested." Monday the 21st, as Winslow writes, they "sounded the Harbour (Plymouth), and found it a very good Harbour for our shipping, we marched also into the Land, and found divers corne fields, and little running brookes, a place very good for scituation, so we returned to our Ship againe with good newes to the rest of our people, which did much comfort their hearts."

This was the landing on Plymouth Rock and this simple account all that contemporaneous history tells of it. December 26 the Mayflower sailed up into the harbor; soon after the whole company went ashore, the beginning of the common house was made and a new Nation was born.

Three disastrous months followed and one of many who fell

by the way was his faithful wife, yet such were the perils and necessities of the situation that but seven weeks elapsed before he married a second wife, Susannah White, who herself had been a widow but twelve weeks.

The period of mourning seems short but the perils surrounding them allowed no yielding to the natural feelings of grief and compelled the union of families for protection and safety. The marriage proved a happy one and Susannah Winslow became famous in history as the wife of one Pilgrim Governor, the mother of another, who was the first native born Governor, and mother also, by her first husband, of the first white child born in New England, Peregrine White. She survived her husband a quarter of a century and died at Marshfield in 1680.

In March the Pilgrims were startled by the appearance among them of the Indian Samoset with his "Welcome Englishmen" and were informed by him of the neighborhood of the Sachem Massasoit and his desire to confer with them. For the delicate and dangerous duty of interviewing the chief and of ascertaining his temper of mind Winslow was selected, and meeting Massasoit a short distance from the settlement he arranged a conference in Plymouth and volunteered to remain with the Indians while Massasoit visited the authorities. Through his tactful address and skill this meeting became an eventful one and resulted in a treaty of peace with the Indians which remained unbroken for fifty-five years, until King Philip's war. It is not too much to say that upon the result of these negotiations largely depended the future of the settlement, for in its weak and forlorn condition peace with the Indian neighbors was of the first importance.

In July it was determined to explore the interior and return the visit of Massasoit at his home near Mt. Hope and Winslow was chosen for that duty with Stephen Hopkins.

The journey through thirty miles of trackless forest was a rough one and perilous from the uncertainty as to the disposition of the Indians on the route, but they reached Massasoit in safety and found him and his people friendly and desirous of extending a hospitable welcome, but as they had just returned from an expedition they were very short of provisions. Winslow quaintly writes "Late it grew, but victualls he offered none; for indeed he had not any, being he came so newly home. So we desired to goe to rest: he layd us on the bed with himselfe and his wife, they at the one end and we at the other, it being onely plancks layd a foot from the ground, and a thin Mat upon them. Two more of his chiefe men for want of roome pressed by and upon us; so that we were worse weary of our lodging then of our journey. . . . . wee desired to keepe the Sabboth at home: and feared we should either be light-headed for want of sleepe, for what with bad lodging, the Savages barbarous singing, (for they use to sing themselves asleepe) lice and fleas within doores and Muskeetoes without, wee could hardly sleepe all the time of our being there."

This promiscuous lodging with its disagreeable accompaniment of friendly but unattractive hosts made the dreary settlement in Plymouth appear a haven of rest.

This was not to be the last nor the most uncomfortable visit of Winslow to Massasoit. In the Spring of 1623 news came of the serious illness of the latter and again Winslow set out with an Indian guide Hobamak and a "gentleman from London," John Hampden. Much has been written of the significance of the supposed comradeship of the famous John Hampden, but more recent investigation has clearly shown that the patriot Hampden was not in this country at the time.

Yet the visit was a remarkable one, for the country of Massasoit's probable successor, Corbitant, had first to be gone through, and he was known to have ambitious projects and not to be over friendly towards the Pilgrims; but Massasoit's home was reached and the evident cordiality of the reception showed how deep was the impression upon the Indians of Winslow's tenderness of heart and gentle bearing. Fortunately he possessed some knowledge of medicine and after most assiduous personal ministration was able to relieve the monarch's suffering and when the time came to depart was followed with most demonstrative evidence of gratitude and friendship.

On the way home he stopped at Swansea and passed the night with Corbitant, finding him a most entertaining host, being, as he says, "a notable politician, yet full of merry jests and squibs, and never better pleased than when the like are returned upon him again" — What a scene for a painter — probably the only one of the Pilgrims who had fun and wit enough to enjoy this rather grim frolic in the woods — imagine the sturdy and scholarly Pilgrim alone in the wilderness with the treacherous chief, sitting over the fire smoking hospitable pipes in the lonely hut and exchanging jokes, all the while suspecting that the jolly savage was hostile and uncertain. Corbitant expressed to him his surprise that he risked the journey, and hinted that he wouldn't have come on his account if he had been sick like Massasoit, became very inquisitive, poked fun at him, and in Indian style tried to draw him out. A full report would be most entertaining but we have only fragments, as for instance when Corbitant asked why when he came to Plymouth they stood upon their guard with the mouths of their pieces presented to him and upon Winslow's shrewdly answering "it was the most honorable and respective entertainment we could give them" and such as they bestowed upon distinguished persons — Corbitant dryly remarked he "liked not such salutations." They parted however in the morning in a cordial way and Winslow returned having gained much important information as to threatened hostile movements and yet leaving a distinct impression upon the Indians of the good will of the settlement and its desire to be on friendly terms with its neighbors.

In September of the same year Winslow sailed in the "Anne" for England as agent for the Colony and while there published his "Good Newes from New England," giving rather a hopeful account of the plantation from the period when the so-called "Mourt's Relation" left off down to September 10, 1623, being really a continuation of the latter book, which it is understood was written by Bradford and Winslow and sent to England in 1622 for publication, its name being derived from the fact of its preface being signed by "G. Mourt."

In March, 1624, he returned with much needed supplies, bringing also the first bull and heifers imported to the Colony.

Another portion of the cargo was less satisfactory, for with him came one John Lyford, an Episcopal preacher with Puritan leanings who contrary to Winslow's advice was selected by a portion of the Adventurers in England. Lyford soon became a thorn in the flesh to the Pilgrims and by his unseemly behaviour and duplicity so aroused the Pilgrim ire that they drove him from the settlement and repudiated all connection with him.

Subsequently Winslow had much trouble over this matter in England and was compelled to expose the disagreeable facts of Lyford's early life to show the man in his true colors and vindicate the Pilgrim action.

For the next few years he was fully occupied with negotiations and business transactions with the Kennebec and other settlements, and in 1627 Bradford, Standish, Allerton, Winslow, Howland, Alden and Prence agreed with the Adventurers in England to take over the whole trade of the Colony for six years, undertaking to pay all debts and arrange for the removal of the rest of the congregation from Holland, Robinson their revered pastor having died.

In 1630 he went to England again as Agent and after his return was chosen Governor in 1633, to succeed Bradford who sought a well earned retirement, and the next year was chosen one of the Assistants, which office he filled for eleven years.

In 1632 Winslow had made an expedition to the Connecticut River and established a trading post near Hartford;—the region being claimed by the Dutch and also by settlers from Dorchester and Cambridge, warm disputes arose in 1635–6 as to ownership;—the Plymouth men had driven out the Dutch and Governor Winthrop having taken up the cause of the Massachusetts men Winslow was sent to negotiate with him. The powerful influence of the larger Colony was too much for Plymouth although a large portion of the latter's claim was conceded, but the reputation that Winslow acquired in Boston was soon shown by the remarkable action of the Massachusetts authorities in requesting him in face of some opposition to represent them in England in the matter of the Dutch complaints, the alleged restriction of the suffrage, and other points.

In 1635 he sailed for England but arrived at an unfortunate time for any one with Puritan or Pilgrim antecedents. Archbishop Laud was Chairman of the Commission before which he was delegated to appear, and, although by his arguments Winslow was able to influence the rest of the Commission, the Archbishop had him arrested and imprisoned for seventeen weeks under charge of being a Separatist and of solemnizing marriages illegally, and he escaped punishment only by influence of friends in high station.

Winslow always charged this imprisonment to the spite of Morton of Merry Mount fame who certainly had no occasion to love the authorities of either Plymouth or Boston.

Perhaps the strongest testimony to the value of Winslow's services is afforded in a letter of one of his bitterest opponents from America, Samuel Maverick a devoted Churchman living at East Boston in a fortified house surrounded by four cannon, who was in violent hostility to the Boston men on account of alleged deprivation of political rights;—he wrote from England —"a dismal change falling out just at that time. and they (the Boston men) sending hither one Edward Winslow a smooth tongued cunning fellow who soon got himself into favor of those then in the supreme power, against whom it was in vain to strive."

Returning in 1636 with enhanced reputation he was again chosen Governor. The religious controversies between the more liberal and the stricter Puritans in Boston were now at their height and the Governor of Plymouth, who was known to hold moderate views, had no easy task to avoid being drawn into them and to answer the sometimes sharp and imperious letters from Boston.

The banishment of Roger Williams from Boston threatened no small embarrassment to Plymouth as he had formerly been the minister there and at first removed only to the edge of their settlement where he had many friends, and it was only by Winslow's tact that trouble was avoided by persuading Williams to move a little farther on into Rhode Island with the suggestion that then "they would remain loving friends together" thus avoiding any dispute with Boston. It is a singular historical fact that the chief cause of Williams leaving the Plymouth ministry was the unpopularity there of his severe and narrow views as to church membership.

The kind relations between Winslow and Williams continued for many years after the latter's removal to Rhode Island and frequent friendly visits were exchanged.

The big hearted and courteous Pilgrim Governor was a difficult man to quarrel with and nothing shows more clearly his genial qualities of mind and heart than his success in dealing with such different elements and retaining the friendship and respect of all, whether it was the authorities in England, the Governor in Boston, the dissenting colonists in Rhode Island or the wild Indian in the forest. With them all he carried himself with unmistakeable high breeding and courtesy, with a tactful shrewdness and with a keen knowledge of men and affairs such as few men in either settlement possessed.

In 1638 he purchased an estate in that part of Duxbury now Marshfield, which he named Careswell in memory of the old home in England and which remained in possession of the family for nearly two centuries, when it became the property and the home of Daniel Webster.

In 1639 we find him associated with Governor Bradford, Endicott and Stoughton in settling the boundaries of the colonies, and in 1643 he was one of the first Commissioners of the Confederated Colonies. The next year he was again the Governor of Plymouth, but the time was approaching when he should look his last upon New England, and find employment in a larger sphere of usefulness in the mother country. The Massachusetts Colony was suffering from the complaints and machinations of Gorton and others in England and needed a strong man to represent them. They sought for Winslow's services "as a fit man to be employed in our present affairs both in regard to his abilities of presence, speech, courage and understanding and being well known to the Commissioners as having suffered imprisonment by the Archepiscopal prelate."

Oliver Cromwell was now head of the State and an agent from New England was sure of quite different reception from formerly, yet the business required a man of large experience and extensive influence and Winslow was recognized in New and Old England as possessing special qualifications. Plymouth acceded to the request of Massachusetts that he should act as their Agent with much unwillingness and with fear that he might meet with inducements in England which would prevent his return, but Winslow regarded it a duty to accept and sailed in 1646. The mission was a difficult and responsible one but he accomplished its object with much address.

Governor Hutchinson says of his missions to England "by his prudent management and the credit and esteem he was in with many of the members of Parliament and principal persons then in power he prevented any prejudice to the Colony."

During the long controversy with Gorton in England Winslow published in reply to Gorton's "Simplicities Defence" a very severe and caustic pamphlet entitled "Hypocrisie Unmasked" with an appendix containing his "Brief Narration," and later when Childs published "New England's Jonah cast up in London" which attacked Winslow personally and arraigned the proceedings in Boston against "divers honest and goodly persons" — he came out with a masterly and crushing reply entitled "New England's Salamander discovered by an Irreligious and Scornful Pamphlet."

He also published while there "The Glorious Progress of the Gospel among the Indians" with extracts from letters of Eliot and Mayhew, and organized the Society for Propagating the Gospel among the Indians.

It was not long before his abilities attracted the attention of Cromwell and he was persuaded to take service under the Protector. In 1652 he was Chairman of the Joint English and Dutch Commissioners to award damages for vessels destroyed in Denmark by the Dutch, and in 1655 he accepted his last Commission as chief of three Commissioners — the others being Admiral Penn and Gen. Venable — to capture the Spanish West Indies and to govern Hispaniola.

The expedition against Hispaniola failed through the blundering of the Admiral and sailed to attack Jamaica, but on the passage Winslow was taken ill and died and was buried at sea May 8, 1655, with a salute of 42 guns. His will was proved in England, most of his property being left to his son Josiah, and a copy of it was printed in the January, 1902, number of this Magazine.

The feeling of the members of the expedition towards him was expressed in these quaint lines written by one of the party.

The Eighth of May, west from 'Spaniola shore,
God took from us our Grand Commissioner,
Winslow by name, a man in Chiefest Trust,
Whose Life was sweet, and Conversation just;
Whose Parts and wisdome most men did excel:
An honour to his Place, as all can tell.

It would be of intense interest could we learn more of the inner home life of a man who appears to have had so many attractive qualities and whose influence over men of very different station and character was so marked, but that part of Pilgrim life exists chiefly in romance and tradition, for none of the Pilgrim histories give more than a glimpse of it.

His picture now in Pilgrim Hall, Plymouth, shows a man with open pleasing countenance, mild eye and firm mouth, with a somewhat rotund and vigorous figure and with a striking air of gentility. There is nothing about it of the conventional Pilgrim, it suggests rather the prosperous and contented man of affairs — but his face strongly indicates a gentle temper and a quiet sense of humor, combined with firm determination. This sense of humor was so strongly developed in the descendants of the Governor and has afforded to the Old Colony so many amusing stories of later incidents that we can safely believe it to have been an inherited trait. One wonders a little if Edward Winslow was ever so much *of* the Pilgrims as *with* them. He does not appear to have been strictly a religionist in the meaning of the day and history does not associate him with religious controversies or actions except perhaps in the severe tracts he published in London in his later years. Calvinist as he was in religious faith he was moderate in his opinions, generally tolerant, and exhibited in that part of his character the same breadth of view and cheerfulness that one finds in his bearing in the more practical details of business.

No one could have gained such influence over the Indians as he undoubtedly acquired unless added to his diplomatic talents were a big heart, unselfish devotion and an unruffled temper, and if that was the key to his success with them, it was equally owing to those qualities added to his great ability, his courage and his frank and manly bearing that he won friendship in the narrow and bigoted circles in Boston, at the English Court even when Charles I and Laud were crushing and persecuting the Puritan element, and, later, with the severely practical and stern Cromwellians. He was a man in advance of his times and in many respects unlike his times and yet his work was of inestimable value to the Pilgrims and no one among them could have exactly filled his position, for he seems to have been specially ordained by Providence as a harmonizer and composer of quarrels and as the fit instrument to lead in delicate negotiations and important affairs requiring no small ability as a diplomatist. He somehow appeals to us of the present day in a little different way from any other of the Pilgrim band for he was not unlike the men of the present generation and his nature seems more gentle and loveable than that of most of his contemporaries, still he must have been a true representative of his people and a faithful exponent of their views, for otherwise he would never have been so trusted while he lived and so sincerely mourned at his early death. Whenever history shall present his life to us more fully than can be done in these pages, when the English records shall be more carefully searched for traces of his work and further evidence obtained of his great capacity and power, we are convinced that we shall then have the picture of a great Pilgrim Governor who added cheerfulness to constancy, gentleness to courage and absolute truthfulness and integrity to very high powers of civic statesmanship.

JOSEPH[2] ALDEN'S WILL AND INVENTORY.

Transcribed from the Original Records,

By George Ernest Bowman.

Joseph[2] Alden, son of John and Priscilla (Mullins) Alden, died at Bridgewater, Mass., on 8 February, 1696/7, as shown by a statement in the record of his inventory, his wife Mary, the daughter of Moses Simmons, surviving him. His will and inventory are recorded in the Plymouth County Probate Records, Volume I, pages 256 and 257. The original documents are missing from the files.

[Joseph[2] Alden's Will.]

[p. 256] These are to publish and Declare to all whome it may concern that I Joseph Alden sen^{r} of ye Town of Bridgwater in ye County of plimouth in New England being of sound judgment and memory Do ordain and make my last will and Testament in maner following my Immortall soul I do Humbly Resign into ye mercyfull hands of Almighty God my creator hoping through ye merrits and mediation of Jesus Christ to obtain pardon and Salvation my Body I Commit to ye Earth from whence it was to be Decently Interred at ye Discretion of my executors and the Rest of my christian friends. And as Touching Such worldly Estate as God hath Blessed me withall I Dispose of it in maner and forme as followeth.

Imp^{r}s I Give to my son Isaac fifty Acres of land which he lives upon . further I Give him Ten acres more which I gave him liberty to take up : more Ten Acres of Swamp . more two acres of upland which he hath taken up in liew of the upland belonging to Coasters kitchen meadows . one Acre more of meadow at Byrams hole which he hath hitherto Enjoyed more I give to him Half my meadow lott in Byrams hole In consideration whereof my will is that he allow to my son Joseph Three acres out of the aforementioned ten acres of Swamp further I Give to my son Isaac Half my Sixty acres of land between Byrams Hole and the Sawmill All which lands above mentioned I Say I Give to him and to his heirs and Assigns for Ever.

Item I Give to my Son Joseph The land whereupon he lives of which have already Given him Assurance by written Deed . further I give to him Twenty Acres lying upon the Great River Below Goodman Bayleys land . ffurther I Give Between my two sons Joseph and John Ten Acres of land to be taken up to be equally Divided Between them which said lands as aforesaid I Give to him and to his Heirs and Assigns for ever. Item I Give to my Deare Wife my Homestead With all the Housing thereupon and all my other lands joyning thereunto more I Give unto her Ten acres of land upon the plaine more two woodlots lying on the left hand of ye way to Thomas Washbourns And my will is That my Son John Shall have the use and Improvement thereof for his and my wife's Comfort during her life time And that after her decease my son John Should enjoy it all Together with half my Sixty Acres above mentioned lying near the Sawmill And half my lott of meadow in Byrams hole All which parcels of land I Say I do give to him and to his heirs and Assigns for Ever : ffurther I Give All my moveables to my wife to dispose of as she shall se Cause I Give to my three sons Isaac Joseph and John all my Right and Interest in ye Majors Purchase and Also in ye undivided lands belonging to my purchase Right to be equally Divided amongst them And finally I do Constitute make and ordaine Mary my wife executrix & my son John Joynt executo^{r} of this my last will & Testament utterly Renouncing Revoking & disclayming all other wils and Testaments whatsoever In witness whereof I have hereunto set my hand and Seal this fourteenth day of December in ye year of our Lord one thousand six hundred ninety and six.

Signed Sealed pronounced and declared in the presence of us y^{e} Subscribers vizt — Joseph Alden sen^{r} his mark & a (seal)

Pallatiah Smith
Thomas Delano
Joseph Hayward

Memorandum pallatiah Smith Thomas Delano and Joseph Hayward the witness here named appeared and made oath before Wm Bradford Esqr Judge of probate on y^{e} 10th day of march 169$^{6}_{7}$ That they were present & saw & heard Joseph Alden the Testator above named Sign Seal & declare y^{e} Instrument above written to be his last will And that to y^{e} best of their Judgment he was of sound disposing mind & memory when he did y^{e} same

Attest Saml Sprague Register

[p. 257] William Bradford Esqr Commissionated &c for y^{e} Granting of y^{e} probate of wils and Letters of Administration within y^{e} County of plimouth &c To all to whome these presents shall come or may concern Greeting Know ye that on the tenth day of march $169\frac{6}{7}$ Before me in plimouth The will of Joseph Alden late of Bridgwater deceased to these presents Annexed was proved approved and allowed who having while he lived and at the time of his Death Goods Chattels Rights and Credits The sd Deceased and his said will in any maner Concerning was committed unto Mary his wife and John his Son Executors in the same will named Well and faithfully to Administer ye same and to make a true and perfect Inventory of all and Singular the Goods Chattels Rights and Credits of ye sd deceased and y^{e} same to exhibit into y^{e} Registers office of y^{e} said County according to law Also to Render a plain and true account of their said Administration upon oath. In Testimony whereof I have hereunto set my hand and the seal of y^{e} sd Office. Dated at plimouth the tenth day of march $169\frac{6}{7}$
Samuel Sprague Register. William Bradford

[Joseph[2] Alden's Inventory.]

The Inventory of y^{e} estate of Joseph Alden sen^{r} who deceased y^{e} 8th of ffebr $169\frac{6}{7}$

	£	s	d
Imp^{r}s : Eleven Shirts	..1	..	.
More Linnen	..2	..	.
More Linnen	..1	10	.
More wearing Cloaths hats and Shoose	..6	16	.
More for Beds and Bed Cloathing	.11	..	.
More cloathing	..2	..	.
More for pewter Brass and Iron vessels and Lumber	..9	10	.
More for Armes and Ammunition	..1	15	.
More for Cart and plows with all iron tooles	..4	..	.
More for Corne and other provision	..5	..	.
More for Cattel horse kind and swine	.28	10	.
More in Debts Due	..1	10	.
More in Books	...	10	.
More in Timber and Boards	..1	..	.
Totall Sum	76	.1	.

This Inventory taken which is y^{e} movable Estate of y^{e} abovesd Joseph Alden decesed by us this 3^{d} of march $169\frac{6}{7}$
John Leonard
Joseph Snow
Samuel Allin Junr

John Alden one of ye executors of ye last Will & Testament of Joseph Alden late of Bridgewater deceased made oath before William Bradford Esqr Judge &c on ye 10th day of march 169$\frac{6}{7}$ that the above Written is a true Inventory of ye Goods Chattels & credits of the said Deceased so far as he yet Knoweth and that if more shall come to his Knowledge he will cause it to be added.

Attest Saml Sprague Register

JOHN[2] DOTY'S WILL AND INVENTORY.

Transcribed from the Original Records,

BY GEORGE ERNEST BOWMAN.

JOHN[2] DOTY, son of Edward and Faith (Clark) Doty, died at Plymouth, and his death is entered on the town records [Vol. I, p. 203] as follows: "John doty senior deceased May 8th 1701." His will and inventory are recorded in the Plymouth County Probate Records, Volume I, pages 341–343. The only original document in the files is the inventory, which is badly stained and somewhat worn on the edges. The copy of the inventory here presented was made from the original document, the illegible places being supplied from the record.

[JOHN[2] DOTY'S WILL.]

[p. 341] The last Will & Testament of John Dotey senr of Plimouth. I being Sick & weake of Body & not knowing how it may Please God to deal with me yet being of disposeing mind & memory do dispose as followeth of my worldly Estate which god has Given me Imprimis I Give to my Eldest son John Dotey a hundred Acres of upland at Doteys Plaine And thirty acres of upland at Indian Pond and a Grant of four acres of meadow. Item I Give to Sarah my wife The third of ye Income or profits of my farme and one Roome in my Dwelling house during her widdowhoode further I Give to my wife Two Cows & one Great Trunk and an jron pott & one ffeather bed with furniture belonging to it.

Item I Give to my four youngest Sons Isaac Dotey & Samuel Dotey Elisha Dotey and Josiah Dotey All my Homestead Housing & upland belongng to ye farme whereon I now live and Ten acres of meadow at Doteys meadow more or less I further Give to my four sons Isaac Samuel Elisha & Josiah All my whole Stock undisposed of vizt oxen Cows & Sheep & Cattell of all sorts not disposed of with all my Implements of Husbandry Provided ye Debts being first Paid. Item I Give to my Daughter Elizabeth Moss a two year old Heiffer Item I Give to my Daughter Martha A ffeather Bed With furniture belonging to it Item I Give ye Qarter Part of my Ketch to my four youngest Daughters Martha Sarah [p. 342] Patience and Desire Item I Give to Martha one Pewter Platter Item I Give all ye Rest of my Household Stuff one third part to my wife & the Remainder to my four youngest Sons vizt Isaac Samuel Elisha & Josiah Dotey And I do make & Appoint my loving wife Sarah Dotey to be ye sole Executrix of this my last Will and Testament And I desire my loving Brother John Rickard to be helpfull to my sd Wife in the management of it This I do acknowledge to be my last Will and Testament whereunto I have set my hand and Seal this fifteenth April 1701

Signed Sealed & The mark **X** of John Dotey sen^r^ (seal)
Delivered In y^e^
presence of
William Ring
Eleazer Ring
William Shurtliff

Plimouth ye third day of June 1701 Before Wm Bradford Esqr Appeared William Shurtliff William Ring and Eleazer Ring ye witnesses to ye within written will and made oath that they were present & saw and heard John Dotey ye Testator within named Sign Seal & declare ye within written Instrument to be his last Will and testament And that to the best of their Judgment he was of sound disposing mind & memory when he did ye same.

Attest Saml, Sprague Register

memorandum That on ye day abovesd y^t^ Sarah Dotey Relict of ye sd John Dotey deceased & sole executrix of ye within written will before Probate & allowance of ye same declared that she did & doth Reserve to her self the benifit of ye law Respecting her dower or thirds in ye Housing & lands of ye sd Deccased any thing to ye Contrary thereof Contained in sd Will.

William Bradford Esqr Commissionated &c for ye Granting of ye Probate of wils & letters of Administration within ye County of Plimouth, To all to whome these presents shall come or may concern Greeting know ye that on ye third day of June Anno Domini 1701 Before me in Plimouth, The Will of John Dotey late of Plimouth husbandman to these presents annexe was proved approved and allowed who having while he lived & at ye time of his Death Goods Chattels Rights & Credits The said deceased & his said Will in any manner Concerning was Committed unto Sarah his wife Executrix in ye same Will Named Well & truly to Administer ye same And to make A true & perfect Inventary of all & Singular ye Goods Chattels Rights & Credits of the sd Deceased and the same to exhibit into ye Registers office of ye sd County according to law Also to Render a true & playn account of her Administration upon oath In Testimony whereof I have hereunto set my hand & ye seal of ye sd office.

Dated at Plimouth ye third day of June An° Dom 1701 — William Bradford (seal)

Saml Sprague Register

[John² Doty's Inventory.]

May : the 17th : 1701

An Inventory of the Estate of John Doty of Plimouth Deceased

Imprmis	£	s	d
To wareing Clothes hatt : Stockins & gloves	007 .	05	06
To : 3 : Shirts & neckcloth & Shoose	01	04	00
In the Lower Roome			
To : 1 : bed : 1 : bolster : 1 : pillow : 2 : blanketts : 2 Sheets : 1 : Coverled	05 :	03 :	00
To 1 : paire Curtains & valliens : 18s : & : 1 : Bedsteed 5 Shillings	01	03	00
To : 1 : old trundle bedsteed : 3s : 1 : old Cupbord : 11s : & 1 table 6 shillings	01	00	00
To : 1 : old Cradle : 5s : one box : 1s : six Chaires : 8s & two old wheeles 6 Shillings	01	00	00
To : 1 : Sheet & old towell : 8s : one Cupbord Cloth : 3s : & four pailes at : 2s	00	13	00
To : 1½ : dozen wooden trenchers : Dishes Cann & tunnell	00	03	03
To : 7 : Spoones : 2s : nine porr[eng]ers 1 bason : 1 : plaite : one beacer & 3 : Cups : 7s :	00	09	00
To : 2 quart potts 4s one [bason 4s] five platters 20s : & 4 : platters : 10s	01	18	00
To Earthen ware 3[s : 8d two Bottles & 1 glass C]upp : 1s 2d	00	0[4	10]
To 1 : great Iron Kittle : 7s : one [little ket]tle 3s : 6d :	00	10	06
To : 1 : Iron pott : 7s : one old Iron pott 3s & 1 : great Iron pott : 13s	01	03	00
To : 1 : warming pan : 5s : one frying pan : 1s : & 1 : Smoothing Iron & heaters 2s	00	08	0[0]
To : 1 : paire Andjrons : 1£ 03s one pair tonges & Slice : 5s	01	08	00

To : 1 : Spitt 3s : two : tramells : 6s : one brass Kittle : 12s : & 1 : Long gunn : 1£ 10s	02	11	00
To : 1 gunn : 10s : two old Swords : 10s : one belt : 3s	01	03	00
To 2 Catouch boxes : 2s : four leads & : 1 : line : 4s 6d	00	06	06
To : 1 : pouch & horns : 1 : pair meettings * : 2s : two Sieves & : 1 : halfe bushell : 2s	00	04	00
To : wooden Lomber : 4s : & one lead & line : 1s	00	05	00
In the Chamber			
To : 1 : bed : 1 : bolster : 1 : blankett : 1 : Coverlid & one old Sheet : 3£ 19s 0d	03	19	00
To : the Smallest Bed & bolster : 1 : blankett : 1 : Rugg & 1 : old Sheet	03	09	00
To : 2 : bedsteeds : 14s : one paire Curtaines & vallienes : 18s :	01	12	00
To 1 : paire fine Sheets : 18s one Sheet : 7s : one towel & : 1 : table Cloth : 3s	01	08	00
To : 4 : Cushenes : 7s : one Small box : 1s : one pair Spectacles : 1s	00	09	00
To : 1 : Small Trunck : 2s : one Great trunk : 9s : one Chest : 5s	00	16	00
To : 2 : pair Cards : 2s : & one Chamber pott : 3s 6d	00	05	06
To : 2 : Chaires : 5s : one Churn : 1s : & About : 30 pound of feathers : 1£ 15s 0d	02	01	00
To : 4 : axes : 8s : one Spade : 5s : three hoes : 8s : & one Sieth & Snaeth : 4s	01	05	00
To : 1 : hamer : 1 : fro : 1 : horse Chaine : 5s : & Some old Iron : 6s :	00	11	00
To : 3 : peices of Eight : 18s & : 1 : paire Stockins : 3s :	01	01	00
To : 6 : oxen : att : 22£ : & 5 : Cowes with their Calves att : 15£	37	[00	00]
To : 3 : Cowes & : 1 : heiffer [3 years] old att : 10 pound	[10	00	00]
To : 4 . heiffers : at 6£ 10s one Bull att : 1£ : 10s : & one old Bull : at : 2£ 05s	10	05	00
To : one : 4 : yeare old : Steere 3£ 8s & 3 yearlings at : 3£ 10s	06	18	00
To : 24 : Sheep : & 8 : Lambs : at : 9£ 15s : & one Mair & Colt . one pound	10	15	00
To : 1 : horse att home : with bridle Saddle & fetters att : 3£ 10s	03	10	00
To : Another horse : forty Shillings : & to : 7 : Swine att : 3£ 05s	05	05	00
To : 1 : Cart : & wheeles bolt & Shackles & Rope Att : 4£ :	04	00	00
To 1 : plow : & Irons bolt & Shackles : at : 12s	00	12	00

* Recorded as "mittons."

To 3 : ox yoaks & Iron Staples & hookes at : 6ˢ : & 2 Chaines at : 10ˢ	00	16	00
To one quarter parts of the Catch his Son John Doty went in 30£ 00ˢ	30	00	00
To : 1 : Cannoo : 15ˢ : & A Croscutt Saw : 8ˢ : & : ⅔ of A hatchel : 8ˢ : & A brake : 2ˢ	01	13	00
	163	03	01

The Estate of John Doty Deceased Is Dr

	£	s	d
To : mʳ John Murdo	01	17 :	8
To : Mʳ Nathˡˡ Thomas	14 .	19 :	8¾
To : Mʳ Thomas palmer for : 2 : Journeys & Medicins	01 :	06 :	0
To Richard Cooper	01 :	00 :	01*
To : Doctor Loreing for Medicins	00 :	16 :	00
To John foster	00	04	06
To Doctor L Barrone	00	06 :	00
To Nathˡˡ Clarke for A Coffin	00 :	06 :	00
To James Barnaby	00	12	08
To : James Winslow	00	17	10
To William Shirtclife	01	02	06
To Samuell King Sener	00	15	06
To Isaac Tinkcom	00	02	00
To John Rickard	05	01	08
To John Rouse	10	00	00
To Samuell Dunham	00	03	00
To Isaac Doty	03	19	00
To Thomas holmes	03	00	00
To hannah Rickard	00	05	00
	46 :	15 :	01¾

Due to yᵉ estate from			
Allexander Cannada	01	02	00
Theophilus Doty	01	05	00
Robert Stanford	00	06	00

An Inventary Taken by us Underwritten

Nathaniel Southworth
John Rickard
John Sturtevant

memorand that on yᵉ 3ᵈ day of june 1701 appeared Sarah Dotey Relict & widdow of yᵉ sd Jnᵒ Dotey deceased & Executrix of his last will & Testament & made oath before William Bradford Esqʳ That yᵉ above & within written is a true Inventary of yᵉ Goods chattels Rights & Credits of yᵉ sd deceased sc

* This is recorded as "1—1—0," but the total, which is the same in both original and record, shows the reading here given to be correct.

far as she knows & that if more shall come to her knowledge it shall be Added

Attest Sam[l] Sprague Regist[r]

CAPTAIN JOSEPH[2] HOWLAND'S WILL AND INVENTORY.

Transcribed from the Original Documents,

BY GEORGE ERNEST BOWMAN.

CAPT. JOSEPH HOWLAND, the son of John and Elizabeth (Tilley) Howland, died at Plymouth in January, 1703/4. This statement is made twice in the records of the First Church (Part III, pages 1 and 6), and his will was dated 23 December, 1703, and the inventory taken 31 January, 1703/4.

The will and inventory are recorded in the Plymouth County Probate Records, Volume II, pages 43-45, but the transcript here presented is taken from the original documents, still preserved in the files. The will is twelve and three-fourths inches wide and sixteen and one-half inches high. It is badly cracked in the creases where it has been folded. The inventory is seven and seven-eighths by twelve inches and it is badly cracked. In a few cases it was necessary to complete the copy by comparison with the record.

The will was evidently written out in 1691, and necessary changes made, and the codicil added, in December, 1703, as shown by the erasures and interlineations noted.

[CAPT. JOSEPH[2] HOWLAND'S WILL.]

Be itt Known To all men by these presents That I Joseph Houland of the Towne of plimouth in the County of New plimouth in New England Being Weake of Body but of perfect and sound Memory and understanding blessed be god yet Considering my frailty and uncertainty of Abiding in this vaile of tears Doe therefore Make and ordaine, and by these presents I doe Make and ordaine these presents to be my last Will and Testament to stand good and to Remaine firme and Inviolable for Ever in Manner and forme ffollowing Inprimis I will and bequeath my Body to the dust and my soule to god that gave it mee in hopes of A Joyfull Resurextion through the Merrits of my Deere Redemer and as for that Estate that that god hath given to mee I dispose of as ffolloweth In primis I doe give unto My Deere and Loveing Wife Elizabeth Howland all My whole Estate both housing uplands and Meadow lands and

Moveables to be for her use and support during her Natturall life* Item I doe give unto my sone Thomas Howland all that my housing uplands and meadowlands that was given to mee By my father in law Capt Thomas Southworth lying in the Towneship of plimouth all which housing and lands I doe give unto my sone Thomas howland after My Wifs decease to him and his heirs for ever as allsoe I doe give unto my sone Thomas howland My long gun : and My Belt and Raper, Item I doe give unto my sone James howland My Now dweling hous and all the upland and medo that I am now posesed of lying in Rockkenook as allsoe 4 Acrees of salt Marsh Meadow lying Neere Jons River bridg on the southerly syde of the Rever all which lands and meadows after my Wifes decease I doe give unto my sone James howland to him and his for Ever (he the said James howland Allowing and paying unto his Three† sisters that is to say lydiah‡ howland Elizabeth howland and Marcy howland to each of them five pounds apece.) as also one Muske[t] and a Cuttleas Item Wereas my sone Nathaniel hath thirty Acrees of uplan be it more or less and two acrees of meadow give to him by his granmother § howland lying on the notherly syde of Jons Rever I alsoe doe give unto him my sone Nathaniel Howland two Acrees of salt marsh meadow out [o]f the barkers that lyeth on the southerly side of Jons Rever ‖ all which meadow I doe give unto my sone Nathaniel Howland to him and his heirs for Ever as also I doe give unto my sone Nathaniel howland A smale gun Item all other lands belonging unto mee that is not herein above disposed of I doe give it unto My deere and loving wife for her to dispose of to sell or otherwise to dispose of for her support and Comfort; lastly I doe Appoint my deer and loveing Wife Elizabeth Howland to be the sole Execatrix of this my last will and testament to pay such debts as I owe and to Receive such debts as is owing unto me to se my Body deacently buryed and to defray the Charg thereof; and I doe Request My two Sons Thomas howland and James howland¶ and Thomas faunce to be the

* "or Widowhood" in the original was crossed out. These two words do not appear in the record.

† "four" was crossed out and "Three" written above.

‡ "Sarah howland," before the word "lydiah," was crossed out.

§ See Mayflower Descendant, III : 55.

‖ "as alsoe two Acrees of upland meadow lying att Jons Rever meadow soe Caled" was crossed out in the original and does not appear in the record.

¶ The words "two Sons Thomas howland and James howland" are interlined in the original, above the words "Brother Isaac howland Edward Sothwoth" which are crossed out and do not appear in the record.

superadvisors of this my last Will and Testament Much Confiding in their love and faithfullnes to be helpfull to my said Execatrix in the acting and disposeing of perticklors according to the tenner here of Thus hopeing that this my last will and testament will be kept Revoaking all former wills eithe verbell or written I the said Joseph Howland hath hereunto sett my hand and affixed my seale; on the 23[d] day of December one thousand sev[n] hundred and three 1703 *

Signed Sealed and declared to be my last will and Testament In presence of us Witneses
Rebecca **R** Standford
her marke
Thomas **A** Palmer
his marke
Ephraim Little

Joseph **J H** houl[d] (seal)
his marke

A Codicill to my Last will.

Item . I do give and bequeath to my daughter mercy howland Six Ewes and my three year old mare to be delivered to her, within twelve months after my decease,

Item I do give to mary the daughter of my daughter Sarah howland deceased five pounds, to be paid to her by my Son James howland at y[e] Same time the five pounds apeice above Express[d] shall become due to my s[d] daughters Lydia Elizabeth & mercy howland.

Item. I do give to my Son James howland all my part of y[e] tackling or Instruments of husbandry, w[ch] wee have used between us.

Witness my hand & Seal y[e] day & year abovewritten.

In presence of us.
Rebecca **R** Standford
her marke
Thomas **A** palmer
his marke
Ephraim Little

Joseph **J H** howland (seal)
his marke

Memorand That M[r] EPhraim Little & Rebeca Stanford two of the Witneses to this above written Instrum[t] made oath that they saw the above named Joseph Howland Signe seale & heard him declare the abovewritten to be his last Will &. Testament

* The date was originally written "January one thousand six hundred ninty and one 1691," but was altered to read as in the text. In the original will the day and month are doubtful and the record has here been followed.

& to the best of their understanding he was of a disposeing mind & memory when he so did & That Thomas Palmer the other Witness then also set to his hand as a witness of the same

before me the 10th day of March 1703

Nathaniel Thomas Judge of Probats

[*On the back of the will.*] Thomas Palmer the other Witness named to this Instrument declared upon his oath that he was p^r^sent with M^r^ EPhraim Little & Rebecca Stanford & heard Mr Joseph Howland declare that a writing which was then p^r^sented was his last Will & Testament & that he set his marke to it as a Witness & he saw Mr Little Steady M^r^ howlands hand when he signed said Will & that to the best of his understanding he was in his Right mind when he so did

before me March 10th 1703

Nathaniel Thomas J Probats

[II : 44 *] Pli : ss Nathaniel Thomas Esqr: Appointed & Comisonated Judge of the Probates of wills & Granting letters of Administration &c: To all unto whome these presents shall Come Greeting Know yee that on the tenth day of March in the year of our Lord one thousand seven Hundred [p. 45] Hundred & three Before me at Plimouth in the County of Plimouth the Will of Capt: Joseph Howland late of Plimouth afores^d^ deceased to these presents annexed was proved approved & allowed who having whilst he lived & at the time of his death Goods Chattels Rights or Creditts in the County afores^d^ And the probate of the s^d^ will & power of Comitting administration of all and singuler the goods Chattels Rights & Creditts of the s^d^ deceased & also the hearing examining & allowing the accompts of the same by virtue thereof appertaining unto me; The Administration of all & singuler the goods Chattels Rights & Creditts of the s^d^ deceased & his will in any manner concerning is hearby Comitted unto Mrs Elizabeth Howland Relict widdow of the s^d^ Joseph Howland & sole Executrix in the same will named Well & faithfully to execute the s^d^ will & to administer the Estate of the s^d^ deceased according thereunto & to make a true & perfect Inventory of all & singuler the goods Chattels Rights & Creditts of the s^d^ deceased & to Exhibitt the same into the Registry of the Court of Probate for the County afores^d^ at or before the twentythird day of June next ensueing & also to render a plaine & true accompt of her said administra-

* Plymouth County Probate Records.

tion upon oath In Testimony whereof I have hereunto set my hand & the seale of the s^{d} Court of Probate dated at Plimouth afores^{d} the day & year first above written.
Nathaniel Thomas Register. Nathaniel Thomas.

[Capt. Joseph² Howland's Inventory.]

An Inventary of the Estate of Capt [Jose]ph howland late of plimouth deseaced Taken & apprised by us under written on the 31 day of January 170$\frac{4}{3}$

Imprimis in his waring apparill & Books	04	10	00
Item in armes at	03	06	00
Item in puter & brass	03	14	00
Item in one small silver Cupp	00	04	00
Item in one bed & furnetur to it & Curtens	08	00	00
Item in two beds & the furniture to them	07	00	00
Item in Iron potts & kettle hangers huks & tongus	01	00	00
Item in a grate table & forme & Cupbard & 4 Chests & a box	04	00	00
Item in Chairs one table & table lining & Earthen ware	02	00	00
Item in one saddle & pillion 2 sives [on]e bag	01	00	00
Item in New Cloath	03	00	00
Item in one pare of small stillards [a]nd a Jarr	00	06	00
Item in 4 barrels & one Tubb	00	10	00
Item in Neete Cattle one yook of oxen	07	10	00
Item in 4 Cows	11	00	00
Item in 2 three year old sters at	03	00	[00]
Item in 2 too year olds & three [calv]es	04	00	0[0]
Item in 24 sheepe at	07	04	00
Item in two Mars at	04	00	00
Item in 3 swine at	00	18	00
Item in Cart & plow and tackling	00	15	00
Item in one spade one ffrow one drawing knife & ax & sith	00	12	00
Item in one pestle & morter & one saw 2 hows & other small Iron tools	00	13	00
Item in 2 spining wheeles	00	08	00

John bradford
John Gray
Thomas ffaunce

Memorandum that on the 10th day of march 170$\frac{3}{4}$ before Nath^{ll} Thomas Esqr : Judge of the Probate of wills &c : Elizabeth Howland Executrix to the last will & testament of her Husband Capt Joseph How[land] late of Plimouth Deceased made oat[h th]at the above written is a true Inve[nto]ry of the Estate of the s^d^ Deceased so fa[r as] she knoweth & when she knoweth of mor[e t]hat she will discover the same

Nath^ll^ Thomas Register

THE SETTLEMENT OF STEPHEN[2] SAMSON'S ESTATE.

Transcribed from the Original Documents,

BY GEORGE ERNEST BOWMAN.

STEPHEN[2] SAMSON (*Henry*[1]) probably died at Duxbury shortly before 31 January 1714/15, when his widow Elizabeth was appointed administratrix.

The final settlement of the estate bears no date, but it is recorded among other matters considered at the probate court held June twenty-first and twenty-second, 1716, and it is probable that one of these dates should be assigned to this settlement.

The following transcripts are all made from the original documents, except in the case of the letter of administration, which is not in the files. All the documents except the bond of the administratrix are on record in the Plymouth County Probate Records, Volume III, pages 342–344 and 421.

[LETTER OF ADMINISTRATION.]

[III : 342] Nathaniel Thomas Esqr Appointed and Comissioned by his Excellency the Governour by & with the Advice & Consent of the Council to be Judge of the probate of Wills & for granting Letters of Administration on the Estates of persons Dec[d] haveing Goods Chattells Rights or Credits in the County of Plymouth within his Majesties Province of the Massechusetts Bay In New England. To Elizabeth Samson Relict Widdow of Stephen Samson Late of Duxborough in the County of Plymouth dec[d] Greeting. Whereas the Said Stephen Samson haveing whilest he Lived and at the Time of his decease Goods Chattells Rights and Credits in the County affores[d] Lately Dyed Intestate whereby the power of Comitting administration and of all disposition of all and singuler the Goods, Chattells, Rights & Credits of the S[d] Deceased, and also the hearing Examining and allowing the Accompts of such Administration; doth Appertain unto me, Trusting therefore in your Care & fidelity I do by these presents Comitt Unto you full power [343] To Administer all and singuler the Goods Chattells Rights and Credits of the said deceased, and well and faithfully to dispose of the same According to Law; and also to ask, gather, Levy, recover & receive all and whatsoever Credits of the Said Deceased which to him whilest he Lived and at the time of his death did Appertain; and to pay all debts in which the said dec[d] stood Bound so far as his goods Chattells rights and Credits Can Extend According to the vallue thereof. And to make a true and perfect Inventory of all and Singuler the goods Chattells rights and Credits of the Said Deceased and to Exhibit the same into the registry of the Court of Probates for the County affores[d] at or before the Tenth Day of March Next Ensuing; and to Render a plain and true Accompt of your said Administration Upon Oath at or Before the tenth Day of June Next Ensuing. And I do hereby Ordain Constitute and Appoint you Administratrix of all and Singuler the goods Chattells rights and Credits Affores[d] In Testimony whereof I have hereunto set my hand and the seal of the said Court of Probates. Dated at Marshfield January the 31[st] 1714.

Nathaniel Thomas

[Bond of Administratrix.*]

Know all men by these p[r]sents that We . Elizabeth Samson Relict widow of Stephen Samson late of Duxbury in the County of Plimouth dec[d] & [†] Samson her son both of Duxbury in

* Transcribed from the original document.

† Space was left for the given name of the son.

the County of Plimouth afores^d are holden & stand firmly bound & obleiged unto Nathaniel Thomas Esqr Judge of the Probate of wills &c in the County afores^d in the full sum of two hundred Pounds Currant money in New England To be paid to the said Nathaniel Thomas his succesors in the said office or assigns To which Payment well & truly to be made we bind ourselves & Each of us our & Each of our heires Executors & Administrators Joyntly & severally for the whole & in the whole firmly by these p^rsents Sealed with our seales Dated the 31st day of January Annoq Dom . 1714.

The Condition of this obligation is such That if the above bounden Elizabeth Samson unto whom Power of Administration of all & singuler the goods Chattells Rights & Credits of the said Stephen Samson her late Husband is Comitted do make or Cause to be made a true & perfect Inventory of all & singuler the goods Chattells Rights & Credits of the said dec^d which have or shall Come to the Hands Possession or Knowlege of her the said Administratrix or into the Hands or Possession of any other p^rson or p^rsons for her & the same so made do Exhibit or Cause to be Exhibited into the Registry of the Court of Probats for the County afores^d at or before the tenth day of March next Ensuing & the same goods Chattells Rights & Credits & all other the goods Chattells Rights & Credits of the s^d dec^d at the time of his death which at any time after shall Come to the hands or Possession of the said Administratrix or into the hands or Possession of any other p^rson or p^rsons for her do well & truly administer according to Law & further do make or Cause to be made a Just & true accompt of her said Administration upon oath . at or before the tenth day of June next Ensuing & the Rest & Residue of the said goods Chattells Rights & Credits which shall be found Remaining upon the said Administrators accompt (the same being first Examined & allowed of by the Judge of Probats for the time being of the said County) shall deliver & Pay to such p^rson or p^rsons Respectively as the said Judge by his decree or sentence Pursuant to law shall Limett & appoint & if it shall hereafter appear that any last will & Testament was made by the said dec^d & the Executor or Executors therein named do Exhibit the same into the said Court of Probats making Request to have it allowed and approved accordingly if the said Eliza Samson above bounden being theronto Required do Render & deliver up the said letter of Administration (approbation of such Testament being first had & made) into the said Court Then this obligati[on] to be void & of non effect or else to bide & Remaine in full force & vert[ue]

Signed Sealed & Delivered
in p^{r}sence of us
John Wadsworth
Caleb Samson

Elizabeth Samson
her mark
Benjamin Samso

[*Endorsed on the back.*]
Elizabth Samsons bond of Administration 1714
She owes 0—9—6

[Appointment of Appraisers.*]

Nathaniel Thomas Esqr Comissioned & Appointed by his Exelence the Govr by & with the Consent of the Councill To be Judge of the Probate of Wills &c in the County of Plimouth within the Province of the Massachusets Bay in New England To Mr John Wadsworth Caleb Samson & Bengamin Pryer all of Duxbury in the County of Plimouth yeomen Greeting you are hereby desired Authorised & appointed to make a due & True Apprizement of all & singuler the lands goods & Chattells of Stephen Samson late of Duxbury afores^{d} deceased whereof he died Seized apprizing Each severall Percell of land as also the Movable Estate by themselves & Return the vallue of Each Percell to me under your hands & upon your oaths to be Taken before me as soon as Conveniently you Can. Dated at Marshfeild January ye 31 . 1714.

Nathaniel Thomas

[Appraisal of the Real Estate.*]

Pursuant to the abovewritten Appointment we the Subscribers have made a due & true apprizement (according to ye best of our Judgments) of the several parcels of land whereof ye within named Stephen Samson dyed Seized, which S^{d} apprizement is as followeth, viz.

	£ s d
All his lands & tenements both Divided & undivided lying within ye township of Dartmouth within ye County of Bristol, to be worth	200–00–00
And his right in ye great Cedar Swamp in ye Majors Purchase his s^{d} right being as we are in-	

* Transcribed from the original document.

formed one half a Share in ye fourth lot in number in the s^d^ Cedar Swamp, to be worth 08–00–00
And his lot in y^e^ upland in y^e^ Second Division of Comons belonging to the towns of Duxborough & Pembroke which he bought of Aaron Soule being the 81st lot in number in s^d^ Division, to be worth 18–00–00
February y^e^ 8th Anno Dom. 171$\frac{4}{5}$

John Wadsworth
Caleb Samson
Benjamin Prior

Plim. ss on the 8th day of february Annoq Dom 1714 The above named John Wadsworth Caleb Samson & Benjamin Pryer made oath that the abovewritten apprizment is a true apprizment of the vallue of the said lands according to their best Judgments before me

Nathaniel Thomas Judge of Probates

[Inventory of the Personal Estate.*]

An Inventory of the Moveable Estate of Stephen Samson late of Duxborough, Dec^d^

	£ s d
Inprimis. To his Apparel	5–05–00
Item. to fourteen yards of new Cloath	3–17–00
Item, to Pewter, knives and forks	1–09–10
Item, to Earthen ware	0–04–00
Item, to Books	0–10–00
Item, to a Table	1–05–00
Item. to two Chests	0–07–00
Item, to Chairs	0–14–00
Item, to Iron potts kettles tramels pothooks warming pan frying pan, &c	1–12–00
Item. to a fire Slice	0–04–00
Item, to Beds Bedcloaths Bedsteads and furniture thereto belonging	11–03–00
Item. to divers Sorts of grain	10–00–00
Item. to neat Cattel and hay	30–00–00
Item. to Sheep	3–00–00
Item. to Swine	2–10–00
Item. to meat with other provisions	4–00–00
Item. to a Loom and furniture	1–05–00
Item, to a Cart Plough & furniture to a team	2–10–00
Item, to an ax, & hoes, &c,	0–06–00
Item, to Sythes pitchforks & Rakes	0–10–00
Item. to barrels buckets and other lumber	0–15–00

* Transcribed from the original document.

Item. to Armes and Amunition &c	2–10–00
Item, to debts due to y^{e} Estate	

The aboves^{d} Inventory was taken by us y^{e} Subscribers, Feb. y^{e} 8th Anno 171$\frac{4}{5}$

John Wadsworth
Caleb Samson
Benjamin Prior

plim. ss. on the 8th day of february Annoq^{e} Dom 1714 Elizabeth Samson Relict widow of Stephen Samson late of Duxbury dec^{d} made oth that the above written is a True Inventory of the goods & Chattells of her late husband So far as she knows & when she knows of More will Cause it to be added before me

Nathaniel Thomas Judge of Probats.

[Settlement of the Estate.*]

Plim ss. The Devision & Settlement of the Estate both lands & Movables of Stephen Samson late of Duxbury in the County of Plimouth deceased To & amongst his Widow & Children as followeth his two Eldest sons Benjamin & John haveing settled on them by Deed in their fathers Lifetime the one half of his lands in Darthmouth & his homestead in Duxbury after their Mothers decease.

The movable Estate as apprized in the Inventory Amounts to the sum of	83	0	0
To be deducted therfrom for payment of Debts Loses Charges & funerall Expences as by the administratrix accompt the sum of	49	7	0
There Remains to devid to the widow & Children	33	13	0
wherof the widows thirds amounts to the sum of	11	4	4
There then Remains of Movables to the Children	22	8	8
To which add the $\frac{1}{2}$ half of his lands at darthmouth Prized at	200	0	0
& a lot of Comon land in Duxbury prized at	018	0	0
& Part of a lot of Cedar Swamp in Pembrook Prized	08	0	0
To be devided amongst six of his Children viz To Conelious, Hannah Mary Elizabeth Dorcass & Abigall	248	8	8
which sum being devided into six shares makes Each.	41	6	8

* Transcribed from the original document.

And the said Hannah Mary & Elizabeth shall have
The lot of Comon land in Duxbury prized at 18 pounds & the part of a lot of Cedar swam in Pembroke prized at 8 pounds to them & their severall heires & assigns for Ever . And the said Cornelious Dorcass & Abigall shall have the 22 pounds in Movables in their Mothers hands in Equall parts

And all the said six Children namely Cornelious Hannah Mary Elizabeth Docass & Abigall shall have all the said half of their fathers lands at Darthmouth in Equall parts to them & their severall & Respective heires & assignes for Ever the said Hannah Mary & Elizabeth paying to the said Cornelious Dorcass & Abigall the sum of forty shillings to be Equally devided amongst them Saving their Mother Dower or thirds in all the said lands Dureing here life.

Done & ordered by me

Nathaniel Thomas Judge of Probats.

[*On the back of the document.*]

The Settlemt of Stephen Samsons Estate 1716
Recorded in the 3d Booke page (421)

ISAAC^{2} HOWLAND'S WILL AND INVENTORY.

Transcribed from the Original Records,

BY GEORGE ERNEST BOWMAN.

ISAAC^{2} HOWLAND (*John*^{1}) died at Middleborough, Mass., on 9 March, 1723/4 *, and his widow Elizabeth died at the same place 29 October, 1727, in the seventy-fifth year of her age.*

Isaac's will is recorded in the Plymouth County Probate Records, Volume IV, pages 408 and 409, and the inventory in Volume V, page 6. The inventory is the only original document left in the files and this has been used in making the copy here presented. It is somewhat worn and the copy has been perfected from the record.

[ISAAC^{2} HOWLAND'S WILL.]

[IV : 408] Know all men by these Presents that I Isaac Howland Senr of the Town of middleboro In ye County of Plymouth In New : England Being at this Present Time weak : & under Bodily Infirmitys yet of Sound & Perfect memory & understanding (Blessed be God for It) Do make & ordain this to be my last Will & Testament to Continue forever firm & Inviolable. Imprimis . I give & Bequeath unto my well beloved wife Elisabeth Howland all my Houshold Stuff of all Sorts for Her Improvement during Her Life : & to dispose of among Her Children as Shee Shall See cause : I also give unto my s^{d} wife Two Cows also She Shall have ye use & Improvement of

* Mayflower Descendant, V : 38.

one Room of my dwelling House . which Room She Pleaseth during Her widdow : hood Item . I give & Bequeath unto my Son Seth Howland, all that my Lott of Land : whereon I now dwell Except that Part thereof which I have formerly given to my Son Nathan by Deed : also I give to my Son Seth my dwelling House Barn & outhouses & fences on s^d^ Land : Excepting ye use & Improvement of ye afores^d^ one Room given to my wife during Her widdow : hood as afores^d^ : also I give to my Son Seth : my thirteen acres & one third Part of an acre of Land . Butting upon ye west Side of ye River . In ye Little Lott Men^s^ Purchase, also I give unto my Son Seth all my Stock of Neat Cattle, Jades & Swine, Except ye afores^d^ two Cows : also I give unto my s^d^ Son Seth, all my Tools & Cart & Ploughs, & all other Tackling for ye Team also I give unto my Son Seth all ye Debts due unto me. & my will is that He Shall Pay all my Just Debts & funeral Charges : & my will Is that my Son Seth Shall Pay as a Legacy unto my two Son^s^ Isaac & Nathan, To each of them thirty Pounds : & unto my four Daughters Priscilla Bennett Jael Southworth, Susannah Wood & Hannah Tinkham to each of them Twenty Pounds Either In money, or good Currant Pay at money Price the one half thereof within one year after my decease, & ye other half thereof within one year after my wifes decease . also my will is that my Son Seth Shall Pay unto his mother ten Pounds a year, yearly during Her widdow : hood Either In money or good Currant Pay at money Price, & also he Shall keep for His mother two Cows : during ye whole Time of Her widdow : hood : & that he Shall find Her Firewood Cut & brought to ye Door So much as She Shall have occasion for during Her widdowhood. Item : I give & Bequeath unto my Son Isaac Howland all my Right & Interest In ye Lands & Swamps In ye Sixteen Shilling Purchase. & In assawamsett Neck. & also one third Part of my Six acre Lott of meadow at winnatuxett meadows. Item . I give & Bequeath unto my Son Nathan Howland my fifty acres of Land, being two five & twenty acre Lotts Butting upon ye great River In ye Six & twenty mens Purchase & also my Lott of Cedar Swamp In s^d^ Purchase, & also my five acres & a Quarter of Swamp Land lying on ye beach Islands at Raven Brook In s^d^ Purchase, & also my one half of five acres & half of meadow In ye upper meadows In s^d^ Purchase : and my will is that all my armes & ammunition Shall be Equally divided amongst my afores^d^ three Sons and my will is that my Son Seth Howland Shall be Sole Executor of this my Last Will & Testament : Thus Hoping that this my last will & Testament will be Performed according to ye true Intent & meaning thereof : I Committ my [409] my Body to ye Dust & my Soul to God that gave It. In Witness whereof I have hereunto Sett my Hand & Seal this Sixth day of Febuary anno Domini one thousand Seven Hundred & Seventeen Eighteen.

Signed Sealed & declared by ye above named Isaac Howland Senr to be his Last Will & Testament In ye Presence of us.
Isaac Howland Senr (Seal)

Jacob Tomson
Joseph Vaughan
Jonathan Inglee.

Plym : ss : aprill 6th 1724 Before Isaac Winslow Esqr Judge of ye Probate of Wills &c the within mentioned Jacob Tomson & Joseph Vaughan made oath that they were Present & did See ye within named Isaac Howland Senr Sign & Seal & heard him declare ye within written to be His last will & Testament & that when he So did he was of a disposing mind and memory according to ye best of their Judgements

as attests Nathaniel Thomas Register

att ye Time aboves^d Jonathan Inglee made oath before ye aboves^d Judge that he was desired by ye within named Isaac Howland to Sett his Hand as a witness to ye within written Instrument . & to ye best of His Judgement he heard him declare that ye within written was His will & that He then was of a disposing mind to ye best of his Judgement . as attests

Nathaniel Thomas Register

Isaac Winslow Esqr Duly appointed & Comissionated to be Judge of ye Probate of wills & for granting of administration In ye County of Plymouth within ye Province of ye Massachusetts Bay In New : England. To all to whom these Presents Shall Come Greeting. Know yee that on ye 1st day of June In ye year of our Lord 1724 Before me at Marshfield In ye County afores^d The Will of m^r Isaac Howland late of middleboro In ye County afores^d deceased . to these Presents annexed was Proved approved & allowed : Who having while He Lived & at ye Time of His death goods Chattels Rights or Credits in ye County afores^d & ye Probate of s^d Will & Power of Comitting administration of all & Singular the goods Chattels Rights & Credits of ye sd deceased, & also ye Hearing Examining & allowing ye accompts of ye Same by virtue thereof appertaining unto me. The administration of all & Singular ye goods Chattels Rights & Credits of ye sd Deceased & His will In any manner Concerning is hereby Comitted unto Seth Howland Son of ye sd deceased & Sole Executor In ye Same will named : Well & faithfully to Execute ye sd Will & to administer ye Estate of ye sd Deceased according thereunto; & to make a true & Perfect Inventory of all & Singular ye goods Chattels Rights & Credits of ye sd Deceased & to Exhibit the Same Into ye Registry of ye Court of Probate for ye County aforesd at or before ye first Day of august next Ensuing : & also to Render a Plain & true accompt of His sd administration upon Oath.

In Testimony whereof I have hereunto Sett my Hand & ye Seal of ye sd Court of Probate : Dated att marshfield aforesd the Day & year first above written

Isaac Winslow

[Isaac[2] Howland's Inventory.]

an Inventory on the Estate of Mr Isaac Howland of Middleburro Senr Latly Deceased both Reall & personall which he Dyed Seized of & is as followeth

Imprs his wearing Cloaths	08	15	00
his arms	01	15	00
his money	06	00	00
His Homstead with 13 acres in a neck of Land Called beaver Dam neck	540	00	00
Two acres ¾ of meadow in the upper meadows	07	00	[00]
Two acres of meadow in Winnetuxit meadows at	25	00	00
Cedar Swamp with a ¼ of a beach Island at	10	00	00
in the Sixteen Shilling purchase Cedar Swamp at	04	00	00
in sd purchase forty four acres at	08	00	00
Twenty five acres in Sd purchase at	16	00	00
assawamsit Lot with 2 acres & ½ in Sd Sixteen Shilling purchase	16	00	00
one bond of 30£ Due to him	30	00	00
4 new milch Cows at	18	00	00
one new milch heifier at	04	00	00
3 farrow Cows at	10	00	00
T[wo old] oxen at	13	00	00
Two young oxen at	10	06	00
one two year old heiffer & 4 year old C[attle]	06	10	00
one horss & Saddle	07	12	00
Ten Swine in the woods at	03	10	00
Eleven Sheep with Six Lambs at	05	00	00

to a bed & beding at	09	06	00
to wooll at	01	00	00
to malt & worsted Combs at	01	09	00
to a table & two Sickles at	00	12	00
to a bed & a Chest at	05	10	00
to a tub box & barrells	00	10	00
to a bed & beding with bedstead & trundle-bedstead & warming pan	10	00	00
to a table & Joynt Stools & table linen & an old Chest at	02	00	00
to pillow beirs & a Chest & four Chairs	01	05	00
to brass Koettles & brass Skillits	04	00	00
to pewter platters & all other pewter vessels	02	00	00
to Iron potts Kettles & trammels	03	01	00
a table wooden Dishes & tinn vessels	00	15	00
traies tubs & old barrels & Spining Wheels	01	03	06
a hatchell old Cards & old Shears	00	09	00
Cart & plow tackling axes & howes at	04	04	00
flax at	00	04	00
to Books	0	14	0
five bushells of barly	1	0	0
12 bushells of oats	1	10	0
11 bushells of wheat	3	10	0
Indian Corn	4	05	0
Indian Corn at	1	15	0
hay	2	05	0
Iron Crow an Iron Dog & a howe	0	09	0

Trully taken by us the Subscribers June ye 6th 1724
John Bennet
William Thomas
Ebenezer Sprout:

September the 17 : 1724

The abovenamed John Bennet William Thomas and Ebenezer Sprou[t] made oath that the above and within written is a Just and equall apprisement of the Estate of Isaac Howland late of Middleborough in the County of Plimoth deceased according to the best of their Judgment.

Before Isaac Winsl[ow Judge of] Probate

since added of Debts due to th[e Estate]

from Peter Benet	[1	17	0]
from Ichabod Padock	0	5	0

[December ye 17th] 1724.

[Seth] Howland Executor named in the last Will and Testement of his father mr Isaac Howland late of Middleborough in the County of Plimoth Deceased; made oath that the Inventory herein presented is a tru and perfect Inventory of the Estate of his father the s^d^ Isaac Howland as far as is Come to his knowledg and if more hereafter appears he will also give it in.

Before Isaac Winslow Judge of Probate

THE SETTLEMENT OF CAPTAIN JONATHAN[2] ALDEN'S ESTATE.

Transcribed from the Original Documents and Records,

By George Ernest Bowman.

Capt. Jonathan[2] Alden (*John*[1]) died at Duxbury in February, 1696/7, and his estate was settled 7 January, 1703/4, on the widow Abigail and three sons and three daughters. The only original papers in the probate files are the bond of the administratrix (which is not recorded) and the inventory, which have been used in making the transcripts here presented. The letter of administration, the inventory and the settlement were recorded in the Plymouth County Probate Records, Volume I, page 255, and Volume II, page 28.

[I : 255 *] William Bradford Esqr Commissionated &c for the Granting of the Probate of wils and letters of Administration within ye County of Plimouth &c. To Abigail Alden Relict and Widdow of Capt Jonathan Alden late of Duxboro Deceased Intestate Trusting in your Care and fidelity I do by these

* Plymouth County Probate Records.

presents Commit unto you full power to Administer all and singular y[e] Goods Chattels Rights and Credits of y[e] said Deceased and Well and faithfully to Dispose of the same according to law And also to Ask gather levy Recover and Receive all and whatsoever Credits of y[e] said Deceased which to him while he lived and at the time of his Death did appertaine and to pay all Debts in which the deceased stood Bound so far as his goods Chattels Rights and Credits Can extend according to y[e] value thereof And to make a true and perfect Inventory of all and Singular the goods Chattels Rights and credits of the said Deceased and to exhibit the same into the Registers office of the aforesaid County at or before the [*] day of [*] next ensuing And to Render a plain and true account of your said Administration upon oath at or before the [*] day of [*] one thousand six hundred ninety & eight And I do by these presents Ordaine Constitute and Appoint you Administratrix of all and singular the goods Chattels Rights and Credits aforesaid In Testimony whereof I have hereunto set my hand and y[e] Seal of y[e] s[d] office

Dated in Plimouth y[e] 8th day of march 169$\frac{6}{7}$

Sam[l] Sprague Regist[r] William Bradford

[Bond of the Administratrix.†]

Know all men by these presents that we Abigail Alden Seth Arnold and David Alden all of Duxborough within y[e] County of Plimouth in his Ma[ties] Province of the Massachusets Bay in New England are holden and Stand firmly bound And obliged unto William Bradford Esq[r] in the full Sum of four hundred pounds Currant money of New England to be paid unto the said William Bradford his Successours in the office of Judge of y[e] probate of Wils and Granting Administrations or Assigns To the true payment whereof We do bind our Selves our heirs Executors and Administrators Joyntly and Severally firmly by these presents Sealed with our Seals. Dated in Plimouth, the 8th day of March 169$\frac{6}{7}$ In the nineth year of his Ma[ties] Reign.

The Condition of this present obligation is Such that if the above Bounden Abigail Alden Administratrix of All and Singular the Goods chattels Rights and Credits of her late Husband Cap[t] Jonathan Alden late of Duxborough aforesaid Deceased Intestate Do make a true and perfect Inventory of all and

* Spaces were left for the day and month, but they were not filled in.

† Transcribed from the original document.

Singular the Goods Chattels Rights and Credits of the said Deceased which have or shall Come to the hands possession or knowledge of ye said Administratrix or into the hands or possession of any other person or persons for her And the same so made do exhibit into the Registers office of the said County at or before the first day of May next ensuing And the Same Goods Chattels Rights and Credits and all other the goods Chattels Rights and Credits of the said Deceased at ye time of his Death which at any time after Shall Come to the hands or possession of the said Administratrix or any other person or persons for her Do well and truly Administer according to law And further do make or cause to be made a just and true account of her said Administration at or before the first day of May which will be in the year of our Lord 1698 And all the Rest and Residue of the said Goods Chattels Rights and Credits which shall be found Remaining upon the sd Administratrix her account the same being first Examined & allowed of by the judge or judges for ye time being of probate of wils and Granting of Administration within the County of Plimouth Shall Deliver and pay unto such person or persons Respectively as the said Judge or Judges by his or their Decree or Sentence pursuant to law shall limmit and appoint And if it shall hereafter Appear that any last will and Testament was made by the said Deceased and the Executo^r or Executo^rs therein named do Exhibit ye same Into the said Court of Probate making Request to have it allowed and Approved Accordingly if the said Administratrix within bounden being thereunto Required do Render and deliver the said letters of Administration Approbation of such Testament being first had and made into the Registers office of ye said County Then this obligation to be void and of none Effect or Else to Remain in full force and vertue.

Signed sealed and delivered in presence of. [*]

Abigail Alden (seal)
Seth Arnold (seal)
David Alden (seal)

[JONATHAN² ALDEN'S INVENTORY. †]

An inventory of the Estate of Captain Johnath Alden late of duxborrough deceased taken this third of march : 1697

to his wearing Clothes and money	44	10	0
to bookes Arms and amunition	04	10	0
to beds beding and table lining	22	14	0

* The bond was not witnessed. † Transcribed from the original document.

to Sheep and Cattle and hors kind and furniture	43	10	0
to Swine	01	00	0
to peuter and bras	04	00	0
to iron were and Coopers and Carpenters tools	04	05	0
to Carts and plows and all other husbandry tools	02	10	0
to 5 Chests and one box	01	10	
to one table Carpet and forme	01	00	0
to Chairs and Cushens	01	10	0
to Spining wheels Cards hichel glass bottles Earthen wear tubs pails and other lumber	03	00	0
to A loome and harnes and fethers	02	10	0
to leather and tobakco and feathers	02	10	0
to provision for the family	05	00	0
to his farme	100	00	0
to meadow at the gurnet	04	00	0
to half a Shear in the maiors purchas	01	10	0
due by bills to the Estate	60	00	0
Totall	309	9	0
lands	105	10	0
Chattels	203	1	0

by us edwarde southworth
John Soule
Seth Arnold

Abigail Alden Administratrix of all & singular the goods Chattels Rights & Credits of her late husband Capt Jonathan Alden deceased made oath before Wm Bradford Esqr Judge &c the 8th day of March $169\frac{6}{7}$ that y^{e} above written is a true Inventory of y^{e} Estate of sd deceased so far as she yet knoweth & that when more shall Come to her knowledge she will cause it to be added.

Attest Saml Sprague Register.

Recorded 1st Book page 255.

[The Settlement of the Estate.]

[II : 28*] Plim ss Plimouth January 7th 1703 By Nathaniel Thomas Esqr : Judge of the Probate of Wills & Distributing & settleing the Estat of persons Dying Intestate &c : in the County of Plimouth

The Distributing & Settlement of the Estate of Capt : Jonathan Alden late of Duxborrough in the County of Plimouth deceased Intestate amongst his widdow & Children Whereas the S^{d} Jonathan Alden died Intestate leaving his Widdow M^{rs}

* Plymouth County Probate Records.

Abigal Alden & three sons & three daughters And his Estate being apprized & vallued by three able freeholders in the said Town of Duxborrough & an Inventory thereof Exhibitted into the Court of Probate on the oath of his said Widdow to whome Administration on his Estate was Comitted & the lands of the said deceased in the S^{d} Inventory being valluued at 105 pounds that is to say the farm whereon the S^{d} Deceased dwelt in Duxborrough at 100 pounds & a parcell of Meadow neare the Gurnett at 4 Pounds & half a share in the Majors Purchase at one pound The said Widdows thirds thereof amounts to the sum of 35 pounds & the Remainder of the vallue of the lands is seventy pounds And the Moveable Estate according to the S^{d} Inventory is vallued at 203$^{£}$ 9^{s} 0^{d} the S^{d} Widdows thirds thereof amounting to 67$^{£}$ 16^{s} 4^{d} there Remains thereof the sum of 135$^{£}$ 12^{s} 8^{d} To which sum add the Remainder of the vallue of the land it will amount to 205$^{£}$ 12^{s} 8^{d} the Eldest sons Double share whereof is 58$^{£}$ 15^{s} 2^{d} & Each other Childs share thereof is 29$^{£}$ 7^{s} 7^{d} And forasmuchas the deviding of the farme would be detrementall to or spoyle the whole & that the widdow & all her other Children of full age are desirous that the Eldest son should have his fathers lands to himself It is therefore ordered & Determined as followeth Viz : That John Alden Eldest son of the said Capt : Jonathan Alden shall have all the lands aboves^{d} Viz : all the farme whereof his father died seized the meadow at or near the Gurnett & the half share in the land called the Majors Purchase To him & his heirs forever saving to the said Widdow his Mother her thirds or Dower therein dureing her life he therefore Paying to his mother the S^{d} Administratrix the sum of 11$^{£}$ 4^{s} 10^{d} which is over his Double Portion of all the said Estate And in Convenient time after the decease of his mother he shall also pay to Each of his two brothers & three sisters the sum of five pounds which will be in the whole with his two shares thirty five pounds the Vallue of his Mothers third part of the said lands And the said Administratrix shall Pay unto Each of her other five Children for their Portion of their fathers Estate the sum of twenty nine pounds seven shillings & seven pence with what they or any of them may have already had from her of their said Portions

Memorandom that whereas the Estate by the Inventory amounts to twenty shillings more then what is above devided it is allowed to the said Administratrix towards the Charges of her Administration

Nathl Thomas Register. Ordered by me Nathaniel Thomas

JAMES[2] SAMSON'S WILL AND THE RECEIPTS OF THE HEIRS.

Transcribed from the Original Document and Records,

By George Ernest Bowman.

James[2] Samson (*Henry*[1]) died at Dartmouth, Mass., between 10 January, 1715/16, the day his will was made, and 7 July, 1718, the date on which the will was proved. The will was recorded in the Bristol County Probate Records, Volume III, page 447, and the receipts of the heirs in Volume IX, pages 440 and 441. The original will is still on file and the copy here presented was made from the original document, as was the executor's bond, which was not recorded. No inventory was found.

[James[2] Samson's Will.*]

In The Name of God Amen The Tenth of January one thousand seven hundred & fiveteen sixteen, & In The Second year

* Transcribed from the original document.

of The Reign of our Soveraign Lord George of Great Britain France & Ireland King &c, I James Samson of Dartmouth In The County of Bristol In The Province of The Massachusetts Bay In New England yeoman being well stricken In years but of Disposing mind & memory thanks be Given to God Therefore Calling to mind The Mortality of my Body & knowing That it is appointed for all men once To Dye Do make & appoint & ordain This my last Will & Testament That is to say Principaly & first of all I give & Recommend my soul Into the hands of God That gave it & my body I Recommend To the Earth to be buried In decent christian Burial at The discretion of my Executors nothing doubting but at the General Resurrection I Shall receive the same again by The mighty power of God, And as touching such worldly Estate wherewith it hath pleased God to Bless me in this life, I give demise & dispose of the same In The following manner & Form, Imprimis I give & bequeath To Hannah my dearly beloved Wife The great Room in my dwelling house being a lower room with the Closet in it to be at her disposeing during her widdowhood together with my best bed & furniture to it, to be & Remain (that is the bed & furniture) to her & her heirs & assignes for ever, Item I give unto my son James together with what I have already given him my long gun & my Cane & that to be his full share of my Estate the same to be to him & his Heirs & assignes for ever, Item I give unto my son Henry all my Farme which I now dwell on (to witt) all my homestead with all the lands I bought of John Howard & also all the land that I lately bought of William Allen both upland & meddow land with all the housing fencing and orcharding their or their unto belonging Excepting the reserve of what I have willed to my wife dureing her widowhood, & then that to return to him all which I give to him & his Heirs & assignes for ever for & In Consideration hereafter mentioned That is to say he paying all my Just debts & funeral Charges with Those legacyes he shall be hereby oblidged unto, & he providing for his Mother all things necessary for her Comfortable subsistance dureing the time of her Widowhood both in sickness & health & pay her funeral Charges after Her decease. Item I give unto my son Joseph all my housing at the long plain so called in sd Dartmouth with the lott of land it stands upon as it is layed out by Benjamin Crane with one seventh part of two thirds of a share of upland after the Eight hundred acre grant as it is already layed out by sd Crane, as also the seventh part of two thirds of a share of Ceader swamp to be & remain to him his Heirs & assignes for ever, Item I give to my Daughter Anna twenty Pounds money to be paid by my son Henry within one year after my decease Item I give to my Daughter Penelopy Twenty Pounds money to be paid by my son Henry within two years & an half after my Decease, Item I give to my Daughter Sussannah twenty pounds money to be paid by my son Henry within four years after my Decease, Item I give unto my Daughter Pricilla five shillings with what she hath already had to be paid by my son Henry within halfe a year after my decease & my will is that all the Legacyes to my Daughters be to them their Heirs & assignes for ever: Item I give to my son Henry (whom I Do hereby make & Constitute my sole Executor of this my last will & Testament All the Remaining part of my Estate of what sort or kind soever To be to him & his Heirs & assignes for ever And I Do hereby Disallow & Revoke all other & former wills By me heretofore made Ratifying & Confirming This & no other to be my last will & Testament In Wittness whereof I have hereunto set my hand & seal the Day & year first above written,

Signed Sealed Published James Samson (seal)
pronounced & Declared By
The said James Samson
as his last will & testament
In Presence of us the subscribers:
Jonath^{n} Delano
Jabez Delano
Nathaniel Delano

Bristol ss July the 7th 1718 then before the hon^{r}able Natha^{l} Paine Esqr Judge of the Probate of wills and Granting of Administrations within the County of Bristol Came Lt Jonathan Delono & Nathal Delono & made Oath that they were present and Did hear and see the said James Samson since deceased signe seal publish & declare the above written to be his last will and Testament & that he was of a Disposeing mind when he so did, and further that Jabez Delano signe as a witness with them at the same time

John Cary Reg^{r}: Nath^{ll} Paine

Bristol ss in the Third book folio 447 : 448 the abovewriten was Entered July 11th 1718 by John Cary Register

[Bond of Executor.*]

Know all men by these presents that we Henry Sampson of the town of Dartmouth in the County of Bristol Executor of the last will and Testament of mr James Sampson late of of Dartmouth deceased Captain John Akin & Phillip Taber both of said Dartmouth in the County of Bristol in New England Are held and stand firmly bound and obliged unto the Honrable Nathal Paine Esqr Judge of the Probate of wills & granting of Letters of Administration within the County of Bristol in the sum of One Thousand pounds Lawfull money of New England To be payed unto the said Nathal Paine his Successor in the said office or Assignes To the true payment whereof we bind our selves our heires Executors & Administrators and Each of us & them Joyntly and severally in the whole and for the whole firmly by these presents sealed with our seals dated this fifteenth day of July Anno Domini 1719 Annoq RRs Georgii Quinto

The Condition of this present obligation is such that if the above Bounden Henry Sampson son of James Sampson and Executor of his last will and Testament Duely proved and allowed and allso Residuary Legatary therein Named Shall & do pay all the Debts and Legacyes, and in all Respect well & duely Execute and perform the said will in all and Every the Articles thereof according to the Tennour true Intent & meaning of the sd Testator And do & perform all & whatsoever is by him as Executor aforesaid Enjoyned : in and by the said will without ffraud Collusion or delay Than this present obligation to be void & of None Effect or Elce to Remain in full forcc & vertuc

Signed sealed and delivered — Henry Samson (seal)
In presence of us witnesses — John Akin (seal)
Samuel baily — Phillip Taber (seal)
John Cary

[Receipts of the Heirs.]

[IX : 440] Duxbury November ye 23d 1727

Then Received of Brother Henry Samson Who is Sole Executor of the Last will and Testament of my Honod Father James Samson Late of Dartmouth Deceased the Sum of

* Transcribed from the original document.

Twenty Pounds in full of what was Given us by the Testator In Said Will I say Received by us as wittness our hands

Benjamin Prince — Abraham Samson (seal)
Miles Samson — Penelope Samson (seal)
her mark

Bristol ss July ye 17 1740 Entered per Stephen Paine Register

Know all men by these Presents that I James Samson of Wells In the County of york In the Province of the massachusets Bay In New England yeoman have Remised Released and forever Quit Claim and by these Presents Do Remise Release and forever Quit Claim to Brother Henry Samson of Dartmouth In the County of Bristol in the Province Aforsaid Husbandman his heirs Executors Administrators all and all manner of Action or Actions Quarrels Controverses Trespasses Damages and Demands whatsoever which by Law or Equity may now or hereafter Arise Concerning Mother Hannah Samsons thirds of the Estate of our father James Samson Late of Dartmouth Deceased or otherwise howsoever I the said James Samson against my Said Brother Henry Samson or which my heirs Executors or Administrators Shall or may Claim Challange or Demand for or by Reason or thing Whatsoever Concerning the Aforsaid third of the Said Estate to the Day of ye Date of these Presents : In Wittness my hand and Seal this Twenty fourth Day of July Anno Domini 1726

Signed Sealed and Delivered — James Samson (seal)
In the Presence of us
Mary Adams
Willm Palmer

Entered per Stephen Paine Register

Dartmouth December ye 11th 1727

Then Received of Brother Henry Samson Who is Whol and Sole Executor of the Last will and Testament of our Honoured father James Samson Late of Dartmouth Deceased the Sum of Twenty Pounds in full of what was Giveen us by the Testator In Said will we Say Received by us Wittness our hands and Seals

In the Presence of — Benjamin Hilmon (seal)
Rebeccah + Samson — Susanah Hilmon (seal)
her mark
John Clark

Entered per Stephen Paine Registr

Dartmouth December ye 8th 1727

Then Received of Brother Henry Samson Who is Sole Executor of the Last will & Testament of my Honoured father James Samson Late of Dartmouth Deceased the House and Land in full of what was giveen me by the Testator in Said will I Say Receivd by me as wittness my hand and Seal

In the Presence of us

[p. 441] Rebecah Samson Joseph Samson

John Rouse

Dartmouth December ye 6 : 1727

Then Received of Brother Henry Samson Who is Whol and Sole Executor of the Last will and Testament of my Honoured father James Samson Late of Dartmouth Deceased the Sum of five Shillings in full of what was given us by the Testator in Said will we Say Received by us as Wittness our hands and Seals

In the Presence of us Solomon Hammond (seal)

Joseph Turner Pricilla Hammond (seal)

William Honar

Bristol ss July ye 17 1740 Entered per Stephen Paine Register

Know all men by these Presents that I Shubal Smith and my Wife Ann Smith of Dukes County in Chilmark yeoman have Remised Released and forever Quitted Claim and by these Presents Do Remise Release and forever Quit Claim unto Brother Henry Samson of Dartmouth In the County of Bristol In the Province of the Massachusets Bay Husbandman his heirs Executors administrators of all and all manner of action or actions Quarrels Controverses Trespasses Damages & Demands whatsoever which by Law or Equity may now or hereafter Arise Concerning our Mother Hannah Samson Thirds of the Estate of our father James Samson Late of Said Dartmouth Deceased or otherwise howsoever we the Said Shubal Smith and Ann his wife against the Said Brother Henry Samson or which we our heirs Executors or Administrators Shall or may Claim Challange or Demand for or by Reason or thing whatsoever Concerning the Aforsaid third of the Said Estate to ye Day of the Date of these Presents In Wittness Whereof We have hereunto Set our hands and Seals this Seventh Day of July Anno Domini 1726

Signed Sealed & Delivered Shubal Smith (seal)

In the Presence of us Ann Smith (seal)

John Hammond her mark

Willm Palmer

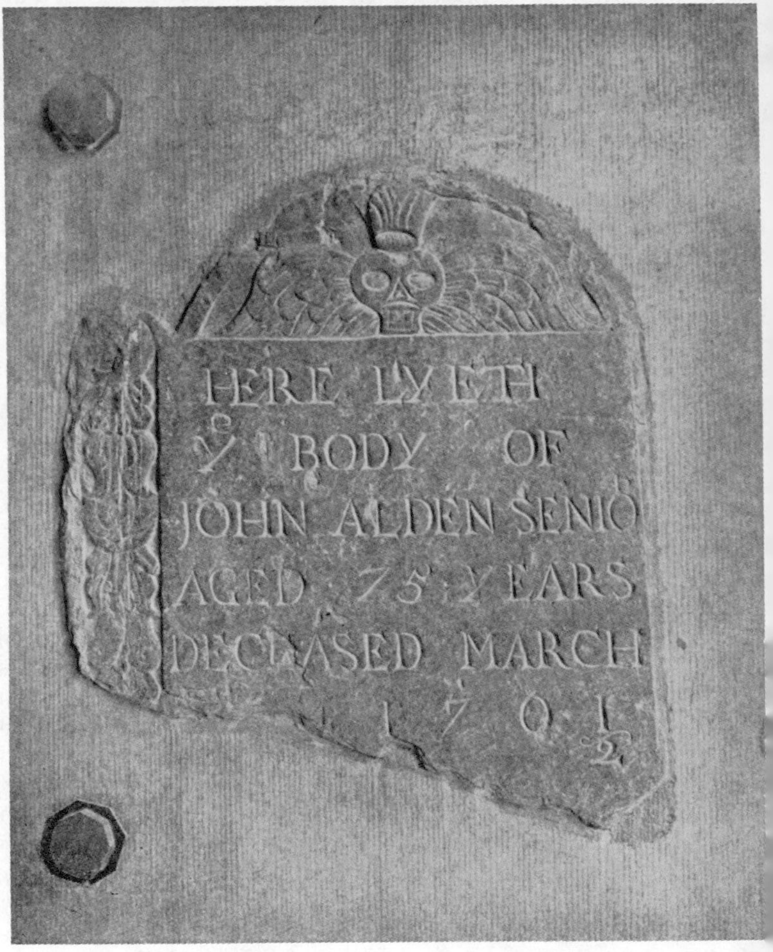

CAPTAIN JOHN[2] ALDEN'S GRAVESTONE

CAPTAIN JOHN[2] ALDEN'S WILL AND INVENTORY AND THE ACCOUNT OF HIS EXECUTORS.

Transcribed from the Original Documents,

By George Ernest Bowman.

Captain John[2] Alden (*John*[1]) died at Boston, Mass., Saturday, 14 March, 1701/2, at five o'clock in the afternoon, aged seventy-five. His gravestone, shown in the accompanying illustration, is now in the porch of the New Old South Church, and is inscribed as follows:

HERE LYETH
Y^{e} BODY OF
JOHN ALDEN SENIO^{r}
AGED 75 YEARS
DECEASED MARCH
[Y]^{e} [1]4 1 7 0 ½

The day of the month is determined by the following entry in Judge Samuel Sewall's Diary:

"Satterday, March 14, 170½ at 5 p.m. Capt. John Alden expired; Going to visit him, I hapened to be there at the time."*

The original will and inventory and the executors' account are still preserved in the files of the Suffolk County Registry of Probate, at Boston, and have been used in making the transcripts here presented.

* Mass. Hist. Soc. Coll., 5th Series, VI: 54.

[Capt. John² Alden's Will.*]

In the Name of God Amen the Seventeenth day of February Anno Domi. 1701 Annoq R Rs Gulielmi Tertii Angliæ &c decimo quarto I John Alden Senr of Boston in the County of Suffolke within his Matys Province of the Massachusetts Bay in New England Mariner being Sick & weak of body but of sound disposing mind and memory (praised be Almighty God for the Same) Do make this my last Will & Testamt in manner and forme following, hereby revoking & making null and void all Wills and Testaments by me at any time heretofore made. First and Principally I humbly commend and resigne my Soul into the hands of Almighty God my Creator, hopeing for the full pardon and remission of all my sins and Salvation through the alone merits of Jesus Christ my Redeemer. My body I desire may be decently buried, at the discretion of my Executors herein after named. And as for that portion of worldly Goods and Estate, which it hath pleased the Lord to bestow upon me. I do give and dispose of the same as followeth That is to say. Imprimis I will That all my just debts & Funeral Expences be well and truely paid or ordained to be paid in convenient time after my decease by my Executors hereafter named, Unto each of whom I give & bequeath the sum of Five pounds, for their care and pains in the sd Trust. Item. After my just Debts, Funeral Expences and Legacys aforesd are paid and discharged, My mind & will is That the whole remainder of my Estate in housing, Lands, money, plate, debts, goods & moveables that is to say, all the remainder of my Estate real & personal wheresoever lying or found, be divided into five equal parts or shares. One fifth part or share whereof I give, devise and bequeath unto my eldest son John Alden forever, one other fifth part or share whereof I give, devise & bequeath unto my Son William Alden for ever. One other fifth part or share whereof I give, devise and bequeath unto my Son Zechariah Alden for ever one other fifth part or share whereof I give, devise and bequeath unto my Daughter Elizabeth Walley for ever, And the other fifth pt. Part or share thereof I give, devise and bequeath unto the Children of my Son Nathaniel Alden deceased, for ever equally to be divided among them And my mind & will is, That my sd Daughter Elizabeth Walley at and upon my decease shall have full, free and quiet possession & seizin of all that piece or parcel of Land which I formerly recovered by Law of James Everel, with all the Edifices and Buildings now thereupon & thereto belonging (being the house wherein I & my sd Daughter

* Transcribed from the original document.

Walley now dwel) Together with the Yard, priviledges and appurtenances to the s[d] house and Land belonging, And the Garden plot adjoyning to the same, that I formerly purchased of Thomas Gross and Elizabeth his Wife, as ℘ Deed may appear, Which s[d] house, Land & premisses my s[d] Daughter Elizabeth Walley shall have hold & enjoy to her, and her heirs and assigns for ever, at the rate or price of four hundred pounds, She the s[d] Elizabeth Walley, her heirs or assigns within the space of three yeares after my decease, paying unto my other Children before named or some of them, as part of their shares or portions before given them of my Estate, such sum or sums as the s[d] house, Land and premisses, at the value or price before mentioned shall amount unto more than one fifth part of my Estate given as is before expressed unto my s[d] Daughter Walley And my mind & will also is That all such sum and sums of money as are due and owing unto my s[d] Daughter Walley from the Estate of my s[d] son Nathaniel Alden dece[d], for any matter or thing whatsoever shall be paid unto my s[d] Daughter Eliz[a] Walley out of the part and share of my Estate herein before bequeathed unto the Children of my s[d] Son Nathaniel. And I order my Executors, upon adjustment of the Accompts thereof with my s[d] Daughter to make payment of the same to her accordingly, out of the said Childrens part or dividend. Item, My mind and will is That if such of my Children unto whom my Brick house and Land in Boston afores[d] which I bought of Samuel Jackson shall, upon the division of my Estate, fall or be allotted, see cause to dwel in the same themselves, Then such Child or Children, during the time that he or they in In their own persons dwel therein, shall have the liberty of using the Kitchen belonging to my other house before mentioned, for washing, brewing and baking, and also liberty of making use of the house of Office, and of the Garden belonging to the s[d] house for the hanging and drying his or their cloaths Lastly I do hereby nominate, constitute & appoint my s[d] Sons John Alden & William Alden to be the Executors of this my last Will and Testament In Witness whereof I have hereunto set my hand & seal the day & year first within written

John Alden (seal)

Signed Sealed, published and Declared by the s[d] John Alden the Testator, as and for his last Will and Testament, in presence of us, who subscribed our names as Witnesses thereto in the said Testators presence

Thomas Savage
Charles Chauncy
Edw[d] : Turfrey

Suffolk Ss. By the Hon[ble] Elisha Cooke Esq[r].
Judge of Probate &c

The beforewritten Instrument being presented as the last Will and Testament of John Alden Sen[r] late of Boston Mariner deced by his sons John Alden and William Alden Executors therein named —

Maj[r] Thomas Savage, Charles Chauncy & Edw[d] Turfrey the three Witnesses to the s[d] Instrum[t] personally appeared before me & made Oath that they did see the s[d] John Alden the Testator, signe seale & declare the same as his last Will & Testament, And that he then was of sound disposing mind to their best discerning, And that they subscribed their names as Witnesses thereto in the s[d] Testators presence

Jurat Cor me Elisha Cooke

Boston April 13th 1702.

[The Letter of Administration.*]

The Probate of the Will of John Alden late of Boston Mariner deced, And Administration granted thereon unto his Sons John Alden and William Alden Executors in the Same Will named.

Elisha Cooke Esq[r] duely appointed and Commissioned to be Judge of the Probate of Wills and for granting Letters of Admin[con] on the Estates of persons deceased, having Goods Chattels, Rights or Credits in the County of Suffolke within his Ma[tys] Province of the Massachusetts Bay in New England. To all unto whom these presents shall come Greeting. Know yee That on the Thirteenth day of April, in the year of our Lord one thousand seven hundred and two . Before me at Boston in the County afores[d] The Will of John Alden Sen[r] late of s[d] Boston Mariner deceased, to these presents annexed, was proved, approved and allowed. Who having while he lived, and at the time of his decease Goods, Chattels Rights or Credits in the County aforesaid, And the Probate of the s[d] Will & power of committing Administration of all and singular the Goods, Chattels, Rights and Credits of the s[d] deceased, and also the hearing, examining and allowing the Accompts of the same, by virtue thereof, appertaining unto me, The Administration of all and singular the Goods, Chattels, Rights & Credits of the s[d] deceased, and his Will in any manner concerning, is hereby committed unto his two sons, John Alden and William Alden Executors in the same Will named; Well

* Transcribed from the Suffolk County, Mass., Probate Records, Vol. XV, p. 5.

and faithfully to execute the s[d] Will, and to administer the Estate of the s[d] deced according thereunto. And to make a true and perfect Inventory of all and singular the Goods, Chattels, Rights and Credits of the s[d] deced, And to exhibit the same into the Registry of the Court of Probate for the County afores[d] at or before the Thirteenth day of October next ensueing, Also to render a plain and true Accompt of their s[d] Administration upon Oath In Testimony whereof I have hereunto set my hand and the seal of the s[d] Court of Probate. Dated at Boston afores[d] the day and year first abovewritten.

Is[a] Addington Reg[rius] Elisha Cooke

[CAPT. JOHN² ALDEN'S INVENTORY.*]

An Inventory of ye Estate of John Alden Sen[r] deceasd

	Dr	*ll*	*s*	*d*
Due from y[e] Estate		317 :	16 :	3
	Cred[t]	*ll*	*s*	*d*
one Wooden house		400 :	0	0
one Brick detto		270	0	0
plate & money		26	6	6
brass ware		09	5	0
iron ware		22	14	0
Rest of ye movibles		69	2	6
Pewter		03	01	6
Debts due to ye Estate ye most of which are desperite		1259	2	1
		2059	11	7

The aboves[d] Estate was apprized by Abraham Blish & William Paine, and the above Inventory exhibited by

Jn[o] Alden Exec[r]

Suffolk Ss By the Hon[ble] Elisha Cooke Esq[r] Judge of Probate &c

John Alden one of the Exec[rs] of the last Will and Testam[t] of his Father John Alden late of Boston Mariner dec[d] exhibited the abovewritten and made Oath That it contains a just & true Inventory of the Estate of his s[d] dece[d] Father so far as hath come to his knowledge and that if more hereafter appears he will cause it to be added

Boston June 2[d] 1702. Jurat Cor me Elisha Cooke

* Transcribed from the original document.

[The Executors' Account.*]

The Accompt of John & William Alden Execut^{rs} : of ye Last Will and Testament of John Alden late of Boston in ye County of Suffolk Marriner Deceac'd as well of and for Such and So much of the goods Chattels and Estate of ye Said Deceac'd as have Come to their hands. As of and for ye payments and Disbursments Out of ye Same as followeth.

The Said Accomptants Chargeth themselves with all and Singular the Goods Chattells and Estate of ye Deceac'd Specified in an Inventory thereof made and Exhibeted into the Registry of ye Court of Probate &c : for S^{d} County, Amounting as ℘ ye Same Inventory apeareth to ye Sume of

				£800	9	6
Rec^{d} more at Sundry Times Since Exhibiting the Inventory, Viz^{tt} off						
Mr James Taylor Treasurer	£18	12	—			
Mr Charles Chauncy	54	10	—			
Mr Daniel Johnnat Rent for ye Brick House	10	10	—			
Mr Simon Willard for Ditto	7	10	—			
Mr Ellis Callander	1	15	2	92	17	2
				893	06	8†
And Petitions for Allowances as followeth.						
for proving ye Will & Charges for prizing ye Estate	£001	1	5			
for a Retaining fee for Mr Dudley	000	12	—			
Presenting & fileing ye Petition for Seling ye Brick House	—	6	—			
Paid Sickness & funeral Charges	050	7	1	52	6	6
Paid Samuel Willard on Bond	100	—	—			
Paid John Campbell on Bond	100	—	—			
to Joshua Windsor for Warehouse room	3	11	11			
to ye Execut^{rs} ℘ Will	10	—	—			
to John Nelson p^{d}	6	—	—			
to M^{r} Dè Chufore p^{d}	5	7	8			
to Doctor Oliver p^{d}	1	13	—			
to Sarah Pemberton p^{d}	2	10	—			
to John Campbell . p^{d} for Intreast mony	3	15	—			
to Samuel Willard . p^{d} for Ditto	6	—	—			
to David Landan work done on ye brick House	1	9	10			
to Eliakim Hutchinson Esqr p^{d}	18	12	—			
to Benj^{a} Elliot p^{d}	11	6	8			
to Eliz^{a} Walley (now Willard)	78	16	9	349	2	10
				401	9	4†
Rests				491	17	4†

Carried Over

Jno Alden

Wm Alden

* Transcribed from the original document.

† In the original document the debit and credit totals, and the balance of £491 17*s* 4*d*, are carried out in a third column at the right.

Suffolk. Ss. By the hon^{ble} Isaac Addington Esqr Judge of Probate &c.

John Alden & Wm Alden Exec^{rs} presented the above written, & made Oath, That it contains a just & true Accompt of their administration on the Estate of John Alden late of Boston Mariner deced, so far as they have proceeded therein, which I do Allow & approve of —

Boston August . 4th 1704. Jurat . Cor . Is^{a} Addington

Brought Over from ye Other Side ye ballance of ye Estate Debts & funerall Charges paid	£491	17	4

N B. Wheras the Within Nam'd John Alden did in his last Will and Testament give and allow unto his Daughter Eliz^{a} : Walley (now (Willard) the preemtion of his Wooden House by Said Alden in his Will Rated at four Hundred pounds She paying to The Other Children or Some of them, as part of their Shares and portions Such Sume or Sumes as Said House Land & premises Shall Amount unto more then one fifth part of his Estate as before given to his Said Daughter Elizabeth Willard, this May Certifie y^{t} y^{e} Said Eliz^{a} : Willard hath paid to John & William Alden Executors of y^{e} Last Will and Testament of John Alden Deceac'd y^{e} full Sume of three hundred one pou^{ds} twelve Shil : 6$\frac{1}{2}$^{d} being y^{e} Over plus of S^{d} House one fifth part of the Estate Deducted

John Alden D^{r}			
to Cash and Sundry Movables	£24	11	6
to ballance p^{d} p^{r} Simon Willard	82	11	4½
	107	2	10½
Supra C^{r}			
By ⅕ part of his Estate	£98	7	5½
By Will Allow'd for Executorship	5	—	—
By his Disburstm^{ts}:	3	15	5
	107	2	10½
William Alden D^{r}			
to Sundry Movables	£8	—	4
to Ballance paid pr Simon Willard	97	3	1½
	105	3	5½
Supra C^{r}			
By ⅕ part his Estate	98	7	5½
By Will Allow'd for Executorship	5	—	—
By his Disburstments	1	16	—
	105	3	5½

Zachariah Alden Dr			
to Sundry Movables	£30	19	7
to ballance paid pr Simon Willard	67	7	10½
	98	7	5½
Supra Cr			
By ye ⅕ ptt of ye Estate	98	7	5½
The Children of Nathl: Alden deceac'd Drs to Eliza: Walley (now Willard) for their Fathrs: Accott	£58	7	10
to John Alden's Disbursments	—	7	—
to ballance pd pr Simon Willard to ye Executors	39	12	7½
	£98	7	5½
Supra Cr			
By ⅕ ptt of the Estate	£98	7	5½
Simon Willard Dr			
to Sundry Movables	£31	6	—
to ye Wooden House	400	—	—
to ye Brick House	280	—	—
to Sundrys Recd: pr him	019	1[5]	2
	731	01	2½
Supra Cr			
By ⅕ part of ye Estate	£98	7	5½
By his Sworne Accott:	95	18	5
By him paid Sarah Pemberton	2	10	—
paid Doctor Oliver	1	13	—
paid John Campbell Intreast money	4	10	—
paid Saml: Willard Ditto	6	—	—
paid Joshua Windsor	3	11	11
paid David Landan for Work done	1	9	10
paid John Campbell Cash	50	—	—
paid John Nelson	6	—	—
paid Dè Chufore	5	7	8
paid William Pain	2	7	—
paid Sundrys for Mourning	6	10	9
paid Saml: Willard on Bond	100		
paid ye Executors by Sundry Charges	1	7	4
	385	13	4½
Paid to John Alden for Ballance	082	11	4½
to William Alden for Ditto	097	1	1½
to Zachr: Alden for Ditto	067	7	10½
to ye Executors for ye Children of Nt Alden deceac'd	098	7	5½
	731	1	2½

Jno Alden
Wm Alden

DAVID[2] ALDEN'S ESTATE.

Transcribed from the Original Documents and Records,

BY GEORGE ERNEST BOWMAN.

DAVID[2] ALDEN (*John*[1]) died at Duxbury, probably not long before 1 April, 1719, the date of the bond given by the administrator, Benjamin Alden of Duxbury. There is no record of the appointment of an administrator, but the original bond is still in the Plymouth County Probate Files. The amount of the bond was £400, and the surety was Samuel Alden of Duxbury. The bond was made out on a printed form, and a part of it reads as follows: "The Condition of this Present Obligation is such, That if the above-bounden Benjamin Alden unto whome is Committed power of administration of the Estate of Mr David Alden Late of Duxborough Afores^{d} deceased." The administrator was required by the bond to bring in an inventory to the Probate Court, of which Isaac Winslow was the judge, on or before 20 June, 1719, and to render an account of his administration on or before 20 September, 1719. The autograph signatures of Benjamin and Samuel Alden are appended to the document, and the witnesses were Henry Gulliford (who signed by a mark) and Anne Thomas.

The inventory of the personal estate and the account of the debts of the deceased were never recorded, but the original documents are in the files and have been transcribed. The inventory of the real estate in Middleborough was recorded, but the original has disappeared.

[INVENTORY OF PERSONAL ESTATE.*]

This is a trew Enventare of ye parsanl Estat of Daved Allden Leat of Duxborogh desest Tacken may ye 12 . 1719 by ous the subcribers

* Transcribed from the original document.

	£	s	d
Emprimos To his waren cloths & books Spectteckels	13	12	00
To 4 beads with thar fornetuer	42	18	06
To spenen whels & cloth & cards	02	12	00
To tabols chests & chers & tronks	03	01	00
To bras ware . . six pounds five	6	05	00
one chafen desh	00	08	00
To peuter vesels & puter ware	04	04	06
To glases of all sorts	00	11	00
To rondellets & barels	00	12	00
To six bushels of ry	01	10	00
To one hafe bushel of solt	00	02	00
one ould bedsted & pece of lathar	00	02	00
2 pelyouns . 2 cushings	00	14	00
Earthen ware	00	04	06
iorn dogs tramels & slis & tongs	01	05	06
teen vasels	00	11	00
iorn vasels & stelyards	03	04	00
Tubs kelors & churn	00	19	06
one spet	00	05	00
Keddoul & sevels 1 sekel	00	05	06
To 4 bags half bushels pals dishes and cans & pegengs	00	09	00
Sex oxen on yoke at	08	00	00
The ledin oxen a	13	00	00
3 pare at	12	00	00
4 cous 2 young calfs	016	15	00
one 3 yer ould ster & 2 tu yer old ons	06	15	00
2 haffors at	04	15	00
one hors saddel & bridels at	04	00	00
2 bore pegs	01	04	00
whels . chans . plougs Al cart and teming tackelen at	06	16	06
other carpenders & horsbendri tols	01	01	0*
to one set of hups & boxes	00	10	*
hors fetars coricome	00	01	*
one goun & 2 sords	01	00	*
one cobard	00	06	0*
one cow bal 3ˢ one grenston 2ˢ both	00	05	00
one stubin sieeth	00	03	00
To other table Lining	01	19	00
to two silver spoons and a pair of wosted Combs	00	18	00
to vials gallepots & Druggs	00	08	00
to a Clock Real and half a hechel	00	09	00
to part of a pair of andjrons	00	04	00

John Alden
Thomas Southworth
John Partridge

* Worn.

May the 22 : 1719

Benjamin Allden Administrator to the estate of mr David Allden late of Duxborough in the County of Plimoth Decased made oath that the within written is a tru and perfect Inventory of the estate of the sd Deceased as far as is Come to his hands and if any more shall after Come to his knowledg he will also give it in : taken before me

Isaac Winslow Judge of Probats

[INVENTORY OF REAL ESTATE AT MIDDLEBOROUGH.]

[IV : 186*] Pursuant to an order from Isaac Winslow Esqr Judge of the probate of Wills &c in the County of Plymouth to us directed. We whose names are hereunto Subscribed have taken a Veiw of the severall parcells of Land whereof Mr David Alden Late of Duxboroug dyed Seized of in the Township of Middleborough, And have made Apprizement of Each perticuler parcell thereof, And According to Our best Judgment the true vallue of Each parcell thereof is as followeth, Namely, Four Lots of Land lying in the purchase of Land Called the Sixteen Shilling purchase, viz.

One Lot Containing 37 Acres being in Number ye 20th Lot in ye Second Allotment in sd purchase, we vallue at	16 — —
One Lot Containing fourty acres being in Number the 49th Lot in sd Second Allotment in sd purchase we Vallue at	25 — —
One Lot in the last Allotment in sd purchase Containing 34 acres being in Number the 29th Lot we Vallue at	18 — —
One Lot in the last Allotment in sd purchase Containing 41 . Acres being in Number the 143. Lot we Vallue at	20 — —
And One Lot in the Neck Called Assawamsett Neck Containing 20 acres being In Number ye 19th Lot in sd Neck we vallue at	18 — —
	£97 — —

The bounds of each of the aforesd Lots may Appear upon the records of ye Aforesd purchase.

Dated at Middleborough May the 20th 1719.

Jacob Tomson, John Bennet, Ichabod Southworth

May ye 22d 1719 John Bennet & Ichabod Southworth two of the abovewritten apprizers made Oath that the Abovewritten

* Plymouth County Probate Records.

is a just & Equall Apprizement of the Land of Mr David Alden late of Duxborough dec^{d} Lying in the Township of Middleborough to the best of their Judgment. Before me.

Isaac Winslow Judge of probates

[Account of David² Alden's Debts.*]

An Account of what is due from the Estate of Mr David Alden late of Duxborough Dec^{d}, ye particulars are as followeth

	£	s	d	
to Mr John Murdock	00	10	08	
to Mr Nathaniel Thomas	07	12	06	
to Thos Delanoe Senr	00	03	00	
to Ben. Delanoe	00	05	00	
to Thos Delanoe Junr	00	14	00	
to Joseph Chanler ye second	01	00	09	
to Joseph Chanler ye third	00	10	00	
to Israel Holms	00	13	08	
to time expended p^{r} ye Administrator	00	16	06	
to Benjamin Alden for work about a sloop	05†	00	00	Anno Dom. 1706
and for mony	06†	00	00	Anno. 1707
more for mony	07†	00	00	Anno. 1707
more for wood payd to a Block maker	02†	00	00	Anno. 1707
more for mony	06†	00	00	Anno. 1708
more for a mare	04†	05	00	Anno. 1708
more for wintering & summering ye stock	20	10	00	
more for sixteen bushels of Corn	02	00	00	
wintering of two piges ‡	0	12	0	
more for malt ‡	0	4	6	
moer for work ‡	0	8	0	
moer for wheat ‡	0	3	6	
to John Allden	0	17	0	
to Benjamin Prior	00	03	00	
for Rates ye last year	01	02	07	
to ye Prizers of the Estate	00	15	06	
to Benjamin Samson	00	12	09	
to William Brewster Junr	01	5	11	

And due to ye aboves^{d} Estate as followeth . viz .

* Transcribed from the original document, which was never recorded.

† The pounds in these items have been crossed out.

‡ These items are on the margin and evidently are additions to the amounts due Benjamin Alden.

	l	*s*	*d*
for one years Rent of the Farm	10	00	00
for one Bull sold to Benjamin Alden	03	00	00
from Peter Hunt	00	15	00
from Ephraim Bradford	00	07	06
moer from Peter Hunt	00	014	00
moer from Beniamen Allden	00	019	00
	15	15	6

Jacob tomson	01	07	00
John bennet	00	14	00
Jekabod Southworth	00	14	00
thomas Southwort	00	03	00
For leters of administeration	00	07	06
For warent of aprisment	00	03	00
For Settelment and recoring	00	11	00
to mor time exspended by administrator	00	09	00

THE ELIGIBLE MAYFLOWER ASCENDANTS AND THEIR MARRIED DAUGHTERS.

THE following list contains the names of the twenty-two heads of Mayflower families from whom descent has been proved,* also the names of all their daughters who are known to have married, with the names of the husbands.

Every line of Mayflower descent that has yet been established has been traced to one of the twenty-two Mayflower Passengers here named, either through a son or through one of the married daughters in this list, which has been prepared by the Editor, merely as a convenient reference table, in consequence of the frequent calls for the names of the Passengers from whom descent can be proved, and the still more frequent letters asking if such and such a person did not marry a daughter of a Mayflower Passenger.

A literal copy of Governor Bradford's list of the Passengers will be found in Volume I (1899) of "The Mayflower Descendant," and in Volume II (1900) is an alphabetical list of the Passengers, giving, as far as then possible, the date and the place of the birth, the marriage and the death of each. Some additional dates, discovered later, may be found in the succeeding volumes.

* The names of William Mullins and John Tilley are omitted from this list to avoid duplication, since the lines of all known descendants of these two men are traced through their respective daughters, Priscilla Mullins, who married John Alden, and Elizabeth Tilley, who married John Howland.

In the following list all names of Mayflower Passengers are printed in capitals.

JOHN[1] ALDEN
  Elizabeth[2] Alden married William Pabodie
  Mary[2] Alden (?) * married Thomas Delano
  Ruth[2] Alden married John Bass
  Sarah[2] Alden married Alexander[2] Standish (MYLES[1])
ISAAC[1] ALLERTON
  MARY[2] ALLERTON married Elder Thomas Cushman
  REMEMBER[2] ALLERTON married Moses Maverick
JOHN[1] BILLINGTON
GOV. WILLIAM[1] BRADFORD
  Mercy[2] Bradford married Benjamin Vermayes
ELDER WILLIAM[1] BREWSTER
  Fear[2] Brewster married (ISAAC[1] ALLERTON)
  Patience[2] Brewster married Gov. Thomas Prence
PETER[1] BROWNE [He left no sons.]
  Mary[2] Browne married Ephraim Tinkham
  Priscilla[2] Browne married William Allen
  Rebecca[2] Browne married William Snow
JAMES[1] CHILTON [He left no sons.]
  Isabella[2] Chilton married Roger Chandler
  MARY[2] CHILTON married John Winslow
FRANCIS[1] COOKE
  Hester[2] Cooke married Richard Wright
  Jane[2] Cooke married Experience Mitchell
  Mary[2] Cooke married John Thomson
EDWARD[1] DOTY
  Desire[2] Doty married (1), William Sherman; (2), Israel Holmes; (3), Alexander[2] Standish (MYLES[1])
  Elizabeth[2] Doty married John Rouse
  Mary[2] Doty married Samuel Hatch
FRANCIS[1] EATON
  Rachel[2] Eaton married Daniel Ramsden†
EDWARD[1] FULLER
DR. SAMUEL[1] FULLER
STEPHEN[1] HOPKINS
  CONSTANCE[2] HOPKINS married Nicholas Snow
  Damaris[2] Hopkins married Jacob[2] Cooke (FRANCIS[1])
  Deborah[2] Hopkins married Andrew Ring
JOHN[1] HOWLAND
  Desire[2] Howland married Capt. John Gorham
  Elizabeth[2] Howland married, (1), Ephraim Hicks; (2), John Dickenson
  Hannah[2] Howland married Jonathan Bosworth
  Hope[2] Howland married Elder John Chipman
  Lydia[2] Howland married James Brown
  Ruth[2] Howland married Thomas[3] Cushman (MARY[2] ALLERTON, ISAAC[1])
DEGORY[1] PRIEST [He left no sons.]
  Mary[2] Priest married Phineas Pratt
  Sarah[2] Priest married John Coombs

* See Mayflower Descendant, Volume V, page 22.

† Also written Ramsdell.

THOMAS[1] ROGERS
HENRY[1] SAMSON
- Dorcas[2] Samson married Thomas Bonney
- Elizabeth[2] Samson married Robert Sprout
- Hannah[2] Samson married Josiah Holmes
- Mary[2] Samson married John Summers
- A daughter, name unknown, married John Hanmore

GEORGE[1] SOULE
- Elizabeth[2] Soule married Francis Walker
- Mary[2] Soule married John Peterson
- Patience[2] Soule married John Haskell

CAPT. MYLES[1] STANDISH
RICHARD[1] WARREN
- Abigail[2] Warren married Anthony Snow
- Anna[2] Warren married Thomas Little
- Elizabeth[2] Warren married Richard Church
- Mary[2] Warren married Robert Bartlett
- Sarah[2] Warren married JOHN[2] COOKE (FRANCIS[1])

WILLIAM[1] WHITE
GOV. EDWARD WINSLOW
- Elizabeth[2] Winslow married, (1), Robert Brooks; (2) Capt. George Corwin

---

THE ESTATES OF WILLIAM^2 MULLINS AND HIS DAUGHTER SARAH^3 (MULLINS) (GANNETT) (SAVILL) FAXON AND OF HER THREE HUSBANDS

Transcribed from the Original Documents and Records

By George Ernest Bowman

William^2 Mullins (*William*^{1}) came to Plymouth Colony some time after his father's death, and his daughter Sarah^3 Mullins married successively Thomas Gannett of Duxbury and Bridgewater, William Savill of Braintree and Thomas Faxon of Braintree, surviving the latter seventeen years. The documents and records relating to the estates of these five persons require so much space it has seemed best to print a part of them in this issue and give the remainder, with the notes on the whole, in the April issue.

ESTATE OF WILLIAM^2 MULLINS

[Appointment of Administrator]

[p. 356 *] Present Jno Leverett Esqr Govr Edwd Tyng esq^r Assist

Administracon to the Estate of William Mullins of Brantry deceased is granted to Thomas Faxton of Brantry in the Right of his wife the s^d Mullins beeing his wifes Father this done March 28th 1674

as Attests ffreeGrace Bendall Record^r

[Inventory of William^2 Mullins]

[p. 357 *] An Inventory of ye Goods & Estate of William Mullins of Brantry Deceased

Imp^{r}mis bedding	5	0	0
It : to wearing apparrell	2	0	0
It to linnen	1	5	0
It : brass peuter Iron potts leaden weights andirons tramell spitt	2	0	0
It to books	—	7	0
It : to two old Chests a Table & form a bottle Case & bottles	1	5	0
It a hat & other lumber	0	5	0
It : Debt due by bill in the hands of John & Benjamin Savell in money	10	0	0
	22	2	0

Taken & a apprized by us 21 March 16$\frac{73}{74}$
Shadrach Thaire Christopher Webb.

* Suffolk County Probate Records, Volume VII.

Present Jno Leverett Esqr Govr & Edw Tyng Esqr Assist March 28 . 1674

Thomas Faxon made Oath that this paper conteyneth a Just & true Inventory of the Estate of his wives Father William Mullins deceased to his best Knowledge & that when hee Knows more hee will discover the same this done as Attests

ffreeGrace Bendall Rec —

[Bond of Administrator *]

Know all men by these p^{r}sents that I Thomas Faxon of Brantry owne & acknowledge myselfe indebted to the Tresurer of the County of Suffolk in the full & Just sume of forty foure pounds currant money of New England for the payment whereof on demand I binde myselfe heirs Executors & Administrato^{rs} firmly by these p^{r}sents as witness my hand & seale In Boston this twentyeight Day of March 1674

The Condicon of this Obligacon is such that if the above bound Thomas Faxson shall well & truly Administer upon the Estate of William Mullins (his Father in law) as far as the Court shall charge him & be accoumptable to this County Court when called for that then this Obligacon to be void & of none efect otherwise to stand & bee in full force & virtue

Signed Sealed & Delivrd in p^{r}sence of
Jno ffreke
ffreeGrace Bendall

Thomas Γ Faxson
his marke.

THOMAS GANNETT'S WILL AND INVENTORY †

[p. 12] The Last Will And Testament of Thomas Gann[att] of Bridgwater late Deceased Exhibited before the cour[t] of Asistants holden Att Plymouthe sixt of August 1655

June the 19th Ann^{o} : Dom 1655

The Last Will and Testament of Thomas Gannatt somtime Inhabitant of Duxburrow; Now liveing in Bridgwater being very weake of body but retaining my pfect sence and memory I comitt my soule to god that gave it and my body to the earth from whence It cam[e] Alsoe I give my goods as followeth; first I give my whole and proper estate houses lands Cattle moveable goods to my wife; onely that such Debts as I owe

* Transcribed from original document.

† Plymouth Colony Wills, Volume II, Part I, pages 12 and 13.

I Desire may bee faithfully Discharged; And I will and give to my brother Mathew Gannatt one shilling six pence to bee payed upon Demand; In Witnes wherof I have sett to my hand;

Thomas Gannatt his mark

Witnes heerof
Willam Brett
Willam Bassett
Thomas haward;

This following was ordered by the Court to be subjoyned to the Will of Thomas Gannett Deceased; recorded in the following page

Wheras the Will above mensioned is apprehended to fall short in fulnes of Law expressions : with reference to the lands Given by Thomas Gannett to his Wife Sarah; soe that shee can not safely make sale of it (as some Conceive) that the pson may not be wronged of her right wee that were witnesses to the said Will Can affeirme upon oath and will if need require; that hee gave the lands to her as the other Moveable goods : as the Will expresseth to be wholly att her Dispose and the Want of Law expression[s] with reference therunto to be Imputed to the Insufficiency of the p^r^son that made the Will being never accustomed to busines of that nature; and the Case being soe that no other healp Could be attained; The p^r^son that made the Will being one of the Witnesses

Witnes Willam Brett
Thomas haward

Plymouth October 28th 1669 *

Wee Willam Brett and Thomas haward of Bridgwater witnesses to the will of Thomas Gannett Deceased; Doe affeirme upon oath That the said Thomas Gannett Did give to his wife Sarah his Lands to be att her Dispose as the other Movable goods Taken upon oath in the Court held att New Plymouth The 28th Day of october 1669 Before mee Thomas Southworth Assistant

An Inventory Taken and made of the goods of Thomas Gannat[t] now Deceased att Bridgwater belonging to the towne of Duxburrow as followeth by Willam Bassett Thomas haward seni^r^ : Willam Brett July 10th Ann^o^ : Dom : 1655 and Exhibited to the court holden att Plymouth the sixt Day of August 1655 on the oath of Sarah Gannatt;

* The foregoing statement is written partly on the inside margin of the twelfth page and partly on the opposite page.

	ll	s	d
Imprimis one Cow	05	00	00
It one Cow	05	00	00
It one Cow	04	10	00
It one heifer	04	10	00
It 3 Calves	02	05	00
It 3 swine	03	00	00
It seaven bushells of Indian Corn	01	01	00
It one muskett	01	00	00
It one shott pouch	00	01	00
It one sword	00	10	00
It one bed	02	10	00
It one bed	01	00	00
It one rugge and blankett	00	06	00
It one Curtaine and fringe	00	06	00
It 2 bolsters	00	08	00
It 2 pillows	00	04	00
It one suite of clothes	01	00	00
It one Coate	00	10	00
It one Iron pott	00	12	00
It one Iron pott	00	07	00
It one brasse kettle	00	06	06
It one felling axe and two hoes	00	04	00
It one hoe	00	03	00
It 3 Iron Wedges	00	06	00
It one frying pan	00	02	00
It pte of one whipsaw	00	04	00
It one Trewell	00	00	09
[p. 13] It one spining wheel	00	02	00
It one Chist	00	10	00
It one Chist	00	04	00
It one box	00	04	00
It five trayes	00	05	06
It one Chaire	00	03	00
It one Cherne	00	04	00
It one earthen pan	00	00	09
It one earthen pan	00	00	09
It one kneading Trough	00	01	06
It 2 pailes	00	02	00
It one seive	00	01	02
It one seive	00	01	02
It one bowle	00	00	08
It one salt box	00	01	00
It one paire of pothangers	00	02	00
It one paire of potthookes	00	01	06
It one brasse ladle	00	01	06
It one grater	00	00	04
It one kandlesticke	00	00	10
It one tinn pan	00	00	10
It one tin pan	00	00	06
It one hammer	00	00	04
It one straining Dish	00	00	04
It 4 pewter spoones	00	00	08
It one pewter platter	00	04	00

It one pewter porringer	00	00	06
It one hatchell	00	10	00
It one Cheespresse	00	02	00
It 2 sythes	00	05	00
It one sneath	00	02	00
It one lamp	00	02	00
It one paire of pincers	00	*	0*
It one paire of scales	00	00	06
It one bell	00	00	06
It one Iron Ringe	00	00	06
It one hook	00	00	06
It one skillett	00	05	00
It 3 baggs	00	06	00
It 20 yards of linnin cloth	02	00	00
It 2 pillowbeers	00	03	00
It one Chaffing Dish	00	01	06
It one tubb	00	02	06
It one tin porringer	00	00	06
It one pewter pott	00	00	09
It 12 pound of shott	00	03	00
It one pitchprong	00	01	04
It one Tubb	00	01	00
It one hoe	00	00	06
It one hoe	00	00	
It 3 earthen potts	00	01	06
It one brush	00	01	02
It one tin pott	00	00	06
It one tin pott	00	00	06
It 2 earthen pots	00	00	04
It one bushell of wheat	00	04	06
It salt	00	01	06
Summa totalis	41	19	0*

[Letter of Administration]

Lres of Adminnestration are graunted unto Sarah the Wife of Thomas Gannett Deceased to Adminnester upon the Estate of the said Gannett and to pay the Debts &c [Court Orders, III : 86, under date of 7 August, 1655.]

WILLIAM SAVILL'S WILL AND INVENTORY

[p. 36†] The last Will & Testament of William Savel Senior : 19 : ffeb : 1668 :

These are to signify that I will & desire that my funerall & debts shall bee discharged out of my sole Estate & that done — I doe give & bequeath to my beloved wife Sarah Savel my House & halfe the Orchard during her life, shee bearing my name — But in Case the heire of this said House, which is my sonn Benjamin Savel, shall give to her yearely while

* Worn. † Suffolk County Probate Records, Volume VI.

shee bares my name, twenty shillings towards hyring of her a Chamber where shee pleases, & in Case shee live in Towne, my Three sonns, John, Samuel Benjamin Savel, shall provide & bring her fowre Coard of wood yearly, (during her name Savel) — And further my Three sonns named shall give unto my wife, a fatt Swine : 80 : weight, & Twenty bushells of Corne during her life bearing my name, And for what movables as a bed & what shee brought I leave with her as her Owne — And her Land & Bridg=water, with two Cowes that was my wives, And the Wintering of them soe long as shee beares my name.

I bequeath & give to my Sonn John Savel, shall have the whole House & barne & shop & tooles, stuffe as Timber pertaining to his trade with the Land also adjoyning, to His House as Pasture & close adjoyning with Dearings Lott, Six Acres upon the Hill, with Three Acres of marsh Land more or less that was Brother Bass — To my Sonn Samuell Savell, Benjamin & William Savell shall have the farme Land Equally divided betweene them, as upland swamp-meadow, & all Appurtenances & Priveledges thereto belonging — But my will is my three Eldest Sonns shall pay the remainder of my debt for Salter farme Each his Proportion alike — my will is that my Sonn John Savel & Benjamin, shall have an Equall Proportion of my stock & the Land at Bridgwater & at Quinipauge therefore they shall pay out their sisters Portions as Expressed — ffor my daughter Hannah Savell my will is that shee shall have my ffowre Acres of Land in the Old feild joyning to Barnabas Derrifeild for a debt of 13£ to her Content, they or Each of them may take the Land — Also I Give fforty pounds to my daughter Hannah to bee paid a yeare after my decease, by my then sonns John, Samuell & Benjamin — To my daughter Sarah Savell I Give 30£ (at Age 21) to bee pd by my Sonns John Samuell & Benjamin & for my movable Goods in my House I Give sonns & daughters an Equall Portion — ffor my Sonn Samuell Savell I Give William Veseys Lott adjoyning to dearings Lott, but this Lott must bee sattisfyed for out of my meadow at the farme, according to Contract before the Divission bee made by my Sonns — And also I give my sonn Benjamin Savell my dwelling House as formerly Expressed & my old barne Orchard & my bit of meadow adjoyning —

This my Will being declared I Give my Sonn John Savell Executo^r with my Brother Samuell Bass, for my daughter Hannah Savell, I leave the Care of her, to my Brother Bass, & my daughter Sarah Savel I leave to my wife but in Case my

Brother Bass & my Sonn John Savel shall see any ill Conveniency [p. 37] to follow my desire is that they shall take her & dispose of her to some sutable place, where shee may bee brought up in the Admonition of the Lord:

my Sonn William Savel is to live as an Apprentice, with his * sonn John Savel untill hee bee 21 : yeares : of Age, my will & Appointment is that in Case y^t^ any of my Sonns : Dye without issue the Land shall returne to the Brethren that survive

Thomas ffaxon Senio^r^, & William needham my will is should see this performed

Witnesses : Samuell Bass — William **W S** Savel
Edward * Quinsey — his marke

29 : July : 1669

Deacon Samuell Bass came into the Court, & publikly renounced his being Executo^r^ to this will & soe made Oath that having subscribed his name as a witnes to this instrument, was present & did at the day of the date thereof signe & publish the same to bee his last will & Testament, that when hee soe did was of a sound mind to his best knowledge.

Edw : Rawson Reccord^r^

26 : Aug^st^ : 1669

Edmond * Quinsey deposed that having subscribed his name as a wittnes to this instrument was present on the day of the date thereof, & did both heare & see Wm : Savel, to signe & publish the same to bee his last will & Testament, that when hee soe did hee was of a disposing mind —

Edw : Rawson Reccord^r^

[Vol. V, p. 148.†] A True Inventory of the Goods & Estate of William Savel, Senio^r^ deceased the 6th of Aprill : 1669 :

Imprs To wearing Apparrell	09	19
To 5 Cowes at 20£ : two Oxen at 10£	30	00
To : 2 : Oxen & Bull Calfe, 11£ . 10 : Swine : 12 : at 12sh	20	10
To : two horse 12£ : & Mares 3£, one horse at 3£	18	00
To bookes 10sh Quishions 25	01	05
To the House & barne & a bitt of meadow	90	00
Johns House Shop barne & Land about 3 Acres	120	00
To Dearings Lott & 6 Acres on the hill & 11 : Acres	66	00
To 3 Acres of salt marsh	30	00
To Land bought of mr Broadstreet	250	00
To 4 Acres of Land upon stony Hill	13	00
To Land at Bridge water 20£. Land at Quinaquagin 10£	30	00
To Land at Bridgwater	37	00

* Sic. † Suffolk County Probate Records.

To bedds Ruggs blanckets & sheets	20	16	
To 5 : Bushells of Rye 20sh : 40 : Bushells of Indian 6£:	07	00	
To : a brass Kettle 3£ 10sh, iron pott 10sh Andirons 20sh	05	00	
To 5 : pewter platters 20sh, bason & Tinn ware 4sh 6d	01	04	6
To spitt & trammells : 11sh, (14)d linnen yarne 25sh	01	16	
To Tables stooles chayres chests & wooden ware	08	04	
To Cart wheeles plow chaynes, with joyners stuffe & Ceder boults	19	03	6
To shooes 8£ 10sh, 4 Axes : 16sh, pickax 18s	10	04	
To sickles wedges 11sh, hand hoe 4sh . flax 10sh . old iron 4sh	01	09	
To . 25 . Acres of English Corne sowed at	25	00	
To : 20 . Acres of Indian planted 15£ : meate 30sh	16	10	
To sacks morter pestel 25sh, 8 : Bushells malt 28sh	02	13	
To : ironing box with heaters & pease hooke	00	04	
	798	17	
Debts due out of the Estate	95	15	6
Due to the Estate	12	08	06

26 : Augst : 1669. Present : major Generall John Leveret mr Edw : Tyng & Reccordr

John Savel deposed that this paper Containes a true Inventory of the Estate of William Savel to the best of his knowledge that when hee knowes more hee will discover it :

Edw : Rawson Recordr :

[Agreement of the Heirs]

Articles of Agreement betweene mrs Savel & her Children :

Articles of Agreement betweene John Savel Samuell Savel & Benjamin Savel of the one part, & Sarah Savell Relict of William Savel deceased of the other party as followeth :

That whereas the Will of Our deceased ffather doth not give soe full sattisfaction to Our mother with Respects to her future maintenance therefore for the Continuance of love & peace betweene us wee John Savel & Benjamin Savel doe hereby bind Our selves that wee will freely pay & performe unto her as foll :

1 : That according to Our ffathers Will, Our mother shall have her whole Estate Returned to her that shee brought to our ffather for her owne use & to dispose of forever with a Chest with drawers & a Cubbert —

2ly : That what the will Expresseth & bindeth us to the performance of for her maintinence wee will truly & faithfully performe, — Also whereas the will Expresseth Twenty bushells of Corne & fowre Cord of wood wee doe hereby Engage to pay itt in these kinds, Three bushells of wheate & three bushells of Rye, & Six bushells of malt & Eight Bushells of

Indian & to pay when shee hath occation, Provided it bee at such times as it will not bee much damage to them — Also whereas the will bindeth us to winter two Cowes for her yearly wee doe hereby Engage to summer them also as wee doe Our Owne yearly during her widdow-hood —

3ly That in Case God soe dispose that Our mother Change her Condition by marriage that then, the former Engagements being voyd wee doe hereby Engage & bind Our selves to pay or Cause to bee paid unto Our mother Sarah Savell the full & just sume of ffowre pounds a yeare, to bee paid Twenty shillings in porke & Three pounds in Corne at price Currant duringe the tearme of her naturall life, Provided that that which is returned to her as her owne Estate shall still Continue soe to bee, her Owne to dispose of forever as formerly Expressed

I Sarah Savel Widdow & Relict of William Savell, deceased, with respect to the above said premisses & Obligations doe hereby declare my selfe to bee sattisfyed & Contented, & doe hereby Engage my selfe that the aforesaid Obligations being performed I will noe way trouble nor molest my Children neither by requiring my thirds of the Estate or suing for the same in a Course of Law or any other way —

[p. 38] And for the true performance of the abovesaid p^r^misses wee both parties doe hereby bind Ourselves, our heires Executo^rs^ Administrato^rs^ & assignes & doe hereunto set Our hands & affix Our seales the : 14 : June : 1669

Signed Sealed & delivered	John Savell & a Seale
in the presence of —	Samuell Savel & a Seale
Thomas ┏ ffaxon	Benja : Savel & a Seale
his marke	Sarah Savel & a Seale
Christopher Webb	

This Agreement Ouned by Sarah Savel & John Savel, in the County Court the 29 : July : 1669 : & by Samuell Savel & Benjamin, the : 26 : August 1669

• As Attests : Edw : Rawson Reccord^r^

THOMAS FAXON'S ESTATE

[LETTER OF ADMINISTRATION]

[Suff. Prob., IX : 19] L^res^ Adm^con^

At a County Court held at Boston . by Adjournm^t^ 23° Decemb^r^ 1680.

ffull power & Authority to Administer all and singular . the goods Estate and Credits of Thomas ffaxton . late of Brantry deced is granted unto Sarah his Relict and Joannah . ffisher . widow his onely daughter . (untill his GrandSon . Thomas ffaxton . come of age when the matter . may bee further considered of) they giving Security to Administer the sd Estate according to Law, and exhibiting an Inventory thereof upon their Oaths Security is accordingly given.

Isa Addington Clr

Isa Addington Clr

[Bond of Administrators *]

Know all men by these presents that Sarah Faxon widdow and Christopher Webb her Surety Joannah Fisher widdow and peter Woodward her Surety stand firmly bound and obliged unto Edward Tyng Esqr Treasuror for the County of Suffolke in the Sume of Eighteen hundred pounds To bee paid unto the sd Treasuror his Successors in sd Office or Assignes in currant money of New : England To the true payment whereof wee do respectively binde and oblige our Selves our heires Execrs and Admrs firmly by these presents . Sealed with our Seales Dated in Boston . 24d Decembr 1680.

The Condicon of this present Obligation is such that if the above bounden . Sarah ffaxon . and Joannah Fisher do well and truly Administer . all and singular the Estate of Thomas ffaxon late of Brantery deced (husband of the sd Sarah and ffather of the sd Joanna) according to Law and shalbee accountable and responsable for the same unto the County Court for Suffolke when called there unto then this Obligation to bee void and of none Effect or else to abide and remain in full force and virtue

Signed Sealed & Delivrd
in ye presence of
Daniell ffisher
Isa Addington Clr

Sarah faxson (seal)
Christopher Webb (seal)
Johan fficher (seal)
Peter Woodward (seal)

[Thomas Faxon's Inventory †]

Braintree the 29th of [Decembr] 1680

An Inventory of the houses [Lands] Chattles goods and estate of Thomas ffax[t]on Deceasd [late] of Braintree

Imprs : house & barne outhouses with the land adioining	400	00	00
It . hollybush . field	050	00	00
to land at Bridgwater	‡	00	00

* Transcribed from the original document.

† Transcribed from the original document, with missing parts supplied from the record in Suff. Prob., IX : 34, 35.

‡ "060" has been crossed out.

It fower oxen	014	00	00
It a house & land at the Towne	008	00	00
It Sixe cowes	015	00	00
It a bull & heifer 3 yeers old	003	00	00
It two calves.	001	00	00
It three horses	009	00	00
It . two mares & two colts	002	00	00
It ten runninge Swine	003	00	00
It fatt Swine	005	10	00
It fower sheep *	001	00	00
It corne & hay in the barne	007	00	00
It beddinge 3 beds as they stand.	008	00	00
It 7 paire of sheets	005	06	00
to provissian butter cheese porck beefe 4 sacks	002	05	00
It linnen	000	17	00
It woolen yerne : woole tow yerne	002	00	00
It 3 chests 3 o[ld be]dsteds	001	00	00
It brasse 7 vessells & peuter 20 peices	004	05	00
It Iron pots tramells potthooks spit andirons tongs Iron peele posnetts frying pan : chasting dish sheep sheers	002	05	00
It paire of Stilliards	000	08	00
It 3 guns 2 swords : cutlash :	001	10	00
It table forme Joynstoole 4 chayrs.	000	15	00
It wooden ware	001	10	00
It bookes	000	12	00
It two chests 2 cubbords	000	15	00
It wearinge aparell . 2 cushions	003	00	00
It cart wheeles cart tire boxes yoke & chaines	005	10	00
It share & coulter	000	07	00
It sett of hoopes for cart wheeles	000	05	00
It axes beetleringes wedgs . sledg . Iron crows	000	16	00
tooles	001	00	00
old Iron	000	10	0
to a cow hide	000	07	02
Due from Jno Brick & Henry Leadbettr . by specially money when the times of paimt Come	300	00	00
Due fro Sam Howard money	003	10	00
Due fro Robert Stanton money	004	00	00
Due from Willm Savell money	010	00	00
The totall	859	03	02

Due from this estate
To Theophilus Curtis
To rates
other debts uncertaine

Taken & aprized by us. Richard Ellis † Samuell Tompson Christopher Webb

The widdows bed as it stands	04	00	00
Twenty sixe sheep . claimed by the grandson Thomas ffaxon.	06	10	00

Apprized by Richard Ellis Samuell Thompson Christopher Webb.

* This entire item was crossed out and does not appear in the record.

† "Jno ffrench senr" has been crossed out and "Richard Ellis" interlined.

Sarah Faxton Admx made oath in Court . 26o Janr . 80 . that this is a just and true Inventory of the Estate of her late husband Thos Faxton deced to her best knowledge and that wn more appeares shee will adde it.

Isa Addington Clr

[Petition of the Widow *]

To the honrd County Court sittinge In Boston by adiourment Decembr 19th 1683

The humble petition of Sarah ffaxen Widow & Relict of Thomas ffaxen late of Brantree Deceasd . Humbly Sheweth .

That whereas your honrs were pleased to grant administration to the estate of sd Thomas ffaxen to myselfe & Joana ffisher his only Daughter untill Thomas ffaxen son of Richard ffaxen Came of age for the preservinge the estate & that now the sd Thomas the sd heire is at full age your petitionr Humbly prays that your honrs would be pleased to ffree your petitionr of administration That the heire may be posesd of the estate your petitionr beinge unable to undergoe such trouble wch will oblige your petitionr evr to pray & subscribe myselfe your Honrs Humble servant

Sarah ffaxen

---

* Transcribed from the original document.

THE ESTATES OF WILLIAM[2] MULLINS AND HIS DAUGHTER SARAH[3] (MULLINS) (GANNETT) (SAVILL) FAXON AND OF HER THREE HUSBANDS

In our January issue we printed the settlements of the estates of William[2] Mullins (*William*[1]) and of his daughter Sarah's three husbands, Thomas Gannett, William Savill and Thomas Faxon. In this issue we give the settlement of Sarah Faxon's estate, with other records relating to her father and herself.

The earliest reference to William[2] Mullins on the Plymouth Colony records is under date of 2 October, 1637, when ten acres of upland were granted to Edmund Hawes at Duxbury, lying across Green Harbor Path next to William Mullins on the south side.*

On 6 April, 1640, ten acres of upland were granted to William Mullins across Green Harbor Path, between the lands of Edmund Hawes and John Tisdall.†

He next appears, as an inhabitant of Duxbury, in the list of males between the ages of sixteen and sixty, taken in August, 1643.‡

Aspinwall's Notarial Record, under the year 1648 (old style), contains the following note about him:

> 15. (11)§ Wm Mullings & John Cuddington did uppon oath testifie that Hugh Burt of Linne was sonne of John Burt some times of Dorking in Surrey deceased and Elder Brother of Tho: Burt late of Dorking aforesd deceased. taken uppon oath before John Winthrop Governor: [Boston Record Com. Reports, xxxii: 190]

* Plym. Col. Rcds., Court Orders, I: 127.

† Ibid., I: 229.

‡ Plym. Col. Rcds., Lists of Freemen, p. 31.

§ 15 January, 1648/9.

Under date of 3 June, 1662, the Colony Court granted him land at what is now Middleborough,* and in the Plymouth Colony Deeds [III : 21] we find that he received the twenty-third lot in the division. This land is probably that mentioned in the will of William Nelson, of Plymouth, dated 31 October, 1673, in which Nelson bequeaths to his son William several tracts of land at Middleborough, including meadow bought of William Mullins.†

"william mullings dyed the 12 m° 12 . 1672,"‡ at Braintree, probably at the house of his daughter, Sarah, the wife of Thomas Faxon. As February was the twelfth month in old style dating, this date should be read 12 February, 1672/3.

As already stated, Sarah³ Mullins was married three times and outlived her last husband. The record of her first marriage, to Thomas Gannett of Duxbury and Bridgewater, has not been found, but her second and third marriages and the deaths of her second and third husbands were recorded at Braintree. The records are as follows:

[I : 125] william Savill and Sarah gannitt were maried the (6) (9) 1655 by maior Autherton of dorchester
[I : 25] william Savill dyed the 2 m° 6 1669
[I : 126] Thomas ffackson & Sarah Savill widow were Maried 7th m° 5th 1670 by Mr Tynge
[I : 35] Thomas ffaxen died Novembr 23th — 1680.

The record of the settlement of the estate of William² Mullins [ante, p. 37] proves that Thomas Faxon's wife Sarah Savill was the daughter of William Mullins. As she was a widow when she married Faxon and the records show that William Savill married "Sarah Gannitt," it is necessary to prove that "Sarah Gannitt" and Sarah the widow of Thomas Gannett were one and the same person. Thomas Gannett died between 19 June and 10 July, 1655, leaving everything to his wife Sarah, except a shilling and sixpence to his brother Matthew Gannett, and in October, 1669 (just after the death of Sarah's second husband, William Savill), the Plymouth Court ordered recorded certain additional evidence § in regard to the terms of Gannett's will, in order to enable the widow to legally dispose of her first husband's lands. That she later conveyed at least part of these lands to her brother-in-law Matthew Gannett, and had also changed her name to Faxon, is shown by the following entry on the "Records of the Purchasers of Bridgewater Book I" [page 22]:

* Court Orders, IV : 19. † Plym. Col. Wills, Vol. IV, Pt. I, p. 54.

‡ Braintree Records, I : 25. § Ante, p. 39.

The Lands of Goody ffackson who was somtime the [*] of Thomas Gannett who was before God tooke him Away an Inhabitaunt And A perchacer hear in the towne of Bridgwater whose lands that are Laide out Are as followeth

And now Mathew Ganuts in the yeare 168$\frac{6}{7}$

The chain of evidence is complete and it has been proved that the widow Sarah Faxon had married successively Thomas Gannett, William Savill and Thomas Faxon. Her will, printed at the end of this article, made 13 August, 1694, and proved 25 November, 1697, states her age as seventy-three years. She was, therefore, born about 1621. As she gave small legacies to her "Cousin, Ruth Webb," who was the daughter of John and Ruth (Alden) Bass, and to her stepson † Benjamin Savill and his wife Lydia, and then directed that the remainder of her estate should be divided among her "nearest relations" it is certain that she left no descendants, and no record has been found to show that she ever bore any children.

The names Mullins, Mullings, Munnings and Manning were badly mixed up by the carelessness of recording clerks, and a study of the original records, the details of which we have not space to give, proves that John Lawton married, in 1659, not "Johanna Mullings widow," ‡ but Joanna the widow of George Munnings. This effectually disposes of the claim that she was the widow of a son of William[2] Mullins.

The Boston records give the marriage, on 7 May, 1656, of a William Mullings to the widow Ann Bell, by Richard Bellingham, Deputy Governor.‡ This was probably William[2] Mullins, although complete proof of his identity has not yet been found. Ann Bell was the widow of Thomas Bell, of Boston, who died 7 June, 1655.‡ The entry, "Anne wife of William Munnings deceased the 4th of December," 1661, probably was intended for Anne "Mullings." ‡

In conclusion I desire to acknowledge the great assistance I have received from Mr. Edward H. Whorf, of our Committee on Publication, who has supplied the transcripts of the Braintree records, made by him from the original volume, and has freely placed at my disposal the results of an exhaustive study of the original records undertaken for the purpose of unraveling the Mullins, Mullings, Munnings and Manning tangle.

* "Husband" was crossed out and "relict" was undoubtedly written above, but all of the latter word except the first letter has been worn off.

† "Son In law" was used at that time in place of the modern term "stepson."

‡ Ninth Report Boston Record Commissioners, pages 51, 56, 71, 81. Also Suffolk Co. Deeds, Vol. III, pages 390–2.

[SARAH FAXON'S WILL *]

The last will and Testament of Sarah Faxson (Widdow of Thomas Faxson late of Braintree Deceas'd :) aged Seaventy three yeares, being weak in body, butt : well In understanding & memory, wch is as followeth

My Soule I give into the hands, of my most gracious god & mercifull father : and Jesus christ my deare redeemer, whom I trust hath redeemed itt, from all iniquity, & from eternall misserie My bodie I give to the earth, to be decently buryed, my worldly goods I give as followeth

Item I give & bequeath, to my well beloved Cousin, Ruth Webb the wife of Peter Webb of Braintree my best feather bed with the broadest bolster & the teaking pillow with the rugg & blanckett and the best paire of Sheets, and a paire of Pillow beers one dowlis one homespun, allso a bellmettle Chafingdish &c : to her & her heirs for ever

Item I give & bequeath to my Daughter In law lidia Savell the wife of Benjamin Savell of Braintree my other feather bead and after her Decease to her Daughter Sarah Savell : &c

The rest of my goods or estate, after funerall Charges are paide to be divided among my nearest relations

And this to be my last will : made the thirteenth day of August one thousand Six hundred ninty & foure, of which will & testament I make and Constitute, my Son In law Benjamin Savell of Braintree executor :

Signed & Sealed In the presence of :
Hannah webb
mary webb

Sarah fexton her mark †

Suffolke ss. By the Honble William Stoughton Esqr Judge of Probate &c

The within written Instrument being presented as the last Will and Testament of Sarah Fexton late of Brantrey Widow dece^d^ by Benjamin Savell Executor therein named. Hannah Webb and Mary Webb the two Witnesses thereto personally appeared before me and made Oath That they were present and did see the s^d^ Sarah Fexton signe and seale, and heard

* Transcribed from the original document in the Suffolk Co., Mass., Probate Files.

† Above this name are what appear to be two attempts of the testatrix to sign her own name. Both have been crossed out.

her publish the same as her last Will and Testament, she being then of sound disposing mind to their best discerning. Boston November 25th 1697.

Jurat Cor Wm Stoughton

[Letter of Administration]

[Suff. Prob., XI : 372]

The Probate of the Will of Sarah Faxon late of Brantrey Widow deced And Administration granted thereon unto Benjamin Savell the Executor in the Same Will named.

William Stoughton Esqr Commissionated by the Governour wth the advice and consent of the Council of his Matys Province of ye Massachusetts Bay in New England For the granting of Probate of Wills and Letters of Administration within the County of Suffolke &c . To all unto whome these presents shall come Greeting . Know yee That on the Twenty fifth day of November in the year of our Lord one Thousand Six hundred ninety Seven Before me at Boston in the County aforesd The Will of Sarah Faxon late of Brantrey within the sd County Widow deced to these presents annexed was proved approved and allowed, Who having while She lived and at the time of her death Goods, Chattels, Rights or Credits in the aforesd County and elsewhere within this Province, For the obtaining whereof The Administration of all and Singular the Goods . Chattels, Rights and Credits the Sd deced and her Will in any manner concerning, was committed unto her Son in Law Benjamin Savell Executor in the Sd Will named . Well & truely [p. 373] Truely to administer the Same, And to make a true and perfect Inventory of all and Singular the Goods, Chattels, Rights and Credits of the sd deced And to exhibit the Same into the Registers Office of the aforesd County according to Law Also to render a plain and true Accompt of his sd Administration upon Oath In Testimony whereof I have hereunto Set my hand and the Seal of the sd Office of Probate Dated at Boston aforesd the day and yeare aforesaid.

Isa Addington Regr Wm Stoughton

THE RECORD OF GOVERNOR BRADFORD'S BAPTISM, ON THE PARISH REGISTER AT AUSTERFIELD

By George Ernest Bowman

Governor William Bradford was born at Austerfield, Yorkshire, England, and in the Parish Register of St. Helen's Church is preserved the following record of his baptism: "William Sone of Willia Bradfourth baptized the xixth day of March Anno dm . 1589." This entry is the last one on the page of the register shown in the accompanying illustration, which is taken from the pamphlet "Austerfield: The Cradle of the Pilgrim Fathers. An Appeal to the American People," issued by the English committee in charge of the restoration of the church in 1897.

The illustration shows the following baptismal records besides that of Governor Bradford, the first two evidently in the year 1587:

"Willia Sone of Robert Bradfourth baptized . 22 . of Septeb
Alice daught^{r} of Willia Bradfourth baptized . 30 . of Noveb
Anno Dom . 1588.
ffrancys Son of Thomas Wright baptized . 27 . of March
Alice daught^{r} of John Richardson baptized . 18 of August.
Alice daught^{r} of Willia Lynsley baptized . 25 of februarie.
William Sone of Willia Wright baptized . 10 . of March.
Anno . Dom . 1589.
Alice daught^{r} of Ralfe Walsh baptized . 27 . of March.
Jane daughter of Robt Stanton baptized . 9 . of May
Guy Son of Bryan Chatbourne baptized . 4 . of October.
Willia & Margaret . Son & daught^{r} of Robt Button baptiz . 12 . of Septem
Jane daught^{r} of George Hanson baptized . 14 of October
Robt Son of Anne Hurton baptized . 5 of december.
Thomas Son of Thomas Morton baptized . first of March"

Willin Sone of Robert Bradfourth baptized. 22. of Septe
Alice daughter of Willin Bradfourth baptized. 30. of Nove
Anno Domi. 1588.
Frances Son of Thomas Wright baptized. 27. of Marc
Alice daughter of John Richardson baptized. 18 of August
Alice daughter of Willin Lynsley baptized. 25 of februarie
William Sone of Willin Wright baptized. 10. of March.
Anno Domi. 1589.
Alice daughter of Ralf Walsh baptized. 27. of March
Jane daughter of Robt Stanton baptized. 9. of May
Guy Son of Bryan Chatburne baptized. 4. of October
Willin & Margret Son & daughter of Robt Button baptiz. 11. of Septem
Jane daughter of George Mansbu baptized. 14 of October
Robt Son of Anne Hirton baptized. 5. of December
Thomas Son of Thomas Morton baptized first of March
William Sone of Willin Bradfourth baptized the
xixth day of March Anno Dom 1589.

THE RECORD OF GOVERNOR BRADFORD'S BAPTISM

In examining these records it is necessary to bear constantly in mind that the dates are in "old style" and that when they were written the year began on the twenty-fifth of March and ended on the twenty-fourth of the following March. This is well illustrated by the following baptisms: Francis Wright was baptized 27 March, 1588, which was the third day of that year; and, nearly a year later, William Wright was baptized, on 10 March, 1588, which was just two weeks from the end of the same "old style" year. Seventeen days after William Wright's baptism, and in the same month, but in the next year, 1589, Alice Walsh was baptized, on 27 March, 1589.

William Bradford was baptized 19 March, 1589, old style, or 29 March, 1590, according to our present calendar; and since it was at that period customary to baptize infants within a very few days of their birth it is safe to assume that he was born in the month of March, 1590, new style, and was, therefore, aged sixty-seven years and nearly two months when he died at Plymouth on Saturday, 19 May, 1657 (new style), just sixty-seven years, one month and twenty days after he was baptized.

Among the baptisms on the page illustrated we find two others which deserve attention — those of William Button and William Wright. I have not been able to identify these two as the William Button, Dr. Samuel Fuller's servant, who died on the Mayflower before she arrived at Cape Cod, and the William Wright who died at Plymouth in 1633; but it is interesting to note that Governor Bradford, Dr. Fuller and William Wright of Plymouth married sisters.

THE SETTLEMENT OF NATHANIEL[2] SOULE'S ESTATE

Transcribed from the Original Documents and Records

By George Ernest Bowman

Nathaniel[2] Soule (*George*[1]) of Dartmouth died intestate and his widow Rose was appointed administratrix. Her appointment was not recorded, but her bond, dated 12 October 1699, is still preserved in the Bristol County, Mass., Registry of Probate. The only other original papers in the files relating to this estate are the inventory, which was not recorded, and the account of the administratrix. The latter document was recorded in Volume II, page 47, of the probate records, and the division of the personal estate on pages 56 and 57 of the same volume.

It probably is merely a curious coincidence that the wife of Nathaniel[2] Soule should be named Rose and that their fourth son should bear the name of Miles, as I have found no evidence that Capt. Standish had either a daughter or a granddaughter named Rose. I have been unable to get any clue to the maiden name of Nathaniel[2] Soule's wife.

[The Bond of the Administratrix *]

Know all men by these presents that we Rose Soul of Dartmouth in the County of Bristoll in the Province of the Masachusett Bay in New-England widow & Relict of Nathaniel Soul late of said Dartmouth Deceased and Joseph Allen & Natheniel Soul Both of said Dartmouth Do stand Bounden unto John Saffin Esqr Judge of Probate of wills &c : within the County of Bristoll in the full sum of three Hundred & Sixty pounds Currant Silver money in New England afores^d^ To be payd to him the said John Saffin or Successor in said office To which Payment well & truely to be made we bind our selves & Either of us by him self Joyntly & Severally for & in the whole our & Either & Every of our heires Executors & Adm^rs^ firmly by these presents Dated in Bristoll this twelveth day of october Ano Domini 1699 & in the Eleventh year of his Majestyes Reigne

The Condition of this present obligation is such that whereas Administration is Granted uto the above Bounden Rose Soul upon the Estate of Nathaniel Soul late of said Dartmouth dec^d^ Intestate If therefore the said Rose Soul Administratrix Shall Bring into the Regist^rs^ office for the County aboves^d^ a true & perfect Inventory of all & Singuler ye goods Chattells Credits & Estate left by the said Dec^d^ at or before the Tenth day of Novemb^r^ Next & shall well & truely Administ^r^ upon & Duely Dispose of all & Singul^r^ the goods Chattells Credits & Estate of the said Dec^d^ to all & Singuler the person & persons to whom of Right it doth pertain according law and shall Render a true & plain accompt of her Administration upon oath at or before the tenth day of November one thousand Seven Hundred without fraud or farther Delay then this obligation to be Null & voyd or Els to stand abide & be in full power force & vertue in the law whatsoever.

Signed sealed & Delivered	the **O** marke
in ye presence of	of Rose Soul. (Seal)
Joseph waterman	Joseph Allen (Seal)
the mark of	nathaniell Soule (Seal)
william **X** Makepeace	

*** Transcribed from the original document, which was not recorded.**

[Nathaniel[2] Soule's Inventory *]

An Inventory of the estate of nathanel Sole desesed of Dartmouth

3 oxen prised at	12	00	00
one ox	1	00	00
7 coues	17	10	00
2 steres 3 yere old	05	00	00
4 hefers 3 yer old	07	10	00
5 hefers 2 yere old	07	10	00
6 yerling	06	00	00
2 booels	02	10	00
6 Calefs	03	00	00
3 sheepe 3 lames	01	7	00
2 horses 1 mar	06	10	00
2 Coonnows	00	10	00
2 goones	00	16	00
Plow taklin ieren bare sith ieren lomber	01	00	00
2 Potes 2 Cetels	00	18	00
1 beede	01	05	00
2 mares 1 hors	04	00	00
one other Bed & furniture	02	10	00
houes and land	120	00	00
Sume	£ 194	16	00

Joseph Allen
Jonathan Devell
nathanel Poter
his mark

Memorandum that Rose Sole Adminis^r : did on the Twelveth Day of Octobr 1699 appear before me Jno Saffin Esqr Judge of Probate of wills &c and made oath to the truth of this Inventory and that when she knowes more she will Reveale it that it may be Recorded

John Cary Regist^r — Coram Jno Saffin

Brought in to be Aded unto ye above written I[nv]entory in Severall stocks of Bees	02	00	0
A Debt aded more octob^r 10 : 1700	01	00	0
	197	16	

[The Account of the Administratrix †]

The Accompt of Rose Soul Administratrix of or unto the Estate of her late Husband Nathaniel Soule late of Dartmouth Deceased Exhibitted this tenth day of october 1700 :

* Transcribed from the original document, which was not recorded.

† Transcribed from the original document, the worn parts being completed from the Probate Records, II : 47.

The said Administratrix is Deb^r :

A by the Inventory upon file the sum of	197	16	0
℣ Contra : Cred^t :			
payd to Doct^r : Arnold :	03	2	8
To m^r Ebenezer Brenton : as p^r Recept	05	16	0
To Thomas waite	02	01	0
To Joseph Allen Junr :	00	10	0
To ffunerall Charges	01	00	0
To procureing Lett^r & bond : & Expences at the same time	00	16	0
To Jonathan Devill	00	02	0
To Nathaniel Potter Junr	00	02	6
To Hugh Mousher	00	03	6
To Provission in the House	02	05	0
To Cloathing for the ffamiley	06	10	0
To Rates payde to Constable Gifford	01	00	0
	£ 23	8	8
To the Ballance of this accompt Remaineing Due thus far as the Accompt is stated the sume of	174	7	4
	£ 197	16	0

Memorandum that on the Tenth Day of octobr 1700 Rose Soal Administratrix of the Estate abovesd appeared before me Jno Saffin Esqr Judge of Probate of Wills &c and made Oath to the truth of this acco[mp]t wch is by me Allowed and approved & [ordered to be] Recorded

John Cary Regist^r : Jno Saffin

Entered & Recorded in ye 2^d Book folio 47 : March ye 19th : day : 1702 By John Cary Regist^r :

[Division of the Personal Estate]

[II : 56 *] Whereas we the subscriberes were Comissioned by John Saffin Esqr Judge of Probate of wills &c . for the County of Bristoll in ye Province of the Massachusett Bay . by a Comission under his hand & seale of his office dated the 16th day of Aprill 1702 to make a Just & Equal Division of the Estate both goods & Chattells left by Natha^ll : Soule late of Dartmoth Deceased

(1) We set forth unto Rose Soul the widow as her Thirds of moveables one Mare two . three year old steers a two year old Bull a two year old Heifer a three year old heifer two Cows, two year old heiffers one year old Bull one yearling steer, to a bed & furniture 2£ : 10^s : 00^d . to Cash 00 11^s 00

* Bristol County Probate Records.

(2) We Divided and set forth unto Nathaniel Soul the Eldest son as his Dubble Portion or share, of sd Goods & Chattells A Brown ox . a black whiteface Cow A Dark brown heyfer, two Connows one Gunn . two pots, one horss whit faced ox . Little Red Cow a brown two year old heifer one bed.

(3) We all Divided & sett forth unto Silvanus Soul the second son as his part of sd Estate one pyed two year old heyfer a young pyed Cow, a black Cow A pyed yearling heifer a Red yearling heifer two stocks of bees

(4) We allso set forth and Divided unto Jacob Soul the Third sonne A Cheery Cow . a Red Cow a two year old heifer, a white faced two year old steere A Red yearling stage Plow Tacklin, Iron Lumber, two sithes a Iron barr & some wooden lumber

(5) We allsoe set forth & Divided unto Miles Soul the fourth son one old Cow a wild Cow a blew Cow . a stock of Bees two Kettles a red yearlin heyfer a black yearling stage & nine shilling Cash whereunto we have set our hands & seales this fifteenth day of May 1702

William Southworth (Seal)
Gershom Woodell (Seal)
Job winslow (Seal)

The totall sum of Each Divission to each Respective party is as followeth vizt

	£	s	d
to ye widow Rose Soul ye sum of	18	02	10
To Nathaniel Soule Eldest son his Dubble portion	14	10	04
To Silvanus Soul his part	07	05	02
To Jacob Soule his part	07	05	02
To Miles Soule his part	07	05	02
suma :	£ 54	08	08

[p. 57] Bristoll Septemb^r^ 10th 1702

This is presented as the Division of the personall Estate of Natha^ll^ Soul late of Dartmouth Dec^d^ : (the Division of the land being suspended for that they are not fully divided by the propriettors of sd town :) which Division as above mentioned being Examined by John Saffin Esqr Judge of Probate of wills &c : within the County of Bristoll is by him Aproved & Allowed thus far and ordered to be putt upon Record :

John Cary Regist^r^ : John Saffin

Thus Entered Octob^r^ . 17th : 1702 by John Cary Record^r^.

THE MAYFLOWER MARRIAGE RECORDS AT LEYDEN AND AMSTERDAM

DURING the month of February, 1905, the Massachusetts Society's former Governor, Mr. Morton Dexter, at the request of the Editor of this magazine personally supervised the photographing of all the marriage records of Mayflower Passengers which have been found at Leyden and Amsterdam. Mr. Dexter has also furnished us with the copies of the Dutch entries and with the English translations.

The marriage records which have been found are as follows: Isaac Allerton's first marriage; William Bradford's first marriage (both Leyden and Amsterdam records photographed); Francis Cooke's; Dr. Samuel Fuller's second and third marriages; Degory Priest's; William White's; Edward Winslow's first marriage. We shall reproduce at least one of these records, with a copy of the Dutch entry and its translation, in each issue until all have been printed.

I. DEGORY PRIEST AND ISAAC ALLERTON

Perhaps the most interesting record is that of a double marriage at Leyden, of Degory Priest to the widow Sarah (Allerton) Vincent and of the latter's brother, Isaac Allerton, to Mary Norris, which forms the subject of our illustration.*

The banns of these two couples were published on the same days, Saturday, 8, 15 and 22 October, 1611, and they were married on Friday, 4 November, 1611.†

Sarah (Allerton) Vincent was Isaac Allerton's sister. After

* Leyden Records, Echt Book B., folio 4.

† All of these dates are in "New Style," adopted by the Dutch in 1583.

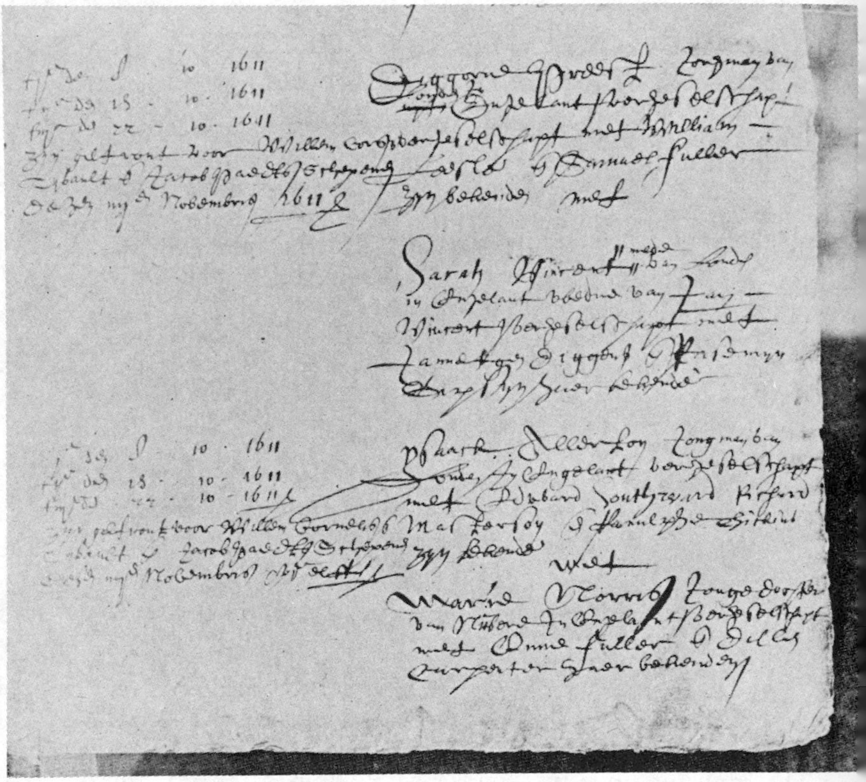

MARRIAGE RECORD OF DEGORY PRIEST AND ISAAC ALLERTON

the death of Degory Priest she married, for her third husband, Godbert Godbertson, whose first marriage was recorded on the same page with Dr. Samuel Fuller's third marriage and will be shown in the reproduction of the latter.

[The Dutch Entries]

t j^{e} de 8 . 10 1611 t ij^{e} de 15 . 10 . 1611 t iij^{e} de 22 . 10 . 1611 zyn getrout voor Willem Corsn Tybault & Jacob Paedts Schepene Dezen iiij^{e} Novembris 1611	Diggorie Preest Jongman van Londe In Engelant Vergeselschapt vergeselchapt met William Leesle & Samuel Fuller zyn bekende met Sarah Vincent mede van Londe in Engelant wedue van Jan Vincent Vergeselschapt met Jannetge Diggens & Rasemyn Gipsyn haer bekende

t j^{e} de 8 . 10 . 1611 t ij^{e} de 15 . 10 . 1611 t iij^{e} de 22 . 10 . 1611 zyn getrout voor Willem Cornelison Tybault & Jacob Paedts Schepene Dese iiij^{e} Novembris xvi^{e} elfte	Isaack Allerton Jongman van Londe In Engelant vergeselschapt met Edward Southward Richard Masterson & Ranulphe Thickins zyn bekende met Marie Norris Jonge dochter van Nubere In Engelant Vergeselschapt met Anne Fuller & Dille Carpenter haer bekenden

[The English Translations]

Degory Priest, unmarried man, from London, in England, accompanied by William Lisle and Samuel Fuller, his acquaintances, with Sarah Vincent, also from London, in England, widow of John Vincent, accompanied by Jane Thickins and Rosamond Jepson, her acquaintances.

They were married before William Cornelison Tybault and Jacob Paedts, sheriffs, this 4th November, 1611.*

Isaac Allerton, unmarried man, from London, in England, accompanied by Edward Southworth, Richard Masterson & Randall Thickins, his acquaintances, with Mary Norris, single woman, from Newbury, in England, accompanied by Anne Fuller and Dille (Priscilla?) Carpenter, her acquaintances.

They were married before William Cornelison Tybault and Jacob Paedts, sheriffs, this 4th November, 1611.*

* The entries "t je de 8 . 10 . 1611" &c. refer to the first, second and third dates of publication of the banns.

GOVERNOR BRADFORD'S ACCOUNT OF NEW ENGLAND *

[THE following lines, having some relation to the soil, the productions and the history of the country are now first printed on that

* These lines (including the introductory note) are reprinted from the "Collections of the Massachusetts Historical Society. For February, 1794," where they follow the concluding portion of Governor Bradford's Letter Book.

account, and not for any poetical beauties to be discovered in them —they may afford some entertainment; and as they seem to be within the views of the Society, they are submitted to the public.]

A Descriptive *and* Historical *Account of* New England *in verse; from a MS. of William Bradford, Governour of Plymouth Colony.*

(A FRAGMENT)

Famine once we had ——————
But other things God gave us in full store,
As fish and ground nuts, to supply our strait,
That we might learn on providence to wait;
And know, by bread man lives not in his need,
But by each word that doth from God proceed.
But a while after plenty did come in,
From his hand only who doth pardon sin.
And all did flourish like the pleasant green,
Which in the joyful spring is to be seen.

Almost *ten* years we lived *here* alone,
In other places there were few or none;
For *Salem* was the next of any fame,
That began to augment New England's name;
But after multitudes began to flow,
More than well knew themselves where to bestow;
Boston then began her roots to spread,
And quickly soon she grew to be the head,
Not only of the Massachusetts Bay,
But all trade and commerce fell in her way.
And truly it was admirable to know,
How greatly all things here began to grow.
New plantations were in each place begun
And with inhabitants were filled soon.
All sorts of grain which our own land doth yield,
Was hither brought, and sown in every field:
As wheat and rye, barley, oats, beans and pease
Here all thrive, and they profit from them raise.
All sorts of roots and herbs in gardens grow,
Parsnips, carrots, turnips, or what you'll sow,
Onions, melons, cucumbers, radishes,
Skirets, beets, coleworts and fair cabbages.
Here grow fine flowers many, and 'mongst those,
The fair white lily and sweet fragrant rose.
Many good wholesome berries here you'll find,
Fit for man's use, almost of every kind,
Pears, apples, cheries, plumbs, quinces and peach,
Are *now* no dainties; you may have of each.

Nuts and grapes of several sorts are here,
If you will take the pains, them to seek for.

Cattle of every kind do fill the land,
Many now are kill'd and their hides tann'd;
By which men are supply'd with meat and shoes,
Or what they can, though much by wolves they lose.
Here's store of cows, which milk and butter yield,
And also oxen, for to till the field;
Of which great profit many now do make,
If they have a fit place and able pains do take.
Horses here likewise now do multiply,
They prosper well, and yet their price is high.
Here are swine, good store, and some goats do keep,
But now most begin to get store of sheep,
That with their wool their bodies may be clad,
In time of straits, when things cannot be had;
For merchants keep the price of cloth so high,
As many are not able the same to buy.
And happy would it be for people here,
If they could raise cloth for themselves to wear;
And if they do themselves hereto apply,
They would not be so low, nor some so high.
As I look back I cannot but smile,
To think how some did themselves beguile,
When called first, went at so high a rate,
They did not think how soon they might abate;
For many then began to look so high,
Whose hopes, soon after, in the dust did lie.
So vain is man! if riches do abide
A little, he's soon lift up with pride.
A cow then was at twenty pounds and five,
Those who had increase could not choose but thrive;
And a cow calf, ten or twelve pounds would give,
As soon as weaned, if that it did live.
A lamb, or kid was forty shillings price,
Men were earnest for them, lest they should rise.
And a milch goat, was at three or four pound;
All cattle at such prices went off round.
In money and good cloth, they would you pay,
Or what good thing else that you would say.
And both swine and corn was in good request,
To the first comers this was a harvest.

But that which did 'bove all the rest excel,
God in his word, with us he here did dwell;
Well ordered churches, in each place there were,
And a learn'd ministry was planted here.

All marvell'd and said, " Lord this work is thine,
In the wilderness to make such lights to shine."
And truly it was a glorious thing,
Thus to hear men pray, and God's praises sing,
Where these natives were wont to cry and yell
To satan, who 'mongst them doth rule and dwell.
Oh, how great comfort was it now to see,
The churches to enjoy free liberty!
And to have the gospel preach'd here with power,
And such wolves repell'd as would else devour;
And now with plenty their poor souls were fed,
With better food than wheat, or angels' bread,
In green pastures, they may themselves solace,
And drink freely of the sweet springs of grace;
A pleasant banquet, is prepar'd for these,
Of fat things, and rich wine upon the lees;
" Eat O my friends, (saith Christ) and drink freely,
Here's wine and milk, and all sweet spicery;
The honey and its comb, is here to be had,
I myself for you, have this banquet made:
Be not dismayed, but let your heart rejoice
In this wilderness, O let me hear your voice;
My friends you are, whilst you my ways do keep,
Your sins I'll pardon and your good I'll seek."
And they, poor souls, again to Christ do say,
"O Lord thou art our hope, our strength and stay;
Who givest to us, all these thy good things,
Us shelter still, in the shadow of thy wings:
So we shall sing, and laud thy name with praise,
'Tis thine own work, to keep us in thy ways;
Uphold us still, O thou which art most high,
We then shall be kept, and thy name glorify,
Let us enjoy thyself, with these means of grace,
And in our hearts shine, with the light of thy face;
Take not away thy presence, nor thy word,
But we humbly pray, us the same afford."

To the north or south, or which way you'll wind,
Churches now are spread, and you'll pasture find.
Many men of worth, for learning and great fame,
Grave and godly, into these parts here came:
As HOOKER, COTTON, DANFORTH, and the rest,
Whose names are precious and elsewhere express'd;
And many among these, you might soon find,
Who in some things, left not their like behind.
But some of these are dead, and others aged be,
Lord do thou supply, in thy great mercy;
How these their flocks did feed, with painful care,

Their labours, love and fruitful works declare;
They did not spare their time, and lives to spend,
In the Lord's work, unto their utmost end:
And such as still survive do strive the more,
To do like them that have gone before:
Take courage then, for ye shall have reward,
That in this work are faithful to the Lord.
Example take hereby, you that shall come,
In after time when these their race have run.

A prudent Magistracy here was placed,
By which, the Churches defended were and graced;
And this new commonwealth in order held,
And sin, that foul iniquity, was quell'd:
Due, right, and justice, unto all was done,
Without delay, mens suits were ended soon.
Here were men sincere, and upright in heart,
Who, from justice and right would not depart:
Men's causes they would scan and well debate
And all bribes and corruption they did hate;
The truth to find out they would use all means,
And so, for that end, they would spare no pains.
Whilst things thus did flourish and were in their prime,
Men thought it happy and a blessed time;
To see how sweetly all things did agree,
Both in the Church and State, there was amity;
Each to the other mutual help did lend,
And to God's honour all their ways did tend,
In love and peace, his truth for to retain,
And God's service how best for to maintain.
Some of these are gone, others do grow grey,
Which doth show us they have not long to stay:
But God will still, for his people provide,
Such as be able, them to help and guide,
If they cleave to him, and do not forsake
His laws and truth, and their own ways do take.
If thou hast view'd the camp of Israel,
How God in the wilderness with them did dwell;
And led them long in that dangerous place,
Through fears and trials for so long a space;
And yet they never saw more of his glory,
Than in this time where he advanced them high.
His great and marvellous works they here saw,
And he them taught, in his most holy law.
A small emblem hereof thou mayest see,
How God hath dealt with these, in some degree,
For much of himself they now here have seen,
And marvellous to them his works have been.

I am loth indeed to change my theme,
Thus of God's precious mercies unto them,
Yet I must do it, though it is most sad,
And if it prove otherwise I shall be glad.
Methinks I see some great change at hand,
That e're long will fall upon this poor land;
Not only because many are took away,
Of the best rank, but virtue doth decay,
And true godliness doth not now so shine,
As some while it did, in the former time;
But love and fervent zeal do seem to sleep,
Security and the world on men do creep;
Pride and oppression, they do grow so fast,
As that all goodness they will eat out at last.
Whoredom and drunkenness with other sin,
Wilt cause God's judgments soon to break in,
And whimsy errors have now got such a head,
And, under notion of conscience, do spread;
So as whole places with them now are stain'd,
Whereas goodness, sometime before hath reign'd.
Where godliness abates, evil will succeed,
And grow apace like to the noisome weed;
And if there be not care, their growth to stop,
All godliness, it soon will overtop.
Another cause of our declining here,
Is a *mixt multitude*, as doth appear;
Many for servants, hitherto were brought,
Others came for gain, or worse ends they sought:
And of these, many grew loose and profane,
Though some are brought to know God and his name.
But thus it is, and hath been so of old,
As by the scriptures we are plainly told;
For when, as from Egypt God's people came,
A mixed multitude got in among them,
Who with the rest murmur and lust did they,
In wants, and fell at *Kibroth Hatavah.*
And whereas the Lord doth sow his good seed,
The enemy, he brings in tares and weed;
What need therefore there is that men should watch,
That satan them not at advantage catch;
For ill manners and example are such,
As others do infect and corrupt much:
Chiefly if they be unstaid and young,
And with all persons do converse among;
Yea some are so wretched and full of vice,
As they take pleasure, others to entice;
And though it be a thing, most vile and bad,
Yet they will do it, and thereat be glad;

And laugh and scoff when any they draw in,
For to do evil, and to commit sin.
But let these, and all profane scoffers know,
That unto God, they do a reckoning owe,
And to account ere long he will them bring,
When they must answer for this, their foul sin.
Was it not enough for them evil to do,
But they must needs cause others do so too?
Herein indeed they act the devil's part,
And if they repent not, with him they'll smart;
For God to such, is a consuming fire,
And they shall perish in his dreadful ire.

But a most desperate mischief here is grown,
And a great shame it is, it should be known:
But why should I conceal so foul a thing,
That, quickly, may our hurt and ruin bring!
For base covetousness hath got such a sway,
As, our own safety, we ourselves betray;
For these fierce natives, they are now so fill'd
With guns and muskets, and in them so skill'd,
As that they may keep the English in awe,
And when they please give to them the law;
And of powder and shot, they have such store,
As sometimes they refuse for to buy more;
Flints, screw-plates, and moulds for all sorts of shot
They have, and skill how to use them, have got;
And mend and new stock their pieces they can,
As well in most things, as an Englishman.
Thus like madmen we put them in a way,
With our own weapons us to kill and slay;
That gain hereof to make, they know so well,
The fowl to kill, and us the feathers sell.
For us to seek for deer it doth not boot,
Since now with guns themselves at them can shoot.
That garbage, of which we no use did make,
They have been glad to gather up and take;
But now they can themselves fully supply,
And the English, of them are glad to buy.
And yet if that was all it might be borne,
Though hereby th' English make themselves a scorn.
But now they know their advantage so well,
And will not stick, to some, the same to tell,
That now they can when they please or will,
The English drive away, or else them kill
Oh base wretched men, who thus for gain
Care not at all, if their neighbours be slain!
How can they think that this should do them good,

Which thus they purchase with the price of blood!
I know it is laid upon the *French* or *Dutch*,
And freely grant that they do use it much,
And make thereof an execrable trade,
Whereby those natives one another invade;
By which also, the Dutch and French do smart
Sometimes, for teaching them this wicked art;
But these both, from us more remote do lie,
And ours, from them, can have no full supply.
In these quarters, it is *English* guns we see,
For French and Dutch, more slight and weak they be;
And these Indians are now grown so wise,
As, in regard of these, theirs they do despise.
Fair fowling pieces, and muskets they have,
All English, and keep them both neat and brave;
And to our shame, speak it we justly may,
That we are not furnished so well as they;
For traders, them will sell at prices high,
Whereas their neighbors, of them cannot buy;
Good laws have been made, this evil to restrain,
But, by men's close deceit, they are made vain.
The Indians are nurtured so well
As, by no means, you can get them to tell,
Of whom they had their guns, or such supply,
Or, if they do, they will feign some false lie:
So as, if their testimony you take
For evidence, little of it you can make.
And of the English, so many are guilty,
And deal under-hand, in such secrecy,
As, very rare it is, some one to catch,
Though you use all due means, them for to watch.
Merchants, shopkeepers, traders, and planters too,
Sundry of each, spare not this thing to do;
Though, many more that do the same abhor,
Whose innocence will one day answer for,
If (which God forbid) they should come to see,
By this means, some hurt or sad tragedy;
And these heathen in their furious mood,
Should cruelly shed our innocent blood.
Lord shew mercy, and graciously spare,
For thy name's sake, those that thy servants are,
And let their lives be precious in thy sight;
Divert such judgments, as fall on them might,
Give them not up into these heathen's power,
Who like the greedy wolves would them devour,
And exercise on them their cruel rage,
With torments great and most salvage;
They are not content their foes only to kill,

But, most inhumanly, torment them they will.
They are men that are skilful for to destroy,
And in others misery, they do take joy.
O Lord take pity on thy people poor,
Let them repent, amend and sin no more;
Forgive, dear Father, what is done and past,
Oh save us still and not away us cast.
Ourselves are weak, and have no strength to stand,
Do thou support us, Lord, by thine own hand;
When we have need, be thou our succour then,
Let us not fall into the hands of men.

When I think on what I have often read,
How, when the elders and Joshua were dead;
Who had seen those great works, and them could tell,
What God had done, and wrought for Israel;
Yet they did soon forget and turn aside,
And, in his truth and ways, did not abide;
But in the next age did degenerate;
I wish this may not be New England's fate.

To you therefore that are for to succeed,
Unto this fair precedent, give you good heed,
And know that, being warn'd, if you do not,
But fall away; God's wrath 'gainst you'll be hot:
For if he spared not those that sinned of old,
But into the hands of spoilers them sold;
How can you think that you should then escape,
That do like them, and will no warning take.

O my dear friends, and children whom I love,
To cleave to God, let these few lines you move,
So I have done and now will say no more,
But remember, God punished them sore.

Melius est peccatum cavere quam emendare.

ISAAC[2] ALLERTON'S WILL

Communicated by MR. WALTER S. ALLERTON

ISAAC[2] ALLERTON, the son of Isaac[1] Allerton and Fear[2] Brewster (*Elder William*[1]), was born at Plymouth about 1630. When his father removed to New Amsterdam in 1638 he remained at Plymouth with his grandfather Elder Brewster, by whom he was being educated, and graduated from Harvard College in 1650, when he joined his father and was associated with him in business at New Amsterdam, New Haven, Virginia and elsewhere. After his father's death at New Haven in 1659 he removed to the plantation which had been acquired about ten years before on the Machoatick River, a small tributary of the Potomac, in Westmoreland County, Virginia, and resided there until his death in 1702. This plantation is laid down on Herrmann's map of Virginia and Maryland, made in 1670, and as a planter Isaac[2] Allerton was successful, and was prominent in the civil and military affairs of the colony. He was a Justice of the Peace, several times a member of the House of Burgesses and of the Governor's Council, and in 1699 Naval Officer and Receiver of the Virginia duties in Westmoreland County, including Yeocomico River. In 1691 Isaac[2] Allerton, John Armistead and Richard Lee the younger refused to take the oath of allegiance to William and Mary and resigned from the Governor's Council, and they were accused of being papists, certainly a strange accusation to bring against the grandson and pupil of Elder Brewster. In 1675 a joint expedition against the Indians was arranged by Virginia and Maryland, and the Virginia troops were commanded by Col. John Washington (great-grandfather of George Washington), Col. George Mason and Major Isaac Allerton, and in 1683 he was Lieutenant-Colonel of the Westmoreland Militia.

Isaac[2] Allerton was first married about 1652, probably at New Haven, but his first wife, of whom little is known except that her first name was Elizabeth, undoubtedly died before his removal to Virginia, where he again married, about 1663, Elizabeth, daughter of Capt. Thomas Willoughby, who was then the widow of Major George Colclough, and who is also said to have had for her first husband Simon Overzee, a Hollander.

[Notes on the Will of Isaac² Allerton]

Cople Parish occupied the lower or eastern part of Westmoreland County. It would seem that in 1702 there was but one church, but at a later date there were two, at Yeocomico in the east, and Nominy in the west.

Sarah Lee was the second child of Isaac² Allerton by his second wife, Elizabeth Willoughby, and must have been born about 1670, for the inscription on the tomb of Hancock Lee says: "and Sarah his last wife, daughter of Isaac Allerton Esq., who departed this life the 17th May, Anno Domo 1731, Aeta 60 years."

From the mention of a grandson Allerton Newton it is generally assumed that Isaac² Allerton had a fourth daughter whose first name is unknown, but it is equally possible that he was the son of Sarah by a first husband, and this would account for the joint devise of lands to them.

Elizabeth Heirs was the eldest child of Isaac² Allerton, and was born at New Haven, September 27, 1653. She married first, December 23, 1675, Benjamin Starr, who died in 1678, and second, July 22, 1679, Simon Eyres, Hyres or Hires.

Frances³ Allerton, who married Capt. Samuel Travers, was probably the youngest child of Isaac² Allerton. Willoughby³ Allerton was probably the first child of Isaac² Allerton and his second wife Elizabeth Willoughby. Like his father he was successful as a planter and prominent in civil and military life in the colony, and died in 1724.

The several bequests of tobacco in this will no doubt appear singular to us at this day, and a young girl who should now receive a thousand pounds upon her seventeenth birthday would no doubt be somewhat surprised, but at that time and in Virginia, where English money was scarce, tobacco was the common currency and measure of value, as beaver skins were at one time in some of the northern colonies.

[Isaac² Allerton's Will *]

In the name of God Amen the 25th day of October in the first year of the reign of our most gracious sovereign Lady Ann, by the grace of God and etc. Annoyi Domini 1702 — I, Isaac Allerton, of the Co. of Westmoreland in the Colony of Virginia, Esqr. being sick and week of body, but of sound and perfect memory thanks be to almighty God for the same, do

* Recorded in Westmoreland County, Virginia, Book 3, page 115. Proved Dec. 30, 1702.

make this my last will and testament in manner & form following, revoking & absolutely annulling by these presents all & every will & wills, testament and none other.

Imprimis I give my soul to God who gave it and my body to the earth from whence it came to be buryed in decent and christian manner as to my executors hereafter named shall be thought meet and convenient there to remain till the joyful resurrection trusting through the merits death and passions of my Saviour Jesus Christ to have full and free pardon for all my sins & to inherit everlasting life. And as tuching the disposition of all such temporal Estate as it has pleased Almighty God to bestow upon me I do order, give and dispose thereof in manner & form following viz.

Item — I give and bequeath the sum of ten pounds sterling to the church of Cople parish to be disposed of by my executors hereafter named for ornament for the sd church. Item — I will that all my just debts be pd duly and punctually. Item — I give bequeath and devise to my dear daughter Sarah Lee & my grandson Allerton Newton two tracks of land lying and being in the County of Stafford . (viz) one track of one thousand & fifty acres and the other track of six hundred acres to be equally divided between them To have and to hold the sd two tracks of land to them the sd Sarah Lee & Allerton Newton and the heirs of their bodies lawfully begotten to be equally divided between them as aforesaid.

Item I give bequeath & devise to my dear daughter Elizabeth Starr als. Heirs who lives in New England six hundred acres of land part of a dividend of one & twenty hundred & fifty acres lying and being on South side of Rappahannock River to her the sd Elizabeth & such of her children as she shall dispose of the same to, but in case the sd Elizabeth be dead before the date of this my will I will & devise the sd six hundred acres of land to her eldest son and to his heirs forever.

Item — I give and bequeath to my sd daughter Elizabeth Heirs the sum of two thousand pounds of tobacco to be pd upon demand. And forasmuch as my daughter Traverse has had a sufficient part or proportion of my estate given her in consideration of marriage I do therefore for memorial sake give unto her three daughters Elizabeth, Rebecca & Winifred Traverse the sum of one thousand pounds of tobacco apeice to be pd them at the yrs of seventeen or the day of marriage which shall first happen. Item — I give and bequeathe to my grandson Allerton Newton the sum of one thousand pounds of tobacco to be pd at the yrs of one & twenty.

Item — I do publish & declare my intent and meaning that the above legacies given to my sd daughter; grandson and grand daughters be deemed & taken to be in lieu & full satisfaction of their filial portions or childs parts of my Estate.

Item — I give bequeath and devise all the remaining part of my land & tenements not above bequeathed how and wheresoever situate & being to my well beloved son Willoughby Allerton and to his heirs forever.

Lastly, I make ordain constitute & appoint my sd son Willoughby Allerton Executor of this my last will and testament to whom I also give & bequeath all my personal Estate, goods & Chattels, real and personal of what kind, sort or quality soever the same be. And in witness that this is my last will and testament I hereunto set my hand and seal the day and year first above written.

Signed sealed & published Isaac Allerton (Seal)
in the prence of
Humphrey Morriss
John Gerrard
Dan[l]. Oceany.

JABEZ² HOWLAND'S WILL AND INVENTORY AND THE AGREEMENT OF THE HEIRS

Transcribed from the Original Records,

BY GEORGE ERNEST BOWMAN

JABEZ² HOWLAND (*John*¹) died at Bristol (now in Rhode Island, but then a part of Massachusetts), probably not long before 6 February, 1711/12, the day his inventory was begun. His will was dated 14 May, 1708, was proved 21 February, 1711/12, and, with the inventory, executors' account and agreement of the heirs, was recorded in the Bristol County Probate Records, Volume III, pages 82, 154, 157, 238. The only original documents now in the files are the account of the executors and six receipts from creditors.

The will mentions by name only the wife Bethiah and the son Jabez, but the agreement of the heirs shows that the "four sons," who were to receive the estate after their mother's death or second marriage, were Jabez, Josiah, Samuel and Joseph, all living at Bristol. It also shows that a daughter Elizabeth had married Nathan Townsend of Newport, R. I., and died, leaving an only son, Nathan.

[JABEZ[2] HOWLAND'S WILL]

[p. 82] In the Name of God Amen I Jabez Howland of Bristol in the County of Bristol in the Province of the Massachuset bay in New England Blacksmith, haveing had Repeated warnings (by the paines of my body offten Returning upon me) of the approches of Death which is the appointed lott & portion of all men (haveing and Returning * my memory and understanding as at other times) Do make & ordaine this to be my last will & Testament: And first & principally I Resigne my soule into the hands of God who gave it, And as to my body I Commend it to the Earth to be Decently buried at the Discresion of my surviveing friends And as Touching my Temporall Estate wherewith it hath pleased God to bless me in this life I give bequeath & Dispose thereof in the following manner & form Item my will is that all my Just Debts & ffunerall Charges be fully sattisfyed in Convenient time after my Decease by my Executors hereafter Named

Item I give & bequeath to my Dear and Loveing wife my whole Estate of what Nature or kind so Ever whether Reall or personall that I shall dye Possessed of or shall belong or appertaine to me in whose hand or Costodie so Ever to be at her sole & absolut dispose, and for her use and Comfort for and Dureing her widowhood or bearing my Name & if my wife shall see cause to Marry then shall she be sattisfyed with her Thirds as the law provides in case of Intestates the Res[t] & Remaining part thereof to be Equally divided to and Among my four sons or those that shall Legally Represent them if any of them should dye: And the like Divission to be made in Case of the Death of my said wife

And of this my last will and Testament I do Nominate make and Ordain my beloved wife Bethiah Howland & my Loveing son Jabez Howland Joynt Executors and I do declare make Null & voyd all other & former wills bequest and Executors by me before this time Named willed or bequeathed declareing this and none but this to be my last will and Testament In Testimony whereof I have hereunto set my hand and seal this fourteent[h] day of May in the seventh year of her

* Sic.

Majesties Reign Annoq Domini seventeen hundred and Eight
Signed sealed pronounced & Jabez Howland (S)
Declared by the above named
Jabez Howland to be his last
will and Testament before
us vizt
Dan Throop William Martin John Cary

Bristol ss In Bristol ffebruary 21st $17\frac{11}{12}$

Then before Natha^{l} Paine Esqr Judge of the Probate of wills &c within the County of Bristol afores^{d} Came & Appeared Dan Throope william Martin & John Cary witnesses to the within written will of m^{r} Jabez Howland Deceased & made Oath that they were present & did see the s^{d} Dec^{d} signe seal and declare the same as his last will and Testament and tha[t] he was of a disposeing mind when he so did
John Cary Reg^{r} Coram Jur^{t} Natha^{l} Paine
Entered Aprill 26 : 1712 By John Cary Reg^{r}

[Jabez² Howland's Inventory]

[p. 154] An Inventory of the Estate of m^{r} Jabez Howland late of Bristol Dec^{d} Taken by us the subscribers the sixth day of ffeb^{ry} $17\frac{11}{12}$ and is as followeth vizt

Imp^{rs} His Silver money Province Bills and Plate at	.45	16	00
more due by bond from Josiah Standish of Boston	.50	00	00
His Cloathing wollen and Linen x^{ta} at	.14	00	00
In the Little Lower Lodging Room four swords & two Bayanits at 3£ & two Canes with a Belt 20^{s}	.04	00	00
Two Bedsteeds Beds and furniture belonging	.11	00	00
Two Guns Powder and Bullets	.02	00	00
A Chest of Drawers one Chest & two boxes	.02	00	00
A table 10sh : 2 Joyntstools 6 Chairs 8sh : an old Case 5s	.01	03	00
A warming Pan 12sh : Looking glass 5sh : & books of all sort 40s	.02	17	00
Glass bottles Drinking glasses & some other smale things	...	10	00
2 Iron potts a skillet & Iron Kettle	001	00	00
3 brass Kettles 4 skillets brass : 5 brass Candlesticks	007	00	00
110 pound pewter at 18^{d} p^{r} pound more old pewter	009	07	00
2 Tramels 3 tongs 2 slices 7 Candlesticks 2 Dogs	001	02	00
one Diaper Table Cloath 6 Diaper Napkins 4 Coarse Table Cloathes and a Duzen & half of Napkins	003	00	00
A Table Cloath & one Duzen of Napkins	000	18	00

Ten Towels 18 Pillowbeers 15 pare of sheets	009	04	00
3 pair Anirons 2 Drippin Pans 2 spits one fendr & frying pan	002	00	00
A screen 5sh. Trayes & old barrills 20sh :	001	05	00
one Table in ye gt Room 2 old forms & a pair of Stiliards	000	15	00
in the gt Chamber 3 feather beds Bedsteeds & furniture	020	00	00
8 Leather Chaires 40sh : a square Table 4 forms 20sh :	003	00	00
in the Porch Chambr one feather bed bedsted & furniture a Looking glass & two Chairs	010	00	00
in the Garet two beds & 2 bolsters & furniture	005	00	00
in the Little Chamber two beds and furniture 8 Chairs & three Chests all at	010	00	00
about 17 yds wosteed shirting 34sh : yarn 18li : 36sh :	003	10	00
one negro man 30li	030	00	00
Shoop Tools Bellows Anvil Beekhorn Vice 2 pair tongs & two hand hammers	005	00	00
In the ware house scales & weights	001	10	00
To 2 Cowes 2 shep & 3 swine	007	00	00
To 3 acres of land Dwelling house & out houseing (Except half the Smith shopp & ye Coopers shoop) with one Commonage	250	00	00
To an 8th part of ye land at ye wharfe formerly Marcht Carys	015	00	00
To a silver Tankard prized at	010	00	00
To Twenty sheep	006	00	00
	549	17	00

Prized & finished by us June 25 : 1713.

Simon Davis
Saml Gallap
John Cary

[p. 155] Bristol ss July the 2d 1713 Then before Collo Nathal Paine Esqr Judge of Probate of wills &c within the County of Bristol Came mrs Bethiah Howland widow Relict of mr Jabez Howland late of Bristol Deceased & Jabez Howland son to ye Decd & both Executors of his last will and Testament : & made Oath that the Inventory within written Containes ye whole of ye Estate both Reall & personall that he the said Deceased Dyed seized of & is Come to their Knowledge and w they Know of more they will Reveal it that it may be of Record herewith

Nathal Paine

John Cary Regr
Entered July 3d : 1713 By John Cary Registr

[Bond of the Executors *]

In the bond of the executors which was dated 21 February, 1711/12, Jabez Howland, of Bristol, is called the eldest son of the deceased. The sureties were Dan Throope and J. Woodbury,† both of Bristol. The executors and sureties all signed their names. The amount of the bond was £800 and the executors were required to present an inventory on or before 10 April, 1712, and an account of their administration on or before 10 April, 1713. The witnesses were William Martin and John Cary.

[The Account of the Executors ‡]

The Accompt of Bethiah Howland & Jabez Howland of Bris[tol] Executors to the last will and Testament of mr Jabez Howland late of sd Bristol Deceased as well of and for so much of the Est[ate] of the said Deceased as is Come to their hands as of & for theyr payments and Disbursments out of the same as ffolloweth &c

The said Accomptonts Chargeth themselves with all & singuler the Goods Chattells & Estate left by the said Deceased Specifye[d] in an Inventory thereof made and Exhibited into the Regrs office for the Court of Probate within the County of Brist[ol] Amounting as by the same Inventory Appeareth

				£	s	[d]
To the sum of				549	17	[00]
Receved since of mr walker	02	10	03			
of Ensigne Reynolds	00	02	10			
of John Haws	00	10	00			
	03	03	01	003	03	01
of mr wofman §	0	9	0		9	
				553	09	01

The Accomptants prayeth allowance for the payment (as well of the severall Debts due by the Deceased at his Death as other Charges ariseing since : which these Accomptants have since payed and Discharged as followeth —

* From the original document.

† In the bond the sureties are written "Dan Throope & Jonathan," a blank being left after "Jonathan."

‡ From the original document.

§ This name on the record [III : 157] reads "Wakman."

				£	s	d
Imp^{rs} To m^{r} william Tickner of Swanzey				01	00	00
To m^{r} John Green of Bristol				01	19	08
To Capt Job Almy of Newport as by his Receipt				17	14	00
To m^{r} william Monro of Bristol as p^{r} Receipt				13	11	08
To m^{r} Christoph^{r} Almy of Newport				01	17	00
To m^{rs} Osborn				02	15	00
To Natha^{l} Paine Esqr				08	02	01
To m^{r} George Monro as p^{r} his Receipt				07	00	00
To ffunerall Charges wine and other Drink *				00	00	00
To 6 Rings for the funerall				03	14	09
To Gloves for the funeral				02	00	00
To proveing the will Recording the will & Inventory				00	12	00
To Doct^{r} ffullton to midicins				00	10	07
more one Ring 12 : 6^{d}				00	12	06
To mourning for m^{r} Townsend				00	17	06
To m^{r} Walker † for Leather and horss hyre				00	13†	00
To m^{r} Bowerman				02	03	00
To Drawing allowing & Registering this accompt				00	10	00
more to Grave stones to m^{r} Stephens	1	10	0			
for the Coffin to m^{r} Church	0	10	0			
for Diging the grave	0	06	0			
	2	06	0 :	02	06	00
				67	05	09

Bristo^{ll} ss By ye Hono^{bl} Nath^{ll} : Paine esqEr . Judge of Probate e^{t}

Mrs Bethiah Howland & . Jabez Howland . presented the above written : and made oath that it Conteines Justt and truc accomp^{tt} of theire Administration on ye estate of m^{r} Jabez Howland . late of Bristoll Decaced so far as they have proceeded : which accomp^{tt} acordeingly I do allow and aprove off : July . 24th . 1713 . Juratt Coram : Nath^{ll} Paine

Bristol ss in the 3^{d} Book fol : 157 July 29th 1713 the above written was Entered by John Cary Reg^{r}

[Receipts from Creditors]

The following original receipts are still preserved in the probate files:

14 March, 1711/12. Receipt from Job Almy to Mr. Samuel Howland for £17, 14s., for rum delivered to the latter's father, Mr. Jabez Howland deceased.

* This item does not appear in the inventory as recorded.

† "Walker" and "13" have been crossed out and this item does not appear in the inventory as recorded.

[not dated] Receipt from William Munro to Widow Bethiah Howland, executrix of Jabez Howland, deceased, for £13, 1s., 8d., for balance of all accounts due. In this receipt the amount appears, both in words and in figures, as here given, but it is incorrectly entered on the account and on the record.

30 January, 1711/12. Receipt from Christopher Almy of Newport to Mr. Samuel Howland for £1, 17s., for a barrell of flour sold to the latter's father, Mr. Jabez Howland, "Last march."

[not dated] Receipt from Mercy Osborne to Widow Bethiah Howland, executrix of Jabez Howland, deceased, for £2, 15s., for balance of all accounts due.

10 May, 1711. Receipt from Nathaniel Paine of Bristol to Mr. Jabez Howland, executor of his father, Mr. Jabez Howland, deceased, for £8, 2s., 1d., in full of all accounts.

June, 1712. Receipt from George Monroe (signed by his mark) to Widow Bethiah Howland, executrix of Jabez Howland, deceased, for seven pounds for balance of all accounts.

[Agreement of the Heirs]

[p. 238] Know all men to whom these presents shall come or any way may Concren that we Jabez Howland Josiah Howland Samuel Howland and Joseph Howland all of Bristol in the County of Bristol sons of our Hon^d ffather m^r Jabez Howland late of Bristoll deceased Agreeable to the will of our s^d ffather & with the Advise & Consent of our Hon^rd mother m^rs Bethiah howland and not without the Best advise of freinds we Could obtain have deliberatly agreed upon and ffully finished a divission and settlement of ye whole Estate Left by our s^d father both Reall and personall (Excepting so much as our said mother hath seen meet to keep in her own hands for her own use dureing her Naturall life) after which the same to be subject to a division as hereafter in this Instrum^t shall be Expressed

Imp^rs We have divided the houselot Containing two acres be it more or less bounded west by hope street North by Charles Street East partly by land belonging to s^d Estate & partly by land of Capt S; davis & southerly by Prison Lane Into four lots or Equall parts allwayes Reserveing Twenty six foot in ye middle of afores^d house lott for a way or passage from the afores^d Hope Street to the Extent of the s^d house lot Eastwards to be left for Common Improvement and fenced out by Josiah Howland and Joseph Howland or their heires or assignes and the End Expiration of three years from and after the Thirtyeth day of march Anno Domini 1714 & upon the Request of any one of the brothers or such as Shall Represent them Desireing the said way may be fenced out The Northward lot by Choice fell to the Eldest Brother Jabez Howland to be to him and to his heires and asignes for Ever The Next Lot on which stands the dwelling house by Choice fell to Josiah Howland to be to to him his heires and assignes for Ever The next lot fell to Joseph Howland the Youngest Brother to be to him his heires and assignes for Ever and the most southermost lot fell to Samuel Howland to be to him his he[ires] and assignes for Ever And whereas according to our Mutuall agreement there hath been a valuation made of the severall lots aforementioned by persons unInterested & mutually Choosen by ye s^d^ Brothers and the lot mentioned to be Josiahs on which the Dweling house standeth being valued at seventy pounds more then the Rest it is hereby mutually agreed by the Rest of the Brothers that the s^d^ Josiah his heires or assignes shall have the space of seven years allowed from the s^d^ Thirtyeth day of march 1714 for the payment of ye said sum Provided that allso he his heires or assignes pay ye Interest of the same yearly and Every year dureing the space of seven years as aforesaid and which moneys & allso the sum ariseing upon the valuation or other wise shall be divided in Equall proportion amongst all the Brothers or such as shall Legally Represent them from time to time and all times as it shall become due

secondly We have made Divission of the acre lot bounded west upon the East End of the house lot before mentioned North by Charles Street East upon High Street and South upon land of Capt Simon [p. 239] Simon Davis : Into five shares or parts the westermost share or part Joyning to the house lot fell by lot to Jabez Howland and the next to Josiah Howland the third lot to Samuel Howland and the fourth to Joseph Howland And the fifth Joyning upon High Street is designed for Nathan Townsend the onely son of our sister Elizabeth dec^d^ to be to us Respectively and to our heires and assignes Respectively for Ever

Thirdly Whereas our said Honored mother hath Choosen the new Room & Buttery adjoyning with so much of the moveables as she hath desired for her own use and benefit Dureing her Naturall life we the s^d^ broth^rs^ do declare our sattisfaction theirwith & that we are Content that it should so Remain in her hand Dureing her life and afterward to be prised & the value thereof to be Equally divided amongst us our heires or assignes — The Little Room or new Room before mentiond at the decease of our said mother to belong to Josiah Howland or his heires He or they paying the value thereof as it shall be prised by men Choosen by all that are interested therein to be divided as above said in Equal proportion

fourthly We the s^d^ Jabez Howland Josiah Howland Samuel Howland and Joseph Howland Do Each of us for ourselves & our Respective heires Execut^rs^ & Adm^rs^ Covenant promise & grant to & with our s^d^ mother in manner and form following that is to say That we will for her Comfortable subsistence pay yearly in money of the Province or other pay to her Content fourteen pounds Every year so long as she shall keep the Negro man in her hands and at her own dispose But if it should so happen said Negro man should Dye be disinabled for Labour or our s^d^ mother should see Cause to part with him to us the s^d^ Brothers, then We further promise and Engage to bear our Equall proportion of Twenty two pounds p^r^ Annum Dureing the Naturall life of our s^d^ Mother and by us to be payd to our said mother and to her acceptance the one quarter of Each of our parts or proportion of the afores^d^ sums at Every quarters End & to the true performance thereof we bind ourselves and Each of us by him Our heires Executors & Administ^rs^ Joyntly & severally to our s^d^ mother in the penall sum of fifty pounds in Currant money to be forfeited and payd to our said mother, if default be made of the quarterly payments as they shall become due from us or any of us And further we say, it is the true Intent and meaning of this agreement that Our said mother shall have the priviledge of water at the well and of some part of ye yard for the laying her firewood & the southwest Corner of the Celler and the like priviledge to be allowed to her assigne[s] if she should see Cause to Remove Else where & put in a Tenant and this priviledg[e] to be allowed freely

fifthly It is further Covenanted and agreed by us the before mentioned Brothers That Notwithstanding in our said ffathers will Nathan Townsend the onely son of our late and onely Sister Elizabeth Townsend late wife of Nathan Townsend of Newport is wholly omitted & Excluded from haveing any part in that Estate left by our said ffather Yet for the love we had to our said sister and which we still have and bear to her late husband and as a Testimony of our Regard & Respect we have to Nathan Townsend Junr : We do hereby bind & oblige our selves severally our and Each of our severall & Respective heires Executors & administ^rs^ by these presents to pay or cause to be payd unto the s^d^ Nathan Townsend only son of our said

Sister Elizabeth Townsend deceased [p. 240] The full sum of forty pounds that is to say Ten pounds Each of us when he shall arive at the age of Twenty one years and then he shall Enter upon Possess and Enjoy the fifth part of the acre lot above mentioned Joyning to High street to be to him his heires & and assignes

Provided Nevertheless that If the said Nathan TownsEnd shall not be content therewith but shall give us trouble in the law then this fifth article shall be voide and of none Effect but the s[d] fifth Lot shall Remain to us our heres and assignes for Ever in Equal proportion Neither shall the s[d] forty pounds be due or Recoverable by vertue hereof but shall Remain with us notwithstanding what is above Expressd

Sixtly It is further agreed and Concluded that upon Condition y[t] Cap[t] Davis his heires or assignes shall see Cause to leave & lay out any part of his land Joyning to the above mentioned acre lot layd out into five shares, for a sufficient way or passage from Charls stret to prison lane then the like quantity for a way shall be taken from the west End of said acree lott and Each five lots to be Lesened in Equall. proportion

Seventhly That the Commonage belonging to our said fathers Estate shall belong to all y[e] Brothers and allso that Right which our s[d] ffather had in y[e] Estate which formerly belonged to m[r] John Cary march[t] and shall be Equally divided or the value thereof to & among the said Brothers or such as shall Legally Represent them

Eightly We ffurther declare by these presents that the moveables or or personall Estate (Excepting what is in the hands of our said mother) have been by us said Brothers have be divided to the sattisfaction of Each of us : And in Testimony that this is our agreement and a full settlement of the said Estate Left by our s[d] ffather we have hereunto set our hands and seals And allso our s[d] Mother Concuring with us in the s[d] division and settlement And hereby to declare her full sattisfaction therein hath with us her four sons Namely Jabez Josiah Samuel & Joseph Howland, set to her hand and seal the Twenty sixt day of November in the first year of our Sovereign Lord Georg King of great Brittain ffrance and Ireland defender of the faith &c Annoq Domini one thousand seven Hundred & fourteen

In presence of us
viz[t] William Monroe
Joseph wardall

Bethiah Howland (S)
Jabez Howland (S)
Josiah Howland (S)
Samuel Howland (S)
Joseph Howland (S)

Bristol ss Novemb^{r} 26 : 1714

Mrs Bethiah Howland m^{r} Jabez Howland m^{r} Josiah Howland m^{r} Samuel Howland & m^{r} Joseph Howland the subscribers to the above mentioned Instrument personally appeared before me underwritten one his Majesties Justices of the peace for the County of Bristol and acknowledged the same to be their free voluntary Act and Deed in ye first year of his Majesties Reign

Natha^{l} Paine

Entered octob^{r} 26 : 1715 by John Cary Recorder

THE WILLS AND INVENTORIES OF GEORGE² SOULE AND HIS WIDOW DEBORAH, WITH THE PETITION OF THE GRANDDAUGHTER MARY COGGESHALL

Transcribed from the Original Documents and Records

By George Ernest Bowman

George² Soule (*George¹*) died at Dartmouth, Mass., probably but a short time before 17 May, 1704, the day his inventory was taken. His widow Deborah died at Dartmouth between the date of her will, 24 January, 1708/9, and the day it was probated, 1 March, 1709/10. The original documents relating to George² Soule's estate have all disappeared from the probate files, but the will, inventory, receipts of heirs and petition of his granddaughter were recorded in the Bristol County Probate Records, Volume II, pages 93, 94 and 96, and in Volume III, pages 585, 586 and 599. Deborah Soule's will and inventory were recorded in Volume II, page 275, and the account of the executrix in Volume III, page 20, but these three original documents, with the bond of the executrix, are still in the files and have been used in making the transcript here presented.

[George² Soule's Will]

[p. 93] The Last will and Testament of George Soule of Dartmouth in the County of Bristoll in New England being of perfect Memory and my understanding not faileing me praises be given to Allmighty God for the same. Doe bequeath my Body to the Earth from whence it Came, and my Soule Unto God that gave it And I do Commend my well beloved wife & Chilldren Unto the Gracious Protection of the Lord, Jesus Christ Humbly Entreating him of his Grace to Replenish them with his holy Spirit so as they may live in the fear of God and Unity of the Spiritt all the dayes of their lives : My will and desire is that all my Lawfull Debts may be truely & Justly payd where and to whom any is oweing and all such debts as is Lawfully due unto me may be Received by my Executors after Named Ittem I do give & bequeath unto my Eldest son William Soule unto him his heires and Assignes for Ever One quarter part of a share of land Divided & undivided scittuated lyeing & being in the said Township of Dartmouth Item I doe give and bequeath unto my son John Soule unto him his heires & Assignes for Ever One Eighth part of a share of land Divided & undivided scittuate lyeing & being in the said Township of Dartmouth Item I Do give & bequeath Unto my son Nathan Soule Unto him his heires and Assignes for Ever One Eighth part of a share of land with my Dwelling house wherin I live at the day of the date hereof onely Reserveing priviledge for his Mother my wife to have free Liberty to Dwell in the said House before given unto my sonne Nathan Dureing the time of her widowhood & priviledge of all sorts of fruits in y^e^ orchard Item I do give & bequeath unto my Daughter Deborah Soule Ten pounds in money : and to be payd unto her by my said sonne Nathan Soule at the age of Eighteen years or at the day of her Marriage = Item I doe give and bequeath unto my three daughters Mary Lydia & Sarah Soule the sum of Thirty pounds in money and three good ffeather beds with furniture belonging to them . that is to be payd by my Executrix and Executor after Named the sum of ten pounds & one feather bed & furniture belonging to it unto Each of them at the age of Eighteen years or at the day of of their Mariage Item I do order Constitute Ordaine and Appoint my dear and Well beloved wife Deborah Soule & my well beloved son William Soule to be my Executrix & Executor to see that this my last will & Testament be truely Executed and fullfilled in all respects to the full meaneing & true Intent thereof in all perticulers = Item I Do desire Request & Impower my Trusty & well beloved freinds Joseph Tripp & George Cadman both of the said Town of Dartmouth to be overseers of this my Last will & Testament & to be helpfull unto my said Executors in the Manageing of their Affaires by their help Advice & Councell in the due Execution of their placces & trust to them Commited, Item I do give and bequeath two overseers five shillings apeice to be payd unto them by my Executors And in Rattifycation & Confirmation that this is my absolute last will & Testament, I have hereunto sett my hand and seale, this Twenty fifth day of the first month March and in the Year of Our Lord one thousand six Hundred Ninety & seven 1697

Signed sealed & owned George Soule (S)
in presence off
Isaace Lawton
John Coggeshall
Elizabeth Coggeshall

Memorandum y^t on ye 30th day of June 1704 then Appeared before Natha^l Byfield Esqr Judge of Probate of wills &c within the County of Bristoll m^r John Coggeshall & m^r Isaace Lawton two of ye wittnesses to the above writen will and did Sollemly declare that they were present & did see George Soule late of Dartmouth, Deceased, signe seale & declare the above written as his last will & testament & that he was of a Disposeing mind when he so did And that they allso see Elizabeth Coggeshall the other witness signe at the same time

John Cary Reg^r Jura^t Coram Natha^l Byfield
July 1st 1704 Entered by John Cary Reg^r

To y^e Judge of Probate of wills = These may Certify the that I am not Capable to come to Bristoll Neither do I accept of what is given to me in my late Deceased Husbands Will but desire that I may have my thirds according to law : and that my son william Soule may proceed in the Execution of his ffathers will

Dated in Dartmouth y^e 22 day of ye 4th month 1704
Deborah Soule

Entered the same 1st day of July 1704 By John Cary Reg^r

[George[2] Soule's Inventory]

[p. 94] Wee whose Names are under written being Elected & Chose by the partyes Concerned to take an Inventory of the Estate of George Soule Deceased late of Dartmouth in the County of Bristoll in New England have to the best of Our Endeavours taken it as ffolloweth

That is to say One halfe of a share of land Devided & undivided throughout the township of Dartmouth with Houseing & Orchard upon it at	400	00	00
one pair of oxen at	008	00	00
Nine Cowes at	020	00	00
2 two year olds	002	15	00
2 Mares & one Coalt	008	00	00
forty four sheep & Twenty two lambs at	015	00	00
six swine at	001	10	00
forty four Goats & ten Kids at	010	00	00
two shairs & 2 Colters & three Chaines at	001	10	00
A Cart & wheels & Yoaks	001	05	00
Axes & saws & augurs with other Iron tools and a bar of Iron	002	14	00
A pair of Andirons 2 tramels a pair of tongs & a slice & a bar of steel	002	03	00
3 iron potts 2 iron Kettles & one Brass Kettle & a pair of Stilliards	002	02	00
A Grinstone a warming Pann a ffrying pann & Grid-iron	001	00	00
A fender & a Gun & a fork & 2 Bottles & 2 jarrs & a Tin pan	000	18	00
3 platters & 2 pots with some old puter & two Candlesticks	001	00	00
three beds with the Beding	018	00	00
A pair money Scales : 11 : Books a Hamer 2 adses 2 Bridles & Sadle	002	00	00
To old Cloathing a Rasor & percell of Yarn 2 pair of Cards	007	10	00
A Loom & Tacklin and a spit a Cart Rope & 2 sifes	004	00	00
7 bushells of Barley 35 Bushells of Indian Corn with some other Corn	005	15	00
three Cheests & some meat & wool & fflax & meal baggs 3 wheels	003	02	00
5 Chaires 8 Barrels 2 Churns 4 Tubbs a Cheespress wth other Lumber	002	08	00
some Leather 15 pounds of fatt & an Earthen pott & ten pounds Tobacco	000	14	00
the whole sum.	591	06	00

We the prizers finished this Inventory the 17th day of may 1704 in Dartmouth

Joseph Tripp
William Wood
George Cadman

[see page 96 an Addition to this Inventory *]

william Soule Executor to the last will & Testament of George Soule late of Dartmouth Decd on the 30th day of June 1704 Appeared before Nathal Byfield Esqr Judge of Probate of wills &c within the County of Bristoll who did Sollemly delare. That the Inventory above written is a true & Just Inventory so far as hath Come to his hand and knowledge (Excepting some few things) and that when he knowes of any more he will Reveale it that it may be herewith Entered and this declaration was made by him as he hoped for help from God.

John Cary Regr   Jurat Coram Nathal Byfield:
Thus Entered July the 1st 1704 By John Cary Regr

[p. 96] William Soul son & Administrator of the Estate Left by George Soule late of Dartmouth in the County of Bristoll Decd Exhibited these perticulers as an Addition to the Inventory upon Record of his said ffathers Estate on the 17th day of Aprill 1705 by the hand of Leiut Little

Imprs money and Debts	2	07	05
to one Cow prised at	1	16	00
to one Conno prised at	0	14	00
To shott moulds & Mustard Bowl	0	02	06
To Butter prised at	0	15	00
To Bees prised at	1	00	00
wosted Combs & Pocket Book prised at	0	15	00
Boards prised at	1	03	08
Sword & looking Glass & sider Mill prised at	0	07	06
three bettle Rings wedges & pitchforks	0	05	00
Joynter & two axcle tree pins & old ax	0	02	06
Hachel prised at	0	01	02
A Combe & 3 ounces of Indigo & a Jugg	0	04	02
Prospect Glass 6d swevl Chain & Dubble Hooks 3s 6d	0	04	00
	9	17	11

This Inventory was taken the 22d day of march 1705

By us Silvanus Soule
Nathaniel Soule

* This note is on the outer margin of the page.

[Receipts of the Heirs]

[III : 585] Received of William Soul of Dartmouth in the County of Bristol in New England Executor of the last will & Testament of his ffather George Soul once of Dartmouth Deceased I say Received by me William Brownel Junor: ten pounds & one feather Bed & furniture belonging to it which Ten pounds & feather bed is the ten pound & feather bed given to Lidia Soule by will she being now wife to me william Brownel in witness whereof I have here unto the sixth day of the sixth month called August in the year of our Lord one thousand seven Hundred & six

Signed and delivered — William Brownel Junr
In presence of — his **X** marke
Henry Howland
William White
Entered October 5th 1719 By John Cary Register

The 30th of the Eleventh month Called January 1710 Recd of will Soule the sum of Ten pounds Currant money of New England which was the Ten pounds which Our ffather George Soule gave to his daughter Mary in his will I say Received by me

Signed in presence of — Joseph Devel
his
Jacob **X** Soule
marke
Mary Soule
Entered October 5th 1719 By John Cary Regr

Dartmouth in the County of Bristol the 25th day of 4th month called June in the year 1707: Received of william Soule Executor of the last will and Testament of his ffather George Soule of Dartmouth deceased ten pounds in money which ten pounds is the ten pounds given to me by my father George Soul in his last will I say Received by me

In presence of us — her
Nathal Soule — Sara : **S** : Soule
Nathan Soule — marke
Entered October 5th 1719 By John Cary Registr

the fifteenth day of the Third month Called may one Thousand seven Hundred & Nineteen then Received of my Brother William Soule the sum of Thirteen pounds one shilling and seven pence which I Receive in full Sattisfaction for and in Liu of the ffeather bed and furniture belonging to it which my ffather George Soule gave to me upon his last will and Testament I say Received by me

In presence of Sarah Soule
Hannah Manchester
Nathan Soule
Entered October 5th 1719 By John Cary Register

[Petition of Joshua and Mary Coggeshall]

[p. 586] Bristol Ss August the 5th 1719

To the Honrable Nathaniel Paine Esqr Judge of Probate of Wills for the County of Bristol Granting Letter of Administrations and settleing Estates of persons Dying Intestate in the said County

The Humble Pittion of Joshua Coggeshall of Dartmouth in the County of Bristol & Mary Coggeshall his wife Daughter of George Soule son of George Soule senr of Dartmouth deceased Humbly showeth

That whereas by one Act or Establishment of this Province made in the Twelfth Year of King William it is Provided and Enacted that any Child or Children not haveing a Legacie given them in the Will of theyr ffather or mother Every such Child shall have a Proportion of the Estate of theyr parents Given and sett out to them as the law directs for the Distribution of Intestate Estates your Pittioner therefore Humbly Informs your honr that [p. 587] That George Soule of Dartmouth Grandfather of your Pittioner Mary Coggeshall Being Seized in his Own Right of a very valuable Estate of lands Rights Goods & Chattells in the Town of Dartmouth on the Twentyh * of march in the year 1697 made his will & Testament in writting in which he gave and bequeathed all his farm Lands Rights and Estate Among his Children then liveing viz William Nathan John Mary Lidia Deborah and Sarah not mention or giveing any Legacy to Mary your Pittioner the Lawfull Child and Representative of George Soule the son of the sd Testator George Soule senr : who was then Deceased allthough said George Soule father of your Petitioner had never any portion of the Estate of his ffather aforesaid in his lifetime Given him or settled upon him

And Now so it is may it Please your Honr that since the makeing of the said Will John Soule One of the sons of the s

* Sic. Compare the date in the will.

George Soule is Deceased without Issue by Meanes of which his part allso by the law is Descended among the surviveing Children and now Ought to be Distributed among them and your Petition^r not being Considered in said will & being now arived to full age is Necessiated to pray your hon^r that the Legatorys and those that are in the Possession of the Estate of the said George Soule Deceased be Citted before your Hon^r at a time Appointed by your Hon^r for hearing the same at which time yor Petition^r will allso appear and produce the Records of the lands & Estate that so yor Hon^r may proceed to sett out to your Petitioner her part & proportion of the s^d Estate as by the aforesaid Act your Hon^r is Enabled and your Petitioner shall pray

Thomas Turner Advocate for the Petitioners

Bristol Ss At a Court of Probate held at Bristol on october 5th 1719

Upon the Reading of the Petition of Joshua Coggeshall and Mary his wife Considering the law of the Province under which the said Mary was Born, A Right if any she had Accrewed mentioned no other then Children, at the time was Omitted or forgotten, which at that time was understood of no other then Imeadiate Children and not Extend to Grand Children

Considering allso the Right of the said Mary if any shee hath lyes fairly at the Common Law it being an Estate in land I Do Dismiss the Petition

Natha^l Paine

Entered October the 6th 1719 by John Cary Register

p. 599] Bristol ss : January the 5th 1719

Joshua Coggeshall for himself and Mary his Wife the Grandaughter of George Soule of Dartmouth Deceased Appealed from the sentence or decree of Natha^l Paine Esqr Judge of Probates given on the fifth of October last To the Governour & Councill and became bound to prosecute his appeal as the law directs

Entered by John Cary Reg^r

[Widow Deborah Soule's Will *]

The 24 day of junuary in the year 1708 or 9

I debrah Soule of dartmouth in the County of bristoll in her maigstey provance of the masathusets bay in new ingland

* From the original document.

wife of george Soule Sener Late of dartmouth desased being very Sick and weak in body but of parfit mind and memory thanks be given to god tharefore Coling to mind the mortolity of my body du make and ordain this my last will and testment that is to Say prinCipllay & first of all I give and bequeth to my daughter Sarah Soule whome I Consitute to be my Sole exacutrix of this my last will and testement all my estate with in dowers and with out paying all lawfull debts and legises itam I give and bequeth to my Son william Soule five shillings itam i give and bequeth to my Son nathan Soule won Shilling item I give and bequeth to my daughter mary divel Six Shillings itan I give and bequeth to my daughter Lediah browniell Six Shillings itam I give and bequeth to mary Soule daughter of my Son george Soule desased three Shillings and I du here by utterly disalow revoke and disanull all and every other form testments wills legeses and bequeths and executors by me in any wis be fore named willed and bequethed rectyfing and confirming this and no other to be my last will and testement in witness whare of I have here unto Set my hand and Seal the day and year above written Sined Sealed as my Last will and testament by the Said debrah Soule in the prence of us the Seubscribers the word in in the third line is interlined before the insealing hereof

Silvanus Soule — her
Jacob Soule — debrah X Soule (Seal
Nathaniel Soule — mark

Memorandum that on first day of march 1709 Then in Bristol Silvanus Soule Jacob Soule & Nathaniel Soule witnesses to the above written will of the said Deceased Deborah Soul Appeared & made Oath (before the Hon^rble^ Natha^l^ Byfield Esq Judge of Probate of wills &c within the County of Bristol) that they were present vizt Silvanus Soule & Jacob Soule & see the said dec^d^ signe seal & declare the above written as her last will & Testament to which they set their hand as witnesses & Natha^l^ Soul vizt that ye Deceased owned the same to be her last will as aboves^d^ : & upon her desire set his hand thereto & further they Swear she was to the best of yr understanding of a Disposeing mind

John Cary Reg^r^ — Jur^t^ Coram N Byfield

Bristol ss In ye 2^d^ Book folio 275 : March 2^d^ 1709-10 Entered By John Cary Register

[Widow Deborah Soule's Inventory *]

Four cattel prized at	06	00	00
Nine sheep at	01	06	00
Won swine at	00	05	00
To beed & beding & Clothen at	07	00	00
Warming pan & puter at	02	00	00
Sheeps wool at	01	09	00
Wosted & yarn prized at	02	10	00
Two poots three cittels & frien pan	01	14	00
Books & Chists	00	10	00
Spining wheals with old lomber	01	17	00
Provision at	00	12	00
to Cash	00	17	00
	26	00	00

An Inventory of the Estate of Deborah Soule Late of Dartmouth Deceased
Nathaniel Soule And
Jacob Soule Prizers

Bristol ss March the first 1709 then Sarah Soule Executrix to the last will & Testament of Deborah Soule Deceased Appeard before the Honerable Natha^{l} Byfield Esqr Judge of Probate &c within the County of Bristol aforesaid & made Oath that the Inventory above written is a Just and true accompt of the Esate of ye s^{d} decead to the best of her Knowledge & when she Knowes of any more she will Reveale it & bring it to the Register that it may be of Record.

John Cary Reg^{r} Jur^{t} Coram N Byfield

Entered March ye 2^{d} 1709–10 By John Cary Register

[Bond of the Executrix *]

The bond of the executrix is on a printed form and is dated 1 March, 1709. The amount of the bond was £60 and the surcties were Nathaniel Soule and Jacob Soule, both of Dartmouth. Nathaniel signed his name to the bond, but Sarah and Jacob made their marks. The witnesses were Samuel Gallup and John Cary. The executrix was required, by the terms of the bond, to present an inventory on or before 10 April, 1710, and an account of her administration on or before 10 April, 1711.

* From the original document.

[Account of the Executrix *]

Bristol ss . March the 7 : $17\frac{10}{11}$

The Accompt of Sarah Soule Executrix of the Last will and Testament of Deborah Soule late of Dartmouth Deceased of her Admistration upon the Estate left by the said Deborah Soule according to the will of the s^{d} Deceased

The said Sarah Execut^{x} Chargeth herself wth the Inventory upon Record being the sum	26	00	00
paid	02	9	4
	23	10	8

The said Executrix Desireth Allowance for such & such much Debts & Legacies payd out of the s^{d} Estate

	£	s	
To Doct^{r} Tallmon Remaining due	00	02	00
To Nicholas Howland for shoes	00	16	04
To my Brother william Soule	00	06	00
A Legacie payd to Mary Devel my sister	00	06	00
& to Lidiah Brownel my sister	00	06	00
Due to be payd to Mary Soul daught^{r} of my late Brother George Soule	00	03	00
to my Brother william Soul	00	05	00
and to my Brother Nathan Soule which they have given me	00	01	00
	02	09	4

Sarah Soul Appeared before me Natha^{l} Paine Esqr Judge of the probate of will &c within ye County of Bristoll and presented this accompt of her Administration upon said Estate & made Oath that the same is true & Just which I have Examined & do allow the same and order it to be of Record the ballence of this account being Twenty three pound Nine shillings and four pence is bequeathed to the said Sarah by the will of her mother Deborah Soul

March 7 . $17\frac{10}{11}$ Juratt Coram Nath^{ll} Paine

This account is Entered in the 3^{d} book for Registring wills folio : 20 : March 3^{d} † $17\frac{10}{11}$ By John Cary Regist^{r}

The will & Inventory to which y^{s} acco^{t} hath Relation is Recorded in the 2^{d} Book folio 275

* From the original document. † Sic.

JOHN^2 SAMSON'S SETTLEMENT OF HIS OWN ESTATE

Transcribed from the Original Records,

BY GEORGE ERNEST BOWMAN

JOHN^2 SAMSON (*Henry*^{1}) is mentioned in his father's will, printed in our second volume; but a long-continued search has failed to reveal any other mention of his name on the records until 1702, when the deed here presented was recorded. By this deed John^2 Samson of Dartmouth, Mass., conveys to his brother James^2 Samson, also of Dartmouth, all of the rights in land at Dartmouth given him by Henry^1 Samson's will. In return for this land James bound himself to provide John with food, raiment and other necessaries as long as he lived.

This deed proves conclusively that John Samson, the son of Henry Samson of the Mayflower, could not have been the person of the same name who, as stated by Vinton, in the Giles Memorial [p. 376], married Mary Pease in 1667 and lived for a time at Beverly, Mass., having three children born there.

As John is called a "Single man" in the deed, it is evident that he had never married and that he had no children, and by this deed he undoubtedly disposed of his entire estate, except possibly a few personal effects.

James² Samson made his will 10 January, 1715/16,* and did not provide for the future maintenance of his brother John. It may safely be assumed, therefore, that John² Samson died before his brother James.

The deed here given was dated 21 May, 1702, and acknowledged 27 May, 1702. It was recorded in the Bristol County Registry of Deeds, Volume III, page 446.

[JOHN² SAMSON TO JAMES² SAMSON]

To all People to whom these presents shall come John Samson of the town of Dartmouth in the County of Bristoll in the Province of the Massachuset Bay in New England Single man sendeth Greeting &c Know yee that I the s^d^ John Samso for & in Consideration That my Brother Jamẽs Samson of the Town of Dartmouth aforesd Yeoman Hath Bound & obliged himself his heires Executors & Administrators to Provide for Keep & Maintaine me the s^d^ John Samson with food Raiment & other Necessarys Dureing the time of my Naturall Life as allso for Divers other Good Causes & Considerations me thereunto Moveing Have given granted Bargained sold Enfeoffed & Confirmed and by these presents Doe fully freely Clearely and absolutely give grant Bargain sell Alien Enfeoffe & Confirm unto him the said James Samson his heires & Assignes for Ever All that my lands both uplands Swamps & meadow Ground which I now have or of Right belongeth unto me Lyeing & being within the Township of Dart [p. 447] Dartmouth aforesd both Divided & undivided which is more perticulerly one Third part of one Whole Share throrowout s^d^ Town both of Divided & undivided both of upland Meadows Swamps & Swampy Ground together with all the standing wood & Timber in & upon all or any of sd lands with all & Singuler the profitts priviledges & Appurtenances thereunto belonging or any wise Appertayning To have and to hold all that my Right title & Interest that I now have . Ever had or of Right ought to have in any of the lands of any sort or Kind within the township of Dartmouth afores^d^ that accrueth to me by the last will & Testament of Henry Samson my Hon^rd^ ffather late of Duxbury Deceased or by any other way or meanes whatso Ever with all the profits priviledges & Appurtenances thereof or thereunto belonging or in any wise appertaining Unto him the said James Samson his heires & Assignes and to the only & alone sole p^r^per Use benefitt & behoofe of him the said James Samson my Brother his heires & Assignes for Ever And

* Mayflower Descendant, VI: 184.

I the said John Samson Do for me myn Executors & Administrators Covenant and Grant to & with the s[d] James Samson his heires & Assignes that att & before the Ensealeing & Delivery of these presents I am the true & Rightfull owner of all the said given & granted p[r]mises and have in my self full power Just Right & Lawfull Authority to give grant & Convey the same in manner & form aforesaid according to the true Intent meaning of these presents and that all the said Bargained premises are to be & at all times hereafter shall Continue to be free & Cleare of & from all former & other Gifts grants Bargaines . sales titles & Encumbrances whatso Ever had made Commited or Done or to be had made Committed Suffered omitted or done by me the said John Samson myn heires or Assignes or from any other person or persons Lawfully Claimeing of from by or under me them or any of them or by myn or their meanes Consent privity or procurem[t]. In witness whereof I the said John Samson have hereunto set my hand & seale this 21st day of may Anno Domini one thousand Seven Hundred & two

Signed sealed & Del[d] John Samson (S)
in presence of
John Perrye
Isaac I Pope
his marke

May the 27th 1702 The above & within mentioned John Samson Personally appeared before me . and Acknowledged the above & within written Instrument to be his Act & Deed
Seth Pope Justice of Peace

Septemb[r] the Eight 1702 Entered by John Cary Record[r],